Wills, Trusts & Probate Administration for the Texas Paralegal

Stonewall Van Wie, III
DEL MAR COLLEGE

WEST PUBLISHING COMPANY
MINNEAPOLIS/ST. PAUL   NEW YORK   LOS ANGELES   SAN FRANCISCO

Production, Prepress, Printing and Binding by West Publishing Company.

 TEXT IS PRINTED ON 10% POST CONSUMER RECYCLED PAPER

COPYRIGHT © 1995 by WEST PUBLISHING CO.
610 Opperman Drive
P.O. Box 64526
St. Paul, MN 55164–0526

ISBN 0–314–04555–4

TABLE OF CONTENTS

CHAPTER 6 ADDITIONAL ESTATE PLANNING DOCUMENTS (POWERS OF ATTORNEY, LIVING WILLS, DESIGNATIONS OF GUARDIAN, ETC.)   113

CHAPTER 7 INTRODUCTION TO TRUSTS   147

CHAPTER 12 PROBATE ADMINISTRATION—MISCELLANEOUS AND ALTERNATIVE PROBATE PROCEDURES   349

CHAPTER 13 PROBATE ADMINISTRATION—CHECKLISTS AND TRANSFERRING ESTATE ASSETS   381

PREFACE

This text has three goals:

1. To provide Texas-specific paralegal course material. The book combines a true paralegal textbook with Texas-specific material.

2. To cover the subject matter as broadly and completely as possible within the restraints of length and expense. Although some might want to consult the Texas Probate Code in tandem with this text, the coverage and summarization of the Code is complete enough that that is unnecessary.

   In addition, the material is presented so completely in the book that instructors can devote more class time to group projects, pair-share-compare exercises, class discussion, and other exercises and assignments rather than having to lecture on the material. This gives time for training in the skills and competencies mandated in SCANS and for exercises designed to increase student thinking and writing abilities.

3. To present the material so that it becomes practical and useful in the real world. The objective is to help legal assistant students acquire skills, competencies, and knowledge that enable them to function immediately with little or no further training in the law office environment.

Flexible Format

This book is designed to be used in a 15-week course. Chapters Three, Nine, or Fifteen may be omitted to fit a shorter course. Or, the material can be divided into two courses—Chapters Two through Nine and Fifteen relate to wills, estates and trusts; Chapters One and Ten through Fourteen relate to probate administration.

Text Organization

The book primarily follows the organization of the Texas Probate Code. Chapter Three, "Estate Planning," serves as an introduction to the use of wills and trusts for estate planning purposes; more detail is given in Chapters Four through Nine. This background helps the reader understand the rather technical discussion of matters like marital deductions and QTIPs. Chapter Fifteen, on estate and gift taxation, is found at the end, so it can easily be omitted if preferred. Because estate and gift taxation is covered in the CLA examination and an understanding of this subject is vital to a legal assistant working in estate planning, the chapter can serve as an excellent resource after the course.

Chapter Organization

Each chapter contains several features designed to aid the learning process.

Chapter Objectives are provided at the beginning of each chapter. These inform the reader of the essential skills and competencies that should be acquired upon completion of the chapter.

A glossary of key terms introduced in the chapter is provided at the beginning of each chapter. This aids the student by introducing the term prior to its use in the text, so that the student does not have to interrupt reading to look up the word. In addition, each key term is printed in boldface when it first appears, to alert the reader to its importance.

Practical tips are included in most chapters. These help students understand how the concepts are used on the job and will serve as a handy resource in their careers.

Ethical considerations are discussed specifically in Chapter Three and generally throughout the text where appropriate.

Examples of practice forms appear in a forms appendix at the end of each chapter but the first. The abundance of forms provided reflects the majority of forms used in actual practice.

Questions and exercises appear at the end of each chapter. They contain:

1. Questions that for the most part require application of the text material to simulated fact situations.
2. Assignments that require application of knowledge gained in the chapter to the preparation of forms and documents actually used in wills, trusts, and probate practice.
3. Assignments that form the basis for class discussion.

Supplemental Material

The Instructor's Manual contains sections relating to each chapter of the text and provides:

1. Suggestions for additional individual and group assignments and projects.
2. Suggestions for class discussion.
3. Citations to additional Texas cases for the purpose of pair-share-compare exercises or class discussion.
4. Exercises to facilitate teaching of critical thinking, creative thinking, and skills of problem solving, decision making, drawing analogies, and categorization.
5. Sample test questions, in short-answer essay format, with answers.
6. Answers to chapter questions.

Acknowledgments

Many persons aided in the writing and polishing of this book. To all of them, I owe a hearty "thank you." First, I wish to thank Laurie Alcala, who labored hard and long to transcribe my dictated notes, which became the first draft. Then, thanks to Don Poenisch, who corrected my grammatical errors.

I owe immeasurable gratitude to my wife, Pamella, for her patience while I wrote this text. Thanks are also due my son, stepchildren, grandchildren, daughter-in-law, and son-in-law, who were also understanding during this period.

I am also grateful to Brenda and Ed Baker, and to T. Mark Anderson, who helped me with probate forms I did not have in my computer. Susannah Mills, a longtime, faithful employee of the State Bar of Texas whom I have known since the early 1970s when I made my first appearance in what were then called "continuing legal education seminars," aided me greatly in getting permission to use State Bar of Texas copyrighted material.

I also want to thank West Educational Publishing for their support in publishing Texas-specific legal assistant textbooks. In particular, I wish to thank Elizabeth Hannan, Patty Bryant, and Caroline Nielsen.

Finally, I would like to acknowledge and thank the following educators, who reviewed the various drafts of this text. Their comments and suggestions were always appreciated.

Donna M. Bobbitt
University of Houston, Clear Lake

Thomas Branton
Alvin Community College

Martin Gewertz
San Antonio College

Susan Hines
San Antonio Court Reporting Institute

David Jaroszewski
Lee College

Carole Olson
El Centro College

Hector Pena
National Career Institute

Tunney S. Robison, J.D.
Center for Advanced Legal Studies

Gene Silverblatt
Central Texas College

DeShaunta Stewart
San Jacinto College North

Leo Villalobos
El Paso Community College

Aida Kennedy Ziemnicki
Southwestern Paralegal Institute

1 INTRODUCTION TO PROBATE LAW AND THE TEXAS PROBATE CODE

CHAPTER OBJECTIVES

Upon completion of this chapter, the student should be able to:

1. Compare and contrast the historical influences on Texas probate law.
2. Determine the court having jurisdiction over a particular probate case or a question incident to or appertaining to the administration of an estate.
3. Determine the correct venue of a probate matter.
4. Determine when the Rules of Civil Procedure are applicable to a probate case.

CHAPTER GLOSSARY

Appellate jurisdiction The jurisdiction to hear appeals, having the power to review, correct, or modify the result of the proceedings in an inferior court.

Application In probate cases, the equivalent of a petition, which is a written statement of a cause of action that when filed in the appropriate court initiates a suit.

Canon law A law, rule, or statute, in general, and of the church, in particular; an ecclesiastical law or statute generally referring to that body of Roman "church" law compiled by the Roman Catholic Church during the Twelfth, Thirteenth and Fourteenth centuries.

Citation In Texas, a written notice to a defendant that suit has been filed against

him and that he must appear and answer by a certain date. In cases other than probate, a copy of the petition is attached to the citation.

Codification The systematic collection and compiling of laws, rules, or regulations. A code is the result.

Collateral attack An attack on a judgment, other than by an appeal of the judgment.

Community property The property acquired by either spouse during the existence of their marriage, other than that acquired by gift, devise, inheritance, recovery for personal injuries, or partition (division) of community property by the spouses.

Concurrent jurisdiction When two or more courts have power over controversies involving the same subject matter, at the same time, and in the same geographical area.

Estate All the assets and liabilities owned and owed by a person. In probate the person is deceased, a minor, or an incompetent.

Exclusive jurisdiction When a court is the only court that can hear and determine a particular controversy.

Executor A person or entity appointed in a will to administer the property of the will maker after his death. Executrix is the feminine form of executor.

Guardian A person appointed by a probate court to administer the property of a minor or of an incapacitated person.

Heir One who is related to a person dying without a will and who receives, by virtue of the statutes of descent and distribution, any or all of the real or personal property of such deceased person.

Homestead The residence of a person, which is protected by the laws of Texas from seizure and forced sale for the satisfaction of debt.

Incapacitated person A minor or an adult who, because of a physical or mental condition, is unable either to provide care for himself or to manage his property; also includes missing persons and persons who must have a guardian in order to receive money from a governmental source. Prior to adoption, in 1993, of the Guardianship Code, incompetent was used to express the same concept.

Jurisdiction The power of a court to determine a controversy, assuming that the court is duly constituted with power over the subject matter of the controversy and that the proper parties are present.

Minutes A book kept by the court clerk for entering memoranda of what takes place in the court. In probate matters the judge makes the entries in the minutes.

Original jurisdiction The power of the court over a lawsuit, when it is first filed, to try it and enter judgment.

Personal representative A generic term to describe any person appointed to administer the estate and property of a deceased person.

Probate The determination by a court that a will has been executed with the formalities required by law to make it valid and that it has not been revoked or otherwise abrogated. In modern usage it refers to any law that concerns the administration of estates.

Probate court Any court exercising probate jurisdiction.

Removal The mandatory transfer of a case from one court to another, both having concurrent jurisdiction. The removal is initiated by the court to which the case is transferred.

Separate property Property acquired by a spouse prior to marriage or by gift, devise, inheritance, recovery for personal injury, or partition of community property.

Statutes of Descent and Distribution The laws that determine who inherits from a deceased person who died without a will; sometimes referred to as intestate succession.

Uniform Probate Code A uniform code approved by the Commissioners on Uniform State Law designed to simplify and make more uniform the probate law of the states. As of this writing 16 states have adopted it. Texas probably will not adopt it as a whole.

Venue The particular county, geographical area, or district in which a case is to be heard; the locality of a suit.

Ward A minor or incapacitated person for whom a guardian has been appointed.

Will An instrument, executed in compliance with state statutes, by which someone disposes of his real and personal property, which is only effective upon his death and is generally revocable during life.

ORIGINS OF TEXAS PROBATE LAW

While most of our current day **probate** law has its origin in the English common law, there are Spanish and Mexican influences as well. The term *probate* comes from the Latin word *probatio*, which means "proof." In early **canon law** (Ecclesiastical or church law), the Latin term referred to the proof of a **will**. The narrow meaning of *probate* therefore refers to the court procedure by which a will is proved to be valid or invalid. The probating of a will is the judicial determination by the court that the will was the lawful, last will and testament of a deceased person, having been executed with all of the formalities and solemnities required.

The word has acquired a broader meaning, generally referring to the legal process whereby the estate of a deceased person or **incapacitated person** is administered. Generally, the administration of an estate involves collecting the assets of the deceased person, paying the liabilities and taxes, and distributing the remaining property to those persons entitled to it either by virtue of inheritance (where there is no will) or by virtue of a will.

English Origins

The church in one sense and the king in another had total control of early probate law in England. By the thirteenth century, the church, through the ecclesiastical courts, had total control over documents disposing of personal property, called *testaments*, and real property, called *wills*. Under the feudal system then in effect in England, all land was owned by the king; individuals were allowed to use the king's land by permission of the king. This permission was called a *feoff*. This system created a *tenancy*, or a type of a lease with ownership characteristics. There was no term to the tenancy; that is, it did not terminate upon any particular event or after the passage of a certain amount of time. The land holder held the land indefinitely, unless he committed a high crime or treason or failed to pay his taxes. When the landholder died, the right to hold his land passed to his **heirs** as determined by the ecclesiastical courts. This finding was certified to the king, who would normally confirm the finding.

Since the Statute of Wills failed to create jurisdiction in any other court in England concerning the probate of wills, wills were self-effectuating. No probate proceedings of any nature were necessary to effectuate a will, although they were still necessary to effectuate a testament under canon law. This distinction between wills and testaments continued in England until 1856, but for some reason it never existed in the laws of most states of the United States, including Texas. In Texas, the disposition of property in a will has always been ineffectual unless the will is first admitted to probate.

Another set of English statutes that had considerable effect on probate law is the **Statutes of Descent and Distribution**. These statutes, which are the subject of Chapter Two, create the law by which it is determined who inherits when someone dies without a will.

The Statutes of Descent and Distribution have always been in statutory form, first in the form of church canons and thereafter in the form of civil statutes. In addition, the administration of the estates of deceased persons or incapacitated persons, and other related matters, have always been the subject of statutes, first church statutes, or canons, and then civil statutes created by the government of England. At present, at least in Texas, probate law is almost entirely statutory in form. The function of the courts is relegated to the interpretation and application of the statutory law. The courts are for the most part barred from the creation of new law or the modification or repeal of old law.

Spanish And Mexican Influences

The laws of Spain provided that property acquired prior to marriage and by gift, through a will, or by inheritance was the **separate property** of the marital partner who acquired it. It further provided that all other property acquired during marriage was owned jointly by both marital partners. This we now refer to as **community property**.

When Mexico achieved its independence from Spain and formed the Republic of Mexico in 1824, it incorporated into its constitution the Spanish community property laws. When Texas formed its first government in 1836, that government chose to adopt the English Common Law as it existed on March 2, 1836. However the Mexican community property concept of marital property was included in one of the earliest constitutions of the Texas Republic and has been included within every constitution adopted by either the Republic or the State of Texas since that date.

The **homestead** laws of the State of Texas are also derived from the constitution of the Republic of Mexico. Texas homestead laws are considerably different from those of all of the other states, being much more stringent, though perhaps not as stringent as the homestead laws in Mexico today. The homestead laws of the State of Texas, like the community property concept of marital property, have had considerable influence on the Texas Probate Code.

TEXAS PROBATE CODE

In 1955, the legislature of the State of Texas codified the probate statutes that existed at that time. This **codification** took effect on January 1, 1956. The Texas Probate Code has undergone many amendments since its adoption, but the foundations of the present code go back to early statutory law created in Texas during the Republic and its early days as one of the states in the United States of America. Most of the important concepts of the Probate Code and the procedure for administrating the estates of deceased and incapacitated persons were found almost word for word in some of Texas' earliest statutes.

The Texas Probate Code has been recognized as being one of the most advanced in the United States. In fact, concepts of the Texas

Probate Code have been copied by other states and by the framers of the **Uniform Probate Code.** Yet, though advanced in its application, the Texas Probate Code is still fairly simple in its language. There is, as in any other area of the law, specialized terminology that can make reading difficult to anyone unfamiliar with that terminology. It includes words and phrases that generally have no meaning outside of probate law. Thus, knowledge of probate terminology is essential to an adequate understanding of Texas probate law and the Texas Probate Code.

Jurisdiction

When a legal assistant has been directed by his supervisor to initiate a probate proceeding, the first determination he must make is where and in which court to file the proceedings. The question of where involves determining proper **venue**, which is discussed in the following section. The question of which court to file the proceeding in involves determining jurisdiction of the courts in the particular county in which proper venue lies.

In the Texas Constitution of 1876, **original jurisdiction** in probate matters was vested in the county court. That same constitution vested **appellate jurisdiction** in probate matters in the district court. Article V, Section 22, of the Constitution gives the legislature the power to alter the jurisdiction of the county court. In the early 1900s, the legislature used this power to create the county courts at law. The legislature also attempted to deprive the county court of all judicial function in any counties that had county courts at law.

The Texas Supreme Court, in 1928, held that the deprivation of probate jurisdiction violated the Texas Constitution, which granted to the county courts jurisdiction in criminal, civil, and probate matters. Section 22, the Court maintained, only conferred power upon the legislature to change the civil and criminal jurisdiction. Later, in 1949, that court, without discussing its earlier opinion, ruled that the legislature could give **concurrent jurisdiction** in probate matters to county courts at law as long as it did not take away the jurisdiction of the county court as provided for in the Constitution.

In 1973, the constitution was amended to give the legislature the power to eliminate the probate jurisdiction of the county courts in counties that have county courts at law. The legislature, so far, has not done so. Consequently, in counties with county courts at law, the county court and the courts at law have concurrent jurisdiction. In some counties, the county judge either refuses probate cases or only hears them in unusual circumstances.

Under the current status of the law, the county judges in counties that have no statutory courts have **exclusive jurisdiction** over uncontested probate matters and concurrent jurisdiction with the district court in contested probate matters. In counties in which there is a county court at law or a statutory probate court, the jurisdiction of the county court is concurrent with the statutory courts'. The district courts have no original jurisdiction over probate matters in such counties.

The term **probate court** as used here and in the Texas Probate Code refers, then, to any of these courts, the county court, county courts at law, statutory probate courts, or other statutory courts when exercising probate jurisdiction. As a result, some lawyers in pleadings and other papers filed in probate court use the generic term *probate court* rather than identifying the specific court in the caption and other places.

Section 4 of the Texas Probate Code provides that the county courts shall have general original jurisdiction over all matters in probate, including the probating of wills, appointment of **guardians** for the benefit of incapacitated persons, the appointment of administrators in the estates of persons dying without a will, and all procedures during the administration of an estate that is not made otherwise independent.

Appellate jurisdiction is vested in the court of appeals. Probate Code Section 5 provides for original concurrent probate jurisdiction over contested matters in the district courts in counties in which there is no statutory court. The statute does not take away any of the constitutional jurisdiction of the county court; it simply provides that the district court has concurrent jurisdiction with the county court in contested probate matters. In counties in which there is no statutory court, it requires that all probate cases be filed in the county court. If some portion of such a case is contested, the county judge on his own motion may (or, upon the motion of an interested party, must) transfer the contested matter to the district court. Even though the contested portion of the probate proceeding has been transferred to the district court, the county court still continues to exercise control over the management of the estate, with the exception of the portion that is being contested. When the district court has determined the contested matter and its judgment has become final, the result is certified back to the county court.

Section 5 also gives the district court jurisdiction over original suits against **executors**, administrators, and guardians. The section also grants concurrent jurisdiction to county courts at law and other statutory courts. Section 5 was amended in 1989 to give statutory probate courts and county courts at law jurisdiction over *inter vivos* (created during life) trusts, charitable trusts, *testamentary* (created in a will) trusts, and trustees.

Section 5(a) gives the statutory probate courts jurisdiction over all matters incident to or appertaining to estates. Most importantly, this statute gives the statutory probate courts, including the county court at law, the power to determine title to land, provided that the estate has or claims an interest in the land, and to hear suits, regardless of the amount in controversy, arising out of claims by or against the estate.

Section 5(b) provides that the statutory courts have, in effect, the power of **removal** from the district courts if a matter incident to an estate is filed in the district court. If such a matter incident or appertaining to an estate is filed in the district court, the statutory court, upon motion of a party to that suit, may have the matter transferred to the probate court.

The guardianship statutes created in 1993 as part of the Probate Code remove guardianships from the effect of provisions in Section 5 and then recreate them in Sections 605 through 609 of the Probate Code.

Venue

Sections 6 and 7 of the Texas Probate Code provide for original **venue** as to estates of decedents; that is, where the suit is to be filed. Venue deals with the locality of the suit, and in state court refers to the particular county in which a lawsuit should be filed. There are 254 counties in Texas, so theoretically there are 254 venues. Texas and most other states have statutes that specify which county a suit must be filed in or, to put it in legal terms, that provide for mandatory venue. Sometimes there is a choice of several counties, and sometimes it is mandatory that a suit be filed in one particular county.

It is easy to forget that the filing of an original **application** in probate is in fact the filing of a suit, because very few probate matters are contested, and most suits are contested. Still, it is true that a probate application is, in effect, a suit. In fact, a probate proceeding is actually a group of individual suits packaged together. Each is initiated by a petition (called an *application* in probate matters), requires citation, and results in final, appealable judgment. The filing and hearing of the original application is one lawsuit that results in a final, appealable judgment. Thereafter, other procedures, which will be discussed in later chapters, are separate lawsuits requiring new citation and resulting in a final, appealable judgment. An example is the procedure to sell property belonging to an estate, which requires that an application be filed and a **citation** issued to interested parties. The judgment, or the decree confirming sale of property, is a final and appealable judgment.

Like the Family Code, the venue provisions dealing with probate are internal, rather than being found in the Civil Practices and Remedies Code, as are the venue provisions applicable to most other civil suits. Also like the Family Code, the venue provisions are mandatory in nature; that is, venue may not be conferred upon a court by consent or inaction. In ordinary civil suits, if a suit is filed in the wrong county, the defendant must object, in the form of a motion to transfer venue, or the court in which it is filed has the power to hear and dispose of the case with no obligation to transfer venue on its own initiative. Consequently, venue can be conferred by consent or inaction.

In both family matters and probate matters the initiating party, called the *petitioner* in family matters and the *applicant* in probate matters, is required to allege affirmatively in the petition or application that the court has venue and then must introduce proof to that effect in the hearing. If the applicant or petitioner fails either to plead or to prove venue, the probate court has the legal responsibility to dismiss (not transfer unless it is done upon the application of a party). Like the Family Code, venue is quasi-jurisdictional in the Probate Code. A judgment is not void or subject to **collateral attack** if it is rendered in violation of the venue provisions, but the court has an affirmative obligation to ensure that the venue provisions are complied with.

Section 6 of the Probate Code provides for venue for the probate of wills and the administration of the estates of *decedents*, or deceased persons, as follows:

1. It provides that venue of suits seeking the probate of wills and the issuance of letters testamentary or the issuance of letters of administration are required to be filed in the county where the deceased resided prior to death, if in fact the deceased had a domicile or fixed place of residence in Texas. Case law indicates that *residence* as used in this statute means the same as it does in other areas of the law. *Residence* is the legal concept of the word rather than the factual concept. Your residence is where you intend to reside, regardless of where you are actually residing at the time. For example, a person moves to Houston for treatment of a disease for which there is not much hope of surviving. The intent is to return home in the event of recovery. That person's residence for the purpose of this statute is the county of origin rather than Harris County.

2. If the deceased person had no domicile or fixed place of residence in this state but died in this state, then venue is either in the county in which the principal estate is located or in the county of death.

One might ask why it would be necessary to probate the estate of a non-Texas resident in Texas. First, the general law in the United States is that a state does not recognize the power of the courts of other states over title to real property located in that state. This is the law in Texas also. Consequently, under the "full faith and credit" provisions of the United States Constitution, there are procedures that must be followed before a state is required to recognize the judicial acts of another state. The procedures that Texas has adopted to comply with the "full faith and credit" provisions of the U.S. Constitution are discussed in Chapter Twelve.

Regardless, if someone dies who is not a resident of the State of Texas but has all or substantially all of his property located there, the necessity of going through a probate procedure in his home state upon death, plus the added cost of going through the procedures provided for in Texas for the recognition of a foreign probate, are a greater expense than if that individual's estate was probated in the state of Texas in the first place.

For example, take an Iowa couple who have been coming to south Texas in the winter for years. Sometime before, they transferred ownership of their farm to their sons and daughters, perhaps retaining a life estate. They own no other real estate in Iowa. They have their money for the most part in a Texas bank or perhaps in joint accounts with their children in Iowa so that the children will have no trouble gaining access to those accounts upon their death. Their only real estate asset is a lot in a trailer subdivision that contains a double-wide trailer from which the axles have been pulled and that is permanently hooked up to utilities. Where is one going to probate the estate? If the estate is probated in Iowa, it could be extremely costly and time consuming, particularly in view of the independent administration that is authorized in Texas (to be discussed in Chapter Ten). If it is probated in Iowa, there is the expense then of going through the recognition procedures in Texas. To avoid the increased expense and delay, one would probate the estate originally in Texas rather than in Iowa.

3. If the deceased person had no domicile or fixed residence in this state and died outside the state, then venue is in any county where the nearest of kin reside or in the county in which the principal property is located if there are no kindred in this state.

4. Section 6 further provides that if an administration is only for the purpose of receiving governmental funds, then venue is in the county where the applicant lives, although citation must be served personally on the mother, father, surviving spouse, and/or adult children of the deceased person.

Section 610, which provides for venue in the case of the appointment of a guardian, is divided into four parts: The first provides for the appointment of a guardian of the person and/or the estate of an incapacitated person; the second provides for the appointment of a guardian of the person and/or the estate of an minor; the third deals with the appointment of a guardian in a will; and the fourth deals with a guardian appointed for a missing person.

The venue provisions for the appointment of a guardian for the person and/or an estate of an incapacitated person state that venue is in either the county in which the incapacitated person resides or in which the person is located on the date the application is filed, or in the county in which his principal estate is located at the time of the application.

Venue with regard to guardians of minors, is in the county where the parents of the minors reside. If the parents do not reside in the same county then venue is in the county in which the parent who is the managing conservator resides. In the case of a joint managing conservatorship, venue is in the county in which the parent who has the greater period of possession and access resides. If only one parent is living, venue is in the county in which that parent resides if that parent has custody. If both parents are dead but the minor had been in the custody of one of them, venue is in the county in which the last surviving parent having custody resided at the time of death. If the parents died simultaneously, then venue is in the county in which both resided if they resided in the same county.

In situations in which a guardian is appointed by a will, a matter that will be discussed later in this text, venue is either in the county in which the will has been admitted to probate, or in the county of the appointee's residence if the appointee resides in Texas, or in the county in which the ward's principal estate is located.

Finally, venue with regard to the estate of a missing person is in the county in which the spouse of the missing person resides. If there is no spouse, venue is in the county in which a parent or child of the missing person resides, or if neither of them exist, in the county where any next of kin resides.

Section 8 of the Texas Probate Code (or Section 611 as to incapacitated persons) provides for concurrent venue and for transfer: If two or more courts have concurrent venue of an estate and an application is filed in both, the court in which the application was filed first shall have jurisdiction to the exclusion of the other.

When probate applications are filed in more than one county, the court in which an application was filed first shall immediately proceed to determine whether it has venue under Sections 6 and 610 of the Probate Code. If it does have venue, the proceeding pending in the other court shall be dismissed. On the other hand, if the court determines that the other court has venue, then the court is required to transfer the proceeding to the other.

Sections 8(c) and 611(c) provide for transfer for the want of venue: If it appears to the court that the proceeding was commenced without venue at any time prior to the final decree, the court shall, on the application of an interested person, transfer the proceeding to the proper county. If there is no application of an interested person, the court is required to dismiss. The transfer for want of venue is accomplished by transmitting to the proper court the entire original file, together with a certified copy of all entries in the **minutes** made by the court lacking such jurisdiction.

Part two of Section 8(c) and Sections 612-614 allow transfers for the convenience of an estate by permitting the court to order proceedings transferred if it appears to the court that it would be in the best interest of the estate to do so.

Citations And Notices

Each part of the Texas Probate Code that relates to an individual procedure to be undertaken during administration of an estate contains a section dealing with the requirements of citation and/or notice under that specific procedure. These requirements will be discussed in later chapters of the book in regard to the individual procedures. However, the Probate Code contains some general provisions relating to citations and/or notices that are applicable to all procedures.

Before discussing those specific sections, a warning is appropriate. Many of the forms books show a form for a citation. In perhaps every county in the State of Texas, the clerk prepares the citation, and not the attorney representing the estate or the applicant. If the legal assistant, believing that the attorney's office must prepare the citation because of the mistaken impression conveyed by the forms book, prepares the citation, it will be useless. However, if the clerk does not follow the usual procedure of mailing a copy of the citation to the attorney's office, the legal assistant should check with the clerk's office to ensure that citation has been properly prepared and posted.

Section 33 is the most important of the statutes relating to citation and notice. It contains a number of different rules concerning both citation and other notices. (Section 632 has virtually the same provisions and is applicable to guardianships.) First, Section 33 provides that, even in those situations in which no citation or notice is required by the Probate Code, the court has discretion to require that notice be given and to prescribe the form and manner of the service and return thereof. Second, it provides that the county clerk shall issue all necessary citations, writs, and processes and all notices that are not required to be issued by the **personal representative** without an order of the court specifying the kind or type, unless such order is required by a provision of the code.

Next, section 33 provides for the contents of citations, writs, and notices, which affects the clerk more than it does someone preparing documents on behalf of an estate or an applicant. This portion of Section 33 has some significance if one claims that citation or other notice is insufficient or defective.

Section 33 goes on to say that if the Code requires a notice to be given or a person to be cited or notified and either no specific method of giving such notice or citing such person is provided or there is an insufficient or inadequate provision therefore, then the court shall by written order direct the form of notice and the manner of service and return.

Section 33 next provides that service of citation and/or notice upon a personal representative, that is, an executor or administrator, shall be by registered or certified mail to the attorney of record for such personal representative or, if there is no attorney, to the personal representative himself.

Section 33 provides for four methods for serving citations and notices:

1. **Personal service.** As in other civil suits, personal service means that the citation is served personally on the person who is to receive it, by a deputy sheriff, constable, or civil process server. If that person is represented by an attorney of record in the probate matters, service may be on the attorney of record rather than on the individual. This citation or notice is returnable at least 10 days after the date of service, excluding the date of service. The Rules of Civil Procedure provide that a citation in a civil case is returnable at 10 A.M. on the Monday following the expiration of 20 days from the date of service, excluding the date of service. This then is a

shortening of the period as required by the Texas Rules of Civil Procedure from 20 days to 10 days and is applicable to all of the methods of service except mailing. The person serving it must endorse on the citation certain information showing the service and the place and time of service, etc. This constitutes proof of service.

2. **Posting.** Most probate notices are posted, although newer code sections are making significant inroads in the number of notices or citations that are served by posting. Posting simply means that the clerk sends the citation to the sheriff or constable, who then takes the citation and posts or tacks it on a bulletin board at the courthouse door or at a place in or near the courthouse where public notices are customarily posted. The sheriff or constable is still required to endorse a return on the citation showing the time and place of posting. The date of posting then becomes the date of service.

3. **Publication.** In ordinary civil suits under the Rules of Civil Procedure, citations served by publication must be published three times. The Probate Code diminishes this to a single publication in a newspaper of general circulation in the county in which the probate proceedings are pending. The actual publication date is the date of service, and the return date is not less than 10 days from that date.

4. **Mailing.** If a citation or notice is required or permitted to be served by registered or certified mail, the clerk is required not only to issue the citation or notice but to mail the same. The citation or notice must be mailed with a restriction to deliver to the addressee only, with return receipt requested. A copy of the citation, together with a certificate of the clerk showing the fact and date of mailing, is required to be filed, and constitutes proof of service. If a return receipt is received, it must be attached to the certificate. If service is made by mail, then the date of mailing constitutes the date of service, but the return date is not less than 20 days later rather than 10 days. If the citation or notice served by mailing is returned undelivered, then a new citation or notice is issued, to be served by posting.

All citations and notices are returnable on the first Monday after service is perfected. Frequently, a firm is engaged to file some form of a probate proceeding, or the firm carries out one of the procedures within the administration of an estate that requires citation and the client is in an extreme hurry. Generally this is because he cannot gain access to bank accounts or other funds that he wants or needs or he is carrying out some transaction that will result in cash, such as sale of an estate asset. At any rate, there is often a rush, and because probate matters are returnable the Monday following the expiration of 10 days from the date of service, the timing of filing becomes important. If the application or other document is filed too late, then a week is lost.

The application can be filed any time in the week prior to the end of Thursday, assuming that the citation is posted before the end of business on Thursday, and end up with exactly the same return date. If the application is not filed timely enough to have citation issued and served by close of business on Thursday but rather is served on Friday, then the return date is a whole week later.

Many clerks have cutoff times on Thursday, so if the application is not filed by then, they will not prepare the citation and get it to the Sheriff for posting prior to the close of business on Thursday. In some counties, this is noon on Thursday and in others it is 3 or 4 o'clock in the afternoon. At least one county requires that the application be filed by close of business on Wednesday.

Section 33 also provides that once an application has been filed, someone interested in either the estate or welfare of a minor or incompetent may file a request with the clerk that such person be notified of any and all or of specifically designated motions, applications, or pleadings filed. The fees and cost for such notices are borne by the persons requesting them, and the clerk can require a deposit. If the clerk's requirements are met, then the clerk must send to that person, by ordinary mail, copies of any documents specified in the request.

Although there are other sections of the Probate Code that deal with citations and notices, the only one important to this discussion is Section 35, which provides that any person who is legally competent and interested in any hearing or proceeding in probate and who is entitled to notice may, in writing, waive notice of that hearing. Section 35 further provides that the guardian of an estate, a guardian ad litem, or a trustee may make such waiver on behalf of the person he represents. Further, a consul or the representative of a foreign government whose appearance has been entered on behalf of any person residing in a foreign country may make such waiver of notice.

Common Law and the Rules of Civil Procedure

Section 32 provides that the rights, powers, and duties of executor or administrator are governed by the principles of common law when those do not conflict with the Probate Code or other statutes of the State of Texas.

Section 22 provides that in all proceedings arising under the provisions of the Texas Probate Code, unless otherwise specified, the Rules of Civil Procedure and the Rules of Evidence shall be applicable to matters relating to discovery, witnesses and evidence.

Section 21 provides that in all contested probate and mental illness procedures in the district court, county court, or statutory probate courts, the parties are entitled to trial by jury.

There are within Chapter One of the Probate Code some miscellaneous sections that affect probate procedure. Among the more important are the following:

1. Section 9 provides that a defect in pleadings cannot affect the validity of any proceedings unless that defect is objected to in a timely manner and brought to the attention of the court.

2. Section 23 requires a judge sitting in probate matters to take judicial actions in open court rather than in chambers (the judge's office). This means the probate judge must render decisions and execute documents in open court that might otherwise be done in chambers. Still, there are some counties in which the judge hears probate matters in chambers.

3. Sections 24, 25, 26, and 27 allow the probate judge the use of ordinary civil sanctions to enforce his orders and decrees. The civil sanctions dealt with in these sections are provided for in the general law applicable to procedure in district and county courts. Section 24 provides for the enforcement of lawful orders against executors, administrators, and guardians by what is referred to as contempt, or attachment and imprisonment, for a period not to exceed three days for any one offense. Section 25 provides for *writs of execution*; that is, orders to a sheriff or constable directing him to seize property and to have it sold at public auction. Section 26 deals with *writs of attachment*; that is, orders to a sheriff or constable directing him to seize specified real or personal property and to deliver same to whomever the court shall specify. Section 27 deals with *specific performance*, which is a writ directed at private individuals directing them to comply with the terms of a legally enforceable contract.

4. Section 31 provides that a Bill of Review, sometimes referred to as an Equitable Motion for a New Trial, may be filed within two years of the decision, order, or judgment complained of. In the event the person was a minor or incompetent, he has two years from the removal of his disabilities to file. The ordinary law applicable to Bills of Review provide that they are available only to those persons who did not receive actual notice of the proceedings that resulted in the order, decree, or judgment complained of. Also, the general law provides that any person who has changed his position in reliance on the judgment, decree or order complained of and who was not a party to the proceeding shall be protected from any setting aside of a decision, judgment, or result by the Bill of Review.

Duties and Responsibilities of Probate Judges

Normally, a judge rendering a decision, order, decree or judgment in a civil suit is protected from liability arising out of that judicial action. This Principle of Judicial Immunity makes a judicial officer absolutely immune from any kind of liability whatsoever arising out of his duties as a judge. In Texas, this principle has been enforced strictly, even in circumstances in which the judge committed an illegal or unconstitutional act in a judicial capacity.

Section 36 of the Probate Code, however, provides that this immunity will not be applicable in probate matters. It makes it the duty of a probate judge to use reasonable diligence to see that estates are properly administered and to examine the condition of each estate annually. It further provides that should damage or loss result to estates or to minors and incompetents through the gross neglect of the judge to use reasonable diligence in the performance of his duty, he shall be liable for the same. Probate Code Section 19 also requires the judge of a court in which probate proceedings are pending to call the docket of all pending estates, both as to the probate docket and the claim docket, and make such orders as are necessary. Consequently, most probate judges are zealous in the review of pending probate matters and in requiring attorneys representing executors, administrators, and guardians to comply with the requirements of the Probate Code in order to protect themselves from liability.

In other civil suits, if the attorney fails to take any action over a period of time, the matter is dismissed for want of prosecution. The probate judge must see that necessary action is taken. In order to meet the duties under the Probate Code, he must review at least annually all pending probate matters to see if the Probate Code requires any action to be taken. If action is required, the judge will generally send a letter to the attorney and to the executor, administrator, or guardian notifying them that such action has not been taken and directing them to do so. If the action is not taken the judge may issue an order directing the executor, administrator or guardian to show cause why he should not be removed or otherwise punished for such neglect.

Probably every attorney who has practiced probate law has faced the situation in which he has lost all contact with the client and some document or action is due, perhaps overdue. The judge sends a notice to the attorney or perhaps even calls the attorney, but the attorney has absolutely no way to contact his client to try at least to get the client to comply. For this reason, client information should be as complete as possible, to aid in tracking down the client who moves without leaving a forwarding address. This should include, at a minimum, the name of the employer, the type of occupation, the name and address of at least one relative who will always know where the client is, and perhaps of at least one other person, say a friend, who could be relied upon to provide information concerning the client's whereabouts.

CHAPTER QUESTIONS AND EXERCISES

1. What courts exercise probate jurisdiction in the county in which you live?

2. Determine venue in the following situations:
   a. An individual dies after surgery at a hospital located in Fort Worth, Texas. He went there for diagnosis, treatment and recuperation, and because he was going to be there a long time he moved his family into a nearby apartment. His home is located in Abilene. You may determine the county in which a city is located by looking in a almanac or a directory of lawyers, among other sources.
   b. An individual dies while in Europe; he was a seaman and at sea for months, sometimes years, at a time. He entered the United

States Merchant Marine Service from Harris County, Texas, to which he returned when he was not at sea. He maintained an apartment in Harris County; however, he owned land and kept his money in a bank in South Padre Island, Texas.

c. An individual dies while on vacation in the State of Montana. He resided in California but, because he had been a resident of Texas prior to moving, all of his assets are located in Texas, primarily in Bexar County. He has close relatives residing in Travis County and in Nueces County.

d. An orphan has inherited his parents' estate which is in need of administration. Consequently, a guardian must be appointed. The orphan now lives in Valverde County with his aunt, although he resided with his parents in Lampasas County prior to his parents' death. The estate is located primarily in Lampasas County.

e. An incompetent is hospitalized at the State Hospital in San Antonio, Texas. His principal estate is located in Kleberg County, although his wife, who is going to apply to be guardian, resides in Nueces County.

f. An orphan's surviving parent died while residing in Pecos County. However, the orphan was not in the custody of the last surviving parent but rather in the custody of his maternal grandparents, who reside in Lubbock County. The estate left to the orphan by the will of the last surviving parent is located in Pecos County. The will appoints as guardian of the person and estate of the orphan a paternal uncle who resides in Hidalgo county.

3. How may citation be served in probate matters? Calculate the return date or the earliest date on which a probate matter could be heard that was filed on June 12 of the current year. If June 12 is not a weekday, use the next weekday date.

4. What are some of the methods by which a court sitting in probate can enforce its orders and decrees? Describe each.

5. Why is it that judges sitting in probate matters are generally more careful to see that all of the required procedures are complied with than for other civil suits?

2 DESCENT AND DISTRIBUTION
(Intestate Succession)

CHAPTER OBJECTIVES

Upon completion of this chapter, the student should be able to:

1. Understanding in general the Statutes of Descent and Distribution.
2. Apply the Statutes of Descent and Distribution in determining heirship under the following circumstances:
   a. Death of a married person who is survived by a spouse and no **descendants**.
   b. Death of a spouse who is survived by a spouse and descendants.
   c. Death of an unmarried person who is survived by children, parents, and/or brothers and sisters.
3. Determine when an **affidavit of heirship** can be used to reflect the passage of title to property upon the death of the owner.
4. Prepare an affidavit of heirship under each of the circumstances referred to in Objective 2.

CHAPTER GLOSSARY

Acknowledgment A statement by a person who has executed an instrument made to an authorized officer (normally a notary public) that she executed the instrument for the purposes and considerations therein expressed.

Adoption A legal process whereby, after termination of the parental rights of the natural parents by either death or legal process, parental rights are created in persons who are not the natural parents of a child.

Advancement Money lent by a parent to a child to be paid back by deducting it from the child's share of the parent's estate.

Affidavit of heirship A written statement of facts, made under oath, as to who the heirs of an intestate decedent are.

Affinity Relationship. In its narrowest sense, a relationship created by marriage; more commonly, any relationship, whether by blood or by marriage.

Ancestor A parent, grandparent, great-grandparent, etc.; someone related in the direct line of ascendancy.

Ascendant Synonym of ancestor.

Collateral kindred Relatives who are neither ascendants nor descendants, such as brothers, sisters, uncles, aunts, nieces, nephews, and cousins.

Community property Property acquired by either husband or wife during marriage, other than by way of gift, devise, descent, recovery for personal injury, or partition of community property.

Curtesy The estate that, under Common Law, a man was entitled to upon the death of his wife; generally, a life estate in one-third of the land that was owned by the wife. Applicable only if children were born of the marriage.

Decedent A deceased person. Used more frequently than any other such descriptive phrase by lawyers and others employed in the legal profession.

Descendants A son or daughter, a grandchild, a great-grandchild, or the like; someone related in the direct line of descent.

Devise The gift of real and/or personal property in a will. It may also be used as a verb. At common law, it referred to a gift of real property only. One who receives a devise is a devisee.

Dower The opposite of *curtesy*; the estate that a widow was entitled to in the property of a deceased husband. Did not require the birth of children.

Escheat The process by which monies and other personal property pass to the state if unclaimed for a certain length of time. This would include any portion of an estate either for which the heirs or devisee could not be determined or located or where there were no heirs.

Half blood When siblings have either the same mother or the same father, but not both.

Intestate To die without a will. It may be used as a noun, an adjective, or an adverb.

Intestate decedent Someone who has died without a will.

Joint tenancy A form of co-ownership of real or personal property in which each co-owner has a right of survivorship by which a deceased co-owner's interest vests in the surviving co-owner(s) rather than passing to the deceased co-owner's heirs or by her will.

Jurat The clause at the bottom of a sworn statement of fact that states who swore, and when, and is signed by a notary public or other officer competent to administer oaths.

Life estate A form of ownership of property in which one person, called a *life tenant*, has the use of and the right to receive the profits from the property during her life (or perhaps during the life of another). Upon the death of the life tenant (or the third person), the ownership of the property either vests in someone else, called a *remainderman*, or reverts to the *grantor* (the person who created the life estate in the first place).

Moiety Half of anything.

Partition The dividing of property or an estate between co-owners so that they no longer own in co-ownership but each owns her specific portion of the property or estate.

Per capita By heads. Denotes a method of dividing an estate so that all who bear the same relationship to an intestate decedent receive an equal share.

Per stirpes By stocks. Denotes a method of dividing the estate of an intestate decedent so that the descendants of a deceased heir take the share that the deceased heir would have received had she survived the decedent.

Remainder What remains of an ownership interest after a lesser ownership interest has been carved out. In this chapter, in connection with life estates, the ownership interest that remains after a life estate is carved out of fee simple title. The remainderman will receive absolute ownership when the person by whose life the estate is measured dies.

Separate property Property acquired by husband or wife prior to marriage and by way of gift, devise, descent, recovery for personal injury, or partition of community property during marriage.

Tenancy in common Co-ownership of real or personal property without a right of survivorship attached to such ownership. Unlike a joint tenancy, when a co-owner dies her interest descends and vests in her heirs or passes by her will.

Title insurance A policy of insurance issued by a title insurance agent on behalf of a title insurance underwriter after searching title to real property. It insures the accuracy of the search against defects in the title.

Whole blood When siblings have the same mother and father.

INTRODUCTION

One task that many legal assistants may be called on to carry out, whether in estate planning, probate, real estate, or other areas, is determinating who inherits from a person who died **intestate**. This requires familiarity with the laws of descent and distribution.

As discussed in Chapter One, the laws of descent and distribution have changed only a little from their beginnings in the custom and tradition of England, which was probably rooted in the Roman Civil Law. Actually, the laws of descent and distribution are not substantially different from those found in the Civil Law countries whose legal heritage came directly from Roman Law. In all of the European countries, the prime ingredient in a determination of who inherits in the absence of a will (once wills were recognized) was **affinity**, or how closely the **decedent** was related to the heirs. Add to this the generally accepted belief that **descendants** were to be preferred over **ascendants** and each country reached approximately the same conclusions as to who inherited.

Most of the Civil Law countries had an added problem to dispose of when the **intestate decedent** was married, because of the different treatment of property acquired during marriage. English Common Law provided that whoever acquired real or personal property owned it, whether or not they were married at the time. The only concession to the other spouse was to be found in the law of **Dower** and **Curtesy**.

The Civil Law countries took a different approach to marital property, or that property acquired during marriage. The philosophy of those countries was that, with some exceptions, property acquired by a spouse during marriage was actually acquired through the efforts of both spouses and was owned, jointly or in common, by both of the spouses. This theory came to be known as the Law of **Community Property** and was adopted by the Republic of Texas as the law of Texas, probably because to have done otherwise would have disrupted the ownership of lands already owned at the time of the creation of the Republic.

As a result of the categorizing of property as either separate or community, the Statutes of Descent and Distribution categorize real or personal property according to whether it was acquired during marriage or outside of marriage. Section 38 of the Texas Probate Code deals with **separate property**, that is, property that was acquired prior to marriage and as a result of gift, devise, descent, recovery for personal injury, or **partition** of community property. Section 45 governs the passage of community property. The other sections in

Chapter 2 of the Texas Probate Code, which is entitled "Descent and Distribution," provide for matters that are collateral to determining inheritance, sometimes relating both to taking property from a decedent's estate by inheritance and by will and sometimes having not much to do with inheritance at all.

Questions of determination of heirship are not limited to the practice areas of probate administration and estate planning. Problems dealing directly with or relating to inheritance arise frequently in real estate, or land title, matters. Sometimes in personal injury litigation, one must deal with matters of heirship. Any other practitioner can also easily find herself in a position in which an assessment of heirship must be made. To function well in the legal practice, students must understand intestate succession.

INTESTATE SUCCESSION—COMMUNITY PROPERTY

For the purposes of legal research in the area of inheritance, it is necessary to understand the application of the terms **per capita** (by heads) and **per stirpes** (by stocks.) Figure 2-1 shows an example of per capita inheritance; Figure 2-2 shows an example of per stirpes distribution. Probate Code Section 43 provides that if the class of possible heirs that will inherit under the Statutes of Descent and Distribution stand in the same degree of relationship to the descendant, they shall inherit per capita. However, when one or more of that class, but fewer than all, have died before the decedent, then the descendants of the deceased shall inherit only the portion of the decedent's estate that the deceased relative through whom they inherit would have received if alive, or such descendants will take per stirpes.

In Figure, 2-1, A, B, and C, being the children of the decedent and all being alive, will inherit per capita, or equally. In Figure 2-2, because of the prior death of A, A's children (A-1 and A-2) inherit only the portion of the estate that A would have inherited, or one-sixth each, that is, one-half of the third of the decedent's estate that A would have inherited had A survived the decedent.

Figure 2-1
Per Capita Inheritance

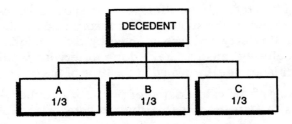

Figure 2-2
Per Stirpes Inheritance

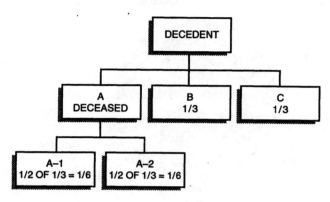

The 1993 amendment to Probate Code Section 45 makes an important change with reference to inheritance of community property. If a spouse dies *prior* to its effective date, September 1, 1993, the surviving spouse will inherit none of the one-half community property interest belonging to the deceased spouse, if the deceased was survived by children or by their descendants. In such case, the children or their descendants inherit all of the deceased spouse's community property, to the exclusion of the surviving spouse. As amended, Section 45 now provides that the deceased spouse's half of the community property passes to the surviving spouse, in the absence of a will, if either:

1. The deceased spouse leaves no children, or their descendants, surviving, or

2. The surviving spouse is the parent or **ancestor** of all of the deceased spouse's children or their descendants.

In the event the deceased spouse is survived by children or descendants who are not the children or descendants of the surviving spouse (i.e., children by a prior marriage), the children or other descendants inherit the community share of the deceased spouse. The surviving spouse keeps the half of the community property she already owns, but inherits none of the decedent's half.

Figure 2-3 illustrates what occurs if the deceased spouse has been survived by children who are not the children of the surviving spouse, where a child has predeceased the decedent and is survived by children of her own or by grandchildren of the deceased. The decedent's half of the community estate is divided into as many slices as there are children of the decedent still alive or children who having predeceased the decedent are survived by children of their own. Since there were three children and A and B are still alive, and since C, although having predeceased, is survived by C-1 and C-2, her children, the decedent's half of the community estate is divided into three slices: one to A, one to B, and one to C-1, C-2, and C-3, per stirpes.

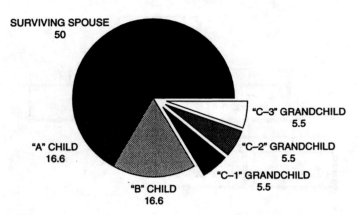

Figure 2-3
Division of Community Estate

It is essential to keep in mind that community property can exist only during a marriage. It ceases to exist at the dissolution of marriage by divorce or by death, and becomes a form of jointly owned property, through not community property. In order for Section 45 to come into play in an intestate death, the decedent must have been married at the time of death. If the decedent was not married at the time of death, Section 45 of the Probate Code cannot apply in any way to the determination of ownership and distribution of the decedent's estate.

When a marriage has been dissolved by divorce but an asset was not divided by the court's decree in the divorce, that asset is owned in a kind of **tenancy in common**. The ownership differs from a tenancy in common in that the Texas Family Code preserves the jurisdiction of the court that decreed the divorce to divide the property equitably (in the best interests of the parties) rather than equally.

To fully understand community property, it is necessary also to be familiar with the Texas Family Code. Texas Family Code Section 5.02 provides that there is a presumption that all property owned during marriage, or at the dissolution thereof, is community property. This presumption would probably also be applicable to the dissolution of marriage by death. To overcome this presumption, it is necessary to trace the ownership of the property back to the inception of title into one of the spouses and to establish that its character at the time of inception was separate or mixed. In other words, one must prove that at the time one of the spouses acquired ownership of the property, that spouse was not married or had received the property by way of gift, devise, inheritance, or the expenditure of separate property funds. For example, mixed property (part community and part separate property) results when a spouse uses separate funds as a down payment but creates a community debt for the payment of the balance of the purchase price. The property would then be separate to the extent of the down payment of separate funds and community to the extent that community indebtedness was created.

The Family Code is also applicable with regard to the definition of marriage; however, it makes no difference in the application of probate law whether the marriage was created in accordance with the statutory formalities or by common law. Recent changes in the Family Code require that a common law marriage be established within one year after the couple separates, or none will exist.

Marriage does not create a blood relationship. When one marries, one does not suddenly bear a blood relationship to the spouse; rather a contractual relationship has been created by operation of law. English Common Law characterized this relationship as the entry into a marital partnership. Partnership law provides that when a partner dies without a will, her blood relations, not the other partner, inherit her partnership interest. Section 45 of the Probate Code provides for the same result, at least to the extent that the decedent leaves children or their descendants surviving who are not also the children of the surviving spouse.

INTESTATE SUCCESSION—SEPARATE PROPERTY

The inheritance of separate property is determined in Section 38 of the Texas Probate Code. Section 38 is divided into two sections: Section 38(a) applies to the passage of separate property upon death where the decedent was not survived by a spouse. Section 38(b) provides for the situation in which a decedent is survived by a spouse and owns separate property at the time of her death.

Section 38(b)

Texas Probate Code Section 38(b) is probably the easier of the two sections to explain. Earlier in this chapter the English Law of Dower and Curtesy was mentioned. When the laws of intestate succession were arrived at in England, divorce was not permitted. English marital property law only had effect when one of the spouses died. The English law provided that property was owned by the spouse who had acquired the property during marriage. Still, the English law recognized that the other spouse had some part in the acquisition of new property, even though it was the separate property of the spouse who acquired it. When the spouse died, the other spouse received some interest in the property of the deceased spouse as compensation, called, in the case of a deceased husband, a dower interest and in the case of a deceased wife, a curtesy interest. This was mandatory and could not be changed by will; nor could property subject to a dower or curtesy interest be deeded away by one of the spouses before death without the consent of the other.

Texas law, in Section 38(b), recognizes this Law Dower and Curtesy, at least to some extent. It applies only to deaths without a will, and only to separate property, and does not affect or encumber the property while both spouses are alive. Remember that Section 38(b) applies only to the situation where the decedent owning separate property leaves a surviving spouse, and applies only to separate property and not to community property. Section 38(b) is then divided into two parts.

Part one of Section 38(b) deals with the situation where the decedent is survived by a child or children or their descendants. In that eventuality, the separate property of the deceased spouse is divided into *real property* (any ownership interest in land) and *personal property* (ownership interest in property other than land). As to the personal property, the surviving spouse receives one-third; and the balance goes to the child or children of the deceased or their descendants. As to the real property, the surviving spouse is entitled to an estate for life in one-third of the land or other real property ownership interests. This is a legal **life estate**, which is the right to the use of, possession of, and the enjoyment of the fruits from said property during the remainder of the life of the *life tenant* (surviving spouse), subject, however, to liability for waste. Upon the death of the surviving spouse, the ownership of the one-third that was subject to the life estate, or the **remainder**, vests in the child or children of the intestate and their descendants; the remaining two-thirds vests immediately in the child or children of the intestate and their descendants.

Part 2 of Section 38(b) provides that if the deceased spouse is not survived by a child, children, or their descendants, then the surviving spouse receives one-half of the decedent's separate real property and all of her separate personal property. This is fee simple ownership, not just a life estate. The remaining half of the real property then passes according to the provisions of Section 38(a), as if the deceased spouse had died leaving no spouse. However, if the decedent is not survived by a mother, father, brothers, sisters, or their descendants (nieces and nephews), then the surviving spouse receives all of the deceased spouse's separate property, both real and personal. Figure 2-4 illustrates the application of Section 38(b), part 1. Figure 2-5 depicts inheritance as provided for in Section 38(b), part 2, where the deceased spouse is survived by a father, mother, brothers, sisters, or the descendants of brothers or sisters. Figure 2-6 illustrates the situation under Section 38(b), part 2, where the deceased spouse is not survived by father, mother, brothers, sisters, or the descendants of brothers or sisters.

Figure 2-4
SECTION 38 (b) (1)
Separate Property Decedent Survived by Children

Separate Real Property

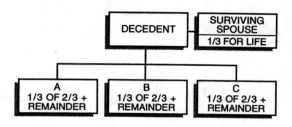

Separate Personal Property

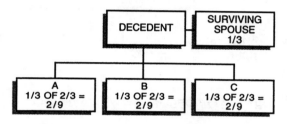

Figure 2-5
SECTION 38 (b) (2)
Separate Real Property No Children

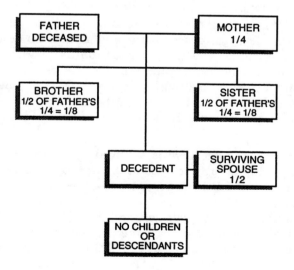

Separate Personal Property No Children

Figure 2-6
SECTION 38 (b) (2)
Separate Real Property No Children

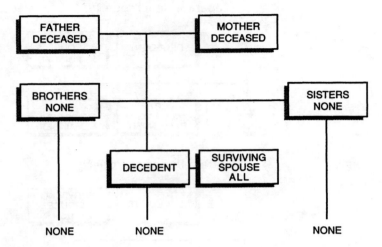

Separate Personal Property No Children

As previously stated, descendants are favored in inheritance law over ascendants. At each level of inheritance it is necessary first to look down from that level for descendants, and then, if no descendants are in existence, to look upwards to ascendants. And, per the prior discussion concerning per capita and per stirpes inheritance, when there is found a level of relationship in which there is a living heir, the inheritance is divided into as many parts as there ever were heirs in that level who are either still alive or survived by descendants who are alive.

In Figure 2-7, the decedent is survived by a wife and no children. His father and mother are deceased at the time of his death, and he had two brothers (B-1 and B-2) and a sister (S-1), but only one brother was still alive at the time of his death. The brother and the sister who predeceased the decedent each left children. Under Section 38(b)(2), half of the real property and all of the personal property passes to the surviving spouse. The one-half of the real property remaining passes according to the provisions of 38(a) (which will be discussed in the next subsection). It would first pass to the mother and father, BUT since the mother and father are deceased, it would then pass to the descendants of the mother and father, which would be the brothers and sisters of the decedent. Since one brother is living, a level of relationship has been reached in which at least one heir is alive. Stopping at that level, the estate is divided into as many portions as the number of original members of that relationship who are either still alive or survived by descendants. This creates three portions. The brother who is still alive receives one of the portions, a third of one-half of the estate of the decedent. The surviving child of S-1 receives the portion that S-1 would have inherited, one-third of one-half, had she been alive at the time of decedent's death. The surviving children of B-2 split the remaining portion, which B-2 would have inherited.

If all the brothers and sisters had survived the decedent, they would have inherited per capita. Because that is not the case, the descendants of the deceased brothers and sisters inherit per stirpes. They receive the share or portion that would have been inherited by their parent had that parent survived the decedent.

Figure 2-7
SECTION 38 (b) (2)
Separate Real Property No Children

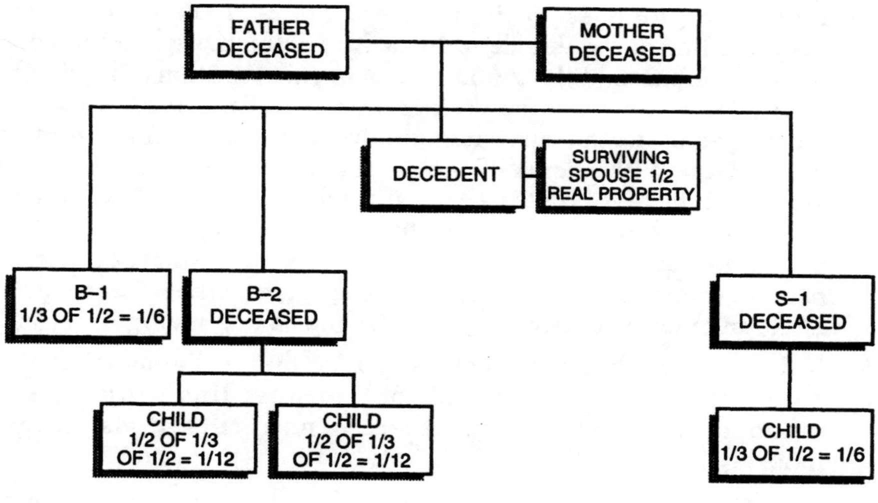

Separate Personal Property No Children

When an heir dies prior to the decedent, the share that she would have inherited passes to her descendants, not by inheritance from the parent, but by inheritance from the original decedent.

Section 38(a)

Section 38(a) provides that upon the death of an intestate who leaves no husband or wife, his estate shall descend and pass in the following order:

1. To his children and their descendants. Figure 2-8 illustrates this with a per stirpes distribution to the children of a deceased child.

2. If there are no children or their descendants, to his father and mother in equal portions. However, if either parent is dead, the estate shall be divided into two equal portions: one passes to the surviving parent of the decedent, and one passes to the brothers and sisters of the decedent or to their descendants. If there are no brothers, sisters, or descendants of brothers or sisters, all of the decedent's estate is inherited by the surviving father or mother. See Figure 2-9, in which both the mother and father are alive, and Figure 2-10, in which one parent has died and decedent is survived by a brother and a sister.

3. If neither father nor mother survives the decedent, to the brothers and sisters and/or their descendants. See Figure 2-11.

4. If there are none of the aforesaid, the estate is divided into two **moieties:** one goes to the paternal line and the other to the maternal line of decedent. In each line, the moiety would go to the grandfather and the grandmother in equal portions. If only one is alive, the moiety is be divided into equal portions, with one portion going to the surviving grandparent and the other portion going to the descendants of the deceased grandparent, that is, the aunts and uncles of the decedent. If there are no such descendants, the entire moiety is inherited by the surviving grandfather or grandmother. If neither grandfather nor grandmother of that particular line survives, the entire moiety goes to their descendants, aunts and uncles of decedent, cousins, and so on. See Figure 2-12.

5. If there are no descendants of the grandfather and grandmother in a particular line, one would look up that line to the great-grandparents. At this point, there is no further division into moieties.

The division into moieties that occurs at the level of the grandparents is permanent, and each moiety stays in the paternal or maternal line until that line is exhausted. If efforts to find ascendants or descendants of ascendants in one line are futile, then the moiety shall pass to the ascendants of the other line. No portion of the estate will **escheat** to the state unless no ascendants are discovered in both lines.

At the level of the great-grandparents of the decedent in the paternal line, there are four great-grandparents. The paternal moiety is then divided into four shares, one to each great-grandparent. However, if any of the great-grandparents has died prior to the decedent, her share will descend and vest to the deceased great-grandparent's descendants. If the great-grandparents have no descendants, the share will go to the surviving great-grandparent.

If one set of great-grandparents is deceased and the other set alive, and there are no descendants on the side of the deceased great-grandparents, the share they would have otherwise received passes to the surviving great-grandparents; if only one is alive, she receives the entire moiety. This is the result only if there is no living descendants of any of the great- grandparents.

Figure 2-8
SECTION 38 (a) (1)
Decedent Survived by Children

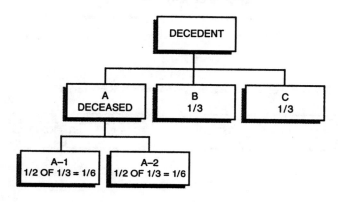

Figure 2-9
SECTION 38 (a) (1)
No Children

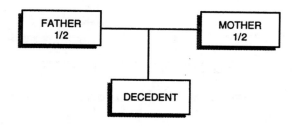

Figure 2-10
SECTION 38 (a)
No Children, One Parent Deceased

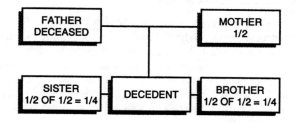

Figure 2-11
SECTION 38 (a)
No Children, Both Parents Deceased

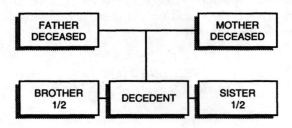

Figure 2-12
SECTION 38 (a)
Both Parents Deceased Without Descendants

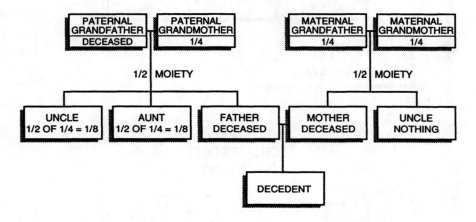

MATTERS AFFECTING THE RIGHT TO INHERIT

There are several other sections of the Probate Code that bear on the right to inherit.

Section 37

Practice in the area of real estate transactions goes hand in glove with practice in the area of probate administration. Probably the most common title defect is that created by the death of a record title holder of real estate. Here is a typical scenario:

A real estate sales contract is brought into a law office in which Jane Smith is selling a house. When title is checked, a copy of the deed is obtained, or an owner's title policy commitment is received from the title company, and it is discovered that title is vested in Ed Smith and wife, Jane Smith. The legal assistant or lawyer calls Mrs. Smith or her realtor™ and is told that Mr. Smith is dead. When asked what has been done about Mr. Smith's estate and she states that everything is taken care of and that Mrs. Smith will bring in the paperwork the next day. The next day, Mrs. Smith shows up in the office and either delivers the original will of Ed Smith, which leaves his entire estate to her, or perhaps produces copies of both a marriage certificate establishing her marriage to Mr. Smith and a death certificate verifying the death of Mr. Smith.

According to Section 37 of the Probate Code, are these things sufficient? Does anything else have to be done in order to properly reflect the passage of title by death as to Ed Smith's one-half interest? Section 37 plainly says that if anyone dies leaving a lawful will, her entire estate will vest immediately in the devisee named in the will. It would seem then that, at least in the first case, since there was a will leaving everything to Mrs. Smith, that Mr. Smith's estate would vest immediately in Mrs. Smith.

The first portion of Section 37 contains some catchwords; specifically the phrase "leaving a lawful will." This refers to the requirement that the will must be executed with all formalities and solemnities required by law and not canceled, revoked, or voided after its execution. The narrow definition of the word *probate* refers to the act of a court in determining that a will is the last and lawful will of a decedent. Therefore, it is the probate court that determines whether a will is lawful. In fact, Section 94 of the Probate Code provides that, except with respect to foreign wills, no will is effectual for the purpose of proving title to real or personal property unless the will has been admitted to probate in this state.

What about the second scenario? Are the copies of the marriage certificate and the death certificate sufficient? Probate Code Section 45 provides that Mr. Smith's children by a former marriage, if any, would inherit his half of the community estate rather than Mrs. Smith. Nothing Mrs. Smith has brought in suggests there are children. Section 37 clearly says that whenever a person dies intestate, all of her estate shall vest immediately in her heirs at law. The question is: How does the legal assistant establish acceptably who the heirs at law of Ed Smith are?

In the second situation, it is more obvious that the information is insufficient to establish the identity of the heirs. Even if Mrs. Smith were to state that Mr. Smith never had any children, such information must be filed of record so that others dealing with title to the land would be placed on notice that title passed by intestacy.

In this situation, there are three methods by which heirship can be determined and shown of record. The first is through an administration of the intestate decedent's estate. This could be either independent or dependent, as will be discussed, respectively, in Chapters Ten and Eleven. The second method is through a determination of heirship as provided by Chapter 3 of the Texas Probate Code, which will be discussed in Chapter Twelve of this text. The third is by an affidavit of heirship, which will be discussed in the last section of this chapter.

Even though the estate vests immediately in the devisee or the heirs, Section 37 provides that if an executor or administrator is appointed in the estate, that executor or administrator shall have the right to possess the estate as it existed at the death of the testator or intestate. This is for the purpose of administration. The executor or administrator has the right, under prescribed circumstances, to sell portions of the decedent's estate for purposes of estate administration.

Section 37A and 37B

Texas Probate Code Section 37A provides a method by which an heir or a devisee may renounce or disclaim all or a portion of the property devised to her in a will, or inherited by her in the case of an intestate death. This disclaimer must be in writing, acknowledged before a notary public, and filed, in the case of a present interest, not later than nine months after the death of the decedent, and in the case of a future interest not later than nine months after the event when the taker of the property is finally ascertained and her interest indefeasibly vested.

The written memorandum of disclaimer must be filed in the probate court in which the decedent's will has been probated or proceedings for the administration of her estate have been commenced. If either the administration has been closed, a year has expired after the issuance of letters testamentary in an independent administration, no will was probated, or there was no administration commenced, then the written memorandum or disclaimer must be filed with the county clerk in the Official Real Property Records. If the provisions of 37A are complied with, the disclaimer becomes effective as of the date of the death of the decedent, and the property disclaimed passes as if the person disclaiming had predeceased the decedent. Section 37A was inserted into the Texas Probate Code to take advantage of provisions of the Internal Revenue Code.

A typical situation in which the disclaimer is used occurs when a will devises a substantial amount of property to an individual. The will provides that if the individual predeceases the testator, the property will go instead to the children of the original devisee. The original devisee doesn't want more money or property, because the income from it will increase her income tax liability and the federal estate tax due upon her death. Through this procedure, she can renounce or disclaim the devise or inheritance, and the property will pass directly to the children and will not be considered a gift by the original devisee. It will never become a part of the original devisee's estate for the calculation of federal estate taxes when the original devisee dies. Should the children be minors and the will does not create a trust for them, a disclaimer will result in the necessity of appointing a guardian to administer the property. This can lead to significant expense.

Section 37B allows a devisee or heir to assign her right in devised or inherited property to a third person. Section 37B provides that the assignment can be filed in the same manner as a disclaimer. Assignment under Section 37B is a gift, not a disclaimer or renunciation. It is therefore subject to gift tax under the Federal Estate and Gift Tax provisions in the Internal Revenue Code. And if it is not subject to the gift tax exclusion, it is carried back into the original devisee's or heir's estate for calculating federal estate taxes upon death. Gift and estate taxes will be discussed more fully in Chapter Fifteen of this text. Although, Section 37A provides that a disclaimer is effective against creditors of the person executing the disclaimer, an assignment under 37B is not effective against creditors of the person who is assigning.

Section 40

Section 40 of the Texas Probate Code provides that, for inheritance purposes, **adoption** is to be treated the same as a natural birth. An adopted child inherits from her adoptive parents, and they from her, just as if she had been born naturally to them. Section 40 also preserves the right of the adopted child to inherit from and through her natural parents while terminating the right of the natural parents to inherit from the child. The Texas Family Code provides that this right of inheritance from and through the natural parents can be terminated in the decree of adoption or termination of parental rights. Generally, the court does terminate inheritance rights from and through natural parents, probably to remove one potential reason for later opening the adoption file.

Section 41(b)

Probate Code Section 41(b) deals with inheritance in regard to heirs of the whole blood and the half blood. This relates to intestate succession where there are **collateral kindred** of both the **whole blood** and the **half blood**—generally, brothers and sisters, some of whom shared two common parents, both mother and father, and others who shared only a single parent, either mother or father. Section 41(b) applies only when someone inherits from a brother or sister related by the half blood.

To illustrate the application of the whole-blood and half-blood rules, assume that a man and a woman are married and have three children. The man dies, then the woman remarries a man and has two more children. In Figure 2-13, the children from the first marriage are depicted as A, B, and C and the children from the second marriage as X and Y. Section 41(b) comes into play when A dies, is not survived by a spouse, has no descendants, and her mother and father have predeceased her also. Probate Code Section 38(a) provides that the brothers and sisters inherit.

B and C share two common parents with A and therefore are related by the whole blood, while X and Y share only a single common parent with A and are related to her by the half blood. Section 41(b) provides that each of the heirs of the half blood inherit only half as much as each of those of the full blood. In other words, the heirs of the whole blood inherit two shares to each share inherited by the heirs of the half blood. To calculate the fractions of inheritance, one adds up the number of shares required to give each whole-blood sibling two shares and each half-blood sibling one share. B and C would each receive two shares, for a total of four. X and Y would each receive one share, for a total of two. Since 4 + 2 = 6, there must be six shares to make the calculations come out right. B and C each get two shares; consequently, they get two-sixths, or one-third, of A's estate.

Figure 2-13
SECTION 41 (b)
Whole Blood and Half Blood

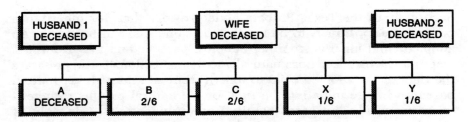

Section 42

The inheritance rights of illegitimate children are covered in Section 42 of the Texas Probate Code, which provides that a child is always a child of her biological or adoptive mother. In other words, a child is always legitimate as to her mother.

With regard to the father, Section 42(b) provides that a child is the child of her biological father if the child either is born under the circumstances described in Section 12.02 of the Family Code, has been adjudicated to be the child of the father by court decree as provided for in Chapter 13 of the Texas Family Code, or was adopted by the father, or if the father executed a statement of paternity as provided in Section 13.22 of the Texas Family Code. The execution of a statement of paternity is of no legal effect under the Texas Family Code, except under Section 12.02, unless a decree of paternity is thereafter entered by the court. It is, however, given legal effect under the Probate Code.

Section 41(b) also gives the probate court the power to determine paternity for the purpose of inheritance only. Should the court find, by clear and convincing evidence, that the decedent was the biological father of the child, then the child would be treated as any other child of the decedent's for the purposes of inheritance.

Section 44

Section 44 deals with **advancements**; which are advances, or loans, against an inheritance. A typical situation would be when a daughter goes to her father to request a loan for the purpose of entering a business. Foreseeing a problem with the daughter's ability to repay the loan, he says to the daughter, "When I die, you will inherit at least

$100,000. Rather than loan you the money and have you repay me, I am simply going to give you an advance on that inheritance." Suppose that the advancement was $50,000. When the father dies, the estate actually amounts to $200,000, half going to the daughter and half to the son. If the probate court determines that the $50,000 was an advancement, it is added to the estate as if the daughter had repaid it, which creates a total estate of $250,000. The estate is divided in half, $125,000 to the son and $125,000 to the daughter. However, since the daughter has already received $50,000 of that, she gets $75,000 and the son gets $125,000.

Section 44 goes on to provide that an inter vivos transfer is not an advancement unless there is a contemporaneous writing by the decedent or an acknowledgment by the heir that the transfer is an advancement. At Common Law, this method of handling advancements was referred to as "bringing the advancement into hotchpot". The term *hotchpot* was also used in Section 44 prior to the 1993 amendments, and will continue to be used in legal circles on the rare occasion when advancements occur. *Hotchpot* refers to the kettle, or hot pot, that hung on a crane in feudal fireplaces or hearths and into which were scraped leftovers from meals. This allowed the cumulative leftovers to be kept hot, preventing spoilage, and providing a hot meal at other than family mealtimes.

Section 47

Section 47 is often referred to as the simultaneous death provision of the Probate Code. In some situations, the survival of one person by another can make a tremendous difference in inheritance, as to who gets property under a will, who gets the proceeds of an insurance policy, or what happens to community property upon the death of the spouses. A couple of examples will illustrate this:

A will provides that a substantial portion of the testator's property goes to X, but that if X predeceases the testator, it goes to Y, who is not related to X. The testator and X die at nearly the same time. If it is determined that X predeceased the testator, Y gets the property. If, on the other hand, it is determined that the testator died before X, then X inherited by reason of his short survival and the property devised to him will pass to X's heirs.

Another example is derived from a trial decided prior to the amendment in 1979 providing for survival by 120 hours. A childless couple was killed in a one-car accident somewhere near San Antonio. All of the couple's property was community property and they had no children. The husband was survived only by brothers and sisters, as was the wife. The medical testimony stated that the injuries to both were so massive that they both had died instantaneously. This testimony was rebutted by photographs showing bloody claw marks on the headliner above the passenger seat where the wife had been seated. Obviously, the wife had lived long enough after her injuries to try to claw her way out of the car.

The old version of Section 47 provided that if the husband and wife died simultaneously, half of the community estate would pass as if the husband had survived and the other half would pass as if the wife had survived. However, the jury found that the wife had survived the husband and in that brief moment the wife inherited the husband's half of the community estate. When she died, both halves went to her siblings, and the husband's siblings received nothing.

In order to prevent this type of occurrence, the legislature amended Section 47 to require survival by 120 hours. The 120 hours was chosen because medical science at that time concluded that if someone survived a traumatic injury by 120 hours and then died, they did not die from the original injury itself but instead from complications caused by either the injury or the treatment. Therefore, the heir must now survive the intestate decedent by at least 120 hours or she will be treated as if she had predeceased the intestate decedent. The same rule applies in other situations: The devisee must survive the testatrix, the beneficiary of an insurance policy must survive the insured, and the joint tenant must survive the other joint tenant, all by at least 120 hours. With regard to community property, unless either the husband or wife survived the other by 120 hours, one- half of the community property would pass as if each had survived the other. Section 47 also allows for changing the effect of the section by specifically providing for such change in a will, life insurance policy, living trust, or **joint tenancy** agreement.

AFFIDAVIT OF HEIRSHIP

Earlier, the affidavit of heirship was mentioned as one of three methods by which the passage of title upon intestacy may be reflected of record. The affidavit of heirship is used primarily to establish the facts of inheritance of the real property of an intestate decedent. In this connection it is important to ensure that requirements of **title insurance** underwriters are complied with so that the affidavit of heirship will be acceptable to such underwriters when real property belonging to the estate is sold.

Prior to the passage in 1993 of the so-called Omnibus Probate Act, there was neither statutory nor case law authorization for the use of affidavits of heirship. Regardless, through custom, the affidavit of heirship has received widespread acceptance by title insurance underwriters and others working with title to real estate.

The 1993 changes to the Probate Code added Section 137(c) to the provisions relating to small estates. (Small estates are discussed in Chapter Twelve.) This provides that an affidavit that meets the requirements of Section 137(a) and is also filed in the deed records will transfer title to the heirs as to homestead only. (Apparently, the legislature forgot that in 1989 they had changed the name of the deed records to "Official Real Property Records.") That subsection further contains language protecting a good-faith purchaser for value relying on such an affidavit from a claim of an undisclosed heir.

One problem that could arise from the passage of Section 137(c) is that underwriters may limit the use of affidavits of heirship to homestead property, whereas they have not done so in the past. Another problem is with the form of the affidavit, which will be discussed shortly.

Title to personal property can sometimes be cleared with the use of an affidavit of heirship. Infrequently, banks will accept an affidavit of heirship for transferring funds that had belonged to the deceased to new accounts in the names of the heirs or simply for allowing the heirs access to those funds. The Texas Department of Transportation uses an affidavit of heirship on a promulgated form for transferring title to motor vehicles from a decedent to an heir. The form is signed by the heirs under oath and contains a place where the heirs can designate an individual to be the title holder.

For the most part, however, one cannot use affidavits of heirship to reflect the ownership of stock, U.S. Savings Bonds, bank accounts, or instruments of indebtedness. To solve all the problems of an estate that owns assets such as these, other methods must be used. Unless the assets have been set up prior to death so they never become an asset of the estate by the use of trusts, joint tenancy, or joint accounts, an affidavit of heirship probably will not be acceptable, and an administration of the estate or determination of heirship may be required.

On many occasions the problems created by the death of a record title holder of real estate will not be dealt with until the heirs try to sell a piece of real property that had belonged to the intestate decedent. In these cases the title insurance agent often will suggest an affidavit of heirship as a possible means of clearing title. The affidavit will have to meet the requirements of the particular title insurance underwriter, generally that it be signed by two disinterested persons, that is, persons who are not heirs and who are not related to the decedent. If, however, Section 137(c) is construed to be mandatory, then the heirs, as well as two disinterested persons, will have to sign the affidavit.

An affidavit of heirship that complies with the requirements of most title insurance underwriters is given in Form 2-1. This form is designed for use when the real property was the homestead of a husband and wife and the husband has died leaving no descendants. Where there is no pending sale of real property or where there is a sale of real property without title insurance, the last paragraph of the form would be deleted. Form 2-2 is an affidavit to be used when a husband has died and been survived by spouse and children. In this event, either the children will be required to convey title to the surviving spouse or all will have to sign the deed to the new purchaser. The children must be adults, or the affidavit of heirship will not solve all problems.

Neither form complies with the requirement of Section 137(c) regarding signatures of the heirs and the listing of all assets and liabilities. Many persons will be reluctant to spread a list of their assets and debts on the public records. If, however, the title insurance underwriters require this, the Small Estate Affidavit found as Form 12-12 (in Chapter Twelve), minus the order of the court, which is unnecessary, complies with 137(c).

If some of the heirs are minors, some lawyers may still use an affidavit of heirship, combining it with either a guardianship or the sale of a minor's interest in real property under Probate Code Section 889(a). Guardianship and the sale of a minor's interest in land will be dealt with later in this text.

The affidavit of heirship can be converted to meet any inheritance situation. Title insurance underwriters, however, have been reluctant to accept them when the chain of inheritance is more distant than brothers and sisters or nieces and nephews. Title underwriters will not accept affidavits of heirship where there is a pending administration or there seems to be a need for an administration. Some underwriters require that four years must have passed since the death of the decedent, though most do not. This four-year requirement is based on a Probate Code provision that requires administration of estates to be opened within four years of death. Some will accept an affidavit of heirship in lieu of the probating of a will, some will not, and some will require the passage of four years before accepting an affidavit instead of the probating of a will.

Most underwriters require the affidavit of heirship to contain the following information:

1. The name of the decedent, preferably as it appears in the deed whereby the decedent took title to the real property involved. If the decedent owns more than one piece of property and the deeds used different names, then "also known as," or "a/k/a," should be used to show all names. The same is true if the deed shows one name and a will shows another.

2. The date of death of the decedent.

3. The name of the surviving spouse, if any. If a spouse has predeceased the decedent referred to in the affidavit and that spouse's estate has been taken care of by either prior affidavit of heirship or probate proceedings, the name of that spouse and a reference to the procedures that cleared title to that spouse should be mentioned.

4. Date of marriage to the surviving spouse and prior marital history.

5. Children born or adopted to the decedent, together with an affirmative statement that these were the only children born to or adopted by or recognized by the decedent prior to death.

6. Regarding children: whether they are adult at the time of the execution of the affidavit, whether they are married and if so to whom, and their residence address. If one of the children predeceased the decedent and left no descendants, that fact should be shown. If the predeceasing child left descendants, their names, ages, spouses, and residence addresses should be shown.

7. A statement as to whether the decedent left a will. If there was a will, the original should be attached as an exhibit to the affidavit of heirship and filed along with the heirship affidavit.

8. A legal description of any real property owned by the decedent. Section 137(c) requires that all assets and liabilities be listed.

9. A statement that there is no necessity for administration on the decedent's estate because there are no unpaid debts and no federal estate taxes or Texas inheritance taxes due against the estate.

The affidavit of heirship must contain a **jurat**, which is the portion of the affidavit signed by the notary public and that starts out "subscribed and sworn." This is necessary for the affidavit to be an affidavit. It is no longer necessary that the affidavit also contain an **acknowledgment**. Forms 2-1 and 2-2 contain an acknowledgment for the purpose of illustration and because many attorneys preparing affidavits of heirship still include an acknowledgment. The acknowledgment is the portion which is signed by the notary public that begins "before me, the undersigned authority."

In the case of an affidavit of heirship being used when the decedent left a will, the requirements of one of the local title agents should be determined. There is a considerable division among underwriters as to the acceptability of affidavits of heirship when there is a will that can be probated. Most underwriters will accept the affidavit of heirship with a will attached if four years have elapsed from the date of the decedent's death. Only a few will accept it within four years. If there is any chance that real property is going to be sold by the current clients within four years, it is necessary to find out if there is a local title insurance agent who will accept the affidavit of heirship with a will attached instead of probating the will. Then deeds will have to be executed not only by those shown as heirs in the affidavit but also by those named devisee in the will. Usually these are the same persons, but not always.

When describing the heirs, it is important that factual terms be used rather than conclusions. Following is an example of language to be inserted in affidavits.

Example 2-14

He was never married. His parents were John Edwards, who died December 2, 1982, and Pearl Edwards who died August 25, 1990. In addition to John Edwards, Jr., three other children were born to John and Pearl Edwards. They are:

Perkin Edwards, who is alive and married to Pasquela Edwards.

Prath Edwards, who died at the age of three and who left no descendants.

Priscilla Edwards Samson, who died April 1, 1979, leaving two children, Sissy Samson and Sam Samson, who are both adults and living at this time.

CHAPTER QUESTIONS AND EXERCISES

1. Who inherits the community property of an intestate decedent?

2. Determine who inherits and in what fractions in the following fact situations:

    a. Sydney Smith dies, survived by his wife and two children. Determine inheritance as to Sydney's separate property.

    b. Charles Carter dies. He never married and has no children. His father and two brothers survive him.

    c. George Grady dies. He never married and has no children. He was an only child and his parents predeceased him. None of his grandparents were alive at the time of this death. All of his uncles and aunts are still alive, three on the paternal side and two on the maternal side.

    d. Sam Spade dies. His wife predeceased him. Three children were born to him, but two of those had already died prior to his death. One child was survived by two children, and the other was survived by three.

3. What is the procedure for and the effect of a disclaimer by an heir or devisee?

4. Darla Daring marries Al Adams. They have three children and then Al accidently ingests rat poison and dies. Darla then has a child out of wed-lock by an unknown male. Finally she marries John Jones, and they have four children. When Darla dies, is there a whole-blood-half-blood situation as to the estate of Darla Daring? Who inherits from Darla, and in what fraction?

5. Continuing the same fact situation as in Exercise 4 above, Darla is now dead. Her children from her first marriage are Al Jr., Darlene, and Ralph. Al Jr. has just died. The child born out of wedlock is named Luvie. The children from Darla's second marriage are Gus, Walther, Aire, and Earl. Who inherits Al Jr.'s estate, and in what fraction?

6. Prepare an affidavit of heirship for the family situation given in Question 2(d). Sam Jr. died intestate April 8, 1992. He owned property described as: "Lot 21, Block TWO (2), Laguna Shores, an addition to the City of Corpus Christi, as shown by map or plat of record in Volume 22, at Page 321, of the Map Records of Nueces County, Texas." Make up any other information or names necessary.

7. Prepare an affidavit of heirship for the family situation shown in Question 2(b).

8. Charles died on February 11, 1987, with a will that left everything to his parents or to their survivor. Is this an appropriate situation for an affidavit of heirship? Explain your answer.

Form 2-1: Heirship Affidavit (No Will)

STATE OF TEXAS   ) (
COUNTY OF NUECES   ) (

HEIRSHIP AFFIDAVIT

BEFORE ME, the undersigned, a Notary Public in and for the State of Texas, on this day personally appeared JOHN CHASE and EDNA BROWN, to me well known, and who, after being by me duly sworn, depose and say that we were well acquainted with PETER SMITH during his lifetime. He was married to PAULA SMITH on July 4, 1946, and was still married to her at the time of his death. They had as issue of this marriage two (2) children, to-wit:

PAUL SMITH, who is married to PEGGY SMITH, and PENELOPE SMITH, who is single, who are adults and living at this time, and there were no other children born to or adopted by the deceased during his lifetime.

PETER SMITH died intestate on January 2, 1992, and no probate has been filed or is contemplated upon his estate, as there are no inheritance taxes due the State or Federal Government, no unpaid bills of any nature, and no necessity for administration of such estate, and no other than the following was owned by the deceased at the date of death:

Lot Two (2), Block Fourteen (14), JOLLYTIME, an Addition in the City of Corpus Christi, Nueces County, Texas, according to map or plat thereof, of record at Volume 37, Page 221, Map Records, Nueces County, Texas.

The undersigned acknowledges that Corpus Christi Title Co. and its underwriter are relying upon the truth of the facts stated in this Affidavit in issuing Owner's and/or Mortgagee's Policies of Title Insurance in connection with its GF# 63,776.

_____
JOHN CHASE

_____
EDNA BROWN

SWORN TO AND SUBSCRIBED before me by JOHN CHASE, on _____, 1994.

_____
Notary Public, State of Texas

STATE OF TEXAS   ) (
COUNTY OF NUECES   ) (

This instrument was acknowledged before me on the _____ day of _____, 1994, by JOHN CHASE.

_____
NOTARY PUBLIC, STATE OF TEXAS

SWORN TO AND SUBSCRIBED before me by EDNA BROWN, on _____, 1994.

_____
NOTARY PUBLIC, STATE OF TEXAS

STATE OF TEXAS   ) (
COUNTY OF NUECES   ) (

This instrument was acknowledged before me on the _____ day of _____, 1994, by EDNA BROWN.

_____
NOTARY PUBLIC, STATE OF TEXAS

PREPARED IN THE LAW OFFICE OF:

RETURN TO:

Form 2-2: Heirship Affidavit (Will)

STATE OF TEXAS   ) (
COUNTY OF NUECES   ) (

HEIRSHIP AFFIDAVIT

BEFORE ME, the undersigned, a Notary Public in and for the State of Texas, on this day personally appeared JOHN CHASE and EDNA BROWN to me well known, and who, after being by me duly sworn, depose and say that we were well acquainted with PETER SMITH during his lifetime. He was married to PAULA SMITH on July 4, 1946, and was still married to her at the time of his death.

They had as issue of this marriage no children and there were no other children born to or adopted by the deceased during his lifetime.

PETER SMITH died on January 2, 1992, leaving a will, the original of which is attached hereto as a Muniment of Title. No probate has been filed or is contemplated upon his estate, as there are no inheritance taxes due the State or Federal Government, no unpaid bills of any nature, and no necessity for administration of such estate, and no other property other than the following was owned by the deceased at the date of death.

Lot Two (2), Block Fourteen (14), JOLLYTIME, an Addition in the City of Corpus Christi, Nueces County, Texas, according to the map or plat thereof, of record at Volume 37, Page 221, Map Records, Nueces County, Texas.

The undersigned acknowledges that Corpus Christi Title Co. and its underwriter are relying upon the truth of the facts stated in this Affidavit in issuing Owner's and/or Mortgagee's Policies of Title Insurance in connection with its GF# 63,776.

_____
JOHN CHASE

_____
EDNA BROWN

SWORN TO AND SUBSCRIBED before me by JOHN CHASE, on _____, 1994.

_____
Notary Public, State of Texas

STATE OF TEXAS   ) (
COUNTY OF NUECES   ) (

This instrument was acknowledged before me on the _____ day of _____, 1994, by JOHN CHASE.

_____
NOTARY PUBLIC, STATE OF TEXAS

SWORN TO AND SUBSCRIBED before me by EDNA BROWN, on _____, 1994.

_____
NOTARY PUBLIC, STATE OF TEXAS

STATE OF TEXAS   ) (
COUNTY OF NUECES   ) (

This instrument was acknowledged before me on the _____ day of _____, 1994, by EDNA BROWN.

_____
NOTARY PUBLIC, STATE OF TEXAS

PREPARED IN THE LAW OFFICE OF:

3 ESTATE PLANNING

CHAPTER OBJECTIVES

Upon completion of this chapter the student should:

1. Apply the purposes and goals of estate planning to client situations.
2. Aid the attorney in estate planning.
3. Know the benefits and drawbacks of the more common estate planning techniques.
4. Recognize some of the more common postmortem estate planning problems.
5. Use a client questionnaire to obtain the information needed for estate planning.
6. Be alert for the common ethical problems in the estate planning field.

CHAPTER GLOSSARY

Beneficiary One who benefits from the act of another or the transfer of property. Includes beneficiary of a trust, beneficiary of a life insurance policy, and beneficiary of an estate.

Checklists Any type of list of actions to be taken, information to be obtained, documents to be prepared or filed, tasks to be completed, etc. Usually particularized to the individual type of legal matter involved.

Client interview form A form of a checklist designed to ensure that the interviewer obtains all needed and relevant information from a client.

Client questionnaire A form given to a client to obtain required information, and to be returned to the attorney upon completion. Use of the questionnaire diminishes the number and length of interviews and involves the client in the legal matter.

Conflict of interest The Texas Disciplinary Rules of Professional Conduct (DR 1.06-1.13) prohibit lawyers from engaging in conduct that would constitute a conflict of interest. This includes dual representation, serving as intermediary between clients, representing clients in a matter in which the lawyer has a personal or financial interest, and representing someone in a matter adverse to a former client. There are exceptions and qualifications to each rule.

Corporation An artificial person or legal entity created under the authority of the laws of a state. The law treats the corporation as a person; it is distinct from its owners (shareholders) and survives their death. Liability of a shareholders is limited to loss of the investment paid the corporation as consideration for their shares.

Credit For income tax purposes, reduces the tax as computed (as opposed to a *deduction*, which reduces the taxable income on which tax is computed).

Deduction An expense that is deductible from gross income in computing taxable income, authorized by the Internal Revenue Code.

Devisee A person to whom either real or personal property is given by will. At common law it related only to a gift of real property in a will.

Donee One to whom a gift is made.

Dual representation Rule 1.06 of the Texas Disciplinary Rules states that a lawyer may not represent opposing parties to the same litigation or multiple parties in the same matter. In the latter situation an attorney may represent multiple parties if he believes that the representation of each client will not materially affect them and if each client consents to the dual representation after a full disclosure of the existence, implications, and possible adverse consequences of the common representation.

Durable Lasting, enduring, or surviving a specified event. When applied to a power of attorney, it means the power of attorney will survive the incompetency of the principal and remain effective during such incompetency.

Duty of confidentiality Section 1.05 of the Texas Disciplinary Rules of Professional Conduct, which regulates the conduct of lawyers and other persons who work in a lawyer's office, states that confidential information includes both privileged information and unprivileged information. *Privileged information* is protected by the lawyer/client privilege as found in the Texas Rules of Evidence and the Texas Rules of Criminal Evidence. *Unprivileged information* includes all other information obtained in the representation of a client. The rule prohibits revealing either kind of confidential information without the client's consent, except under very limited circumstances.

Estate planning The arranging of a person's property and financial affairs, which takes into account the law of wills, insurance, property, taxes, trust, and so on to gain maximum benefits while carrying out the person's wishes concerning the ultimate disposition of his property.

Estate taxes A tax upon death imposed on an estate rather than on the persons receiving the property. As used in this book, the U.S. Estate Tax imposed by the federal government under authority of the Internal Revenue Code.

Exemption-equivalent trust A trust, generally with a spouse as beneficiary, funded by property, either given or devised, that is claimed as a credit under the Federal Estate Tax Unified Credit, and hence it is free from estate tax. Because it does not vest in the spouse, it does not become a part of the spouse's estate; consequently, the trust property is not taxed when he dies either, and his estate can use its credit to shelter his property. Also known as *bypass trust*, or *credit shelter trust*.

Gift A voluntary transfer of property made gratuitously or without consideration. The elements of a valid gift are: intention of the donor, capacity of the donor, delivery to the donee or to someone on behalf of the donee, and acceptance by the donee.

Gift taxes A tax imposed on the transfer of property by gift, to be paid by the donor, not the donee.

GRAT An acronym for *grantor-retained annuity trust*. This is a variation on the GRIT, calling for payment of a fixed amount regardless of the amount of principal or income (but meeting IRS minimums) and allowing GRIT benefit even when the grantor's family will be the ultimate recipients.

GRIT An acronym for *grantor-retained income trust*. A trust in which the grantor (settlor) retains the right to receive the income from or the use of the trust property for a period of time. At the end of that period, ownership passes to someone other than the grantor and his family (unless the trust property is the grantor's personal residence, in which case it may pass to family). If the grantor survives the trust term, the value of the property is removed from the grantor's estate and the gift in trust is subject to gift tax on the property's present value. Present value equals market value at the time of the gift minus the grantor-retained interest, calculated via a table contained in the tax regulations.

GRUT An acronym for *grantor-retained uni-trust*. A variation on the GRIT that allows GRIT benefits even if the gift is ultimately to the grantor's family. It requires a fixed percentage of the net fair market value of the trust assets to be paid at least annually to the grantor.

Inheritance tax A tax imposed on the right to acquire property by inheritance or testamentary gift rather than being imposed on the estate. Texas uses the inheritance method of imposing death taxes, at least to the extent that it imposes any taxes whatsoever upon death.

Inter vivos Between the living, or from one living person to another.

Joint survivorship Description of a joint tenancy. However, under the Texas Probate Code it is now possible for spouses to attach joint survivorship characteristics to community property so that when one of the spouses dies, the property passes by operation of law to the surviving spouse.

Joint tenancy A form of co-ownership. Joint tenants have the same ownership interest and the same undivided possession, which they acquire at the same time under the same instrument. The primary distinguishing characteristic is survivorship: When one of the joint tenants dies, his interest passes by operation of law to the surviving joint tenants, until ultimately the entirety will be owned by the last surviving joint tenant. Upon the death of the last joint tenant, the entirety passes to his heirs or devisees.

Life insurance A contract between the holder of a policy (*owner*) and an insurance underwriter in which the company, in return for premium payments, agrees to pay a specified amount (*face amount*) to the designated beneficiary upon the death of the insured, who may be either the owner or a third party.

Limited liability company A form of business organization characterized by limited liability, management by managers, limitations on the ability to transfer ownership interests, and tax treatment as a partnership.

Limited partnership A type of partnership composed of one or more general partners who manage it and are personally liable for its debts, and one or more limited partners who invest in it and share profits but who do not participate in management and have no liability beyond loss of their investment.

Marital deduction A deduction from federal gift tax and federal estate tax on transfers by one spouse to another either by gift or by will. The deduction is unlimited for spouses dying after 1981.

Partition of community property The division of community property between spouses so that the resulting ownership is separate rather than community.

Partnership A business owned by two or more persons that is not organized as a limited partnership, limited liability company, or corporation.

Personal residence trust A GRIT in which the trust assets are the grantor's personal residences (limited to two). The grantor's family may be the ultimate recipients.

Post-nuptial agreement An agreement between spouses made after marriage. It can take the form of separation agreements, agreements in contemplation of divorce, and property divisions where there is no intention to separate or divorce. In Texas it is generally used in connection with the last, which is restricted by the community property provisions in the Texas Constitution.

Power of attorney A written appointment of an agent; an instrument in writing whereby one person, as principal, appoints another as agent (attorney in fact) and delineates the agent's authority.

Premarital agreement An agreement between prospective spouses to become effective upon marriage. As part of the Texas Family Code, Texas has adopted the Uniform Premarital Agreement Act, which sets forth the requirements and procedures relative to premarital agreements. Sometimes called an *antenuptial agreement*.

QTIP An acronym for a *qualified terminable interest property*. A trust or legal life estate that takes advantage of the marital deduction. It requires that an election be made by the executor of the estate of the settlor; that the surviving spouse have a right to receive all income from the trust, and that he not be given the power of appointment with respect to trust assets.

Representation letter A letter from lawyer to client in which the attorney accepts the duty of representing the client. It explains and confirms the fee arrangement and the acts to be performed for such a fee, and makes any disclosures required by the standards of professional conduct. Also called an *engagement letter*.

Settlor One who creates and funds a trust. The Texas Trust Code uses this term, while the Internal Revenue Code uses the term *grantor*. Also called a *creator*, *donor* and *trustor*.

Significant date list A specialized checklist of dates for completion of legal matters. It is often broken down into significant dates, which are self-imposed deadlines, and critical dates, which are dates imposed by the Probate Code, the Rules of Civil Procedure, the Internal Revenue Codes, etc.

Spendthrift trust A trust that prohibits the sale, transfer, and mortgaging by the beneficiary of his interest. It also has the effect of protecting the interest against the beneficiary's creditors.

Spreadsheet A multicolumned worksheet used by accountants and bookkeepers. With computer software, refers to a program that organizes data into rows and columns, simulating a hardcopy spreadsheet and automatically performing calculations.

Testamentary trusts A trust created by a will that takes effect upon the testator's death and the probate of his will.

Trust A legal entity created by intention of the creator (*settlor*,) and subsequent transfer of property to a person, termed the *trustee*, who holds and manages the trust assets, as a fiduciary, for the economic benefit of the beneficiaries.

PURPOSES AND GOALS OF ESTATE PLANNING

The basic purposes of **estate planning** can be divided into three areas:

1. **Ensuring that the wishes of the testator are carried out upon death.** This includes the disposition of the client's estate upon his death, the avoidance of disputes or will contests, the provision of care for dependents and others to whom the client feels some

obligation (either moral or legal), the disposal of the client's body or the type of funeral, and the preservation of the estate after meeting obligations of support so that the property passes to those whom the client intends to ultimately receive it.

2. **Minimizing the costs of death and incompetency.** This includes the cost of probate proceeding and the liability for **estate taxes**, **inheritance taxes**, **gift taxes**, and sometimes even income taxes during the client's life. This has to be balanced against the cost of estate planning, which can be significant.

3. **Providing for incompetency and/or disability.** This includes preparation of such things as **durable powers of attorney**, directives to physicians, health powers of attorney, designations of guardians, and sometimes the use of **inter vivos** trusts.

In accomplishing these purposes there are goals that are desirable in specific instances of estate planning. Some of these are:

1. **Avoiding disputes and contests.** This may involve the use of clauses to prohibit contests in wills and **trusts**, explanations contained in wills and trusts, or separate documents explaining the reasons why certain dispositions have been made, and the use of business organizations, with severe restrictions on the sale and/or management thereof.

2. **Maintaining liquidity and protecting family assets.** In planning the estate, one must not lose sight of the fact that the client and the client's family are still alive and will need income in the future. This means that catastrophic health care costs, reverses in the economic well-being of the client, divorce, and other similar catastrophes must be considered in the planning for death and incompetency. This may very well involve the creation of business organizations such as family **partnerships**, family **limited partnerships**, close **corporations** and the new **limited liability companies**. In addition, it may necessitate **premarital agreement** and/or **postnuptial agreements**, **partitions of community property**, **joint tenancies**, annuities, and trusts to set aside resources for education, support, and maintenance that are out of the reach of creditors. It also involves planning to preserve assets during life and to satisfy estate and inheritance taxes upon death, which may involve things such as inter vivos trusts, **life insurance** trusts, **exemption-equivalent trusts**, qualified terminable interest property, and a number of other procedures.

3. **Protecting the beneficiaries' and devisees' interests** from loss in divorce or seizure by creditors.

4. **Retaining control over and management of client assets**, while planning for optimum savings in estate tax and other taxes.

5. **Preserving client assets** such as large farms, ranches, and even businesses, so as to prevent sale or division. The famous King Ranch was transferred into a family corporation, with one of the goals being the prevention of division.

6. **Remaining as flexible as possible** to change the estate plan as required by changed circumstances.

7. **Preparing an estate plan** in which all of the elements are tied together in a unified pattern, not only during the life of the client but also upon and after the death of the client.

Clearly, estate planning is an immensely complex and difficult undertaking. It requires knowledge in many areas of the law, such as business organizations, family law, tax law, real property law, probate law, trust law, insurance law, and, to lesser degrees, many others. The legal assistant, in order to work effectively in this area, must have a good working knowledge of the Texas Probate Code and related case law, the Texas Business Corporation Act, the Texas Limited Liability Company Act, the Texas Partnership Act, the Texas Revised Limited Partnership Act, the Texas Trust Code and cases, the Texas Property Code and not only the cases but the traditions and customs exercised in the practice of real estate law, the Uniform Commercial Code, and the Texas Family Code and related cases. In estate planning, all of this knowledge, plus knowledge in areas such as insurance law and tax law, are important to meeting the goals of the client efficiently and ethically.

THE LEGAL ASSISTANT'S ROLE

Any time there is a paper-intensive area of practice, much client contact, and much information to be received and collated, legal assistants should be used. This diminishes the cost to the client and frees the attorney to do the things that only an attorney may do. The area of estate planning meets all of these criteria. The use of legal assistants is not only appropriate but necessary in a heavy estate planning practice.

The functions that a legal assistant might participate in during the planning of a client's estate are the following:

1. Attending client interviews.

2. Obtaining the financial and asset information needed to develop the estate plan.

3. Putting the information obtained into a usable format, or perhaps inputting the information obtained from the client and other sources into a computer to make use of sophisticated estate tax planning software.

4. Participating in the creation and upgrading of document assembly programs, **checklists**, questionnaires, formatted correspondence, billing practices, and other time-saving and expense-reducing procedures.

5. Preparing **spreadsheets**, flowcharts, and other charts showing the analysis of savings of estate tax, gift tax, and income tax. Doing accounting calculations.

6. Preparing drafts of wills and trust agreements.
7. Preparing summaries of lengthy documents to aid client understanding.
8. Drafting bills to clients.
9. Preparing a multitude of documents, including:
   a. Premarital and postnuptial agreements.
   b. Designations of guardian.
   c. Partition and exchange agreements.
   d. Powers of attorney.
   e. Directives to physicians and durable powers of attorney for health purposes.
   f. Insurance trusts and split dollar insurance agreements.
   g. Business organizations of all kinds and types.
   h. Promissory notes and security agreements.
   i. Codicils, appointments, and resignations of trustees and other representatives.
   j. Revocation of powers of attorney and trusts and other such documents.
   k. Inter vivos, or living trusts.
   l. Deeds, mortgages, and stock powers.
10. Obtaining information on and changing beneficiaries and ownership of insurance policies.
11. Serving as notary public or witness during the execution of documents.
12. Participating in the editing of draft documents.
13. Handling client contact.
14. Obtaining information needed for the planning and execution of the estate plan from a myriad of sources, including employers, life insurance companies, and banks.

The legal assistant does not have to understand the law or the practices well enough to make decisions or to advise the clients. In fact, legal assistants are prohibited by state law from doing this. An attorney is prohibited by the Rules of Professional Responsibility from letting a legal assistant give legal advice. However, the legal assistant working in this area must understand the documents and the clauses so as to be able to prepare drafts and to participate in the editing of those drafts and to understand how the various documents correlate and work together to achieve the ultimate purposes and goals.

The legal assistant course of study will aid in the understanding of all the areas of the law needed for background in estate planning, but the legal assistant should also be prepared to use the law library, take courses in a local legal assistant program, attend continuing legal education seminars offered by the State Bar of Texas and others, and read anything that touches on estate planning. This is not only an initial step to competency in estate tax planning but also a necessary part of maintaining competence, because of the rapid changes in applicable laws.

In spite of the complexities, estate planning and probate administration can be one of the most satisfying areas of practice. Estate planning is not involved only with money; much of it is involved with human emotions and the execution of clients' wishes for the future. Dealing with grateful clients gives legal assistants a sense of self-worth that can only come from knowing they have done their job well and benefited other human beings.

ESTATE PLANNING TECHNIQUES

There are many different techniques and procedures in estate planning. It would be impossible to catalog them all or to discuss all of the relevant law and its applications. Therefore, this textbook will discuss only the major estate planning techniques—wills, trusts, and some miscellaneous documents and the tax law. What follows is a brief discussion of those techniques and their purpose or goals. There are other techniques, and new ones will be developed in the future. Some of the techniques and vehicles to be covered here will be discussed in further detail later in this text.

Gifts

The 1976 Tax Reform Act and the 1981 Economic Recovery Tax Act took away many of the benefits of making lifetime **gifts**. (This subject will be discussed more in Chapter Fifteen.) Nonetheless, there remain at least two advantages to the making of lifetime gifts. The first advantage is that gifts up to $10,000 annually per **donee** are excluded from federal gift tax and therefore estate tax. This allows the taxpayer and his spouse, if any, each to give to individuals the sum of $10,000 per year, which removes that $10,000 from each of their estates for purpose of calculating federal estate tax. Amounts paid directly to providers of education for tuition and to providers of medical care for such care are also excluded from gift taxes.

Additionally, for the purpose of estate tax, the value of an asset is generally fixed at the date of death, whereas the value of a gift is fixed at the time of the gift. If the taxpayer or client makes a gift of property that is subject to rapid appreciation or growth, the value of the asset is determined at the time of the gift. For example, an asset worth $30,000 at the time of the gift that grows to a value of $100,000 at the time of death, yields to the estate a tax savings in the amount of the tax that would have been assessed on the difference of $70,000. Actual tax savings, depending on the size of the entire estate, could approach $37,500.

GRITS, GRATS, GRUTS, PRTS, QPRTS, AND OTHER LIVING TRUSTS

These gifts may be made directly to the donee or to an inter vivos trust, or living trust, of which the taxpayer/client is the trustee. The taxpayer/client retains management of and control over the gifted assets or funds. In addition, to avoid the creation of a separate taxpaying entity, the taxpayer/client may retain the right to receive all of the income from the trust during his life. The income will then be included within the income of the grantor, and he, rather than the trust, will pay the income tax on it.

These gifts could also be to a life insurance trust (which will be discussed shortly) so as to provide liquidity to the estate. Also, the gift could be to a **GRIT** (grantor-retained income trust), a **GRAT** (grantor-retained annuity trust) or a **GRUT** (grantor-retained uni-trust), any of which can reduce the taxable value of the gift to zero while removing a valuable asset from the estate for the purpose of estate tax calculations. Even a client's home and vacation home can be given to a PRT (**personal residence trust**) or a QPRT (qualified personal residence trust), and the trust will receive the benefit of treatment as a GRIT. These will be discussed more fully in Chapter Nine.

Exemption-Equivalent Trust

The exemption-equivalent trust (sometimes called a *credit shelter trust*, or *bypass trust*) is the amount of an estate's net assets that are exempt from gift and/or estate taxation. That figure is currently $600,000. For the purposes of example, assume that the taxpayer/client accumulated, together with his wife, community property in excess of $600,000 but less than $1.2 million. When the taxpayer dies, his half of the community property will be less than $600,000, inasmuch as the entirety is less than $1.2 million. However, if nothing further is done, the estate will become a part of the spouse's estate. When she dies there is a possibility that her estate will exceed $600,000 and be subject to taxation.

To avoid this, estate planners often create an exemption-equivalent trust in the taxpayer/client's will. The will provides that a trust be created upon death and then devises all or a portion equal to $600,000 of the taxpayer/client's estate to the trust. Generally, the trust provides that the surviving spouse receive all of the income during her life and that upon her death the assets remaining in the trust be divided amongst the children.

The husband's half of the community estate never becomes a part of the wife's estate, so that when she dies her estate is still less than $600,000 and there is no tax due. Consequently, the children receive from the mother's estate and from the father's trust an amount in excess of $600,000, with no estate tax levied on it.

This is often used even when the estate exceeds $1.2 million. Even if the husband will owe estate tax on his estate, it is still of benefit to put $600,000 into an exemption-equivalent trust, because doing so keeps that much money out of the spouse's estate and saves estate tax, at least to the extent of the $600,000. The spouse is entitled to the income from the trust during her life, and it passes to the children or other beneficiaries upon her death. This alone can save as much $300,000 in estate tax.

Marital Deduction and QTIPs

The **marital deduction** basically allows a person to leave an unlimited amount of qualified assets to his spouse. Although the same will go into the surviving spouse's estate, there will be no federal estate tax paid by virtue of the first spouse's death. However, at the time the surviving spouse dies, federal estate tax will be paid on the entire estate, both the portion that was her community property and the portion she received from the predeceasing spouse. Consequently, the marital deduction allows the deferment of estate tax until the last surviving spouse dies.

Sometimes the **deduction** is used in connection with what is referred to as a **QTIP**, or qualified terminable interest property. This can be the creation of either a trust or a legal life estate with reference to the predeceasing spouse's estate. Under this provision, the first spouse dying leaves his estate either in a legal life estate or in a trust, with the income to go to the surviving spouse during her life. The marital deduction then defers the estate tax until the last spouse dies, but the surviving spouse gets only the income from the trust during her life, and the assets are kept together and cannot be sold by the surviving spouse so that they ultimately will vest in the persons that the predeceasing spouse intended, normally the children.

Life Insurance Trusts

Life insurance trusts are used primarily to create liquidity. The procedure is to create an inter vivos trust and either transfer existing insurance to it or suggest or request that the trustee use whatever assets have been conveyed into trust to purchase life insurance on the client's life. The beneficiaries will generally be the children of the client. Then the client uses the $10,000 annual gift tax exclusion to continue making gifts each year into the life insurance trust. The trustee uses this money to pay the annual premiums on the life insurance. When the originator of the trust—called the **settlor**, or grantor—dies, his remaining estate will pass through an exemption-equivalent trust and a marital deduction trust to his surviving spouse, with no tax consequences. When the surviving spouse dies, the life insurance, which was paid at the death of the original spouse and is then in the trust, becomes the property of the children, and the proceeds can be used to pay the federal estate tax due upon the last dying spouse's estate, with no additional tax consequences to the estate because the money passed to the children as a gift rather than by virtue of the parent's death. There are some rigid requirements provided by tax law that must be com-plied with in order to make this work. This provides liquidity to pay for federal estate and inheritance taxes as well as cash for other purposes.

Inter Vivos (Living) Trusts

Inter vivos trusts are used to avoid costs of probate. They make a much better vehicle for providing for the incompetency or disability of the client than do powers of attorney. Everyone accepts the authority of a trustee to act on behalf of a trust, whereas many refuse to accept a power of attorney.

Trusts, either inter vivos or testamentary, are also used to provide support for a spouse, often a second spouse, during his life, while preventing the trust assets from vesting in that spouse (in which case the assets might pass to the spouse's heirs or devisees, a subsequent spouse) so that upon his death the assets pass to the children and/or grandchildren of the client.

Premarital and Post-nuptial Agreements

Premarital and postnuptial agreements serve many purposes. One is to move property subject to rapid appreciation into the ownership of the spouse anticipated to survive, without the necessity of making a gift. These agreements can also create **joint survivorship** or joint tenancy agreements, which avoid the cost of probate and expensive estate planning.

Business Organizations

Business organizations are used to move the ownership of assets and the receipt of income from one family member to another and to make gifts, while still retaining control and management. Some business organizations also add a new dimension, limited liability. This can prevent the loss of all of a family's assets when a profit-making venture goes sour.

Spendthrift and Sprinkling

Spendthrift trusts can be used to protect a loved one against his own bad budgeting and economic management by ensuring that the trust assets are exempt from seizure by his creditors.

Sprinkling (sometimes called *spraying*) provisions in trusts can allow for the trustees to spend more money on some beneficiaries than on others, thereby enabling the trustees to adjust to events, such as the catastrophic illness or divorce of one of the beneficiaries, which might come up after the client's death and require higher expenditures for one beneficiary than for another.

POST MORTEM ESTATE PLANNING

Estate planning does not come to an end with the death of the client. There are a multitude of elections, choices, and procedures that can reduce or defer federal estate or income taxes, even if no estate planning has occurred prior to the death. In fact, some estate planners create plans that depend on the making of elections. For instance, the amount of the marital deduction depends on how much is claimed as a deduction on the federal estate tax return. If the marital deduction amount is to be left to the spouse in a trust containing QTIP provisions, there must be a QTIP or partial QTIP election made in the U.S. Estate Tax Return. The planner, then, can create a will or a trust that names the wife beneficiary as to the entirety of the husband's estate in a marital deduction trust with QTIP provisions. The planner also creates an exemption-equivalent trust and provides that if a partial QTIP election is made, waiving the marital deduction as to a portion of the husband's assets, such assets will become a part of the exemption-equivalent trust. Then, when the husband actually dies, the executor or trustee can choose how to fund the marital trust and the exemption-equivalent trust by making the elections.

There are many elections required or allowed by tax law that make a difference in how much estate tax is paid, when it is paid, and how much income taxes will be due with the final return for the year of the decedent's death or the fiduciary return due each year thereafter until the estate is closed or the trust terminated. These choices are important not only because of their effect on the estate, but also because of the effect on beneficiaries. An election can reduce the net percentage of the estate received by one beneficiary and increase it for another, or increase the tax burden (estate, income, or generation-skipping) for one and decrease it for another. Further, it can delay the receipt by the beneficiaries of their share of the estate. These decisions can create **conflicts of interest** between the attorney representing the estate and the various parties who have an interest in the estate. .

CHECKLISTS, CLIENT QUESTIONNAIRES AND INTERVIEW FORMS

Estate planning, even in its simplest form, involves a lot of detail and often the obtaining of large amounts of information concerning family relationships, client assets and finances, and expectations for the future. Because of this, it is an area that lends itself well to the use of checklists to avoid overlooking needed information and the use of **client questionnaires**, which involve the client in obtaining some of the information, thereby diminishing the time expenditure of the lawyer and the legal assistant.

This book will not attempt to provide forms for all of the possible checklists, lists of significant or critical dates, client questionnaires, and **client interview forms** that may be useful in the estate planning practice. There are numerous publications that contain these. Any professional development program on the drafting of wills, the drafting of trusts, and estate planning invariably contains one or more client questionnaires or checklists. A publication by the State Bar of Texas called *Texas Probate System* contains a number of **significant date lists**, checklists, interview forms, and client questionnaires.

Commercial software used in estate planning and document assembly programs for the preparation of wills, **testamentary trusts**, and inter vivos trusts come with written checklists that can be ordered from the software producer or printed through the software.

In fact, some of the document assembly programs are checklists within themselves. In order to prepare the first draft, the user must enter information and answer questions asked by the program. The user can merely call it up on a computer terminal. As questions are asked or information is requested by the program, he obtains the information from the client sitting at the desk across from him and enters it immediately into the computer. As for information the client does not have on hand, a handwritten note can remind the client to obtain it or a "print screen" command can generate a printout of the screen containing the unanswered questions, which can then be given to the client.

When the client brings in the missing information, the person responsible can immediately access the file already created for the client in the document assembly program, and input the information. Then not only is the information stored, but a simple command will produce a first draft of the document needed for that particular client. Examples of documents produced on such document assembly programs are included with later chapters.

Almost all authorities agree on the benefits of the client questionnaire. One example can be found at the end of this chapter as Form 3-1. Other forms can be found in *Texas Probate System* and several recent estate planning programs by the State Bar of Texas.

As legal assistants (and, for that matter, lawyers) get more deeply involved in estate planning, they will generally discover that even the best client questionnaires available from other sources do not meet all of their needs and must be modified to some extent. Even though an attorney may adopt a client questionnaire discovered in one of these publications, it will doubtless be amended until it is unrecognizable after a while.

The client questionnaire is meant to involve the client in the process of estate planning, to decrease the time expenditures of the lawyer and the legal assistant (thereby decreasing the cost to the client), and to protect the lawyer or firm against possible grievances or malpractice suits. This may take the form of either a client questionnaire or a letter of instructions to the client concerning what information he must obtain for the attorney.

It is impossible for attorneys and legal assistants to do an adequate and accurate job of estate planning, particularly for larger estates, unless they have detailed and complete lists of assets—probate or nonprobate assets—in which clients have any ownership interest, along with information on expected future assets. Failure to obtain this information because of negligence by the lawyer or legal assistant can make the lawyer liable for malpractice should such failure cause loss or damage by way of costs or increased estate, inheritance, gift or income taxes. Questionnaires are essential to make sure that all avenues have been considered in the estate planning and that all clauses necessary or desirable have been considered for possible inclusion in the documents prepared in carrying out the estate plan.

Checklists, questionnaires, interview forms, and significant or critical date lists in probate administration will be discussed in Chapter Thirteen.

ETHICAL CONSIDERATIONS

The three most important areas of ethics to be concerned with in estate planning are competency, the **duty of confidentiality**, and **dual representation**.

Competency

Estate planning changes yearly because of changes in tax laws. Estate planners and others are continually attempting to discover new tax *avoidance* techniques; meaning the use of tax law provisions to reduce taxes. This should not be confused with tax *evasion*, which is an illegal failure to pay taxes.

As fast as new tax avoidance techniques are discovered, the Internal Revenue Service attempts to counter them, through legislation or regulation or court cases. The federal government's need for tax revenue creates an ever-changing body of law. Plus the U.S. Congress creates major modifications in the Internal Revenue Code every three to five years, particularly in the area of estate and gift taxation. With the passage of the 1976 Tax Reform Act, many said estate planning for the purpose of decreasing federal estate taxes was a thing of the past. Others said it was of no further benefit to make gifts for the purpose of reducing taxes. Although estate planners had to be tremendously innovative, they appear to have proven both claims untrue. As tax law changes, one trust, such as the Clifford Trust, ceases to exist as a tax-saving vehicle and others, such as the GRIT, GRAT, and the GRUT rise out of its ashes.

Because of the continual changes in tax law and in estate planning techniques, everyone on the estate planning team must keep current, both by attending legal seminars and by reading in sources of the most recent law.

Confidentiality

Estate planners have access to a tremendous amount of information about each client that must be kept confidential. This includes not only financial and asset information, but also information about personal things such as divorce intentions, illegitimate and unrecognized children, prior marital history, extramarital dalliances, business reversals, and threatened bankruptcy. If these topics are talked about outside of the office, it can lead to severe personal and financial troubles for the client and his lawyer, e.g., grievances, lawsuits, and loss of business reputation. Any legal assistant discovered revealing confidential information about a client can expect immediate termination. The legal assistant, like the lawyer, cannot speak of anything concerning a client that is learned in the office. In fact, he even cannot speak of the fact that a client is a client other than to persons employed in the office.

The duty to preserve the confidentiality of client information goes further than not speaking of it outside of the office. It requires the legal assistant, before inviting a client into his office or work area, to make sure there are no documents on his desk that reveal any confidential information. In addition, the legal assistant should never leave anyone alone at a desk or table or in an office where there is easy access to files or documents relating to other clients. The legal assistant should not talk to a client or to someone about a client on the telephone while someone else is in within hearing distance. Extreme care must be taken not to leave files or other documents where outsiders might stumble on them. This applies also to the use of copy machines, especially where nonemployees have access to the copy machine.

A new problem is the use of the fax. It is easy for faxed material to be misdirected by simply misdialing a number. It is also possible for faxed documents to be intercepted, although that would be unlawful. Thus, every law office should be extremely careful about what is sent by fax, particularly when it comes to sensitive information relating to a client.

Dual Representation/Conflict of Interest

Dual representation in estate planning is a very sensitive area. In most estate planning situations, more than one client may be involved. Even where there appears to be only a single client, others may be involved in the estate planning to whom a court may find a duty of loyalty and fiduciary care. Many times, elderly people, particularly, are brought into a law office by someone who is to be a beneficiary. Although the estate planning is done for the elderly person, the intended beneficiary presumes that he is being represented also.

With regard to spouses, the legal assistant should be alert to signs of conflict, fraud, double dealing, or advantage taking. Representation of both parties in estate planning under such circumstances may be construed to be representing adverse parties in violation of the Texas Disciplinary Rules.

Many real estate lawyers who handle a real estate sales transaction for both the seller and the buyer are now requiring that the parties execute **representation letters** in which the parties acknowledge that the attorney has advised them concerning dual representation and conflicts of interest, and that they consent to the attorney representing both of them. Many of these letters go on to say that if in fact a true conflict arises between the parties, the attorney will be paid for all services rendered to that time and will then decline any further representation of either party.

An adaptation of such a letter may be in order when a law firm is engaging in joint estate planning for two persons, perhaps husband and wife, parent and child, friends, or persons in a relationship other than marriage. The opportunity for adverse interests exists almost as frequently in estate planning as it does in real estate transactions.

The legal assistant should be alert for signs of conflict or adversity between parties for whom the firm is doing estate planning, and immediately advise the responsible attorney if any are observed.

Legal Advice

The legal assistant is barred from representing himself as an attorney or from allowing someone to form a false belief to such effect. He is further prevented from giving legal advice. With regard to the first restriction, unless the lawyer has at the initial interview clarified who the legal assistant is and explained that assistant's role, the legal assistant should, at first contact with the clients, make it abundantly clear that he is not a lawyer. It is probably also a good idea for the legal assistant to describe the role of the legal assistant and to explain exact-ly what he will be doing in connection with the representation of those clients.

The prohibition against giving legal advice is probably both the hardest to define and the hardest to observe. Exactly where advising clients regarding facts and procedures ends and advising them as to the law begins is difficult to ascertain. The practicing legal assistant should probably make such decisions leaning toward the broadest possible interpretation of the term legal advice so as to avoid any indication whatsoever of engaging in the unauthorized practice of law. It is a good practice to seek guidelines from the supervising attorney as to what may and may not be told to a client in connection with the gathering of information, the formulation of the plan, and the carrying out of the plan.

Perhaps even harder is avoiding the natural tendency to respond to a question before thinking through the ramifications of answering such a question. The urge to answer, accompanied by the desire to feel important and to respond to people's needs, can produce what, upon reflection, is legal advice. Each legal assistant must learn to deal with this tendency in his own way, but must remain constantly vigilant to avoid even the appearance of giving legal advice.

CHAPTER QUESTIONS AND EXERCISES

1. What do you think the most important purpose of estate planning is? Explain your answer. Has it an intellectual basis or an emotional one? Has some experience in your background influenced you in making such a decision?

2. Do some outside reading or other investigation to discover a method or technique of estate planning not discussed in this chapter. Fully explain this method or technique.

3. What are some additional roles for a legal assistant in estate planning?

4. What sections of the Texas Family Code deal with premarital agreements? With postnuptial agreements?

5. State every benefit you can think of about the making of lifetime gifts. Now state every detriment or drawback.

6. State every benefit you can think of about the use of checklists. Now state every detriment or drawback.

7. How many ways can computers be of benefit in estate planning?

8. Define legal advice. Defend your definition.

9. With the aid of another classmate, role-play a client interview using a client questionnaire.

Form 3-1: Estate Planning Questionnaire

(If estate non-taxable use through page 4)

CONFIDENTIAL

ESTATE PLANNING QUESTIONNAIRE

_____

Client

_____

Date

DOCUMENTS TO BE ATTACHED

	Attached or N/A
1. Existing wills of both spouses...	_____
2. Existing Powers of Attorney of both spouses...	_____
3. Income tax returns for past three years	_____
4. Business agreements and documents regarding interest in corporations, partnerships and sole proprietorships..	_____
5. Prenuptial or postnuptial agreements (including joint tenancies with right of survivorship)...	_____

FAMILY INFORMATION

1. **Personal:**   **Client**   **Spouse**

   a. Name _____ _____

   b. Home address _____ _____

   c. Home phone _____ _____

   d. Employer & Business address _____ _____

   e. Business phone _____ _____

   f. Birth Date _____ _____

   g. Place of birth (citizenship) _____ _____

   h. Social Security Number _____ _____

   i. Date and place of marriage _____ _____

2. **Your Children**

            Name and Address   **Birth Date**

   a. _____ _____

   b. _____ _____

   c. _____ _____

   d. _____ _____

3. **Particulars regarding your grandchildren:**

   Their Parents   **Names of Grandchildren**   **Birth Date**

   a. _____ (1) _____ _____

      _____ (2) _____ _____

      _____ (3) _____ _____

   b. _____ (1) _____ _____

      _____ (2) _____ _____

      _____ (3) _____ _____

Form 3-1: (continued)

FAMILY INFORMATION, CONTINUED

4. **Parents**

	Client	Spouse

Father: _____ _____
           Name   Birth Date   Name   Birth Date

           _____ _____
                    Address   Address

Mother: _____ _____
           Name   Birth Date   Name   Birth Date

           _____ _____
                    Address   Address

5. **Other dependent persons—names, addresses, and relationships:**
_____
_____
_____
_____
_____

ADVISERS

Names, addresses, and telephone numbers:

1. Attorney: _____
2. Accountant: _____
3. Life insurance adviser: _____
4. Banker and trust officers: _____
5. Stockbroker: _____
6. Executor: _____
7. Substitute Executor: _____
8. Trustee: _____
9. Substitute Trustee: _____
10. Designated guardian for children: _____
11. Substitute guardian: _____
12. Investment adviser: _____
13. Physician: _____
14. Attorney in fact (business): _____
15. Attorney in fact (medical): _____
16. Designated guardian for self or spouse: _____
17. Person to be barred as guardian or self or spouse: _____

DISTRIBUTION OBJECTIVES

1. At death, how do you want your estate distributed?
_____
_____
_____

2. (a) At what age do you want your children to receive their portion of the estate?
_____
_____

Form 3-1: (continued)

DISTRIBUTION OBJECTIVES, CONTINUED

(b) Do any of your children have special educational, medical or financial needs?

_____
_____
_____

4. Do you contemplate making future gifts in excess of $10,000?

_____
_____

5. Do you wish to make bequests to your church or synagogue or to any other charitable organization?

_____

Furnish details:

_____
_____

6. If none of your children are living at the time of your spouse's death, do you want your estate to go to:

Your family?_____.   Spouse's family?_____.   Elsewhere?_____.

7. Will your spouse continue to live in present home?

_____

ASSETS

1. Did you or your spouse own any substantial separate property before marriage?

_____
_____

2. Have any gifts or inheritances been received by either you or your spouse separately or do you expect any in the future?

_____
_____

3. Would you or spouse have any problem (emotional or otherwise) with entering a postnuptial agreement for purpose of tax reduction?

_____
_____

CASH AND PERSONAL EFFECTS

Type and Number	Bank	Amount	If Joint Account State Kind and Name of Joint Owner
Bank accounts:		$	
_____	_____	_____	_____
_____	_____	_____	_____
_____	_____	_____	_____
_____	_____	_____	_____
_____	_____	_____	_____
Certificate of Deposit:			
_____	_____	_____	_____
_____	_____	_____	_____
_____	_____	_____	_____
_____	_____	_____	_____

Total: $ _____

Form 3-1: (continued)

CASH AND PERSONAL EFFECTS, CONTINUED

Fair Market Value

Automobiles $ _____
Household furnishings   _____
Jewelry   _____
Collections (Arts, etc.)   _____

Other items of significant value   _____

_____   _____
_____   _____
_____   _____

Miscellaneous personal effects   _____
                                       Total: _____

LIFE INSURANCE POLICIES (AND ANNUITIES)

Life Insurance Provided by Employer:

	Policy #1	Policy #2	Policy #3
Company			
Policy			
Type			
Insured			
Owner			
Beneficiary			
Contingent Beneficiary			
Face Value			
Amount of Loan			
Employee's Contribution			

Other Life Insurance:*

	Policy #4	Policy #5	Policy #6
Company			
Policy			
Type			
Insured			
Owner			
Beneficiary			
Contingent Beneficiary			
Face Value			
Current Cash Surrender Value			
Amount of Loan			
Annual Premium			

*Include policies on life of spouse and children. Attach additional pages if needed.

Form 3-1: (continued)

STOCKS*

Company and Type	Ownership	Number of Shares	Date of Purchase or Acquisition	Basis	Total Current Market Value
_____	_____	_____	_____	_____	$_____
_____	_____	_____	_____	_____	_____
_____	_____	_____	_____	_____	_____
_____	_____	_____	_____	_____	_____
				Total:	$_____

BONDS AND TREASURY NOTES

					$_____
_____	_____	_____	_____	_____	_____
_____	_____	_____	_____	_____	_____
_____	_____	_____	_____	_____	_____
_____	_____	_____	_____	_____	_____
_____	_____	_____	_____	_____	_____
_____	_____	_____	_____	_____	_____
_____	_____	_____	_____	_____	_____
_____	_____	_____	_____	_____	_____
				Total:	$_____

REAL ESTATE
(Use additional sheets if necessary)

	Property 1	Property 2
Legal description (Please attach copy of Deed, Note and Deed of Trust)		
Location	_____	_____
Personal Residence? (primary or secondary, and period of occupancy and ownership)	_____	_____
in Names of:	_____	_____
Rate of Acquisition	_____	_____
How acquired (gift, purchase, etc.)	_____	_____
Cost Basis	_____	_____
Accumulated Depreciation cost recovery*	_____	_____
Current Market value	_____	_____
Encumbrances: Name of current holder	_____	_____
Amount	_____	_____
Monthly payments (principal & interest)	_____	_____
Interest rate	_____	_____
Remaining period of loan	_____	_____
Annual interest	_____	_____
Annual taxes	_____	_____
Annual income (gross)*	_____	_____
Annual depreciation cost recovery*	_____	_____
Annual costs (maintenance, etc.*)	_____	_____
Annual net income*	_____	_____

*Income producing property only

Form 3-1: (continued)

CLOSELY HELD BUSINESS INTERESTS

(Use separate sheet for each business interest)

Name _____ Percent Owned _____

Type of entity:

Corporation _____ Partnership _____ Sole Proprietorship _____

Is interest jointly owned with spouse? _____

Has he or she participated in the business? _____

Your estimate of the fair market value of your interest _____

_____

Your tax basis for your interest _____

Do you have any plans to dispose of a business interest during your lifetime? _____

If so, please describe _____

_____

What are your wishes as to disposition of ownership after death:

1. Transfer to family _____
2. Sale to co-owner of business _____
3. Sale to key-employee _____
4. Other _____

Is there a buy/sell, shareholders or redemption agreement?

Yes _____   No _____

Please provide financial statements and tax returns for the previous 5 years and a copy of any buy/sell redemption agreements.

MISCELLANEOUS

Do you own any other assets? _____

If so give full explanation including type, location, value, name of co-owners, whether vested or contingent, etc.

_____

_____

RETIREMENT, DISABILITY AND DEATH BENEFITS

If you have any interest in a pension, profit-sharing, stock bonus, self-employed retirement plan, individual retirement account or deferred compensation plan, or any other similar type of benefit, attach copies and complete the following:

Company	Type of Plan and Benefits*
_____	_____
_____	_____
_____	_____
_____	_____
_____	_____

*List beneficiary of death benefit and form of payment.

SOCIAL SECURITY

Estimate basic social security benefit for self and spouse _____

_____

Form 3-1: (continued)

OTHER ASSETS

Description	Fair Market Value	Basis
Incentive stock options:	$ _____	$ _____
	_____	_____
Nonqualified stock options:	_____	_____
	_____	_____
Property paid for services and subject to a substantial risk for forfeiture:	_____	_____
	_____	_____
Stock appreciation rights:	_____	_____
	_____	_____
Other	_____	_____

Note: Include other assets such as a remainder, reversionary, or income interest in a trust and copies of documents. Also include the source and approximate amount of any expected inheritance.

LIABILITIES
(Not previously listed)

Creditor	Secured By	Interest Rate	Due Date	Repayment Schedule	Current Balance
___	___	___	___	___	___
___	___	___	___	___	___
___	___	___	___	___	___
___	___	___	___	___	___
___	___	___	___	___	___
___	___	___	___	___	___
___	___	___	___	___	___
___	___	___	___	___	___
___	___	___	___	___	___
___	___	___	___	___	___
___	___	___	___	___	___
___	___	___	___	___	___
___	___	___	___	___	___
___	___	___	___	___	___
___	___	___	___	___	___
___	___	___	___	___	___

Form 3-1: (continued)

ANNUAL EXPENDITURES

Standard of Living: $ _____

Food   _____

Mortgage payments or rent   _____

Real estate taxes   _____

Entertainment   _____

Miscellaneous (clothing, utilities, etc.)   _____

Other:

    Income taxes   _____

    Saving and investment   _____

    Other loan payments   _____

    Education   _____

    Life insurance premiums   _____

    Keogh plan contributions   _____

    Unusual expenditures: _____

    _____   _____

    _____   _____

    Total annual expenditures: $ _____

GIFT DATA

Gifts Made to Others:

Have you made any gifts other than to charities in any one year before 1982 to any one or more persons which exceeded $3,000.00, if made by you alone ($10,000 if after 1981) or $6,000 ($20,000 if after 1981) if jointly made by you and your spouse.

                YES _____ NO _____

If gift tax returns were filed, please furnish copies.

If gift tax returns were not filed, describe the gift, date, fair market value, and to whom given _____

_____

_____

Have gifts been made by creating a trust? _____YES _____ NO _____

If so, provide trust document.

Have gifts been made under the Uniform Gift to minors Act?

                YES _____ NO _____

If you or your wife are the custodian, please give details on the property.

_____

_____

REMARKS

_____

_____

_____

_____

4 EXECUTION AND REVOCATION OF WILLS

CHAPTER OBJECTIVES

Upon completion of this chapter, the student should be able to:

1. List the statutory requirements relating to the validity of a will.
2. Distinguish between statutory (formal) wills, holographic wills, and nuncupative wills.
3. Determine the competency of a witness to a will.
4. Determine the competency of a person who is to execute a will.
5. Define *self-proving affidavit*, and list the requirements as to validity.
6. Know how a will is revoked.
7. List and explain the possible grounds of a will contest.
8. Describe the process by which wills are amended.

CHAPTER GLOSSARY

Anti-lapse statute A statute providing that a devise to a predeceased devisee passes to the descendants of the predeceased devisee, thereby preventing a lapse of the devise, which would result in its passing by intestate succession.

Attest To act as a witness, to bear witness, to sign a document certifying that it is genuine.

Cancellation The writing of words indicating an intent to revoke across the face of a will.

Codicil A document that amends, adds to, explains, or revokes an existing will. It is not a will and does not by implication revoke a prior will; rather, it and the existing will must be read together in order to determine the testator's intentions.

Credible In regard to a subscribing witness to a will, competent to appear and testify that the will was executed in accordance with all legal requirements. A witness who receives some benefit in a will may not be credible.

Holographic will A will that is entirely handwritten by the testator and is excepted from the statutory requirement that it be witnessed by two credible persons.

Insane delusion A belief based on facts that do not exist and that no reasonable person would believe. It destroys testamentary capacity.

Joint will A single testamentary document which is executed by two or more persons with the intent that it serve as the will of each of them.

Mutual will A will that contains provisions reciprocal with those of another person's will.

Nuncupative will An oral will spoken by the testator. It is only applicable to personal property and does not require witnesses unless the property exceeds $30 in value.

Pretermitted child A child, unintentionally omitted from a will by the testator, who was either living at the time of the execution of the will or born after the making of the will (*afterborn*).

Publication The declaration by the testator/testatrix to the witnesses that the will is his/her last will and testament.

Reformation A court-ordered correction of a written instrument causing it to comply with the original intentions of the parties.

Revocation With regard to wills, a subsequent act or writing by a testator/testatrix done or made with the intent to void or render inoperative an existing will.

Self-proving affidavit An affidavit attached to a will that, if executed by the testator/testatrix and the witnesses, dispenses with the necessity of the witnesses' appearing and testifying when the will is offered for probate.

Sound mind Testamentary capacity, which is required of a testator/testatrix for a valid will. Generally, the testator must know and understand the nature and extent of his property and be capable of forming a donative intent based on semireasonable facts.

Statute of frauds A statute, first enacted in England in 1677, that required certain legal acts to be expressed in a written document. In regard to wills, it also required witnesses. Present law places the requirements of a will in the Texas Probate Code rather than in the Statute of Frauds.

Statutory will A will that meets the requirements of the statute prescribing the elements essential to a valid will, including the requirement of being witnessed by two credible persons. Sometimes referred to as a *formal will*.

Subscribe Literally, to sign under; to sign at the bottom or end of a document.

Testator/testatrix A *testator* is a man who is executing or has executed a will. The term is generally only used to refer to a living person. *Testatrix* is the feminine form.

WHO MAY EXECUTE A WILL

In this chapter three kinds of wills will be discussed:

1. Statutory, or formal, wills.
2. **Holographic wills**.
3. **Nuncupative wills**.

As with other legal documents, in order to create a valid will, the person who executes it must have legal capacity. Section 57 of the Texas Probate Code provides the standards of legal capacity as for all three kinds of wills: Before someone can execute a valid will, she must be 18 or older, or have been or be lawfully married, or be a member of the armed forces or maritime services, and be of **sound mind**. The requirement that a **testator/testatrix** be either 18 or have been or be lawfully married simply incorporates the already existing law regarding when a minor comes of age. Similar provisions are found in the Texas Family Code and elsewhere in the statutes of the State of Texas.

The original 1540 English Statute of Wills gave the power to direct the disposition of real estate upon death without any kind of qualification as to soundness of mind. That statute was amended two years later, providing that "idiots" and persons not of "sane memory" could not make valid wills. Most states, including Texas, require that the testator "be of sound mind." The courts have interpreted "soundness of mind" as something different from "incompetency" as defined elsewhere in the Probate Code. These cases also have said that the capacity to make a will may exist even when the person lacks capacity to execute a valid contract [Hamill v. Brashear, 513 S. W.2d 602 (Tex. Civ. App.-Amarillo, 1974 writ ref'd nre)], but see Bach v. Hudson, 596 S.W.2d 673 (Tex. Civ. App.-Corpus Christi, 1980 no writ). A 1886 Supreme Court opinion said as follows:

> If at the time of making his will, he was capable of understanding the nature of the business he was engaged in, the nature and extent of his property, and the person or persons to whom he meant to convey it, and the mode of distributing it among them, and was not under the influence of an **insane delusion**, which affected the disposition of his property, which he was attempting to make, this is sufficient, and he would have what is called testamentary capacity. [Vance v. Upson, 1 S.W. 179 (TEX. 1886)]

This quotation is still an adequate description of testamentary capacity, or the soundness of mind required in order to execute a valid will.

A will may be held invalid for lack of mental capacity, in spite of the fact that the testator was not incompetent as that term is defined elsewhere in the Probate Code. In the quotation in Vance v. Upson this is referred to as *insane delusion*. The Probate Code generally defines *incompetent persons* as those who are mentally incompetent to care for themselves or to manage their property or financial affairs. In 1964, the Supreme Court said,

> A person who is entirely capable of attending to his business affairs may nevertheless have his mind so warped and deranged by some false and unfounded belief that he is incapable of formulating a rational plan of testamentary disposition. [Lindley v. Lindley, 384 S.W.2d 676 (TEX. 1964)]

Texas courts have defined *insane delusion* as "the belief of a state of supposed facts that do not exist, and which no rational person would believe" [Knight v. Edwards, 264 S.W.2d 692 (TEX. 1954)]. An example might be the totally unreasonable belief of spousal infidelity that induces the testatrix to omit her husband from her will.

Obviously, lack of capacity, whether because of age or unsoundness of mind, constitutes the basis on which many wills being offered for probate have been contested. At the end of this chapter some other grounds for the contest of wills that do not directly relate to soundness of mind or age will be discussed.

STATUTORY OR FORMAL WILL

Prior to the enactment in of the 1677 **Statute of Frauds** in England, the only statutory requirement affecting the validity of a will was that it be in writing. The Statute of Frauds added the requirement that it be signed by the testator, or some other person at his direction and in his presence, and witnessed by three or four **credible** witnesses.

When Texas first adopted statutes concerning wills and intestacy in 1840, it copied those statutes almost entirely from statutes of the State of Virginia, which closely followed the English statutes. Since no major change has been made since 1840 in Texas law concerning the validity of wills, it can be said that our law of wills follows the English law of 1677. The nuncupative will was provided for in the Statute of Frauds of 1677, but that statute made no provision for a holographic will. Such provision is taken from the Virginia statutes, having its origin in Roman and then French Civil Law. The English statute had recognized a holographic will only in the case of wills conveying personal property.

Section 59 of the Probate Code contains the current requirements for the execution of a **statutory will** (formal will). Section 59 has two parts. The first deals with requirements regarding the validity of the will and the second deals with the so-called **self-proving affidavit**, which is optional.

The first portion of Section 59 states the requirements of a valid will:

1. The will must be in writing.
2. The will must be signed by the testator or by someone else on his behalf, in his presence, and at his direction.
3. If not wholly in the testator's writing, the will must be witnessed by at least two credible witnesses above the age of 14.
4. The witnesses must **subscribe** (sign under) their name to the will while in the presence of the testator.

It makes no difference what kind of writing the will is in, be it pencil, ink, typewriter, braille, code, or a foreign language. Nor does the testator need to be capable of reading what is written. (Most authorities agree that a will written in some recognized system of shorthand would be valid.) And a will does not necessarily have to be written on paper. (There have been instances in other states of wills written on chalkboards or slates, inscribed upon a bedpost or other structure; one was even written on a woman's slip!) Some authors have maintained that the testator's voice recorded on audiocassette or on videotape could, because of the state of modern technology, be determined by a court to be a writing. These authors see little difference between the inscription of braille on paper and magnetic impressions on recording tapes. No case in Texas has made such a ruling. And although some other states have statutorily provided for the videotaping of wills, Texas has not done so. Consequently, to rely on the belief that a court would reach a determination that a videotape qualifies as a writing would be extremely hazardous.

As to the requirement that a will be signed by the testator, it is fairly clear that the signature need not be in handwriting, as an early case determined that a typewritten signature on a will fulfilled this requirement [Zarusa v. Schumaker, 178 S.W.2d 542 (Tex. Civ. App.-

Galveston, 1944 no writ)]. Other states have upheld the validity of signatures made with a rubber stamp or even by the impressing of the testator's fingerprint.

A number of Texas cases have agreed that the testator who is unable to sign his own name may execute a will by mark and that the mark would be considered a valid signature [Guest v. Guest, 235 S.W.2d 710 (Tex. Civ. App.-Ft. Worth, 1951 writ ref'd nre)]. Initials or a first name have been held to be sufficient. For instance, in a 1921 Civil Appeals opinion, a will signed "your brother Ed" was held to be valid [Barnes v. Horne, 233 S.W. 859 (Tex. Civ. App., 1921 no writ)].

In addition to signing her own name, the testatrix may direct another person to sign her will for her, provided the act of signature is performed within the presence of the testatrix. No requirement is made that the testatrix be incapable of signing her own name, although it would be unusual for someone physically capable of signing her own name to have her signature written by some other person. An early English case, Lemayne v. Stanley, dealt with a will in which the only place the testator's signature appeared was in the opening statement, with no signature at the end of the will. The court found it a valid will, holding that the English statute did not provide a requirement as to where the will should be signed and that therefore a signing in any portion of the will was sufficient. Texas cases have reached a similar result where the signature occurred in the body of the will or on the back of the paper upon which the will was written [In re Estate of Brown, 507 S.W.2d 801 (Tex. Civ. App.-Dallas, 1974 no writ)].

In another line of cases, the testator failed to sign on the blank provided at the end of the will but signed only on the blank provided at the end of the self-proving affidavit. The courts found that the will was not signed, reasoning that the self-proving affidavit was not a part of the will [Boren v. Boren, 402 S.W.2d 728 (TEX. 1966)]. Because of these cases, when Section 59 was amended in 1991, a provision was included that a signature on the self-proving affidavit is to be considered a signature on the will. However, if the signature on the self-proving affidavit is used as the signature on the will, the will cannot be considered to be self-proved.

From the very beginning of its probate law, Texas has required only two witnesses. A number of other states require three. Because of this, some attorneys in Texas advocate the use of three witnesses to a will so that it will meet the requirements of those states. This is unnecessary, however, since all of the states that require three witnesses also have a provision preserving the validity of a will executed in another state with only two witnesses, provided the law of the state in which it was executed requires only two witnesses.

The Texas statute requires that the will be **"attested"** by two or more credible witnesses and further requires that they subscribe their names in their own handwriting. The word subscribed means, literally, "to sign under," that is, to sign at the bottom. The word attest is generally defined as "to bear witness." The witness, by signing the will, certifies compliance with the required formalities of execution of the will.

The statute does not require that the testator sign or execute the will in the presence of the witnesses. In fact, case law has indicated that the testator may sign the will either before or after (as long as it is immediately after) the witnesses subscribe their names and that such signing need not be in the presence of the witnesses [Venner v. Lanton, 244 S.W.2d 852 (Tex. Civ. App.-Dallas, 1951 writ ref'd nre); Ludwick v. Fowler, 193 S.W.2d 692 (Tex. Civ. App.-Dallas, 1946 writ ref'd nre)]. Generally it is assumed that the witnesses attest that the testatrix has declared to them that the document is her will and that she has signed it as such.

Texas cases conflict as to whether **publication** is essential to the validity of a will. *Publication* means that the testatrix declares to the witnesses that the document signed by her is intended by her to be her last will and testament. No such requirement appears in the first part of Section 59, where the requirements of a valid will are set forth. The self-proving affidavit is required, in the second portion of Section 59, to include the following statement:

> The said _____, testator, declared to me and to the said witnesses in my presence that said instrument is his last will and testament, and that he had willingly made and executed it as his free act and deed.

Also, the Texas statute does not require that the testator request the witnesses to attest and subscribe the will. The language of the self-proving affidavit says:

> And upon their oaths, each witness stated further that they did sign the same as witnesses in the presence of the said testator and at his request.

The only cases to determine the matter have not required that there be an expressed declaration, but have found that the testator's silence and acquiescence in the witnesses' subscribing to the will was sufficient [Kveton v. Keding, 286 S.W. 673 (Tex. Civ. App.-Galveston, 1926 writ dism'd)].

Further, Section 59 requires that the witnesses subscribe their names in the presence of the testator. There is no requirement, however, that the witnesses subscribe in the presence of each other. Most authorities see the phrase "in the presence of the testator" as relating to the physical capability of the testator to see the witnesses at the time they sign, regardless of whether the testator did in fact see them sign. A Texas case dealt with a fact situation in which the testator could not see the will at the time the witnesses signed because the witnesses' bodies were between him and the will itself. However, the court seemed to feel it was sufficient that he could see the witnesses, rather than the document itself, at the time they signed, and held that the will was subscribed by the witnesses in the presence of the testator [Earl v. Munday, 227 S.W.2d 716 (Tex. Civ. App.-El Paso, 1921 writ ref'd)].

As to the witness's signature, a mark is sufficient, though a rubber stamp or other facsimile signature probably would not be, because the statute requires that the witness subscribe her name in her own handwriting. It is possible this express language, which was added in 1947, might even eliminate signature by mark, although no case has addressed the situation. Also, it should eliminate the subscription of the witness's name by another person.

With regard to the location of the witnesses' names, in several cases the witnesses have signed someplace other than the extreme end of the will. In one case they signed in the body of the will but after the main dispositive provisions, and in another case their signatures appeared in the attestation clause itself. In another case they appeared under the terminology "witnesses to his mark," and in yet another case the signatures of the witnesses appeared in the margin of the instrument. In each of these cases the will was held to be valid.

In the adoption of the Probate Code in 1955, a provision was added to Section 59 allowing a will to be made self-proved. This is not mandatory; it is optional, although it would be difficult to imagine why anyone would leave such an important provision out of a will in this day and age. It should be noted that the only time a notary public becomes involved with a will is with the self-proving affidavit. To be valid, a will does not have to be executed before a notary public, and in fact execution before a notary public adds nothing to its validity. A self-proving affidavit, however, does have to be executed and sworn to before a notary public.

The only remaining question concerning the validity of a will is the requirement that the witnesses be credible. The word *credible*, as used in the statute, does not mean "believable." Rather, it means "competent, or eligible to testify in court." Lack of mental capacity and conviction of a felony made a witness incompetent to testify at common law. Although the incompetency of a witness created by her conviction as a felon has been removed in Texas, it is probably still the law that an incompetent witness is not a credible witness.

Section 61 was added to solve some of the problems created by court decisions prior to the adoption of the Probate Code. It provides that should a person who is subscribing witness also be a devisee in the will and if the will cannot be established by other means, that is, by the testimony of other witnesses who are credible, then the devise in favor of that witness in the will is declared void. The witness will be allowed, and, in fact, compelled, to give her testimony as if such devise had never been made. The statute does provide that if a witness would have been entitled to a share of the estate had the testator had no will, the devisee/witness will still receive the share that she would have been entitled to in the event of intestacy not to exceed what she was left in the will. Section 62 also deals with this particular issue: If the testimony of an interested witness can be corroborated by one or more disinterested and credible persons who can testify that the testimony of the subscribing witness with an interest is true and correct, then the witness shall not be regarded as an incompetent or noncredible witness.

Whenever a will is being executed, it is best that the legal assistant assure herself that none of the witnesses have any interest whatsoever in the will and that there is no possible way that it could be found that they have some interest under the will. In most law offices it is office staff who serve as the witnesses, and they would rarely have any interest. There is a question whether the attorney, who is named to be attorney for the estate of the testatrix in the will and who serves as either witness or notary public, would be credible as a witness or competent to act as notary.

HOLOGRAPHIC WILL

Section 60 deals with the exception pertaining to holographic wills. The word *holographic* comes from the Greek for "wholly written." As applied to wills and other legal documents it means that the document is written wholly in the handwriting of the testator.

Although a large number of states do not recognize a holographic will, Texas does. Section 60 provides that if a will is written wholly in the handwriting of the testator, the attestation by subscribing witnesses can be dispensed with. Section 60 further provides that a holographic will may be made self-proved by the attachment of a self-proving affidavit. The self-proving affidavit, in the case of a holographic will, is an affidavit by the testator to the effect that the instrument is his will, that he was at least 18 when he signed it or was or had been lawfully married or a member of the armed forces, that he was of sound mind, and that he has not revoked the instrument.

The holographic exception removes only the requirement that the will be attested by two subscribing witnesses. All other requirements of a will that have been discussed, except as they pertain to the witnesses, are still mandatory for the holographic will. It must be signed, and the same law already discussed is applicable to the placement of the signature on a holographic will. It need not be published, because publishing is the declaration to the witnesses, and since there are no witnesses there can be no declaration. The law already discussed concerning competency and testamentary intent is applicable to the holographic will. Texas courts have held that an undated holographic will may be probated. If the date is written in by some person other than the testator, the date will be considered mere surplus and not essential to the validity of the will.

It makes no difference with what the testator writes or upon what he writes; however, it must be by his hand, and mechanical reproduction is not sufficient. It cannot be typewritten; it must be printed or written in script by the hand of the testator.

Sometimes on holographic wills there will be matters written or typed by other persons. Texas has applied a "surplusage" theory to these problems. If what is added in the hand of another or typewritten is mere surplusage and the will can stand alone without it , it will be disregarded, and the will is eligible for admission to probate. If, on the other hand, the added writing forms an essential part of the will, the will will not be found to be wholly in the handwriting of the testator [Maul v. Williams, 69 S.W.2d 1107 (Tex. Comm'n. App., 1934 Holding approved)].

Obviously, a law office is not going to be preparing a holographic will. However, many attorneys have dictated a holographic will over the phone to a client, generally one who is in the hospital, scheduled for surgery from which she might not recover and who has never made a will. This should only be done in circumstances in which it is impossible to prepare a formal will and to have it executed prior to whatever event is going to take place. Also, some clients getting ready to make a trip or in the middle of a divorce may want an immediate will, without expense, to serve until they can make decisions concerning what they want in their will. In this case an attorney might advise the client on how to prepare a valid holographic will. The legal assistant should not give such advice, for this would violate the ethical rules concerning the conduct of a legal assistant.

NUNCUPATIVE WILL

The nuncupative will existed at Roman Civil Law and also under Spanish and Mexican law. However, the nuncupative will of Roman, Spanish, and Mexican law is not related to the nuncupative will recognized in Texas. The oral testament of personal property came out of the custom and tradition of England, and even during the Twelfth, Thirteenth and Fourteenth centuries, when English law prohibited the passage of real property by will, the ecclesiastical courts of England were enforcing oral wills.

The nuncupative will is an oral statement made with testamentary intent at a time when the testator has the capacity to execute a will. The nuncupative will is totally ineffective with respect to real property, inasmuch as anything that transfers an interest in real property must be in writing. Further, a nuncupative will is only effective for personal property not exceeding $30.00 value, unless it is proved by three credible witnesses that the testator asked them to witness his testamentary words or to bear testimony that such words are in fact his will.

Few lawyers have ever had to probate a nuncupative will, and its importance is slight.

REVOCATION AND AMENDMENT OF WILLS

Section 63 provides that a will can be revoked only by a subsequent will, by a **codicil**, by a declaration in writing that is executed with the formalities required by the statute, or by the testator's destroying or canceling the will or causing that to be done in his presence.

The first portion of Section 63 states that a will may not be revoked except by subsequent will, codicil, or declaration in writing with like formalities. The words *like formalities* have been construed to mean that the testatrix has the capacity to make a will, that is, she meets the age requirements and is of sound mind. Further, the document must show the intent of the testator to revoke the prior will. Lastly, *like formalities* means that the instrument must be eligible for probate. It does not mean that a formal will can only be revoked by a document executed with all the formalities required of a formal will or that a holographic will may only be revoked by a holographic will.

The Texas courts have held that a will may be revoked by a subsequent will with inconsistent provisions even though that will contains no revocatory language [Thomason v. Gwin, 184 S.W.2d 542 (Tex. Civ. App.-1944 writ ref'd wom)]. The practice of most attorneys is to include a revocatory provision in each will prepared.

Texas has never required any specific means of destruction. Any ripping, tearing, obliteration, or burning that leaves the document unreadable, done with the intent of revoking, is sufficient [Simpson v. Neely, 221 S.W. 2d 303)Tex. Civ. App.-Waco, 1949 writ ref'd)].

Cancellation involves writing across the face of the will the word *canceled* or *revoked* or something else indicating the testator's intention to revoke the prior will. Remember that the physical act of destruction, or cancellation, must be made or done with the intent of revoking the prior instrument. Accidental destruction does not revoke the instrument. However, nonproduction of the will creates a presumption of **revocation**. Should the will bear the word *canceled* or *revoked* or be cut in two and then pasted back together, there will be a presumption of revocation by destruction or cancellation. This presumption can be overcome by proof that such destruction was accidental. For instance, if the testatrix thought she was destroying an older will and then when she realized her mistake she taped it back together, there would be no revocation.

There are two instances in which wills or portions of wills may be revoked by operation of law. The first is found in Section 69, which provides that, if the testator is divorced after the making of a will, all provisions of the will in favor of the divorced spouse and appointing such spouse to any fiduciary capacity under the will are void and of no effect.

Second, Section 57 has the effect of revoking portions of the will in the event that a testator has a child born after the making of his last will. The child so born is termed a **pretermitted child**. Section 67 provides that if the testator has one or more children living when he executes the will and no provision is made for any such child, the pretermitted child succeeds to the portion that the child would have inherited had the testator died intestate, provided that portion of the estate is not devised to the parent of the pretermitted child. If the will does make provision for children who were alive at the time of the executed will, the pretermitted child is entitled to receive a portion equal to that of the other children. If the testator had no child alive, the pretermitted child receives that portion the child would have inherited had the testator died without the will, providing that portion is not devised to a parent of the pretermitted child.

As has been previously mentioned, a will may be revoked by a codicil. But a codicil has other uses also. In fact, the most common use of a codicil is to amend a prior will without revoking it. Codicils can be used to explain or clarify provisions of an existing will, to delete from an existing will one or more provisions without revoking the will itself, to alter or modify one or more provisions of the will, or to add provisions to the will. A codicil should not rewrite a will substantially. Instead, a new will should be prepared and executed that replaces and revokes the prior one.

Many lawyers believe that codicils should not be used to amend wills. They say that it is too easy to suppress a codicil and offer the will for probate as if the codicil had never been executed. Instead, they recommend and sometimes even insist that the client execute a new will that cancels the old. In addition, they supervise the complete obliteration of the old will.

Some wills have been amended multiple times by complicated codicils. After several involved amendments it can be difficult, perhaps impossible, to determine the testamentary intent of the testator. Many clients, however, believe that a codicil is less expensive to prepare than a new will. This may be accurate in the case of a long, complicated will that is to be amended only in a minor way. But it is generally not true for a simple will. Also, computers in the law office now ease the task of creating new wills, particularly if the old will is still stored on disk in the office.

Some question exists as to the effect of a revocation of a codicil that changes a will. Does the revocation of the codicil reinstate the will as originally executed? Although there might not be a definite answer to this question, there is no doubt that revocation of a later will that revokes an earlier will does not reinstate the earlier will. Rather than revoke by codicil, it is far safer to execute a new will containing the same provisions as the older one.

An example of a codicil is found at the end of this chapter as Form 4-1.

MISCELLANEOUS MATTERS CONCERNING THE EXECUTION & EFFECTIVENESS OF WILLS

Prior to 1979, there were a considerable number of cases concerning so-called joint wills and/or mutual wills. A **joint will** is one in which two people make a single will; and a **mutual will** is one in which there are mutual provisions in the wills of two persons. The problem was that if the will was joint and mutual, there was a presumption that the testator intended the will to become a contract, and therefore the surviving testator could not revoke following the death of the first testator.

This area of the law was put to rest by the adoption in 1979 of Section 59(a). This section provides that a contract to make a will or devise or not to revoke a will or devise, if executed or entered into after September 1, 1979, can only be established if the will itself contains provisions stating that a contract does exist and further states the material provisions of the contract. Section 59 also provides that the execution of a joint will or reciprocal wills does not by itself suffice as evidence of the existence of a contract.

Sometimes people will want some sort of a contractual provision in a will, often a prohibition against revocation by the surviving person. Section 59(a) allows a testator in a will to devise property to the trustee of any trust that is in existence before or comes into existence concurrently with or after the execution of the will. This is a "pour over" clause, because it pours over the assets that pass under the will into the corpus of the trust.

Section 68 provides for the prior death of a devisee. This is sometimes referred to as the **antilapse** statute. Generally, at common law if a devisee died prior to the testator, the gift to that devisee lapsed and it passed by intestacy. The antilapse provisions of Section 68 do two things:

1. They prohibit lapse in a case in which the devisee is a descendent of the testator or a descendant of the testator's parent. In the event such a devisee dies prior to the testator, the gift does not lapse but rather passes to the surviving descendants of the devisee.

2. They state that if, in fact, a devise does lapse, such devise or bequest becomes a part of the residuary estate and, assuming there is a residuary clause, as will be discussed in the next chapter, the lapsed gift will be added to the residuary passing to the residuary devisee.

Section 68 then says that if the residuary estate is devised to two or more persons and the share of one lapses, the deceased devisee's share passes to the surviving devisees. Finally, if all residuary devisees are deceased, the residuary estate passes as if the testator had died intestate.

The 1993 Omnibus Probate Bill added a provision requiring that descendants of the devisee survive the testator by 120 hours in order to receive benefits under the antilapse statute. It also provides some nonexclusive language to include in wills to override the effects of the antilapse statute. For example, a devise "to my surviving children" will benefit only those children who actually survive the testator, and will not pass to descendants of a predeceasing child. It also provides that a class gift will not pass to the descendants of a member of the class who was deceased at the time that the testatrix executed her will.

WILL CONTESTS

A considerable number of will contests, that is, legal actions to have a will declared void, are based on the lack of a requirement that a testator be of sound mind when he executes a will. Other will contests are based on the claim that the will fails to meet one or more statutory or case law requirements. A number of will contests, however, are based on the traditional contractual defenses of mistake, duress, and undue influence.

Mistake is divided into mistake in the factum and mistake in the inducement. *Mistake in the factum* is generally defined as a mistake that occurs when a testatrix is in error or mistaken as to the identity or the contents of the document she is signing that later is offered as her will. It may be that she does not realize she is signing a will but thinks she is signing some other type of document, or it may be that she intends to sign a will and by mistake signs an old version that has been abandoned. Also, the will may contain, without the knowledge and against the desires of the testatrix, a gift to a particular person, or the testatrix may believe that the will does contain a gift to a particular person though it does not.

A will is not subject to **reformation**, so the only action a court can take is to strike the unintended clause or, when the mistake involves the entire document, to declare the document null and void. To obtain this kind of relief, it is necessary first to overcome the presumption that the testator knew and understood the contents of the wills.

Mistake in the inducement has been defined as a mistake that exists when the testator is not in error as to his belief concerning the identity of the instrument or the contents of the instrument that he is signing but as to some fact outside of the will or as to the legal effect of the will. Some of the cases concern falseness of a friend or the moral habits of one of the devisees named in the will or the marital status of one of the devisees or perhaps the death or continued life of one of the devisees. The courts have generally refused to give any relief in the situation where there is a mistake in the inducement.

Fraud as applied in will cases is no different than fraud applied as a defense to contracts. There must be a representation that has the effect of deceiving the testator about some material fact, that representation must have been made with intent to deceive and the testator must have relied on that representation.

Fraud is broken down into fraud in factum and fraud in the inducement. *Fraud in factum* occurs when the testator is deceived as to the identity or the contents of the instrument he is signing. The courts generally have had no difficulty at all in determining the invalidity of a will under these circumstances.

Unlike mistake, the courts have routinely ruled that a will is invalid where it was a result of *fraud in the inducement*. This is because of the intentional conduct of the deceiver and the fact that such behavior destroys testamentary intent.

The grounds of will contests known as *undue influence* are a mixture of duress and fraud. In fact, duress and fraud are sometimes mixed together in discussion of undue influence. Generally speaking, undue influence, as distinguished from ordinary duress, involves moral coercion. In many cases, the facts constituting undue influence appear to come within the definition of duress. Generally, undue influence is a more subtle influence than duress. It might be a constant begging or whining (as opposed to threats) by the actor until the testator no longer has any free will. It might be continual persuasion and argument, particularly of a moral type, to the point that the testatrix does not know what she wants and acquiesces to the actor.

Many of the cases dealing with undue influence require the actor to be in some fiduciary or confidential relationship to the testator. This is a relationship that creates a belief or feeling by the testator that the person advising him would only do so with the best interest of the testator in mind and would certainly not do anything to harm the testator. This includes not only the traditional fiduciary-type relationships such as guardian and ward, attorney and client, trustee and beneficiary, agent and principal, and minister and congregation, but also close family relationships and, probably, close business relationships. An example is the will contest in the Sarita K. East Estate and the testimony concerning the actions of Brother Leo, Mrs. East's spiritual adviser and confidante. This particular prominent and protracted contest of the wills of Sarita K. East, a descendant of the founder of the King Ranch, has been in the news many times over the past 15 or so years. (See various news accounts, including those that appeared in the *Wall Street Journal* and the *Corpus Christi Caller-Times*.)

Duress is generally divided into emotional duress and physical duress. *Physical duress* involves physical acts that would cause harm or threaten harm to the testator unless the testator executes the will. *Emotional duress* is sometimes almost indistinguishable from undue influence.

All of these concepts, under the proper facts, can constitute grounds to contest the probate of the will, either at the time it is offered from probate or thereafter as provided for in the Probate Code. A successful contest of a will or revocation of an earlier will has the effect of reinstating the earlier will. This was the result in the Sarita K. East will contest.

CHAPTER QUESTIONS AND EXERCISES

1. How did the passage of the Statute of Wills and the Statute of Frauds in England affect the law concerning wills?

2. Suppose an individual becomes obsessed with the belief that his children are attempting to kill him for his money; although this is in fact totally. Acting on this mistaken belief, the individual makes a will that omits his children from any benefits. Assuming the will meets all other requirements of law, is the will valid and enforceable? Explain your answer.

3. A will is offered for probate. The only place the testatrix's signature appears is at the end of the self-proving affidavit. Is the will valid? Would it make any difference if the will were offered for probate prior to September 1, 1991? Explain your answers.

4. During the probate of a will, it becomes necessary to have the original witnesses to the will appear and testify. In their testimony

the witnesses admit that the testatrix never stated to them in any form or fashion that the document was her will, but that they presumed it was because the lawyer had asked them to come in to witness a will (although the lawyer's statement was not in the presence of the testatrix). In fact, the witnesses testify that there were no words spoken by the testatrix, nor did they see her sign the will. Assuming that the will meets all other requirements of law, is the will valid and admissible to probate? Explain your answer.

5. Suppose witnesses are necessary to prove the validity of a will when it is offered for probate. They testify that when the attorney instructed the testator to sign the will, the testator picked up his poodle, pressed its paw into an ink pad, and stuck the paw on the will in the area of the signature line, saying at the same time, "This is my last will and testament and by this act I am executing it as such." Is the will valid and admissible to probate? Explain your answer.

6. What is the effect of the self-proving affidavit?

7. Suppose a witness to a will is also named as a substitute independent executrix. She is to serve as independent executrix if the first-named independent executor dies, refuses to serve, or resigns. When the will is offered for probate, the originally named independent executor files an application requesting that he be named independent executor. It becomes necessary to establish the will by the testimony of the witnesses, and when the witness, who was also named as substitute independent executrix, attempts to testify, an objection is made that she is not a credible witness. Is she or is she not credible? Discuss your answer.

8. Suppose a holographic will contains no signature at the end or anywhere else, except in the first line, which says: "I, Joe Testator, being of sound mind and disposing intent, do hereby make this my last will and testament." If other requirements are satisfied, is the will valid and admissible to probate? Explain your answer.

9. Suppose Testator dies in a fire that starts in his bedroom. Witnesses say that, shortly prior to retiring for the night, he had a violent argument with a friend, who was also a beneficiary in his will, and announced that he was going to revoke his will and cut the friend out of it. Testimony by the fire marshall indicates that the fire started in the drawer of a bedside table. Witnesses further testify that the testator always kept his will in that drawer. An attempt is made to probate the will by proving its contents by extraneous testimony. Is there a problem with the admission of the will to probate? If so, what is the problem? Explain your answer.

10. In a will, suppose that a testatrix leaves $10,000. to her nephew. Prior to the testatrix's death the nephew dies, leaving as his heir a son. The will provides that the residuary of the testatrix's estate goes to the her spouse. Upon the testatrix's death, who receives the $10,000? Would it make any difference if the devise had been to an uncle who was survived by one son? Explain your answer.

Form 4-1: Codicil to a Will

FIRST CODICIL TO THE LAST WILL AND TESTAMENT OF PETER SMITH

I, Peter Smith, of Corpus Christi, Nueces County, Texas do make, publish and declare this to be the first codicil to the last will and testament executed by me on the 12th day of January, 1994, in the presence of Jane Brown and Martha Green.

Paragraph Second is hereby amended to read as follows:

I give, devise and bequeath to my beloved children, or the survivors of them, all the rest, residue, and remainder of my property of every kind and description of which I may die seized and possessed or in which I may have an interest, whether real, personal or mixed and wherever situated.

Paragraph Third is hereby deleted.

In all other respects, I ratify and confirm all of the provisions of my said will.

IN TESTIMONY WHEREOF, I sign, publish and declare this instrument to be the first codicil to my last will and testament, said codicil consisting of this page and the succeeding page, this _____ day of March, 1994.

_____

The foregoing instrument, consisting of this and the preceding page was signed, published and declared by Peter Smith, the Testator, to be the first codicil to his last will and testament in our presence, and we at his request and in his presence and in the presence of each other have hereunto subscribed our names as witnesses, this_____ day of March, 1994, at Corpus Christi, Texas.

_____ residing at _____
_____ residing at _____

STATE OF TEXAS   ) (
COUNTY OF NUECES   ) (

BEFORE ME, the undersigned authority, on this day personally appeared PETER SMITH, _____ , and _____ , known to me to be the Testator and the witnesses, respectively, whose names are subscribed to the annexed or foregoing instrument in their respective capacities, and all of said persons being by me duly sworn, the said PETER SMITH, Testator, declared to me and to the said witnesses, in my presence that said instrument is the First Codicil to his Last Will and Testament and that he had willingly made and executed it as his free act and deed for the purposes therein expressed; and the said witnesses, each on their oath, stated to me and in the presence and hearing of the said Testator that the said Testator had declared to them that said instrument is the First Codicil to his Last Will and Testament, and that he executed the same as such and wanted each of them to sign it as a witness; and upon their oaths, each witness stated further that they did sign the same as witnesses in the presence of the said Testator and at his request; and that he was at that time eighteen (18) years of age or over, and was of sound mind and that each of said witnesses was then at least fourteen (14) years of age.

_____
PETER SMITH

_____

_____
WITNESSES

SUBSCRIBED AND SWORN BEFORE ME by the said PETER SMITH, Testator, and by the said _____ and _____ , witnesses, this the _____day of March, 1994.

_____
Notary Public for the State of Texas.

5 DRAFTING AND EXECUTION OF WILLS

CHAPTER OBJECTIVES

Upon completion of this chapter, the student should be able to:

1. Conduct an interview of a client, and obtain the information needed to prepare a will for that client.

2. Recognize and understand the nature and effect of standard will clauses.

3. Prepare simple wills for single persons, for married couples, and for married couples with children.

4. Direct the execution of a will.

CHAPTER GLOSSARY

Attestation clause The clause at the end of a will in which the witnesses certify (attest) that they have witnessed the will in conformity with state statutes.

Beneficiary In regard to trusts, the person for whose benefit property is held in trust. In regard to wills, a person named to receive specific property.

Bequest At common law, the transfer of personal property by will. Under the Texas Probate Code, both the transfer of personal property and the transfer of real property.

Class gift A gift (by will) to a group of persons, uncertain in number at the time of the gift, to be determined at some future time, who all share equally.

Corpus Body. In regard to trusts, the principal of the trust or the property the

settlor put into the trust originally, which may have changed during the trust.

Execution The signing of a document.

Executor Someone appointed in a will to carry out the directions, request, and dispositions of the testator after his death.

Exordium and publication clause The introductory clause of a will. Also called *preamble*.

General bequest In a will in which there is no specific bequest, the gift of the entire estate to a named person, persons, or a class of persons.

Guardian A person legally charged with responsibility for the care and management of the person and/or estate of a someone considered incapable of managing his own affairs, such as a minor or an incapacitated person. Guardians are normally appointed by the Probate Court.

Independent executor An executor who can sell property belonging to the estate, pay creditors, distribute the estate to the devisees, and so on without first obtaining approval and consent from the Probate Court.

In terrorem clause A clause in a will that threatens devisees with forfeiture of their bequests if they contest the validity of all or any part of it.

Legacy At common law, a gift of personal property by will. Under the Texas Probate Code, interchangeable with the word *devise* in referring to the gift of both real and personal property by will.

Pour over The funding of a previously existing trust by assets devised to the trust in a will.

Power of appointment The right to designate the persons who shall enjoy the use of property in the future.

Residuary clause In a will, a clause that disposes of that portion of the estate that has not been disposed of by a specific bequest.

Specific bequest or devise A gift, by will, of specific articles of personal property or specifically described real estate.

Sprinkling The unequal distribution of income to the beneficiaries of a trust. Allows the trustee to spend the income to meet the needs of the beneficiaries even if the result is an unequal distribution. Sometimes referred to as *spraying*.

Testimonium clause In a will, a concluding clause that describes those who executed the will and the date of execution.

INTRODUCTION

Exactly when the legal assistant is brought into contact with the client concerning the preparation of wills will vary from office to office, though such involvement should be as early as possible. The client's first contact is generally with the attorney. However, with the approval of the supervising attorney, the legal assistant alone can conduct the initial interview, provided the client needs no legal advice concerning his choices in making the will.

If the initial interview is to be with the attorney, the legal assistant is usually brought into the interview at the very beginning. Once the fee is established, gathering of necessary information is often left to the legal assistant.

One of the first things that must be determined is whether the client's potential estate is significant enough to suggest estate planning. In a number of firms this is done by having the client, either on his own or with the aid of a legal assistant, fill out a lengthy checklist concerning family data and current assets and liabilities (including reasonably anticipated accessions to wealth, such as inheritances and early retirement allowances. In at least one trial in Texas an attorney was sued for malpractice after the death of a client by the devisees named in the will. The contention was that the attorneys had failed in their obligation to look into the size of the possible estate and to suggest methods for reducing federal estate taxes. The evidence indicated that the attorneys suggested delving into such matters but that the clients had insisted the estate was not large enough to worry about and that they only wanted a simple will. Although the jury in this case held in favor of the attorney, in general the expense of such a suit is best avoided.

A number of attorneys insist that if the client does not complete the lengthy checklist concerning financial data, they will either refuse to represent him or require that the client sign a statement waiving, on behalf of himself and his devisees, any future liability by reason of the client's refusal to engage in estate planning.

The Estate Planning Questionnaire in Chapter Three (Form 3-1) is of the type that could be used for gathering the data necessary to determine whether estate planning should be suggested. Even if the checklist is not totally filled out by the client because either he refuses to do so or a rough determination has indicated that his estate is not taxable, then the portion of the checklist that relates to the will itself, the devisees, the **executor**, the trustee, the **guardians**, etc., is still useful in the initial interview.

When obtaining information about assets, the legal assistant should not forget to ask about nonprobate assets, such as life insurance payable on the death of the client, employment benefits (including life insurance, which is often forgotten by the employee,) retirement plans, individual retirement accounts, and interests in trust. These are still subject to estate tax and may necessitate estate planning even though the portion of the estate that will pass by the will does not.

Assuming the client knows to whom he wants to leave the property and who is to be executor, guardian, or trustee, the legal assistant will normally assume sole responsibility for the remainder of the interview.

INFORMATION GATHERING—THE INTAKE INTERVIEW

The nature of the interview is probably less important in the preparation of wills and trusts than it is with probate administration. In the case of probate administration, the client generally has recently lost someone close. In either situation, the legal assistant should appear competent and knowledgeable. This can be best accomplished via careful preparation and rehearsal. The use of a checklist with which the legal assistant is already quite familiar can enhance the interview situation.

The duties of legal assistants for obtaining information in the preparation of wills and testamentary trusts include the following:

1. Obtain the name and residence of all persons to be named in the will—devisees, executors, trustee, guardians, and beneficiaries and remaindermen of the trust. Sometimes the client will not understand the function of each of these representatives. The legal assistant's supervising attorney should define how far the legal assistant can go in explaining these representative capacities, but a simple, plain-language definition of each probably does not constitute giving legal advice.

2. Be alert, as the client talks about these persons, to indications of fear of conflict between the devisees, advancements, persons who for some reason may be unable to handle their own financial affairs, and any other emotional or personal situation that might affect the preparation of the will.

3. Find out the client's desires as to the final disposition of his property. Ask the client if there is any specific property that is to go to a particular person. Sometimes the client may state that everybody knows who gets what. This response is unacceptable. Unless the client can be encouraged to be more specific without the legal assistant's explaining the law, the lawyer will have to be brought into the discussion.

4. Get information that will provide for contingent devisees in the event the primary devisees die before the client and the client does not immediately change his will. Also, get names for substitute executors, guardians, and trustees. Most attorneys prefer wills to provide for at least one level of substitute or alternate devisee, executor, guardian, or trustee. Some attorneys want to go even further.

5. Check the ages of all primary and contingent beneficiaries. If some are minors, a trust, a devise under the Uniform Gift to Minors Act, or some other procedure should be included in the will to provide for the management of the estate until the minor devisees are mature enough to take care of it themselves. Even where the beneficiaries are adults, if they are young, dependent or sheltered, the client should be queried as to whether they are able to manage their own financial affairs. If not, a trust should be considered.

6. Make sure all names are spelled correctly. It is astonishing how many different ways common names are spelled. For example, *Ann* is sometimes also spelled *Anne, An* or *Ayn. Elizabeth* is sometimes spelled with an *s*, sometimes with a *z*. Have the client spell out each name.

7. Make sure no relative is omitted from the will. In Texas, children of the will maker have no absolute right of inheritance. Any relative can be omitted from a will. Many clients have been told they should leave a small amount of money to a child, such as one dollar, if they are otherwise going to cut that child out of the will. This is acceptable, but unnecessary under Texas law. However, if a client is making an *unnatural devise*, (a devise that deliberately omits persons, such as a spouse or children, that one would normally expect a testator to make provision for), the legal assistant may want to advise considering a gift of one dollar or an affirmative statement that a particular person is being deliberately omitted and an explanation of why the unnatural devise is being made. The unnatural devise may be used as evidence that the testator was not of sound and disposing mind at the time of the **execution** of the will. If the explanation is reasonable, then this can be used as proof in a will contest that the testator was competent.

8. If trusts are going to be provided for in the will, must get information from the client concerning the expenditure of funds by

the trustee on behalf of the beneficiaries during the trust. This would include: whether the trustee can make unequal distributions to beneficiaries (called *sprinkling* or set limitations or expansions on the rights and responsibilities of the trustee; whether the trustee has the power to invade the **corpus** of the trust (or to spend the principal of the trust as well as the income for the benefit of the **beneficiary**); and whether to include spendthrift provisions. Also, information must be obtained as to when the trust shall vest or come to an end and the remaining principal and income distributed to the remaindermen.

9. Give the client a written list of needed information that the client did not bring. A date should be set for a follow-up interview at which time the client will provide the information still needed.

10. If the law office mails a draft of the will to the client to review prior to coming in to execute it, tell the client about this and explain how the client may go about notifying the office of corrections or changes. Also, discuss whether the client will have to call for an appointment to execute the will or when the client may come in to execute the will. If the office does not follow this procedure, explain whatever procedure the office follows for client review of the will and how the client will be notified. Give the client some idea of when the work will be completed. The client may have some deadline, such as a extended trip, or some other reason to have the will executed quickly.

11. Make sure that the anticipated fee has been adequately explained, especially if the legal assistant is not present at the initial conference. It may be necessary to bring the attorney back into the discussion unless, through some office procedure or policy, the legal assistant knows what the charge will be and is authorized to tell the client.

INITIAL CONSIDERATIONS OF THE PREPARATION OF A WILL

The will should be in a single typeface; however, if the law firm has a computer with a choice of fonts, the will can be dressed up as long as everything fits together. If boldface or different-sized type is selected, the same font should be used.

Many clients expect double margin ruled paper, will covers, and will envelopes. If the law office does not use will covers, the attorney's name, address, and phone number should appear. This encourages future business for the attorney. Often, executors (including banks) and principal devisees will engage the same attorney who prepared the will to probate it if they know who that attorney is.

If the legal assistant has to draft language for the will because he cannot find the needed language in any form book or in previous wills drawn up by the firm, he must do this with the utmost care. The language should harmonize with that in the remainder of the will. To ensure that the added language reflects the client's desires properly and is clearly written, the legal assistant should request at least one other person in the firm, perhaps several persons, to read it before the will is submitted to the attorney for approval. The plainer the language, the more likely the clause will be interpreted in accordance with the client's wishes. Also, if the legal assistant finds an acceptable clause in a forms book, the wording should be amended as needed to harmonize with the rest of the will.

Unless there is a **general bequest**, a **residuary clause** should always be included. (General bequests and residuary clauses will be discussed later in this chapter.) There have been many horror stories about the drafters of wills who failed to include a residuary clause, with the result that the testators died partially intestate.

Erasures and corrections should be avoided. In this day of word processors and computers, this is easy to do. The will must be carefully proofread for typographical errors that could change the meaning of the will. (There is even a very early Texas Supreme Court decision based wholly upon the placement of a semicolon. The case is so old that it does not appear in *Southwestern Reporter*.) If, in fact, erasures or corrections are necessary, the legal assistant should have the client initial each erasure or correction when he executes the will.

Full data on everyone named should be stated in the will, preferably at least the city or county of residence, if not a street address. Also the relationship to the client should be spelled out. This sets the stage for the gift and provides a reason for it, which can be used in a will contest to establish competency. A trial lawyer can point to the fact that the testator knew the addresses of the devisees and other persons named in the will as further evidence of competency. However, the prime reason such information is included is to make it easier to locate these people in the event they are not readily available at the time of the death of the testator. Obtaining witnesses' addresses is particularly important, in case the self-proving affidavit (discussed later in this chapter) fails and the witnesses are needed to establish the validity of the will at the time of probate.

The following are the relevant events common to the drafting of a will:

1. Conducting the client intake interview.
2. Gathering data from the client via checklists.
3. Analyzing of the information obtained from the client to determine whether estate planning techniques should be used and which clauses to insert.
4. Preparing a preliminary draft.
5. Reviewing the draft with the supervising attorney and making changes suggested by him.
6. Delivering the draft to the client for review.
7. Preparing the final draft.
8. Supervising the execution of the will by the client.

Although these events will differ slightly from client to client, they will all occur to some degree. The initial interview may be only a telephone call. The checklist may contain only the names of devisees and executors. The analysis may take a very short time, and the review of the draft with the client may consist of mailing it to him and telling him to look it over. In other cases, the intake interview may last an hour or more, the checklist may be 20 or 30 pages long, and the analysis may consist of multiple conferences with the attorney responsible for the will, research, and multiple conferences with the client. The client's review of the initial draft may require the attorney's presence and may take over an hour.

ANATOMY OF A STANDARD WILL

The following is a list of clauses that are fairly standard in Texas wills. Some will not be included in every will or will be combined with another clause or will be found in a different order. Often there will be additional clauses to make the will fit the particular needs and situation of the testator or testatrix.

1. Preamble (**exordium and publication clause**).
2. Clause revoking prior wills.
3. Provision for the payment of debts.
4. Appointment of **independent executor**.
5. Instructions for funeral and burial arrangements.
6. **Specific bequests or devises**.
7. Residuary clause, often creating a testamentary trust.
8. Appointment of guardian for minor children, if applicable.
9. Afterborn children provision.
10. **In terrorem clause**.
11. **Testimonium clause**.
12. Testator's signature.
13. **Attestation** clause.
14. Witnesses' signatures and addresses.
15. Self-proving affidavit.

Preamble (Exordium and Publication Clause)

The exordium and publication clause states that the testator intends the document to be a will that takes effect and disposes of his property upon his death. Its purpose is to declare that the testator has the capacity to make a will and the freedom and intention to do so and that the testator understands the document is his last will and Testament.

Example 5-1: Preamble

I, John Smith, of Corpus Christi, Nueces County, Texas, being of sound and disposing mind, and not acting under the influence of any person whatsoever, do hereby make and publish this my last will and testament.

Revocatory Clause

Sometimes following and sometimes combined into the exordium and publication clause is a clause revoking all prior wills and codicils. Most of the will forms published for use in Texas contain such a clause, frequently combined into the exordium and publication clause.

Example 5-2: Revocatory Clause

I do hereby expressly revoke all prior wills and codicils heretofore made by me.

Clause Directing Payment of Debts

Following the revocatory clause frequently is found a provision requiring the independent executor to pay debts. This clause is probably not needed, because the Texas Probate Code already imposes this responsibility on the independent executor.

Example 5-3: Clause Directing Payment of Debts

I direct that all my just debts shall be paid as soon as they might accrue.

or

I direct my independent executor hereinafter named to pay all my just debts, all the expenses of the administration of my estate, the expenses of my last illness, and expenses for my funeral and burial prior to distribution of any of my estate to my devisees.

Appointment of Independent Executor

Next comes a clause that appoints an independent executor. In some wills this is placed after the residuary clause. Texas provides that a testator may appoint an independent executor in a will. (More will be said about the independent executor in Chapter 10.) The appointment of an independent executor saves considerable costs to the estate and carries out the wishes of the testator more quickly in the event of his death. There is no situation imaginable that would justify not using this procedure. If the testator is worried that the person he has selected cannot be trusted or that a conflict will arise between the named executor and the devisees, the testator can name co-executors or an executor who has no interest in the estate at all or, if the estate is large enough, the trust department of a bank (a trust department receives the same consideration as any other executor and, consequently, the estate must be large enough for it to make a profit for its services).

Probate Section 145 provides as follows:

Any person capable of making a will may provide in this will that no other action shall be had in the county court in a relation to the settlement of his estate than the probating and recording of his will, and the return of an inventory, appraisement, and list of claims of his estate.

Most lawyers feel that the clause covering the appointment of the independent executor should use the language of the statute. However, there is at least one case indicating that the statutory language is not necessary but requires the testator to show an intention that the executor be independent of the court's control. Many forms now in circulation do not use the language of the statute but merely refer to the executrix as an independent executor (some do not even do that much).

The legal assistant should make sure that the will form contains language waiving the requirement of a bond. Unfortunately, there are a number of wills in forms books for use in Texas that fail to contain language waiving the bond of the independent executor.

A relatively recent case has confirmed what some already thought to be the law: An executor, unless otherwise authorized by the will, only has the authority to sell or lease property of the estate, without first seeking permission of the court, if the purpose is to carry out the administration of the estate [*Gatesville Redi-Mix, Inc. v. Jones*, 787 S.W.2d 443 (Tex. App.-1990 writ dnd)]. "Carrying out the administration" means that the purpose may be to pay the claims of creditors or to distribute the estate to the devisee. There is an indication in that case that a sale of property by an executor, unless the will expressly authorizes the executor to sell real or personal property of the estate whenever he deems it advisable, may be set aside unless it can be established that the sale was in furtherance of the administration of the estate. There are two versions of a clause (see Examples 5-4 and 5-5), that authorize such discretionary sale. The second version gives the executor all of the powers given to a trustee under the Texas Trust Code; including the authority to sell.

Example 5-4: Appointment of Executor With Discretionary Power of Sale

I hereby appoint my wife, Paula Smith, of Nueces County, Texas, independent executrix of this, my last will and testament, and in the event she should predecease me or is unable to perform said office, I hereby appoint my brother, Pavel Smith of Harris County, Texas, independent executor of my last will and testament; I further direct that no bond be required of my wife or said substitute and that no other action shall be had in the county court in relation to the settlement of said estate than the probating and recording of this, my will, and return of the statutory inventory, appraisement, and list of claims due or owing by me at the time of my death. I hereby authorize and empower my independent executor to mortgage, sell, dispose of, deliver, and convey any portion of my estate, real or personal, at public or private sale, for any price, on any terms, and in any manner that may seem to her best, or to lease, pledge, or otherwise manage any and all of my property.

An alternate provision to use in place of the last sentence of Example 5-4 is given in Example 5-5:

Example 5-5: Powers of Trustee

I do hereby direct that my said independent executrix shall have all the powers and rights of a trustee as provided in the Texas Trust Code.

Provisions for Funeral and Burial

Only a few testators have any specific directions to make concerning their funeral and burial. It is probably best not to suggest that they put specific directions for funeral and burial arrangements in their will. It is not clear just how efficient the directions concerning funeral and burial in a will are to be. Some states provide that the next of kin of the decedent has the final say as to funeral and burial arrangements, regardless of what the will says. In Texas this has always been assumed to be the case. Texas statutory law specifies who has the right to determine the place of burial, the prior right being in the surviving spouse. No statute or case, however, addresses what happens when a probated will provides otherwise.

Some years ago, the news media told of a case probated in northwest Texas in which the decedent provided in her will that she be buried in her Porsche, wearing her favorite negligee, with her fur coat draped around her shoulders, and wearing a lot of jewelry. The general or residual devisees were unhappy at the thought of burying over $100,000 of property. The executor announced his intentions to comply with the decedent's request, so the devisees stormed into Probate Court. The Probate Court held that the executor alone had the choice as to whether to comply with the funeral and burial instructions contained in the will. The executor was not bound to follow the instructions, but having determined to follow them could not be second-guessed by a court or devisees. The Probate Court held, however, that extravagant funeral or burial instructions could not be used to subvert the rights of creditors. Apparently, the case was not appealed.

Another provision that may be included within the funeral and burial clause concerns making anatomical gifts. Although there is nothing wrong with doing this, the body may be embalmed by the time anyone even looks at the will, and may be buried long before the will is probated. If someone requests this, he should be advised to tell all who would have a close knowledge of his death that the will makes an anatomical gift and also to specify the gift on his driver's license, as allowed by Texas statute.

Example 5-6: Funeral and Burial Clause

I direct that my funeral be conducted according to the rites of the Protestant Episcopal Church of the United States of America, in the church of which I am a member at the time of my death, and by the rector or assistant rector of said church. I further direct that my coffin shall remain closed at all times so that I may be remembered as I was when I was alive.

Specific Bequests

Specific bequests are not as common as one might think. The majority of wills contain a general bequest to the spouse and then, in the event of the spouse's predeceasing the testator, to children and/or other relatives. Only infrequently do people want to make specific bequests.

In wills that set up marital trusts and family trusts to take advantage of the marital deduction, the house in which the testator and his spouse resided, the furniture, and the automobile and personal effects are often specifically devised to the spouse.

In some states, the words **legacy** and **bequest** refer to a gift of personal property and the word *devise* refers to a gift of real property. This distinction has been removed both by the Texas Probate Code and by the Uniform Probate Code, primarily because it was a trap for the unwary. The Uniform Probate Code uses devise, exclusively, for all purposes. Although the Texas Probate Code does not mandate use of *devise*, it is found there almost exclusively, and lawyers tend to use it most of the time. The legal assistant dealing with clients or lawyers from other states should make them aware of the meanings of these words.

The specific devises should be located in the will ahead of the residual or general devises, or, at the very least, the residual devise should be conditioned specifically on the specific devises. If a general bequest or residuary clause is placed first in a will and contains no conditions concerning specific bequests, then the entire estate has been disposed of, including any property mentioned later in specific bequests. This could render the specific bequests ineffective.

For the same reason, a clause providing for a marital deduction must come ahead of the residual devise. The marital deduction can be an estate tax savings device. Although a full discussion of the marital deduction provision involves the subjects of taxes and trusts, a short discussion of it is appropriate at this point.

In the Tax Reform Act of 1976, a marital deduction equal to the greater of $250,000 or one-half of the marital estate was established for property passing to a spouse from a decedent. This was designed to equalize noncommunity property states, in which the husband owns substantially all of the marital property, with community property states, where each spouse owns one-half of the marital property. The act also provided a tax break for estates in community property states under certain circumstances.

The Economic Recovery Act of 1981 provided for an unlimited marital deduction. It also made similar provision in the gift tax sections, allowing, for an unlimited deduction for gifts to a spouse, provided that the marital deduction is claimed by filing a gift tax return. This becomes a necessary estate planning tool in the avoidance of tax.

In order to draft specific bequests, the legal assistant must make sure he understands the intention of the testator. For example, if a testator wants to leave his 1993 Buick Riviera to a named individual and the legal assistant puts a clause in the will specifically leaving the 1993 Buick Riviera to the named person, but the testator sells the car prior to his death, the devise would be considered void. The devisee would receive nothing, because the testator did not own a 1993 Buick Riviera at his death. If the testator simply intended the named person to get whatever car he owned at the time of his death and was not expressing himself clearly, then the intentions of the testator would be thwarted by the will. A clause should appear in the will saying "I give and devise the automobile that I may own at the time of my death to _____."

Along these same lines, real estate should always be described by its legal description and not by a street address or something even more vague. Title insurance underwriters sometimes refuse to give effect to a real estate description that is too vague to determine what property was intended to be devised. Often, wills devise "the home in which I reside at the time of my death." This clause is generally sufficient, although a title underwriter may require that the executor deed the property to the named devisee or that some additional proof be provided that the real property to be sold was the home in which the decedent resided at the time of death.

Sometimes the testator desires to leave personal effects, jewelry, furniture, etc. to a class of individuals, such as children, brothers, sisters, or grandchildren. This often occurs when the testator is unable to make up his mind concerning who exactly shall have what. There are at least two methods of handling this. One is to create a minitrust for the items, allowing the trustee discretion as to which member of the class gets which article of personal property. The second method is to use a **power of appointment**, generally to the executor. A power of appointment in this circumstance transfers the decision as to who will get each specific item from the testator to the independent executor.

Example 5-7: Specific Bequest

I give, will, and devise to the following named people the sums of money and/or articles of personal property as shown hereafter:

1. To my sister, Penelope Peters—the sum of $10,000 and any furs that I may own at the time of my death.
2. To my son, Peter Peters, Jr.—the automobile that I own and use for my personal use at the time of my death.
3. To my friend, Nancy Naismith—the pottery that I purchased in Nuevo Laredo.

Example 5-8: Specific Bequest

I give, will, and devise all my personal effects, jewelry, clothing, and antique furniture to my grandchildren: Paul Peters III, Pauline Peters, and Pearl Peters. I hereby give the authority to my independent executor herein above named to determine which of my grandchildren shall receive the specific articles constituting this devise, directing him only to attempt as equal a division between said grandchildren as is possible, understanding that a mathematically exact division will be impossible.

Residuary Clause

The residuary clause provides for the disposition of all assets of the estate, after providing for debts and administration expenses, that are not otherwise bequeathed. If any portion of a decedent's estate is not disposed of by a specific bequest and there is no residuary clause, that portion of the estate will pass by intestacy. A residuary clause disposing of "all the rest, residue and remainder of the property that I may own at the time of my death" includes the following kinds of properties:

1. Property the testator has omitted from the specific bequests.

2. Property which the testator has forgotten he owns or perhaps owns but does not know that he owns.

3. Remainder or reversionary interests owned by the testator.

4. Property acquired by the testator after the execution of a will.

5. Real or personal property disposed of in a specific bequest that has lapsed because the beneficiary died before the testator and the antilapse statute does not apply.

6. Property the original of which was specifically bequeathed but that has changed by reason of sale and repurchase.

7. Bequests forfeited by a beneficiary who violates an in terrorem clause.

A residuary clause should provide for as many contingent beneficiaries as are needed under the client's particular circumstances to be sure he will not die intestate in regard to any part of his estate.

In a **pour over** will, the beneficiary of the residuary estate is the trustee of an inter vivos trust, or a trust created during the testator's lifetime. Section 58 of the Texas Probate Code recognizes such provisions. For some reason, the trust may not be in existence at the time of the testator's death, possibly because it has been revoked or because all the trust property has been lost and, consequently, the trust has failed for lack of assets. The will should provide for a contingent residual devisee.

Some residuary clauses are simple, leaving everything to a single person; others leave the residuary estate to multiple persons; still others leave the residuary estate to a class of persons. **Class gifts** can be dangerous. Generally, a class gift to the children of the testator causes no problems. For example, a testator might make a class gift to "my grandchildren." This is a class gift because it identifies the devisees by relationship rather than by name. What happens if the testator dies while his children are still within childbearing age? Must the gift be postponed until it can be definitely ascertained how many grandchildren there will be (more grandchildren could be born after the death of the testator)? The class gift raises questions concerning when membership in the class is determined— at the date of the execution of the will, at the date of the testator's death, or at some subsequent date?

A number of Texas cases deal with class gifts. An examination of such cases and the common law concerning class gifts is beyond the scope of this text. It is important that the basis for determining the class be specified in the will. For instance, rather than "I give to my grandchildren," use "I give to my grandchildren who are alive and in being upon the date of my death."

A distinction needs to be drawn between a general bequest and a residuary clause. A general bequest is used in a will in which there are no specific bequests. It says something like "I give, will, and devise all of my property to X, Y, and Z, share and share alike." If a general bequest is drafted so as to ensure that all of the property of the testator is disposed of, whether owned at the time of the will or acquired thereafter, no residuary clause is necessary. A number of very careful attorneys will follow a general bequest, which gives all of the testator's property to named beneficiaries, with a residuary clause to the same named beneficiaries. Texas case law says that a residuary clause is to be given the broadest possible interpretation, to avoid intestacy. No such law exists concerning a general bequest. Some attorneys use a residuary clause, which traditionally contains the words "rest, residue, and remainder," instead of a general bequest.

Example 5-9: General Bequest

I give, devise, and bequeath to my beloved wife, Paula Peters, all of my property of every kind and description of which I may die seized or possessed or in which I may have an interest, whether real, personal, or mixed, and wherever situated.

Example 5-10: Residuary Clause

I give, devise, and bequeath to my beloved wife, Paula Peters, all the rest, residue, and remainder of my property of every kind and description of which I may die seized and possessed or in which I may have an interest, whether real, personal, or mixed, and wherever situated.

Example 5-11: Contingent Residuary Clause

If my said wife, Paula Peters, should predecease me, then I give, devise, and bequeath all or the rest, residue, and remainder of my property of every kind and description of which I may die seized or possessed or in which I may have an interest, whether real, personal, or mixed, and wherever situated, to my children, Paul Peters and Penelope Peters Smith, share and share alike.

Many times, particularly with younger married couples, the contingent residuary clause provides for a trust for minor children, perhaps even for children who are above the age of minority but whom the testator feels may not yet be capable of handling their own funds.

Example 5-12: Contingent Residuary Clause Allowing Texas Trust Code to Provide for Powers, Rights, Duties, and Responsibilities of a Trustee

Notwithstanding the proceeding provisions of this section. If any of my surviving children are under the age of thirty (30) years at the date of my death, I give my entire residuary estate, in trust, as the trust estate of a single trust to be held, managed, and distributed as follows:

The trustee shall distribute to my children or the issue of a deceased child of mine, at intervals as it may determine, so much of the trust income and principal as will adequately provide for their necessary or reasonable health, education, maintenance, and support, considering all sources of income available to them to the knowledge of the trustee. Any such distributions need not be made equally among them and shall not be charged against a share of a distributee (or any person taking such distributee's share by representation) upon the termination of the trust. When all of my surviving children have obtained the age of thirty (30) years of age, or died, the trust shall terminate and the then-remaining trust estate shall be distributed in fee simple and free of trust to my children in equal shares. If any child of mine shall not then be living but leaves issue then surviving, the share of the trust estate that would otherwise pass to such deceased child of mine shall pass, per stirpes and not per capita, to the then-surviving issue of such deceased child of mine. If any child of mine is deceased without leaving any surviving issue, no share shall be created on behalf of such deceased child. If none of my children or their issue are then surviving the remaining trust estate shall be distributed to such of my heirs as would be determined under the Texas Statutes of Descent and Distribution.

I appoint Pavel Peters as my trustee, and if he fails to qualify or ceases to act, I appoint Peggy Smith as successor trustee. I further direct that no bond be required of either of them.

Also, the residuary clause, or for that matter even a specific bequest, may take advantage of the provisions of the Texas Uniform Gift to Minors Act. The devise would leave the property to a custodian for the benefit of named minors under the Uniform Gift to Minors Act. The custodian has the same rights, powers, duties, and responsibilities as a trustee under the Texas Trust Code. The main distinguishing factor between a gift under the Uniform Gift to Minors Act and a gift in trust as just described is that under the Uniform Gift to Minors Act entitles the testator to give the power to appoint a custodian to a designated person under the will. For instance, he can make a gift for the benefit of the minors, and empower the minister of his church to appoint a custodian to take care of the property, with the appointment to be made after the probate of the will.

Example 5-13: Uniform Gift to Minors Act

I give, devise, and bequeath under the Texas Uniform Gift to Minors Act for the benefit of my minor children, Paul Peters and Penelope Peters Smith, to a custodian under said Uniform Gift to Minors Act. I hereby empower John Wesley, Pastor of the Second Avenue Methodist Church, to appoint any person whom he may chose, including himself, as custodian for the benefit of said minor children.

All devises, whether general or residuary, should provide for prior or simultaneous death by specifying contingent bequests in case the devisee dies at the same time as or prior to the testator, as in Example 5-11.

Appointment of Guardian

Texas Probate Code Section 117 allows the last surviving parent of minor children to appoint a guardian for his minor child or children. It further provides that, if the person appointed as guardian is not disqualified, he shall also be appointed guardian of the estate after the death of the surviving parent. Section 195 provides that, if a will is made by a surviving parent and directs that the guardian or guardians therein appointed serve without bond, no bond shall be required.

One must be very sure that the form chosen waives the necessity of a bond. Just eliminating the bond can be a significant cost savings. Many bonding companies are collecting the bond in the case of a guardian for a minor child for the full term of the guardianship. This means the bonding company will require payment in advance, with an appropriate discount for prepayment, of the bond premium for each year the guardianship will remain open until the majority of the minors. Thus, if the minor was thirteen (13) years of age at the time the guardianship was open, the bonding company would require five years of premium paid in advance.

Example 5-14: Appointment of Guardian

I appoint Perkin Peters to act as the guardian of the person of my minor child, Paul Peters, and further request that the Probate Court appoint him as guardian of the estate of said minor. I direct that no bond be required of him.

Only the surviving parent has the right to appoint a guardian. Since it is possible for either the husband or the wife to be the surviving parent, this provision should go into both wills. The legal assistant should be aware that where the parents are divorced, this provision will not prevent the exspouse from getting custody of the child, nor will it be effective if that exspouse survives the client. The Probate Code provides that a parent is the natural guardian of the child and has priority over all others. If a client wants to prevent the exspouse from obtaining control of the children's devise, a trust can be established.

After Born (Pretermitted) Children

It is common to provide for pretermitted, or afterborn, children. It is best to include a section that addresses the rights of an afterborn child even if the client is single or apparently past childbearing age.

Example 5-15: Afterborn Children Provision

In the event any other child or children are born to or adopted by me after the execution of this will, it is my intention that such a child or children shall share equally with my children herein named and be included in the provisions of this will, share and share alike.

If the will is to use a trust to carry out its intent, the provisions of the trust could appear after the clause shown in Example 5-15. The residuary clause would leave the property to the trust or trusts created, and provide clauses relating to the payment of income during the existence of the trust, the powers, duties, and responsibilities of the trustee, vesting, etc. Testamentary trusts are generally created to ensure that the estate is properly managed for the benefit of someone the testator believes is otherwise unable to manage for himself or to insure that the estate remains intact until it gets to the ultimate intended beneficiary while providing for someone's support in the interim. In addition, there are limited uses of a testamentary trust for saving estate taxes on either the immediate estate or the estate of the surviving spouse. Clauses in testamentary trusts are generally the same as in inter vivos trusts. (Further discussion of trust clauses is deferred to Chapters 7-9.)

In Terrorem Clause

An in terrorem clause provides for the forfeiture of a devise to any devisee if the devisee contests the validity of the will. Some of these clauses go further and forfeit the interest of anyone who institutes any judicial proceeding, including will contests, and will constructions, or who attempts to create constructive or resulting trusts as to the assets of the estate.

For an in terrorem clause to have any effect, the devisee who is threatened with forfeiture must be devised a sufficient amount to make forfeiture a real threat. If the entire will is invalidated, the devisees will take any interest that they would have taken by intestacy, unless there was a prior will. If a particular devisee is also one who will take by descent and distribution and the amount devised in a will is considerably less than what the devisee would have received had the testator died intestate, then the risk of contesting the will may be worthwhile. If the beneficiary has nothing to lose, or very little to lose, by contesting the will, the forfeiture clause is meaningless.

In a fairly recent decision, a Texas court has affirmed that forfeiture of rights under the terms of a will will not be enforced where the contest of the will was made in good faith and upon reasonable cause [*Hammer v. Powers*, 819 S.W.2d 669 (Tex. App.-Fort Worth, 1991 no writ)]. In this case, a videotape of the testatrix signing the will was used to prove testamentary capacity.

The clause in Example 5-16 attempts to prevent the bringing of any kind of judicial proceeding concerning the will rather than just a contest of all or a portion of it. It also seeks to overcome the existing law and to make forfeiture applicable even when the judicial proceeding is brought in good faith and with probable cause. Although no cases have construed such a provision, the probate courts probably would honor the expressed intention of the testator as stated in the in terrorem clause. There are dicta in Texas cases indicating that the in terrorem clause can be extended to include judicial proceedings other than those that contest the validity of the will. There are no cases, however, indicating that an in terrorem clause will be effective even when the proceeding has been brought in good faith and with probable cause. In construing wills, normally courts bow to the testator's intention. However, the courts "abhor a forfeiture."

Example 5-16: In Terrorem Clause

I vest in my personal representative the authority to construe this will and to resolve all matters pertaining to disputed issues and controverted claims. I do not want to burden my estate with the cost of a litigated proceeding to resolve questions of law or fact unless that proceeding is originated by my personal representative or with the personal representative's written permission. Any other person, agency, or organization who shall originate (or who shall cause to be instituted) a judicial proceeding to construe or contest this will or to resolve any claim or controversy in the nature of reimbursement, constructive or resulting trust or other theory that, if assumed as truth, would enlarge (or originate) the claimant's interest in my estate, shall forfeit any amount to which that person, agency, or organization is or may be entitled, and the interest of any such litigant or contestant shall pass as if he or she or it had predeceased me.

These directions shall apply even though the person, agency or organization shall be found by a court of law to have originated the judicial proceedings in good faith and with probable cause, and even though the proceeding may seek nothing more than to construe the application of this no-contest provision.

Testimonium Clause

The testimonium clause states that the testator has signed the will freely and requests the witnesses to sign as witnesses. Since the testimonium clause generally repeats what has been covered in the opening paragraphs, it may not be necessary to a modern will. Again, it is much easier to include it than take the chance that it later may be considered essential to the validity of the will.

Testator's Signature

Following the testimonium clause comes the testator's signature. (Execution will be dealt with later in this chapter.) This is not the only place that the testator signs; for he signs again following the self-proving affidavit, and almost all authorities say the testator should sign or initial each page of the will. Some attorneys provide lines for such initials or signatures at the bottom or in the left margin of each page of the will not otherwise having a signature line. If the testator signs by mark, it is advisable to have witnesses to his mark, as in other legal documents. To the left of the testator's signature line should be placed two other signature lines, headed "witnesses to his mark" The witnesses should sign there, and the legal assistant should make a slight alteration of the self-proving affidavit to show that the witnesses saw the testator affix his mark and that he acknowledged to them and the notary that it was his mark.

Attestation Clause

There is no case law clarifying what the prerequisites of an attestation clause are. The one included in Form 5-2 (at chapter's end) and in Example 5-17 is traditional in Texas and elsewhere.

Example 5-17: Attestation Clause

The above instrument was published as his last will and Testament subscribed by Paul Peters, the testator, in our presence, and we, at his request, in his presence, and in the presence of each other, sign and subscribe our names hereto as attesting witnesses.

Witnesses' Signatures

Texas (and most states) require two witnesses. However, at least two other states require three witnesses. Some lawyers routinely use three witnesses, as a precautionary measure, even though it is unnecessary, as discussed in Chapter Four. In any case, the client should be advised that if he moves to another state, he should see an attorney there to determine if the will meets that state's requirements, and probably have a will executed in accordance with that state's statutes.

Most lawyers want the witnesses' names and addresses typed on the will. In some offices it can be determined in advance who the witnesses will be and to have their names and addresses typed on the will. If the office has computers or dedicated word processors, then it is relatively easy, when the client comes in to execute his will, to determine who the witnesses will be and their addresses and to print the last pages after filling in this information. Some attorneys add the names and addresses with the standard typewriter after execution, despite the warnings by experts that no additions or corrections be made after a will has been executed. It is doubtful that the mere addition of typed names and addresses after the execution of a will would affect its validity. It is important that addresses be shown for each witness, should it become necessary to find the witnesses to prove the will for probate.

Self-Proving Affidavit

Finally, comes the self-proving affidavit. It's exact form was changed by amendment to Section 59 of the Texas Probate Code, effective September 1, 1991. The legal assistant should be extremely careful when using forms books, because many contain the old version of the self-proving affidavit. To determine whether it is the old form or the new, look at the jurat at the very end. The new form is sworn to by the testator and the witnesses, whereas the old form was acknowledged by the testator and sworn to by the witnesses. A current self-proving affidavit is attached to each of the wills contained in the Forms Appendix of this chapter.

SAFEKEEPING OF WILLS

At the execution of a will, clients will often ask what they should do with the original. There are three choices in Texas. One is to deposit the will with the county clerk as provided in Texas Probate Code Section 71. This has no legal significance; it is simply a safe keeping service offered by the county clerk. The problem with this procedure is that often a testator moves, and in the flurry of moving fails to remember to withdraw the will from the county clerk's office and to take it with him. After a few such moves, no one will ever think to check with the county clerk's office where he lived 10 years before. Also, whoever is looking for the will may be unaware of the testator's former residence. Finally, because only a few wills are filed with the county clerk's office, the family, and even the attorney, may neglect to check with the county clerk's office. A part of the procedure of depositing the will is enclosing it in a sealed wrapper that states who may withdraw it upon proof of death. The person named on the envelope should be the executor named in the will, not the attorney. If the will is to be deposited with the county clerk, both the person named as executor and the principal devisee should be notified of that fact.

The second choice is for the client to keep the will in his safe-deposit box. Whereas earlier in Texas history safe-deposit boxes were automatically sealed upon notification of death, this is no longer the case. Someone with joint access can get into a safe-deposit box. However, if the bank is aware of the death, it will want to inventory the contents of the box in case of later problems.

Probate Code Sections 36C-36F provide procedures by which the contents of a safe-deposit box can be examined by a spouse, a parent, a descendant, or a person designated as executor in a will (a copy is sufficient proof), either with or without a court order. The will will be delivered to the named executor.

The safe-deposit box is as good a place to store the will as any, particularly since it is often used for other valuables a client will not forget when moving. Even if he does forget the will, he will receive a notice from the bank when it wants the next rental payment on the box. Again, however, the client should be advised to tell other persons where the will is located.

Finally, the client may simply put the will wherever he keeps his other important papers, whether it be a special drawer in his desk at home, a file at his office, or a safe at his office or home. Close family members will know where important papers are kept; but if they don't, they should be so advised. Many law firms furnish the client with extra copies of the will and suggest that he give one whomever is named executor and one to the principal devisee, with a notation on the copy as to where the original is being kept.

EXECUTION OF WILLS

If the client has accepted the final draft of the will and there are no further matters to discuss, only the formal execution of the will remains. There is no ethical or legal reason for the attorney to be involved in this procedure. Although some attorneys want to be present because they believe that fosters better client relations, many have nonlawyer personnel handle the execution of all simple wills. Ethical provisions allow a legal assistant to do any act, under the supervision and at the direction of an attorney, that an attorney can do, except appear in court, give legal advice, or represent himself to be an attorney. One purpose for legal assistants is to diminish the attorney's time spent with the client. Delegation to the lowest-paid competent employee is good management. The execution of a will does not require the presence of an attorney, provided no explanation of the will is required.

Most law firms have specially trained secretaries or legal assistants supervise the execution of a will. Probably, the legal assistant, being the best-trained employee, should supervise the execution and serve as notary public. Although the person who supervises the execution need not be the notary public, this only makes sense because then only one person is asking questions.

The self-proving affidavit itself makes a nice script for the execution of a will. The notary can simply go down the self-proving affidavit and ask the questions which it requires to be declared. The notary public must administer an oath to the testator and the witnesses.

For years, notary publics have been skipping this essential formality. In a recent Texas case, a notary public was asked, concerning an affidavit, if she had administered an oath to the affiant executing the affidavit (the affidavits were designed to be used in connection with a motion for summary judgment). The trial court ignored the notary's public answer that no such oath had been administered. The appellant court reversed the summary judgment, indicating that there was a possibility the affidavits did not qualify as affidavits because the affiants were not sworn prior to executing them. Further, the statute requires the administration of an oath.

If the legal assistant is to supervise a will's execution, he must explain his position in the law firm and that he is not an attorney. In addition, the legal assistant must not explain the will or give legal advice; this only the attorney may do.

Example 5-18: Oath of Affiants Prior to Execution of an Affidavit

Do you and each of you solemnly swear to tell the truth in connection with the execution of this will, so help you God?

The conversation might continue as follows:

> Do you declare to me and the witnesses that this instrument is your last will and testament and that you have willingly made and executed as your free act and deed?

> Mr. Testator, please state to the witnesses that this instrument is your last will and testament and that you have executed it as such and that you wish each of them to sign as witnesses.

> Mr. and Mrs. Witness, does each of you state to me under oath in the presence and hearing of Mr. Testator that Mr. Testator declared to you that this instrument is his last will and testament and that he has executed the same as such and that he wishes each of you to sign as witness?

Then the witnesses sign.

> Mr. and Mrs. Witness, do you state further that you have signed the document as witnesses in the presence of the testator and at his request?

> Mr. Testator and Mr. and Mrs. Witness, does each of you state to me that Mr. Testator is over the age of 18 years of age and is of sound mind and that each of the witnesses is at least 14 years of age?

As stated earlier, this format is not the only way for a will to be executed. Some firms prepare exact scripts for legal assistants; in others, the attorney may rehearse the legal assistant; and in yet others the legal assistant is given no guidance at all. If this last is the case, then the script in Example 5-18 can be of use.

CHAPTER QUESTIONS AND EXERCISES

1. What information should be gathered in preparation for the drafting of a will?

2. What information should be gathered in preparation for the drafting of a testamentary trust as a part of a will?

3. For what purposes may an independent executor sell property belonging to the estate? What must be done so the independent executor can sell property whenever he feels it is in the best interest of the estate to do so?

4. What is a residuary clause? When and why is it inserted in a will?

5. What is a class gift? What problems can be created by using a class gift in a will? How can such problems be solved?

6. Who may appoint a guardian of a minor child? Can a bond of such a guardian be waived? If so, how?

7. What is an in terrorem clause? Are such clauses enforced by the Texas Courts?

8. Draw up a checklist to fit the following circumstances (use your imagination as to names and other information needed):

The clients are husband and wife. They are in their early 30s and they have two very young children. They both work for relatively high salaries and have recently bought a house. Their assets, probate and not probate, come nowhere close to being taxable should one of them die in the near future. They want to leave everything to each other and then to their children.

9. Draft a will to fit the circumstances described in Exercise 8. If you have been assigned Exercise 8 by your instructor, then use the checklist and the information he provides. Otherwise, make up any needed details such as names and places.

10. Using your own family situation, draft a will, either for yourself or for a family member.

11. Draft a will for the following circumstances, supplying the names and other information (the oldest brother should be the executor and the youngest the substitute.)

The client is a single man with no children. He wishes to leave his automobile, a 1990 Oldsmobile, to a male friend. He also wishes to leave his collection of stamps to his younger brother and his little black addressbook to his older brother.

Form 5-1: Simple Will

LAST WILL AND TESTAMENT OF PETER SMITH

THE STATE OF TEXAS	) (	KNOW ALL MEN BY THESE
COUNTY OF NUECES	) (	PRESENTS:

That I, PETER SMITH, of the County of Nueces, State of Texas, being in good health, of sound and disposing mind and memory and above the age of Eighteen (18), do make and publish this my Last Will and Testament, hereby revoking all Wills, by me at any time heretofore made.

FIRST: I direct that all my just debts shall be paid as soon as they might accrue.

SECOND: I give, devise and bequeath to my beloved wife, PAULA SMITH, all the rest and residue of my property of every kind and description of which I may die seized or possessed or in which I may have an interest, whether real, personal or mixed and wherever situated.

THIRD: If my said wife, PAULA SMITH, should predecease me, then I give, devise and bequeath all the rest and residue of my property of every kind and description, of which I may die seized or possessed or in which I may have an interest, whether real, personal or mixed and wherever situated, to my children, PAUL SMITH and PENELOPE SMITH HALL share and share alike.

In the event any of my said children should predecease me, then the share herein devised and bequeathed to said deceased beneficiary shall descend to his child or children surviving him, in equal parts, per stirpes; should such deceased beneficiary die without having child or children surviving him, then the share herein devised and bequeathed to said deceased beneficiary shall vest in my surviving children.

FOURTH: In the event any other child or children are born to or adopted by me, after the execution of this Will, it is my intention such child or children shall share equally and be included in the provisions of this Will, share and share alike.

FIFTH: I hereby appoint my wife, PAULA SMITH, Independent Executrix of my Will, and in the event that she should predecease me or is unable to perform said office, I hereby appoint JOAN SMITH, Independent Executrix of my Will, and I direct that no bond shall be required of her or said substitute and that no other action shall be had in the County Court in relation to the settlement of said estate than the probating and recording of this, my Will, and the return of statutory inventory, appraisement and list of claims of said estate and all claims due or owing by me at the time of my death. I hereby authorize and empower my said Independent Executrix to mortgage, sell, dispose of, deliver and convey any portion of my estate, real or personal, at public or private sale, for any price, on any terms and in any manner that may seem to her best, or to lease, pledge or otherwise manage any and all of my property.

This I make and publish as my Last Will, hereunto signing and subscribing my name, this _____ day of _____, 1992, in the presence of _____ , and _____ , who attest the same at my request.

_____
PETER SMITH, Testator

The above instrument was now here published as his Last Will and signed and subscribed by PETER SMITH, the Testator, in our presence, and we, at his request, in his presence, and in the presence of each other, sign and subscribe our names hereto as attesting witnesses.

_____   _____

_____   _____
WITNESSES   ADDRESSES

Form 5-1: (continued)

THE STATE OF TEXAS   ) (

COUNTY OF NUECES   ) (

BEFORE ME, the undersigned authority, on this day personally appeared PETER SMITH, _____ , and _____ , known to me to be the Testator and the witnesses, respectively, whose names are subscribed to the annexed or foregoing instrument in their respective capacities, and all of said persons being by me duly sworn, the said PETER SMITH, Testator, declared to me and to the said witnesses, in my presence that said instrument is his Last Will and Testament, and that he had willingly made and executed it as his free act and deed for the purposes therein expressed; and the said witnesses, each on their oaths, stated to me and in the presence and hearing of the said Testator that the said Testator had declared to them that said instrument is his Last Will and Testament, and that he executed the same as such and wanted each of them to sign it as a witness; and upon their oaths, each witness stated further that they did sign the same as witnesses in the presence of the said Testator and at his request; and that he was at that time eighteen (18) years of age or over, and was of sound mind and that each of said witnesses was then at least fourteen (14) years of age.

_____
PETER SMITH

_____

_____
WITNESSES

SUBSCRIBED AND SWORN BEFORE ME by the said PETER SMITH, Testator, and by the said _____ and _____ , witnesses, this the _____ day of _____ , 1992.

_____
Notary Public for the State of Texas.

Form 5-2: Simple Will With Trust for Minor Children

LAST WILL AND TESTAMENT OF PETER SMITH

THE STATE OF TEXAS	) (	KNOW ALL MEN BY THESE PRESENTS:
COUNTY OF NUECES	) (	

That I, PETER SMITH, of the County of Nueces, State of Texas, being in good health, of sound and disposing mind and memory and above the age of Eighteen (18), do make and publish this my Last Will and Testament, hereby revoking all Wills, by me at any time heretofore made.

FIRST: I direct that all my just debts shall be paid as soon as they might accrue.

SECOND: I hereby appoint my wife, PAULA SMITH, of Nueces County, Texas, Independent Executrix of this my Last Will and Testament, and in the event that she should predecease me or is unable to perform said office, I hereby appoint PERKIN SMITH, Independent Executor of my Last Will and Testament; I further direct and provide that no bond be required of her or said substitute and that no further action shall be had in the County Court in relation to the settlement of my estate than the probating and recording of this my Last Will and Testament and the return of the statutory inventory and appraisement and list of claims. I hereby authorize and empower my said Independent Executor to mortgage, sell, dispose of, deliver and convey any portion of my estate, real or personal, at public or private sale, for any price, on any terms and in any manner that may seem to him best, or to lease pledge or otherwise manage any and all of my property.

THIRD: I give, devise and bequeath to my beloved wife, PAULA SMITH, all the rest and residue of my property of every kind and description of which I may die seized or possessed or in which I may have an interest, whether real, personal or mixed and wherever situated.

FOURTH: If my said wife, PAULA SMITH, should predecease me, then I give, devise and bequeath to JOHN SMITH, as trustee, all the rest and residue of my property of every kind and description, of which I may die seized or possessed or in which I may have an interest, whether real, personal or mixed and wherever situated, such property to pass in trust, for the following purposes and on the following terms and conditions.

A. My Trustee shall take, hold, manage, invest and reinvest said property, shall collect the income therefrom, and shall make such disbursements therefrom to my minor children, PAUL SMITH and PENELOPE SMITH and any other children hereinafter born or adopted to me, or the survivors of them as hereinafter provided, hereinafter called beneficiaries, or to the legally appointed guardian of their estate which said Trustee shall deem necessary for the health, education, support, and maintenance of my said Beneficiaries, and said Trustee shall have the exclusive management and control of said estate, in accordance with the terms hereof.

B. In addition to the powers heretofore enumerated, my Trustee shall have the following powers in the administration of said estate;

1. The Trustee shall take over, hold and manage all the properties conveyed here in trust as soon as applicable.

2. The Trustee shall have full power to mortgage, sell, transfer, convey, rent, lease for oil or other minerals, trade, exchange and otherwise manage all the properties of this trust as if the Trustee were the owner thereof.

3. The Trustee shall have full power to continue to operate any business in which I may be engaged at the time of my death, with full power to borrow money mortgage, sell, trade or exchange such properties on such terms as the Trustee deems best.

4. The Trustee shall have full power to invest any cash in such bonds, stock and securities as the Trustee sees fit; to retain, invest in or exercise rights for its own corporate stock, to hold cash without investing it; to mortgage such securities; to sell, trade, or exchange any of them at any time and from time to time, and reinvest the proceeds from such sale or other property as if the Trustee was the owner. By way of further power, and not in any manner restricting the other powers herein granted, my Trustee shall have the power to invest any funds coming into the Trustee's possession in stocks of any company in which I now own stock regardless of whether or not the Trustee shall also own stock therein or be an officer or director thereof, and in so doing shall not in any manner be held guilty of violation of this trust or of the Texas Trust Act.

5. The Trustee shall have the right to expend such part of the principal of or income from said trust estate as, in its discretion, shall deem necessary or proper for the health, education, support or maintenance of my said beneficiaries, and, in the performance of said trust, said Trustee shall have the powers, duties and responsibilities now set out in Section 25 of the Texas Trust Act. Said Trustee shall have the right and authority to distribute all or any part of said trust estate to my Beneficiaries at such time or times in such amount or amounts and for such purposes as it in its sole discretion may deem to be in the best interests of said Beneficiaries having expressly in mind that I intend that such monies be used by my Beneficiaries, if it be needed, for health, education, support or maintenance, said Trustee being charged with the responsibility of determining that such expenditures are necessary and judicious.

Form 5-2: (continued)

6. My Trustee shall have full power to lend money to or advance funds to or buy assets from my said estate for the purposes of paying inheritance or estate taxes, or for paying the debts of my estate.

7. With regard to all policies of insurance on my life which designate any Trustee hereunder as Beneficiary, my Trustee shall have full power:

   (a) to execute and deliver receipts and other instruments and to take such action as may be appropriate to obtain possession and control of such policies.

   (b) to execute and file proofs of claim required to collect the proceeds thereof, and the receipt of my Trustee shall constitute full acquittance to insurance companies for all proceeds so paid; provided, however, that my Trustee shall be under no legal obligation to institute legal proceedings for the collection of proceeds of any policy until and unless it has been indemnified to its satisfaction for all costs and expenses, including attorney's fees.

   (c) to elect, in its discretion, any optional modes of settlement available to it under said policies.

   (d) to receive insurance proceeds and to administer and distribute same as principal in accordance with the dispositive provision of this will.

   (e) to use the proceeds of insurance policies in the purchase from my estate of such assets as the Trustee deems advisable without being limited to assets authorized by law for the investment of trust funds.

8. Having acted in good faith, the Trustee shall not be liable for mistakes in judgment.

9. By enumeration of powers, it is not intended to limit the Trustees' power. On the contrary, so far as possible, it is intended to give the Trustee all the powers of an owner to manage and preserve the trust estate for the beneficiaries named.

10. No person shall be required to look to the appli catio n of any properties or money paid to the Trust ee to the purposes of this trust. The recital of facts in any conveyance or instruments executed by the Trustee shall be conclusive evidence that the recitals are true and shall be accepted in all courts without further proof.

11. No bond shall be required of Trustee.

C. My Trustee shall distribute the said trust estate in the following manner:

Upon the Thirtieth (30) birthday of the youngest of my said Beneficiaries, the Trustee shall divide the remainder of the trust estate into two equal portions and shall distribute one portion to each Beneficiary, upon which this trust shall terminate absolutely.

In the event that any of my said children should die before reaching the age of distribution hereunder, and with children surviving either of them, then the portion herein devised and bequeathed to such deceased Beneficiary shall be distributed to and become the property of the children of such deceased Beneficiary; in the event such deceased Beneficiary leaves no child or children surviving him, then his share shall pass to the remaining children.

FIFTH: In the event I am the last surviving parent, I nominate and appoint PERKIN SMITH as Guardian of the person and estate of PAUL SMITH and PENELOPE SMITH if they are still minors at the date of my death, and I direct that no bond shall be required of him.

This I make and publish as my Last Will, hereunto signing and subscribing my name, this _____ day of _____, 1992, in the presence of _____, and _____, who attest the same at my request.

_____
PETER SMITH, Testator

The above instrument was now here published as his Last Will and signed and subscribed by PETER SMITH, the Testator, in our presence, and we, at his request, in his presence, and in the presence of each other, sign and subscribe our names hereto as attesting witnesses.

_____

_____   _____
      WITNESSES   ADDRESSES

Form 5-2: (continued)

THE STATE OF TEXAS   )   (

COUNTY OF NUECES   )   (

      BEFORE ME, the undersigned authority, on this day personally appeared PETER SMITH, _____ , and _____ , known to me to be the Testator and the witnesses, respectively, whose names are subscribed to the annexed or foregoing instrument in their respective capacities, and all of said persons being by me duly sworn, the said PETER SMITH, Testator, declared to me and to the said witnesses, in my presence that said instrument is his Last Will and Testament and that he had willingly made and executed it as his free act and deed for the purposes therein expressed; and the said witnesses, each on their oath, stated to me and in the presence and hearing of the said Testator that the said Testator had declared to them that said instrument is his Last Will and Testament, and that he executed the same as such and wanted each of them to sign it as a witness; and upon their oaths, each witness stated further that they did sign the same as witnesses in the presence of the said Testator and at his request; and that he was at that time eighteen (18) years of age or over, and was of sound mind and that each of said witnesses was then at least fourteen (14) years of age.

_____
PETER SMITH

_____

_____
WITNESSES

      SUBSCRIBED AND SWORN BEFORE ME by the said PETER SMITH, Testator, and by the said _____ and _____ , witnesses, this the _____ day of _____ , 1992.

_____
Notary Public for the State of Texas.

6 ADDITIONAL ESTATE PLANNING DOCUMENTS (Powers of Attorney, Living Wills, Designations of Guardian, etc.)

CHAPTER OBJECTIVES

Upon completion this chapter, the student should be able to:

1. Compare and contrast the benefits and drawbacks of durable powers of attorney.

2. Draft a durable power of attorney.

3. Know how and when to prepare a directive to physicians and a durable power of attorney for health care.

4. Prepare a designation of guardian, and describe the its benefits.

5. Discuss the laws creating "community property with the right of survivorship," and prepare the required documents.

6. Explain the use of community property partition agreements and other marital agreements in connection with estate planning.

CHAPTER GLOSSARY

Agent One who acts for or in place of another (principal), often establishing contractual relationships between the principal and third parties.

Attorney in fact An agent whose authority is granted by a written power of attorney.

Community property with right of survivorship Community property to which has been attached the right of survivorship, meaning that upon the death of one spouse the interest passes by operation or law to the surviving spouse.

Conveyances Any instrument in writing by which any interest in land is created.

Deed A conveyance whereby title to realty is transferred (conveyed) one to another.

Deed of trust An instrument that in some states (including Texas) takes the place of a mortgage as to realty. It conveys an interest in land to a trustee to secure repayment of a debt. Foreclosure is by private sale.

Directives to physicians A set of written instructions, authorized by the Texas Natural Death Act, directed to treating physicians concerning whether a terminal patient wants life-saving or life-prolonging treatments.

Durable power of attorney An instrument authorizing another to act as one's agent or attorney, which will remain effective in the event of the disability of the principal.

Durable power of attorney for health care A power of attorney that survives incompetency and that authorizes an agent to make medical decisions when the principal is incapacitated.

Incompetent The 1993 Guardianship Code replaces the word *incompetent* with *incapacitated*. However, many forms and statutes continue to use *incompetent*.

Living will A document that governs the withholding or withdrawing of life-sustaining treatment from a patient who is immediately terminal and who is not able to make decisions concerning her treatment.

Mortgage An instrument creating an interest in realty that provides security for the repayment of a debt or the performance of some other duty. Foreclosure is only by suit.

Principal The source of authority; one who has authorized or directed another (agent) to act for her benefit, subject to her control, so that the acts of the agent become binding on the principal.

Title insurance agent One who issues title insurance policies as agent of an underwriter.

Title insurance underwriter A party who assumes risk by issuing a contract of title insurance for a premium. *Title insurance* is a policy issued by a title company after searching the title, representing the state of that title, and ensuring the accuracy of the search against claims or defects.

Universal power of attorney Appoints an agent who is empowered to do all the acts that a principal can do personally and that may be delegated to another.

DURABLE POWER OF ATTORNEY

The word *attorney* comes from the French for "agent." A power of attorney, then, is the appointment of an agent by an individual, called a **principal**. This agent is sometimes referred to as an **attorney in fact** to distinguish her from an *attorney at law*, which is altogether different. A written power of attorney is necessary only when one or more of the tasks that the agent is going to perform on behalf of the principal are required to be in writing under the Statute of Frauds.

An obscure English rule known as the *Equal Dignities Rule* requires that if an agent is appointed to carry out a task on behalf of a principal that involves entering into an agreement required to be in writing by the Statute of Frauds, the appointment must be in writing also. Obviously, powers of attorney that authorize an agent to execute **deeds** and **conveyances** or contracts concerning real estate must be in writing, because the ultimate document to be executed by the agent must be in writing. However, a more important reason that powers of attorney are in writing is to constitute written evidence, or proof, of the appointment as agent.

Adding the word *durable* when describing a power of attorney means the power of attorney will survive and be exercisable by the agent in the event of the disability or incompetence of the principal. Until 1971, it was debatable whether or not a power of attorney in Texas survived the disability or incompetence of the principal. Although no Texas cases existed, cases from other states, including California, indicated that a power of attorney was voided by the incompetence of the principal.

This durable power of attorney, often referred to as a **living will** by attorneys before **directives to physicians** became known by that term, was often recommended by attorneys involved in estate planning to provide a vehicle for dealing with the incompetency of the client, in much the same way that a will provides for death. This was true even though no one could be sure that the power of attorney executed by the client would in fact be effective upon the client's incompetency.

In 1971, the legislature added to the Texas Probate Code Section 36A, which originally provided that if a written power of attorney contained words similar to "this power of attorney shall not terminate on disability of the principal" or other words showing the principal's intention that the power not terminate upon disability, the power of attorney would not terminate upon incompetency or disability. Regardless of what the Texas law was prior to that time, there is no doubt that since the passage of Section 36A, a power of attorney will survive the incompetency of the principal only if it contains such a provision.

The inclusion of words indicating the intent of the principal that the power not terminate upon incompetency is still a requirement for a power of attorney to be durable, even in the 1993 act (which will be discussed shortly). In 1989, additional requirements were included that became effective September 1, 1989. The 1989 amendment to Section 36A required that in order to be durable, in addition to containing words showing an intention not to terminate upon incompetency, the instrument creating the power of attorney had to be:

1. In writing.
2. Signed by the principal, who must be an adult.
3. Witnessed and signed by two persons 18 years of age or older (not required after adoption of the Durable Power of Attorney Act in 1993).
4. Filed for record in the county in which the principal resides, except for a power of attorney executed for medical care (not required after adoption of the Durable Power of Attorney Act in 1993).

The 1989 amendment provided that a **durable power of attorney** will not lapse because of the passage of time unless some time limitation is specifically contained in the power of attorney itself. In addition, it required a power of attorney to terminate upon the qualification of a guardian. Although the statute did not specifically say whether it was referring to a guardian of the person or a guardian of the estate, it was presumed that the statute referred to a guardian of the estate. If a guardian is appointed, not only will the power of the attorney in fact or agent terminate upon the qualification of such guardian, but the attorney in fact or agent must deliver to the guardian any assets of the estate of the ward (principal) that are in her possession, and must account to the guardian for any transactions she conducted.

These two provisions concerning lapse and the effect of the appointment of a guardian are also found in the 1993 Durable Power of Attorney Act. In fact, that act makes it clear that only the appointment of a guardian of the estate can terminate a power of attorney. The 1993 Durable Power of Attorney Act is based on the Uniform Powers of Attorney Act. It is incorporated into the Probate Code as Chapter XII and is found in Sections 481 through 506. It repeals and replaces Section 36A of the Probate Code as of September 1, 1993, while preserving the validity of any power of attorney executed prior to that date in accordance with Section 36A.

The 1993 statute also makes several important changes in the law applicable to powers of attorney. First, with regard to validity, it eliminates the requirements that a power of attorney be witnessed and be filed of record (although one to be used in a real estate transaction should be filed). However, it adds a requirement that the power of attorney be acknowledged before a notary public or other officer having the authority to take acknowledgments and administer oaths.

Second, it provides that an affidavit by the attorney in fact stating that she has no knowledge of the death of the principal, revocation by the principal, or termination by the appointment of a guardian is conclusive proof and may be relied on. In addition, an affidavit by the attorney in fact that the principal is disabled or incapacitated constitutes conclusive evidence of the disability or incapacity.

Next, while not providing for a method of revocation, the act does state that no revocation will be effective against a third party who relies on the power of attorney unless the third party has actual knowledge of the revocation. This provision, when taken together with the one allowing absolute reliance on affidavits by the attorney in fact, may make powers of attorney more acceptable.

Finally, the act adopts a statutory form of a power of attorney while reserving the right to use other forms. (The statutory form is found appended to this chapter as Form 6-1.)

Though a detailed discussion of the statutory form is not appropriate in this text; two matters bear relevance to estate planning. First, some believe that the statute authorizes so-called "springing" powers of attorney, or powers of attorney that have no effect until the principal becomes disabled or incapacitated. In fact, the statute states nothing one way or the other. However, the statutory form, in Alternative B near the end of the form, says, "This power of attorney becomes effective upon my disability or incapacity." It could therefore be argued that only by using the statutory form and choosing Alternative B can a springing power be created.

Second, if the principal initials (and thereby grants) power H— estate, trust, and other beneficiary transactions, then one of the powers attached automatically to H by Section 499 is to transfer (pour over) all or any part of the assets of the principal to a revocable trust created by the principal as settlor. This grants pour-over powers to the attorney in fact without specifically providing for them.

Most attorneys recommend that durable powers of attorney, declarations of guardianship and medical powers of attorney or directives to physicians be executed as a part of overall estate planning. Since the preparation of all these documents increases the attorney's fees, some attorneys are reluctant to bring up the subject. However, failure at least to advise the client concerning the benefits and drawbacks of powers of attorney, medical powers, directives to physicians, and appointments of guardians may be construed as professional negligence.

Even when inter vivos trusts are created, most experts have indicated that a durable power of attorney should be prepared containing a pour-over provision (discussed in the previous chapter) to deal with the possibility that the client acquires assets after the creation of the inter vivos trust and fails to transfer or convey them to the inter vivos trust. If that client becomes **incompetent**, she will die with those after-acquired assets still in her estate rather than in the living trust. This will necessitate the probate of a will, which most estate planners prepare in connection with an inter vivos, or living, trust, a cost that such a trust is designed to avoid. The statutory form provides for pour-over. If one is not using the statutory form, a clause such as that in Example 6-1 should be added.

Example 6-1

If, in the event of my disability or incompetency, I own real or personal property of any nature whatsoever then I hereby authorize and direct my said attorney in fact to transfer and/or convey all such real or personal property that I may own at such a time to an inter vivos trust created by me on the _____ day of _____, 19___ and known as the _____ Trust.

The primary benefit of the durable power of attorney is to appoint someone who has the authority to manage any assets of the client upon the client's incompetency. This avoids the necessity of appointing a guardian, which can be an expensive process. Further, there may be some disability of the principal that prevents her from taking care of her own property but that does not constitute incapacity (incompetency) as defined in the statutes.

In this century, life expectancy has increased tremendously, as has the incidence of mental incompetence due to aging and diseases that normally strike only the aged. Therefore, the use of powers of attorney becomes a vital part of estate planning. Unfortunately, they are not widely accepted. Many banks, savings and loans, **title insurance underwriters**, and others have refused to accept a power of attorney in the event of the incompetency of the principal. Their refusal is based on documented events of misuse of powers of attorney by those appointed as attorney in fact. These institutions simply do not want to incur the possible liability or court costs, even if they prevail.

What effect the 1993 Durable Power of Attorney Act will have on increasing the acceptability of powers of attorney is not clear yet. One eminent authority, Stanley M. Johanson of the University of Texas Law School, recommends putting a clause in a durable power of attorney providing that the attorney in fact either may or even must file suit against any institution that refuses to accept the power of attorney if the refusal causes injury or damage to the principal's estate. This opinion is based on language found in Section 36A that does not appear in the 1993 act. However, it is likely that many lawyers will continue to use similar language in powers of attorney, at least to the extent that they do not switch over to the statutory form.

This is an interesting area of the law, and a lot of estate planners eagerly await a suit against someone who causes injury or damage by refusing to accept a power of attorney. The first of these cases may very well be against a **title insurance agent** who refuses to allow an attorney in fact appointed under a properly executed durable power of attorney, without the creation of a guardianship and the resulting court granted authority of the guardian, to sell the real property. In such a situation one could easily allege a duty under the statute, a breach of the duty, and injury (economic loss in the form of attorney's fees and other costs of the guardianship), proximately caused by the refusal to accept the power of attorney. There is a growing opinion among estate planners that institutions that customarily refuse powers of attorney may be incurring more liability by refusing to accept the powers than by accepting them.

A general power of attorney, or **universal power of attorney**, not in the statutory form, is attached to this chapter as Form 6-2. General (universal) power means that the power of attorney creates an authorization by the principal allowing the agent to do any and all contractual or other acts that the principal herself could do. A durable power of attorney, when created, must be universal (genera) because no one has any idea at the time of its creation what transactions may become necessary upon the incompetency of the principal.

In this regard, there is some common law from other states, relating to powers of attorney, and some case law in Texas, relating to other documents, that if the authorizing provisions attempt to list specific powers, then the specific grants of authority control over the general grant of authority. The result is that the general power of attorney is thwarted, and the attorney in fact has only the powers listed in the power of attorney. For this reason many attorneys do not list specific powers in a power of attorney which is intended to be universal (general), fearing such a list would destroy the grant of general powers. The 1993 act provides that listing specific powers in the statutory form does not diminish a general grant of powers.

A specific grant of authority is probably essential in a power of attorney if the attorney in fact might execute deeds or conveyances. Although there is no relevant case law in Texas, there is case law in many other states, including California, that a power of attorney is ineffective to grant authority to the attorney in fact to execute contracts for the conveyance of land or to execute deeds, conveyances, **mortgages**, or **deeds of trust** unless that authority is specifically given in the power of attorney. Consequently, it would be extremely unwise to prepare a power of attorney, other than in the statutory form, that does not specifically authorize the attorney in fact to execute deeds, conveyances, deeds of trust, and mortgages.

LIVING WILL

As stated earlier, at one time many attorneys referred to the power of attorney as a living will because it appointed someone to manage a client's assets in the event of the client's incompetency, much the same as a will appoints someone to manage and take care of a client's assets in the event of the client's death. In the late '60s or early '70s a nationally syndicated advice columnist applied the term *living will* to a document giving instructions concerning the use of medical devices and procedures to prolong life artificially. The term stuck to those instruments, which had no legal force whatsoever, and is still applied today.

A majority of the population appears to desire to execute some sort of instructions dealing with the use of such techniques, but not very many know how to obtain such a document or at least how to obtain a document that might have some legal effect. Most hospitals have the forms available and supply them on request. However, by the time someone goes into the hospital it may already be too late.

Texas has adopted two sets of statutes dealing with this particular problem. One creates and authorizes a directive to physicians; the other provides for a **durable power of attorney for health care**. The first is found in the Natural Death Act, Sections 672.001-672.021 of the Health and Safety Code. The medical power of attorney is provided for in Sections 135.001-135.018 of the Civil Practices and Remedies Code.

The Natural Death Act provides for the execution of written directives to physicians. Such directives may be executed by any competent adult, who must sign the written directive in the presence of two witnesses. The act requires the witnesses to sign the directive and states that they *may not be*:

1. Related to the declarant by blood or marriage.
2. Entitled to any part of the declarant's estate after the declarant's death under a will or codicil executed by the declarant or by operation of law.
3. The attending physician.
4. An employee of the attending physician.
5. An employee of the health care facility in which the declarant is a patient if the employee is providing direct patient care to the declarant or is directly involved in the financial affairs of the facility.

6. A patient in the health care facility in which the declarant is a patient.

7. A person who, at the time the directive is issued, has a claim against any part of the declarant's estate after the declarant's death.

The act further allows the declarant to designate a person to make treatment decisions for the declarant in the event the declarant becomes comatose, incompetent, or otherwise mentally or physically incapable of communication. The declarant is required to notify the attending physician of the existence of a written directive; but the act says that if the declarant is unable to do so, then another person may notify the attending physician of the directive's existence. Upon notification, the attending physician is required to make the directive a part of the declarant's medical record.

The act provides a form for a written directive, which is not mandatory. A directive prepared pursuant to the act in the statutory language is attached to this chapter as Form 6-3. Section 672.005 of the Health and Safety Code says that such a directive may be issued orally in the presence of the attending physician and two witnesses. Upon such a declaration, the physician is required to make a note of the directive in the declarant's medical records and to have the witnesses sign the entry. Further, Section 672.006 provides that a spouse (if the spouse is an adult), the parents, or a legal guardian may execute a directive on behalf of a qualified patient who is less than 18 years of age. However, the expressed instructions of a competent patient, including one younger than 18 years of age, supersede the effect of the directive.

If an adult, qualified patient has become comatose, incompetent, or otherwise mentally or physically incapable of communication and has designated a person to make a treatment decision under the act, then the attending physician and the designated person shall make a treatment decision to withhold or withdraw life-sustaining procedures. If, however, the patient has not designated a person to make a treatment decision, the act says that the attending physician shall comply with the directive unless the physician believes the directive does not reflect the patient's present desire.

If an adult, qualified patient has not executed or issued a directive and is comatose, incompetent, or otherwise physically or mentally incapable of communication, then the attending physician and the patient's legal guardian may make a treatment decision. If the patient does not have a guardian, the attending physician and at least two persons from the following categories and in the priority listed may make a treatment decision that could include a decision to withhold or withdraw life-sustaining procedures:

1. The patient's spouse.

2. A majority of the patient's reasonably available adult children.

3. The patient's parents.

4. The patient's nearest living relative.

This decision must be made in the presence of at least two witnesses who are subject to the same restrictions listed on page 119.

The act states that prior to withholding or withdrawing life-sustaining procedures from a qualified patient, the attending physician must:

1. Determine that the patient's death is imminent or will result within a relatively short time without application of those procedures.

2. Note that determination in the patient's medical records.

3. Determine that the proposed steps are in accord with the act and the patient's desires.

Section 672.003 allows that a declarant to include directions other than those provided in the statutory form of written directive.

The act goes on to:

1. Provide for revocation of the directive by either canceling, defacing, obliterating, burning, tearing or destroying it, signing and dating a written revocation, or orally stating the declarant's intent to revoke. This revocation requires a new entry in the patient's medical records.

2. Provide that the directive does not impair or invalidate the patient's life insurance policies.

3. Limit the liability of a physician, health facility or health professional who in some way participates in the withholding and withdrawing of life-sustaining provisions in accordance with the act.

4. Limit the liability, both civilly and criminally, of a physician, health care facility, or health care professional who refuses to act in accordance with the directive.

5. Provide for criminal penalties if someone conceals or defaces or damages another person's directive without that person's consent or in some manner falsifies or forges a directive or conceals knowledge of revocation and thereby causes the withholding or withdrawing of life-sustaining procedures.

Chapter 135 of the Texas Civil Practice and Remedies Code covers a durable power of attorney for health care, and requires that it must be in substantially the same form as provided for in the statute. Form 6.4 at the end of this chapter shows this statutory form.

In addition, the Civil Practice and Remedies Code states that a durable power of attorney for health care is not effective unless the principal signs a statement that she has received a disclosure statement in statutory form and has read and understood its contents. This disclosure must be signed prior to the execution of the power of attorney. The disclosure form is provided for in Section 135.015. It is attached to this chapter as Form 6-5.

The statute states that a person cannot exercise the authority of agent while serving as:

1. The principal's health care provider.

2. An employee of the principal's health care provider unless the person is a relative of the principal.

3. The principal's residential care provider.

4. An employer of the principal's residential care provider unless the person is a relative of the principal.

The two witnesses required by the act are required to affirm that the principal:

1. Appeared to be of sound mind to make a health care decision.

2. Stated in the witnesses' presence that she was aware of the nature of the durable power of attorney for health care and signed the document voluntarily and free from any duress.

3. Requested that the witnesses serve as witnesses to the execution of the document.

A witness is ineligible or incompetent to act as a witness if she is:

1. The agent.

2 The principal's health care or residential care provider or the provider's employee.

3. The principal's spouse or heir.

4. A person entitled to any part of the principal's estate upon the death of the principal under a will or deed in existence or by operation of law.

5. Any other person who has claim against the estate of the principal.

The statute says that if the principal is physically unable to sign, another person may sign the durable power of attorney for health care with the principal's name, providing it is done in the principal's presence and at her direction.

Unlike durable powers of attorney for other purposes, the appointment of a guardian does not automatically suspend the durable power of attorney for health care purposes. Rather, the act says that the Probate Court shall determine whether to suspend or revoke the authority of the agent designated in the durable power of attorney for health care. However, until the court does so, only the guardian has authority to make health care decisions. The statute protects anybody who, not having actual knowledge of the appointment of a guardian, allows decisions to be made by the agent appointed in the power of attorney.

The care provider is required to consult with the agent appointed and to follow the agent's directives to the extent consistent with the desires of the principal and the durable power of attorney without verifying that the directive is consistent with the principal's wishes or religious or moral beliefs. The statute further holds that if the health care or residential care provider finds it impossible to follow a directive, she must immediately notify the agent so the agent can select another provider who will follow the directives.

As in the Natural Death Act, there are provisions dealing with the limitations of liability of the physician, health care or residential care provider and agent.

The statute recognizes the validity of a durable power of attorney for health care provisions executed in another state or jurisdiction, provided that instrument complies with the law of the state or jurisdiction in which it was executed.

Finally, the statute recognizes the possibility of conflict with the Natural Death Act and provides that to the extent a durable power of attorney for health care conflicts with a directive executed under the Natural Death Act, the instrument executed later in time controls. A physician can act on the agent's directive under a durable power of attorney for health care and is then not required to comply with the Natural Death Act.

Physicians often do not want to make the decision themselves, which is what the directive requires them to do. Rather, the physician wants someone else to instruct her to withhold or withdraw life-sustaining procedures. Many attorneys believe that both the medical directive and a durable power of attorney should be executed simultaneously. Then the person appointed as agent in the durable power of attorney for health care can first present the directive to physicians or health care providers and, if they refuse to honor it then present the durable power of attorney for health care, which has more general acceptance than the directive to physicians.

One matter that is often overlooked in estate planning for younger married couples or single parents with minor children is the preparation of a power of attorney giving an agent the authority to make health care decisions concerning the minor children. Many times parents do not think of the need for such a power of attorney until they decide to go on an extended trip, leaving their children in the care of others. It is a good policy at least to suggest this power of attorney. Although no statutory authority exists for it, Section 35.01 of the Texas Family Code gives implied authority. It lists who may consent to the medical treatment of a minor in the absence of the parents or other person having primary power to consent as provided elsewhere in the Family Code, including: "an adult who has the care and control of the minor and has written authorization to consent from the person having power to consent as otherwise provided by law." This section appears to allow the parents, managing conservator, or other person having power to consent under other provisions of the Family Code to give written authorization, but only to a person who, at the time that medical consent is needed, has care and control of the minor.

A general power of attorney to make medical decisions for minor children executed by the parents would probably not be effective unless at the particular time the minors were in the actual physical care and control of the agents appointed in the power of attorney. However, when parents routinely leave their children in the care of the same persons, it is appropriate that they execute powers of attorney to allow those persons to give consent to medical treatment for the children.

DESIGNATION OF GUARDIAN

Section 118A of the Texas Probate Code allows a competent adult to designate by a written declaration who shall serve as guardian of either her person or her estate in case she becomes incompetent or to disqualify persons from serving as guardian of the person or estate. It requires the declaration to be attested to by at least two credible persons 14 years of age or older who are not named as guardian or alternative guardian in the declaration. A self-proving affidavit signed by the declarant and the witnesses attesting to the incompetence of the declarant and the execution of the written declaration must be attached. The self-proving affidavit constitutes prima facie evidence that the declarant was competent at the time of execution and that the guardian will serve in the best interest of the ward.

This section further provides that unless the court finds that the guardian is disqualified or will not serve in the best interest of the ward, the court is required to appoint the person named in a written declaration as guardian in preference to those who might otherwise be entitled to serve as guardian under the code. It also provides that the court may not appoint a person who is disqualified from serving as guardian in such a written declaration.

The declaration may be revoked by the declarant via the same methods provided for by Section 63 for the revocation of a will, and is automatically revoked if the declarant designates her spouse to serve as guardian and is subsequently divorced from that spouse.

The statute gives a suggested, but not mandatory, form. An example of the statutory form is attached as Form 6-6 at the end of this chapter.

No estate planning is complete unless a declaration of guardian is prepared and executed by each of the clients. As mentioned earlier in this chapter, when an inter vivos trust has been prepared and all of the client's assets in existence at that time have been transferred into the trust, a power of attorney should still be prepared for the likelihood that the client will acquire additional property that she neglects to have conveyed into the trust.

Also discussed earlier in this chapter was the law that a power of attorney is voided by the appointment of a guardian. The client's wishes as to who will manage her property upon incompetency might be thwarted by someone's obtaining guardianship in the event of incompetency and thereby voiding the power of attorney. To avoid this, a designation of guardian should be executed that appoints as guardian the same person named in the power of attorney, with the same substitute or alternatives. Further, the client should give some serious thought as to whether to disqualify persons who might be high in the order of preference provided by the Probate Code.

COMMUNITY PROPERTY WITH THE RIGHT OF SURVIVORSHIP

At common law, the joint tenancy was the preferred form of co-ownership. *Preferred* means that unless the co-owners expressed what form of co-ownership they were holding under or unless the person who conveyed ownership to the co-owners expressed in what form of ownership the property would be held, the common law presumed it was a joint tenancy, provided that it met all of the prerequisites for the existence of the joint tenancy.

What distinguishes a joint tenancy from most other forms of co-ownership is that when one co-owner dies, her ownership interest, instead of descending to and vesting in her heirs or devises, passes to the other joint owners. The last surviving joint owner will own all of the real property or personal property, and her interest then will pass to her heirs or devisees upon death.

The early Texas legislature, in an overreaction to this rule, created a statute that prohibited joint tenancy. That statute was then incorporated into the current Texas Probate Code as the first sentence of Section 46(a). In 1969, the legislature deemed that property could be held in joint tenancy if the joint owners agreed in writing that the interest of any joint owner who died passed to the surviving joint owner or owners. That amendment further provided that no such agreement would be inferred from the mere fact that property is held in joint ownership.

Almost immediately, some spouses attempted to create joint tenancy property out of community property. That is, they tried to change the nature of community property so that upon the death of one, the ownership of that undivided half of the community property would automatically pass to the surviving spouse. Almost as quickly, the Supreme Court of Texas declared that Section 46 was unconstitutional to the extent that it might be used to change the nature of community property. This then allowed non-spouses, and spouses with separate property, to create joint tenancies, but prohibited spouses from using community property to create joint tenancies. Thereafter, the portion of the Constitution of the State of Texas dealing with separate and community property (Article 16, Section 15) was amended to allow spouses to partition between themselves their community property. The Supreme Court then created what is sometimes referred to as the "Texas Two-Step." (This will be discussed in more detail in the following section.)

In 1987, Article 16, Section 15, of the Texas Constitution was amended again to allow spouses to agree in writing that all or part of their community property will become the property of the surviving spouse upon the death of one of the spouses. In 1989, Section 46 of the Probate Code was amended by adding a subsection (b) that held that subsection (a) would not apply to agreements between spouses regarding their community property, but rather those agreements would be governed by Chapter 11 of the Probate Code. Chapter 11, Part

3, was then adopted by the legislature in 1989 to permit spouses to agree between themselves that all or part of their community property, either existing or to be acquired later, would become the property of the surviving spouse upon the death of one of the spouses.

Those sections dealing with **community property with right of survivorship** begin at Probate Code Section 451 and continue through Section 462. They state that an agreement creating a right of survivorship in community property must be in writing and signed by both spouses and, to be effective, must include one of the following phrases:

1. "With right of survivorship."
2. "Will become the property of the survivor."
3. "Will vest in and belong to the surviving spouse."
4. "Shall pass to surviving spouse."

The statute further says that any agreement may be revoked in accordance with the terms of the agreement; and if the agreement does not provide a method for revocation, it may be revoked by written instrument delivered to the other spouse. Because of this, it is strongly suggested that the written agreement between the spouses state that the agreement may only be revoked by an instrument in writing, recorded in the official real property records of a named county.

The Probate Code protects anyone who purchases real or personal property from a person claiming ownership under such a written agreement if more than six months have expired after the date of the death of one of the spouses, provided that they have been furnished an original or a certified copy of the agreement or that one is recorded in the county in which the real property is located and the purchaser had no notice that the agreement had been revoked.

In addition, the Probate Code supplies an abbreviated procedure by which a court having probate jurisdiction can adjudicate the validity of the agreement creating the right of survivorship in community property.

Several title insurance underwriters in the State of Texas have created underwriting rules by which they will accept the validity of an agreement creating a right of survivorship in community property. This is conditioned on the requirements that the transaction occur more than six months after the death of the deceased spouse, that the surviving spouse execute an affidavit that the agreement creating survivorship rights has not been revoked, and that the purchaser execute an affidavit that he has no knowledge or notice of revocation. If the transaction is to occur in less than six months, the underwriters require an adjudication as provided in the Probate Code.

The execution of an agreement between spouses creating a right of survivorship in community property does not otherwise change in any way the nature of the ownership of the community property. It still remains community property, and the spouses' rights concerning management and control or disposition of the property are not affected unless the agreement provides otherwise. A form for such an agreement is given at the end of this chapter as Form 6-7.

JOINT TENANCY

The previous section mentioned the "Texas Two-step." As stated earlier, in the early 1980s the Constitution was amended to allow spouses to:

> By written instrument from time to time partition between themselves all or part of their property, then existing or to be acquired or exchange between themselves the community property of one spouse or future spouse in any property for the community interest of the other spouse or future spouse in other community property then existing or to be acquired, whereupon the portion or interest set aside to each spouse shall be and constitute a part of the separate property and estate of such spouse or future spouse; spouses may also from time to time, by written instrument, agree between themselves that income or property from all or part of the separate property then owned or which thereafter may be acquired by only one of them, shall be the separate property of that spouse; if one spouse makes a gift of property to the other that gift is presumed to include all income or property which might arise from that gift of property; and spouses may agree in writing that all or part of their community property becomes the property of the surviving spouse on the death of the spouse.

The last portion produced the agreement creating community property with a right of survivorship that is discussed in the preceding section. The first phrase is what will be discussed in this section, and the entirety—but particularly the first, second, and third phrases—shall be discussed in the following section.

The constitutional amendment allowed spouses to enter into an agreement to partition the property they owned at the time of execution of the agreement and property to be acquired in the future. The effect, assuming the spouses agree to partition all of their community property, is to do away totally with any community property, at least whatever exists at the time of the agreement, and to convert it to the separate property spouse. (Remember that the preexisting law held that a joint tenancy with the right of survivorship could be created only by unmarried persons or by married spouses out of their separate property.)

In applying these two rules of law, the Supreme Court of Texas created the so-called "Texas two-step." The first step is for the spouses to enter into a partition agreement, partitioning whatever property that they want to hold in a joint tenancy. Then, the spouses enter into a joint tenancy agreement for that same property, which is valid because the joint tenancy is being created from the separate property that had been created by the partition agreement.

Also, the constitutional amendment allows the partition of property to be acquired in the future. Such a partition agreement could perhaps state that any property acquired would be owned as separate property

by the spouse in whose name it was acquired or who physically purchased and paid for it, regardless of the source of the funds. This sort of
thing should only be done between spouses who trust each other fully,
because it could lead to fraud and the hiding of income in order to
acquire property that would be separate. Some agreements have gone
so far as to state that any wages, salaries, profits, or other income
earned by either spouse would be the separate property of the spouse
earning it. Some commentators believe that such an agreement goes
further than the constitutional amendment contemplated. However, as
will be discussed in the following section, the Uniform Premarital
Agreement Act, as adopted by Texas in 1987, indicates that it may
be interpreted broadly enough to allow the division of future income,
at least for agreements entered into prior to and in contemplation
of marriage.

Sections 5.51-5.56 of the Texas Family Code, which are applicable
to agreements entered into after marriage, were created in 1987 at the
same time as the Uniform Premarital Agreement Act was adopted.
Those sections, however, use language that is not as broad as that in the
Uniform Premarital Agreement Act and, in fact, limit application to the
terminology found in the constitutional amendment quoted earlier.
However, cases that have been determined based on those acts seem to
apply the same law to premarital agreements and so-called post-nuptial
agreements. Also, the language in both provisions of Family Code
concerning the division of future income is almost identical, and the
statutes regulating post-nuptial agreement have adopted the definition
of *property* from the Uniform Premarital Agreement Act: "an interest,
present or future, legal or equitable, vested or contingent, and real or
personal property, *including income and earnings*."

Both of those acts also apply new standards for enforcement. They
require that such agreements may not be set aside by the court unless
the court finds that one party did not execute the agreement voluntarily
or that the agreement was unconscionable at the time it was executed,
provided also that the party claiming the agreement was
unconscionable prove she was not given a fair and reasonable
disclosure, did not voluntarily and expressly waive in writing any right
to disclosure, and did not nor reasonably could have had an adequate
knowledge of the property or financial agreements. This changed the
then-existing law of Texas (that the proponent of a post-nuptial
agreement prove its validity), giving the party challenging the
premarital agreement the burden of proving that it was
unconscionable. It also established conscionability as the legal standard
of enforcement, changing the existing law (in which the legal standard
was fairness or unfairness).

A discussion of Texas Family Law may seem out of place in a text
dealing with Texas Probate Law. But the fact is that since the
constitutional amendment that allowed partition and the resulting
"Texas two-step" estate planners have made the "Texas two-step" an
essential part of estate planning. The legal assistant engaged in
preparing instruments may be required to create community property

partition agreements for some portion of the client's property, or even all of it, and an agreement of joint tenancy. These kind of agreements are sometimes used to avoid probate without the need of an inter vivos trust, and often also to effectuate interspousal gifts. A partition and exchange between spouses that also incorporates some other post-nuptial agreements and an agreement between spouses to hold property in joint tenancy with the right of survivorship are found at the end of this chapter as Form 6-9. A form of a agreement to hold in joint tenancy is attached as Form 6-8.

MARITAL AGREEMENTS

The creation of survivorship as between spouses in community property and the creation of joint tenancy by way of a partition and exchange agreement that converts community property into joint tenancy property have already been discussed. Both premarital and post-nuptial agreements are also used by estate planners.

Estate planning sometimes occurs in contemplation of marriage. In fact, for persons who have never been married but possess a good deal of property and for those who have been previously married and possess property, planning for death or incompetency is a much more valid use of premarital agreements than is planning for a divorce. In addition, after marriage, even spouses who did not accumulate much property prior to marriage may desire to have specific items of what is currently their community property passed to children by a former marriage or even to children of the current marriage. Although a widow's election will, which has already been discussed, may be used to accomplish this purpose, a much more certain method is the post-nuptial agreement, with a will executed at the same time, that disposes of the property partitioned between the spouses.

Probably the most important reason for using premarital agreements and post-nuptial agreements or partition agreements between the spouses is to ensure that property passes, upon death of one of the spouses to the persons to whom that spouse desires it to go. These agreements also serve to avoid legally the imposition of estate taxes and to avoid the cost of probate. A post-nuptial agreement is attached at chapter's end as Form 6-9. Some premarital agreements use language similar to that found in Form 6-9 and go beyond what some experts in family law believe is permissible under the Texas Constitution and perhaps even the Family Code. A more conservative form may be found in the *Texas Family Practice Manual*, published by the State Bar of Texas.

BUSINESS ORGANIZATIONS

This text will not attempt to explain the law of business organizations or how they differ and are created. For many years, however, estate planners have used the creation of family-owned business organizations as a way legally to avoid current income taxes, gift taxes, and estate taxes and to avoid seizures of property by creditors in the event of a reversal of finances.

In the past, a favored vehicle was the family corporation. At least one prominent attorney practicing in the field of estate planning prepares a family limited partnership for almost all of his wealthier clients. It is foreseeable that the new limited liability company will also be used as an estate planning vehicle, since by a simple change in the organization one can create a company with all of the limited liability aspects of a corporation while being taxed either as a partnership (without the necessity of complying with Subsection S of the Internal Revenue Code) or as a corporation. Further, one can provide for management by the members or by a designated manager or managers. Due to the versatility of the limited liability company, it will probably become a favored vehicle of attorneys creating business organizations for the purpose of estate planning. The legal assistant should therefore be familiar with the law of business organization, including but not limited to the following:

1. How to create each of the major business organizations recognized in Texas.

2. The operation and management of each of the business organizations recognized in Texas.

3. Amendment and dissolution of business organizations under Texas law.

4. The management structure permissible for business organizations under the laws of Texas.

5. Income taxation of business organizations under the laws of Texas.

6. The law concerning interstate operations.

It is very likely that a legal assistant working in estate planning will be called on to prepare the documents that create, organize, and establish ownership of one or more types of business organization.

CHAPTER QUESTIONS AND EXERCISES

1. What is a power of attorney? What is required in order to make it durable? Why is it a part of estate planning?

2. What are the problems concerning the acceptability of a power of attorney? What can be substituted for a power of attorney that is more acceptable?

3. What is a living will? Where are the Texas statutory provisions for a living will found?

4. What requirements are there as to the witnesses to a directive to physicians?

5. How may someone designate a guardian in the case of incompetency? How may someone disqualify someone as her guardian?

6. What is community property with the right of survivorship? How is it created? How may it be revoked?

7. What is a joint tenancy? Can property owned as community property be converted to joint tenancy property? How?

8. As a minimum estate plan for the following circumstances, what documents would you execute, and why? (Note: This exercise involves material from prior chapters.)

   A client comes to your law firm and, after discussion, you find that he and his wife have adult children and can reasonably expect to own about $900,000 in total community property at the death of the first of them.

Form 6-1: Statutory Durable Power of Attorney

POWER OF ATTORNEY

NOTICE: THE POWERS GRANTED BY THIS DOCUMENT ARE BROAD AND SWEEPING. THEY ARE EXPLAINED IN THE DURABLE POWER OF ATTORNEY ACT, CHAPTER XII, TEXAS PROBATE CODE. IF YOU HAVE ANY QUESTIONS ABOUT THESE POWERS, OBTAIN COMPETENT LEGAL ADVICE. THIS DOCUMENT DOES NOT AUTHORIZE ANYONE TO MAKE MEDICAL AND OTHER HEALTH-CARE DECISIONS FOR YOU. YOU MAY REVOKE THIS POWER OF ATTORNEY IF YOU LATER WISH TO DO SO.

I, **JOHN SMITH**, 1414 Monolle, Turkey, Texas, my social security number being 000-00-0000, appoint **PAULA SMITH** as my agent(attorney in fact) to act for me in any lawful way with respect to the following initialed subjects:

TO GRANT ALL OF THE FOLLOWING POWERS, INITIAL THE LINE IN FRONT OF (N) AND IGNORE THE LINES IN FRONT OF THE OTHER POWERS.

TO GRANT ONE OR MORE, BUT FEWER THAN ALL, OF THE FOLLOWING POWERS, INITIAL THE LINE IN FRONT OF EACH POWER YOU ARE GRANTING.

TO WITHHOLD A POWER, DO NOT INITIAL THE LINE IN FRONT OF IT. YOU MAY BUT NEED NOT, CROSS OUT EACH POWER WITHHELD.

INITIAL

_____   (A)   real property transactions;

_____   (B)   tangible personal property transactions;

_____   (C)   stock and bond transactions;

_____   (D)   commodity and option transactions;

_____   (E)   banking and other financial institution transactions

_____   (F)   business operating transaction;

_____   (G)   insurance and annuity transactions;

_____   (H)   estate, trust, and other beneficiary transactions;

_____   (I)   claims and litigation:

_____   (J)   personal and family maintenance;

_____   (K)   benefits from social security, Medicare, Medicaid, or other governmental programs or civil or military service;

_____   (L)   retirement plan transactions;

_____   (M)   tax matters;

_____   (N)   ALL OF THE POWERS LISTED IN (A) THROUGH (M). YOU NEED NOT INITIAL ANY OTHER LINES IF YOU INITIAL (N).

SPECIAL INSTRUCTIONS:

ON THE FOLLOWING LINES YOU MAY GIVE SPECIAL INSTRUCTIONS LIMITING OR EXTENDING THE POWERS GRANTED TO YOUR AGENT:

NONE _____

_____

_____

_____

_____

_____

_____

_____

UNLESS YOU DIRECT OTHERWISE ABOVE, THIS POWER OF ATTORNEY IS EFFECTIVE IMMEDIATELY AND WILL CONTINUE UNTIL IT IS REVOKED.

Form 6-1: (continued)

CHOOSE ONE OF THE FOLLOWING ALTERNATIVES BY CROSSING OUT THE ALTERNATIVE NOT CHOSEN:

(A) This power of attorney is not affected by my subsequent disability or incapacity.

(B) This power of attorney becomes effective upon my disability or incapacity.

YOU SHOULD CHOOSE ALTERNATIVE (A) IF THIS POWER OF ATTORNEY IS TO BECOME EFFECTIVE ON THE DATE IT IS EXECUTED.

IF NEITHER (A) NOR (B) IS CROSSED OUT, IT WILL BE ASSUMED THAT YOU CHOSE ALTERNATIVE (A).

I agree that any third party who receives a copy of this document may act under it. Revocation of this durable power of attorney is not effective as to a third party until the third party receives actual notice of the revocation. I agree to indemnify the third party that arise against the third party because of reliance on this power of attorney.

If any agent named by me dies, becomes legally disabled, resigns, or refuses to act, I name the following (each to act alone and successively, in the order named) as successor(s) to that agent:

JOHN SMITH, JR., AND PENELOPE SMITH _____

Signed this _____ day of _____, 19<u>94</u>.

                                              _____
                                              JOHN SMITH

State of _____

County of _____

This document was acknowledged before me on _____
              (date)

by_____.
          (name of principal)

                                              _____
                                              (signature of notarial officer)

(Seal, if any, of notary)

                                              _____
                                              (printed name)

                                              My commission expires:_____

THE ATTORNEY IN FACT OR AGENT, BY ACCEPTING OR ACTING UNDER THE APPOINTMENT, ASSUMES THE FIDUCIARY AND OTHER LEGAL RESPONSIBILITIES OF AN AGENT.

(AUTHOR'S COMMENT: The grammatical and logical inconsistencies are those of the Texas Legislature. This includes telling the principal that he must chose "above" when the alternatives are below and requiring printed name and expiration date of the notary's seal when such information is required to be printed within the seal.)

Form 6-2: General Durable Power of Attorney

POWER OF ATTORNEY

Date: January 17, 1992

Principal: PETER SMITH

Principal's Mailing Address: 1412 Bullmoose, San Juan Hill, Texas 79231

County of Residence of Principal: Rough Rider County, Texas

Agent: PAULA SMITH

Agent's Mailing Address (including county): 1412 Bullmoose, San Juan Hill, Rough Rider County, Texas 79231

Successor Agent: PETER SMITH, JR.

Successor Agent's Mailing Address (including county): 252 Yellowstone Pkwy, Rough Rider County, Texas 79231

Effective Date: Immediately

Termination Date: Upon death of Principal

Property: Any and all property owned by Principal or in which Principal has an interest.

Powers Given:

1. Do any act and exercise any power that Principal could do personally or through any other person, and to indemnify and hold harmless any third party who accepts this Power of Attorney and acts in reliance thereon.

2. Lease, mortgage, encumber, sell, or convey the property for any price or any terms.

3. Execute and deliver any legal instruments including Bills of Sale, Warranty Deeds, Promissory Notes or Deeds of Trust relating to the sale or purchase of Property.

4. Release notes, deeds of trust, and other legal instruments, pertaining to the Property.

5. To collect and receipt in Principal's name all monies and funds of whatever nature and source, and access to any safe-deposit box held in Principal's name. To write checks upon any bank account in Principal's name for whatever bills or necessities accrued by Principal.

6. To sell, assign and transfer any shares of capital or corporate stock standing in my name on the books of any corporation, and for that purpose to make and execute all necessary acts of assignment and transfer, including the power and the duty in such a case, to deliver the certificates representing such shares, to endorse thereon the assignment of such shares and/or contemporaneously, to deliver this power of attorney, and to transfer and do all acts proper to accomplish the transfer of such shares on the books of said corporation.

7. Do everything and sign everything necessary or appropriate to accomplish the powers set out.

Principal appoints Principal's Agent to act for Principal in accordance with the power with respect to the Property, and Principal ratifies all acts done pursuant to this appointment. Agent's authority shall begin on the effective date and end on the termination date unless revoked sooner by Principal's written statement recorded in the office of the county clerk of the county where the Power of Attorney is recorded. This power of attorney shall not terminate on disability of the Principal.

If the Agent named ceases to serve as my Agent due to death, incapacity, or resignation, Principal appoints the named successor Agent as successor Agent to have all of the powers described herein. The successor Agent may evidence the death, incapacity or resignation of the original Agent, and third parties may rely thereon, by an acknowledged written statement signed by the successor Agent which (i) states the facts relating to the death, incapacity, or resignation of the former Agent, and (ii) is filed for record in the office of the County Clerk of the County where the power of attorney is recorded.

Principal binds Principal and Principal's heirs and personal representatives to indemnify and hold Agents harmless from all claims, demands, losses, damages, actions, and expenses that Agent may sustain or incur in connection with carrying out the authority granted to Agent in this power of attorney. Such indemnity shall apply whether the claims, demands, losses, damages, actions or expenses or other liability arises in whole or in part from the negligence of Agent.

_____

PETER SMITH

Form 6-2: (continued)

STATE OF TEXAS   §

COUNTY OF ROUGH RIDER   §

    This instrument was acknowledged before me on _____, 19_____, by **PETER SMITH**.

                                             _____

                                           Notary Public, State of Texas

Form 6-3: Directive to Physicians

DIRECTIVE TO PHYSICIANS

Directive made this 3rd day of June, 1992.

"I, **PAULA SMITH**, being of sound mind, willfully and voluntarily make known my desire that my life shall not be artificially prolonged under the circumstances set forth in this directive.

"1. If at any time I should have an incurable or irreversible condition caused by injury, disease, or illness certified to be a terminal condition by two physicians, and if the application of life-sustaining procedures would serve only to artificially postpone the moment of my death, and if my attending physician determines that my death is imminent or will result within a relatively short time without the application of life-sustaining procedures, I direct that those procedures be withheld or withdrawn, and that I be permitted to die naturally.

"2. In the absence of my ability to give directions regarding the use of those life-sustaining procedures, it is my intention that this directive be honored by my family and physicians as the final expression of my legal right to refuse medical or surgical treatment and accept the consequences from that refusal.

"3. If I have been diagnosed as pregnant and that diagnosis is known to my physician, this directive has no effect during my pregnancy.

"4. This directive is in effect until it is revoked.

"5. I understand the full import of this directive and I am emotionally and mentally competent to make this directive.

"6. I understand that I may revoke this directive at any time."

PAULA SMITH
San Juan Hill, Rough Rider
County, Texas

I am not related to the declarant by blood or marriage. I would not be entitled to any portion of the declarant's estate on the declarant's death. I am not the attending physician of the declarant or an employee of the attending physician. I am not a patient in the health care facility in which the declarant is a patient. I have no claim against any portion of the declarant's estate on the declarant's death. Furthermore, if I am an employee of a health facility in which the declarant is a patient, I am not involved in providing direct patient care to the declarant and am not directly involved in the financial affairs of the health facility.

WITNESS

WITNESS

Form 6-4: Durable Power of Attorney for Health Care

DESIGNATION OF HEALTH CARE AGENT

I, **PETER SMITH** appoint:
Name: **PAULA SMITH,**
Address: 1412 Bullmoose, San Juan Hill, TX 79231
Phone: (000) 000-0000

as my agent to make any and all health care decisions for me, except to the extent I state otherwise in this document. This durable power of attorney for health care takes effect if I become unable to make my own health care decisions and this fact is certified in writing by my physician.

LIMITATIONS ON THE DECISION-MAKING AUTHORITY OF MY AGENT ARE AS FOLLOWS:
None

DESIGNATION OF ALTERNATE AGENT.

(You are not required to designate an alternate agent but you may do so. An alternate agent may make the same health care decisions as the agent if the designated agent is unable or unwilling to act as your agent. If the agent designated is your spouse, the designation is automatically revoked by law if your marriage is dissolved.)

If the person designated as my agent is unable or unwilling to make health care decisions for me, I designate the following persons to serve as my agent to make health care decisions for me as authorized by this document, who serve in the following order:

A. First Alternate Agent
   Name: **PETER SMITH, JR.**
   Address: 252 Yellowstone Pkwy, San Juan Hill, TX 79231
   Phone: (111) 111-1111

B. Second Alternate Agent
   Name: **PENELOPE SMITH**
   Address: 721 Monolle, San Juan Hill, TX 79231
   Phone: (222) 222-2222

The original of this document is kept at 1412 Bullmoose, San Juan Hill, TX 79231.

The following individuals or institutions have signed copies:
   Name: Dr. Ashmosh Nefrititi
   Address: 521 Egyptian, San Juan Hill, TX 79231
   Name: Rough Rider County Memorial Hospital
   Address: 911 Hospital Road, San Juan Hill, TX 79231

DURATION

I understand that this power of attorney exists indefinitely from the date I execute this document unless I establish a shorter time or revoke the power of attorney. If I am unable to make health care decisions for myself when this power of attorney expires, the authority I have granted my agent continues to exist until the time I become able to make health care decisions for myself.

(IF APPLICABLE) This power of attorney ends on the following date: N/A

PRIOR DESIGNATIONS REVOKED.

I revoke any prior durable power of attorney for health care.

ACKNOWLEDGMENT OF DISCLOSURE STATEMENT.

I have been provided with a disclosure statement explaining the effect of this document. I have read and understand that information contained in the disclosure statement.

(YOU MUST DATE AND SIGN THIS POWER OF ATTORNEY.)

I sign my name to this durable power of attorney for health care on 3rd day of June, 1994, at San Juan Hill, TX 79231.

_____
PETER SMITH

_____
(Print Name)

Form 6-4: (continued)

STATEMENT OF WITNESSES:

I declare under penalty of perjury that the principal has identified himself or herself to me, that the principal signed or acknowledged this durable power of attorney in my presence, that I believe the principal to be of sound mind, that the principal has affirmed that the principal is aware of the nature of the document and is signing it voluntarily and free from duress, that the principal requested that I serve as witness to the principal's execution of this document, that I am not the person appointed as agent by this document, and that I am not a provider of health or residential care, an employee of a provider of health or residential care, the operator of a community care facility, or an employee of an operator of a health care facility.

I declare that I am not related to the principal by blood, marriage, or adoption and that to the best of my knowledge I am not entitled to any part of the estate of the principal on the death of the principal under a will or by operation of law.

Witness Signature: _____

Print Name: _____ Date: _____

Address: _____

Witness Signature: _____

Print Name: _____ Date: _____

Address: _____

Form 6-5: Information Concerning the Durable Power of Attorney for Health Care

INFORMATION CONCERNING THE DURABLE POWER OF ATTORNEY FOR HEALTH CARE

THIS IS AN IMPORTANT LEGAL DOCUMENT. BEFORE SIGNING THIS DOCUMENT, YOU SHOULD KNOW THESE IMPORTANT FACTS:

Except to the extent you state otherwise, this document gives the person you name as your agent the authority to make any and all health care decisions for you in accordance with your wishes, including your religious and moral beliefs, when you are no longer capable of making them yourself. Because "health care" means any treatment, service, or procedure to maintain, diagnose, or treat your physical or mental condition, your agent has the power to make a broad range of health care decisions for you. Your agent may consent, refuse to consent, or withdraw consent to medical treatment and may make decisions about withdrawing or withholding life-sustaining treatment. Your agent may not consent to voluntary impatient mental health services, convulsive treatment, psycho-surgery, or abortion. A physician must comply with your agent's instructions or allow you to be transferred to another physician.

Your agent's authority begins when your doctor certifies that you lack the capacity to make health care decisions.

Your agent is obligated to follow your instructions when making decisions on your behalf. Unless you state otherwise, your agent has the same authority to make decisions about your health care as you would have had.

It is important that you discuss this document with your physician or other health care provider before you sign it to make sure that you understand the nature and range of decisions that may be made on your behalf. If you do not have a physician, you should talk with someone else who is knowledgeable about these issues and can answer your questions. You do not need a lawyer's assistance to complete this document, but if there is anything in this document that you do not understand, you should ask a lawyer to explain it to you.

The person you appoint as agent should be someone you know and trust. The person must be 18 years of age or older or a person under 18 years of age who has had the disabilities of minority removed. If you appoint you health or residential care provider (e.g., your physician or an employee of a home health agency, hospital, nursing home, or residential care home, other than a relative), that person has to choose between acting as your agent or as your health or residential care provider; the law does not permit a person to do both as the same time.

You should inform the person you appoint that you want the person to be your physician and give each a signed copy. You should discuss this document with your agent and your physician and give each a signed copy. Your agent is not liable for health care decisions made in good faith on your behalf.

Even after you have signed this document, you have the right to make health care decisions for yourself as long as you are able to do so and treatment cannot be given to you or stopped over your objection. You have the right to revoke the authority granted to your agent by informing your agent or your health or residential care provider orally or in writing or by your execution of a subsequent durable power of attorney for health care. Unless you state otherwise, your appointment of a spouse dissolves on divorce.

This document may not be changed or modified. If you want to make changes in the document, you must make an entirely new one.

You may wish to designate an alternate agent in the event that your agent is unwilling, unable, or ineligible to act as your agent. Any alternate agent you designate has the same authority to make health care decisions for you.

THIS POWER OF ATTORNEY IS NOT VALID UNLESS IT IS SIGNED IN THE PRESENCE OF TWO OR MORE QUALIFIED WITNESSES. THE FOLLOWING PERSONS MAY NOT ACT AS WITNESSES:

(1) the person you have designated as your agent;

(2) your health or residential care provider or an employee of your health or residential care provider;

(3) your spouse;

(4) your lawful heirs or beneficiaries named in your will or a deed; or

(5) creditors or persons who have a claim against you.

I have received, read and understand the above information concerning the durable power of attorney for health care.

_____
PETER SMITH

Form 6-6: Declaration of Guardian in the Event of Later Incompetence or Need of Guardian

DECLARATION OF GUARDIAN

I, **PETER SMITH**, make this Declaration of Guardian, to operate if the need for a guardian for me later arises.

1. I designate **PAULA SMITH** to serve as guardian of my person, **PETER SMITH, JR.** as first alternate guardian of my person, **PENELOPE SMITH** as second alternate guardian of my person.

2. I designate **PAULA SMITH** to serve as guardian of my estate, **PETER SMITH, JR.** as first alternative guardian of my estate, **PENELOPE SMITH** as second guardian of my estate.

3. If any guardian or alternate guardian dies, fails, or refuses to qualify, or resigns, the next alternate guardian succeeds the prior named guardian and becomes my guardian.

4. I expressly disqualify the following persons from serving as guardian of my estate:

JOHN SMITH

SIGNED this 3rd day of June, 1992.

_____
PETER SMITH

_____   _____
WITNESS   **WITNESS**

Form 6-6: (continued)

Self-Proving Affidavit

Before me, the undersigned authority, on this date personally appeared the declarant, and
_____ and _____ as witnesses, and all being
duly sworn, the declarant said that the above instrument was his Declaration of Guardian and that he
had made and executed it for the purposes therein expressed. The witnesses declared to me that they are
each 14 years of age or older, that they saw the declarant sign the declaration, that they signed the declaration as witnesses, and that the declarant appeared to them to be of sound mind.

_____

PETER SMITH

_____   _____

AFFIANT   **AFFIANT**

Subscribed and sworn to before me by the above named declarant and affiants on this _____ day
of _____ , 19_____ .

_____

Notary Public, State of Texas

Form 6-7: Survivorship Agreement for Community Property
(Pursuant to Chapter 11, Part 3, Texas Probate Code)

SURVIVORSHIP AGREEMENT FOR COMMUNITY PROPERTY

DATE: November 22, 1993

SPOUSES: PETER SMITH and PAULA SMITH

PROPERTY: Lot Two (2), Block One (1), Sunnyside Addition, an addition in the City of San Juan Hill, Texas, as shown by the map or Plat Records of Rough Rider County in Volume 12, at page 334 of the map records of Rough Rider County, Texas

Spouses own the property and for valuable consideration agree with each other as follows:

1. As long as the property remains community property, then on the death of either spouse, the interest of the spouse who dies will become the property of the surviving spouse and will not descend or be vested in the heirs, devisees, or legal representatives of the deceased spouse.

2. Spouses will after this date own the property in the same manner as joint tenants with right of survivorship.

3. This agreement may be revoked by a written instrument signed by both spouses, by a written instrument signed by one spouse and delivered to the other spouse, or by the disposition of any of the property by one or both spouses if such disposition is not inconsistent with applicable law.

_____
PETER SMITH

_____
PAULA SMITH

STATE OF TEXAS

COUNTY OF ROUGH RIDER

This instrument was acknowledged before me on the _____ day of _____ by **PETER SMITH** and **PAULA SMITH**.

_____
Notary Public, State of Texas

Form 6-8: Joint Tenancy Agreement

(Pursuant to 46 (a), Texas Probate Code)

SURVIVORSHIP AGREEMENT

DATE: November 22, 1993

OWNERS: **PETER SMITH** and **PAULA SMITH**

PROPERTY: Lot Three (3), Block One (1), Morningside Addition, an addition in the City of San Juan Hill, Texas, as shown by the map or Plat Records of Rough Rider County in Volume 22, at page 222 of the map records of Rough Rider County, Texas

Owners own the property jointly and for valuable consideration agree with each other as follows:

1. If no severance occurs before the death of any Owner, then on the death of **PETER SMITH** and **PAULA SMITH** Owners, the interest of the joint Owner who dies shall survive to the surviving joint Owners.
2. Owners will after this date own the property as joint tenants with right of survivorship.
3. This agreement is binding on Owners and Owners' respective heirs and personal representatives.

_____
PETER SMITH

_____
PAULA SMITH

STATE OF TEXAS

COUNTY OF ROUGH RIDER

This instrument was acknowledged before me on the _____ day of _____ by **PETER SMITH.**

_____
Notary Public, State of Texas

STATE OF TEXAS

COUNTY OF ROUGH RIDER

This instrument was acknowledged before me on the _____ day of _____ by **PAULA SMITH.**

_____
Notary Public, State of Texas

Form 6-9: Post-nuptial Agreement

MARITAL AGREEMENT

This agreement is made by **PETER SMITH** and **PAULA SMITH**. We are already married, and we are making this agreement to set out in writing our understandings concerning this marriage. We agree as follows:

1. Intent

   It is our desire that conflicts regarding financial matters be minimized in our marriage, and this agreement is intended to prevent such conflicts. We make and execute this agreement voluntarily and without the intention to defraud preexisting creditors.

2. Disclosure

   Each of us has provided a fair and reasonable disclosure of that party's property and financial obligations to the other party. Each of us hereby voluntarily and expressly waives in writing any right to further disclosure of property or financial obligations of the other party. Further, each of us has or reasonably could have had adequate knowledge of the property and financial obligations of the other party.

3. Confirmation of Separate Property

   (a) Separate Property of Husband. All property listed in Schedule A is stipulated and agreed to be the separate property of Husband.

   (b) Separate Property of Wife. All property listed in Schedule B is stipulated and agreed to be the separate property of Wife.

4. Partition of Community Property

   (a) Property to Husband. Husband shall own, possess, and enjoy as his sole and separate estate, free from any claim of Wife, the property listed in Schedule C; and Wife partitions to Husband all that property, together with any insurance policies covering that property and any escrow accounts that relate to that property; and Wife grants, releases, and confirms to Husband and to his heirs and assigns all right, title, and interest in and claims to that property, to have and to hold the same, with all and singular the hereditaments and appurtenances thereto belonging forever.

   (b) Property to Wife. Wife shall own, possess, and enjoy as her sole and separate estate, free from any claim of Husband, the property listed in Schedule D; and Husband partitions to Wife all that property, together with any insurance policies covering that property and any escrow accounts that relate to that property; and Husband grants, releases, and confirms to Wife and to her heirs and assigns all right, title, and interest in and claims to that property, to have and to hold the same, with all and singular the hereditaments and appurtenances thereto belonging forever.

5. Earnings and Income

   (a) Income or Property Derived from Separate Property. All the income or property (whether from personal effort or otherwise) arising from the separate property owned at the date of this agreement by either of us, or that may later be acquired, shall be the separate property of the owner of the separate property that generated that income, increase, property, or revenue.

   (b) Earnings. All salary, earnings, and other compensation for personal services or labor received or receivable by either of us, now or in the future, shall be the separate property of the party who performed the services or labor and received or is due to receive the salary or other compensation.

6. Liabilities

   All liabilities and obligations (contingent and absolute) of either of us that exist at the date of this agreement shall be enforceable against and discharged from the separate property of the party who incurred the particular liability or obligation and shall not be enforceable against or dischargeable from the property of the other.

7. Future Property

   (a) Jointly Owned Property. It is our intent that from the date of this agreement, we will from time to time by mutual agreement have the opportunity to acquire jointly owned separate property but not own any community property. Any jointly owned property will be jointly owned by our respective separate estates. Any property that is acquired by either of us from the date of this agreement, regardless of the source of consideration exchanged for the property, will be owned only as separate property of the party in whose name the title is taken and will be free of any claim of reimbursement on the part of the other. If the evidence of reimbursement on the part of the other. If the evidence of title reflects both our names, that property will be owned by us as joint tenants with right of survivorship.

Form 6-9: (continued)

(b) Credit Purchases. Any property purchased on credit will be the separate property of the party in whose name the title is taken. If there is no evidence of title, the party to whom the credit was extended shall own the property and be solely responsible for paying any purchase-money indebtedness with that party's separate funds. If title to the property is taken in both our names, we shall both be responsible for paying any purchase-money indebtedness with our respective separate funds.

8. Reimbursement

Any payment or contributions by one of us to satisfy the debts or otherwise benefit the separate estate of the other shall not give rise to a claim for reimbursement or an interest in any property purchased by those payments unless we otherwise agree in writing. Any right of reimbursement that may arise during our marriage for payments or contributions made to the other's separate estate to the extent any payment is made by one for the benefit of the other shall be presumed to be a gift to the other party's separate estate.

9. Divorce

In the undesired event that our marriage is dissolved by divorce, each party shall receive the following:

(a) all separate property belonging to that party and

(b) one-half of all community assets (if any exist, it being our intent that we will have only separate property).

10. Death

If our marriage is dissolved by death, the survivor shall retain his or her separate property and one-half of all community assets plus any property that may be left to the survivor as a result of the other party. Each party waives any homestead rights that party could assert in the other party's separate property.

11. General

(a) No Third-Party Beneficiary. This agreement is for our exclusive benefit and not for the benefit of any third party.

(b) Heirs and Assigns. This agreement is enforceable by our executors, administrators, and heirs and is intended to be binding on our respective estates.

(c) Amendment. We reserve the right to amend or rescind this agreement, but any such amendment or rescission must be in writing and signed by both of us.

(d) Severability. If a part of this agreement is not enforceable, the rest of this agreement will be enforceable.

12. Representation by Attorneys

(a) Independent Counsel. Each party was represented by independent counsel in connection with this agreement.

(b) Full Understanding. We both acknowledge that we have carefully read and understand this agreement. We each understand that our marital rights and property may be adversely affected by this agreement.

13. Execution

This agreement is signed and voluntarily executed on the date of the acknowledgments shown below to be effective on the date of signing.

_____   _____
PETER SMITH   PAULA SMITH

APPROVED AS TO FORM:

_____   _____
ATTORNEY FOR PETER SMITH   ATTORNEY FOR PAULA SMITH

Form 6-9: (continued)

STATE OF TEXAS   §

COUNTY OF ROUGH RIDER   §

    This instrument was acknowledged before me on _____, 19____, by
PETER SMITH.

_____
Notary Public, State of Texas

STATE OF TEXAS   §

COUNTY OF ROUGH RIDER   §

    This instrument was acknowledged before me on _____, 19____, by
PAULA SMITH.

_____
Notary Public, State of Texas

ATTORNEYS' CERTIFICATES

I am the attorney for **PETER SMITH** in the above Marital Agreement. I have consulted with my client
about this agreement and explained its terms to him, and my client understood and voluntarily executed
the agreement after consulting with me.

_____
ATTORNEY FOR PETER SMITH

I am the attorney for **PAULA SMITH** in the above Marital Agreement. I have consulted with my client
about this agreement and explained its terms to her, and my client understood and voluntarily executed
the agreement after consulting with me.

_____
ATTORNEY FOR PAULA SMITH

7 INTRODUCTION TO TRUSTS

CHAPTER OBJECTIVES

Upon completion of this chapter, the student should be able to:

1. Apply the basic provisions of the Texas Trust Code to fact situations.
2. Name the statutory and common law prerequisites to the creation of a valid trust.
3. List the purposes and goals in creating trusts.
4. List and define the various classifications of trusts.
5. Name the required parties to trusts, and explain their capacity, or lack thereof, and their rights and responsibilities.

CHAPTER GLOSSARY

Active trust A trust in which the trustee has duties and responsibilities in the execution of the trust or in the management of the trust property.

Blind trust A device used to give management of assets to another while retaining no control over the management. Also describes the situation where title to real property is transferred into a person as trustee but the conveyance identifies neither the trust nor the beneficiaries.

Charitable remainder trust A trust in whose assets are distributed to a charity upon termination of the trust.

Consideration An element necessary to the existence of a contract; a profit or benefit received by one party as an inducement to enter the contract, or a detriment or forbearance suffered by the other party to the contract.

Constructive trust A trust created as a fiction by courts exercising equitable powers, to avoid the effects of fraud, malfeasance, or unfair or unjust behavior. The court rules that a person who has acquired legal title by inequitable, unfair, or unjust means holds such title as trustee for those harmed.

Crummy provisions Provisions named after the case of *Crummy v. Commissioner* (Ninth Circuit Court of Appeals) that if annual gifts are to be made to a trust, usually to take advantage of the $10,000 gift tax exclusion, the gift will qualify as an absolute gift if the beneficiary is given the right to receive, on demand, the gift amount each year. The right to the annual gift may be lost if no demand is made.

Cy-pres A rule used in the construction of written instruments. In the case of charitable trusts, the rule is applied to prevent the failure of the trust should the group that benefits from the trust cease to exist. The court will identify another group with needs as close as possible to those of the original group and continue the trust for the benefit of the succeeding group.

Distribution The act of paying the cash or transferring the property constituting the trust property to the beneficiaries, both remainder and income beneficiaries, of the trust.

Equitable title The ownership interest of one who has the real and beneficial use and ownership of property even though actual title may be vested in someone else.

Express trust A trust created in express terms or by a positive act of the parties, but usually by an instrument in writing.

Gestation The time from conception to birth. In legal usage, the period of gestation is conclusively presumed to be nine months.

Gratuitously Done or accomplished without consideration.

Implied trust A trust created by implication of law. Constructive trusts and resulting trusts are examples.

Income beneficiary The person or persons entitled to receive the income from a trust during its existence.

Invasion of corpus The act of a trustee in distributing to the income beneficiary, in addition to the income, a portion of the principal, or the trust property. Such an act must be authorized in the document creating the trust.

Legal title Record ownership, as opposed to equitable ownership. The owner has title to the property but has no other rights or benefits unless he also owns the equitable title.

Passive trust A trust in which the trustee has no duties or responsibilities. The courts of most states ignore the trust and hold that title, both legal and equitable, vests in the beneficiaries.

Private trust A trust established for the benefit of named persons or a class of persons who are identifiable from the terms of the trust document.

Public trust A trust created to benefit either the public generally or a large group that matches a certain description.

Qualified minor's trust A trust created pursuant to Section 2503(c) of the Internal Revenue Code, which provides that a gift to a trust will be considered the gift of a present interest if the trust property and income can be expended for the benefit of the minor prior to his reaching the age of 21 and if the entire principal will vest in him on his twenty-first birthday or in his estate if he dies prior to that.

Remaindermen In connection with trusts, the person who receives the trust property when the trust comes to an end, or terminates. Sometimes referred to as *remainder beneficiary*. (*Remainder* is defined in Chapter Two.)

Resulting trust A trust that arises out of implication of law, when legal title is transferred or conveyed but the intent appears or is inferred that beneficial ownership is in someone other than the one holding legal title.

Revocable trust A trust that the settlor reserves the right to revoke. Under IRS rules, a trust is revocable if the grantor reserves any right to modify the trust.

Rule against perpetuities A rule in the Texas Trust Code prohibiting the creation of an interest in property that will not vest within the life of a person in being at the time, plus 21 years, plus the period of gestation (nine months).

Sovereign immunity A doctrine that prevents the bringing of a suit against the government without its consent, based on the common law principle "The king can do no wrong." The federal government has generally waived its immunity; Texas has waived immunity in certain tort cases.

Testamentary Relating to a will or testament. In the case of trusts, it means the trust is created in a will and will not become effective until after the death of the testator.

Totten trust A trust created by the opening of a bank account in which the owner of the account acts in trust for another. It can be revoked by closing the account.

Trust property The property originally transferred or later added to a trust by the settlor, as it might change, increase, or decrease during the existence of the trust. Also referred to as *res*, *corpus*, *principal* and *trust estate*.

Uni-trust A trust in which the trustee is required to pay annually to the beneficiary a fixed percentage of the market value of the trust assets.

INTRODUCTION

In 1983, the Texas Legislature revised the existing Texas Trust Act and placed it as Subtitle B of Title 9 of the Texas Property Code. Title 9 of the Texas Property Code is labeled "Trusts," and Chapter A of Title 9 contains what was formally referred to as the **Blind Trust** Act. Subtitle C contains miscellaneous provisions dealing with employees' trusts and the attorney general's participation in proceedings involving charitable trusts. Subtitle B contains what Section 111.001 states may be cited as the Texas Trust Code, even though that subtitle refers to itself as "The Act" several times afterwards. The act does not substantially vary the common law, but rather preserves the common law to the extent that it is not in conflict with the code itself.

Because Texas is one of the few states having a comprehensive trust act, trust instruments in Texas are often much lengthier than necessary because they come from form books published for use throughout the United States. In most other states, there are no trust acts that specify things like the powers, duties and responsibilities of the trustee, how **trust property** is to be dealt with, and how trusts are revoked or terminated. Accordingly, trust forms go into great detail concerning subjects unnecessary in a trust instrument prepared for use in Texas. Although the instrument could be made substantially shorter by simply incorporating the code or letting the code apply without expressed reference, it is easier to use the form unchanged. There is a benefit to spelling out in detail all of the rights, duties, responsibilities, limitations, etc. within the instrument: The parties can simply consult the trust instrument to settle a disagreement or for guidance. They do not need to know the Texas Trust Code or to consult an attorney to find out what the code says on a particular question.

CREATION AND VALIDITY OF TRUSTS

Section 112.001 of the Texas Trust Code says that a trust may be created by:

1. A declaration by the owner of property that he holds the property as trustee for another.

2. The inter vivos (during life) transfer of property by the property owner to another as trustee for a third person or for himself.

3. A **testamentary** transfer of property by the owner thereof to another person as trustee for a third person.

4. An appointment under a power of appointment to another as trustee for the donee of the power or for a third person.

5. A promise to another whose rights under the promise are to be held in trust for yet a third person.

Many commentators seem fascinated by the argument about whether Texas case law mandates that the settlor or creator of the trust manifest an intention to create a trust. The issue seems to be put to rest by Section 112.002 of the Texas Trust Code, which states that a trust is created only if the settlor manifests an intention to do so.

Although Section 112.003 of the Trust Code provides that **consideration** is not required in order to create a trust, it does say that a promise to create a trust in the future is enforceable only if all the requirements of an enforceable contract are present, including consideration.

The Trust Code also contains a Statute of Frauds (Section 112.004) that specifies that a trust in either real or personal property is enforceable only if there is some written evidence of the terms of the trust that bears the signature of either the settlor or the settlor's authorized agent. The statute goes on to detail two exceptions in the case of personal property. The first is when trust property is transferred to a trustee who is neither the settlor nor a beneficiary of the trust if simultaneously with the transfer the transferor expresses an oral intention to create a trust. The second exception is when there is a declaration in writing by the property owner stating that he holds the property as trustee for another or for the owner and another. This declaration does not have to provide the trust terms.

The Trust Code states that a trust cannot be created unless there has been some property transferred to the trust. Property may be added to existing trusts from any source, unless the addition is either prohibited by the terms of the trust or is unacceptable to the trustee.

Sections 112.007 and 112.008 deal with capacity of the parties to the trust. The first section deals with the capacity of the settlor or creator of the trust, who is required to have the same capacity as required of a person transferring property, executing a will, or creating a power of appointment. It would appear, therefore, that the prerequisites for capacity to execute a valid will are also applicable to the execution of a valid trust. As discussed in Chapter Four, those prerequisites are that the testator be either 18 years of age or be or have been lawfully married or be in the armed forces, and be of sound mind. It would appear further that the Texas will cases defining the term *sound mind* are applicable to a determination of the capacity of a settlor or creator of a trust.

Section 112.008 deals with the capacity of the trustee and requires that the trustee have legal capacity to take, hold, and transfer the trust property. This would seem to eliminate anyone under the age of 18 or who had not otherwise been emancipated. Some authors seem to believe that a minor can serve as a trustee if appointed. However, although a minor has the capacity to take and hold property, a minor does not have the capacity to transfer property. Consequently, it would seem that the statute prevents a minor from acting as trustee.

However, the appointment of a minor as trustee probably would not invalidate the trust. Unless otherwise provided in the trust instrument, it would probably be necessary for the court to remove the trustee and appoint a successor. This section also provides that a trustee is not disqualified from acting as trustee if the person named as trustee also is a beneficiary or the settlor or creator of the trust.

Some states require that for a trust to come into existence the trustee must accept in writing the obligations under the trust. The Texas statutes do not go to this length. Section 112.009 does state that a signature of the trustee on the trust instrument or on a separate written acceptance constitutes conclusive evidence that he has accepted the trust. It provides that if the person named as trustee exercises any powers or performs any duties under the trust, acceptance is presumed. The statute goes on to say that a person who does not accept the trust incurs no liability whatsoever with respect to the trust, and a person named as alternate in the trust or selected by a method prescribed in the trust may then accept the trust. If there is no alternate named in the trust, or no provision for selecting an alternate, the court shall appoint a substitute trustee upon the petition of any interested person.

Although these provisions do not mandate a written acceptance, they do suggest that it would be good practice to have a trustee's written acceptance for each inter vivos (during life) trust executed at the time of or shortly after the execution of the trust itself. With regard to a testamentary trust, a trust created by a will, an acceptance should be executed shortly after the will is admitted to probate. A form of an acceptance is included at the end of this chapter as Form 7-1.

Section 112.031 states that a trust may not be created for an illegal purpose, nor may it require the trustee to commit any criminal or tortious act or any act contrary to public policy. Section 112.032 provides that a so-called passive trust (which will be discussed later) is void, and title to any real property attempted to be placed in such a trust vests directly and immediately to the beneficiary.

Finally, regarding the creation and validity of trusts, is Section 112.036, entitled the **rule against perpetuities**. This is a very old statute and provides that if there is a division of title into legal and the equitable, the **legal title** and the **equitable title** must come back together or vest within 21 years after some life in being at the time of the creation of the interest, plus the period of **gestation**, or 9 months. Section 112.036 makes the rule against perpetuities applicable to trusts, which was one of the prime applications to the rule when originally adopted in the common law. Although the rule against perpetuities has application in the division of title of property into multiple interest, one of its objectives was to prevent property from being placed into trust forever. Consequently, as will be mentioned later, one of the standard provisions in a testamentary trust or an irrevocable trust is a perpetuities provision. A sample provision follows.

Example 7-1: Perpetuities

In no event will the term of this trust continue for a term greater than twenty-one (21) years after the death of the last survivor of settlor and all relatives of settlor living on the effective date of this trust agreement. A continuation of this trust by the exercise of the power of appointment will be construed as the creation of a separate trust and the extending of the rule against perpetuities to the maximum extent permitted by law. The court of jurisdiction is deliberately to construe and apply this provision to validate an interest consistent with settlors intention and may reform and construe an interest according to the doctrine of cy pres.

PURPOSES OF CREATION OF TRUSTS

There are many reasons why trusts are created and many objectives accomplished by creating trusts. For example, one might create a trust:

1. **To provide support for dependents or family members**, including parents, children, grandchildren, and spouse. This most commonly is accomplished through a testamentary trust created in a will. However, inter vivos trusts are established for the same purpose.

2. **To keep the settlor's property intact for later distribution.** Often a trust created for this purpose provides support for someone to whom the settlor feels obligated, such as a spouse, without transferring to that person absolute ownership. Consequently, the settlor's property can be retained for a class of persons to which the settlor ultimately desires it to go,. This commonly is used when the settlor has entered into a second marriage: Although he desires to provide for the support, maintenance, and care of his spouse, assuming she survives him, he does not want the property to vest in that spouse because it may then vest in the heirs or relatives of the spouse rather than in his own heirs or relatives. Consequently, a trust is created that allows the expenditure of income, and perhaps even of principal of the trust (commonly referred to as **invasion of**

corpus), during the life of the surviving spouse for that spouse's support, maintenance, care, and medical treatment. It provides that upon the death of the surviving spouse the remaining principal, or trust property as it is called by the statute, will vest in the settlor's children, grandchildren, or other **remaindermen**.

3. **To prevent the expenditure of funds until some goal of the settlor is met.** A common use of such a trust is to provide for the college education of minor children. This goal can sometimes be met while at the same time providing estate planning against gift and inheritance taxes for the settlor's estate, such as through the use of a **qualified minor's trust** under Internal Revenue Code Section 2503(c).

4. **To provide professional financial management** for those inexperienced in the handling of money or who lack capacity to manage their own financial affairs. This could be minor children or a spouse who is disabled, either physically or mentally, or who because of lack of education or experience cannot manage his own funds.

5. **To avoid the cost and delay of probate.** As previously mentioned, although this may be a reason for creating a trust, it probably should not be the sole reason in Texas. The Texas Probate Code provisions on independent administration reduce the costs of probate in Texas enough that it is probably cheaper to probate than to prepare the type of trust necessary to avoid the cost of probate. However, if combined with some other purpose, the cost-reducing or -eliminating effects of inter vivos trusts are an added benefit.

6. **To reduce present income taxes.** Although the Internal Revenue Service has lowered the chance for using a trust for this purpose by prohibiting income splitting through what is known as a Clifford Trust, possibilities still exist. For instance, an individual could create a **charitable remainder trust** under the provisions of Internal Revenue Code Section 170(f)(2)(A). These can be in the form of a *CRAT* (charitable remainder annuity trust), a *CRUT* (charitable remainder uni-trust), or a charitable lead trust, sometimes referred to as a charitable income trust. These provisions allow an individual to obtain current deductions for charitable contributions by placing property in trust while retaining the right either to receive some income during the settlor's life or to receive the property back after a period of years.

7. **To provide for disability or incompetency.** In our earlier discussion of this subject (Chapter 6) the point was made that a trustee operating under an existing trust agreement has much wider acceptance than does an attorney in fact operating under a power of attorney.

8. **To provide for professional management or management by others.** Many times, trusts, particularly **revocable trusts**, are created by persons who no longer want the time involvement and responsibility of managing their own properties. They may even

have a fear that because of age they have lost or are beginning to lose the mental sharpness required to manage property. They may then desire either to turn over the management of their property to professional managers, including trust departments of banks, or perhaps to turn over management of their assets to those who will receive the assets upon their death. Many larger farmers, ranchers, and business owners have placed assets into a revocable trust naming as trustees, those persons who would receive the properties upon death of the settlor as trustees. The trust provides for the expenditure of income for the care, support, maintenance, and well-being of the settlor during the rest of his life. In either situation, the settlor can then divorce himself from the cares and tribulations of running the business or operating the farm or ranch while receiving the income necessary for continued enjoyment of life. If the settlor becomes dissatisfied either with the trust arrangement or with the trust management, he can simply revoke it, remove the trustee and appoint a new trustee, or modify the trust to obtain the desired result.

9. **To reduce the incidence of gift, estate, and inheritance taxes.** This is often a major purpose in creating of certain kinds of trusts. Trusts such as GRITs (grantor-retained interest trusts), GRATs (grantor-retained annuity trusts), GRUTs (grantor-retained **unitrusts**), PRTs or QPRTs (personal residence trusts or qualified personal residence trusts), and trusts with **Crummy provisions** allow the transferring of assets, with little or no gift tax consequences, out of the settlor's estate, thereby reducing the taxable estate and the resulting estate inheritance taxes. (These subjects will be discussed in greater detail in the following chapters.) Gifts of property subject to rapid appreciation into a trust can reduce the incidence of estate and inheritance tax while allowing control of the property to be retained by the settlor because the value of the property will be fixed, subject to some exceptions, at the time of the gift rather than at the time of death. Consequently, property that might end up being valued at $500,000 at the time of death can be given away while the value is still $100,000 and the settlor can retain control of the property by naming himself as trustee. These types of trusts have some complex drafting requirements in order to obtain all of the benefits while the grantor also retains control.

CLASSIFICATION OF TRUSTS

All trusts may be divided into two categories, expressed and implied. **Express trusts** are created by voluntary action of the owner of property and are represented either by a written document or by an oral declaration in the limited instances allowed by Section 112.004 (which has previously been discussed). The express trust embodies a deliberate action of the settlor and is classified as either private or public, active or passive and inter vivos or testamentary.

Private Trusts vs. Public Trusts

A **private trust** is created by expressed intention between a person who has the capacity to be a settlor and one who has the capacity to be a trustee, for the financial benefit of certain named beneficiaries. Private trusts constitute a majority of all trusts. These are the type of trusts that primarily will be discussed in this text.

A **public trust** or charitable trust, is an express trust established for the purpose of accomplishing social benefits for the public or community. Although charitable trusts are public trusts, the beneficiary of a charitable trust need not always be the general public. The trust fund must be designated for the benefit either of the general public or of a reasonably large, indefinite class of persons who may be personally unknown to the settlor, e.g. the deaf. The true test of a creation of a valid public trust is not the indefiniteness of the persons aided by the trust, but rather the amount of social benefit that accrues to the public. Also, the purposes of the charitable trust must not include profit making by the settlor, the trustee, or any other person.

The law will not allow the charitable trust to fail even though its purposes have been accomplished or its beneficiary no longer exists unless the settlor clearly intended it to end at that time. As an example, if the trust was to help AIDs sufferers and the medical community seeking a cure, the courts would apply the doctrine of **cy-pres**. This doctrine, which comes from the French phrase *cy-pres comme possible*, meaning "as near as possible," holds that the trust continues to exist for the benefit of an organization whose purpose is as close as possible to the purpose originally intended by the settlor. The attorney general of the State of Texas has the jurisdiction to enforce public and charitable trusts.

Active Trusts vs. Passive Trusts

An **active trust** is an express trust that can be either public or private. The features that distinguish an active trust from a **passive trust** are the obligations of management and administration that the active trust imposes on a trustee. **Implied trusts** are passive trusts.

The passive trust implies that the trustee is merely holding the trust property for the beneficiary, with no obligation or power to administer the trust. In other words, the passive trust commissions the trustee to perform, at most, only minor acts of a mechanical or formal nature and often creates no duties whatsoever. The passive trust has been abolished in most states, including Texas, either because the state courts have interpreted the law so as to incorporate the old English Statute of Uses as a part of that state's common law or by passing statutes, such as Section 112.032 of the Texas Trust Code, which provides that title to real property held in trust vests directly in the beneficiary if the trustee has neither powers nor duties relating to the administration of the trust.

Inter Vivos Trusts vs. Testamentary Trusts

Inter vivos trusts and testamentary trusts are both express trusts. As the names imply, they are created at different times in the settlor's life. The term *inter vivos* pertains to a gift made in trust between living persons. The term *testamentary* pertains to a gift in trust made after death as a part of the last will and testament that becomes effective upon the admission of the will to probate.

Otherwise, inter vivos trusts differ little from testamentary trusts. Both are widely employed as means of conserving property for the benefit of surviving spouses and/or children and other family members. The inter vivos trust offers some estate planning benefits over the testamentary trust because it allows the settlor to see how well the trust operates by creating a revocable trust while the settlor is still alive that may be either modified or revoked if the settlor is dissatisfied with it. In addition, there are provisions available for increased savings of estate tax, gift tax, and even current income tax through an inter vivos trust that are not available through a testamentary trust. By the same token, the testamentary trust allows the settlor to enjoy the full benefits of ownership of his property until his death.

Implied Trusts

Implied trusts are not tangential to this text because they relate neither to estate planning nor to probate administration. However, as the opposite of express trusts, they deserve a short discussion.

Implied trusts are divided into constructive trusts and **resulting trusts**. Resulting trusts are created by the inferred or presumed intention of the owner of property. There are three situations in which an implied resulting trust may occur:

1. When one person's money has been paid for an investment in land or personal property but for some reason legal title is conveyed to another person, the law implies that a resulting trust, referred to as a *purchase money resulting trust*, has been created for the benefit of the person who paid the consideration. Generally, proof by clear and convincing evidence is required, and the law places the burden of proof on the person seeking to have the resulting trust implied.

2. When a settlor attempts to create an express private trust **gratuitously** and the trust fails or is declared void for any reason other than for having an illegal purpose, a resulting trust arises for the benefit of the settlor. This allows the settlor to recover the trust property from the trustee in the event of the invalidity of the trust.

3. If the trust property exceeds what is necessary for the purposes intended by the settlor and the trust makes no provision for a remainderman, a court may establish a resulting trust for the benefit of the settlor or the settlor's successors in interest, heirs, or devisees.

Constructive trusts are not created by the stated intent of the settlor, nor are they created by the implied or presumed intent of a property owner whose acts cause a court to enforce a resulting trust. Constructive trusts are a creation of the courts of equity for the purpose of rectifying a wrong or preventing the unjust enrichment of a wrong-doer. An example out of family law is the creation of a constructive trust in the husband when he has fraudulently transferred community property, or even the separate property of the wife, to himself and has by the expenditure of the property enhanced the value of his own separate property that is adjudged by the court to be held in trust.

Even though both the resulting trust and the constructive trust are passive trusts, the Statute of Uses, or its modern counterpart found at Section 112.032 of the Texas Trust Code, do not apply.

Other Trust Classifications

In addition to the classifications just discussed, there are scores of others based on the purposes, benefits, and other elements of trusts. These include GRITs, GRATs, GRUTs, PRTs, QPRTs, spendthrift trusts, pour-over trusts, business trusts, Totten (or savings bank trusts), qualified trusts for minors, and charitable remainder trusts. (Many of these will be discussed in the next two chapters.)

Business trusts are created by settlors as an alternative to creating corporations or other business organizations. Often referred to as *Massachusetts trusts*, they are not recognized in Texas, with the exception of the so-called real estate investment trust, or REIT. These trusts, however, are related more closely to business organizations than to the topics of discussion in this text.

In the **Totten trusts**, or savings bank trust, the settlor has placed money in a bank or savings and loan under his name (or sometimes the name of another) in trust for a named beneficiary. Such deposits allow the depositor or trustee to withdraw money during the depositor's life and allow the remaining balance to be transferred to the beneficiary upon the depositor's death. The depositor, or the grantor, can revoke the trust by withdrawing the entire amount prior to death. Since banks in Texas have been using joint survivor accounts, which accomplish the same results without creating a trust, Totten trusts have not been in great use in Texas although they are recognized by Sections 436-450 of the Texas Probate Code.

PARTIES TO THE TRUST

One may convey property in trust to another for the benefit of a third person. Although three parties often participate in the creation of a trust, the law demands the involvement of at least two. The same person cannot be sole trustee and sole beneficiary, thus holding both legal and equitable title, which would defeat the separation-of-title mechanism inherent in every trust.

Settlor

The settlor is the person who creates the trust. This person is also referred to as the *creator*, the *grantor*, or the *trustor*. Provided the settlor manifests a clear intent to establish the trust, no particular words are needed to create a trust. To be a settlor, an individual must either own a transferable interest in real or personal property or have the right or power to transfer a property interest, have contractual capacity, and show a clear intention to create a trust.

Some trusts are created without a settlor. These *constructive trusts*, as discussed before, are forms of implied trusts, created and controlled by the courts to remedy wrongful, dishonest, unconscionable, or fraudulent behavior.

Once a settlor creates a trust, and assuming he does not appoint himself as trustee or beneficiary, he has no further rights, duties, or liabilities in the trust administration. He may, however, have a reversionary interest at the termination of the trust; and while alive he may expressly retain the right to revoke or modify the trust, in which case the trust is said to be *revocable*. A revocable trust does not allow the settlor to pass income from himself to another under the existing tax laws. In other words, a revocable trust is not sufficient to save taxes. However, by the same token, if used for other purposes, it may save the expense of filing income tax returns because it does not become a separate tax-paying entity.

The right or power to select the trustee normally belongs to the settlor, but that right may be given to the beneficiary or to another person. This is referred to as a *power of appointment*.

Trustee

Any natural person having the legal capacity to take, hold, own, and transfer property may be a trustee. The law of many states is that a minor or insane person may take, hold and own property and consequently can be a trustee. However, the duties of a trustee involve entry into contracts and, since a minor's contract is voidable, the courts may remove a minor as trustee upon the request of the beneficiary. As discussed before, the Texas statutes require that the trustee be able to transfer property. A minor cannot transfer property he owns. Consequently, there is some doubt in Texas as to whether a minor or an insane person can be a trustee.

The trustee must be either a natural person or a legal entity. Although many states have entities called *trust companies* that serve as trustee even though they are not banks, in Texas only banks possessing trust powers are authorized to act as trustee.

A city cannot act as trustee of a private, expressed trust, but may act only as trustee of a public trust. The federal government and the state, or one of its political subdivisions, may act as trustee, but because of the doctrine of **sovereign immunity** cannot be sued by the beneficiary.

Regarding aliens and nonresidents, Texas law makes no prohibition as to individuals, but does as to corporations. Section 112.008 of the Texas Trust Code says that if a trustee is a corporation, it must have the power to act as trustee in this state. Section 105(a) of the Texas Probate Code says that if a bank or trust company, organized under the laws of the District of Columbia or any territory or state of the United States other than the State of Texas, desires to be appointed or to serve in the State of Texas as a trustee, it may do so if the District of Columbia, territory, or other state grants authority to Texas banks to serve in like fiduciary capacity. However, before qualifying or serving in the State of Texas, the trustee must meet the requirements of Section 105A(b) of the Probate Code.

There may be co-trustees; if so, they hold in joint tenancy unless otherwise provided in the trust agreement. Because of this and the rule that a person may not confer joint tenancy on himself and another (because the joint tenancy would lack the unities of time and title) it is necessary for an owner to convey to a straw man, or dummy, who will then reconvey to the co-trustees, one of whom would be the settlor. This may still be the law in Texas; at least it is the way that many attorneys still do it today.

A sole trustee may not be the sole beneficiary, but a beneficiary may be a co-trustee. This prevents merger of interest so as to destroy the trust as referred to earlier. Specific provisions dealing with merger are found at Section 112.034 of the Texas Trust Code.

Normally the settlor will name or appoint a trustee in the trust instrument itself. If he does not, a trustee may be appointed by the court.

Since the trust imposes burdens on the trustee, the trustee has a right to renounce or reject the trust, possibly by either words or conduct. But having once rejected the trust, the named trustee cannot thereafter change his mind. As referred to earlier, in the absence of a definite acceptance or rejection, any positive act will confirm acceptance. However, failure to do or to say anything within a reasonable time will be construed as a disclaimer. Probably the best course of conduct is to have either the disclaimer or the acceptance in written and recordable form.

After accepting the duties of the trust, the trustee can be relieved of the duties of the trust by:

1. The settlor (if that power is retained by the settlor in the written trust instrument).
2. Death.
3. Removal by the court.
4. Resignation.

The trustee may be removed either in accordance with the terms of the trust or upon petition of an interested person after a hearing. The court may remove a trustee and deny part or all of his compensation if the trustee materially violated or attempted to violate the terms of the trust and the violation or intended violation resulted in material financial loss, or if the trustee has become incompetent or insolvent or at the discretion of the court for any other cause. Causes for removal that have been found by the courts are: lack of capacity; commission of a serious breach of trust; refusal to give bond when bond is required; refusal to account for expenditures, investments, and the like; commission of a crime (particularly one involving dishonesty); long or permanent absence from the state; showing favoritism to one or more beneficiaries; and unreasonable failure to cooperate with co-trustees.

Some states require a qualifying act by the trustee, such as the taking of an oath, the execution of a formal acceptance of the trust, or the execution of a bond. Texas does not require such a formal qualifying act unless it is required by the trust instrument. Texas does, however, require that a trustee other than a corporate trustee must give a bond, unless otherwise provided in the trust document. The bond must be payable to each person interested in the estate, conditioned on the faithful performance of the trustee's duty, in such an amount and with such sureties as required by the court. This bond must be deposited with the clerk of the court that issued the order requiring the bond.

Interestingly enough, however, there is no procedure provided for the setting of a bond. The section dealing with bonds (113.058 of the Trust Code) does say that an interested person may bring an action to increase or decrease the amount of a bond or to substitute or add sureties. It further states that failure to comply does not make the trust void or voidable or otherwise affect an act or transaction of a trustee with any third person. It would appear, therefore, that unless there is a waiver of a bond in the trust agreement, an individual trustee must give bond, but that the trustee can assume his duties and act until some action is brought into court not only to set the amount of the bond but to require the trustee to file a bond. This having been done, if the trustee refuses to give the bond, there is little doubt that he may be removed for such refusal.

There is law from some other states with statutes somewhat similar to Texas' that any person interested in the estate may demand that the trustee obtain a bond in a reasonable amount; should the trustee fail to comply with the demand, he is subject to removal. In those some of the states that require a formal qualifying act, the trustee can be removed for failing to take the qualifying acts; in others the trustee does not become the trustee at all until he takes the qualifying act, so that if he fails to take it the office is considered vacant and no removal is necessary. There is no law in Texas concerning whether the trustee is simply subject to removal or whether the office of trustee is considered vacant if the trust agreement makes a formal act a condition to the taking of office by the trustee.

The trustee is entitled to receive a reasonable compensation for acting as trustee, unless the terms of the trust provide otherwise. If the agreement says there shall be no compensation, there will be none and the trustee must choose whether or not to accept the trust. If the trustee is a bank having trust powers, the compensation would be its customary charge for performing such services.

Generally, banks offer two options—a percentage of the gross estate to be paid each year or a larger percentage of the income earned each year. The settlor may choose in the trust instrument between these two methods. The legal assistant should confer with the trust officer at the bank the settlor names as trustee to find out their current methods of charging for trust services. If there is a choice, he should confer with the settlor, allowing the settlor to choose the option. (Whenever a legal assistant is drafting a trust instrument that involves a bank as trustee, he should remain in close contact with one of the trust officers and allow the trust officer to review a draft of the proposed trust document, with a view toward suggesting changes.)

If nothing is said in the trust document, and provided that the trustee has no interest in the trust as settlor, beneficiary, or remainderman, then the court, upon request, will set a reasonable compensation. If the trustee commits a breach of trust, the court may in its discretion deny him all or any part of his compensation.

In addition, the trustee is entitled to reimburse himself from trust principal or income for advances made for the convenience, benefit, or protection of the trust and expenses incurred while administering or protecting the trust. To secure this right of reimbursement, the trustee is given a lien against trust property.

Also, a trustee who incurs personal liability for a tort committed in the administration of a trust is entitled to have the claim paid from trust property if the trustee has not paid the claim, and to indemnification from trust property if the trustee has paid the claim, provided:

1. The trustee was properly engaged in the business activity of the trust, and the tort is common incident to that type of activity.

2. The trustee was properly engaged in the business activity for the trust, and neither the trustee nor any agent of the trustee has committed actionable negligence or intentional misconduct in incurring the liability.

3. The tort increased the value of the trust property; in other words, the tort was to the benefit of the trust.

The Texas Trust Act details the powers and responsibilities of the trustee when the trust instrument is silent concerning those powers and responsibilities. For most of the provisions of the act, if there is a conflict between the trust instrument and the act, the trust instrument prevails. In addition, a trustee may be given discretion to carry out an act that is not contemplated by the Texas Trust Code, for instance, discretionary invasion of corpus. *Invasion of corpus* means that the trustee, acting within his discretion, has the right and power to expend not only income but also principal for the benefit of the **income beneficiary**.

Trustees have the duty to carry out the terms of the trust as required by the trust agreement or by Section 113.056 of the Texas Trust Code. They become personally liable for any loss sustained by failure to perform the duties of the trust, unless the failure can be justified under the doctrine of reasonability. There is no personal liability if the trustees have exercised the degree of care that persons of ordinary prudence, discretion, and intelligence exercise in the management of their own affairs, in regard not to speculation but to the permanent disposition of their funds, considering the probable income and the probable increase in value and the safety of their capital. That section goes on to say that the determination as to whether a trustee has exercised due care with respect to an investment decision shall take into consideration the investment of *all* assets of the trust over which the trustee had management and control rather than just a single investment.

Under Section 113.051, a trustee, in the absence of any contrary terms in the trust agreement or in the Trust Code itself, is required to perform all the duties imposed on trustees by the common law. These duties are generally stated as:

1. **The duty to use ordinary, reasonable skill, and prudence.**

2. **The duty of loyalty;** meaning:
    a. Avoiding conflicts of interest.
    b. Avoiding self-dealing. In fact, the Texas Trust Code specifically prohibits self-dealing in Sections 113.052 and 113.053. And Section 113.059 adds that a settlor may not relieve a corporate trustee from those provisions. This would seem to indicate that the trustee may authorize self-dealing if the trustee is a noncorporate trustee. A provision authorizing self-dealing is often used in connection with a trust providing support, care, and maintenance to a spouse in which the spouse also serves as trustee.
    c. Not profiting personally, other than to recover compensation allowed by contract or as set by the court or customarily charged. One exception allows a financial institution to receive compensation directly or indirectly on account of its services performed, whether in the form of sharing commissions, fees, or otherwise. Such compensation is in addition to its compensation as trustee, provided such compensation does not exceed customary or prevailing amounts charged to persons other than trusts.
    d. Acting for the sole and exclusive benefit of the beneficiaries.

3. **The duty to take possession of, protect, and preserve trust property.** This includes:
    a. Keeping trust property insured.
    b. Keeping trust property maintained.
    c. Placing cash in insured bank accounts.

    d. Safeguarding valuable papers.

    e. Paying taxes assessed against trust property.

    f. Avoiding the commingling of trust property with individually owned property.

    g. Selling property to avoid deterioration.

    h. Collecting debts owed to the estate.

4. **The duty to make trust property productive,** including immediately investing trust assets in income-producing accounts or investments and selling nonproducing assets. The Texas Trust Code lists no real limitations or requirements concerning investments and, in fact, says that a trustee may acquire and retain every kind of property and every kind of investment that persons of ordinary prudence, discretion, and intelligence acquire or retain for their own account. The trust agreement may name restrictions or even mandate the types of investments that the trustee may make.

5. **The duty to pay income and principal to the named beneficiary.** Unless the trust provides otherwise by allowing discretionary invasion of the corpus, the trustee can only pay income to the beneficiaries during the existence of the trust. This also is applicable to the payment of the corpus, or principal, of the trust to the remaindermen at the termination of the trust. In some states the remaindermen are called *remainder beneficiaries*, and what has to this point been referred to as beneficiaries are called income beneficiaries. The Texas Trust Code does use the term *income beneficiaries*, but never uses *remaindermen* or *remainder beneficiaries*. In the several places that it does talk about distributions upon termination, it refers to those entitled to such distribution simply as beneficiaries.

6. **The duty to account.** The trustee has a duty to render accounting at reasonable intervals to those who are interested in the trust, including the settlor and the beneficiaries. This means retaining trust documents and records, securing vouchers for all expenditures and disbursements, and keeping complete and accurate books. Section 113.051 of the Trust Code says that a beneficiary may, by written demand, request the trustee to deliver to each beneficiary a written statement of accounts covering all transactions since the last accounting or the creation of the trust, whichever is later. If the trustee fails or refuses to deliver an accounting within a reasonable time after the demand, the beneficiary of the trust may file suit to compel the trustee to render an accounting. A trustee is not obligated or required to account more frequently than every 12 months, unless more frequent accounting is required by the court. Section 113.152 details what such accounting shall show. Included is a listing of all trust property, a complete account of receipts, disbursements, and other transactions, a listing of all property being administered, the cash balance on hand and the name and location of the depository where it is kept, and all known liabilities.

The Texas Trust Code lists the powers that a trustee possesses in managing the trust; however, Sections 113.002 and 113.024 gives what are generally referred to as the *implied powers*. The first such section states that the trustee may exercise any powers, in addition to the powers authorized by the Texas Trust Code, that are necessary or appropriate to carrying out the purposes of the trust. The second section holds that the powers, duties, and responsibilities provided by the Texas Trust Code do not exclude any implied powers, duties, or responsibilities that are not inconsistent with the Texas Trust Code.

There are some powers that case law indicates must be given specifically to trustees in the trust document if the trustees are to have the powers. Some of these are:

1. **The power to sprinkle,** which is the discretionary right of the trustee to prefer one beneficiary over others in the distribution of income. This allows the trustee to adjust to changed circumstances that create a situation in which a particular beneficiary has an increased need for support, care, or maintenance.

2. **The power to invade the corpus.** This allows the trustee to expend sums of principal as well as income for the support, care, and maintenance of a beneficiary.

3. **The power to self-deal.** This has already been discussed; however, self-dealing may be desirable when the income beneficiary of the trust is the decedent's surviving spouse who is also serving as trustee. The spouse may, for instance, find it beneficial when acquiring a new residence to borrow money from the trust. Or, the trust, to gain cash funds to pay taxes, may need to sell assets the surviving spouse does not want to sell. The provision in the trust document allowing self-dealing enables the surviving spouse to purchase the assets from the trust, thereby meeting both the needs of the trust and the desires of the spouse.

There are other less important powers not provided by the Texas Trust Code that do not accrue to a trustee unless specifically given in a trust. Careful drafting of a trust requires considering all of the powers needed under the client's circumstances and including specific authorizations to exercise such powers be included within the trust instrument.

The trustee is liable to the beneficiary, as provided by Section 114.001 of the Texas Trust Code, for any damages arising from a breach of trust or for a failure to meet the standards of reasonability, which has already been discussed. Such damages would include the loss of profits that would have accrued to the trust estate but for the default of the trustee.

The beneficiaries have certain remedies should a trustee breach the trust:

1. The beneficiary can maintain a suit to compel the trustee to reimburse the trust for any loss or depreciation in value of the trust property caused by the trustee's breach or for any profit made by

the trustee by reason of such breach or for any profit that would have accrued to the trust estate had there been no breach.

2. The beneficiary can obtain an injunction to compel the trustee to refrain from doing any act that would constitute a breach.

3. The beneficiary can trace and recover trust property that the trustee has taken wrongfully, unless it has been acquired for value by a bona fide purchaser.

4. The beneficiary can request the court to remove a trustee and to appoint a successor trustee.

5. The beneficiary can sue for specific performance to compel the trustee to perform the duties created by a private trust agreement.

The trustee also faces liability to a third party for breaching contracts or the commission of torts. In addition, the trust property may be subject to seizure arising out of a judgment based on a tort committed by the trustee if the trustee was properly engaged in a business activity for the trust and the tort is common to that kind of activity, or if the trustee was properly engaged in a business activity for the trust and neither the trustee nor his agent has committed actionable negligence or intentional misconduct or the tort increased the value of the trust property and therefore benefited the trust.

Section 114.084 of the Trust Code provides that if a trustee makes a contract that is within his power as trustee to make and some cause of action arises, the plaintiff may sue the trustee in his representative capacity, and a judgment is collectible against the trust property. The plaintiff may sue the trustee individually if the trustee made the contract and the contract does not exclude the trustee's personal liability. The addition of "trustee" or "as trustee" after the signature of the trustee who is a party to a contract becomes prima facie evidence of an intent to exclude the trustee from personal liability.

At common law a trustee is liable for a breach of contract by the trust because it was he who made the decision to breach or to cause the breach. He can be reimbursed by the trust to the extent that the contractual action benefited the trust, but not otherwise. This means that the trustee is at risk if he engages in a breach of contract. A breach is generally the result of a conscious decision made by the trustee; consequently, the common law provides that he is therefor responsible for it.

The language in Section 114.084 could be construed to modify that common law, although it can be argued that the restriction on the trustees personal liability does not apply when the damages arise out of a conscious breach by the trustee. Rather, it seems to create the type of limitation on liability that runs in favor of an agent of a fully disclosed principal. There is a difference; that is, when an agent enters a contract on behalf of a fully disclosed principal, it is the principal who breaches the contract and not the agent. At any rate, the statute does create a question as to whether the common law rule is still in effect.

Beneficiary

The beneficiary is the recipient either of the trust property upon termination or of benefits during the existence of the trust. Every valid private trust must have a beneficiary, who must be identified well enough that the trustee can determine, within the period of the rule against perpetuities, who the beneficiary is. An exception is a charitable trust, in which the beneficiaries may be members of the public at large or a particular class of the public.

Any persons, including infants, aliens, and insane persons may be the beneficiaries of a trust. Legal entities may be the beneficiaries of a trust, as may federal, state, and local governments.

Although beneficiaries must be identified, they need not be identified by name. Class designations are sufficient. Use of "my grandchildren" is sufficient, while "my friends" is too vague. The words "my family" and "my relatives" have been construed to mean those who would inherit by descent and distribution.

The beneficiary owns equitable title to the trust property for a period of time that may be limited to a term of years or for the life of the beneficiary. The beneficiary of a trust is free to alienate (sell) his interest, subject to restrictions provided in the trust instrument. These restrictions are called *spendthrift provisions*. One of the prerequisites of a spendthrift trust is that the beneficiary's interest and the income or the principal of the trust may not be voluntarily or involuntarily transferred prior to payment or delivery of the interest to the beneficiary by the trustee. If the trust does not have spendthrift provisions and the beneficiary sells his interest, the purchaser of that interest or the transferee gets only the rights of that beneficiary. Creditors of the beneficiary may seize his interest in the trust, although the spendthrift trust is an exception.

Beneficiaries' rights, other than the right to an accounting and some of the other things that have already been discussed, are totally determined by and found in the trust instrument.

The Trust Code, at Section 114.031, discusses the beneficiary's liability to the trustee if the beneficiary has:

1. Misappropriated or otherwise dealt with the trust property.
2. Expressly consented to, participated in, or agreed with the trustee to be liable for a breach of trust committed by the trustee.
3. Failed to repay an advance or loan of trust funds.
4. Failed to repay a distribution or disbursement from the trust in excess of that to which the beneficiary is entitled.
5. Breached a contract to pay money or deliver property to the trustee to be held by the trustee as part of the trust.

This section also states that, unless provided otherwise by the agreement, the trustee is authorized to offset a liability of the beneficiary to the trust estate against the beneficiary's interest even if the trust contains a spendthrift provision.

Section 114.05 provides that a beneficiary who has legal capacity and is acting on full information can release any past violation or breach by the trustee and, further, can relieve a trustee from any future duty, responsibility, restriction, or liability regarding the beneficiary. That section does except the duties, restrictions and liabilities imposed on corporate trustees but only as to Sections 113.052 and 113.053, which are the self-dealing statutes. The release must be in writing and must be delivered to the trustee.

Liability is incurred by the trustee if he makes a distribution to a beneficiary or if the beneficiary wants the trustee to make a distribution that is not contemplated by the trust. An example is the purchase of a new sports car or airplane when the trust purposes are to provide for the support, care, and maintenance of the beneficiary. If the beneficiary wants the trustee to act in a way that may be beyond his legal ability or is in violation of a duty or restriction provided by the Trust Code or the trust document, then the trustee should get a written release or other agreement from the beneficiaries to relieve the trustee of such duties, responsibilities, restrictions, or liabilities. Since minor beneficiaries cannot give such consent, no deviation from the terms of the trust would be permissible. See Form 7-2 at the end of this chapter.

TRUST PROPERTY

The trust property is the property that is transferred to the trustee to hold for the benefit of another. It is sometimes called the *res, corpus, principal,* or *subject matter* of the trust. The Texas Trust Code uses the words *trust property*.

Any transferable interest in an object subject to ownership may become trust property. This includes real or personal property. Consequently, it could be a fee simple interest in land, a co-owner's interest in land, a mortgage, a life estate, a right to remove minerals, a business interest, promissory notes, stocks and bonds, trade secrets, copyrights, patents, cash, or any other form of property subject to ownership.

On the other hand, a nontransferable interest may not be the subject of a trust. Examples of such interests are government pensions, interest in an existing spendthrift trust, and tort claims for personal injury.

A trust involving the transfer of only personal property may be created orally, but one involving real property requires a written agreement.

The trust agreement must include the purpose of the trust, the length of time the trust will last, and a description of and conveyance of the trust property. It must also include the names of the trustees and beneficiaries, and must list the powers, rights, responsibilities of the parties, including how much the beneficiaries are to receive and when they are to receive it. No particular form or language is necessary, as long as these elements are included. If some, but not all, of these elements are missing, most of them can be supplied by the court or are supplied by the Texas Trust Code.

Concerning real property, either the trust instrument must contain a conveyance or there must be separate conveyances executed by the settlor. Regarding personal property, delivery of possession is normally sufficient.

No trust can exist unless some trust property is conveyed to or transferred to the trust. The definition of the trust requires the division of property into legal and equitable. Some commentators, in interpreting Probate Code Section 58(a), which authorizes unfunded life insurance trusts, say that the section also authorizes the creation of a trust that owns no property other than that anticipated as a devise under a will. If they are correct, no trust can exist until the will is probated and the property devised by the will is thereby vested in the trust. However, Section 112.005 of the Texas Trust Code clearly states that no trust can be created unless there is trust property.

CHAPTER QUESTIONS AND EXERCISES

1. Under what circumstances may a trust come into existence without being created in a written document?

2. Who are the parties to an express trust? May one person hold more than one capacity in a trust? Explain your answer.

3. Explain the difference between an express trust and an implied trust, between an active trust and a passive trust, and between a public trust and a private trust.

4. If anything, what must a trustee do to act as a trustee in Texas?

5. Does a trustee have to post a bond in Texas? Explain your answer.

6. What should a legal assistant do when the trust department of a bank is to be named as trustee in a trust document the legal assistant is drafting?

7. What are the contractual and tort liabilities of a trustee?

8. What are the statutory and common law duties of a trustee?

9. What are the "implied powers" of a trustee? What are the powers that are not implied, regardless of the circumstances indicating a need for such powers?

10. Does a beneficiary have the right to sell his interest in a trust? What does the purchaser of such interest receive? When is the beneficiary prohibited from selling his interest?

Form 7-1: Acceptance by Trustee

ACCEPTANCE BY TRUSTEE

DATE:

THE TRUST:

TRUSTEE:

SETTLOR:

DATE OF THE TRUST:

Trustee acknowledges appointment as trustee of the trust, accepts appointment, and agrees to perform the duties and undertake the responsibilities according to the terms and conditions of the trust and applicable law.

_____

TRUSTEE

Form 7-2: Receipt and Release

RECEIPT AND RELEASE

DATE:

THE TRUST:

TRUSTEE:

SETTLOR:

DATE OF THE TRUST:

BENEFICIARY:

TRUST PROPERTY:

Beneficiary acknowledges that the distribution of the trust property made or to be made by Trustee is at the request of Beneficiary or Beneficiary consents to the same. If such distribution is being made to Beneficiary, Beneficiary hereby acknowledges receipt.

Beneficiary further acknowledges that such distribution is in accordance with the law and the terms and conditions of the Trust. To the extent that such distribution may be violative of the terms and conditions of the Trust or the law pertaining thereto, Beneficiary waives all rights in connection therewith.

Beneficiary releases and discharges Trustee from any liability arising out of such distribution and agrees to indemnify Trustee as to any liability, cost or expense arising from such distribution.

_____
BENEFICIARY

8 TESTAMENTARY TRUSTS

CHAPTER OBJECTIVES

Upon completion of this chapter, the student should be able to:

1. Apply the marital deduction and the exemption-equivalent in planning for estate tax avoidance or deferral.

2. Draft a will for spouse and minor children devising the entire estate to the spouse, with a contingent residuary trust for minor children.

3. Prepare a will with a bypass trust, which takes maximum advantage of the marital deduction in a direct gift to the spouse.

4. Prepare a will with a bypass trust and a QTIP trust utilizing the marital deduction.

5. Obtain all of the information necessary to prepare the above wills through client interviews and by requesting information from other sources.

CHAPTER GLOSSARY

Bequest A gift by will of personal property at common law. In Texas it includes gifts of real property.

Contingent residuary clause A will clause that gives the residual estate to a person or persons, but only if some other named person or persons (primary beneficiaries) have predeceased the testatrix.

Direct skip A gift to or for the benefit of a person or persons who are at least two generations below that of the donor. This is one of the three situations in which the generation-skipping transfer tax (GSTT) is imposed.

Primary residuary clause A will clause that gives the residual estate to a person or persons subject to no contingencies other than that they be alive at the time of the testatrix's death.

Residuary trust A trust created by and funded in the residuary clause of a will.

Situs Location or place. Generally, the tax situs of personal property is in the taxing district in which it is located, and of personal property where the owner is domiciled. The situs of a trust is usually where the trustee performs her duties.

Unified credit A credit against both estate and gift tax, officially called the Unified Transfer Tax. It is currently in the maximum amount of $192,800, which shelters up to $600,000 of taxable estate. Further discussion of the unified credit is found in Chapter Fifteen.

Unified Transfer Tax A federal tax levied on the transfer of property by reason of death or gift.

INTRODUCTION

The testamentary trust may very well be the most frequent form of trust drafted by attorneys. It is more or less standard when drafting wills for a couple with minor children or a for single parent with minor children, to create a residuary trust in the event that the surviving spouse has predeceased the testatrix or that the testatrix is not married at the time of her death, in order to provide for minor children. Testamentary trusts are also used extensively in estate planning to effectuate estate and inheritance tax savings or to defer tax until the death of a surviving spouse.

A testamentary trust is a trust created in a will that becomes effective upon the probate of the will. Probate Code Section 37 provides that when a person dies, leaving a lawful will, all of her estate vests immediately in the devisees and legatees of the estate, subject to the payment of debts of the testatrix. The assets of the estate remain in the possession of the executor or administrator for the purposes of administration. If a devisee in a will is a trust or the trustee of a trust that has not been funded, the trust comes into existence when the will is admitted to probate. Active administration of the trust property may be delayed until debts are paid by the executor.

After describing some of the frequently used types of testamentary trusts, this chapter will cover standard and nonstandard provisions for testamentary trusts. With a few exceptions, the same clauses are used in testamentary trusts as in inter vivos trusts. The only real difference between the basic form of the testamentary versus the inter vivos trust is that the testamentary trust is created in a will, whereas the inter vivos trust is a separate, self-sustaining document. Consequently, to the extent standard provisions for trusts are discussed in this chapter, they will not be discussed again in the next chapter, dealing with inter vivos trust.

RESIDUARY TRUSTS

A **residuary trust** is simply a trust created by either the **primary residuary clause** or the **contingent residuary clause** of a will. This is probably the most frequent kind of testamentary trust found in wills. It is distinguished by the fact that the residuary clause of a will, as discussed in Chapter Five, makes a bequest of the entire residuary estate to a trust or trustee. It is not a pour-over provision, leaving the residual estate to an existing trust; rather, the will creates the trust to which the residuary clause devises the testator's estate.

The primary residuary clause refers to the **bequest** that is intended to take effect upon the testatrix's death, barring the predecease of any of the devisees named in the will. The contingent residuary clause refers to the bequest created by the residuary clause that is designed to go into effect if the primary beneficiary of the will has predeceased the testatrix. This latter case is commonly a husband-wife will, with a contingent residuary clause creating a trust for the benefit of minor children in the event the spouse predeceases the testatrix.

Many different forms are provided by form books and other sources for simple wills containing residuary trusts for minor children. An example of one such form is attached at the end of Chapter Five as Form 5-2. Another, prepared using document assembly software, is attached to this chapter as Form 8-3.

The forms vary considerably in length. Some incorporate provisions of the Texas Trust Code by reference or simply allow the Texas Trust Code to apply without referring to it. Some duplicate many of the provisions that may already be in the Texas Trust Code, and do not vary or modify the application of the Texas Trust Code at all. As referred to before, there are two schools of thought concerning whether it is better (1) simply to incorporate the Texas Trust Code by reference or to allow the Texas Trust Code to supplement the testamentary trust, or (2) to have every provision, even those that merely mimic the Texas Trust Code, contained in the instrument creating the trust, in this case a will.

CREDIT SHELTER BYPASS TRUSTS (EXEMPTION-EQUIVALENT BYPASS TRUSTS)

A credit shelter bypass trust, or exemption-equivalent bypass trust, is a trust funded with the *exemption equivalent*, utilizing the **unified credit** to diminish estate taxes. *Exemption equivalent* is the language used in the Internal Revenue Code, which refers to the amount of a decedent's estate that is not subject to estate tax by virtue of the unified credit. In order to avoid taxing small estates, the U.S. Congress has allowed a tax credit in the calculation of federal estate and gift taxation, or the **unified transfer tax**. It is called "unified" because the same credit is available in either gift or estate tax. If all or any portion of it is used to avoid gift tax, then to whatever extent it has been used, it is not available to shelter against federal estate tax.

The maximum unified credit will shelter $600,000 of estate assets. This is referred to as the *exemption equivalent*. This explains why *exemption equivalent* and *credit shelter* are used in the names of these kinds of trusts. "Bypass" refers to the fact that the trust bypasses and does not vest in the estate of a surviving spouse. Therefore, that amount is not added to the estate of the surviving spouse, and additional estate tax is avoided.

This form of trust allows a surviving spouse to receive the interest and other income from assets of the deceased spouse equal to the exemption equivalent of $600,000 while not allowing actual ownership of the $600,000 of estate assets to vest in the surviving spouse. This permits $600,000 of the first dying spouse's estate to bypass the estate of the surviving spouse so that the $600,000 does not become a part of the surviving spouse's estate. It therefore avoids increasing the tax on the surviving spouse's estate.

Assume that two spouses have accumulated $1 million in community assets. When the first spouse dies, she owns $500,000 in assets, or half the community property. The exemption equivalent is $600,000. Consequently, there is no tax owed on the estate of the first spouse to die, inasmuch as the estate does not exceed $600,000. If the first spouse devises all of her estate to the surviving spouse, that $500,000 will be added to the surviving spouse's estate, who will then have an estate equal to $1 million. When the surviving spouse dies, there will be federal estate tax due on the excess of the estate over the exemption equivalent, or $400,000. This assumes that the surviving spouse does not die within a fairly short time after the surviving spouse, which would bring into effect other forms of credits (to be discussed in Chapter Fifteen). Of course, this example also assumes that the surviving spouse doesn't spend the amount received from the other spouse prior to her death.

What the exemption equivalent bypass (credit shelter bypass) trust does is create a testamentary trust and devise all of the testator's estate, or at least $600,000 worth of assets, to a trust from which the surviving spouse receives only income during her life. The trust does not have to give all of the income to the surviving spouse; rather, the distribution of income can be left to the discretion of the trustee, pursuant to IRS standards.

In addition, a trustee may be given discretion to convey trust principal to the spouse, and the will may specify a standard for making distributions. The will may even give the trustee unlimited power for invasion of corpus for the benefit of the spouse, provided the spouse is not the trustee making that decision. The spouse may serve as a co-trustee, as long as he does not have discretion to determine what distributions will be made to himself. The trust will continue until the death of the spouse, at which time the remaining assets will pass to the testatrix's descendants, or the trust may be continued until the descendants reach ages at which the testator believes they will be competent to manage their own finances.

This type of trust is often used in connection with a second type of trust, also created in the will, that takes advantage of the marital deduction and that may, in addition, create a qualified terminable property interest. (These two matters will be respectively discussed in the following two sections.)

If the surviving spouse lives a reasonably long time after the first spouse, the $500,000 put into the bypass trust, as in the above example, may have appreciated in value until it is worth more than $1 million. The appreciation, as well as the original principal of the trust, never becomes a part of the surviving spouse's estate. This can create considerable estate tax savings when the surviving spouse dies.

There are different ways to fund the exemption-equivalent trust. The devise in the will can contain a specific bequest of the exemption-equivalent amount to the trust, with the remainder going to the surviving spouse, either outright or in trust. The marital deduction will defer tax on the latter amount until the surviving spouse dies. (An example of a clause using a bequest, the amount of which is determined by the then-existing exemption equivalent, with an outright gift of the remainder is found at upcoming Example 8-1.)

Next, the testator can leave to the bypass trust an amount substantially more than the exemption equivalent. The estate will owe estate tax on the amount in excess of the exemption equivalent that was devised to the bypass trust. The advantage of this type of a arrangement is that the excess placed in the bypass trust will normally be property that is subject to rapid appreciation. This prevents not only the $600,000 but also the additional property from ever going into the surviving spouse's estate. Consequently, not only is the exemption-equivalent amount sheltered, but also the appreciation in value of both the exemption-equivalent amount and the excess.

The third way to fund the bypass trust is simply to leave all of the estate in a marital deduction bequest, to create a bypass trust, and to provide that it will only come into existence if the surviving spouse executes disclaimers under Probate Code Section 37(a). Then the surviving spouse can decide what properties, if any, to place in the bypass trust. The spouse will execute disclaimers meeting the requirements of Section 37(a) of the Probate Code and describing the property to be placed into the bypass trust. The spouse therefore waives any interest whatsoever in the property, which, because of the provisions in the will, automatically goes into the bypass trust. A disclaimer form is found at Form 8-2.

MARITAL DEDUCTION TRUSTS

A marital deduction trust is a trust funded with property, whose value is deducted in the calculation of estate taxes per the marital deduction provision of the Internal Revenue Code.

Under current Internal Revenue Code provisions, each spouse has an unlimited marital deduction. That is, when calculating the taxable estate, the amount of qualifying property left to a surviving spouse by a predeceasing spouse may be deducted from the gross estate of the predeceasing spouse. If the predeceasing spouse left her entire estate to the surviving spouse, in most cases the marital deduction would result in a taxable estate of zero.

The marital deduction does not avoid the tax altogether, but merely defers it because the property is added to the surviving spouse's property, and the portion of the estate not expended will be taxed when the surviving spouse dies.

The unified credit and the marital deduction are also available with regard to gift taxation. A bypass trust and a marital deduction trust can be set up inter vivos as well as in the last will and testament of the spouses. This is not commonly done but does occur. Also, if the surviving spouse is not a U.S. citizen, the marital deduction is limited to $100,000.

Normally, a marital deduction trust will also be a qualified terminable interest property trust, or a QTIP. (This will be discussed in the next section.) Sometimes, however, the testatrix may feel that the surviving spouse will need not only the interest that accrues from the marital deduction property but also the ability to invade the corpus of the trust. A provision in the trust document allowing the discretionary invasion of corpus prevents the trust from qualifying as terminable interest property.

There is no prohibition concerning the spouse's being the trustee of a marital deduction trust because the funds that constitute the trust property could have been devised to her outright rather than in trust. In addition, in a QTIP, if created properly, the trustee has no discretion concerning distributions. She cannot invade the corpus and must distribute all of the income at least annually. Generally, the trust property that goes into the trust will all be property that was not placed into the exemption-equivalent or bypass trust.

QUALIFIED TERMINABLE INTEREST PROPERTY (QTIP)

Qualified terminable interest property, or QTIP, is property that passes from a decedent in which the surviving spouse has a qualifying income interest for life and for which an election has been made by the executor under IRC 2056(b)(7). "Qualifying income interest for life" means that the surviving spouse is entitled to receive all income of the trust or from the qualifying property, payable at least annually, and that no person has the power during the life of the surviving spouse to appoint any of the property to some person other than the surviving spouse. A QTIP can be created either in the form of a trust or in the form of a legal life estate. The most common QTIP is in the form of a trust.

The trust provisions must mandate the payment of all income to the surviving spouse as income beneficiary during the remainder of her life. Also, in order for property to qualify as QTIP, an election must be made by the executor of the first spouse's estate at the time of the filing of the estate tax return. This is in addition to an election to treat property under marital deduction provisions, which must also be made at the time of the filing of the estate tax return for the predeceasing spouse's estate.

If, upon the death of the surviving spouse, the principal of the QTIP trust passes to a qualified charity, then none of the assets will be subject to estate tax at any time, either upon the death of the first spouse or upon the death of the second spouse. This allows a maximum saving of federal estate tax, perhaps eliminating tax altogether on both estates, because there is no limit to charitable deductions with regard to estate tax. This would usually be used by spouses who had no close relatives to whom they desired to leave the bulk of their estate.

The QTIP election for the marital deduction trust allows two basic benefits:

1. It ensures that the qualified terminable interest property will qualify for the marital deduction.

2. It allows the testatrix to control the ultimate disposition of her property so that, although the surviving spouse will have ample income for his support and maintenance during his life, the property will ultimately vest in those persons in whom the testatrix desires that it vest. If these ultimate recipients, or remainder beneficiaries, are in the third generation (the testatrix's grandchildren), or further removed, the QTIP trust creates a **direct skip**, making the estate of the testatrix subject to the generation skipping transfer tax (GSTT). (This subject will be discussed in some detail in Chapter Fifteen.)

TESTAMENTARY TRUST PROVISIONS

The trust provisions that are found in both testamentary trusts and inter vivos trusts, whether irrevocable or revocable, will be discussed here. Standard provisions can be found in the forms attached to this chapter as Forms 8-1 and 8-3, and also in Form 5-2 in Chapter Five. In addition, examples of provisions are contained within the remaining body of this chapter.

Devise to the Trust

The wills in each of Forms 8-1 and 8-2 contain provisions for a devise to trust. If there is not to be any estate tax planning carried out in connection with the drafting of the will, such as the creation of an exemption-equivalent or bypass trust or a bequest taking advantage of the marital deduction, but instead a contingent trust is being created to provide for minor children, then a devise such as Example 8-1 might be used.

Example 8-1: Outright Gift of All Property to Wife Contingent Gift to Children With Trust

I give all of the rest and residue, and remainder of my property, whether I may own the same outright or merely have an interest therein, whether my ownership may be legal or equitable, which I may own now or may herein after acquire to my wife, if she survives me. If she does not survive me, I give my residuary estate above described to my children, in equal shares. If any child of mine shall predecease me but issue of such deceased child of mine survive me, the share of my estate that otherwise would pass to such deceased child of mine shall pass, per stirpes and not per capita, to the issue who survives me of the deceased child of mine. If any child of mine is deceased without leaving any surviving issue, no share shall be created on behalf of such deceased child.

Not withstanding the preceding provisions of this section, if any surviving children are under the age of thirty (30) years at the date of my death, I give my entire residuary estate as above described to my trustee, in trust, as a trust estate of a single trust to be held, managed, and distributed as follows:

> My trustee shall distribute to my children, or the issue of a deceased child of mine, at intervals as he may determine so much of the trust income and principal as will adequately provide for their necessary or reasonable health, education, maintenance, and support, considering all sources of income available to them to the knowledge of the trustee. Any such distributions need not be made equally among them and shall not be charged against the share of the distributee (or any person taking such distributee's share by representation) upon the termination of the trust. When all of my surviving children have obtained the age of thirty (30) years of age, or died, this trust shall terminate and then the remaining trust estate shall be distributed in fee simple and free of trust to my children in equal shares. If any child of mine shall then not be living but leaves issue then surviving, the share of the trust estate that would otherwise pass to such deceased child of mine shall pass per stirpes and not per capita to the then-surviving issue of such deceased child of mine. If any child of mine is deceased without leaving any surviving issue, then no share shall be created on behalf of such deceased child.

Example 8-1 devises the residuary estate to the trustee without naming the same. A clause appointing the trustee must therefore be inserted in the will at some later point. Some clauses name the trustee, and then add after her name "as trustee only subject to the terms and conditions hereafter contained." Others also name the trust using language such as "I give the remainder of my estate to the trustee to be held as the trust estate of a trust to be named the 'Smith Children Trust.'"

If the legal assistant is not working from a unified form and instead is piecing together a will, she should be extremely careful in reading each piece of the will to make sure that contingencies created by each clause are in accord. For instance, if the devise is directly into a named trustee, then in a later clause there is no need to appoint an original trustee, but there is a need to name successor trustees. If, on the other hand, the devise is just to the trustee, without naming the trustee, the later clause that appoints trustees must appoint the original as well as the successor trustees.

Also, as referred to in earlier chapters concerning the preparation of wills, if clauses are being taken from different sources, it is necessary to coordinate the language. For instance, the legal assistant might pick a clause that refers to representatives and then in some other clause defines the word *representative* to include the trustee appointed by the will. Then she may find a clause from yet another source that uses the word *trustee* instead of *representative*. If she decides to use *representative*, then either she has to add a clause defining *representative* that includes the word *trustee* or she must refer to each fiduciary by its proper name. That is, when referring to an executor she uses the term *executor*, when referring to a trustee, the word *trustee*, and when referring to a guardian, the word *guardian*. It doesn't make any difference which is chosen, providing uniformity is maintained through the entire will.

Name of the Trust

Most of the forms provided for the more complicated wills containing bypass trusts and QTIP trusts name the trusts, often with a name that indicates the function of the trust. For instance, a bypass trust may be called a bypass trust, a credit shelter trust, or an exemption-equivalent trust. It may have the last name of the testatrix added to it, e.g., "Smith Bypass Trust." Very commonly, a trust used as an exemption-equivalent bypass is referred to as a *family trust*, with the name of the testatrix added to it, such as "Smith Family Trust." A trust used as a depository for the marital deduction bequest is often referred to as a *marital trust*, preceded by the last name of the testatrix or sometimes by the full name of the testatrix's spouse. Some forms refer to Trust A and Trust B, or A, B, and C. These forms are often called to as AB trust wills or ABC trust wills.

Where multiple trusts are to be created, it is vital that they be given names that distinguish them from each other. Whoever is drafting a will must keep firmly in mind which trust is which, because it is very easy to lose track, particularly when working with a strange form. If the drafter makes requirements of only one trust that need to be made of the others, as well, the desired tax effect may be lost for all of the trusts.

Appointment of the Trustee

Many times the testatrix desires help in determining who to make trustee: an individual, or a bank having trust powers as trustee or perhaps co-trustees. This decision depends on the capabilities of those she is considering.

If they are simply good and dependable people but lack financial or investment experience, then a corporate trustee should be chosen. As previously explained, the only corporate trustee permissible under the present laws in the State of Texas is a bank having trust powers. The officer of the bank (trust officer) who is assigned responsibility for a particular trust cannot follow the income beneficiaries around to determine what their particular needs are at any particular time. She must rely on someone else's assessment, often one or more of the beneficiaries themselves. Beneficiaries can be very persuasive if they want something bad enough. Yet banks are concerned about being sued by the beneficiaries if they refuse to make a distribution the beneficiary desires but that may not match the testatrix's intentions, such as expensive sports cars, airplanes, and long sojourns in Europe.

To solve this problem, co-trustees often will be appointed, one an individual having close personal knowledge of the needs, desires, and activities of the beneficiary, and the other a bank having trust powers. Then the powers will be divided between the co-trustees, with the individual trustee making distributions and the corporate trustee handling the investments and other financial management. This gives the best of both worlds.

When dealing with a QTIP trust, all of the income must be paid to the surviving spouse, and the only function a trustee has is investment and management. A corporate trustee may be the best choice.

The lawyer or the legal assistant cannot and should not make the choice of trustee for the testatrix. However, the functions of the trustee and the possible problems with overindulgence or an opposing tendency can be pointed out to the testatrix, with suggestions towards solving the problem. It should be clearly understood that a single trustee has the obligation both to invest and manage the trust property and to make distributions. If these distributions are discretionary, the pull between the two duties may be more than a single trustee can really handle with the ease that the testatrix requires.

When appointing a trustee, it is necessary to consider also whether or not the trustee will receive compensation. Remember that the Texas Trust Code states that the trustee shall receive a reasonable compensation, unless the trust provides otherwise. If the trustee is to receive no compensation, the trust should state this. If the amount of the compensation is to be limited, then the trust should state expressly how the compensation will be calculated.

Remember also that a bond is required of a trustee by the Texas Trust Code, unless waived. If the person to serve as trustee has been carefully selected by the testatrix, a bond is an unnecessary expense. Therefore, it is almost a standard rule that the bond be waived by the trust agreement.

Finally, successor trustees should be appointed. In the past it was necessary only to appoint a successor trustee for individuals; it was presumed that banks would remain forever. With the recent flurry of bank failures, it has been discovered that successor trustees should be perhaps appointed, even for corporate fiduciaries.

There are two scenarios in the event of a bank failure. In the first, the bank fails, the Federal Deposit Insurance Corporation appoints a receiver, the depositors are paid off to the extent of federal deposit insurance, and the receiver attempts to collect loans and to recover other assets for the payment of other debts and stockholder interest after the FDIC has recovered insured amounts paid. In this scenario, the trustee ceases to exist, and unless a successor trustee is named in the will, it will be necessary to file a proceeding in court to have a successor trustee appointed.

In the second scenario, rather than simply liquidating the failed bank, the Federal Deposit Insurance Corporation transfers the beneficial assets of the failed bank to some other entity. In this case, it is possible for the FDIC to split the regular banking functions and the trust functions of the bank and to transfer them to different entities. This occurred in the case of the MBank failures. When the testatrix appointed the bank, she assumed that the trustee would be the same bank with which she had done business, and in fact would be the bank with which her beneficiaries also did business. With this type of split it is very possible that the trust assets of the bank will be transferred to a bank company that does not perform regular banking functions, only trust functions, which may not be at all what the testatrix desires. In several cases in which the beneficiaries were unhappy with the trust's being transferred by the FDIC to some other entity, they attempted to stop the transfer and to have a successor trustee appointed by a state court. In these suits the trial court found that the FDIC had the power to transfer the management of that trust to whatever entity it chose and that the beneficiaries had no say in the matter.

In light of such cases, it would seem advisable, when a named trustee is a corporate fiduciary, for the trust document to provide that in the event of the failure of the bank, regardless of whether it is to be rehabilitated under a conservatorship, with its assets (including trust assets) being transferred to another entity, or whether it is to be liquidated, that the trustee's existence be considered to have ended. The document should provide for the appointment of a successor trustee either by the beneficiaries or by the state courts.

Another way to handle this problem would be to give the beneficiaries the power to remove a trustee and to appoint a successor. Such a provision, which is often used, should contain a power authorizing the oldest current adult beneficiary or the guardian of the oldest minor beneficiary to remove a corporate trustee and to appoint as successor a bank having trust powers. Form 8-1 contains a clause allowing all adult beneficiaries to remove the trustee.

A number of trust documents use a "trust committee," which is appointed by the document, to deal with such matters as removal of a trustee, oversight of the trustee, and appointment of successor trustees.

A very simple provision appointing a trustee to serve without compensation and without bond is given in Example 8-2.

Example 8-2: Appointment of Trustee

I appoint Paula Smith as my trustee, and if she fails to qualify or ceases to act, I appoint Peter Smith, Jr., as successor trustee. My said trustees shall serve without compensation and no bond shall be required of either of them.

Distribution of Income and Principal

One set of provisions that must be very carefully considered are those that would provide for the distribution of income and principal, both during the existence of the trust and upon termination. There are many reasons for this including fulfilling the goals of the testator, providing for a harmonious relationship between the trustee and the beneficiaries, and avoiding adverse estate tax consequences.

With regard to the last of these, it is mandatory under the QTIP provisions that all income be distributed to the surviving spouse. She can, if she desires, disclaim or waive the right to receive part of the income, but the trustee must have an absolute duty to disburse all of the income to her. In other situations, if the surviving spouse is the sole trustee, giving her discretion as to how much income to disburse and whether to invade the corpus of the trust may have adverse tax consequences. Therefore, the drafter must be careful to ensure that the provisions relating to distributions of income during the existence of the trust are consistent with the estate tax code sections, regulations, and decisions.

Distributions of the corpus at termination also have to be watched. For instance, giving the surviving spouse a power of appointment to determine who will receive the principal of the trust upon termination of the trust will disallow the trust from electing QTIP status. Generally speaking, the time and method of termination of the trust also are dealt with in the provisions that cover distributions of income or principal during the life or existence of the trust. Examples of distribution and termination provisions are found in both of the will forms attached to this chapter (Forms 8-1 and 8-3) and also in Example 8-1.

The testatrix might also want to direct some special distributions; for instance, for education purposes at the beneficiaries' request. That is, she might direct the trustee to make whatever distributions the beneficiaries request as long as they are related to the furtherance of the beneficiaries' education. This allows the beneficiaries, rather than the trustee, to choose the educational institution they are going to attend and what and how many degrees to pursue.

Other provisions are used when the trust is going to remain in existence until the beneficiaries are rather far along in age. Some trusts maintain the trust corpus, disbursing only income, until the beneficiaries reach the age of 30-35 or 40-45. The testatrix may want to consider special distributions of income or principal for purposes such as the acquisition of a house or the starting of a new business.

Termination

The termination provisions of the trust instrument or will establish when the trust will end, thereby reuniting legal title and equitable title, and who will receive legal title and equitable title upon termination. As mentioned earlier, the termination provisions are often combined with provisions relating to the distribution of income and principal during the term of the trust. In yet other trusts, the termination provisions will appear at the very end of the trust, sometimes labeled "vesting."

The termination provisions are not difficult to draw up in most instances; however, they do need to be well defined. The drafter should avoid termination provisions that use words like "my family." In most instances individual names should be used, and the drafter should always consider the possibility that the persons named to take the property upon termination may die prior to termination. The courts have generally held that the members of a class who will take upon termination of a trust are determined at the time of termination. Therefore, a clause saying that "upon termination my trustee shall divide my estate equally among my children" or even directing that the trust be divided into as many shares as the testatrix has living children without providing for the death of those children may lead to problems if any of the children die prior to termination. Thus, it is necessary to find out from the client what she desires in the event one or more of the remainder beneficiaries die prior to termination of the trust.

Powers of the Trustee

The Texas Trust Code gives the trustee the following powers, unless the trust agreement denies the trustee such powers or limits them:

1. The power to retain, without regard to diversification of investments and without liability for depreciation of loss resulting from the retention, any property that constituted the initial trust corpus or is later added to the trust.

2. The power to receive additions to the assets of the trust.

3. The power to acquire all or a portion of the remaining undivided interest in property in which the trust holds an undivided interest.

4. The power to manage the trust and invest and reinvest in property of any character on such conditions and for such a length of time the trustee considers proper, notwithstanding that the time may extend beyond the term of the trust.

5. The power to deposit funds in banks that are subject to supervision by the state or federal government.

6. The power to invest, continue, or participate in the operation of any business or other investment enterprise in any form, including sole proprietorships, partnerships, limited partnerships, corporations, and associations.

7. The power to manage real property, including a long list of particular acts that could be carried out in reference to the management of such property.

8. The power to contract to sell, sell and convey, or grant options to sell real or personal property, either at public auction or at private sale or for cash or for credit or for part cash and credit with or without security.

9. The power to lease real and personal property for any term, with or without options to purchase, and with or without conveyances relating to the erection of buildings.

10. The power to enter into mineral transactions.

11. The power to purchase insurance of any kind, form, or amount to protect the trust property or the trustee.

12. The power to pay taxes or assessments.

13. The power to borrow money from any source, including a trustee, to purchase money on credit, and to mortgage, pledge or in any other manner incumber all or any part of the assets of the trust.

14. The power to manage securities.

15. The power to hold stock and other securities in the name of a nominee.

16. The power to employ attorneys, accountants, agents, and brokers reasonably necessary in the administration of the trust estate.

17. The power to settle claims by or against the trust estate or the trustee.

18. The power to abandon property that the trustee considers burdensome or worthless.

19. The power to make distributions for minors or incapacitated beneficiaries, either to the beneficiary directly or to a guardian or by paying the monies direct or to a custodian under the Texas Uniform Gift to Minors Act or reimbursing the person who is actually taking care of the beneficiary.

20. As long as the trust is not a charitable remainder uni-trust, annuity trust, or pooled-income fund intended to qualify for a tax deduction under Section 664 of the Internal Revenue Code, the power to provide a residence for the beneficiary and to pay funeral expenses

of a beneficiary who at the time of the beneficiary's death was eligible to receive distributions from the trust estate.

21. The power to appoint ancillary trustees to act outside of the estate, including the power to remove them if necessary.

The drafter of a trust instrument, including a testamentary trust, may want to consider specifically giving the trustee additional powers, even though some of them may be implied under Section 113.024 of the Texas Trust Code, such as:

1. The power to give guarantees, including the guarantee of a loan to a beneficiary.

2. The power to employ and rely on investment advisors.

3. The power to lend money, including to beneficiaries.

4. The power to delegate the trust powers, especially in the case of a temporary absence or illness.

5. The power to hold assets other than stock and securities in nominee form.

6. The power to self-deal so that the trustee can purchase from the trust, sell to the trust, and borrow money from the trust.

In addition, it may be advisable:

1. To give the trustee broad discretionary powers concerning the distribution or retention of income.

2. To provide a procedure for the resignation of the trustee. Section 113.081 of the Texas Trust Code says that a trustee may resign in accordance with the terms of the trust instrument or by petitioning a court for permission to resign as trustee. Most trust forms contain a clause allowing the trustee to resign by giving 30 days' written notice to the beneficiaries.

3. To allow the trustee to commingle trust estates; that is whether originally created or as a result of a splitting of a trust by the trustee, allowing the trustee to commingle the funds and hold them as a common fund, with a separate trust owning undivided interest therein. This can give the trusts increased purchasing power, lending power, and the power to purchase stocks in round lots, as well as other benefits.

Responsibilities and Compensation of the Trustee

Most trust instruments provide a reasonable compensation for the trustee. However, if the trustee is going to have duties in addition to those normally borne by trustees, for instance, the operation of a business, then the client may want to set up additional compensation and also to add language that protects the trustee from the extra liability created by the operation of or investment in businesses.

Most trust instruments, when dealing with a member of the family as trustee, particularly a wife or a child, will add specific provisions absolving the trustee from any liability whatsoever. This is an attempt to prevent or defuse litigation between members of the family arising out of disagreements concerning how the trust is managed or how income is distributed. A clause negating the trustee's liabilities for ordinary acts of negligence is found in the will in Form 8-3. In addition in various paragraphs located throughout that form there are other negations of liability in regard to the trustee.

Miscellaneous Provisions

The drafter of a trust instrument or a will that includes a testamentary trust may want to consider additional miscellaneous clauses, such as the following:

1. A perpetuities savings clause (this was discussed in Chapter 7).

2. A spendthrift provision, to protect the beneficiaries from their own unwise sale of their interest or execution upon their interest by their creditors.

3. A clause enabling the trustee to terminate a small trust when the cost of maintaining the trust exceeds what is reasonable.

4. A clause that specifies the **situs** of the trust, for the purposes of local taxation and the law that will be applied in litigation concerning the trust, and that empowers the trustee to change the trust situs.

5. A provision allowing the trustee to purchase life insurance on the life of any of the parties to the trust, including the settlor and the beneficiaries.

6. Provisions providing for the removal of the trustee and the appointment of successor trustees.

7. A clause that gives the trustee the power to deal with the testatrix's estate in terms of purchasing from the estate or lending to the estate or making distributions to the estate for the purpose of paying loans or mortgages or taxes.

8. A provision giving the trustee discretion to make tax elections (to be discussed in Chapter 7).

9. Clauses that alter obligations to account to the beneficiaries, such as requiring the trustee to deliver an accounting quarterly.

10. A clause giving the power to sprinkle (as discussed earlier).

This is not an exhaustive list. When drafting a new form of trust, the best way to ensure that all clauses have been considered is to look into every single trust and every form book or other book or manual on trusts. If someone else hasn't thought of it, either it is not important or there is little possibility that the drafter could be held liable for malpractice for failing to include it.

There are other types and variations of testamentary trusts used in estate planning in addition to those covered in this chapter. Only the most commonly used testamentary trusts, in their simplest form, have been presented here. The legal assistant who wants to be employed by an estate planning specialist will, in all likelihood, have to delve deeper into this subject.

CHAPTER QUESTIONS AND EXERCISES

1. Explain the use of a bypass trust and its effect on federal estate tax.

2. When may the marital deduction be claimed? How much can be claimed? What is the effect of claiming the marital deduction on federal estate taxes?

3. What is a QTIP trust, and what are its benefits?

4. When might co-trustees be appointed? (Do not limit yourself to the examples in the book. Imagine other fact situations in which the use of co-trustees would be beneficial.) Explain your choices.

5. What eventualities should be considered with reference to the appointment of a corporate trustee? What choices are available in such eventualities?

6. Using as a form the checklist found in Form 8-4, relating to the powers of a trustee, prepare a checklist designed to ensure that a legal assistant obtains all the information necessary to setting up the trust provisions of a will containing tax planning testamentary trusts.

7. Using one of the forms provided in this book, prepare a will that incorporates a bypass trust, of which the spouse is the income beneficiary and the children are the remainder beneficiaries, with an outright gift to the spouse that seeks to take advantage of the marital deduction. Make up necessary names, dates, and addresses. There should be a specific gift to the spouse, of the home, automobiles, furniture and furnishings of the home, and all personal effects of testator and spouse. The trustee is to be a bank, and there are three children.

8. Using a form you have found in a form book or other source, prepare a will that incorporates both a bypass trust and a QTIP trust, taking full advantage of the marital deduction. There are no specific devises. The trustee is to be a bank and is to be given discretionary power to invade the corpus of the marital deduction trust only to provide for the support, care, and maintenance of the spouse. As to the bypass trust, the trustee will have the power to invade the corpus for both spouse and children for any reason. The children will be the remainder beneficiaries of both trusts. Make up any additional information needed.

9. Prepare a will for a client with a spouse and three children. She wants to create a bypass trust with all as income beneficiaries and the children as remainder beneficiaries. The remainder of her estate she wants to leave to her spouse. If the spouse predeceases her, she wants to create a single trust for the children. The trust is to vest at age 25 for two of the children. However, the third child will need continued guidance for the rest of his life, so the client wants the trust to continue for that child until his death. Upon the death of that child, the trust will vest and be divided between the other two children or their descendants. A bank and the oldest child, who is 18, will be co-trustees. She wants spendthrift and sprinkling provisions and discretionary power for invasion of corpus. You will need to be innovative with one of the furnished forms, or find a form in some other source.

Form 8-1: Will With Bypass Trust and Outright Gift of Remainder to Surviving Spouse

(Form authored by Steve R. Akers and Jenkins & Gilchrist, P.C.; this form is based on a will form in the Ameritrust Will and Trust Manual, published by Ameritrust Texas, N.A.)

LAST WILL AND TESTAMENT
OF
PETER SMITH

THE STATE OF TEXAS	) (
COUNTY OF NUECES	) (KNOW ALL MEN BY THESE PRESENTS THAT:

I, Peter Smith, a resident of Nueces County, Texas, hereby make and declare this to be my Last Will, and revoke all other Wills and Codicils previously made by me.

FIRST
IDENTITY OF TESTATOR'S FAMILY

I declare that I am married to Paula Smith and that all references in this Will to Paula Smith are references to her. I have two children, now living, whose names are Peter Smith, Jr. and Penelope Smith. All references in this Will to my children are references to them.

SECOND
FUNERAL ARRANGEMENTS AND PAYMENT OF DEBTS

I direct that my body be buried in a manner suitable to my circumstance in life at the time of my death. I further direct that all my just debts, funeral expenses, and expenses in connection with the administration of my estate be paid as soon after my death as practicable, except that any debt or expense secured by a mortgage, pledge or similar encumbrance on property owned by me at my death shall not be paid by my estate, but that such property shall pass subject to such mortgage, pledge, or similar encumbrance.

THIRD
PROPERTY BEING DISPOSED

It is my intention by this Will to dispose of one-half of the community property owned by my wife and myself, and of any separate property that I may own at the time of my death. However, I hereby elect not to exercise any power of appointment exercisable by a Will which I now have or which may hereafter be conferred on me; no provision of this Will shall be construed as an exercise in whole or in part of any such power.

FOURTH
BEQUESTS AND DEVISES

I give the following properties to the following persons:

(1) Personal Effects: All my jewelry, clothing, household furniture and furnishings, chinaware, silver, pictures, works of art, books, personal automobiles, boats, and other tangible articles of a personal nature, not otherwise specifically disposed of by this Will, together with any insurance thereon, to my wife, Paula Smith, or, if she has predeceased me, to my children then living, share and share alike; provided, however, if any of my children have predeceased me but issue of such deceased child of mine survive me, the share that would otherwise pass to such deceased child of mine shall intend pass, per stirpes and not per capita, to the then surviving issue of the deceased child of mine. While this bequest is absolute, it is my wish that any memorandum I may leave addressed to my executor indicating my desire with respect to the disposal of these items, or any of them, shall be regarded.

(2) Residue:

    (a) If my wife survives me by one hundred eight (180) days, the rest, remainder and residue of my estate shall be divided into two (2) parts, one (1) part consisting of property to be transferred to my wife outright and free of Trust; and the other part to be held in the "By-pass Trust", to be administered and disposed of as provided in Article FIFTH hereof.

        (i) The part to be transferred to my wife outright and free of Trust will consist solely of assets qualifying for the Estate Tax Marital Deduction, and the amount of such property to be so transferred shall be computed by reducing the remainder of my estate eligible for the unlimited Marital Deduction under the Federal Estate Tax Law by the amount, if any, needed to increase my taxable estate to the largest amount, which, after allowing for the Unified Credit, will result in no Federal Estate Tax being imposed upon my estate and no tax on generation-skipping transfers with respect to which I am the deemed transferor being payable to reason of my death.

        (ii) The part to be transferred to the "By-pass Trust" shall consist of the balance of my residuary estate, after establishing the amount and identity of the assets to be transferred to my wife outright and free of Trust under the preceding Subparagraph (i) hereof.

    (b) If my wife does not survive me by one hundred eighty (180) days, I give, devise and bequeath all of the residue of my estate, real, personal and mixed, wherever situated to the Trustee of the "By-pass Trust" to be held, administered and distributed in accordance with the provisions hereof.

Form 8-1: (continued)

FIFTH
BY-PASS TRUST

The portion of my estate to be held under the terms hereof in the "By-pass Trust" shall be transferred to my wife, Paula Smith, of Dallas, Texas and Rough Rider National Bank, of Dallas, Texas as Co-Trustees (hereinafter referred to in the singular as "Trustee"), in Trust, to be held, administered and distributed in accordance with the following provisions:

A. PAYMENT AND DISTRIBUTION OF INCOME AND PRINCIPAL

   (1) <u>Payments During Paula Smith's Lifetime</u>: The Trustee, during the lifetime of my wife, shall make the following payments:

      (a) The Trustee shall pay to or apply for the benefit of my wife so much of the net income from the Trust Estate during her lifetime, in monthly or other convenient installments, as the Trustee in its discretion deems advisable for her proper care, support, and maintenance in the standard of living to which she was accustomed at the time of my death.

      (b) The Trustee shall pay to, or apply for the benefit of each of my children, so much of the remaining net income in such manner and in such proportions as it, in its absolute discretion, deems proper and advisable.

      (c) The Trustee shall also pay to my wife such additional amounts out of the principal of the Trust Estate as are reasonably required for her support in her accustomed manner of living at the time of my death. My wife need not exhaust her other income in order to be entitled to receive such payments.

   (2) <u>Wife's Power to Direct Sale of Home</u>: If any interest in the home occupied by my wife and myself as our principal residence at the time of my death is distributed to the Trustee, the Trustee is authorized and directed to allow her to use and occupy it as her residence without payment of any rent during her lifetime or as long as she desires to do so. The Trustee shall pay the taxes, assessments, insurance, maintenance costs, costs of ordinary repairs and replacements, and costs of reasonable improvements for the home during its occupancy by my wife from the income or principal of the Trust Estate as the Trustee, in its discretion, shall determine. With the written consent of my wife, or when she ceases to occupy the home, the Trustee may sell the home and, on her written request the sale proceeds shall be used by the Trustee to purchase, acquire, or build a substantially similar home or, if my wife desires, a home of lesser value; title to the property shall be taken in the name of the Trustee and my wife shall be allowed to occupy the home on the terms set forth hereinabove. If my wife does not request the acquisition of another home, the Trustee shall invest proceeds of any such sale and shall administer and distribute the income and principal of such funds under the terms of this Will, exclusive of this Paragraph. The word "home" as used in this Section, means the home originally distributed to the Trustee and any other home acquired in lieu thereof.

   (3) <u>Income Received During Probate</u>: All income received during the probate administration and distributed by my Executor to the Trustee, less an amount equal to any family allowance paid to my wife and my children, shall be paid to my wife by the Trustee; the income not paid to her under this provision shall be retained by the Trustee and treated as principal of the Trust Estate.

   (4) <u>Continuance of Trust Upon Death of Paula Smith</u>: On the death of my wife, the balance of the Trust Estate shall remain in Trust for the benefit of my children, if they are then surviving, and the Trustee shall hold, administer, and make distribution from said Trust in accordance with the following provisions.

B. PAYMENT AND DISTRIBUTION OF TRUST ESTATE AFTER DEATH OF PAULA SMITH

   (1) <u>Administration of Single Family Trust</u>: After the death of my wife, the entire Trust Estate shall be administered as one (1) until no child of mine is living who is under the age of twenty-five (25) years. Until that time, the Trustee shall apply the net income and principal of the Trust Estate as follows:

      (a) So long as any of my children are under the age of ^C, the net income of the Trust shall be paid to, or applied for the benefit of, any or all of my children at such times and in such amounts as my Trustee, in its discretion, deems necessary for their support, welfare, maintenance, and education. In the event the income shall be insufficient to provide any of my said children with adequate maintenance, support, welfare, or education; the Trustee may invade the principal of this Trust for this purpose; payments of income and principal to a child pursuant to the Paragraph shall not be taken into account in any later division of the Trust Estate into shares for distribution to my children or children of a deceased child of mine.

      (b) The Trustee may pay more to, or apply more for, some beneficiaries than others and may omit distribution to some beneficiaries entirely during the continuance of the Trust.

Form 8-1: (continued)

(c) The Trustee, in exercising its discretionary authority with respect to the payment of income or principal of the Trust Estate to any beneficiary, shall take into consideration any income or other resources available to such beneficiary from sources outside of this Trust that may be known to the Trustee. The Trustee may accept as final and conclusive the written statement of the beneficiary receiving payments as to other available income or resources. The determination of the Trustee with respect to the necessity of making payments out of income or principal to any beneficiary shall be conclusive on all persons howsoever interest in the Trust.

(d) The Trustee shall accumulate and add to principal, any net income of the Trust not paid out in accordance with the discretion hereinabove conferred on the Trustee.

(e) In the event any child of mine predeceases me or dies prior to the termination of this Trust, the interest of such child in the trust shall cease; except that, if such deceased child of mine is survived by any children, then the Trustee may pay net income of the Trust to, or apply the same for the benefit of, such children of a deceased child of mine in such amount or amounts as the Trustee, in its discretion may determine for support, welfare, and maintenance. Payments out of income or principal to a child of a deceased child of mine pursuant to this Paragraph shall not be taken into account in any later division of the Trust Estate into shares for distribution to my children or children of a deceased child of mine.

(2) <u>Termination and Distribution of Trust</u>: When no child of mine is living who is under the age of twenty-five (25) years, the Trust shall terminate and the Trustee shall immediately distribute the balance of the Trust Estate, in equal shares, to my children then living. However, if any child of mine not then living has issue then surviving, an equal share of the Trust Estate shall be distributed to the then surviving issue of each such deceased child of mine, per stirpes and not per capita.

(3) <u>Definitions</u>: The following terms, as used in this Will, mean:

(a) The term "children" includes adopted children and any who may hereafter be born or adopted.

(b) The term "issue" means lawful blood descendants in the first, second, or any other degree of the ancestor designated, and includes legally adopted children.

(c) All references to the "Trust" or the "Trust Estate", unless otherwise specifically provided for herein, refer to each of the separate Trusts herein provided for, respectively, and the Trust Estate of each Trust.

(d) The term "education" means both college and postgraduate study at any accredited institution of the beneficiary's choice for any period of time that, in the Judgment of the Trustee, is advantageous to the beneficiary; the Trustee shall provide adequate amounts for all related living and travel expenses of the beneficiary within reasonable limits.

(4) <u>Maximum Duration of Trust</u>: All of the Trusts provided for herein shall in any event terminate on the death of the last survivor of all my children in being at the time of my death.

(5) <u>Beneficiaries' Other Means of Support</u>: The Trustee, in exercising its discretionary authority with respect to the payment of income or principal of the Trust Estate to any beneficiary, except my husband, shall take into consideration any income or other resources available to such beneficiary from sources outside of this Trust that may be known to the Trustee. The Trustee may accept as final and conclusive the written statement of the beneficiary receiving payment as to other available income or resources. The determination of the Trustee with respect to the necessity or advisability of making payments out of income or principal to any beneficiary shall be conclusive on all persons howsoever interested in the Trust.

(6) <u>Alleviation of Guardian's Burden</u>: In making the aforesaid payments for the welfare, support, maintenance, and education of each of the aforesaid beneficiaries, the Trustee shall give a liberal interpretation to the discretionary authority conferred by this Will so as to alleviate any burden on the guardian of the person of the child and on the guardian's family that might be caused in any way by the presence of the child in the guardian's home.

(7) <u>Alienation and Attachment of Beneficiary's Interest</u>: No beneficiary or remainderman of any Trust shall have any right to alienate, encumber, or hypothecate his or her interest in the principal or income of the Trust in any manner, nor shall any interest of any beneficiary or remainderman be subject to claims of his or her creditors or liable to attachment, execution, or other process of law.

(8) <u>Distribution on Failure of Trust</u>: If on termination of the administration of my probate estate there has been no distribution in Trust to the Trustee and events have occurred which would require the Trustee under the terms of this Will to make immediate distribution of all property, my Executor shall perform all of the acts necessary to complete such distribution and for that purpose shall have all of the powers granted by this Will to the Trustee.

Form 8-1: (continued)

C. GENERAL ADMINISTRATIVE POWERS OF TRUSTEE

In order to carry out the purposes of the Trust established by this Will, the Trustee, in addition to all other powers granted by this Will or by law, shall have the following powers over the Trust Estate, subject to any limitation specified elsewhere in this Will:

(1) Retention of Assets: To retain any property received by the Trust Estate for as long as the Trustee considers it advisable.

(2) Investments: To invest and reinvest in every kind of property and investment which men of prudence, discretion, and intelligence acquire for their own accounts.

(3) Management of Securities: To exercise, respecting securities held in the Trust Estate, all the rights, powers and privileges of an owner, including, but not limited to, the power to vote, give proxies and to pay assessments and other sums deemed by the Trustee necessary for the protection of the Trust Estate; to participate in voting trusts, pooling agreements, foreclosures, reorganizations, consolidations, mergers, and liquidations, and in connection therewith to deposit securities with and transfer title to any protective or other committee under such terms as the Trustee may deem advisable; to exercise or sell stock subscription or conversion rights; to accept and retain as an investment any securities or other property received through the exercise of any of the foregoing powers, regardless of any limitations elsewhere in this instrument relative to investments by the Trustee.

(4) Form of Ownership of Trust Property: To hold securities or other Trust property in the name of the Trustee under this Trust or in the Trustee's own name or in the name of a nominee or in such condition where ownership will pass by delivery.

(5) Business Interests: To continue and operate, to sell or to liquidate, as the Trustee deems advisable at the risk of the Trust Estate, any business or partnership interests received by the Trust Estate.

(6) Sell and Exchange: To sell for cash on deferred payments at public or private sale, to exchange, and to convey any property of the Trust Estate on such terms and conditions as the Trustee may deem advisable.

(7) Division of Trust Estate: On any division of the Trust Estate into separate shares or Trusts, to apportion and allocate the assets of the Trust Estate in cash or in kind, or partly in cash and partly in kind, or in undivided interests in the manner deemed advisable in the discretion of the Trustee.

(8) Abandonment of Trust Assets: To abandon any Trust asset or interest therein in the discretion of the Trustee.

(9) Option: To grant an option involving disposition of a Trust asset and to enter into an agreement for an option for the acquisition of any asset by the Trust Estate.

(10) Lease: To lease any real or personal property of the Trust Estate for any purpose for terms within or extending beyond the duration of the Trust.

(11) Personal Management: To manage, control, improve, and repair real and personal property belonging to the Trust Estate.

(12) Development of Property: To partition, divide, subdivide, assign, develop, and improve any Trust property; to make or obtain the vacation of plats and adjust boundaries or to adjust differences in valuation on exchange or partition by giving or receiving consideration; and to dedicate land or easements to public use with or without consideration.

(13) Repair, Alter, Demolish, and Erect: To make ordinary and extraordinary repairs and alterations in buildings or other Trust property, to demolish any improvements, to raze party walls or buildings, and to erect new party walls or buildings as the Trustee deems advisable.

(14) Borrowing and Encumbering: To borrow money for any Trust purpose from any person, firm, or corporation on the terms and conditions deemed appropriate by the Trustee and to obligate the Trust Estate for repayment; to encumber the Trust Estate or any of its property by mortgage, deed of trust, pledge, or otherwise, using whatever procedures to consummate the transaction deemed advisable by the Trustee.

(15) Natural Resources: To enter into oil, gas, liquid or gaseous hydrocarbon, sulphur, metal and any and all other natural resource leases on terms deemed advisable by the Trustee, and to enter into any pooling, unitization, repressurization, community, and other types of agreements relating to the exploration, development, operation, and conservation of properties containing minerals or other natural resources; to drill, mine, and otherwise operate for the installation and operation of absorption and repressuring plants; and to install and maintain pipelines.

(16) Insurance: To procure and carry at the expense of the Trust Estate, insurance of the kinds, forms, and amounts deemed advisable by the Trustee to protect the Trust Estate and the Trustee against hazard.

(17) Enforcement of Hypothecations: To enforce any deed of trust, mortgage, or pledge held by the Trust Estate and to purchase at any sale thereunder, any property subject to such hypothecation.

(18) Extending Time of Payment of Obligations: To extend the time of payment of any note or other obligation held in the Trust Estate, including accrued or future interests, in the discretion of the Trustee.

(19) Adjustment of Claim: To compromise, submit to arbitration, release with or without consideration, or otherwise adjust claims in favor of our against the Trust Estate.

Form 8-1: (continued)

(20) <u>Litigation</u>: To commence or defend at the expense of the Trust Estate, any litigation affecting the Trust or any property of the Trust Estate deemed advisable by the Trustee.

(21) <u>Administration Expenses</u>: To pay all taxes, assessments, compensation of the Trustee, and all other expenses incurred in the collection, care administration, and protection of the Trust Estate.

(22) <u>Termination by Trustee of Small Trust</u>: To terminate, in the discretion of the Trustee, any separate Trust held for an income beneficiary and remainderman if the fair market value of the separate Trust at any time becomes less than Five Thousand Dollars ($5,000.00) and, regardless of the age of the income beneficiary, to distribute the principal and any accrued or undistributed net income to the income beneficiary, or to his guardian, conservator, or other fiduciary.

(23) <u>Distribution</u>: On any partial or final distribution of the Trust Estate, to apportion and allocate the assets of the Trust Estate in cash or in kind, or partly in cash and partly in kind, or in undivided interests in the manner deemed advisable in the discretion of the Trustee and to sell any property deemed necessary by the Trustee to make the distribution.

(24) <u>General</u>: To do all the acts, to take all the proceedings, and to exercise all the rights, powers, and privileges which an absolute owner of the property would have, subject always to the discharge of its fiduciary obligations; the enumeration of certain powers in this Will shall not limit the general or implied powers of the Trustee; the Trustee shall have all additional powers that may now or hereafter be conferred on it by law or that may be necessary to enable the Trustee to administer the Trust in accordance with the provisions of this Will, subject to any limitations specified in this Will.

D. OPERATIONAL PROVISIONS

(1) <u>Determination of Income and Principal</u>: The Trustee shall determine what is income and what is principal of each Trust established under this Will, and what expenses, costs, taxes and charges of any kind whatsoever shall be charged against income and what shall be charged against principal in accordance with the applicable statutes of the State of Texas as they now exist and may from time to time be enacted, amended, or repealed.

(2) <u>Trustee's Fees</u>: The Trustee shall receive a reasonable fee for the ordinary and extraordinary services rendered by it.

(3) <u>Waiver of Trustee's Bond</u>: No bond for the faithful performance of duties shall be required of any person named in this Will as Trustee.

(4) <u>Limit of Trustee's Liability</u>: No Trustee appointed under this Will shall at any time be held liable for any action or default of it or its agent or of any other person in connection with the administration of the Trust Estate, unless caused by its own gross negligence or by a willful commission by it of an act in breach of trust.

(5) <u>Choice of Law</u>: The validity and administration of any Trust established under this Will and all questions relating to the construction or interpretation of any such Trust shall be governed by the laws of the State of Texas.

(6) <u>Successor Trustee</u>: If my wife, Paula Smith, is unable or unwilling to act or to continue to act as Co-Trustee, then I appoint Arthur Brown, as the Co-Trustee with the same powers, rights, obligations, discretion, and immunities.

(7) <u>Removal of Trustee</u>: The legally competent adult beneficiaries and the guardian or guardians of any legally incompetent beneficiaries of the Trusts established hereunder may, by mutual consent, agree to remove any Trustee acting hereunder from its position as such, by giving thirty (30) days written notice of same to the Trustee. In such case, such beneficiaries shall mutually appoint as Successor Trustee, such an individual or corporation as will qualify, when considered as a whole along with the other Trustee or Trustees which will be acting as such, as an "Independent Trustee" under Section 674(b)(8) of the Internal Revenue Code of 1954.

(8) <u>Delegation of Record Keeping, Accounting, and Safekeeping to Corporate Fiduciary</u>: All records, books of account, inventories, and accountings in connection with the administration of the Trusts created herein shall be prepared solely by my Corporate Trustee and my Corporate Trustee shall be responsible for the care and safekeeping of all moneys and securities included in the Trusts. My individual Trustee shall be relieved of all liability with regard to duties specifically delegated to my Corporate Trustee. However, in no event will my Corporate Trustee be responsible for determining the accuracy of any accounting procedures utilized by my Executor, if other than the Corporate Trustee, in determining the amount to be distributed from my Estate to the Trustee hereunder or the property of such a distribution.

(9) <u>Authority of Individual Fiduciary to delegate Power to Corporate Fiduciary</u>: My individual Trustee may, at any time, delegate to my Corporate Trustee, any or all of the powers or duties, discretionary or otherwise, exercisable by or required of the individual Trustee in this Will, and may revoke such delegation at any time thereafter, and such delegation or revocation shall be affected by a written instrument duly acknowledged and filed with my Corporate Trustee.

SIXTH
PAYMENT OF DEATH TAXES

All estate, inheritance, and succession taxes, together with any interest and penalties thereon, payable as a result of my death and imposed with respect to property passing under this Will, shall be paid out of the residue of my estate. All estate, inheritance, and succession taxes, together with any interest and penalties thereon, payable as a result of my death and imposed on property passing outside of this Will

Form 8-1: (continued)

shall be equitably pro-rated among the persons to whom such property was transferred or to whom any benefit therein accrued; my executor shall take whatever action is necessary to collect such taxes and charges from such persons, and may withhold such taxes and charges from any property that may be distributable to such persons.

SEVENTH
EXECUTOR

(1) <u>Appointment</u>: I appoint my wife, Paula Smith, as the Independent Executrix of this Will. If she is unable or unwilling to act or to continue to act in that capacity, then I appoint Arthur Brown, as the Independent Executor of this Will. I direct that no action shall be taken in any court in the administration of my estate other than the probating and recording of this Will and the return of an inventory, appraisement, and list of claims of my estate. My Independent Executrix, whether original, substitute, or successor, is hereafter referred to as my "Executor".

(2) <u>No Bond Required</u>: No bond or other security shall be required of any Executor appointed in this Will.

(3) <u>Powers</u>: My Executor shall have, in extension and not in limitation of the powers given by law or by other provisions of this Will, the following powers with respect to the settlement of my probate estate:

    (a) <u>Same Powers as Trustee</u>: To exercise with regard to the probate estate, all of the powers and authority conferred by this Will on the Trustee over the Trust Estate.

    (b) <u>Employment of Attorneys, Advisers, and Other Agents</u>: To employ any attorney, investment adviser, accountant, broker, tax specialist, or any other agent deemed necessary by my Executor; and to pay from my estate reasonable compensation for all services performed by any of them.

    (c) <u>Determination of Income and Principal</u>: To pay as income, the whole of the interest, dividends, rent, or receipts from property, whether wasting or not and although bought or taken at value above par, but if it is deemed advisable when property is bought or taken at a value above par, a portion of the income may be retained to offset such loss to the principal; to treat as income or principal or to apportion between them, stock dividends, extra dividends, right to take stock or securities, and proceeds from the sale of real estate, although such real estate may have been wholly or partly unproductive; to charge to income or principal or to apportion between them, custodians' compensation, brokers' commissions, agents' compensations, attorneys' fees, insurance premiums, repairs and improvements, taxes (income, estate, inheritance, or any other taxes), depreciation charges, and all executor's compensations; generally to determine all questions as between income and principal or to apportion between them, any receipt or gain and any charge, disbursement, or loss as is deemed advisable in the circumstances of each case as it arises, notwithstanding any statute, rule of law, or determination of any court.

    (d) <u>Where Estate Property Kept</u>: To keep any or all of the property of my estate at any place or places in Nueces County, Texas, or elsewhere within the United States or abroad or with a depository or custodian at such place or places.

    (e) <u>Income Tax Returns</u>: To join with my wife or her executor or administrator in filing any income tax return for the income of my said wife and myself for any period for which such a return may be permitted, and to agree with my said wife or her executor or administrator:

        (i) As to how the burden of the liability for any income tax, or interest thereon, arising out of the filing of a joint return by my Executor and my said wife or her executor or administrator, shall be borne as between my estate, my said wife or her estate; and

        (ii) As to who, as between my said wife or her estate and my estate, shall be entitled:

            (A) To any refund or credit of any income tax, or interest thereon, based on the filing of a joint return by my said wife and myself or by my executor and my said wife or her executor or administrator;

            (B) To any refund or credit of any amount paid on account of any joint declaration of any estimated income tax filed by my said wife and myself, and of the interest on any such refund; and

            (C) To the benefit of any payment made by my said ^C and myself on account of any joint or separate declaration of any estimated income tax.

    (f) <u>Distribution of Estate</u>: When paying legacies or dividing or distributing my estate, to make such payments, division, or distribution wholly or partly in kind by allotting and transferring specific securities or other personal or real properties or undivided interests therein as a part of the whole of any one or more payments or shares at current values in the manner deemed advisable by my executor.

All of the above powers may be exercised from time to time in the discretion of my executor without further order or license.

EIGHTH
GUARDIANS

(1) <u>Appointment</u>: If my wife does not survive me, then I appoint Arthur Brown, as the guardian of the person of each of my minor children and I request that he seek appointment as the guardian of their estates.

(2) <u>No Bond Required</u>: No bond or other security shall be required in any jurisdiction of any guardian appointed in this Will for the performance of his duties as guardian.

Form 8-1: (continued)

NINTH
WILL CONTESTS

If any beneficiary or remainderman under this Will in any manner, directly or indirectly, contests or attacks this Will or any of its provisions, any share or interest in my estate or in the estate of any Trust established by this Will given to that contesting beneficiary or remainderman under this Will is revoked and shall be disposed of in the same manner provided herein as if that contesting beneficiary or remainderman had predeceased me without issue.

TENTH
GENERAL

(1) <u>Number and Gender Defined</u>: As used in this Will, whenever the context so indicates, the masculine, feminine, or neuter gender, and the singular or plural number, shall each be deemed to include the others.

(2) <u>Effect of Inoperative, Invalid, or Illegal Provision</u>: If any provision of this Will or of any Codicil thereto is held to be inoperative, invalid, or illegal, it is my intention that all of the remaining provisions thereof shall continue to be fully operative and effective so far as is possible and reasonable.

(3) <u>Headings</u>: The headings above the various provisions of this Will have been included only in order to make it easier to locate the subject covered by each provision and are not to be used in construing this Will or in ascertaining my intentions.

(4) <u>Will Not Contractual</u>: My wife and I are executing wills at approximately the same time in which each of us is the primary beneficiary of the Will of the other. These Wills are not being made because of any agreement between my wife and myself. Either Will may at any time be revoked at the sole discretion of the maker thereof.

IN WITNESS WHEREOF, I have hereunto signed my name to this my Last Will and Testament, typewritten on 17 pages, including the self-proving affidavit, each of which I have initialed, in the presence of the undersigned Witnesses, who at my request, and in my presence and in the presence of each other, signed their names as Witnesses this the 23rd day of November, A.D., 1993.

_____
Peter Smith

SIGNED, DECLARED, AND PUBLISHED BY Peter Smith, as his Last Will and Testament, in the presence of us, the attesting Witnesses, who have subscribed our names in the presence of Peter Smith, and in the presence of each other, at his special instance and request this the 23rd day of November, A.D., 1993.

_____

_____
Witnesses

THE STATE OF TEXAS   ) (
COUNTY OF NUECES   ) (

BEFORE ME, the undersigned authority, on this day personally appeared Peter Smith, Testator, _____, and _____, known to me to be the Testator and the Witnesses, respectively, whose names are subscribed to the foregoing instrument in their respective capacities, and, all of said persons being by me duly sworn, the Testator declared to me and to the said Witnesses in my presence that the said instrument is his Last Will and Testament, and that he had willingly made and executed it as his free act and deed; and the said Witnesses, each on his oath, stated to me, in the presence and hearing of the said Testator, that the said Testator had declared to them that the said instrument is his Last Will and Testament, and that he had executed the same as such and wanted each of them to sign it as a Witness; and upon their oaths each Witness stated further that they did sign the same as Witnesses in the presence of the said Testator at his request; that he was at that time eighteen (18) years of age or over and was of sound mind; and that each of said Witnesses was then at least fourteen (14) years of age.

_____
Peter Smith

_____

_____
Witnesses

SUBSCRIBED AND SWORN TO BEFORE ME by the said Peter Smith, Testator, and by the said _____, and _____, Witnesses, this the day of November, A.D., 1993.

_____
Notary Public, State of Texas

Form 8-2: Disclaimer

State of Texas) (
County of Rough Rider) (

The undersigned hereby renounces and disclaims all of her right, title and interest in and to the following described real property located in Rough Rider County, Texas:

The undersigned's interest arises out of the will of Peter Smith, dated November 22, 1992, and filed for probate on March 2, 1993, in County Court at Law No. 2 of Rough Rider County, Texas, under Cause No. 93-1254-2.

This Disclaimer is made pursuant of Section 37A of the Texas Probate Code and shall be irrevocable.

DATED THIS _____ DAY OF _____, 1993.

_____
Paula Smith

State of Texas) (
County of Rough Rider) (

BEFORE ME, the undersigned authority, on this day personally appeared Paula Smith, known to me to be the person whose name is subscribed to the foregoing instrument, and acknowledged to me that she executed the same for the purposes and considerations therein expressed.

GIVEN UNDER MY HAND AND SEAL OF OFFICE This _____ Day of _____, 1993.

_____
Notary Public, State of Texas

Form 8-3: Will With Pour-Over Provision and Contingent Trust for Minor Children

This will was prepared using PRODOC™, Document Assembly Software for Legal Professionals and the Wills Module, both distributed by Automated Legal Systems, of Universal City, Texas, Allan Schoolcraft, President.

LAST WILL AND TESTAMENT

OF

Peter Smith

I, Peter Smith, of the County of Nueces and the State of texas, being in good health, of sound and disposing mind and memory, do make and declare this instrument to be my Last Will and Testament, hereby expressly revoking all former Wills and Codicils made by me at any time heretofore, and intending hereby to dispose of all the property of whatever kind and wherever situated which I own, or in which I have any kind of interest at the time of my death.

I.

IDENTITY OF THE FAMILY

My wife's name is Paula Smith. All references in this Will to my "spouse" or to my "wife" are to her. At the time of the execution of this Will, I have two children, namely, Peter Smith, Jr. and Penelope Smith. If subsequent to the execution of this Will there shall be a child or children of mine born, or a child adopted by me on or before the child is eighteen (18) years of age, and if such child or children, or issue thereof, shall survive me, then in such event, such child or children, or issue thereof, shall share in the benefits of my estate equally and to the same extent as my children hereinabove named and their issue; and the provisions of this Will shall be deemed modified to the extent necessary to effectuate such intention.

II.

PAYMENT OF EXPENSES

I direct that all the expenses of my last illness, my funeral expenses, and my just personal debts, including any inheritance taxes, transfer taxes, and estate taxes which may be levied by the United States Government or by any state by reason of my death, shall be paid by my Independent Executrix out of the residue of my estate as soon as conveniently may be done; provided that my Independent Executrix, in such Executrix's sole discretion, may distribute from time to time any real or personal property in my estate which at my death is subject to a lien securing an indebtedness upon it without discharging said indebtedness, if in my Independent Executrix's judgment, the condition of my estate so requires. The distributee shall then be considered as having received my estate's equity in the property.

III.

DISPOSITION OF ESTATE

A. I give, devise and bequeath all of my estate to the Trustee of **THE SMITH FAMILY LIVING TRUST** established on June 1 _____, 1994, to be administered according to the terms and conditions of the Trust Agreement governing that trust, as amended or restated from time to time. If **THE SMITH FAMILY LIVING TRUST** is not in existence at the time of my death, I give, devise and bequeath all of my estate of whatsoever kind and wheresoever situated as hereinafter provided in this Article.

B. If **THE SMITH FAMILY LIVING TRUST** is not in existence at the time of my death and if my wife, Paula Smith, survives me, I give, devise and bequeath all of my estate of whatsoever kind and wheresoever situated to my wife, Paula Smith. If my wife, Paula Smith, does not survive me, I give, devise and bequeath all of my estate to my children, in equal shares, Peter Smith, Jr. and Penelope Smith; provided, however, that if a child of mine shall not then survive me, but should leave issue then surviving me, such then surviving issue shall take, per stirpes, the share that such deceased child would have taken by surviving me, or if none is then living, then said share shall be distributed my then living child or his or her issue, per stirpes, or if none of my descendants is then living, then said share shall be distributed as provided in the paragraph below.

C. I may provide instructions in a Letter to my Independent Executrix as to the disposition of some of my personal and household effects. While I hope that my family will abide by my wishes as expressed in the Letter, it is merely an expression of my wishes and is not intended to alter the absolute nature of any bequest contained in this my Will.

D. Any other property of mine that has not been disposed of under any other provision of this Will shall go and be distributed to my heirs-at-law. Their identity and respective shares shall be determined in all respects as if my death had occurred immediately following the happening of the event requiring such distribution, and according to the laws of Texas then in force governing the distribution of the estate of an intestate.

IV.

DEFINITION OF SURVIVAL

Any legatee, devisee, donee, person or beneficiary with respect to all or any part of my estate who shall not survive until ninety (90) days after the date of my death, or until this Will is probated, whichever occurs earlier, shall be deemed to have predeceased me, and shall be treated for all purposes herein as though such person had predeceased me.

Form 8-3: (continued)

V.
CONTINGENT TRUST

In the event that any beneficiary has not reached the age of twenty-one(21) years, then in such event I give, devise and bequeath the share or shares of such beneficiary to my Trustee, IN TRUST NEVERTHE-LESS, for the uses and purposes hereinafter set forth.

A. My Trustee, in such Trustee's discretion, shall distribute to or for the benefit of each beneficiary, as much of the income, and in addition, so much of the corpus of each separate per stirpes share or trust created for that particular beneficiary as my Trustee shall consider necessary or advisable for his or her health, support, education, and maintenance.

B. Any income or corpus not so distributed or used shall be separately accumulated for each beneficiary. Upon attaining the age of eighteen(18) years, each beneficiary shall have the option of withdrawing for his or her separate share one-third (1/3) of the property then constituting his or her separate trust estate. Upon attaining the age of twenty(20) years or any time thereafter, each beneficiary shall have the option of withdrawing one-half (1/2) of the remaining property then constituting his or her separate trust estate. Upon attaining the age of twenty-one(21) years or any time thereafter, each beneficiary shall have the option of withdrawing the remaining balance of the property then constituting his or her separate trust estate. Each beneficiary shall be advised of his or her options ninety (90) days prior to his or her respective birthdays when such options shall arise. Furthermore, any beneficiary intending to exercise any of his or her options to withdraw, shall give the Trustee at least sixty (60) days' written notice of such intent. The Trustee may, in the Trustee's sole discretion, waive all or any portion of such sixty (60) days' notice. In the meantime, during the pendency of each trust, the Trustee shall have the same powers, discretions, duties and responsibilities that the Trustee has generally with respect to this trust as to administration and distributions.

C. If any beneficiary of the trust shall die before complete distribution of his or her share, then upon the death of such beneficiary the share of such beneficiary as then constituted shall be distributed equally to said deceased beneficiary's children or his or her issue, per stirpes, as provided in Sections A and B above; or if none is then living, then said share shall be distributed to my then living child or his or her issue, per stirpes; or if none of my descendants is then living, then said share shall be distributed as provided in the paragraph below.

D. Any share or portion of a share of any trust created hereunder or any other property of mine that has not been disposed of under any other provision of this Will shall go and be distributed to my heirs-at-law. Their identity and respective shares shall be determined in all respects as if my death had occurred immediately following the happening of the event requiring such distribution, and according to the laws of the State of Texas then in force governing the distribution of the estate of an intestate.

VI.
APPOINTMENT OF TRUSTEE

I nominate, constitute and appoint Rough Rider National Bank, of Dallas to act as Trustee of the trust created in Article V herein.

VII.
TRUSTEE POWERS

The trusts created or arising by virtue of this, my Last Will and Testament, shall be governed by and administered in accordance with the following provisions:

A. The Trustee during the continuation of each trust shall have the sole and complete right to possess, control, manage, and dispose of each trust estate and the said Trustee shall have the powers, rights, responsibilities and duties given to or imposed upon trustees by the Texas Trust Code as such Code now exists.

B. The Trustee shall at all times keep proper records and books of accounts which shall be open to the inspection of the beneficiaries at all reasonable times.

C. The Trustee shall act without bond of any kind, and shall be liable only for gross negligence, fraud or defalcation.

D. The Trustee shall have full power, in the Trustee's discretion, to litigate, compromise, adjust and settle all claims arising out of or in connection with the trust and property of the trust, and the Trustee may employ counsel and other agents in the discharge of duties and determine and pay them a reasonable compensation.

E. The Trustee shall be entitled to pay out of the trust estate or to be reimbursed for any and all legitimate expenses incurred in the management of the trust estate.

F. The Trustee shall have the sole discretion to determine what is income or corpus of each respective trust, and shall apportion and allocate all receipts, credits, disbursements, expenses, and charges to income or corpus as the Trustee shall deem proper.

G. The Trustee may resign by sending an acknowledged written notice to the trust beneficiaries thirty (30) days prior to resignation.

H. As compensation for its services hereunder, my Trustee or its successor shall be entitled to charge the same fees customarily charged for similar services in other trusts at the time the services are rendered.

Form 8-3: (continued)

VIII.
APPOINTMENT OF EXECUTOR

I hereby nominate, constitute and appoint my wife, Paula Smith, as Independent Executrix of my estate.

If any individual Independent Executor or Executrix becomes unable to discharge his or her duties under this Will because of accident, physical or mental illness or deterioration, or other cause and does not resign, then upon certification in a form sufficient for the recording of a deed in the State of Texas by two medical doctors (neither of whom is a beneficiary under this Will) affirming that each has examined the Independent Executor or Executrix and that each has concluded, based on such examination, that the Independent Executor or Executrix is unable to discharge his or her duties under this Will, the Independent Executor or Executrix shall cease to serve, as if he or she had resigned, effective the date of the certification.

It is my will and desire and I hereby direct that in the administration of my estate, my Independent Executrix or any successor shall not be required to furnish any bond of any kind and that no action shall be had in any court in the administration of my estate other than the probating of this, my Last Will and Testament, and the filing of any Inventory, Appraisement and List of Claims of my estate that may be required.

IX.
POWERS OF EXECUTOR

The estate created or arising by virtue of my death and this instrument, my Last Will and Testament, shall be governed by and administered in accordance with the following provisions:

A. I hereby grant unto my Independent Executrix or any successor named above, full power and authority over any and all of my estate and they are hereby authorized to sell, manage, and dispose of the same or any part thereof, and in connection with any such sale or transaction, make, execute and deliver proper deeds, assignments and other written instruments and to do any and all things proper or necessary in the orderly handling and management of my estate.

B. My Independent Executrix or any successor named above, shall have full power and authority to compromise, settle and adjust any and all debts, claims and taxes which may be due from or owing by my estate.

C. My Independent Executrix or any successor named above, shall have full power and authority to deal with any person, firm, or corporation including any trusts or trust estate created by this, my Last Will and Testament.

D. My Independent Executrix or any successor named above, shall have full power to borrow money at any time and in any amount from time to time for the benefit of my estate, from any person, firm, or corporation or from any bank or trust company and to secure the loan or loans by pledge, deed of trust, mortgage or other encumbrances on the assets of the estate and from time to time to renew such loans and give additional security.

E. As compensation for her services hereunder, my Independent Executrix or any successor named above shall be entitled to charge the same fees customarily charged for similar services in other estates at the time the services are rendered.

X.
APPOINTMENT OF GUARDIANS

In the event that any child of mine has not reached the age of eighteen (18) years at the date of my death, and my wife is not then alive, then in such event, I nominate and appoint my brother, Paul Smith, to act as Guardian of the person and the estate of said minor child or children, and I direct that no bond or other security shall be required of the Guardian.

XI.
SPENDTHRIFT PROVISION

No interest of any beneficiary in the corpus or income of my estate or of any trust created herein shall be subject to assignment, alienation, pledge, attachment, or claims of creditors of such beneficiary and may not otherwise be alienated or encumbered by such beneficiary, except as may be otherwise expressly provided herein.

XII.
MAXIMUM TERM OF TRUST

If any trust created hereunder shall violate any applicable Rule Against Perpetuities or any similar rule or law, my Trustee is hereby directed to terminate said trust on the date limited by such rule or law and thereupon the property held in such trust shall be distributed to the persons then entitled to share such income, notwithstanding any provision of this Will to the contrary.

XIII.
IN TERROREM CLAUSE

If any beneficiary under this Will shall in any manner contest or attack this Will or any of its provisions, any share or interest in my estate given to such contesting beneficiary under this Will is hereby revoked and shall be disposed of as part of the residue of my estate.

Form 8-3: (continued)

XIV.
WILLS NOT CONTRACTUAL

My spouse and I are executing Wills at approximately the same time in which each of us may be a primary beneficiary of the Will of the other. These Wills are not executed because of any agreement between my spouse and myself. Either Will may be revoked at any time in the sole discretion of the maker thereof.

XV.
DEFINITIONS AND INTERPRETATIONS

For purposes of interpretation of this, my Last Will and Testament, and the administration of the estate and any trusts established herein, the following provisions shall apply:

A. The words "child, children, descendants, issue," and similar terms shall be deemed only to include children born to, or adopted (on or before eighteen years of age) in, a lawful marriage.

B. When a distribution is directed to be made to any person's descendants "per stirpes," the division into stirpes shall begin at the generation nearest to such person that has a living member.

C. The use of the masculine, feminine or neuter genders shall be interpreted to include the other genders, and the use of either the singular or the plural number shall be interpreted to include the other number, unless such an interpretation in a particular case is inconsistent with the general tenor of this instrument. Any references herein relating to my Independent Executrix shall include her successors regardless of the gender of the successors.

D. This Will shall be probated in accordance with the laws of Texas, and should any provisions of the same be held unenforceable or invalid for any reason, the unenforceability or invalidity of said provision shall not effect the enforceability or validity of any other part of this Will.

IN TESTIMONY WHEREOF, I hereunto sign my name to this, my Last Will and Testament, consisting of _____ ( ) typewritten pages (including the pages containing the attestation clauses and the self-proving affidavit), each of which pages I am initialing or signing for the purpose of identification, all in the presence of the undersigned, who witness the same at my request, on this _____ day of _____, 1994.

_____
Peter Smith
Testator

ATTESTATION

The foregoing instrument was, on this the _____ day of _____, 1994, made and published as the Last Will and Testament of Peter Smith, Testator, and is signed and subscribed by the said Peter Smith, in our presence, and we, the undersigned, at his request, and in his presence, and in the presence of each other, sign and subscribe our names hereto as attesting witnesses.

_____   _____
WITNESS   WITNESS

_____   _____
STREET   STREET

_____   _____
CITY AND STATE   CITY AND STATE

Form 8-3: (continued)

SELF-PROVING AFFIDAVIT

STATE OF TEXAS   *

COUNTY OF NUECES   *

                        *

        BEFORE ME, the undersigned authority, on this day personally appeared Peter Smith, _____ and _____, known to me to be the Testator and the witnesses, respectively, whose names are subscribed to the annexed or foregoing instrument in their respective capacities, and all of said persons being by me duly sworn, the said Peter Smith, Testator, declared to me and to said witnesses in my presence that said instrument is his Last Will and Testament and that he had willingly made and executed it as his free act and deed for the purposes therein expressed; and the said witnesses, each on his oath stated to me in the presence and hearing of the said Testator that the said Testator had declared to them that said instrument is his Last Will and Testament and that he executed same as such and wanted each of them to sign it as a witness; and upon their oaths, each witness stated further that they did sign the same as witnesses in the presence of the said Testator and at his request; that said Testator was at that time eighteen (18) years of age or over (or being under such age, was or had been lawfully married, or was then a member of the armed forces of the United States or of an auxiliary thereof or of the Maritime Service) and was of sound mind; and that each of said witnesses was then at least fourteen (14) years of age.

_____

Peter Smith
Testator

_____

Witness

_____

Witness

       SUBSCRIBED AND ACKNOWLEDGED before me by the said Peter Smith, Testator, and **SUBSCRIBED AND SWORN TO before me** by the said _____ and _____, Witnesses, this the _____ day of _____, 1994.

_____

Form 8-4: Partial Testamentary Trust Checklist

Section _____
Powers of the Trustee.

1. Limitations on statutory authority:

2. Lend money to beneficiaries. yes / no. Limitation:

3. Purchase residence for beneficiaries. yes / no

4. Delegation of trust powers. yes / no. Limitations:

5. Power to self-deal. yes / no. Limitations:

6. Power to engage investment advisors. yes / no

7. Power to terminate. yes / no. Limitations:

8. Power to divide/merge. yes / no. Limitations:

9. Power to purchase life insurance. yes / no. Income beneficiary/Remainder beneficiary. Limitations:

10. Power to pool trust funds. yes / no

11. Power to sprinkle. yes / no. Amount sprinkled to remainder beneficiary to be charged against remainder interest. yes / no

12. Power to give guarantees. yes / no

13. Hold assets other than stocks and securities in nominee form. yes / no

14. Power to change situs of trust. yes / no. Limitations:

9 INTER VIVOS TRUSTS

CHAPTER OBJECTIVES

Upon completion of this chapter, the student should be able to:

1. Understand the purpose, benefits, and detriments of grantor living trusts.

2. Structure a grantor living trust to achieve maximum tax benefits and to meet other client objectives/goals.

3. Prepare the instruments necessary to effectuate a living trust and to achieve the client's goals.

4. Appreciate the uses and benefits of insurance trusts, and know how to comply with the Crummy requirements.

5. Understand the application of the various types of grantor-retained interest trusts and their usefulness in enhancing the benefits of inter vivos gifts.

6. Structure a children's or grandchildren's trust to ensure maximum benefit under estate and gift tax laws and minimum impact of the GSTT.

7. Understand the benefits of charitable remainder trusts.

8. Structure educational trusts and other gifts ensuring the education of a descendant.

CHAPTER GLOSSARY

Adjusted basis For calculating of capital gains tax on the sale of a capital asset, adjusted basis equals the cost of acquisition of the asset, plus additions, minus allowable depreciation. Also known as *adjusted cost basis*.

Ancillary administration The administration of an estate in a state other than the state in which the decedent was domiciled and administration first opened.

Annual gift tax exclusion The amount of money or value of property (currently $10,000) that can be given to any donee annually that is excluded from (does not incur) gift tax and that is not carried back into the donor's estate for the calculation of the Unified Transfer Tax.

Grantor living trust A trust in which the grantor reserves control to the extent that he continues to be treated as the owner of both the trust assets and income for income tax purposes. In the normal grantor trust, the grantor reserves control by being the sole trustee or by reserving the power to revoke the trust. Also called *living trust* and *revocable inter vivos trust*; named *grantor trust* in the Internal Revenue Code and regulations.

Insurance trust A trust in which the corpus consists in whole or in part of life insurance payable to the trust upon the death of the insured.

Midterm rate A percentage provided by the treasury tables for calculating the value of a grantor-retained interest in an irrevocable term trust, such as a GRIT. It estimates the annual rate of return of income to the grantor. This rate is multiplied by the number of years of the term of the trust, with the amount of the gift reduced by the resulting factor, being the amount of the retained interest. Also known as midterm *adjusted federal rate (AFR)*.

Present interest A gift to which ownership (legal or equitable) has passed absolutely to the donee and in which the donor has retained no incidents of ownership.

QTIP election In order to receive the benefits of the QTIP provisions on amounts deducted from the gross estate of a decedent under the marital deduction, the executor must elect QTIP status by making a declaration on Form 706, U.S. Estate Tax Return.

Straight life insurance Insurance on which premiums at a level rate are collected throughout the life of the insured. It builds up a cash reserve that may be withdrawn upon cancellation (*cash surrender value*) and that may be borrowed against (*cash loan value*). Also referred to as *whole life insurance*.

Taxable distribution Distribution of either corpus or income during the existence of a trust that is subject to the GSTT.

Taxable termination Distribution of the remainder, upon termination of a trust, that is subject to the GSTT.

Taxpaying entity An Internal Revenue Service term for any person, legal entity, or other organization or association they consider an entity and therefore liable for federal taxes and for filing tax returns.

INTRODUCTION

Inter vivos trusts are trusts created and funded during the life of the settlor. It is impossible to list and discuss all possible variations of inter vivos trusts, due to limitations of space. Neither, for the same reason, is it possible to attach to this chapter all the different kinds of forms as examples. Even if an attempt had been made to do so, by the time the book was published, either the tax laws would have changed or some estate planner would have developed a new technique using trusts in estate planning. As a result, this chapter deals only with the highlights and uses of selected inter vivos trusts, those that have withstood the test of time and are likely to be in use for a few years to come. And any of the trusts or provisions thereof discussed here and the tax benefits they provide may be the subject of new or amended regulations or sections of the Internal Revenue Code or rulings by the Internal Revenue Service that take away, modify, or limit any possible tax benefits. The estate planning legal assistant not only must remain current concerning new laws and new rulings and decisions, but also must stay abreast of pending changes.

Because this area of the law is subject to rapid change, which can apply retroactively, it is good practice management to maintain some kind of a database by which the estate planner can immediately determine which prior estate plans have either been adversely affected by a change in the law or could benefit from a revision. Some of the more expensive software designed for preparing inter vivos trusts and wills also have a built-in database through which a user can retrieve the names and file numbers of all clients for whom documents have been prepared using that software, plus the date the documents were prepared. When a new law becomes effective and its effective date has been determined, a search can be made of the database to learn which clients will be affected or benefited by the change in the law. It seems unlikely that an attorney would be held liable for failing to notify a client of a change in the law. However, if the attorney retrieves the name of all past clients affected by a law change and sends them a newsletter concerning the change and its effect on their particular estate plan, the clients probably will return to the attorney to have their estate plan amended to comply with or receive the benefits of such changes, thereby producing additional income for the office.

Inasmuch as the Internal Revenue Code uses the term *grantor* rather than *settlor*, *grantor* is used in this chapter.

GRANTOR LIVING TRUSTS

The **grantor living trust**, also known as the *family living trust* and the *revocable living (inter vivos) trust*, has become quite popular and is the subject of many seminars and sale promotions by attorneys and other estate planners. If the grantor living trust is prepared properly and all assets of the grantor are transferred into the trust, both at the time the trust is created and thereafter, then the grantor living trust avoids probate.

This can have a number of advantages. First, it affords to the survivors of the grantor privacy that is not possible when it becomes necessary to probate a will. Where there is a full administration of a decedent's estate, one of the requirements of the probate code is that the executor or administrator file an inventory, appraisement, and list of claims showing all the personal property that was owned by the decedent on the date of his death, wherever located, and all of the real property owned by the decedent located in the State of Texas. The inventory must also show all debts owed to the estate and the market value of all listed assets. This is information the beneficiaries of the estate often would prefer not be made public.

Second, avoiding probate saves the cost of probate. This may not be a significant benefit in Texas inasmuch as the cost of probate in Texas is considerably lower than in other states. In fact, in an attempt to sell grantor living trusts in Texas, at least one financial advisor publishes the average cost of probate in three or four states but not that in Texas. Only as a footnote to the charts showing the probate cost relative to the total assets in the estate does it state that the cost in the reader's state may be higher or lower.

Most attorneys probably charge more for preparing a grantor living trust and the necessary accompanying documents than for a will and probate combined. If cost is the only motivating factor, in most instances it will cost the client less to have wills prepared and ultimately to pay the costs of probate. This may be true even for very large estates, where numerous and varying types of assets will need to be transferred into the trust in order to avoid probate effectively. Because the number of assets and the amount of variations of the assets generally increase with the size of the estate, so does the cost of transferring the assets into the trust.

Third, the living trust is a much more effective way to provide for incompetency than is the power of attorney. (This has previously been discussed.) The expenses of a guardianship can far exceed the expenses of probating a will, and the client will eventually die, thereby adding probate costs to the guardianship costs. Consequently, in the event of incompetency, a living trust can significantly reduce costs.

A fourth benefit of the probate-avoiding feature of a grantor living trust comes when the client owns property located in other states. In this situation, it might be necessary not only to probate that client's estate upon his death in Texas, but to open an **ancillary administration** in each of the other states and perhaps even foreign countries in which that client owned property at the time of his death. Ancillary administration is nearly as expensive, and in fact can be more expensive, than original probate in Texas. If one multiplies the cost of probate by the number of states in which probate proceedings will have to be begun, it can well end up that the cost of a grantor living trust and the necessary accompanying documents may be considerably less than the cost of probate.

Prior to 1981, it was detrimental to use the living trust because the IRS considered the trust as a separate **tax-paying entity**. A separate tax return had to be filed for the trust, yet there was no benefit from tax splitting because income tax had to be paid at the grantor's tax rate, increasing the cost of tax accounting and preparation. Effective 1981, the tax law was changed to provide that if the grantor is a trustee and the trust is revocable, then the trust is not a separate tax-paying entity. The tax identification number of the trust is the social security number of any one of the grantors.

The grantors of a grantor living trust can be either unmarried individuals or married individuals dealing with their separate property or their share of the community property. In the most common situation, in which both husband and wife are dealing with all of their separate and community property, the grantor living trust can be written to give maximum credit shelter and to make use of the marital deduction. In addition, QTIP provisions can be used, as discussed in the previous chapter. In fact, the same clauses for credit bypass trusts or exemption-equivalent trusts as discussed in reference to testamentary trusts are applicable with only minor modifications to living trusts in general and in particular to the grantor living trust.

The grantor living trust, as commonly drawn, becomes irrevocable at the death of the first spouse for that spouse's contributions to the trust property. The trust can then provide that the interest of the deceased spouse, retained in trust for the benefit of the surviving spouse, will qualify as a QTIP and that an election can be made by the trustee that will qualify the transfer for the unlimited marital deduction. The trust may provide for a partial **QTIP election** and allow the trustee to divide the trust assets into separate trusts to reflect the partial election.

In the alternative, the trustee can choose to continue the trust as is, with the percentage of the whole representing the portion elected as QTIP maintained so as to reflect the proportionate share of increase and decrease in the property and to divide it between the elective QTIP property and the non-elective property. This allows the property not elected to qualify as a bypass, credit shelter or exemption-equivalent trust. Then, if the total trust property and all other assets of the spouses that might pass by reason of the death of one of the spouses does not exceed $1.2 million at the time of the first spouse's death, the trustee will simply refuse to make a QTIP election. Since the total assets of both spouses do not exceed $1.2 million, the portion passing by reason of the death of the first spouse will not exceed $600,000. This is less than the exemption equivalent of $600,000. If no QTIP or marital deduction election is made, the property will qualify as a bypass and there will be no estate tax on the estate of the first spouse to die, since the assets of that portion of the trust do not vest in the surviving spouse. The assets will never become a part of his estate. Assuming that his estate remains approximately the same for the remainder of his life, when he dies he also will have less then $600,000. Consequently, neither estate will be subject to federal estate tax.

If, on the other hand, the combined marital estate exceeds $1.2 million, the trustee can make a partial QTIP election on the portion that exceeds $600,000 to qualify that amount for the marital deduction. This election can be made for all or any part of the property that meets the QTIP requirements. A partial election must be a defined fraction of the entire trust or other property. The fraction may be defined via a formula in a clause stating that the numerator of the fraction will be the amount, if allowed as a marital deduction, that results in the least possible federal estate tax being payable by reason of the first spouse's death, and the denominator will be the value, for estate tax purposes, of the property that becomes trust property. Then the trustee only has to determine the value of the decedent's interest in the trust assets and other property, make that figure the denominator and $600,000 the numerator, and reduce the resulting fraction to its lowest common denominator. This effectively removes estate assets equal to $600,000 from the QTIP portion of the trust. Then by either separating the trust or just separating the funds within the trust, the $600,000 that does not go into the QTIP becomes a bypass trust. When the surviving spouse dies, that property which is held as a bypass trust will pass directly to the remainder beneficiaries without ever going into the spouse's estate. The bypass amount will never be included within the surviving spouse's estate upon death for the purpose of calculating tax. The portion to which the partial election was made will be considered part of the surviving spouse's estate upon his death.

The marital deduction does not avoid the tax; it simply defers it until the last spouse dies. The qualified terminable interest property provisions are not intended to save estate tax but rather to allow the owner of property to pass to a surviving spouse property that qualifies for the marital deduction while allowing that owner to control its ultimate disposition. The property can pass in absolute gift, vest in the surviving spouse, and still qualify for the marital deduction. The purpose for the QTIP is to allow the first spouse to choose the ultimate remainder beneficiaries.

It would also be possible to draft the trust in such a way that upon the first spouse's death a bypass trust and a marital deduction trust with QTIP provisions would automatically be set up. The reason for not doing this in most grantor living trusts is that neither the grantors nor the estate planner can be absolutely sure what kind of assets the grantors will have upon the death of the first of them. The methods described here allow the trustee, by making either an election, a partial election, or no election at all, to adjust to the actual assets on hand at the time of the first spouse's death.

It is important to include spendthrift provisions in a grantor living trust. A spendthrift provision, as discussed in prior chapters, protects the beneficiaries by preventing seizure of trust assets by the beneficiaries' creditors. Such a provision also prohibits sale of any interest in the trust by the beneficiaries. The Texas Trust Code indicates that spendthrift provisions can never be applied so as to protect the grantor from his own debts. When the first spouse dies, the trust, to the extent of the contributions by the deceased spouse, becomes irrevocable for the benefit of the surviving spouse. This is a trust created not for the benefit of the grantor but for the benefit of another person. Consequently, spendthrift provisions would be effective to protect the irrevocable portion of the trust from the imprudence or debts of the surviving spouse/beneficiary.

When preparing a grantor living trust, it is essential also to prepare a pour-over will and a power of attorney with pour-over provisions. The pour-over will is prepared so that upon the death of the first spouse, any assets that spouse has acquired that either were not transferred to the trust, could not be transferred to the trust, or were acquired after the creation of the trust and not transferred to the trust would simply pour over directly into the trust. Another way of saying this is that a will must be prepared in which the devisee of all property is the grantor living trust already in effect.

The goal of the power of attorney is more or less the same, although it provides for incompetency rather than death. If a spouse has acquired assets, either before or after the trust, that were not transferred into the trust and the spouse then becomes incompetent, an attorney in fact will be needed to administer those assets. The attorney in fact probably should be the same person as is appointed trustee of the grantor living trust. The pour-over provision allows the attorney in fact to transfer assets to the trust.

The statutory form of power of attorney [if "(H) estate, trust, and other beneficiary transaction" is selected] provides for pour-over. If the statutory form is not used, a provision such as Example 9-1 should be inserted into the form.

Example 9-1

Peter Smith and Paula Smith of _____ herewith have created a revocable inter vivos trust that is called the Smith Living Trust. I specifically authorize my attorney in fact to make transfers to said trust of any of my property that has not been transferred to the trust or otherwise acquired by the trust, especially during any period in which I may be disabled. As to my interest in said trust, my attorney will not have the authority to revoke or amend the Smith Living Trust, as to my percentage of ownership therein.

Ideally then, in the event a spouse becomes incompetent, the attorney in fact appointed in the power of attorney (being the same person as the trustee) would immediately transfer any assets into the trust.

When the trust document, pour-over wills, and powers of attorney have been signed, it is necessary to transfer all assets of the grantors into the trust. This is essential to the usefulness of the trust. It is at this task that the legal assistant may spend the most time. First, a careful and complete listing of every asset the grantors own must be prepared by the legal assistant, one that not only lists the assets but fully describes them. In some instances the legal assistant will need to obtain the original instruments reflecting the ownership of assets, such as deeds, automobile titles, and stock certificates. Phone calls and letters may be necessary to obtain things like change-of-beneficiary forms from life insurance carriers, managers of pension and retirement funds, and depositories of individual retirement accounts, and stock-transfer forms from transfer agents. The clients will have to be given instructions concerning the changing of ownership of bank accounts and other transactions that they must do personally. The legal assistant should instruct the client to obtain copies of the completed bank signature cards or other proof that the client has carried out the instructions, for the law firm's file.

Deeds to the real estate have to be prepared, executed, and filed of record, and copies will have to be sent to the companies holding any mortgages. It will also be necessary to have the names of the insured on existing casualty insurance on such real property changed to reflect the name of the trust. Stock powers will have to be executed and sent, along with the original stock certificate, to the appropriate transfer agents. Change-of-beneficiary forms will have to be signed, executed, and transmitted. Oil and gas royalty interests may have to be transferred, automobile titles changed, and so on. Sometimes more time is spent doing these things than in preparing the instruments. One must remember that the grantor living trust loses some of its purpose unless every single asset owned by the clients ends up being owned by the trust.

Prior to September 1, 1993, there was substantial question as to what effect transferring the homestead into a trust had, as to both the protection and the ad valorem tax exemptions that homestead creates. Some Texas cases implied that such transfer would not cause the loss of the homestead protection, and a fairly recent case said so directly. However, as to the tax exemption, there was no guidance, and tax assessor-collectors of local taxing districts were taking opposing stances. Effective September 1, 1993, the Texas Legislature created an amendment to the Tax Code stating that the conveyance of the homestead into a revocable trust, a PRT, a QPRT, or a testamentary marital trust does not cause the loss of the homestead exemption.

INSURANCE TRUSTS

The **insurance trust** is an irrevocable trust to which the grantor transfers ownership of a life insurance policy on his life or that, when funded by the grantor, purchases a life insurance policy on the life of the grantor. This is often done to ensure that the ultimate beneficiaries of the grantor either will have the liquidity with which to pay the estate taxes due on his estate or on his surviving spouse's estate or will have funds to lend to the estate for paying federal estate taxes.

Two provisions of the Internal Revenue Code are applicable to the transfer of an insurance policy already owned by the grantor. The first, Section 2035, provides that if the original purchaser of the policy is the insured and the insured dies within three years after the transfer of the policy to a trust, all of the proceeds derived from the payment of the policy will be brought back into the estate for tax purposes. There is some tax law that indicates that if the original purchaser of the policy is the trust, even though the premium payments may be made with money that has been given to the trust by the insured, if the insured dies within three years of the policy purchase the policy proceeds will still be excluded from the insured's estate. Therefore, the trustee must be given the express discretion in the trust document either to purchase or not to purchase life insurance on the grantor's life. If the trustee is required to purchase life insurance, it is very possible that the three-year exclusion rule will be applied. The grantor and the trustee may have an understanding prior to the creation and funding of the trust, but it should not be put in writing, to avoid contractually binding the trustee. If (a) the grantor merely funds a trust with cash, (b) the trust provisions allow, but do not require, the trustee to purchase life insurance on the grantor's life, (c) the grantor does not pay the premiums directly to the insurance company, (d) the insured transfers to the trust more than the exact amount of the premium, and (e) the insured allows a lapse of time before the trustee actually purchases the policy, then existing law will support the position that the three-year rule in Section 2035 does not apply.

The second applicable provision of tax law is the gift tax provision. The transfer of an existing policy will be a gift equal to the present value of the policy. Assuming that the policy is for **straight life insurance** or whole life insurance, the present value is equal to its *cash surrender value*, that is, the amount of money that will be given back to the owner if the owner cancels the policy. The cash surrender value is reduced by any loans made by the insurance company to the owner in the amount of the principal and accrued interest owed.

One way to reduce the cash surrender value to zero or almost zero is to borrow from it a maximum amount. However, if, rather than giving an existing policy to the trust, a trust is set up that is funded with cash and meets all the requirements previously referred to, then the only gift will be the amount of money given, which would usually be within the **annual gift tax exclusion** amount.

It is generally important that the initial gift to the insurance trust and subsequent gifts necessary to pay premiums made to the insurance trust qualify for the annual exclusion under the gift tax provisions. Internal Revenue Code Section 2503(b) provides that whether a transfer to a trust qualifies for the $10,000-per-donee annual gift tax exclusion depends on whether the gift is of a **present interest**. If it is not, under the code provisions it does not qualify for the gift tax exclusion.

This requires the use of the so-called Crummy provisions, the origin of which was discussed in Chapter Three. In the Crummy case, the gift into a trust was ruled to be a present interest because the beneficiaries had a right of withdrawal. Since then there have been many revenue and private letter rulings construing the effect of Crummy. These decisions have required that the withdrawal right be almost absolute. The decisions do allow the power to restrict withdrawal to the greater of $5,000 or 5 percent of the value of the trust principal, which is known as the "five-and-five" rule.

Some estate planners believe that it is dangerous to put any restriction on the right of withdrawal, maintaining that it is safer to leave it up to the beneficiaries' judgment, after having advised them that the purpose is to provide funds, via life insurance benefits, to pay estate tax. Further, the beneficiaries are advised that if the funds to pay the premiums are not available within the trust, then the life insurance policy will lapse for nonpayment, and there will be no funds with which to pay estate tax. Since it is very important to the grantor to maintain the life insurance, there can be a provision included directing that future gifts shall not be subject to withdrawal rights if the beneficiary decides to thwart the purpose of the trust by withdrawing funds under the mandatory withdrawal provision. Future gifts will then not qualify for the annual gift tax exclusion, but the grantor can make gifts of money into the trust to ensure that the insurance policy stays in effect.

In addition to the beneficiaries' having a right of withdrawal, they must be given actual notice each time a gift is made into the trust that is subject to withdrawal, and must have a reasonable opportunity to exercise the right of withdrawal. There is some indication, particularly in the case of minor children, that a single notice that the grantor will make future gifts in a specified amount at specified times is sufficient. If gifts are continued after the minor beneficiaries reach majority, new notice will have to be given, either through their guardian, if they have one, or to their natural parent, which should be the parent other than the grantor if there is such a parent. Some estate planners believe that the beneficiaries may waive future notices. Others suggest that such a waiver may be dangerous and that notices should be sent to the beneficiaries each time a gift to the trust is made. The form for a notice of deposit is found attached to this chapter as Form 9-2.

In addition to other problems and requirements created under the Crummy rule, there is a problem as to whether the right of withdrawal may be made to lapse regarding a particular deposit of funds if the beneficiary elects not to withdraw it within a given time. Such a provision, particularly if used with a five-and-five restriction on the right of withdrawal, may create additional gift tax complications. Again, many estate planners prefer to use an unlimited right of withdrawal, with no lapse due to failure to withdraw, thereby leaving to the beneficiaries the choice of whether to continue the insurance in effect, by allowing the money necessary to pay the premium to stay in the trust.

GRIT, GRAT, GRUT, PRT AND QPRT

All of these forms of trust make use of the same tax savings laws and, therefore, will be discussed together. They are all based on the original GRIT, or grantor-retained income trust, rules, one of whose benefits is that the value of the gift for the purposes of gift tax is reduced by the retained interest of the grantor. The GRIT allows a client to make a substantial gift into a trust, the value of which is be reduced by the grantor's right to receive income from the trust assets during the term of the trust. This requires that the trust be a term trust, that the ownership of the assets placed into trust pass to the remainder beneficiaries upon the expiration of the term, and, further, that the grantor survive the term of the trust. An example is where the grantor creates a trust and funds it with $1.7 million in assets. The trust provides that it is for a term of 10 years and that upon the expiration of that term, the assets will pass to the named remainder beneficiaries; that is, the grantor will no longer have any interest in those assets at all.

Assets transferred into the GRIT become a gift subject to gift tax. The GRIT rules provide that the value of the gift will be reduced by subtracting the grantor's retained interest, except as specified. The value of the retained interest is determined by treasury tables. If, in fact, the federal **midterm rate** applicable at the beginning of the trust is close to 11 percent, then (using the treasury tables) the retained interest of the grantor would be approximately $1.1 million. By using the Unified Gift Tax Credit with an exemption equivalent of $600,000, there would be zero gift tax. Therefore, the client can transfer approximately $1.7 million, provided the federal midterm rate is high enough, to a trust with absolutely zero gift and estate tax consequences, assuming that the grantor survives the trust term. The grantor, however, has depleted his unified credit, so it will not be available to shelter any part of his estate.

One of the catches to the GRIT rule is that the grantor must survive the term of the trust. The longer the term of the trust, the more value to the grantor's retained interest, but also the greater chance that the grantor will die prior to the expiration of the term. If this happens, the entire value of the assets in the trust will be placed in the grantor's estate for the purpose of calculating estate tax. Once estate tax is calculated, then any gift tax paid at the time the grantor transferred the property into trust will be credited against the tax.

Section 2702 of the Internal Revenue Code, which was part of the Omnibus Budget Reconciliation Act of 1990, has the effect of negating some of the benefits of the GRIT. That section values the retained interest at zero if the remainder beneficiaries are members of the grantor's family and the grantor or another family member retains an interest in the trust. Family members include the grantor's spouse, any ancestors or lineal descendants of the grantor or the spouses of any ancestors or lineal descendants, the brothers or sisters of the grantor, and any spouse of a brother or sister of the grantor.

There are exceptions created to this rule in the case of a qualified annuity interest or a qualified uni-trust interest and also in the case of a personal residence GRIT or a qualified personal residence GRIT. These exceptions then provide the basis for the personal residence trust (PRT), the qualified personal residence trust (QPRT), the GRAT (grantor-retained annuity trust), and the GRUT (grantor-retained uni-trust.)

The GRAT and GRUT have to meet some highly technical requirements, the scope of which is beyond the purpose of this text. However, a qualified annuity means the grantor retains an irrevocable right to receive a fixed amount in each taxable year of the term. The fixed amount must be a stated dollar amount, payable periodically but not less frequently than annually and only if the amount paid in one year does not exceed 120 percent of the amount payable in the preceding year or a fixed fraction of the initial fair market value of the property transferred to the trust. This last also has to be payable periodically but not less frequently than annually and only if the amount produced by application of the fraction does not exceed 120 percent of the amount payable in the preceding year.

The GRUT, on the other hand, in order to qualify must provide that the grantor has an irrevocable right to receive, at least annually, a fixed percentage of the net fair market value of the trust assets as determined annually. One advantage of the GRAT or GRUT is that, although the trust must fix the term, the term may be for the life of the term holder. Also, by IRS rule, the death of a grantor during the term does not necessarily require inclusion of the entire amount of the trust assets in the grantor's gross estate.

With regard to the PRT and the QPRT, Section 2702 provides an exception to the zeroing-out of the grantor's retained interest. This is in the case of a GRIT into which is placed the residence of a grantor, who retains the right to use the residence for a stated number of years, after which the residence passes to the named beneficiaries, who can be family. If the grantor survives the term of the trust, the property passes to the remainder beneficiaries, with no additional tax, and is not included in the grantor's estate. On the other hand, if the grantor does not survive the term of the trust, the property is included in the grantor's estate, but a credit is given for any gift tax paid at the time the trust was established.

Personal residence is defined as the principal residence of the term holder and one other residence, as defined in other statutes. This allows the creation of a trust containing both the grantor's homestead and a vacation or summer home, or the creation of two trusts, one with the homestead and the other with the vacation home.

With these trusts, although the grantor can retain use of the residence during the term of the trust, title must pass absolutely to the remainder beneficiaries upon the expiration of the term of the trust. In this case, the value of the gift will be the market value of the personal residences, less the retained interest, again calculated according to the treasury tables.

If the grantor desires to retain possession of the residence after expiration of the term, he can enter into a lease with the remainder beneficiaries, or he can repurchase the residence from the trust prior to termination. The latter course of action results in cash ending up in the trust rather than in the house.

The main difference between the PRT and the QPRT is that in the QPRT the grantor is able to put additional assets into the trust. This is limited to cash which is not to exceed the amount required for the payment of trust expenses, including mortgage payments, either already incurred or reasonably expected to be paid within six months from the date the cash is contributed to the trust, for improvements to be paid within six months or for the purchase of a replacement residence within three months. In addition, a QPRT is permitted to hold improvements to the residence and proceeds from the sale of the residence or from insurance policies payable as a result of damage to the residence.

The definition of personal residence excludes personal property but includes such improvements to real property as used by the term holder for residential purposes. The amount of land is limited to what is reasonably appropriate for residential purposes. A 200-acre farm with house, barns, pens, fences, storage area, etc. would not qualify, because it includes assets in excess of what may be considered reasonably appropriate for residential purposes.

Finally, although Section 2702 zeroes-out the value of the retained interest of the grantor in a GRIT in which the beneficiaries are the family members of the grantor, it continues the effectiveness of a GRIT established with beneficiaries other than members of the grantor's family. As an example, the grantor can create a GRIT for nieces and nephews, who do not come within the definition of the grantor's family members.

CHILDREN AND/OR GRANDCHILDREN TRUSTS

The trusts dealt with here could also be for a spouse or for any relative or friend. The trust is designed to be a receptacle for gifts, both of property subject to rapid appreciation on which the grantor pays the gift tax or for which he uses a portion of his unified credit and of gifts that qualify for the annual $10,000 exclusion.

The annual exclusion includes all gifts, such as special-occasion gifts like birthday, Christmas, or other holiday gifts. For most clients, the annual gift to such a trust will be less than $10,000, to retain some of the $10,000 exclusion to shelter birthday and other gifts. If, on the other hand, the beneficiary of the trust is not a person to whom the grantor makes such gifts, the grantor can give the full $10,000 to the trust each year. If the trust is established by both husband and wife, then the husband and wife combined can give up to $20,000 each year to the trust. By establishing a separate trust for each child or grandchild or other individual, the grantors can make such gifts to each trust, thereby transferring from their assets to the trust $20,000 per year multiplied by the number of trusts, with no tax consequence and without using any portion of either of their unified credits. For example, with three children, the grantors could transfer $60,000 per year from their ownership to the childrens'. If both grantors lived an additional 20 years, this would have the effect of transferring $1.2 million out of the estate of the grantors to the children, with no gift or estate tax consequences. This alone would produce an estate tax savings of as much as $660,000.

In order to qualify the gifts to the trust for the annual tax exclusion, the trust must contain Crummy provisions. Notice must be given to the beneficiaries of their right to withdraw any nontestamentary gifts made to the trust.

The trust will be authorized to purchase life insurance on the life of one or both of the grantors and will be given the power to lend money to the estate of the last surviving grantor for the purpose of paying federal estate tax. If this is done, the tax savings can be even larger, although the trust corpus will be depleted by the premiums necessary to purchase life insurance. There is no reason why the purchase of life insurance has to be limited to just the amount needed to pay federal estate taxes. The life insurance can be in an amount far beyond that, thereby providing a much larger tax-free estate and increased tax savings to the ultimate recipients.

The estate planner will want to add spendthrift provisions to the trust to protect the beneficiaries from creditors seizing trust assets. He may very well want to have pour-over devises in the will, naming the trust as devisee. In this manner, no creditor can ever acquire right to seize any portion of the monies given on behalf of or devised to that particular beneficiary. It is for this reason that these trusts are often used for spouses as well as for children and grandchildren.

The typical trust is for a child and for the children of that child. As generally created, the trust is irrevocable and is designed to continue for the life of the children. During his life, the beneficiary has the right to the income of the trust; however, the principal of the trust can be used also for his needs, if the trust contains a provision allowing the invasion of the corpus by the trustee. Also, the typical child beneficiary has the right by the power of appointment contained in the trust to appoint the remainder beneficiaries who will receive the trust property upon his death, though this is often limited to his children, grandchildren, relatives, or charitable organizations.

This last feature is not necessary, and the trust can specify who is to be the remainder beneficiary. This trust will be subject to the generation-skipping transfer tax (GSTT) (which will be discussed in detail in Chapter 15). It is possible to draft the trust so as not to be subject to the GSTT by giving the power to the child of the grantor, who is the income beneficiary, to withdraw the entire corpus of the trust during the beneficiary's life. This typically provides that the beneficiary has the right to withdraw the principal of the trust in a number of installments, often three. An example would be a provision allowing the beneficiary to withdraw one-third of the value of the trust property at age 25, another third at age 35, and the entire remaining principal at age 45. This right of withdrawal is in addition to the right of withdrawal required to qualify with the Crummy decision. If the beneficiary elects not to make such withdrawals, that amount will continue in trust, passing to his children unless he exercises his power of appointment in some other fashion.

The reason the beneficiary child is given a power of appointment to determine the remainder beneficiaries is to allow that child to adjust to facts that come into existence after the creation of the trust that the grantor may have not been able to foresee and that, because the trust is irrevocable, the grantor has no power to adjust to. This power of appointment would typically allow the child who is the immediate beneficiary of the trust to state that the trust will not terminate upon his death but will continue for his children for a specified period of time.

As mentioned earlier, it is not necessary to create the power of appointment; however, since the purpose is to avoid generation-skipping transfer taxes, it is generally suggested to include, in addition to the right of withdrawal just discussed, the power to appoint the remainder beneficiaries upon termination. Even though the trust for children and grandchildren may be subject to the GSTT, the GSTT allows a lifetime $1 million exclusion to each donor. Thus, spouses could make a $2 million generation-skipping transfer in the form of a trust for the benefit of grandchildren without incurring generation-skipping transfer tax.

If the trust constitutes a "direct skip" (see Chapter Fifteen), the value of the gift is determined at the time of the gift, and therefore appreciation of the trust assets can result in the grandchildren's receiving far more than $2 million, none of it subject to the GSTT. On the other hand, if the trust is drawn so that the gift to the grandchildren constitutes a **taxable distribution** or a **taxable termination**, the value of the gift will not be determined until it is made, which means the $2 million originally placed in the trust and any appreciation in value or income not distributed to someone else would be added to the $2 million, resulting in a liability for GSTT.

The benefits of the trust discussed here are as follows:

1. The trust constitutes a vehicle for gifts of property subject to rapid appreciation in value, thereby fixing the value of the gift at the time the gift is made rather than at the time of death of the grantor.

2. Because it contains Crummy provisions, it also becomes a vehicle for making tax-free gifts within the annual $10,000 gift tax exclusion.

3. Because the trust is also a life insurance trust, it may own life insurance on the life of either the beneficiaries' parent or the beneficiary.

4. The child can be trustee of the trust, provided that distributions to the child are limited to income and principal, but only such principal as is necessary to provide for the beneficiary's health, education, support, and maintenance.

5. Because the trust contains spendthrift provisions, it protects the assets of the trust from seizure by creditors of the beneficiary or of the beneficiary's spouse, from seizure by the creditors of the remainder beneficiaries, from division in beneficiaries' divorce proceedings, and against such unexpected catastrophic losses as failure of business, tort liability, and unknown liability incurred by marriage or entry into a business relationship. The spendthrift provisions of a trust protect the assets of the trust even against the Internal Revenue Service.

6. The trust is designed to pass to third-generation beneficiaries (grandchildren) the maximum amount allowed by law, free of federal estate tax and with the smallest possible GSTT.

CHARITABLE REMAINDER TRUSTS

The charitable remainder trust is a transfer tax exclusion vehicle. If properly created and funded, it can increase the grantor's spendable income, avoid capital gains tax, reduce the grantor's income tax, reduce the grantor's estate tax, pass additional wealth to the grantor's beneficiary, and be a significant gift to charity.

The use of the charitable remainder trust is complicated and must be properly documented. There are many ways to structure the charitable remainder trust. It can be arranged as a charitable remainder annuity trust or charitable remainder uni-trust. It can even reverse the traditional GRIT, GRAT, and GRUT configuration by giving the retained income to a charity, thereby receiving a charitable contribution equal to the annuity over the term of the trust or the uni-trust distributions over the period of the trust.

In its simplest form, however, the grantor or grantors (if husband and wife) create a charitable trust with someone other than themselves as trustee. The trust is irrevocable and provides that all income during the life of the grantors or their survivor shall be paid to the grantors. The trust terminates upon the death of the last of the grantors, and the remainder beneficiary is a tax-exempt charity.

Because of the gift in trust to the charity, the grantors are entitled to an income tax deduction equal to the present value of the gift. "Present value" means the same as previously discussed with reference to the GRIT rules. This is, in fact, a GRIT with a charitable remainder. The trust then pays the income to the grantors for the remainder of their life or the life of their survivor, and, upon termination, there is no estate tax because there is an unlimited deduction against estate tax equal to the amount of gifts to qualified charities.

The client might say, "I want to give my property to my children. I don't want to give it all to a charity, or even a significant amount of it, and so the charitable remainder trust is of no benefit to me." However, consider the following example: One creates a charitable trust and puts in it property worth a million dollars, with the result that, upon the death of the last grantor, the charity receives $1 million worth of property. But the trust also generates $1 million worth of property that passes to the children, while the grantor still receives income during his life and an income tax deduction for the charitable donation.

This is a situation in which the grantors own property in which they have a very low **adjusted basis** and that has appreciated greatly in value. Perhaps they no longer want to manage this property, or perhaps the time is right to sell it to obtain maximum profit. If they sell, they may have federal income taxes of $250,000 or more. Then, in addition, assuming they keep the remainder of the $750,000 intact and defer the tax on that $750,000 via a marital deduction when the surviving spouse dies, the estate tax may be as high as $375,000. The $1 million has been reduced to $375,000 because of income and estate taxes.

On the other hand, if they place that property in a charitable remainder trust and the trustee then sells the property, since the charitable trust is tax exempt, it pays no tax on the sale whatsoever. In addition, the husband and wife will receive a tax deduction for the gift to the charitable trust that might approximate $200,000 to be spread over several years. They will receive higher income from the charitable trust than if they had sold the property themselves and had to pay the tax on it and then invest the remainder. A portion of this income will be tax sheltered by the charitable deduction. If they use a portion of their tax savings and perhaps a portion of the trust income, if necessary, to make gifts into a life insurance trust that purchases a $1 million life insurance policy that pays on the death of the last of them, then they have given to the charity a million dollars, will leave at least a million dollars to their children, and will receive income for the remainder of their life in excess of what they would have received had they simply sold the asset and invested the balance remaining after the payment of capital gains tax.

EDUCATIONAL TRUSTS

An educational trust can be either in the form of a Section 2503(c) trust or in the form of the Crummy trust. The 2053(c) trust requires that the trust principal and income be expended by, or for the benefit of, the beneficiary before he attains the age of 21. To the extent it is not expended, the trust principal and income pass to the beneficiary when she obtains the age of 21. If the beneficiary dies before age 21, the trust principal and income must be payable to his estate.

The Crummy trust can be made to continue after the 21st birthday of a minor provided that Crummy rights of withdrawal are a part of the trust. The 2053(c) trust cannot be made to extend beyond the 21st birthday and consequently is often used for an educational trust, based on the assumption that the children will have nearly completed their education by the age of 21. A 2053(c) trust can be used for grandchildren or other direct lineal descendants as well as for children and will qualify for the GSTT exclusion.

An alternative for providing for the education of a child or other direct lineal descendant to make gifts pursuant to the Texas Uniform Gift to Minors Act; these will also qualify for the annual exclusion. However, under the Uniform Gift to Minors Act, the child is entitled to absolute ownership of the funds upon reaching his 18th birthday. This may not adequately take care of educational needs.

Another way is by outright gifts. The annual exclusion from gift tax is $10,000, but in addition, payments to an educational organization as tuition for the education of a donee and payments to any person who provides medical care for the donee are excluded. The GSTT, like the gift tax, has an annual exclusion of $10,000, so the gifts can be for the education of a grandchild as well as of a child.

CHAPTER QUESTIONS AND EXERCISES

1. Using the discussion in the chapter and Form 9-1, prepare an outline, with a short explanation or summary, of the clauses or provisions of Form 9-1.

2. Discuss the relative benefits and detriments of a grantor living trust. Be critical, and look for benefits and detriments other than those discussed in the chapter. Be prepared to support your conclusions in a class discussion.

3. Using the text material, class discussion, and Form 9-1, prepare a checklist designed to obtain all of the information needed to prepare a grantor living trust, collateral documents, and property transfers to the living trust. Again, be prepared to support your work in a class discussion.

4. List all documents needed to carry out the purposes and goals of a grantor living trust, together with all assets that a grantor might own that would require transfer to the trust. Do not limit yourself to those discussed in the book. See if you can identify types or kinds of assets not identified in this chapter.

5. Be prepared to discuss in class the steps that a legal assistant will need to take in order to transfer assets to a living trust.

6. Explain the use of insurance trusts to provide liquidity, enhance assets, and take advantage of the gift tax annual exclusion.

7. Explain fully the application of the Crummy rule to gifts to trusts designed to take advantage of the gift tax annual exclusion.

8. Using the chapter discussion, Form 9-1, and any other trust forms either in the book or elsewhere, list the steps you would take to change Form 9-1 from a grantor living trust to an insurance trust. As to new or modified clauses, be specific setting out the language changed or added.

9. Discuss the applicability, benefits, and limitations of GRITs.

10. Explain briefly the various types of grantor-retained interest trusts.

11. Explain fully the use of children's/grandchildren's trusts.

12. List various ways in which a client may make provision for the educational needs of descendants while achieving a tax advantage.

13. Explain the benefits of a charitable-remainder trust.

Form 9-1: Living Trust

This living trust was prepared using PRODOC™, Document Assembly Software for Legal Professionals and the Wills Module, both distributed by Automated Legal Systems, of Universal City, Texas, Allan Schoolcraft, President.

THE SMITH LIVING TRUST

THIS AGREEMENT OF TRUST is made and executed at San Juan Hill, Rough Rider County, Texas, on this the _____ day of _____, 1994, by and between PETER SMITH and PAULA SMITH, hereinafter referred to as "Settlors", or as "Settlor" when reference is made to only one of them, and PETER SMITH and PAULA SMITH, hereinafter referred to as Trustees, of this trust known as **THE SMITH LIVING TRUST**.

WITNESSETH:

WHEREAS, the Settlors wish to establish a revocable trust by transferring the assets described on the attached Schedule A to the Trustees to hold and administer upon the terms and conditions set forth in this Trust Agreement; and

WHEREAS, Settlors contemplate that they may, by inter vivos document, transfer other assets and property to the Trustees, to be added to the trust estate; and

WHEREAS, the Trustees are willing to hold and administer such property as they may receive upon the terms and conditions set forth in this Trust Agreement;

NOW, THEREFORE, in consideration of the mutual covenants herein contained, the Settlors and the Trustees do hereby agree as follows:

ARTICLE I.
Trust Estate

Settlors have conveyed, transferred, and assigned and do by these presents convey, transfer, and assign unto the Trustees the assets and properties described on Schedule A attached hereto and made a part hereof. Such assets and properties shall be held, administered, and distributed as a revocable, amendable trust, subject to the provisions hereof, for the uses and purposes hereinafter set out. Settlors or any other person or persons may by a written document, by a Will, or by naming the Trustees as beneficiary of life insurance or employee benefit plan proceeds, deliver to the Trustees at any time and from time to time additional assets and properties acceptable to the Trustees, which additional assets and properties shall be held, administered, and distributed pursuant to this Trust Agreement. No gift, change or transfer of community property or separate property interests is intended by the terms of this trust during the joint lives of Settlors. Investment or income-producing assets and property added to this trust during the joint lives of Settlors, and the income therefrom, shall be considered as community property of Settlors by the Trustees unless when delivered said property is designated in writing to be the separate property of one of the Settlors. The Trustees shall maintain records and accounts to appropriately identify such property, with all income being designated and identified as the community property of Settlors; provided, however, that the Trustees shall have no duty to characterize property of the trust as community or separate property and shall have the right to rely on representations of Settlors, or either of them, as to such property's character. Any property subsequently withdrawn from the trust estate shall have the same character as community or separate property which it would have had if it had never become a part of the trust estate.

ARTICLE II.
Identification of Beneficiaries

The primary beneficiaries of this trust are the Settlors, PETER SMITH and PAULA SMITH. After the surviving Settlor's death and pursuant to the terms of Article VII below, the trust may continue for the benefit of the children of Settlors, namely PETER SMITH, JR. and PENELOPE SMITH.

ARTICLE III.
Revocability of Trust

This trust is revocable during Settlors' joint lives. Settlors shall have the power and right to amend, modify or revoke, in whole or in part, this agreement or any terms or provisions thereof by notice in writing delivered to the Trustees. Such amendment, modification or revocation shall be effective immediately upon delivery to the Trustees, except that changes with respect to the Trustees' duties, liabilities or compensation shall not be effective without the Trustees' written consent. Settlors shall further have the power and right to require and direct the Trustees to distribute to Settlors or to any other person designated by Settlors any property or properties held by the Trustees hereunder; provided, however, either Settlor shall have the unlimited right during the time that both Settlors are living to withdraw all or any part of the trust corpus which is the separate property of such withdrawing Settlor. Upon the death of first Settlor to die, the then remaining trust estate shall be divided as provided in Article V below. Thereupon the trust estate designated by the name of the deceased Settlor shall be irrevocable and not subject to amendment or change by the surviving Settlor or any person whomsoever. The trust estate designated by the name of the surviving Settlor shall continue to be revocable and subject to amendment, modification or revocation, in whole or in part, as provided above.

Form 9-1: (continued)

ARTICLE IV.
Distributions While Both Settlors Are Living

If during the joint lives of Settlors there shall be transferred to the Trustees, to be held in accordance with the terms of this Trust Agreement, investment or income-producing assets, then so long as both Settlors shall live, there shall be distributed to or for the benefit of Settlors so much of the trust income and corpus as Settlors shall from time to time direct in writing. Initially and until further written notice from Settlors to the Trustees, the Trustees shall distribute to Settlors the net trust income. In the event of the incapacity of either Settlor or both of them then, notwithstanding any prior written instructions to the contrary, the Trustees may distribute to or for the benefit of either or both of Settlors so much of the trust income and corpus as the Trustees shall determine, in their sole discretion, to be necessary and appropriate to provide for the health, maintenance and support of Settlors. Any income not so distributed shall be added to corpus. The Trustees shall, for the purpose of this Article IV, be the sole judge of a Settlor's incapacity; no judicial determination shall be required and the Trustees shall incur no liability to any person whomsoever for making distributions to or for the benefit of Settlors, or either of them, upon the Trustees' determination of a Settlor's incapacity.

ARTICLE V.
Distributions Upon Death of First Settlor to Die

Upon the death of the first Settlor to die, the trust estate shall be disposed of as follows:

A. If one Settlor shall survive the other Settlor by ninety (90) days, the trust estate shall be divided into two (2) separate trust shares, each trust share being composed of the respective Settlor's one-half (1/2) community property interest and all of such Settlor's separate property interest in the trust, and such trust shares shall be designated as the "THE PETER SMITH TRUST" and "THE PAULA SMITH TRUST". Except as otherwise specifically provided herein, "THE PETER SMITH TRUST" and "THE PAULA SMITH TRUST" shall be deemed and referred to for the purposes herein as one trust and any distributions of income or corpus by the Trustees on behalf of the surviving Settlor shall be made equally from each trust. The trust estate shall continue to be held, administered and distributed for the following uses and purposes, and subject to the following provisions, conditions and limitations:

   A. Income. During the life of the surviving Settlor, the Trustee shall pay to the surviving Settlor, at such intervals as the Trustee may determine, so much or all of the net income as the Trustee, in the Trustee's sole and absolute discretion, deems necessary and appropriate to provide for the health, maintenance, and support of the surviving Settlor in accordance with his or her station in life. Any income not distributed shall be accumulated and added to the corpus of the trust.

   B. Special Distributions of Corpus. If at any time during the existence of the trust, the net income which shall be distributed to the surviving Settlor under the terms hereof shall not be adequate in the opinion of the Trustee for the surviving Settlor's health, maintenance and support in accordance with his or her station in life considering all other sources of income available to him or her, then the Trustee may make supplemental distributions of corpus out of the trust directly to the surviving Settlor to the extent and in the manner that the Trustee may deem advisable. Distribution of the entire corpus of the trust is authorized if the Trustee shall determine such distribution to be in the best interest of the surviving Settlor in accordance with the foregoing standard.

   C. Reserve for Taxes and Obligations. Upon the death of the surviving Settlor, the Trustee shall be authorized to withhold from distribution an amount of property sufficient, in the Trustee's judgment, to cover any liability that may be imposed upon the Trustee or the trust for estate, excise, or inheritance taxes attributable to the inclusion of the trust property in the surviving Settlor's estate and to pay such liabilities out of the trust. The Trustee is further authorized, in the Trustee's sole and absolute discretion, to withhold from distribution, as much property that is sufficient to pay any of the surviving Settlor's obligations (including all taxes) or expenses with respect to the administration of his or her estate and to pay such obligations or expenses out of the trust. Any payment made pursuant to this paragraph may be paid directly or made to the legal representative of the surviving Settlor's estate, as the Trustee deems advisable. Upon the Trustee being satisfied that the Trustee no longer has any liability with respect to such taxes, and that the Trustee need not pay such liabilities, obligations and expenses, the balance of such withheld property shall be distributed in accordance with the applicable provisions of the preceding paragraph. The Trustee's selection of assets to be sold to make payments pursuant to this paragraph, and the tax effects thereof, shall not be subject to question by any beneficiary hereof. Likewise, neither the trust nor any trust beneficiary shall be entitled to reimbursement from the surviving Settlor's estate or his or her heirs or devisees on account of any payment made pursuant to this paragraph.

Form 9-1: (continued)

ARTICLE VI.
Distributions Upon the Death of the Last Settlor To Die

Upon the death of the surviving Settlor, the entire trust estate shall be distributed, subject to the following provisions, conditions and limitations, and subject to restrictions imposed upon distribution because of age as hereinafter provided, outright and FREE FROM TRUST, in equal shares, to Settlors' children, PETER SMITH, JR. and PENELOPE SMITH. Provided, however, the share of a deceased child of Settlors shall be distributed outright and FREE OF TRUST to the issue, per stirpes, of such deceased child, subject to restrictions imposed upon distribution because of age as hereinafter provided, or if said deceased child of Settlors has no issue surviving, then the share of such deceased child shall be distributed outright and FREE OF TRUST to the child of Settlors surviving at the time of the death of the last Settlor to die, or his or her issue, per stirpes. If the children of Settlors, and their issue, should die prior to the death of the Settlor who is the last to die, the then remaining corpus and undistributed income of THE PETER SMITH TRUST shall be distributed outright and FREE OF TRUST to the heirs-at-law of PETER SMITH and the then remaining corpus and undistributed income of THE PAULA SMITH TRUST shall be distributed outright and FREE OF TRUST to the heirs-at-law of PAULA SMITH. Provided, however, if both PETER SMITH and PAULA SMITH shall die simultaneously or at any time prior to the division of the trust estate as hereinabove provided, the then remaining corpus and undistributed income of the combined trust estate shall be divided into two (2) separate trust shares, each trust share being composed of the respective Settlor's one-half (1/2) community property interest and all of such Settlor's separate property interest in the then remaining trust, and each separate trust share shall be distributed outright and FREE OF TRUST to the heirs-at-law of its respective Settlor. The identity and respective shares of such heirs (as hereinafter defined in Article XIII) shall be determined in all respects as if the deaths of the Settlors had occurred immediately following the happening of the event requiring such distribution, and according to the laws of the State of Texas then in force governing the distribution of the estate of an intestate.

ARTICLE VII.
Restrictions Upon Distribution Because of Age

In the event that any beneficiary has not reached the age of twenty-one(21) years, then the Trustee shall hold the share or shares of such beneficiary, IN TRUST NEVERTHELESS, for the uses and purposes hereinafter set forth.

A. The Trustee, in the Trustee's discretion, shall distribute to or for the benefit of each beneficiary, as much of the income, and in addition, so much of the corpus of each separate, per stirpes share or trust created for that particular beneficiary as the Trustee shall consider necessary or advisable for his or her health, support, education, and maintenance.

B. Any income or corpus not so distributed or used shall be separately accumulated for each beneficiary, or his or her issue, and the separate, per stirpes share or trust distributed to said beneficiary when he or she reaches the age of twenty-one(21) years, at which time the Trustee shall transfer, convey, deliver and pay over to said beneficiary, FREE FROM TRUST, all of the property then constituting his or her trust estate.

C. If any beneficiary of a share or trust being held for his or her benefit shall die before complete distribution of his or her trust estate, then upon the death of such beneficiary, the share or trust shall be distributed outright and FREE OF TRUST to the issue, per stirpes, of such deceased beneficiary, subject to restrictions imposed upon distribution because of age as hereinabove provided, or if said deceased beneficiary has no issue surviving, then the share of such deceased beneficiary shall be distributed outright and FREE OF TRUST to the child of Settlors surviving at the time of the death of the last Settlor to die, or his or her issue, per stirpes.

D. Any share or portion of a share of any trust that has not been disposed of under any other provision of this Trust Agreement from THE PETER SMITH TRUST shall be distributed outright and FREE OF TRUST to the heirs-at-law of PETER SMITH and any share or portion of a share of any trust that has not been disposed of under any other provision of this Trust Agreement from THE PAULA SMITH TRUST shall be distributed outright and FREE OF TRUST the heirs-at-law of PAULA SMITH. The identity and respective shares of such heirs (as hereinafter defined in Article XIII) shall be determined in all respects as if the deaths of the Settlors had occurred immediately following the happening of the event requiring such distribution, and according to the laws of the State of Texas then in force governing the distribution of the estate of an intestate.

Form 9-1: (continued)

ARTICLE VIII.
General Provisions Relating to the Trustees

All of the provisions of this Article VIII are applicable to all trusts and shares created by this Trust Agreement.

A.   Joint Control. Except as otherwise stated herein, in any event when two trustees are serving, the rights, powers, duties and discretions of the trustees shall be exercisable jointly, except for the original, initial Trustees, PETER SMITH and PAULA SMITH, each of whom may act singly without the joinder of the other. In any event when more than two trustees are serving jointly hereunder, unless otherwise stated herein, the rights, powers, duties and discretions shall be exercisable by a majority vote of the trustees then serving.

B.   Succession of Trustees During the Lifetime of Both Settlors. The initial Trustees of the trust created by this Trust Agreement shall be PETER SMITH and PAULA SMITH. If either PETER SMITH or PAULA SMITH should fail or cease to serve as Trustee for any reason, the other Settlor shall continue to serve singly as Trustee. If both PETER SMITH and PAULA SMITH should fail or cease to serve as Trustees for any reason, then PETER SMITH, JR. shall serve as successor Trustee. If PETER SMITH, JR. should fail or cease to serve as Trustee for any reason, then a successor trustee shall be appointed in the manner and with the qualifications pursuant to the terms of this Trust Agreement set forth in the paragraph below entitled "APPOINTMENT OF SUCCESSOR TRUSTEES".

C.   Succession of Trustees After Death of First Settlor To Die. Upon the death of the first Settlor to die, the surviving Settlor shall serve singly as Trustee of both trusts hereinabove created as "THE PETER SMITH TRUST" and "THE PAULA SMITH TRUST". If the surviving Settlor should fail or cease to serve as Trustee for any reason, then PETER SMITH, JR. shall serve as successor Trustee. If PETER SMITH, JR. should fail or cease to serve as Trustee for any reason, then a successor trustee shall be appointed in the manner and with the qualifications pursuant to the terms of this Trust Agreement set forth in the paragraph below entitled "APPOINTMENT OF SUCCESSOR TRUSTEES".

D.   Removal of Trustees. The Settlors, or the surviving Settlor, (including the legal guardian or legal representative of a Settlor, in the case that a Settlor is under legal disability), or after the death of both Settlors, a majority of the trust beneficiaries (including a beneficiary's natural or legal guardian or legal representative, in the case that a beneficiary is under legal disability) who might then be entitled to receive a distribution from the trust estate, shall have the power to remove any trustee and successor trustees then serving hereunder and further, the power to appoint a successor trustee. If a trustee is removed, such trustee must be replaced by another trustee in the manner and with the qualifications pursuant to the terms of this Trust Agreement set forth in the paragraph below entitled "APPOINTMENT OF SUCCESSOR TRUSTEES". Such removal shall be by a written document, duly executed and acknowledged by the removing parties and by the successor trustee appointed as the replacement trustee, and shall be filed for record in the Real Property Records of Nueces County, Texas. The successor trustee shall promptly deliver a copy of such recorded document to the trustee being removed and then serving and the delivery of such recorded document shall immediately deprive the removed trustee of all powers as trustee hereunder. No purchaser or other person dealing with any trustee serving hereunder is obligated to examine the County records and such person or persons shall be protected in all transactions made with any trustee serving hereunder, whether or not any such replacement has taken place.

E.   Resignation of Trustees. Any trustee serving hereunder is authorized to resign by filing a document, duly executed and acknowledged by the resigning trustee, for record in the Real Property Records of Nueces County, Texas, which filing shall immediately deprive such resigning trustee of all powers as trustee hereunder; provided, nevertheless, that at least thirty (30) days prior to filing such document, the resigning Trustee shall give written notice thereof to the Settlors, or the surviving Settlor, (including the legal guardian or legal representative of a Settlor, in the case that a Settlor is under legal disability), or after the death of both Settlors, a majority of the trust beneficiaries (including a beneficiary's natural or legal guardian or legal representative, in the case that a beneficiary is under legal disability) who might then be entitled to receive a distribution from the trust estate.

F.   Appointment of Successor Trustees. If any trustee appointed or serving pursuant to this Trust Agreement should fail or cease to serve as trustee for any reason and no trustee has been named in this document to serve as successor, or if all successor trustees named herein have failed or ceased to serve for any reason, then the Settlors, or the surviving Settlor, (including the legal guardian or legal representative of a Settlor, in the case that a Settlor is under legal disability), or after the death of both Settlors, a majority of the trust beneficiaries (including a beneficiary's natural or legal guardian or legal representative, in the case of a beneficiary under a legal disability) who might then be entitled to receive a distribution from the trust estate, shall have the power to appoint, as successor trustee, any national or state bank or trust company possessing trust powers and having a capital, surplus and undivided profits of at least Twenty Million Dollars, or any individual regardless of domicile. Such appointment shall be made by a written document, duly executed and acknowledged by the

Form 9-1: (continued)

appointing parties and by the successor trustee being appointed, and shall be filed for record in the Real Property Records of Nueces County, Texas. If a successor trustee is not appointed as herein-above provided, then a court of competent jurisdiction shall appoint a successor trustee with the qualifications set forth above, and the costs associated with such a court proceeding shall be paid from the trust or trusts for which the successor trustee is appointed.

G. Relinquishment of Powers. Any trustee may release or relinquish any one or more of any powers, rights or privileges which, in the trustee's judgment, unless released or relinquished, might result in adverse consequences to the trust estate or any beneficiary because of changes in law or interpretation of the law. Any such release or relinquishment shall be made by a written document, duly executed and acknowledged by said trustee, and shall be filed for record in the Real Property Records of Nueces County, Texas. After any power has been so released or relinquished, it shall never again be exercised by such trustee.

H. Compensation and Bond. Any trustee serving hereunder shall be reimbursed for any and all expenses incurred while acting as trustee of the trust created pursuant to the provisions hereof, and in addition any corporate trustee shall receive fair and reasonable compensation for services as trustee in accordance with the corporate trustee's regular fee schedules as published from time to time. No trustee serving hereunder shall be required to furnish bond or any other security, and all rights, powers, authorities, privileges and discretions herein conferred upon any trustee authorized to serve hereunder shall be exercised without the supervision of any court, it being intended that so far as can be legally provided the trustee serving shall be completely free of all court supervision of any kind, including the requirements of any accounting; provided, however, that the then serving trustee shall furnish an accounting to any beneficiary or guardian of any beneficiary upon reasonable demand made therefor.

I. Powers and Duties of Successor Trustees. On the appointment and qualification of any successor trustee, the same duties shall devolve on and the same rights, powers, authorities, privileges, and discretions shall inure to such successor trustee as to the Trustees originally designated hereunder. All rights, powers, authorities, privileges and discretions shall be exercised without the supervision of any court. No successor trustee shall have any duty, responsibility, obligation or liability whatsoever for the acts, defaults or omissions of any predecessor trustee. Any successor trustee named herein shall be responsible only for the assets delivered by the preceding trustee, or his or her legal representative, and may accept as correct the statements of such predecessor, or his or her legal representative, that these constitute all of the assets of the trust estate, without any duty to inquire into the administration or accounting by the preceding trustee. No successor trustee shall be held responsible for and by reason of any act or omission of a predecessor in trust.

J. Reorganization of any Corporate Trustee. Any corporation or national or state banking association that shall succeed to all or the greater part of the assets of any corporate trustee serving hereunder by purchase, merger, consolidation, or otherwise, shall succeed to all the rights, duties, and functions of such corporate trustee as trustee under all trusts governed by this Trust Agreement for which the corporate trustee is then serving or may serve as trustee.

ARTICLE IX.
General Provisions Relating to the Trust

A. Situs of Trust. The trusts created herein shall be deemed Texas trusts and shall, in all respects, be governed by the laws of the State of Texas. However, if the Trustees, in the Trustees' sole discretion, determines that a change of situs would be beneficial to the purposes of any separate trust established by this Trust Agreement, the Trustees shall have the discretion and authority to change the situs of any such trust to another state. Formal notice of any change of situs may be given by filing of record a written declaration in the Real Property Records of Nueces County, Texas. If the situs of any such trust is changed to another state, then the trust shall, in all respects, be governed by the laws of the state which is the new situs. No such change of situs shall be authorized herein, however, which would result in a termination of the trust for federal tax purposes.

B. Small Trust Provision. Any provision of this Trust Agreement to the contrary notwithstanding, any trustee, other than a beneficiary hereof, shall have the discretionary power to terminate any separate trust created by this Trust Agreement whenever the continued management thereof is no longer economical because of the small size of such trust, taking into consideration financial or other special advantages to the beneficiary or beneficiaries of continuing the trust estate. Upon the termination of any trust estate, the then remaining corpus and undistributed income shall be distributed outright and free of trust to the Settlors as their interests may appear, if both of them are then living; otherwise to the surviving Settlor, if living; otherwise to the beneficiaries thereof, or to a custodian named for a beneficiary under a Uniform Gifts to Minors Act, or to the beneficiaries' legal representatives in proportion to their respective presumptive interests in the trust or share at the time of such termination. Upon such distribution and delivery, the said trust or share shall terminate and the Trustee then

Form 9-1: (continued)

serving shall not be liable or responsible to any person or persons whomsoever for so acting. The Trustee then serving shall not be liable for failing or refusing at any time to terminate the trust or a share thereof as authorized by this paragraph.

C. <u>Merger of Trusts</u>. If any time the Trustee of any trust created pursuant to this Trust Agreement shall also be acting as Trustee of any other trust created hereby, or by a Will for the benefit of the same beneficiary or beneficiaries upon substantially the same terms and conditions, the then serving Trustee is authorized and empowered, if in such Trustee's discretion such action is in the best interest of the beneficiary or beneficiaries of the trust created hereunder, to transfer and merge all of the assets then held under such trust created pursuant to this Trust Agreement to and with such other trust and thereupon and thereby to terminate the trust created hereby. Such Trustee is further authorized to accept the assets of the other trust which may be transferred to such trustee of the trust created hereunder and to administer and distribute such assets and properties so transferred in accordance with the provisions of this Trust Agreement. If the component trusts differ as to contingent beneficiaries and the contingency occurs, the funds may be distributed in such shares as the Trustee, in the Trustee's sole discretion, shall deem necessary to create a fair ratio between the various sets of remaindermen. If any trust created in this Trust Agreement is merged with any trust created under any other document, such merged trust shall not continue beyond the date on which the earliest maximum term of the trusts so merged would, without regard to such merger, have been required to expire. Settlors further direct that, as to any property belonging to any trust estate at any time (including a merged trust) as to which under the laws of any state applicable to said property that trust is required to be terminated at any time prior to its normal termination date, the trust as to that particular property shall terminate at the time required by the laws of said state.

D. <u>Perpetuities Provision</u>. Notwithstanding any other provisions of this Trust Agreement to the contrary, any trust herein created, if it has not previously terminated, shall terminate twenty-one (21) years after the death of the last to survive of the Settlors and all the lineal descendants of the Settlors living on the date of this Trust Agreement. Upon such termination, the remaining assets and property of the trust shall be delivered and distributed, outright and free of trust, to the person or persons to whom the income of the particular trust may be distributed at that time. If the income of a particular trust may be distributed to more than one person at that time, the then serving Trustee shall divide the assets and properties between such persons in such proportions between them as said Trustee shall determine, in the Trustee's sole discretion, to best carry out the Settlors' intentions as expressed in this document.

E. <u>Spendthrift Provision</u>. No beneficiary shall have the right or power to anticipate, by assignment or otherwise, any income or corpus given to such beneficiary or any portion thereof; nor, in advance of actually receiving the same, shall any beneficiary have the right or power to sell, transfer, encumber or in anywise charge same; nor shall such income or corpus, or any portion of same, be subject to any divorce, execution, garnishment, attachment, insolvency, bankruptcy or other legal proceeding of any character, or legal sequestration, levy or sale or in any event or manner be applicable or subject, voluntarily or involuntarily, to the payment of such beneficiary's debts or other obligations.

ARTICLE X.
Powers of the Trustees

The Trustees shall have and may exercise the following rights, powers and privileges with respect to each trust created by this document, unless specifically limited by other provisions of this document:

A. <u>General Powers</u>. The Trustees may sell, exchange, alter, mortgage, pledge or otherwise dispose of trust property; borrow any sum believed by the Trustees to be necessary or desirable for protecting the trust or any part thereof, making any income or corpus payment or distribution, or for any other purpose which in the Trustees' opinion may be appropriate; pay all reasonable expenses; execute obligations, negotiable and nonnegotiable; join in, by deposit, pledge, or otherwise, any plan of reorganization or readjustment of any investments of the trust, and vest in a protective committee or other legal entity such power as in the Trustees' opinion may be desirable; and sell for cash and/or credit all or any part of the trust property.

B. <u>Distributions</u>. The Trustees shall have full power and authority to make all partitions, divisions and distributions contemplated by any of the provisions of this Trust Agreement. Any partitions, divisions or distributions may be made by allocating assets and property proportionately in kind or by allocating undivided interests therein in kind. Any partition, division, or distribution made by the Trustees in good faith shall be binding and conclusive on all interested parties. In the event that a beneficiary shall, in the opinion of the Trustees, be incapacitated by reason of age, illness, or any other cause at the time of a particular distribution, the Trustees may apply the distribution for the benefit of such beneficiary in any manner that the Trustees may deem advisable, whether by payment of such beneficiary's expenses or to any such beneficiary, the legal or natural guardian, the person having custody of such beneficiary or any other person deemed suitable by the Trustees. Should any property be distributable hereunder to a minor person, the Trustees may make the distribution to a custodian for such person under the Uniform Gifts to Minors Act of Texas or any other state.

Form 9-1: (continued)

C. <u>Conservation of Trust Properties</u>. The Trustees may hold, manage and conserve any and all properties transferred to the trust and may take any action that the Trustees may deem necessary or appropriate, including the exercise of all rights and powers that a prudent owner would exercise in managing and conserving properties of a like kind.

D. <u>Investment in Securities</u>. The Trustees may buy, sell or trade any security of any nature (including stocks, stock rights, warrants, bonds, debentures, notes, certificates of interest, certificates of indebtedness and options) or any other things of value issued by any person, firm, association, trust, corporation or body politic whatsoever.

E. <u>Securities and Margin Accounts</u>. The Trustees may buy, sell and trade in securities of any nature, including covered and uncovered options on margin and, for such purposes, may maintain and operate margin accounts with brokers and may pledge any securities with brokers as security for loans and advances made to the Trustees.

F. <u>Investment in Real Estate and Personal Property</u>. The Trustees may, at such cost and upon such terms as the Trustees may deem advisable, purchase or otherwise acquire real estate and personal property of any kind and hold, manage and conserve the same in whatever manner the Trustees may deem best; lease such property under a lease or leases to commence at once or in the future and for any period of time, even though such period may extend beyond the duration of the trust; renew and extend leases; partition, exchange, release, convey or assign any right, title or interest of the trust in any real estate or personal property owned by the trust; plat real estate and lay out and dedicate streets, alleys and ways; and improve and erect buildings on any real property (in addition to or substitution for buildings at any time existing thereon).

G. <u>Investment in Oil, Gas and Other Mineral Interests</u>. The Trustees may purchase or otherwise acquire oil, gas and other mineral interests, leases, royalties, overriding royalties, production payments, oil payments, gas payments, net profit overriding royalties, and net profit interests; grant, make and release oil, gas and other mineral leases, subleases and farmouts; enter into development and drilling contracts, operating contracts and utilization agreements; make arrangements for present or future pooling of any interest in oil, gas or other mineral properties and for secondary recovery projects, and exercise with respect to any and all oil, gas and other mineral properties all rights and powers that a prudent owner would have with respect to properties of a like kind.

H. <u>Investment in Undivided Interests</u>. The Trustees may, for any trusts created under this Trust Agreement, jointly hold, manage and invest in one or more assets, properties or consolidated funds, in whole or in part, as the Trustees may determine. As to each asset, property or consolidated fund, division into the appropriate shares need be made only on the Trustees' books of account, in which each trust shall be allotted its proportionate part of the principal and income of the asset, property or fund and charged with its proportionate part of the expenses thereof. No such holding shall, however, defer the vesting in possession of any estate created by this Trust Agreement.

I. <u>Investment in Partnerships</u>. The Trustees may purchase or otherwise acquire an interest in any partnership conducting a lawful business, transfer trust property to any partnership which will conduct or is conducting any lawful business, or become either a general or limited partner of any such partnership.

J. <u>Power to Organize or Continue Business</u>. The Trustees may continue any business (whether a proprietorship, corporation, partnership, limited partnership or other business entity) which the trust may own or in which it may be financially interested for such time as the Trustees may deem to be in the best interests of the trust; employ in the conduct of any such business such capital out of trust as the Trustees may deem proper; borrow money for use in any such business alone or with other persons financially interested in such business, and secure loans by a mortgage, pledge or any other manner of encumbrance of not only the trust's property and interest in such business but also such portion of the trust outside of such business as the Trustees may deem proper; organize, either alone or jointly with others, new corporations, partnerships, limited partnerships or other business entities and convey to it or them trust property or any part thereof; and generally exercise with respect to the continuance, management, sale or liquidation of any business which the trust may own or in which it may be financially interested, or of any new business or business interest, all the rights and powers which a prudent owner of any such business would have.

K <u>Selection and Retention of Investments</u>. Any property acquired by the Trustees and at any time constituting any part of the trust shall be deemed a proper investment, and the Trustees shall be under no obligation to dispose of or convert such property. Investments need not be diversified, may be of a wasting nature, and may be made or retained with a view to possible increase in value. The Trustees may invest all funds available for investment at any time that the Trustees may deem advisable in such investments as the Trustees may be permitted to make pursuant to the terms hereof. The Trustees, unless otherwise herein specifically prohibited, shall have as wide a latitude in the selection,

Form 9-1: (continued)

retention and making of investments as any individual would have in retaining or investing his or her own funds and shall not be limited to nor bound or governed by any statute or regulation respecting investments.

L. Holding Title to Investments. The Trustees may hold title to investments in the name of the Trustees or a nominee. If the trust owns assets located in a jurisdiction in which the Trustees cannot be authorized to act, then the Trustees may appoint any national bank authorized to act in such jurisdiction as Trustees of such assets and confer on such Trustees any power as may be necessary in the premises, but, in any event, such Trustees shall account for all net income and/or net proceeds from the sale of such assets to the Trustees acting hereunder.

M. Power to Make Loans. The Trustees may make loans, secured or unsecured, in such amounts, upon such terms, at such reasonable rates of interest, and to such persons, firms or corporations as the Trustees may deem proper and appropriate; provided, however, that the Trustees shall not be empowered to make any loan to any person or corporation then serving as Trustees hereunder.

N. Power to Vote Stock. The Trustees may vote shares of stock in person or by proxy, with or without power of substitution; exercise and perform any and all rights, privileges and powers inuring to the holder of any stock or security comprising at any time a part of the trust, and exercise by agent or attorney-in-fact any right appurtenant to any property or matter in which the trust may be interested.

O. Protection of the Trust Estate. The Trustees may protect, perfect and defend the title to any trust property; sue and be sued; enforce any bonds, mortgages or other obligations or liens owned by the trust; compromise, arbitrate, or otherwise adjust claims in favor of or against the trust; waive or release rights of any kind; and abandon any property considered by the Trustees to be worthless.

P. Notes, Mortgages, and Foreclosures. The Trustees may, at any time, reduce the rate of interest payable on any bond, note, or other security owned by the trust; continue mortgages upon and after maturity, with or without renewal, or extend the same upon such terms as seem advisable to the Trustees without reference to the value of the security at the time of such continuance; modify or release any guaranty or mortgage; as an incident to collection of any bond or note, foreclose and bid in the property at foreclosure sale, acquire the property by deed from the mortgagor or obligor without foreclosure and retain the property so bid in or taken over without foreclosure.

Q. Insurance. The Trustees may carry such insurance coverage (in stock companies or in mutual companies), including public liability, property damage and life insurance, for such hazards and in such amounts as the Trustees may deem advisable. With respect to life insurance, the Trustees may acquire life insurance on the life of any beneficiary or on the life of any person in whom a beneficiary has an insurable interest from any company in such amount and type as the Trustees may deem advisable, pay all premiums from either income or principal, and designate as beneficiary the Trustees of the trust. With respect to all insurance policies held in the trust estate, unless the Trustees shall arrange for the automatic application of dividends in reduction of premium payments, dividends shall be treated as a return of corpus and applied to the payment of such premiums.

R. Employ and Compensate Agents and Representatives. The Trustees may employ, appoint, remove and compensate, out of income or corpus or in such proportion between income and corpus as the Trustees may deem proper, agents or other representatives, including accountants, brokers, attorneys-at-law, attorneys-in-fact, investment counsel, investment brokers, realtors, rental agents, geologists, engineers, and other assistants and advisers as deemed by the Trustees to be helpful in the proper administration of the trust, without liability for any neglect, omission, misconduct, or default of such agent or representative, provided such agent or representative was selected and retained by the Trustees with due care.

S. Establish and Maintain Reserves. Out of rents, profits, or other income received, the Trustees may set up reserves for taxes, assessments, insurance premiums, repairs, improvements, depletion, depreciation, obsolescence and general maintenance of buildings or other property.

T. Power to Determine Income and Corpus. Stock dividends and capital gains shall be treated as corpus. Except as herein specifically provided, the Trustees shall determine in accordance with general principles of federal tax law the manner in which expenses are to be borne and receipts credited between corpus and income and what shall constitute income, net income and corpus. In determining such matters, the Trustees may give consideration to, but shall not be bound by, the provisions of the Texas Trust Code.

U. Liability of Third Party. No purchaser at any sale made by the Trustees or person dealing with the Trustees is obliged to see to the application of any money or property paid or delivered to the Trustees or to inquire into the expediency or propriety of, or the authority of the Trustees to enter into and consummate, any transaction.

V. Documents. The Trustees may execute and deliver any deeds, conveyances, assignments, leases, contracts, stock or security transfer powers, or any other written document of any character appropriate to any of the powers or duties herein conferred upon the Trustees.

Form 9-1: (continued)

W. <u>Transactions with Beneficiaries and Fiduciaries</u>. The Trustees is authorized to enter into any transaction permitted by this Trust Agreement, even though the other party to that transaction is a beneficiary; the estate of a beneficiary; a trust created by or for the benefit of a beneficiary, whether living or deceased; the estate of either Settlor; a personal representative of any estate, including that of either Settlor; or a Trustees of any trust, including the Trustees under this Trust Agreement acting individually; except to the extent that the Texas Trust Code, as amended, or any successor statute may expressly prohibit Settlors from authorizing any corporate Trustees serving hereunder from engaging in any such transaction. The Trustees is authorized, but not directed, to lend trust funds to the personal representatives of the Settlors' estates upon such security and for such time and at such rate of interest as the Trustees, in their sole discretion, deems proper, and to purchase any assets from the personal representatives of the Settlors' estate for such sums and on such terms as the Trustees may deem appropriate or proper; provided, however, that the Trustees shall be required to act in all such matters on the same basis as it would in dealing at arm's length with an unrelated third party.

X. <u>Reserve for Taxes and Obligations</u>. Upon the date of the first Settlor to die, the Trustees shall be authorized to withhold from distribution of principal in accordance with this Trust Agreement an amount of property sufficient, in its judgment, to cover any liability that may be imposed upon the Trustees or the trust estate for estate, inheritance or other taxes attributable to the estate of the first Settlor to die or to meet any obligations (including all taxes) of such Settlor or expenses with respect to the administration of his or her estate, and to pay such liabilities, obligations and expenses out of the trust created hereunder. Upon the Trustees being satisfied that they no longer has any liability with respect to such taxes and that they need not pay such liabilities, obligations and expenses, the balance of such withheld property shall be distributed in accordance with the applicable provisions of this Trust Agreement. Neither the trust estate nor any trust beneficiary shall be entitled to reimbursement from the estate of such Settlor, or his or her heirs or devisees, on account of any payment made pursuant to this paragraph.

Y. <u>Powers Cumulative</u>. Except as herein otherwise provided, the powers conferred upon the Trustees shall not be construed as in limitation of any authority conferred by law, including but not limited to the Texas Trust Code (including any amendments thereto) and its successor statute or statutes, but as in addition thereto.

ARTICLE XI.
Provisions Relating to Life Insurance Policies

A. <u>Rights Reserved in Policies and Benefit Plans</u>. The Settlors reserve to themselves during their joint lifetimes, and may receive or exercise without the consent or approval of the Trustees or any beneficiary hereunder, all benefits, payments, dividends, surrender values, options, rights, powers and privileges with respect to the policies listed in the attached Schedule A, and any other policies or any benefit plans which may be made payable to the Trustees hereunder, including, but not limited to, the following:

1. The power, as provided in Article I above, to add the proceeds of any other policies of insurance and any benefit plans to the operation of the trust by making such policies and benefit plans payable to the Trustees;

2. The right to receive or apply dividends or distributive shares of surplus, disability benefits, surrender values or the proceeds of matured endowments;

3. The power to obtain and receive from the respective insurance companies such advances or loans on account of policies as may be available;

4. The power to exercise any option, right or privilege granted in any policy or benefit plan;

5. The power to borrow on, sell, assign or pledge any policy or rights under any benefit plan;

6. The power to change the beneficiary of any policy or benefit plan;

7. The power to withdraw a policy or benefit plan from the operation of this trust in order to exercise a reserved power or for any other purpose;

8. The power to change the beneficiaries under this Trust Agreement, their respective shares and plans of distribution; and

9. The power to convert any policy of insurance into another form or forms of insurance.

It is the intent of the parties hereto that as to the life insurance policies listed on the attached Schedule A, the Trustees shall receive only the proceeds payable at the death of the insured Settlor subject to all loans and charges against such proceeds as may have accrued during such Settlor's lifetime, and the Settlors shall, during their joint lifetimes, retain all other contractual benefits, powers and options under such policies and benefit plan. Upon the death of the first Settlor to die, the rights and powers described in this Article XI shall pass from the surviving Settlor to the Trustees.

Form 9-1: (continued)

B. **Duty Regarding Policies and Premium Payments.**

1. **Settlors' Duties.** It is the Settlors' intention to pay all premiums, assessments, or other charges necessary to keep all policies owned by them and payable to the Trustees in force, but the Settlors shall be under no duty to do so and shall sustain no liability to anyone if Settlors should permit any policies within operation of the trust to lapse for nonpayment of premiums, assessments, or other charges, or otherwise permit the policies, or any of them, to become uncollectible.

2. **Trustees' Duties.** The Trustees shall be under no obligation, during the lifetime of the Settlors, to pay any premiums, assessments, or other charges necessary to keep the policies in force, nor shall the Trustees be under any obligation to ascertain whether the same have been paid, or to notify any person of the non-payment of premiums. The Trustees shall keep safely all policies deposited with the Trustees, and shall, at the request of the Settlors, execute such releases and other documents as shall be required to permit the Settlors to exercise any options, privileges, or powers reserved to the Settlors hereunder.

C. **Trustees' Duties Upon Insured Settlor's Death.** As soon as practicable after the death of an insured Settlor, the Trustees shall make such proofs of death as shall be required under any policies of insurance then within the operation of this Trust Agreement and payable to the Trustees, and the Trustees shall receive such sums of money as shall be due to the Trustees under the terms of such policies of life insurance, including double indemnity benefits, and hold the same, in trust, for the uses and purposes hereinafter set forth. To facilitate the receipt of such sums of money, the Trustees shall have the power to execute and deliver receipts and other documents, to compromise or adjust disputed claims in such manner as the Trustees, in the Trustees' sole discretion, may deem just, and to take such steps as the Trustees, in the Trustees' sole discretion, shall deem necessary and proper for collection thereof; provided that if payment on any policy is contested, the Trustees shall not be obligated to take any action for collection unless and until the Trustees shall have been indemnified to the Trustees' satisfaction against any loss, liability, or expense, including attorney's fees; and provided further, that the Trustees may, in the Trustees' sole discretion, use any funds in the Trustees' hands, whether corpus or income, to pay the costs and expenses, including attorney's fees, of bringing action for the collection of the proceeds of any policy hereunder, and the Trustees may be reimbursed for any advances made for such purposes. Upon payment to the Trustees of the amounts due under the policies of insurance payable hereunder, the insurance companies issuing such policies shall be relieved of all further liability hereunder, and no such insurance company shall be under any responsibility to see to the performance of the trust created hereby.

To the extent permitted, the Trustees shall have the right to negotiate and receive proceeds from employee benefit plans in any manner the Trustees may deem prudent and consistent with the tax (estate, generation-skipping, income, and other) and other objectives of any trust established hereunder and its beneficiaries; provided, however, if such proceeds would be otherwise exempt from federal estate taxes in whole or in part, the Trustees shall not elect to receive, use or expend such otherwise exempt proceeds in such a manner as will subject them to federal estate taxation in a Settlor's estate without the written consent of the personal representative of that Settlor's estate.

ARTICLE XII.

Acceptance by the Trustees

The Trustees, by executing this Trust Agreement, hereby accepts the trust created by this Trust Agreement and covenants to faithfully discharge all duties of the Trustees hereunder.

ARTICLE XIII.

Definitions and General Provisions

The following definitions and provisions are applicable to this Trust Agreement:

A. **Children and Descendants.** The terms "child, children, descendants, issue" and similar terms shall be deemed only to include children born to, or adopted (on or before eighteen years of age) in, a lawful marriage. A posthumous child shall be considered as living at the death of his parent.

B. **Heirs.** The "heirs" of a person shall include those persons who would have inherited the personal property of a deceased person had such deceased person died intestate at the time of such distribution, unmarried and domiciled in Texas, under the laws of the State of Texas then in force, taking shares as prescribed by such applicable laws.

C. **Beneficiary.** A "beneficiary" is a person who is entitled to distribution assets hereunder.

D. **Trust.** Except as provided otherwise by the context of this document, the word "trust" as used herein shall include any and all trusts created hereunder.

E. **Trust Estate.** The term "trust estate" means all assets, however and whenever acquired, including income, which may belong to a trust at any given time.

Form 9-1: (continued)

F. Trustees. The term "Trustees" shall include within its meaning any trustee and all trustees serving from time to time hereunder and shall refer both to the original Trustees and to any successor or substitute thereof.

G. Code. The term "Code" refers to the Internal Revenue Code of 1986, as amended, and corresponding provisions of any subsequent federal tax laws.

H. Other Terms. The use of any gender includes the other genders, and the use of either the singular or the plural includes the other.

I. Per Stirpes. When a distribution is directed to be made to any person's issue or descendants, "per stirpes," the division into stirpes shall begin at the generation nearest to such person that has a living member.

ARTICLE XIV.

Binding Effect

This Trust Agreement shall extend to and be binding upon the heirs, executors, administrators, legal representatives and successors, respectively, of the parties hereto.

ARTICLE XV.

Captions Not Interpretive

The captions that have been used to designate the various articles, paragraphs and subparagraphs in this Trust Agreement are solely for convenience in reading and ease of reference and shall not be construed in any event or manner as interpretive or limiting the interpretation of the same.

IN WITNESS WHEREOF, this Trust Agreement was executed on this the _____ day of _____ , 1994.

_____

PETER SMITH, Settlor

_____

PAULA SMITH, Settlor

_____

PETER SMITH, Trustee

_____

PAULA SMITH, Trustee

Form 9-1: (continued)

THE STATE OF TEXAS   *
                                                      *
COUNTY OF ROUGH RIDER   *

    BEFORE ME, the undersigned authority, in and for the State of Texas, on this day personally appeared PETER SMITH, in his capacity as Settlor, known to me to be the person whose name is subscribed to the foregoing document, and acknowledged to me that he executed the same for the purposes and consideration therein expressed and in the capacity therein stated.

    GIVEN UNDER MY HAND AND SEAL OF OFFICE on this the _____ day of _____ , 1994.

_____
Notary Public, State of Texas
Printed Name of Notary:

_____
My Commission Expires: _____

THE STATE OF TEXAS   *
                                                      *
COUNTY OF ROUGH RIDER   *

    BEFORE ME, the undersigned authority, in and for the State of Texas, on this day personally appeared PAULA SMITH, in her capacity as Settlor, known to me to be the person whose name is subscribed to the foregoing document, and acknowledged to me that she executed the same for the purposes and consideration therein expressed and in the capacity therein stated.

    GIVEN UNDER MY HAND AND SEAL OF OFFICE on this the _____ day of _____ , 1994.

_____
Notary Public, State of Texas
Printed Name of Notary:

_____
My Commission Expires: _____

THE STATE OF TEXAS   *
                                                      *
COUNTY OF ROUGH RIDER   *

    BEFORE ME, the undersigned authority, in and for the State of Texas, on this day personally appeared PETER SMITH, in his capacity as Trustee, known to me to be the person whose name is subscribed to the foregoing document, and acknowledged to me that he executed the same for the purposes and consideration therein expressed and in the capacity therein stated.

    GIVEN UNDER MY HAND AND SEAL OF OFFICE on this the _____ day of _____ , 1994.

_____
Notary Public, State of Texas
Printed Name of Notary:

_____
My Commission Expires: _____

Form 9-1: (continued)

THE STATE OF TEXAS   *
                                                *
COUNTY OF ROUGH RIDER   *

BEFORE ME, the undersigned authority, in and for the State of Texas, on this day personally appeared PAULA SMITH, in her capacity as Trustee, known to me to be the person whose name is subscribed to the foregoing document, and acknowledged to me that she executed the same for the purposes and consideration therein expressed and in the capacity therein stated.

GIVEN UNDER MY HAND AND SEAL OF OFFICE on this the _____ day of _____ , 1994.

_____
Notary Public, State of Texas
Printed Name of Notary:

_____
My Commission Expires: _____

Form 9-1: (continued)

SCHEDULE A
TO THE SMITH LIVING TRUST
DATED _____, 1994

Initial Assets: All of Settlors' interests in and to the following described properties:

REAL PROPERTY:
   Parcel #1
   ADDRESS: 1412 Bullmoose
            San Juan Hill, Texas
   LEGAL DESCRIPTION: Lot Two (2), Block One (1), Sunnyside Addition, an addition in the City of
                      San Juan Hill, Texas, as shown by the map or plat records of Rough Rider
                      County in Volume Twelve (12), at Page Three Hundred Thirty-Four (334) of
                      the Map Records of Rough Rider County, Texas.

ALL HOUSEHOLD FURNISHINGS OWNED BY SETTLORS

MOTOR VEHICLES:

   Vehicle #1
   Description: 1994 Lexus, Motor ID # 0N876D4898GK23

CASH IN BANKS:

   Account #1
   Institution: Rough Rider National Bank
   Account type: checking
   Account/CD #: 09301167012

   Account #2
   Institution: Rough Rider National Bank
   Account type: certificate of deposit
   Account/CD #: 384760289

INSURANCE:

   Policy #1
   Insurer: Reliable Life Insurance Company
   Policy #: 000879356407

   Policy #2
   Insurer: Reliable Life Insurance Company
   Policy #: 00000785428946

Form 9-1: (continued)

SECURITIES:

Security #1
Description: 1200 shares of the common stock of Falty Medical
                       Supply Company, Certificate # 3674

Security #2
Description: 2400 shares of Greater West Texas Utility
                       Company, Certificate # 73506

_____
PETER SMITH, Settlor

_____
PAULA SMITH, Settlor

_____
PETER SMITH, Trustee

_____
PAULA SMITH, Trustee

Form 9-2: Crummy Notice to Beneficiary

Peter Smith, Jr.
129 Teton Village Rd.
Jackson, Wy. 12345

RE: Peter Smith, Jr. Trust

Dear Mr. Smith:

On the 12th day of September, 1993, Peter Smith, as grantor of the Peter Smith, Jr. Trust, made an additional deposit to the corpus of said trust in the amount of $10,000.00.

Rough Rider National Bank, the trustee of said trust, has received and receipted for such deposit.

Accordingly, pursuant to the terms and conditions of the trust, you are notified that you have a right to withdraw such sum of money and an additional amount not to exceed $5,000.00 or 5% of the trust assets, whichever is greater.

Rough Rider National Bank

By:_____
   John Roosevelt
   Trust Officer

Form 9-3: Grantor-Retained Annuity Trust

THE PETER SMITH GRANTOR-RETAINED ANNUITY TRUST

THIS TRUST AGREEMENT is effective this _____ day of July, 1992, by and between **PETER SMITH** of Rough Rider County, Texas, hereinafter called the "Grantor," and **ROUGH RIDER NATIONAL BANK** of Rough Rider County, Texas, hereinafter called the "Trustee."

WITNESSETH

That the Grantor has this day delivered to the Trustee his interest in the property described in Schedule "A" attached hereto and the Trustee agrees to hold, administer and distribute the property contributed by the Grantor, as the corpus of a trust for the benefit of the Grantor in accordance with the terms and provisions hereinafter set out.

SECTION 1.
NAME OF TRUST

1.1 Name of Trust. This Trust shall be known as the **PETER SMITH GRANTOR RETAINED ANNUITY TRUST.**

SECTION 2.
TERM OF TRUST AND DISTRIBUTION TO GRANTOR

2.1 Trust Term. The Trust held under this Section 2 for the Grantor shall terminate upon the earlier of (i) the death of the Grantor of the Trust, or (ii) Ten (10) years from the date of this Agreement (the "Fixed Term"). Upon the termination of the Trust, the Trustee shall distribute the principal of the trust estate, as it is then constituted, in accordance with the provisions of Section 3.

2.2 Payment of Annuity Amount. The Trustee shall pay to the Grantor in each taxable year of the Trust during the trust term an annuity amount equal to 8.5% of the net fair market value of the assets of the Trust as of this date. The annuity amount shall be paid in equal quarterly amounts from the income, and to the extent income is not sufficient, from principal. Any income of the Trust for a taxable year in excess of the annuity amount shall be added to principal. If the net fair market value of the trust assets is incorrectly determined, then within a reasonable period after the value is finally determined for Federal tax purposes, the Trustee shall pay to the Grantor (in case of an undervaluation) or received from the Grantor (in case of an overvaluation) an amount equal to the difference between the annuity amount or amounts properly payable and the annuity amount or amounts actually paid, plus interest on such amounts computed at the rate required by the applicable Treasury Department Regulations or, if there are no such regulations, the rate used for valuing annuity interests under Section 664 of the Internal Revenue Code of 1986 ("the Code"), compounded annually.

2.3 Pro Ration of Annuity Amount. In determining the annuity amount, the Trustee shall pro rate the same on a daily basis for a short taxable year and for the taxable year of the Grantor's death.

SECTION 3.
TERMINATION OF TRUST

3.1 Death Prior to Expiration of Fixed Term. If the Grantor dies prior to the expiration of the Fixed Term of this Trust, upon the Grantor's death, the principal of the deceased Grantor's Trust, as it is then constituted, shall be paid over to on equal shares to **PETER SMITH, JR.** and **PENELOPE SMITH,** if either dies prior to expiration of the fixed term then such beneficiaries share will be paid to the children of such predeceasing beneficiary.

3.2 Grantor Survives Fixed Term. If the Grantor survives the Fixed Term of his Trust, the remaining property of the surviving Grantor's Trust shall be distributed to **PETER SMITH, JR.** and **PENELOPE SMITH,** if either dies prior to expiration of the fixed term then such beneficiaries share will be paid to the children of such predeceasing beneficiary.

SECTION 4.
CONTINGENT TRUSTS

4.1 Contingent Trusts for Minor Beneficiary. The share of any beneficiary or distributee hereunder who is under the age of twenty-five (25) years shall be held in trust for such beneficiary until he or she attains the age of twenty-five (25) years in accordance with the following provisions:

A. Until the beneficiary attains the age of twenty-five (25) years, the Trustee may pay to the beneficiary, or apply on his or her behalf, so much of net income or principal as is necessary for the support, health and education of such beneficiary, while a minor, either directly or by making payment of distribution thereof to the parent, guardian, custodian or other legal representative, wherever appointed, or to such beneficiary or to the person with whom such beneficiary shall reside, or to such beneficiary personally.

B. Upon the beneficiary attaining the age of twenty-five (25) years, the Trustee shall distribute the remaining balance of the trust to such beneficiary and the trust shall terminate; provided, however, if the Trustee, in its sole discretion, determines that a beneficiary has a physical or mental infirmity or illness, or a beneficiary is financially insolvent, the Trustee shall have the right to

Form 9-3: (continued)

delay making any installment distribution until such time as the beneficiary no longer suffers from such physical or mental infirmity or illness and is not financially insolvent. If the Trustee defers making the distribution of principal under this paragraph, the, for the duration of such beneficiary's trust, the Trustee shall distribute to such beneficiary, or shall apply on the beneficiary's behalf, the entire net income of the beneficiary's trust and, in addition, the Trustee may distribute to the beneficiary, or apply on such beneficiary's behalf, so much of the principal as is necessary to provide adequately for such beneficiary's health, support and education and for the health of such beneficiary's children.

C. In case a beneficiary shall die before distribution of all the property held under this section for his or her benefit, the remaining trust fund shall be distributed to such beneficiary's then living descendants, per stirpes; and if none, to such beneficiary's brothers and sisters who are Grantor's descendants in equal shares, or to the then living descendants of any deceased brother or sister, per stirpes, and if none, to Grantor's then living descendants, per stirpes. If at the time of such distribution any such individual is an income beneficiary of any trust under this Agreement, the share of such individual shall be added to the corpus of his or her trust fund as an integral part of the trust, to be administered and distributed in accordance with all the terms, conditions, and limitations applying to the trust.

4.2 If No Surviving Descendants. If all of Grantor's descendants shall die prior to the complete distribution of the trusts created in this Agreement, then, upon the happening of such event, all assets held by the Trustee shall be distributed to those persons then living who are entitled to take from the Grantor, under the Texas laws of descent and distribution then in effect, assuming in the case of the Grantor's heirs that the Grantor had died immediately before the death of his last surviving descendant.

SECTION 5
TRUSTEE PROVISIONS

5.1 Appointment of Trustee. **Rough Rider National Bank** shall serve as Trustee of the trust created under the terms of this Trust Agreement. Should **Rough Rider National Bank** fail, refuse or otherwise cease to act as Trustee, **Yellowstone State Bank** shall serve as the successor Trustee.

5.2 Rights and Liabilities of Trustee. The Trustee of any trust created under this Trust Agreement shall have the following rights and liabilities:

A. **Freedom from Court Supervision.** No proceedings shall be had in any court of any jurisdiction with respect to the administration of any trust created under this Trust Agreement.

B. **Waiver of Bond.** No bond or other security shall be required in any jurisdiction of any person or entity named in this Trust Agreement as Trustee or successor Trustee.

C. **Limit of Liability.** No Trustee or successor Trustee appointed under this Trust Agreement shall at any time be held liable for any action or default of such Trustee or successor Trustee if done in good faith and without gross negligence.

D. **Compensation of Trustee.** Each individual Trustee shall serve without compensation. Each corporate Trustee shall be entitled to reasonable compensation for services rendered. Each Trustee shall be reimbursed for reasonable expenses incurred in connection with its duties as Trustee.

E. **Successor Trustee.** Any successor Trustee shall possess and exercise all powers and authority conferred upon the original Trustee.

5.3 Right to Resign; Right or Removal; Appointment in Case no Successor Named. Any Trustee may resign by giving the adult beneficiary, or the natural guardian of a minor beneficiary, reasonable notice. If at any time an appointed Trustee should, for any reason, resign, fail or cease to act as Trustee hereunder or be removed and, at the time, should no successor Trustee be otherwise appointed in a manner provided for by this Agreement, then, within a reasonable time, the adult income beneficiary (or, if there is no adult income beneficiary or if the adult income beneficiary fails to act, a county or probate judge in the county in which the trust corpus is located), in his individual capacity, shall appoint a qualified bank as the successor Trustee.

5.4 Qualified Bank as Successor. A qualified bank to serve as a successor Trustee of any trust established under this Agreement must be a national bank with trust powers.

SECTION 6
ADMINISTRATION OF TRUST

6.1 General Powers of Trustee. In addition to the powers granted elsewhere in this Trust Agreement, but subject to any limitations stated elsewhere herein, the Trustee of any trust shall have the following powers, which may be exercised free from court supervision, and which shall exist until all of the assets of the trust have been distributed:

A. **Management.** The Trustee may hold property unproductive of income.

Form 9-3: (continued)

B. **Transfers, Loans.** The Trustee may lease, sell, transfer, exchange, partition or encumber in any manner (including with purchase money mortgages) all or any part of the assets of any trust estate, and may loan or borrow money in any manner (including by joint and several obligations) with or without security.

C. **Dealing With Third Parties.** The Trustee may deal with any person or entity regardless of relationship or identity of the Trustee to or with that person or entity and may hold or invest all or any part of any trust in common or undivided interests with that person or entity. The Trustee may purchase any interest in any ranch property (including any interest held directly or indirectly through a partnership or corporation) from any other person or entity including the Trustee for cash or on credit terms.

D. **Agents, Employees.** The Trustee may employ and compensate agents and other employees, and may delegate to them any and all discretion and powers.

E. **Claims, Controversies.** The Trustee may maintain and defend any claim or controversy by or against the trust without the joinder or consent of any beneficiary.

F. **Income and Principal.** The Trustee may allocate receipts and expenses between income and principal of the trust estate in accordance with applicable local law, and pay from the income or principal of the trust estate, as the case may be, the expenses properly chargeable to the income or principal of the trust estate and permitted by Treas. Reg. 25.2702.

During the Fixed Term of this trust the percentage depletion allowed under the Internal Revenue Code shall be allocated to the Grantor.

G. **Powers Under Changed Conditions.** The Trustee may exercise such powers as may be necessary or desirable in the management and control of the trust estate, whether or not such powers are of like kind or character to those enumerated in this instrument, to enable the Trustee to act under changed conditions, the exact nature of which cannot now be foreseen.

H. **Execution of Documents.** The Trustee may execute and deliver agreements, assignments, bills of sale, contracts, deeds, leases, notes, powers of attorney, warranties, covenants, guaranties, receipts, releases, discharges, acquittances, and other papers or documents reasonably necessary or desirable to carry out the powers granted to a trustee.

I. **Additional Powers.** In addition, the Trustee shall have the rights, privileges and powers now or hereafter granted to a trustee under the Texas Trust Code as it presently provides or as it may be amended.

J. **Distributions.** During the term of the trusts, to make any distribution from the trusts (i) to the beneficiary; (ii) if the beneficiary is under a legal disability or, if the Trustee determines that the beneficiary is unable to manage properly his or her affairs, to a person furnishing support, maintenance, or education for the beneficiary or with whom the beneficiary is residing, for expenditures on the beneficiary's behalf; or (iii) if the beneficiary is a minor to a custodian for the beneficiary as selected by the Trustee under the Uniform Gifts to Minors Act of any state. Alternatively, the Trustee may apply all or a part of the distribution for the beneficiary's benefit. Any distribution under this paragraph shall be a full discharge of the Trustee with respect thereto.

6.2 Spendthrift Provision. No interest of any beneficiary of any trust created under this Trust Agreement shall be transferable, assignable, or subject to the claims of any beneficiary's creditors. It is the intent of the Grantor that the property of such trusts, including any income distributed to any beneficiary be the separate property of the beneficiary.

SECTION 7.
SPECIAL RULES

7.1 Additional Contributions. Neither the Grantor nor any other person may make contributions to the trust in addition to the original contribution to this trust.

7.2 No Commutation. The interest of the Grantor in this Trust created under shall not be commuted.

7.3 Amounts Payable to Other Persons. The Trustee is prohibited from making distributions to the Trust to or for the benefit of any person other than the Grantor prior to the expiration of the Fixed Term.

7.4 Texas Laws to Govern. All questions concerning the meaning and intention of any terms of this Trust Agreement, it validity, or administration of any powers created in this Trust Agreement shall be determined in accordance with the laws of the State of Texas. The trusts created herein shall be deemed Texas trusts and shall, in all respects, be governed by the laws of the State of Texas.

7.5 Headings. The headings of the various provisions of this Trust Agreement have been included only in order to make it easier to locate the subjects covered by such provisions and are not to be used in construing this Trust Agreement or ascertaining the Grantor's intentions.

Form 9-3: (continued)

7.6 <u>Other Terms Used in This Trust Agreement</u>. Pronouns, nouns and terms as used in this Trust Agreement shall include the masculine, feminine, neuter, singular and plural form wherever appropriate to the context. Whenever used in this Trust Agreement:

A. <u>Children</u>. The term "child" or "children" means the immediate lawful, lineal descendants by blood or adoption of the persons referred to who are living at the time they must be ascertained in order to give effect to the reference to them; provided that a person who is adopted while sixteen (16) years or older shall not be included as a child hereunder.

B. <u>Trustee</u>. The term "Trustee" or "Trustees" shall refer to the then acting Trustee or trustees, whether original or successor, individual or corporate, acting individually or with another, and regardless of gender.

C. <u>Code</u>. The term "Code" shall mean the Internal Revenue Code of 1986, as amended, together with temporary, proposed and final regulations issued thereunder, as amended.

7.7 <u>Irrevocability of Trust</u>. This Trust shall be irrevocable and shall not be altered, amended, or revoked or terminated by the Grantor or any other person.

7.8 <u>Intent of Grantor</u>. The Grantor intends that this trust be treated as a "Grantor Retained Annuity Trust" in that the Grantor has retained a "Qualified Interest" as defined in 2702(b)(1) of the code and the regulations thereunder. The Trustee shall take no action inconsistent with the treatment of this trust on the Grantor's retained interest as a "Qualified Interest" under above described Code or its regulations.

SIGNED AND DATED as of the first date hereinabove stated.

_____
PETER SMITH

THIS TRUST AGREEMENT IS HEREBY ACCEPTED.

ROUGH RIDER NATIONAL BANK

By: _____

Its _____

10 PROBATE ADMINISTRATION– INDEPENDENT ADMINISTRATION

CHAPTER OBJECTIVES

Upon completion of this chapter, the student should be able to:

1. Obtain all relevant information from a client needed to prepare the necessary documents used in an independent administration.
2. Prepare the various applications filed to initiate independent administrations.
3. Determine the filing fees, cause the application to be filed, have citation issued and served, and set the hearing on an independent administration.
4. Prepare all relevant documents needed both at the independent administration hearing and in order for the independent administrator to qualify.
5. Gather the information needed to prepare an inventory, appraisement and list of claims.
6. Cause notices to creditors to be mailed and published.
7. Prepare distribution deeds to and receipts and releases from the heirs or devisees.
8. Close an estate.

CHAPTER GLOSSARY

Administration of an estate The process of gathering the assets of the estate, collecting the claims due it, paying the claims of creditors of the estate, and distributing what is left to the distributees.

Allegation An assertion, claim, or statement of a party to a lawsuit, made in a pleading, setting out what that party intends to prove.

Bond A form of surety or guarantee containing the promise of a third party to pay, up to the penalty amount of the bond, any damages caused by a personal representative's defaulting in the faithful and competent performance of her duties.

Claims Per Probate Code Section 3(c): The debts/liabilities of a decedent created prior to her death, the debts/liabilities incurred in the administration of the estate of either a decedent or a ward, including funeral expenses, tombstone expenses, administration expenses, estate and inheritance taxes, expenses for the maintenance and support of a minor or incompetent, and debts due or owed to the estate.

Court coordinator An individual employed to manage a court's calendar or docket. Among other duties, she sets hearings and trials, or assigns a date and time for them.

Court cost deposit A sum of money required to be paid to a court clerk when a legal proceeding is filed. Includes statutorily required and authorized fees and an estimate by the clerk of fees to be charged during the progress of the proceedings. The clerks of some counties have adopted a pay-as-you-go plan under which the initial deposit covers anything filed within the first 90 days. Thereafter, if anything is filed or some action is requested, additional fees must be paid before the document can be filed or the action taken.

Dependent administration Estate administration in which the personal representative of the estate is under the close supervision and control of the court and is not allowed independent action.

Distributee Per Probate Code Section 3(j): A person entitled to a portion of an estate of a decedent under a lawful will or under the statutes of descent and distribution. Generally replaces the terms *heirs* and *devisees*, after the commencement of a probate proceeding. At common law, and in some other states, it referred only to heirs.

Independent administration Estate administration in which the personal representative is free from court control and may take independent action; administration either by an independent executor or an independent administrator.

Inheritance tax A tax imposed upon inheritances. The amount is determined by how much each devisee or heir receives from an estate or by virtue of death, and is subtracted from the inheritance or devise against which it is imposed. It is the form of death tax imposed by most states, including Texas. Texas has repealed the inheritance tax except to the extent of the federal credit.

Letters Written certification by the county clerk that a personal representative has been duly appointed by the court and has qualified by filing an oath and a bond (if a bond is required). Displayed by the representative to third parties to establish her authority. Includes letters testamentary, letters of administration, letters of temporary administration, and letters of administration with will annexed.

Minor Per Probate Code Section 3(t): A person under the age of 18 who is not or has not been lawfully married and whose disabilities of minority have not been removed for general purposes in a court proceeding.

Muniment of title Evidence, in the form of a document, of the passage of title from one person to another.

Oath A solemn declaration by a person in which she signifies that she is bound in conscience to perform certain duties, faithfully and truly.

Setting The date and time set for hearing before the court or a trial.

Subpoena A written order to appear at a certain place and time and to give testimony.

Trial amendment An amendment to pleadings that is made after the deadline for the completion of pleading, normally during the trial itself. Allowed only at the discretion of the judge, under guidelines imposed by the Rules of Civil Procedure.

Verified Sworn as true by the attaching to a pleading of an affidavit of the party filing the pleading.

Written proof A narrative statement of the testimony required to be given in connection with an original proceeding in probate that is signed under oath before the court clerk and filed with the clerk.

INTRODUCTION

For 100 years, Texas was the only state that allowed a procedure similar to what in Texas is called **independent administration**. In Gammel's Law (an early compilation of Texas Statutes), language substantially identical to the present Section 145B of the Probate Code was included. In a case decided in 1884, the Texas Supreme Court said:

> An independent executor, in performing acts in relation to the settlement of an estate may do, without an order, every act which an executor administering an estate under the control of the court may do with such an order." [Lumpkin v. Smith, 62 TEX 249 (1884)]

Yet, despite the fact that the language of Section 145B has been around since the earliest Texas laws, and despite the early pronouncement of the Supreme Court of Texas, many lawyers have been unaware of the existence of this procedure.

Section 45B says:

> Any person capable of making a will may provide in his will that no other action shall be had in the county court in relation to the settlement of his estate other than the probating and recording of his will, and the return of an inventory, appraisement, and list of **claims** of his estate.

This early independent administration required that there be a will and that the will both name an executor and provide that there should be no other action in the county court other than the probating of the will and the return of the statutory inventory, appraisement, and list of claims. The addition of this language required that, when the will was probated, the executor would act independent of the Probate Court.

At the time of the adoption of the current Probate Code in the 1955 legislative session, effective September 1, 1956, no other state had a procedure that resembled the independent administration provided for in Section 145 of the Probate Code. In the 1970s, a few states adopted similar procedures based on the Texas statutes. In addition, the Uniform Probate Code now provides for an informal probate administration, allowing the relaxation or elimination of some of the probate procedures normally required in a formal probate administration.

Texas has not adopted the Uniform Probate Code. However, effective September 1, 1993, it has adopted part of the informal administration procedures; that is, informal probate. The usefulness of this procedure is still uncertain in Texas (as will be discussed in Chapter Twelve). The procedures adopted by these other states and by the Uniform Probate Code are, in general, more complicated and the statutes longer and more difficult to read and understand than those found in the Texas Probate Code.

In 1977, the Texas Legislature substantially enlarged the scope of independent administration. The Probate Code was amended to allow an independent administration in almost every situation in which the devisees/heirs agree to an independent administration. Prior to September 1, 1977, independent administration had been allowed only when an independent executor was named in the last will and testament of the decedent.

Another amendment, in 1979, effective August 27, 1979, enlarged the scope of Section 145 to include every situation in which agreement of the devisees/heirs could be obtained. An independent administration could be created not only in a situation where there was a will and that will nominated an independent executor, but also where a will existed that did not provide for an executor, where there was a will that did not make the executor independent, or where there was no will at all. In addition, Section 145 gives the Probate Court authority to waive the **bond** generally required of an executor or administrator.

The primary and most immediate purpose of the filing of a probate administration is to have a personal representative appointed to administer the estate.

The Probate Code defines *personal representative* to include the following:

1. **Executor:** The executor (masculine) or executrix (feminine) is the person designated in the last will and testament of the decedent to collect and gather the estate, pay the claims of creditors, and distribute the assets to the devisees as provided and directed in the will.

2. **Administrator:** The administrator (masculine) or administratrix (feminine) is the person appointed by the Probate Court to administer the estate of an intestate decedent. An administrator with will annexed is appointed by the court when the will does not name an executor or the executor named in the will is unable, fails, or refuses to qualify as executor.

3. **Temporary Administrator** A temporary administrator or administratrix is appointed for a definite and short period of time by the Probate Court to handle emergency situations, such as making application for employment benefits on behalf of dependents, safeguarding property belonging to the estate, or obtaining the will of the decedent from the possession of some third person.

This chapter and the following will discuss only the executor, the administrator, and the administrator with will annexed. Temporary administrators will be discussed in Chapter 12.

The executor and administrator may be either independent or dependent. An executor or administrator is independent if the procedures required in Section 145 are complied with; she is dependent if the provisions of Section 145 cannot be complied with. The difference basically is that the independent executor or administrator does not have to seek, in formalized procedures, permission of the court to do such things as pay the claims of creditors, set and pay allowances to widows and other dependents, and make distribution of the assets to the devisees (in the case of an executor) or heirs (in the case of an administrator where there is no will).

Because the independent executor or administrator does not have to go through these procedures and is not subject to many of the other statutes relating to the **administration of an estate**, independent administration is considerably cheaper and less time consuming. The creation of an independent administration instead of a dependent administration can reduce the attorney's fees and court costs from thousands of dollars to hundreds of dollars. In addition, it is impossible to close and distribute the assets of the estate to the persons entitled to them in a **dependent administration** until one year has elapsed since the appointment of the administrator. The independent administrator can make distribution the day following appointment, in an appropriate case.

A personal representative appointed by the court must qualify for that post. A personal representative qualifies by filing an **oath** and a bond, if a bond is required. (These will be discussed later in this chapter.) Once the personal representative qualifies, she is issued **letters** by the clerk of the court. These are called *letters testamentary* in the case of an executor, *letters of administration* in the case of an administrator, and letters of *administration with will annexed* in the case of an administrator with will annexed. The letters are the badge of authority of the executor or administrator. The personal representative of the estate gives a copy of the letters to banks, stock-transfer agents, title insurance companies, and relevant others to prove her authority to act on behalf of the estate.

Probate Code Section 77 specifies an order of appointment of executors and administrators, and any failure to follow this prescribed order must be justified. The first in order of preference is the person named as executor in the will of the deceased, the second is the surviving husband or wife, and the third is the principal devisee or legatee of the testator. If no executor is named in the will, or there is no will, then the highest in preference is the surviving spouse. The surviving spouse can waive her right to serve under Section 79 and appoint another qualified person, regardless of the order of preference that person is assigned by Section 77. On the other hand, if the surviving spouse simply refuses to serve, then the next order of preference is the principal devisee or legatee.

Any such refusal to serve must be documented, generally by an instrument in writing in which the spouse renounces her right to serve. If there is no executor, no will, and no surviving spouse, the principal devisee can indicate her refusal to serve by written document, in which case the court will go to the next category, which is any devisee or legatee. This category is followed by the nearest of kin, a creditor, any person of good character, and, finally, anybody.

Section 78 of the Probate Code lists the disqualifications to serve as executor or administrator. Disqualified persons are **minors**, incompetents, convicted felons, nonresidents (unless they have appointed a resident agent to accept service of process), corporations not authorized to act as a fiduciary in this state, or any other person whom the court finds unsuitable.

APPLICATION

The first step in any administration, whether independent or dependent, is the filing of an application. The statutes dealing with the contents of the application do not distinguish between independent administration and dependent administration. The statutes do, however, distinguish between applications for the probate of a written will and applications for letters of administration, where no will, written or oral, is known to exist.

Sections 81 and 82 are the primary sections of the Probate Code setting out requirements for these applications. Section 81 requirements concern an application for letters testamentary where there is a probate of a will. It applies to the probate of a written will, of a written will not produced, and of a nuncupative will. Section 82 requirements deal with applications for letters of administration where no will, either written or oral, is alleged to exist.

The legal assistant should be extremely familiar with the current requirements of both Section 81 and Section 82. The legislature periodically adds requirements to both statutes that are not picked up by many of the form books for years after the change. For instance, in 1987 a requirement was added that the Social Security numbers of the applicant and the decedent be shown as to both code sections. There are at least two form books published for use in the State of Texas that still do not show this requirement in either the main volume or the pocket parts. Another example: In 1989, a further requirement was added requiring that an application for letters testamentary show whether or not the state, governmental agency of the state, or charitable organization is named by the will as devisee. Almost none of the form books published for Texas reflect this change. It is so frequently left out of applications that the judges in some counties have printed up **trial amendments** adding the language to the application. When attorneys attend court with their client to prove the validity of the will, the clerk hands them the trial amendment and asks them to sign it and file it. At one time some county clerks were (and probably still are) rejecting applications that do not show the social security numbers. At least one county clerk was rejecting applications for letters testamentary unless the **allegation**, concerning whether the state or a charity is named as a devisee, was contained in the application.

It is up to the legal assistant to check any form she uses, particularly in probate, against the current requirements of the statutory or procedural law. A form for application for the probate of a will and the issuance of letters testamentary, where the will names an executor and provides that she be independent, is found as Form 10-1. A form for an application for letters of independent administration with will annexed is attached to this chapter as Form 10-2, and a form for an application for letters of independent administration is attached as Form 10-3.

When a will does not appoint an independent executor or does not appoint any executor at all, or the named executor refuses or is unable to serve, then similar changes need to be made to the application for the probate of a will and issuance of letters testamentary as made in the application for letters of administration in order to change it to an application for letters of independent administration with will annexed.

If an application is made that an administration be made independent, the consent of all devisees and/or heirs must be submitted. A form for such consent is found at Form 10-4.

Section 81 requires that the application for letters testamentary contain:

1. The name and domicile of each applicant.

2. The name, age (if known), and domicile of the decedent, and the fact, time, and place of death. In alleging the domicile of the decedent, one should be careful to remember that the domicile of the decedent also controls the place of venue. The fact of death is presented simply by an allegation that the decedent is dead.

3. Facts showing the court has venue. (Venue is discussed in Chapter 1.) The normal venue is based on the residence of the decedent at the date of death. An allegation should be made here that the defendant resided and was domiciled in the appropriate county at the time of death.

4. A statement that the decedent owned real or personal property, or both, and describing these generally, including the probable value. Most form books and most lawyers meet this requirement by alleging that the decedent owned real and personal property of a probable value in excess of or less than the amount at which **inheritance tax** became due. For instance, at one time an heir of the first class did not owe inheritance tax until the inheritance exceeded $25,000, so the allegation in many form books said that the estate's property either did or did not exceed $25,000. Later, an estate did not owe inheritance tax until the total estate exceeded $200,000, and some form books use this amount. Probably the most common allegation is that the decedent owned real and personal property in excess or not in excess of $50,000, with no explanation for that amount. Some probate judges consider this allegation insufficient. Although these judges may not reject the application, they may request that the application at least describe real property and give approximate market values for real property.

5. The date of the will, the name and residence of the named executor, if any, or if none were named, then the name and residence of the person to whom it is desired that letters be issued, and also the names and residences of the subscribing witnesses, if any. If there is no executor named in the will, then the person to whom letters are issued will be an administrator with will annexed and the letters will be termed "letters of administration with will annexed." In order to convert this application from an application for probate of written will for letters testamentary to an application for probate of written will and for letters of administration with will annexed, one simply changes the name of the letters every place found, replaces the word *executor* with *administrator with will annexed* and adds the allegation that a necessity exists for the administration of the estate, including facts that show such necessity. The latter is a requirement of an application for letters of administration.

6. A statement about whether any children born or adopted after the making of a will survived the decedent, plus their name This relates to Section 67 of the Probate Code which deals with *pretermitted children* (children born to a testator after the testator has executed the will that is probated as his last will and testament).

7. A statement that the executor, applicant, or other person to whom it is desired that letters be issued is not disqualified by law from accepting letters. This relates to Section 78, which was discussed earlier in this chapter.

8. A statement about whether the decedent was ever divorced, and, if so, when and from whom. This relates to Section 69 of the Probate Code, which voids devises to a spouse upon a divorce between the spouses.

9. The Social Security numbers of the applicant and the decedent.

10. Whether the state, a governmental agency of the state, or a charitable organization is named by the will as devisee.

The Rules of Civil Procedure affecting pleadings also apply to applications of probate. Each allegation has to be in a separately numbered paragraph and must be signed by the attorney representing the applicant. Under the signature line must be typed the attorney's name, address, telephone number, state bar number, and fax number. Some forms for applications have a signature line only for the applicant. This does not comply with the Texas Rules of Civil Procedure, which require the signature of the attorney, if there is one. Also, as required in the Texas Rules of Civil Procedure, the application must be on letter-size paper.

Section 81(b) adds some additional requirements to be alleged in the application if the written will cannot be produced in court because it has been lost, accidentally destroyed, or the like. In such case the application must also state:

1. The reason the will cannot be produced.

2. The contents of the will.

3. The date of the will, and the executor appointed therein if any.

4. The name, age, marital status, address, and relationship to the decedent of each devisee and of each person who would inherit as an heir in the absence of a valid will.

The allegation regarding why the will cannot be produced will have to explain the reason for nonproduction in a manner consistent with its being accidentally lost or destroyed rather than deliberately destroyed so as to cause its revocation. Section 85 of the Probate Code says that if a written will cannot be produced in court, the cause of its nonproduction must be proved and such proof must be sufficient to satisfy the court that it cannot, with reasonable diligence, be produced, and the contents of the will must be substantially proved by the testimony of a credible witness who has read it or heard it read. Commonly, proof is a copy of the will from the attorney's file. The requirement of alleging the heirs is in case the court wants to give those heirs personal notice so they have an opportunity to appear and to contest the probate.

In addition, Section 81(c) provides some additional allegations in the case of nuncupative wills. In the opening paragraph, it says that the application shall contain all applicable allegations required with respect to written wills and, in addition, must allege the substance of the testamentary words spoken and the names and residences of the witnesses to the speaking of the will.

An application for letters of administration when no will, written or oral, is alleged to exist must contain most of the same information as required of the application for letters testamentary. In addition, there must be an allegation as to the fact of intestacy and of the name, age, marital status, address, and relationship of each heir to the decedent. Finally, it must be alleged that a necessity exists for administration of the estate, including the facts that show such necessity. Section 178(b) states that a necessity exists if there are two or more debts outstanding against the estate or it is desired to have the county court partition the estate amongst the **distributees**. These two instances of necessity are not exclusive, and other instances can be established or alleged in the application.

Section 81(a) stipulates that the original will be filed along with the application for probate. Thereafter, the will is to remain in the custody of the county clerk unless removed by order of the court. Section 90 of the Probate Code says that the original will can only be removed to another place for inspection, and the person removing the will must give a receipt for it. It is a good idea to advise the client of this requirement, because otherwise she may think she will get the will back.

Section 72 of the Probate Code states that the probate of the will of a living person is void. Further, if the death of the person can be proved by circumstantial evidence, a will may be admitted to probate and letters granted, but no distribution can be made until after three years from the date the letters are granted. This statute also details what happens if the presumably dead person reappears and claims the estate.

Section 73 stipulates that no will is to be admitted to probate after four years from the date of the testator's death, unless the party applying for such probate is not in default by failing to present it within that period. Regardless of whether or not there is default, no letters testamentary can be issued where a will is admitted to probate after the four years. The will may be admitted to probate only as a **muniment of title** (to be discussed in Chapter 12).

Section 74 requires that all applications for the grant of letters testamentary and of administration be filed within four years of the death of the testator or intestate. Section 94 states that no will is effectual until probated.

Once the application has been prepared, the legal assistant will need to arrange to file the application together with the original will. Many attorneys and firms do not trust the U.S. Postal Service and prefer the application and will to be filed by hand. Often, this will be done by the legal assistant or a runner. Whoever does it, a check must be obtained, payable to the county clerk, in the amount of the required **court cost deposit**. Whether the monies are advanced by the firm and an operating account check is written, the monies are collected from the client and a trust account check is written, or the client writes a check to the county clerk is a question of firm policy.

Almost all county and district clerks publish schedules of required court cost deposits, and the legal assistant should have a schedule for each county in which the law firm customarily files probate matters. If the application is being filed in a county for which the legal assistant does not have a schedule, then a phone call should be placed to the county clerk to determine the court cost deposit for that particular type of probate matter.

The legal assistant should also learn from the county clerk what the cutoff time is for posting probate citations. Section 128 of the Probate Code provides that, where an application is for probate of a written will that is produced in court or for letters of administration, citation is to be by posting. If the application is for probate of a written will not produced or of a nuncupative will, citation shall be by personal service. As discussed in Chapter 1, the clerk prepares the citation, not the legal assistant.

As discussed in Chapter 1, the citation must be posted or served by Thursday afternoon in order to get the earliest hearing date. Because many attorneys wait until the last minute to file, numerous county clerks have established specific cutoff times, and any citation posted on a Thursday must be filed prior to that cutoff time. Cutoff times range from noon to 4:00 P.M. Some may be set for earlier than noon. The legal assistant needs to know the cutoff times of all the county clerks with whom the firm customarily files probate matters.

The original application with the attorney's signature on it and the original will and a check for the court cost deposit are forwarded to the county clerk's office. In most counties, there is no need to send a copy to have file stamped. The county clerk will forward to the attorney a copy of the prepared citation, which will show the cause number (as will the fee receipt) and the earliest date on which the hearing can be held, which is 10:00 A.M. on the Monday following the expiration of 10 days from the posting or service of citation.

If the application of the will and the court cost deposit check are to be mailed, an appropriate enclosure letter should be included; a sample is found at Form 10-5. Most firms want the letter to go by certified mail, return receipt requested, if not registered, to protect the original will as much as possible.

THE HEARING

Immediately after receiving a copy of the citation, or its posting in those counties where the clerk does not mail out a copy, the legal assistant should begin to arrange for a **setting**. The procedure for obtaining a setting on an uncontested probate matter, which does not require an order of the court, varies from county to county. In some counties, one calls the **court coordinator** or administrator, in others the county clerk, and in yet others the judge's secretary. A number of counties, have set times of the week during which the court hears probate matters, and one simply shows up and places her name on a list. Immediately on obtaining employment, the legal assistant should find out her firm's procedure for obtaining a setting in the county in which she works (and perhaps surrounding counties, depending on the firm's practice).

Generally speaking, the attorney will attend the hearing on the application by herself and will not take the legal assistant along. The hearing is too simple to justify having two persons in court. As it stands now, a legal assistant may not participate actively in a probate hearing. No change in that rule is expected, even though such hearings are fairly routine and could easily be handled by a legal assistant.

There is still plenty for the legal assistant to do in preparation for the hearing. First of all, with regard to proof to be heard at the hearing, Section 84 of the Probate Code provides that if the will is self-proved, there need be no further proof of the execution with the formalities and solemnities and under the circumstances required to make it a valid will. Consequently, it is necessary only to take the applicant, who can usually testify concerning all of the facts necessary to be introduced into evidence. This consists primarily of proof as to each item alleged in the application.

If the will is not self-proved, it must be proved by the sworn testimony of one or more of the subscribing witnesses. If the subscribing witnesses are not residents of the county and not subject to a **subpoena**, it must be proved by either the written or the oral deposition of at least one of them. If none of the subscribing witnesses can be found or they are deceased or beyond the jurisdiction of the court, the will can be proved by two witnesses to the signature of one or both of the subscribing witnesses or of the testator. It will be up to the legal assistant to arrange for the attendance in court of the necessary witnesses. If the testimony of subscribing witnesses is necessary and they are not within the county, the legal assistant must arrange for their deposition by written interrogatories, which is the usual method. The procedure for taking such depositions on written interrogatories is provided for in the Texas Rules of Civil Procedure as modified by Section 84(c), which says that a deposition for the purpose of establishing a will may be taken in the same manner as provided elsewhere in the Code for the taking of depositions where there is no opposing party. This is a reference to Section 22 of the Probate Code, which provides that if there is no opposing party or attorney of record on whom notice and/or copies of interrogatories may be served, then service may be had by posting notice of intention to take depositions for a period of 10 days, as provided in the Code governing posting of other notices, and that a commission to take the deposition will issue after 10 days from the date on which the notice is filed with the clerk.

Section 22 further allows the judge of the court to file cross-interrogatories if she so desires.

The need to produce a subscribing witness in court has declined, because very few people are dying who have wills executed prior to the adoption of the Probate Code section providing for a self-proving will. There are a few wills with defective self-proving affidavits, primarily because one of the form books contained a defective self-proving affidavit. If this happens, then it is the same as if the will is not self-proved, so witnesses must be produced. Regardless, the need to produce witnesses to prove up a will is very small, and the need to take a witness' testimony by deposition is even smaller. Form 10-6 shows a letter arranging for a witness to be present.

The best way to arrange for the applicant or the witnesses to attend court is by telephone, followed up by a letter of confirmation so there can be no question as to whether the phone call was made.

The applicant or the witnesses might be nervous. If the legal assistant has attended probate hearings, she will find it quite easy to allay these fears. If, however, the legal assistant has never attended probate hearings, probably the best way to soothe the client or witnesses is to reassure them that the attorney will brief them prior to the hearing and that they will only be asked simple questions like "Is it true that your name is Jane Smith?"

The legal assistant will also need to see to the preparation of legal documents that must be carried to the courthouse by the attorney. These are at least two in number and generally three:

1. An order admitting the will to probate, if there is a will, and granting letters, either testamentary or of administration, as the case may be.

2. A **written proof**.

3. The oath to be signed by the personal representative, assuming that the person who is applying to be the personal representative will be present in court, which is not always the case.

Orders that go along with the applications are found in Forms 10-7, 10-8, and 10-9. Examples of oaths are found in Forms 10-13, 10-14, and 10-15.

Many law firms want the name of the judge typed under the signature line exactly the way the judge signs. If the legal assistant does not know who the judge is or how she signs her name, the legal assistant is going to have to ask someone else in the law firm or find a copy of another order signed by the judge. Some firms are not so particular, and under each signature line they simply put "Judge Presiding." It is important, however, that at the end of the order and before the signature line, the order recite, "Signed and ordered entered this _____ day of _____, 19____." or, "Ordered entered this _____day of _____, 19____." Some judges will accept the mere statement of "entered this _____ day of _____, 19____." This order is in fact a final judgment that is appealable.

The next document required to be prepared for the attorney to take to court is what is generally called a written proof. This is in compliance with Section 87 of the Probate Code, which requires that all testimony taken in open court with regard to an application of probate of will shall be put in writing at the time it is taken, and shall be subscribed and sworn to by the witness or witnesses, and then filed with the clerk.

Although Section 87 requires written proof in connection only with an application of probate of will, many probate judges also require it in connection with an application for administration of an intestate decedent's estate, in which case it is called "Proof of Death and Other Facts." The written proof is a narrative statement of the evidence that is to be proffered by the witnesses. Forms of written proofs are found in Forms 10-10, 10-11, and 10-12.

Notice that rather than being signed before a notary public, they are signed before a deputy county clerk. In smaller counties, the county clerk herself may be the one who attends court during the hearing on the application. The clerks of courts have the power to administer oaths and take acknowledgments relative to matters pending in the court. No notary publics will be present, even though some form books have prepared the signature line of the officer administering the oath for a notary public rather than for a deputy county clerk. If the attorney shows up in court with a written proof or (as will be discussed later) an oath that requires a notary public, she may very well have to find a typewriter in the county clerk's office to prepare a new written proof or to amend the one she has so it properly reflects that it is the deputy county clerk administering the oath rather than the notary public. If she shows up without a written proof, she will have to pay the court reporter to take down and transcribe the testimony.

The third document the legal assistant will need to prepare is the oath of the personal representative. If the person who is to become personal representative is going to be present in court, the oath can be signed, before the deputy county clerk, immediately after the court enters. If, on the other hand, the person who is going to be the personal representative will not be present in court, the oath will have to be signed later, and before a notary public. The legal assistant should therefore determine whether or not the prospective personal representative will be present in court. If so, the oath should be prepared to be executed before a deputy county clerk, as shown in Forms 10-13 and 10-14. If not, then the oath should be prepared for execution before a notary public, as shown in Form 10-15.

Even though an order has now been entered directing the issuance of letters, no letters will actually issue until the personal representative qualifies. Section 189 of the Probate Code provides that a personal representative shall be deemed qualified when she has taken and filed her oath and made the required bond, if one is required, and had the bond approved by the judge and filed with the clerk. If no bond is required, then the representative shall be deemed qualified when she has taken and filed the oath. The personal representative must qualify within 20 days of the entry of the order. Failure to do so, however, only subjects the personal representative to possible removal and the appointment of a substitute.

Inasmuch as an independent executor or administrator will be required to file a bond only infrequently, the discussion of bonds is deferred to Chapter 11.

INVENTORY AND APPRAISEMENT

The independent executor or administrator is subject to the same requirements concerning the filing of an inventory, appraisement, and list of claims as the dependent executor or administrator. The Probate Code sections relating to the inventory, appraisement, and list of claims are Sections 248 through 261. Section 250 requires that the personal representative file with the clerk of the court, within 90 days after her qualification, a **verified**, full and detailed inventory of all the property of the estate that has come into her possession and knowledge. The inventory must include all real property of the estate situated in the State of Texas and all personal property of the estate wherever situated. The representative must set out in the inventory the appraisement, or the fair market value, of each item as of the date of death. Further, the inventory is to specify what portion of the property is separate property and what portion community property. If the property is owned in common with others, the interest owned by the estate shall be shown, together with the names and relationships of the co-owners.

Section 251 requires that there shall be made out and attached to the inventory a full and complete list of all claims due or owing to the estate. This is not a list of debts owed by the estate, but rather debts owed <u>to</u> the estate; that is, they are assets of the estates, not liabilities.

Some attorneys also list in the inventory any claims that are due and owing by the estate, including the debts that existed at the time of death, that arose by reason of death, or that have become due by reason of administration of the estate. This practice relates back to a time when the Probate Court determined whether the estate owed inheritance tax and, if so, the amount. Because inheritance tax was imposed on the net estate, that is, the assets of the estate minus the liabilities of the estate, the probate judge could not determine the amount of inheritance tax due unless the debts owed by the estate were also set out in the inventory, appraisement, and list of claims. The setting out of claims or debts owed by the estate is not required by the Probate Code and is no longer necessary.

The list of claims must show the name of each person indebted to the estate and her address, the nature of the debt (whether by note or by bond or written obligation), the date of the indebtedness and the date it became due or will become due, the amount, the rate of interest, and whether the claim is separate or community property.

Attached to the inventory, appraisement, and list of claims is an affidavit, subscribed and sworn to before an officer authorized to administer oaths, that the inventory and list of claims is a true and correct statement of the property and claims of the estate that have come to the knowledge of the personal representative. Some of the forms have separate oaths attached to the inventory and appraisement and to the list of claims. Probably because Section 250 says the inventory and appraisement shall be verified and Section 252 says attached to the whole thing shall be an affidavit swearing to both the inventory and the list of claims. The more modern practice appears to be to have a single affidavit in which the personal representative swears to the accuracy of both the inventory and appraisement and the list of claims.

At one time in the history of Texas probate law, the market value of the items of real and personal property shown in the inventory was determined by two appraisers appointed by the court. The use of the appraisers was made mandatory by the Probate Code, even though it was not necessary in smaller estates. For estates in which appraisers were really not necessary, even though required by the Probate Code, the judges often appointed deputy county clerks as the appraisers. The law-yer prepared the inventory and appraisement, putting in the figures that she and the client established, took it to the county clerk, found the deputy county clerks that had been appointed by the court, had them sign it, and paid to them the $5 fee set by Section 253 of the Probate Code.

Sometime later, Section 248, which had required the appointment of appraisers, was amended to provide that the court could, with just cause, dispense with the necessity of appraisers. This required an affirmative finding in the order granting letters that appraisers were unnecessary and therefore were dispensed with. Thereafter, Section 248 was changed to its present language, which states that the court will appoint appraisers only if it deems it necessary. Nothing is required to be put into the order granting the letters unless the court finds it necessary to have appraisers. Generally, the only time this happens is when some interested party asks the court to appoint appraisers. Section 248 provides for the appointment, when necessary, of not less than one and no more than three disinterested persons to appraise the property of the estate. These will normally be people who have some specialized knowledge concerning the value of real property or personal property in the county of probate.

Section 255 provides that when the inventory, appraisement, and list of claims is filed, the judge of the court shall examine and approve or disapprove it. If approved, the judge issues an order to that effect, normally attached to the inventory, appraisement, and list of claims (see the sample inventory and list of claims provided in Form 10-16.) If disapproved, the judge enters an order to that effect and requires the return of another inventory, appraisement, and list of claims.

There are other provisions in the Probate Code requiring an additional inventory and appraisement if new property is discovered or if someone objects that property or claims have not been included or that the appraisement is unfair. Section 149(c) stipulates that an independent executor or administrator may be removed as executor or administrator if she fails to return, within 90 days after qualification, an inventory, appraisement, and list of claims.

Finally, Section 261 provides that the inventory, appraisement, and list of claims may be used in evidence but shall not be conclusive evidence.

In an estate where there is some bickering and maneuvering, games can be played with an inventory and appraisement. For instance, if the independent executor or dependent executor knows that one of the devisees or heirs particularly wants an article of personal property or perhaps a piece of real property and is insisting that she receive that particular piece of property, she can inflate its value on the inventory and appraisement. Likewise, if the executor or representative wants a particular piece of property for herself, she can deflate is value slightly. The legal assistant should be alert for these types of games, and should remember that the firm she works for does not represent just the executor or the administrator, but also has ethical responsibility and civil liability to the heirs or devisees and, perhaps, even the creditors. This is similar to the kind of problems attorneys can get into when they create business organizations: Once the business organization is created, the attorney represents the business organization and not those who engaged the attorney to create it. It is easy to think of the personal representative as the only client because it is she who came into the office, entered into a fee agreement with the firm, and is the only one with whom there was contact. However, she is not the only client. Care should be taken by the legal assistant that she and the firm do not get caught up in these kinds of games and end up in conflict with other persons with an interest in the estate.

Whenever the estate is required to file a United States Estate Tax Return, most attorneys prefer to defer the filing of the inventory, appraisement, and list of claims until the return is prepared, so the inventory conforms to it. (Forms of a motion and order postponing the due date of the inventory may be found in Chapter 11.)

PAYMENT OF CLAIMS

The independent executor or administrator is not required to do anything after the filing of the inventory, appraisement, and list of claims. As we will see later, the independent executor may close the independent administration by affidavit, and under certain circumstances may be required either to give a bond or to make an accounting after 15 months from the date the administration was created. The only requirement for the interim period is that contained in Section 146 of the Probate Code: The independent executor must receive and classify claims and allow and pay or reject claims in the same order of priority, classification, and proration as required by Part Four of Chapter 8 of the Probate Code, beginning at Section 294.

Although Section 146 does not specifically require the giving of notices, as do the aforementioned claims procedures, there are a number of attorneys who believe that the independent executor or administrator must comply with the requirements regarding notice to creditors. Nothing in the Probate Code expressly demands the independent executor or administrator to do so. In fact, it appears that if the independent executor or administrator were required to give notices, some such language would have been placed in Section 146.

Regardless, most attorneys probably do follow the notice requirements. These are set out primarily in Sections 294 and 295. Section 294 requires a notice to creditors to be published in some newspaper printed in the county in which the letters were issued. The notice must include the time of the issuance of letters, the address to which claims may be presented, and instructions as to the representative's choice that the claims be presented either to him personally or to him in care of the representative's attorney. The notice need be published only once. When it has been published, the newspaper will attach a publisher's affidavit to a copy of the printed notice, and an employee will sign and swear to the facts contained in the affidavit. Then it will be sent back to the attorney who placed the ad, who should immediately file it in the clerk's office. In addition, if the decedent had been paying some form of taxes to the Comptroller of Public Accounts, then a notice must be sent to the Comptroller by certified or registered mail.

Section 295 requires that within four months of receiving letters the representative must give notice to each and every person who had a claim for money that was secured by a deed of trust, a mortgage, or a vendor's, mechanic's, or other contractor's lien on real estate belonging to the estate. In addition to this notice, and also within the same period of time, notice must be given to each person having an outstanding claim for money against the estate of which the representative has knowledge. These notices must be given by certified mail or registered letter, with return receipt requested, addressed to the record holder of the indebtedness at her last known post office address. Copies of the notice, together with the return receipt and an affidavit of the representative, are to be filed in the Probate Court. A copy of the notice to be published in the newspaper is found at Form 10-17, a copy of a letter forwarding the notice to the publisher is at Form 10-18, and a form letter to creditors in compliance with Probate Code Section 295 is found at Form 10-19. The attorney's affidavit is found at Form 10-19A, and the letter to general creditors is found at Form 10-20.

Sections 241-247 of the Probate Code cover the compensation for and recovery of expenses by a personal representative. Form 10-21 presents a motion for payment of independent executrix fees and costs. The legal assistant should be familiar with how the exact fee amounts are arrived at, as stipulated in Section 241(a) with regard to executors and administrators.

SALE OF REAL PROPERTY

Chapter Five included a discussion concerning the power of an independent executor to sell real property belonging to the estate of a decedent, unless that power was included in the will. In an independent administration where there is no will, there is obviously no such clause. Consequently, where the will contains no clause granting discretionary power of sale or where there is no will, a problem exists in regard to the power of an independent administrator to sell real property belonging to the estate, unless the sale can be adequately shown to be for the purposes of the administration of the estate.

Title underwriters have adopted a rule whereby they will not insure a sale of real property by an independent administrator, except where authorized by an appropriate clause in a will, unless:

1. It is adequately demonstrated that the sale is for the purposes of administration, such as for the payment of the debts of the estate.

2. All devisees named in the will to receive the property join in the execution of the deed.

3. The independent administrator goes through the procedures to get court permission to sell the property (see the next chapter). The Probate Code does not authorize such a procedure in an independent administration, but the probate courts generally have been cooperative.

CLOSING THE ESTATE

Section 151 of the Probate Code provides that the independent executor may close the independent administration by affidavit. As in other statutes, the word *may* indicates discretion. The independent executor/administrator may choose to close or not to close the administration by affidavit. Again, attorneys and law firms differ in their practice. A number of lawyers consider it appropriate not to close the estate. Generally, these are individuals who have previously had a problem in an estate where, many years after the estate either was or could have been closed, assets have been discovered that either were difficult to deal with because the estate had been closed or were easy to deal with because the estate had not been closed. Sometimes, survivors, years later, find stock certificates they had not known the deceased possessed, or the county tax office sends a letter threatening a suit for unpaid taxes on property that no one knew that the decedent owned. These can be handled very easily if the independent administration is not closed.

Section 153 provides that the executor may receive new letters testamentary at any time before the authority of an executor has been terminated by the closing of the estate, either by affidavit, as provided for in Section 151, or by action by the distributees, as dealt with in Section 152. If some property is discovered, the executor/administrator simply has to go to the county clerk's office and get new, currently dated letters testamentary, with which she can handle the necessary transfers. This is true even when property or assets of the estate are discovered years later. Even if the estate has been closed, there is usually some way to handle newly discovered assets. But it is not going to be as easy, and sometimes it will be impossible, because of deaths, disappearances, etc.

If a decision is made to keep the estate open, the legal assistant should be sure that deeds are prepared for the independent executor/administrator to sign conveying all real property owned by the estate to the devisees named in the will. This is necessary because as long as the estate is open, the executor/administrator is entitled to possession of assets of the estate for the purpose of administration. If the devisees desire to sell, they will have to get the independent executor/administrator to sign a deed to them at that time or to join in the deed to the purchaser. Some may not be very happy about having to do this. On the other hand, if the estate is closed, that fact, in itself, divests the executor/administrator of the right to possess any of the assets of the estate, and the will serves as a muniment of title and vests title to all real property in the named devisees.

If the firm or attorney the legal assistant works for follows the practice of closing the independent administration when it is believed that all creditors have been paid and all property has been distributed to the persons entitled to it, then the estate is closed by filing a closing report verified by an affidavit showing:

1. The property of the estate that came into the hands of the independent executor.

2. The debts that have been paid.

3. The debts, if any, still owed by the estate.

4. The property of the estate, if any, remaining on hand after the payment of debts.

5. The names and residences of the person to whom the property of the estate has been distributed.

The executor must file signed receipts or other proof of delivery of property to the distributees named in the closing report, if the closing report shows there was property remaining on hand after the payment of all debts and claims.

There is no requirement for approval by the court; rather, Section 151(b) states that the filing of the affidavit and proof of delivery automatically terminates the independent administration and the power and authority of the independent executor. Further, when the affidavit has been filed, persons dealing with properties of the estate or claims against the estate shall deal directly with the distributees. Section 151(c) uses the same language as used with reference to the probate of wills as a muniment of title to indicate that the filing of the affidavit alone and by itself is sufficient to vest title in the distributees.

An example of a closing affidavit is found in Form 10-22. A receipt, to be signed by the distributees, is at Form 10-23; a distribution deed is at Form 10-24.

Section 152 allows the devisees or distributees to force an independent executor/administrator to close an estate by filing a verified report, stipulated in Section 151, at any time after the estate has been fully administered and there is no longer any need for an independent administration.

Although not dealing with the closing of the estate, Sections 154 and 154(A) of the Texas Probate Code deal with the continuation of an estate where an independent executor/administrator either dies, resigns, fails to qualify, or is removed from office with things still to be done in the estate. The court has the power in this circumstance to appoint a successor administrator if none is provided for in the will of the decedent. This administrator will be dependent, unless, under Section 154(A), all of the distributees, or devisees and/or heirs, agree to the appointment of a successor independent executor. The successor can be made independent by virtually the same procedure that an original administrator could have been made independent under Section 145 of the Probate Code. An example of a form for application for successor administration is attached to this chapter as Form 10-25.

CHAPTER QUESTIONS AND EXERCISES

1. State the circumstances under which an independent administration may be created.

2. What are the differences between an application for probate of a will and for letters testamentary and an application for letters of administration?

3. What is the order of preference for persons to be chosen to serve as executor or administrator?

4. What must be sent to the courthouse with the original application to probate a will?

5. What are the requirements of the Texas Rules of Civil Procedure concerning the signature on a probate application?

6. What are the duties of the legal assistant concerning the hearing on the probate application?

7. What must be included in the inventory, appraisement, and list of claims?

8. What commission or fee is an executor allowed to charge the estate for her services?

9. What notices are given creditors in the administration of an estate?

10. What is the procedure for closing an independent administration?

11. Prepare an application to be filed in your county for the following situation: Harry Hanson had a self-proven will dated November 22,

1972. He had no children born after the making of the will and was not divorced prior to his death on February 2 of this year. He named his wife, Harriet, as independent executrix and left his entire estate to her. He owned only his community property interest in the home, the usual personal property, and bank accounts. Make up any additional names, address, numbers, or other necessary information.

12. Repeat Exercise 11, except this time Harriet has predeceased and the will appoints Harry, Jr., as substitute independent executor.

13. For the following circumstances, prepare the necessary documents to create and independent administration, adding whatever information is needed to complete the document:

    Syd Stewart dies in your county without a will. He leaves only community property and is survived by his wife and two adult children. His heirs do not want the added expense of a dependent administration and bond.

14. Prepare an "enclosure letter" forwarding the documents prepared in Exercise 12 to the courthouse in the county in which you reside. Include in your letter the actual name and address of the county clerk.

15. Prepare the documents needed at the hearing for the application required to be prepared in Exercise 11.

16. Prepare the documents needed at the hearing for the application required to be prepared in Exercise 13.

17. Prepare an inventory, appraisement, and list of claims with reference to the facts given in Exercise 11. The description of the real property and banks should be localized to your county. There are two vehicles, one checking account, one savings account, and a certificate of deposit in the same bank where the checking account is. Decedent also had a vested interest in a pension and profit-sharing plan at his place of employment. Include the usual things that people own (referred to in question 11), such as furniture and furnishings, personal effects, and clothes. Supply all other information you might need.

Form 10-1: Application for Probate and Letters Testamentary

NO. _____

IN RE ESTATE OF	§	IN THE COUNTY COURT
PETER SMITH,	§	AT LAW NO. _____
DECEASED	§	ROUGH RIDER COUNTY, TEXAS

APPLICATION FOR PROBATE OF WILL PRODUCED
IN COURT AND FOR ISSUANCE OF LETTERS TESTAMENTARY

TO THE HONORABLE JUDGE OF SAID COURT:

PAULA SMITH, Applicant, for the purpose of probating the written will of **PETER SMITH**, deceased, and for issuance of Letters Testamentary, furnishes the following information to the Court:

I.

Applicant is interested in this estate and is an individual domiciled in and residing at 1412 Bullmoose, San Juan Hill, Texas 79231, Rough Rider County, Texas.

II.

Decedent died on March 3, 1992, in San Juan Hill, Rough Rider County, Texas at the age of 87 years.

III.

This Court has jurisdiction and venue because deceased was domiciled and had a fixed place of residence in this county at the time of death.

IV.

Decedent owned real property as part of the community estate described generally as a house and lot located at 1412 Bullmoose, San Juan Hill, Texas 79231, more particularly described as:

Lot Two (2), Block One (1), Sunnyside Addition, an addition in the City of San Juan Hill, Texas, as shown by the map or Plat Records of Rough Rider County in Volume 12, at page 334 of the map records of Rough Rider County, Texas

Decedent owned personal property as part of the community estate described generally as household goods, personal effects, clothing, cash, tools, and 1991 Chevrolet Lumina APV, vehicle I.D. #3CZL42810M213. All of such property has a probate value of in excess of $500,000.00.

V.

Decedent left a valid, unrevoked, written will bearing decedent's signature and dated June 19, 1964, which is filed with this application.

VI.

Decedent's will named his spouse, **PAULA SMITH**, whose residence address is 1412 Bullmoose, San Juan Hill, Texas 79231, Rough Rider County, Texas, to serve without bond or other security as Independent Executrix.

VII.

The subscribing witnesses to the will and their address are:

Selma Secretary, 123 President, San Juan Hill, Texas.

Rhonda Runner, 12C Whitehouse Blvd., San Juan Hill, Texas.

VIII.

No child was born to or adopted by decedent after the making of the will.

IX.

Applicant is not disqualified by law from accepting letters.

X.

Decedent was never divorced.

XI.   ⟶ TAKE OUT

Decedent's Social Security number was 280-92-4242 and Applicant's Social Security number is 420-26-4340.

XII.

The will provides that no action be had or taken by the Probate Court other than probating the will and filing an inventory and appraisement of the estate and a list of claims.

521453

Form 10-1: (continued)

XIII.

The will was made self-proved in the manner prescribed by law.

XIV.

The will contains no provision which makes any devise in favor of the State of Texas or any governmental agency or charitable organization.

WHEREFORE, Applicant requests that citation be issued to all persons interested in this estate as required by law, that the will be admitted to probate, that letters testamentary be issued to the person named in paragraph VI, and that such other and further orders be made as the Court may deem proper.

Respectfully submitted,

TEDDY & FRANKLIN

_____

JOHN TEDDY

State Bar No. 00000100

5155 Teton Pkwy., Suite 206

P.O. Box 186

Corpus Christi, TX 79421

(512) 555-1234 Telephone

(512) 555-5678 FAX

ATTORNEY FOR THE ESTATE

Form 10-2: Application for Probate and Letters of Independent Administration with Will Annexed

NO. _____

IN RE ESTATE OF	§	IN THE COUNTY COURT
PETER SMITH,	§	AT LAW NO. _____
DECEASED	§	ROUGH RIDER COUNTY, TEXAS

**APPLICATION FOR PROBATE OF WILL PRODUCED
IN COURT AND FOR ISSUANCE OF LETTERS OF INDEPENDENT
ADMINISTRATION WITH WILL ANNEXED**

TO THE HONORABLE JUDGE OF SAID COURT:

PETER SMITH, JR., Applicant, for the purpose of probating the written will of **PETER SMITH**, deceased, and for issuance of Letters Testamentary, furnishes the following information to the Court:

I.

Applicant is interested in this estate and is an individual domiciled in and residing at 706 Capitol, San Juan Hill, Texas 79231, Rough Rider County, Texas.

II.

Decedent died on March 3, 1992, in San Juan Hill, Rough Rider County, Texas at the age of 87 years.

III.

This Court has jurisdiction and venue because deceased was domiciled and had a fixed place of residence in this county at the time of death.

IV.

Decedent owned real property as part of the community estate described generally as a house and lot located at 1412 Bullmoose, San Juan Hill, Texas 79231, more particularly described as:

Lot Two (2), Block One (1), Sunnyside Addition, an addition in the City of San Juan Hill, Texas, as shown by the map or Plat Records of Rough Rider County in Volume 12, at page 334 of the map records of Rough Rider County, Texas

Decedent owned personal property as part of the community estate described generally as household goods, personal effects, clothing, cash, tools, and 1991 Chevrolet Lumina APV, vehicle I.D. #3CZL42810M213. All of such property has a probate value of in excess of $500,000.00.

V.

Decedent left a valid, unrevoked, written will bearing decedent's signature and dated June 19, 1964, which is filed with this application.

VI.

Decedent's will named his spouse, **PAULA SMITH**, whose residence address is 1412 Bullmoose, San Juan Hill, Texas 79231, Rough Rider County, Texas, to serve without bond or other security as Independent Executrix. **PAULA SMITH** died on February 11, 1978, and the Last Will and Testament of **PETER SMITH** appoints no substitute executor.

VII.

The subscribing witnesses to the will and their address are:

Selma Secretary, 123 President, San Juan Hill, Texas.

Rhonda Runner, 12C Whitehouse Blvd., San Juan Hill, Texas.

VIII.

No child was born to or adopted by decedent after the making of the will.

IX.

Applicant is qualified and not disqualified by law from accepting letters.

X.

Decedent was never divorced.

XI.

Decedent's Social Security number was 280-92-4242 and Applicant's Social Security number is 420-26-4340.

XII.

All devisees named in such will have filed a consent to the appointment of applicant as administrator with will annexed and further agreeing that no action be had or taken by the Probate Court other than probating the will and filing an inventory and appraisement of the estate and a list of claims.

Form 10-2: (continued)

XIII.

The will was made self-proved in the manner prescribed by law.

XIV.

The will contains no provision which makes any devise in favor of the state or any governmental agency or charitable organization.

WHEREFORE, Applicant requests that citation be issued to all persons interested in this estate as required by law, that the will be admitted to probate, that Letters of Administration with Will Annexed be issued to the person named in paragraph VI, andthat such other and further orders be made as the Court may deem proper.

Respectfully submitted,

TEDDY & FRANKLIN

JOHN TEDDY
State Bar No. 00000100
5155 Teton Pkwy., Suite 206
P.O. Box 186
Corpus Christi, TX 79421
(512) 555-1234 Telephone
(512) 555-5678 FAX

ATTORNEY FOR THE ESTATE

Form 10-3: Application for Letters of Independent Administration

NO. _____

IN RE ESTATE OF	§	IN THE COUNTY COURT
PETER SMITH,	§	AT LAW NO. _____
DECEASED	§	ROUGH RIDER COUNTY, TEXAS

APPLICATION FOR LETTERS OF INDEPENDENT ADMINISTRATION

TO THE HONORABLE JUDGE OF SAID COURT:

PAULA SMITH, applicant, makes this application for letters of administration of the estate of **PETER SMITH**, deceased, and furnishes the following information to the Court:

1. Applicant is interested in this Estate and is an individual domiciled in and residing at 1412 Bullmoose, San Juan Hill, Texas 79231.

2. Applicant is entitled to Letters of Administration and is not disqualified by law to act as administratrix.

3. Decedent died intestate on March 3, 1992, in San Juan Hill, Rough Rider County, Texas, at the age of 87 years, have not elapsed since decedent's death.

4. This Court has jurisdiction and venue because decedent was domiciled and had a fixed place of residence in this County on the date of death.

5. Decedent owned real and personal property described generally as a home, bonds, automobile, cash, household goods, and personal effects of a probably value in excess of $25,000.00.

6. The name, age, marital status, and address if known, and the relationship, if any, of each heir to the decedent, or each person with a potential interest in the real estate of the decedent, are as follows:

   NAME: PAULA SMITH   AGE: Adult
   ADDRESS: 1412 Bullmoose, San Juan Hill, TX 79231
   MARITAL STATUS: Widow
   RELATIONSHIP TO DECEDENT: Wife

   NAME: PETER SMITH, JR.   AGE: Adult
   ADDRESS: 252 Yellowstone Parkway, San Juan Hill, TX 79231
   MARITAL STATUS: Single
   RELATIONSHIP TO DECEDENT: Son

   NAME: PENELOPE SMITH   AGE: Adult
   ADDRESS: 721 Monolle Drive, San Juan Hill, TX 79231
   MARITAL STATUS: Married
   RELATIONSHIP TO DECEDENT: Daughter

7. The children born to or adopted by decedent were:
   As shown in paragraph #6.

8. Decedent was divorced from JANE SMITH on or about April 5, 1931, in Corpus Christi, Texas. No children were born of that union.

9. A necessity exists for administration of the Estate because there are at least two debts against the estate.

10. There is no need for appointment of appraisers.

11. All of the distributees of the decedent have agreed on the advisability of having an independent administration and collectively designate **PAULA SMITH**, a qualified person, to serve as Independent Administratrix. The distributees request that no action be had in this Court in relation to the settlement of the decedent's estate other than the return of an inventory, appraisement, and list of claims of the decedent's estate.

12. All of the distributees of the decedent consent to this application, and all of the distributees waive the issuance and service of citation, which waiver will be filed herein.

13. Applicant and distributees further request that bond be waived.

Form 10-3: (continued)

PRAYER

Applicant prays that citation issue as required by law to all person interested in this estate.

That applicant be appointed Independent Administratrix of this estate;

That Letters of Independent Administration be issued to Applicant;

That appraisers not be appointed;

That no action be had in this Court in relation to the settlement of the decedent's estate other than the return of an inventory, appraisement, and list of claims against the decedent's estate;

That bond be waived;

And that all other orders to be entered as the Court may deem proper.

Respectfully submitted,

TEDDY & FRANKLIN

JOHN TEDDY
State Bar No. 00000100
5155 Teton Pkwy., Suite 206
P.O. Box 186
Corpus Christi, TX 79421
(512) 555-1234 Telephone
(512) 555-5678 FAX

ATTORNEY FOR THE ESTATE

Form 10-4: Consent to Independent Administrator and Waiver of Certification

NO. 23814-2

IN RE ESTATE OF	§	IN THE COUNTY COURT
PETER SMITH,	§	AT LAW NO. TWO
DECEASED	§	ROUGH RIDER COUNTY, TEXAS

WAIVER OF CITATION

STATE OF TEXAS	§
COUNTY OF ROUGH RIDER	§

BEFORE ME, the undersigned authority, on this day personally appeared **PETER SMITH, JR.** who being by me duly sworn, upon oath stated:

"I, **PETER SMITH, JR.**, am the adult son and heir and devisee of **PETER SMITH**. My mailing address is 252 Yellowstone Parkway, San Juan Hill, Texas. I have been given a copy of the Application for Letters of Independent Administration that has been filed in this cause, and I have read it and understand it. I hereby waive the issuance and personal service of citation in accordance with Rule 35 of the Texas Probate Code. I agree to all that is stated therein and that the matter may be taken up and considered by the Court without further notice to me. I consent to and request that **PAULA SMITH** be appointed independent Administratrix of the Estate of **PETER SMITH**, Deceased. I request that no action be hand in this Court in relation to the settlement of this estate other than the return of a statutory inventory, appraisement and list of claims. I further request that bond be waived.

_____
PETER SMITH, JR.

SUBSCRIBED AND SWORN TO BEFORE ME this _____ day of _____, 19____.

_____
Notary Public, State of Texas

Form 10-5: Letter in Closing Application

May 4, 1992

Rough Rider County Clerk
Rough Rider County Courthouse
1200 Main
San Juan Hill, TX 79421

     RE: Estate of **PETER SMITH**, Deceased
           County Court at Law
           Rough Rider County, Texas

Dear Sir:

    You will find enclosed with this letter the Application for Probate Will and for Letters Testamentary together with the original will of **PETER SMITH** to be filed among the papers for the above estate.

    Also enclosed is our check in the amount of $125.00 in payment of the court cost deposit.

Yours very truly,

JOHN TEDDY

JT:la

Enclosure

Form 10-6: Information Letter to Client

(Reprinted from Texas Probate System, copyright State Bar of Texas, with permission.)

May 11, 1992

Mrs. Paula Smith
1412 Bullmoose
San Juan Hill, TX 79231

RE: Estate of **PETER SMITH**

Dear Mrs. Smith:

The Application for Probate of will and for Issuance of Letters Testamentary was filed in Cause No. 23814-2 in the County Court at Law No. Two of Rough Rider County, Texas on May 4, 1992 and a copy is enclosed for your review. A hearing has been set for the probate of said will on May 21, 1992 at 1:30 p.m.

At the probate hearing, it will be necessary for you to appear for the purposes of presenting testimony relating to the death and family history of **PETER SMITH**. You will find enclosed a copy of the affidavit setting forth your proposed testimony with respect to the death and family history of **PETER SMITH**.

You will also find enclosed a copy of the document entitled "Oath" which will be presented to, sworn to and executed by you in the presence of the Clerk of the County after the will is admitted to probate.

Assuming no complications arise at the hearing for probate, the last Will and Testament will be admitted to probate on May 21, 1992. I have enclosed a copy of the proposed Order which will be presented to the Judge. At that time you will qualify as Independent Executrix of the Estate, which will entitle you to receive Letters Testamentary.

These Letters Testamentary represent evidence of your appointment as Independent Executrix and grant you full authority to act for and on behalf of the Estate. A copy of said Letters will be forwarded to you for your use in opening a checking account. Any checking or savings accounts opened for the Estate should be styled "Estate of **PETER SMITH**, Deceased, **PAULA SMITH**, Independent Executrix.

The information contained on the following pages is set forth to help you to more fully appreciate the office of Independent Executrix. Although it may appear to be lengthy, I am sure you will find it interesting as well as informative.

First of all, you should be aware of the meaning of "Independent Executrix." An "Executrix" is the person appointed in the will of the Decedent to carry out the desires of the Decedent as expressed in that will and to administer the estate of the Decedent.

The word "Independent: means that the Executrix may act independent of control by the court and is required only to present the will for probate and to file the required Inventory, Appraisement and List of Claims with the Court. Without the use of the word "Independent," virtually all of the Executor's duties and actions would be subject to prior approval by the Court since a mere Executrix is required to obtain court approval for virtually every action. This is obviously a cumbersome and expensive procedure and since you are an Independent Executrix, we will not need to seek court approval for your actions.

An Independent Executrix has broad powers, limited only be the will and the Texas Probate Code, and unless limited by either of said documents, the Executrix may, without Court approval, do anything which an ordinary Executrix or Administrator could o with Court approval.

In your capacity as Independent Executrix, you are the Decedent's representative for the purpose of terminating the Decedent's affairs. This involves the assembly and collection of the Decedent's assets, the payment of debts, expenses of administration, and taxes, and the distribution of the remaining assets to those beneficiaries named by the Decedent's will.

The first step in this journey is for us to have the will admitted to probate. Once this has been accomplished, the administration phase of the Estate will begin. The Executor will need to prepare an inventory of the assets of the Estate, collect debts due to the estate, determine the liabilities of the Estate, and pay the Decedent's enforceable debts and taxes.

Within one month from the date of the filing of your Oath as Independent Executrix, we must publish notice to the general creditors of the Estate. I will prepare that notice and will have it published in an appropriate newspaper.

Within four (4) months after that same date, the Executrix must send notice by registered mail to any secured and general creditors. I will prepare such a notice for each such creditor, if any, and will forward them to you for proper signature and mailing.

Form 10-6: (continued)

Within ninety (90) days after such date, we must file an Inventory, Appraisement and List of Claims, including proper and complete descriptions of the various assets together with accurate valuations of the assets, as of the date of Decedent's death, unless an extension of time for filing is obtained.

Where a Decedent's gross estate (that is all separate property plus Decedent's one-half of the community property) exceeds $600,000.00, a Federal Estate Tax Return must be filed and estate taxes must be paid within nine months after the date of death. For purposes of this return, we can value the estate as of the date of death or as of six months after the date of death. As I do not prepare these tax returns, I would urge you to consult your Certified Public Accountant for preparation of those items.

A final income tax return for the decedent for the year 1992 must be filed and taxes must be paid on or before April 15, 1993, reporting all income earned in 1992, prior to the date of death. A Fiduciary Income Tax Return for the Decedent's Estate (Form 1941) will be required in all years in which the income of Decedent's Estate exceeds $600.00. the beginning date of the first year is the date of Decedent's death (1992) and it may end on December 31 of the same year, or at the end of any other month that does not exceed one year from the date of Decedent's death. Please consult you tax advisor regarding any need for the preparation and filing of such returns.

After all known debts and taxes of Decedent and of Decedent's Estate have been paid, the Executrix may then distribute the remaining assets to the appropriate beneficiaries named in the will.

By way of partial summary, let me point out that the administration of this Estate is an essential and very important process. The administration clears title to real estate, it settles legitimate debts (and wipes out others) and it will establish a new income tax basis for the property in the Estate. It also permits the distribution of property to the persons entitled to receive same under the terms of the will.

I look forward to working with you in this matter. Please call me if you have any questions with respect to the information set forth herein or if I can be of any assistance to you.

Respectfully submitted,

TEDDY & FRANKLIN

JOHN TEDDY
State Bar No. 00000100
5155 Teton Pkwy., Suite 206
P.O. Box 186
Corpus Christi, TX 79421
(512) 555-1234 Telephone
(512) 555-5678 FAX

ATTORNEY FOR THE ESTATE

JT:la

Enclosures

Form 10-7: Order Granting Letters Testamentary

NO. 23814-2

IN RE ESTATE OF	§	IN THE COUNTY COURT
PETER SMITH,	§	AT LAW NO. TWO
DECEASED	§	ROUGH RIDER COUNTY, TEXAS

ORDER PROBATING WILL AND AUTHORIZING LETTERS TESTAMENTARY

On this day, came on to be heard the written application of Applicant, **PAULA SMITH** to probate the will of **PETER SMITH**, deceased, and for letters testamentary. In support of the application, there was presented in open court the will filed with the Court on April 14, 1992.

The Court, having heard the evidence and having reviewed the will and the other papers on file in this cause, finds that all of the statements and allegations contained in the application are true.

The Court further finds that citation and notice as required by law were issued, served, and returned in the manner and for the length of time required by law.

The Court further finds that it has jurisdiction and venue over this estate.

The Court further finds that at the time of executing the will dated June 19, 1964, the decedent was of sound mind and was at least 18 years of age, and that the instrument was provided by law and made self-proved as executed with the formalities and solemnities and under the circumstances required by law to make it a valid will, and that no objection to or contest of the probate of the will has been filed.

The Court finds that **PETER SMITH** died at the age of 87 years on March 3, 1992 in San Juan Hill, Rough Rider Count, Texas, that the will was not revoked by decedent, that four years have not elapsed since the death of the decedent, that no child was born to or adopted by the decedent after the making of the will, and that the decedent was not divorced after the making of the will.

The Court further finds that **PAULA SMITH** was named as the Independent Executrix in the will, and is a resident of and domiciled in San Juan Hill, Texas, and is not disqualified to serve as Independent Executrix under the will.

The Court further finds that the will is entitled to be admitted to probate and that the Independent Executrix is entitled to the issuance of letters testamentary.

The Court further finds that the will provides that no bond be required of the Independent Executrix and that no action be had in the Probate Court with respect to the estate of **PETER SMITH**, deceased, except to probate the will and return and cause to be filed and approved an inventory, appraisement, and list of claims.

IT IS, THEREFORE, ADJUDGED, AND DECREED that the will of **PETER SMITH**, deceased, dated June 19, 1964, and on file with the Court, be and is hereby admitted to probate and record as the last will of **PETER SMITH**, deceased, and that the will, together with the application for probate and the testimony given in these proceedings, be recorded in the minutes of this Court.

IT IS FURTHER ORDERED that **PAULA SMITH** be and she is hereby appointed as Independent Executrix of the estate of **PETER SMITH**, deceased, and that letters testamentary issue upon her taking the oath required by law, without the posting of any bond.

SIGNED AND ORDERED entered this _____ day of _____, 19_____.

_____

JUDGE PRESIDING

Form 10-8: Order Granting Letters of Administration with Will Annexed

NO. 23814-2

IN RE ESTATE OF	§	IN THE COUNTY COURT
PETER SMITH,	§	AT LAW NO. TWO
DECEASED	§	ROUGH RIDER COUNTY, TEXAS

ORDER PROBATING WILL AND AUTHORIZING LETTERS OF ADMINISTRATION WITH WILL ANNEXED

On this day, came on to be heard the written application of Applicant, **PETER SMITH, JR.** to probate the will of **PETER SMITH**, deceased, and for letters testamentary. In support of the application, there was presented in open court the will filed with the Court on April 14, 1992.

The Court, having heard the evidence and having reviewed the will and the other papers on file in this cause, finds that all of the statements and allegations contained in the application are true.

The Court further finds that citation and notice as required by law were issued, served, and returned in the manner and for the length of time required by law.

The Court further finds that it has jurisdiction and venue over this estate.

The Court further finds that at the time of executing the will dated June 19, 1964, the decedent was of sound mind and was at least 18 years of age, and that the instrument was provided by law and made self-proved as executed with the formalities and solemnities and under the circumstances required by law to make it a valid will, and that no objection to or contest of the probate of the will has been filed.

The Court finds that **PETER SMITH** died at the age of 87 years on March 3, 1992 in San Juan Hill, Rough Rider Count, Texas, that the will was not revoked by decedent, that four years have not elapsed since the death of the decedent, that no child was born to or adopted by the decedent after the making of the will, and that the decedent was not divorced after the making of the will.

The Court further finds that **PAULA SMITH** was named as the Independent Executrix in the will, but died on February 11, 1978 and no substitute for her was provided for in the will.

The Court further finds that all devisees named in the will have consented to the appointment of **PETER SMITH, JR.** as Independent Administrator and have requested that no bond be required of him.

The Court further finds that the will is entitled to be admitted to probate and that **PETER SMITH, JR.** is entitled to the issuance of letters of independent administration with will annexed.

The Court further finds that no bond be required of the Independent Administrator with will annexed and that no action be had in the Probate Court with respect to the estate of **PETER SMITH**, deceased, except to probate the will and return and cause to be filed and approved an inventory, appraisement, and list of claims.

IT IS, THEREFORE, ADJUDGED, AND DECREED that the will of **PETER SMITH**, deceased, dated June 19, 1964, and on file with the Court, be and is hereby admitted to probate and record as the last will of **PETER SMITH**, deceased, and that the will, together with the application for probate and the testimony given in these proceedings, be recorded in the minutes of this Court.

IT IS FURTHER ORDERED that **PETER SMITH, JR.** be and he is hereby appointed as Independent Administrator with will annexed of the Estate of **PETER SMITH**, deceased, and that letters issue upon his taking the oath required by law, without the posting of any bond.

SIGNED AND ORDERED entered this _____ day of _____, 19_____.

_____
JUDGE PRESIDING

Form 10-9: Order Granting Letters of Independent Administration

NO. 23814-2

IN RE ESTATE OF	§	IN THE COUNTY COURT
PETER SMITH,	§	AT LAW NO. TWO
DECEASED	§	ROUGH RIDER COUNTY, TEXAS

ORDER GRANTING LETTERS OF INDEPENDENT ADMINISTRATION

On this day the court heard the Application For Appointment of Independent Administratrix and for Letters of Administration filed by **PAULA SMITH**, in the Estate of **PETER SMITH**, deceased.

The Court heard the evidence and reviewed the documents filed herein and finds that the allegations contained in the application are true; that notice and citation have been given in the manner and for the length of time required by law; that decedent is dead and that four years have not elapsed since the date of decedent's death; that this court has jurisdiction and venue of the decedent's estate; that decedent died intestate; that there is a necessity for administration of this Estate; that the application for Letters of Independent Administration should be granted; that applicant is entitled by law to be appointed Independent Administratrix of this Estate and is not disqualified from acting as such Administratrix and is qualified to receive Letters of Independent Administration; and that no interested person has applied for the appointment of appraisers and none are deemed necessary by the Court.

IT IS ORDERED that a bond in the sum of _____ , payable and conditional as required by law shall be required (it is ordered that no bond be required of said Independent Administratrix) and that upon the taking and filing of the oath required by law, Letters of Independent Administration shall issue to **PAULA SMITH** who is appointed Independent Administratrix of this Estate.

SIGNED AND ORDERED entered this _____ day of _____ , 19_____ .

_____
JUDGE PRESIDING

Form 10-10: Proof of Death by Other Facts

NO. 23814-2

IN RE ESTATE OF	§	**IN THE COUNTY COURT**
PETER SMITH,	§	**AT LAW NO. TWO**
DECEASED	§	**ROUGH RIDER COUNTY, TEXAS**

PROOF OF DEATH AND OTHER FACTS

On this day, **PAULA SMITH** personally appeared in open court, and after being duly sworn, deposed and said:

I.

PETER SMITH, decedent, died on March 3, 1992, in San Juan Hill, Rough Rider County, Texas, at the age of 87 years, and four years have not elapsed since the date of decedent's death.

II.

Decedent was domiciled and had a fixed place of residence in this county at the time of death.

III.

The document now shown to me and which purports to be decedent's will dated June 19, 1964, was never revoked so far as I know.

IV.

No child was born to or adopted by decedent after the making of the will.

V.

Decedent never divorced.

VI.

The Independent Executrix named in this will is not disqualified by law from accepting letters testamentary or from serving as such, and is entitled to such letters.

SIGNED AND ORDERED entered this _____ day of _____, 19_____.

_____
PAULA SMITH

SUBSCRIBED AND SWORN TO BEFORE ME by **PAULA SMITH** this ____ day of _____, 19____, to certify which witness my hand and official seal.

_____
CLERK OF THE COUNTY COURT
Court of Rough Rider County, Texas

By: _____
Deputy

Form 10-11: Proof of Death and Other Facts (Will Annexed)

NO. 23814-2

IN RE ESTATE OF	§	IN THE COUNTY COURT
PETER SMITH,	§	AT LAW NO. TWO
DECEASED	§	ROUGH RIDER COUNTY, TEXAS

PROOF OF DEATH AND OTHER FACTS

On this day, **PETER SMITH, JR.**, Affiant, personally appeared in Open Court, and after being duly sworn, deposes and says that:

1. "**PETER SMITH**, Decedent died on March 3, 1992 in San Juan Hill, Rough Rider County, Texas at the age of 87 years.

2. "Decedent was domiciled and had a fixed place of residence in this County at the date of death.

3. "The document dated June 19, 1964, now shown to me and which purports to be Decedent's will was never revoked so far as I know.

4. "No child or children were born to or adopted by Decedent after the date of the will.

5. "Decedent was never divorced.

6. "The Executor appointed in such will is deceased and **PETER SMITH, JR.** is qualified and not disqualified to serve as Independent Administrator with will annexed.

7. "All of the distributees of the Estate of **PETER SMITH** have consented to the creation of an Independent Administration."

SIGNED this _____ day of _____, 19_____.

_____
AFFIANT

SWORN TO AND SUBSCRIBED BEFORE ME by **PETER SMITH, JR.** this _____ day of _____, 19____ , to certify which witness my hand and seal of office.

_____
CLERK OF THE COUNTY COURT
Court of Rough Rider County, Texas

By: _____
Deputy

Form 10-12: Proof of Death and Other Facts (No Will)

NO. 23814-2

IN RE ESTATE OF	§	**IN THE COUNTY COURT**
PETER SMITH,	§	**AT LAW NO. TWO**
DECEASED	§	**ROUGH RIDER COUNTY, TEXAS**

PROOF OF DEATH AND OTHER FACTS

On this day, **PETER SMITH, JR.**, Affiant, personally appeared in Open Court, and after being duly sworn, deposes and says that:

1. "**PETER SMITH**, decedent died on March 3, 1992 in San Juan Hill, Rough Rider County, Texas, at the age of 87 years and four years have not elapsed since the date of Decedent's death.

2. "Decedent was domiciled and had a fixed place of residence in this County at the date of death.

3. "So far as I know and believe, Decedent did not leave a will.

4. "A necessity exists for the administration of this Estate.

5. "All of the distributees of decedent have consented to the appointment of affiant as independent administrator.

6. "The Applicant for Letters of Independent Administration is not disqualified by law from accepting Letters of Independent Administration or from serving as Independent Administrator and is qualified and entitled to such Letters."

SIGNED this _____ day of _____, 19_____.

_____
PAULA SMITH

SWORN TO AND SUBSCRIBED BEFORE ME by **PAULA SMITH** this _____ day of May, 1992, to certify which witness my hand and seal of office.

_____
CLERK OF THE COUNTY COURT
Court of Rough Rider County, Texas

By: _____
Deputy

Form 10-13: Oath of Executrix

NO. 23814-2

IN RE ESTATE OF	§	IN THE COUNTY COURT
PETER SMITH,	§	AT LAW NO. TWO
DECEASED	§	ROUGH RIDER COUNTY, TEXAS

OATH OF EXECUTRIX

I do solemnly swear that the writing which has been offered for probate is the last will of **PETER SMITH**, so far as I know or believe, and that I will well and truly perform all the duties of Independent Executrix of that will of the Estate of **PETER SMITH**, deceased

_____
PAULA SMITH

SUBSCRIBED AND SWORN TO BEFORE ME this _____ day of _____, 19____, to certify which witness my hand and official seal.

_____
CLERK OF THE COUNTY COURT
Court of Rough Rider County, Texas

By: _____
Deputy

Form 10-14: Oath (Will Annexed)

NO. 23814-2

IN RE ESTATE OF	§	IN THE COUNTY COURT
PETER SMITH,	§	AT LAW NO. TWO
DECEASED	§	ROUGH RIDER COUNTY, TEXAS

OATH

I do solemnly swear that the writing which has been offered for probate is the last will of **PETER SMITH** so far as I know or believe, and that I will well and truly perform all the duties of Independent Administrator with Will Annexed of the Estate of **PETER SMITH**, Deceased.

_____

PETER SMITH, JR.

SUBSCRIBED AND SWORN TO BEFORE ME by **PETER SMITH, JR.** this _____ day of May, 1989, to certify which, witness my hand and seal of office.

_____

CLERK OF THE COUNTY COURT
Court of Rough Rider County, Texas

By: _____
Deputy

Form 10-15: Oath (Independent Administration)

NO. 23814-2

IN RE ESTATE OF	§	IN THE COUNTY COURT
PETER SMITH,	§	AT LAW NO. TWO
DECEASED	§	ROUGH RIDER COUNTY, TEXAS

OATH

I do solemnly swear that the writing which has been offered for probate is the last will of **PETER SMITH** so far as I know or believe, and that I will well and truly perform all the duties of Independent Administratrix of the Estate of **PETER SMITH**.

_____
PAULA SMITH

SUBSCRIBED AND SWORN TO BEFORE ME by **PAULA SMITH** this _____ day of _____ , 19_____, to certify which, witness my hand and seal of office.

_____
Notary Public, State of Texas

Form 10-16: Inventory, Appraisement, and List of Claims

NO. 23814-2

IN RE ESTATE OF	§	IN THE COUNTY COURT
PETER SMITH,	§	AT LAW NO. TWO
DECEASED	§	ROUGH RIDER COUNTY, TEXAS

INVENTORY, APPRAISEMENT, AND LIST OF CLAIMS

Date of Death: March 23, 1992

The following is a full, true and complete Inventory and Appraisement of all personal property and of all real property situated in the State of Texas, together with a List of Claims due and owing to this Estate as of the date of death, which have come to the possession or knowledge of the undersigned.

INVENTORY AND APPRAISEMENT

Real Property (See Schedule A)	$ 132,211.00
Stocks and Bonds (See Schedule B)	504,384.00
Mortgages, Notes and Cash (See Schedule C)	499,877.65
Insurance Payable to Estate (See Schedule D)	.00
Jointly Owned Property (See Schedule E)	.00
Miscellaneous Property (See Schedule F)	82,213.00
TOTAL	$2,018,685.65

LIST OF CLAIMS

1. Noted dated October 2, 1988, made payable to Decedent by Bob Buyer, and wife Barbara Buyer in original principal amount of $85,000.00. Bearing interest at 11%, secured by a first lien on real property located at 1202 Lincoln Memorial, San Juan Hill, Texas.

The foregoing Inventory, Appraisement and List of Claims should be approved and ordered entered of record.

Respectfully submitted,

TEDDY & FRANKLIN

_____

JOHN TEDDY
State Bar No. 00000100
5155 Teton Pkwy., Suite 206
P.O. Box 186
Corpus Christi, TX 79421
(512) 555-1234 Telephone
(512) 555-5678 FAX

ATTORNEY FOR THE ESTATE

THE STATE OF TEXAS	§
COUNTY OF ROUGH RIDER	§ **KNOW ALL MEN BY THESE PRESENTS THAT:**
	§

I **PAULA SMITH**, having been duly sworn, hereby state on oath that the foregoing Inventory and List of Claims is a true and complete statement of all the property and claims of the Estate that have come to my knowledge.

_____

PAULA SMITH
Independent Executrix

SWORN TO AND SUBSCRIBED BEFORE ME by the said **PAULA SMITH** on this the _____ day of June, 1992, to certify which witness my hand and seal of office.

_____

Notary Public, State of Texas

ORDER

The foregoing Inventory, Appraisement and List of Claims of the above Estate having been filed and presented and the Court having considered and examined the same and being satisfied that it should be approved and there having been no objections made thereto, it is in all respects APPROVED and ORDERED entered of record.

SIGNED AND ENTERED on the _____ day of _____, 19_____.

_____

Judge Presiding

Form 10-16: (continued)

SCHEDULE A—REAL PROPERTY

Community

Description	One-half Market Value
Lot Two (2), Block One (1), Sunnyside Addition, San Juan Hill, Rough Rider County, Texas, also known as 1412 Bullmoose, San Juan Hill, Texas.	$132,211.00

Separate

Description	Market Value
None	

Form 10-16: (continued)

SCHEDULE B—STOCKS & BONDS

Community

Description	One-half Market Value
1. 1,000 shares New York Utility $132.00 per share, Common, NYSE CUSIP No. 932478 102	$176,000.00
2. 20,000 shares of Rough Rider Mineral Corp., $65.00 per share	$350,000.00
3. 3,922 Shares, Allied Chemical Corp. $72.00 per share, held as employers' contribution in employee account in the Allied Chemical Employee Stock Purchase Plan	78,384.00

Separate

Description	One-half Market Value
None	

Form 10-16: (continued)

SCHEDULE C—MORTGAGES, NOTES AND CASH

Community

Description	One-half Market Value

1. Checking Account
    #2500-512-0
    First City—San Juan Hill, N.A. $ 37,523.13

2. C.D.
    #210093
    First City—San Juan Hill, N.A. $125,132.12

3. C.D.
    #000137492
    San Juan Hill Savings Bank, F.S.B $337,222.40

Separate

Description	One-half Market Value

None

Form 10-16: (continued)

SCHEDULE D—INSURANCE PAYABLE TO ESTATE

Community

Description   One-half Market Value

None

Separate

Description   One-half Market Value

None

Form 10-16: (continued)

SCHEDULE E—JOINTLY OWNED PROPERTY

Community

<u>Description</u>   <u>One-half Market Value</u>

None

Separate

<u>Description</u>   <u>One-half Market Value</u>

None

Form 10-16: (continued)

SCHEDULE F—MISCELLANEOUS PROPERTY

Community

Description	One-half Market Value
1. 1991 Chevrolet Lumina APV Vehicle ID #3C2L42810M21B	$ 8,213.00
2. Clothing and Personal Effects	3,200.00
3. Jewelry	15,000.00
4. Wood Working Tools	12,000.00
5. Furniture & household Goods	46,000.00

Form 10-17: Published Notice to Creditors

NOTICE TO ALL PERSONS HAVING CLAIMS
AGAINST THE ESTATE OF PETER SMITH

Administration of the Estate of **PETER SMITH**, deceased, has been commenced by the issuance of Letters Testamentary to **PAULA SMITH** on May 21, 1992, by the County Court at Law of Rough Rider County, Texas, acting in Cause No. 23814-2, styled in Re Estate of **PETER SMITH**, Deceased, in which court the matter is pending.

All persons having claims against the Estate are hereby notified to present them to the undersigned in care of John Teddy, Attorney at Law, P.O. Box 186, Corpus Christi, Texas 79421, within the time prescribed by law.

_____
PAULA SMITH
Independent Executrix of the
Estate of **PETER SMITH**, Deceased

Form 10-18: Enclosure Letter to Publisher

June 3, 1992

Rough Rider County Gazette
P.O. Box 270
San Juan Hill, Texas 79421

Dear Sirs:

Enclosed please find the Notice required in the **PETER SMITH** Estate to be published for one day only. Please bill us.

It is necessary for us to file a copy of the printed notice, together with the sworn affidavit of the publisher to the effect that the notice was published as provided in the Texas Probate Code. Please return these to us at your earliest convenience.

Thank you for your cooperation. If there are further questions, please let me know.

Sincerely,

JOHN TEDDY

BT:la

Enclosure

Form 10-19: Notice to Secured Creditors

June 3, 1992

Ajax Loan Company
8300 Main
San Juan Hill, Texas 79421

RE: Estate of **PETER SMITH**
     Deceased, No 23814-2
     County Court at Law No. Two
     Rough Rider County, Texas

Gentlemen:

Our records tentatively indicate: (1) that you have a claim against the estate which is secured by a deed of trust, mortgage, vendor's, mechanic's, or other contractor's lien upon real estate belonging to such estate; and (2) that the instrument creating, extending, or transferring such lien was duly recorded prior to the death of the decedent named above in the county in which the real estate covered by such lien is situated, or prior to the time at which title vested in an heir or devisee.

Since you appear to have such claim under our records, notice is hereby given to you that you are required to present such claim to the undersigned at the address shown below within the time limits prescribed by applicable law.

Original Letters Testamentary upon such Estate were issued on May 22, 1992, in the above numbered and entitled Estate. Your claim should be directed as follows:

Paula Smith
c/o **JOHN TEDDY**
P.O. Box 186
San Juan Hill, Texas 79421

Very truly yours,

_____
PAULA SMITH,
Independent Executrix

Form 10-19A: Proof of Service of Notice Upon Claimants Against Estate

NO. 23814-2

IN RE ESTATE OF	§	IN THE COUNTY COURT
PETER SMITH,	§	AT LAW NO. TWO
DECEASED	§	ROUGH RIDER COUNTY, TEXAS

PROOF OF SERVICE OF NOTICE UPON CLAIMANTS AGAINST ESTATE

STATE OF TEXAS	§
COUNTY OF ROUGH RIDER	§

BEFORE ME, the undersigned authority, on this day personally appeared **PAULA SMITH** and after being duly sworn, stated that:

The attached notices are copies of the notices which were sent by Certified Mail, Return Receipt Requested to the creditors at such addresses as reflecting in such notices in compliance with Section 295 of the Texas Probate Code. The Return Receipt is attached to the notice.

_____
PAULA SMITH

SUBSCRIBED AND SWORN TO BEFORE ME by **PAULA SMITH** on this 3rd day of June, 1992.

_____
Notary Public, State of Texas

Form 10-20: Notice to All Creditors Other Than Secured Creditors

June 3, 1992

Edward Johnsonany
109 N. Main
San Juan Hill, Texas 79421

RE: Estate of **PETER SMITH**
      Deceased, No 23814-2
      County Court at Law No. Two
      Rough Rider County, Texas

Gentlemen:

    Our records tentatively indicate that you have a claim against the estate.

    Since you appear to have such claim under our records, notice is hereby given to you that you are required to present such claim to the undersigned at the address shown below within the time limits prescribed by applicable law.

    Original Letters Testamentary upon such Estate were issued on May 22, 1992, in the above numbered and entitled Estate. Your claim should be directed as follows:

Paula Smith
c/o **JOHN TEDDY**
P.O. Box 186
San Juan Hill, Texas 79421

Very truly yours,

_____
PAULA SMITH,
Independent Executrix

Form 10-21: Motion of Payment of Independent Executrix Fees and Expenses

NO. 23814-2

IN RE ESTATE OF	§	IN THE COUNTY COURT
PETER SMITH,	§	AT LAW NO. TWO
DECEASED	§	ROUGH RIDER COUNTY, TEXAS

**MOTION FOR PAYMENT OF
INDEPENDENT EXECUTRIX FEES AND EXPENSES**

TO THE HONORABLE JUDGE OF SAID COURT:

NOW COMES **PAULA SMITH**, Independent Executrix of this Estate, and moves that she receive an Order from the Court granting her fees for estate administration pursuant to Probate Code Section 241 and reimbursement for her reasonable and necessary expenses incurred by her herein and for which she has not been previously reimbursed:

I.

Pursuant to Texas Probate Code Section 241, the personal representative of an estate is entitled to a commission of five per cent (5%) on all sums she may actually receive in cash and the same per cent on all sums actually paid out in cash in the administration of the Estate.

II.

PAULA SMITH, as Independent Executrix of this Estate, has received the sum of $152,000 in cash, which sum is reflected in Exhibit A attached hereto. The five per cent (5%) commission on this sum is $2,650.00.

III.

PAULA SMITH, as Independent Executrix of this estate, has paid out the sum of $11,020.00 in cash to claimants, as shown in Exhibit A. The five percent (5%) commission on this sum is $551.00.

IV.

The total of the sums in paragraph II and III do not exceed five per cent (5%) of the gross fair market value of the Estate.

V.

PAULA SMITH, as Independent Executrix of this Estate, has incurred necessary and reasonable expenses in the preservation, safekeeping, and management of this Estate, and in collecting or attempting to collect claims or debts, and in recovering or attempting to recover property to which the Estate has a title of claim, in the sum of $125.00, which is reflected in Exhibit B attached hereto. These expenses are allowed to be reimbursed to the Executrix pursuant to Section 242 of the Texas Probate Code.

VI.

Sufficient funds are on hand in the estate to pay the fees and expenses set out above.

WHEREFORE, the Executrix requests the Court to enter an Order authorizing payment of each of the foregoing amounts, which total the sum of $3,326.00 from the Estate.

Respectfully submitted,

TEDDY & FRANKLIN

JOHN TEDDY
State Bar No. 00000100
5155 Teton Pkwy., Suite 206
P.O. Box 186
Corpus Christi, TX 79421
(512) 555-1234 Telephone
(512) 555-5678 FAX

ATTORNEY FOR THE ESTATE

Form 10-22: Affidavit Closing Independent Administration

NO. 23814-2

IN RE ESTATE OF	§	IN THE COUNTY COURT
PETER SMITH,	§	AT LAW NO. TWO
DECEASED	§	ROUGH RIDER COUNTY, TEXAS

CLOSING AFFIDAVIT

Now comes **PAULA SMITH**, Independent Executrix in the Estate of **PETER SMITH**, Deceased and presents hereby his verified account for final settlement and would respectfully show that Court that property listed on the Inventory on file herein contains all the property of the Estate and the Applicant would show the Court the following:

1. There has been no additional property belonging to the Estate that has come into the hands of this Independent Executrix;

2. The property has been distributed to the beneficiaries designated in the will;

3. All debts of the Estate have been paid;

4. There are no debts or expenses still owing by the Estate;

5. No property of the Estate still remains on hand;

6. The persons entitled to receive such Estate are the beneficiaries designated in the will of **PETER SMITH**, Deceased.

7. No advancements or payments have been made by the Independent Executrix from this Estate other than the distribution of the assets as specified in the will.

The Applicant herein, **PAULA SMITH**, Independent Executrix of the Estate of **PETER SMITH**, Deceased respectfully requests that this Estate be closed and that she be discharged from her trust.

_____

PAULA SMITH

SWORN TO AND SUBSCRIBED before me by **PAULA SMITH**, on this _____ day of _____, 19_____.

_____

Notary Public, State of Texas

Form 10-23: Receipt by Distributee

NO. 23814-2

IN RE ESTATE OF	§	IN THE COUNTY COURT
PETER SMITH,	§	AT LAW NO. TWO
DECEASED	§	ROUGH RIDER COUNTY, TEXAS

RECEIPT AND RELEASE

WHEREAS, **PETER SMITH** died in Nueces County, Texas on March 3, 1992, with a valid will; and

WHEREAS, **PAULA SMITH** applied for and was granted Letters Testamentary as Independent Executrix of the Estate on May 21, 1992; and

WHEREAS, the undersigned beneficiary is entitled to a share of the Estate of **PETER SMITH**; and

WHEREAS, the Independent Executrix of the Estate, upon the advice of her attorney, has requested the execution and delivery of this Receipt and Release to evidence distribution to the beneficiary of his share of the estate pursuant to the terms of the Last Will and Testament of **PETER SMITH**.

NOW, THEREFORE, the beneficiary acknowledges receipt of all of the property from the **PETER SMITH** Estate to which he is entitled and acknowledges receipt of all legacies and bequests to which he is entitled.

In addition, the beneficiary does hereby give the Estate of **PETER SMITH**, Deceased, and the said **PAULA SMITH**, in her representative capacity as the duly qualified and acting Independent Executrix of the Estate of **PETER SMITH**, a full and complete release and acquittance from any further liability to the undersigned as a beneficiary and the undersigned further hereby ratifies and confirms each and every act performed by the said **PAULA SMITH**, as Independent Executrix of the Estate of **PETER SMITH**, Deceased.

Beneficiary further agrees that the Estate of **PETER SMITH** may be closed at any time without any further notice to her.

EXECUTED this _____ day of June, 1992.

_____
PENELOPE SMITH

STATE OF TEXAS	§
COUNTY OF ROUGH RIDER	§

This instrument was acknowledged before me on this the _____ day of June, 1992 by **PENELOPE SMITH**.

_____
Notary Public, State of Texas

Form 10-24: Distribution Deed

ESTATE OF PETER SMITH, DECEASED

DISTRIBUTION DEED

STATE OF TEXAS	§	
COUNTY OF ROUGH RIDER	§	**KNOW ALL ME BY THESE PRESENTS:**

WHEREAS, **PETER SMITH** died in Rough Rider County, Texas, on March 3, 1992; and

WHEREAS, **PETER SMITH** left a written will dated June 19, 1964, which was admitted to probate under Cause No. 23814-2 in the County Court at Law No. 2 of Rough Rider County, Texas, by Order dated June 19, 1964; and

WHEREAS, **PAULA SMITH**, Independent Executrix was granted Letters Testamentary of the Estate of **PETER SMITH**, Deceased, and qualified as Independent Executrix and

WHEREAS, the below described property has been devised to the following pursuant to Article II of the will: 50% to **PETER SMITH, JR.**; 50% TO **PENELOPE SMITH**; and

WHEREAS, the Independent Executrix, pursuant to the terms of the will, desires to grant, convey, release and distribute to said Beneficiaries all of the below-described property free from all the Independent Executrix's possessory rights in and authority over such property;

NOW, THEREFORE, in consideration of the premises **PAULA SMITH**, Independent Executrix of the Estate of **PETER SMITH**, Deceased acting herein pursuant to the terms of the will, hereby GRANTS, CONVEYS, RELEASES AND DISTRIBUTES to **PETER SMITH, JR.** 50%; **PENELOPE SMITH** 50%, whose address is P.O. Box 3264, San Juan Hill, Texas 79321, all of the following described property located in Rough Rider County, Texas.

Lot Two (2), Block One (1), Sunnyside Addition, an addition in the City of San Juan Hill, Texas, as shown by the map or Plat Records of Rough Rider County in Volume 12, at page 334 of the map records of Rough Rider County, Texas

TO HAVE AND TO HOLD the Property, subject to the matters herein set forth, together with all and singular the rights and appurtenances thereto in anywise belonging, unto Grantee and Grantees's successors and assigns forever; and Grantor does hereby bind Grantor and Grantor's successors to WARRANT AND FOREVER DEFEND all and singular the Property, subject to the matters herein set forth, unto Grantee and Grantee's successors and assigns, against every person whomsoever lawfully claiming or to claim the same or any part thereof, by, through, or under Grantor, but not otherwise.

This conveyance, the Property, and all of Grantor's warranties are subject to the following:

1. Taxes and assessments on the Property, the payment of which is assumed by Grantee.

2. Any and all existing leases covering oil, gas or other minerals and all outstanding royalty and mineral interest in and to the oil, gas and other minerals situated in, on or under the Property.

3. Any and all covenants, conditions, easements, rights-of-way and restrictions affecting the Property as evidenced by instruments filed in the public records of Rough Rider County, Texas, to the extent the same are valid and still in force and effect.

4. All statutes, ordinances, regulations and laws of any municipality or other governmental authority having jurisdiction over the Property.

DATED this _____ day of _____, 19____.

_____

PAULA SMITH
Independent Executrix of the Estate of
PETER SMITH, Deceased

STATE OF TEXAS	§
COUNTY OF ROUGH RIDER	§

This instrument was acknowledged before me on the _____ day of June, 1992 by **PAULA SMITH**, Independent Executrix of the Estate of **PETER SMITH**, Deceased.

_____
Notary Public, State of Texas

PREPARED IN THE OFFICE OF:
JOHN TEDDY
5155 Teton Pkwy., Suite 206
Corpus Christi, TX 79421

Form 10-25: Application for Appointment of Successor Administrator

NO. 23814-2

IN RE ESTATE OF	§	IN THE COUNTY COURT
PETER SMITH,	§	AT LAW NO. TWO
DECEASED	§	ROUGH RIDER COUNTY, TEXAS

APPLICATION FOR APPOINTMENT OF SUCCESSOR REPRESENTATIVE AND FOR ISSUANCE OF LETTERS OF INDEPENDENT SUCCESSOR ADMINISTRATION

PETER SMITH, JR., applicant, makes this application for appointment as successor representative of the Estate of **PETER SMITH**, deceased, and for issuance of Letters of Administration, and furnishes the following information to the Court:

I.

Applicant is interested in this Estate and is an individual domiciled in and residing at 252 Yellowstone parkway, San Juan Hill, Texas 78231.

II.

Applicant is entitled to be appointed successor representative, is entitled to Letters of Administration, and is not disqualified by law to act as Administrator.

III.

PAULA SMITH, Independent Administratrix of this Estate died on March 12, 1990.

IV.

Decedent **PETER SMITH** died intestate on March 3, 1992, leaving no lawful will to provide for the naming of a successor representative.

V.

This Court has continuing jurisdiction and venue because decedent was domiciled and had a fixed place of residence in this County on the date of death.

VI.

The name, age, marital status, and address if known, and the relationship, if any, of each heir to the decedent, or each person with a potential interest in the real estate of the decedent, are as follows:

NAME: PETER SMITH, JR.   **AGE:** Adult
ADDRESS: 252 Yellowstone Parkway, San Juan Hill, TX 79231
MARITAL STATUS: Single
RELATIONSHIP TO DECEDENT: Son

NAME: PENELOPE SMITH   **AGE:** Adult
ADDRESS: 721 Monolle Drive, San Juan Hill, TX 79231
MARITAL STATUS: Married
RELATIONSHIP TO DECEDENT: Daughter

VII.

The children born to or adopted by decedent were:
As shown above.

VIII.

Decedent was divorced from JANE SMITH on or about April 5, 1931, in Corpus Christi, Texas.

IX.

A necessity exists for administration of the Estate because there are continuing payments being made to the Estate from the sale of real property and distributions to the heirs must be made.

X.

There is no need for the appointment of appraisers.

XI.

All of the distributees of the decedent agree on the advisability of having a successor independent administration and collectively designate **PETER SMITH, JR.**, a qualified person, to serve as Successor Independent Administrator. The distributees request that no action be had in this Court in relation to the settlement of the decedent's estate other than the return of an inventory, appraisement, and list of claims of the decedent's estate.

Form 10-25: (continued)

XII.

All the distributees of the decedent join in this application, and all of the distributees waive the issuance and service of citation.

XIII.

Distributees further request that bond be waived.

WHEREFORE, Applicant prays that citation issue as required by law to all persons interested in this Estate; That Applicant be appointed Successor Independent Administrator of this Estate; That Letters of Successor Independent Administration be issued to Applicant; That appraisers not be appointed; That no action be had in this Court in relation to the settlement of the decedent's estate other than the return of an inventory, appraisement, and list of claims against the decedent's estate; That bond be waived; and that all other orders to be entered as the Court may deem proper.

Respectfully submitted,

TEDDY & FRANKLIN

JOHN TEDDY
State Bar No. 00000100
5155 Teton Pkwy., Suite 206
P.O. Box 186
Corpus Christi, TX 79421
(512) 555-1234 Telephone
(512) 555-5678 FAX

ATTORNEY FOR THE ESTATE

11 PROBATE ADMINISTRATION– DEPENDENT ADMINISTRATION

CHAPTER OBJECTIVES

Upon completion of this chapter, the student should be able to:

1. Prepare, in a dependent administration, applications, orders of the court, written proofs, oaths, inventories, notices to creditors, and other relevant documents.

2. Prepare (if necessary) and arrange for an administrator's bond.

3. Request exemptions and allowances, and prepare all the necessary documentation.

4. Manage the claims procedure and prepare necessary documents.

5. Prepare all documents in connection with the procedure to sell real estate.

6. Understand the procedure for closing a dependent administration, and prepare all necessary documents.

CHAPTER GLOSSARY

Accounting Rendition of an account, either voluntary or by order of the court. An *account* is a statement, in writing, listing debts and credits or receipts and disbursements, along with dates and other clarifying information.

Commissioners An officer of the court appointed expressly to hear facts and report to the court.

Decree In England, a decree was issued by a court of equity, as opposed to a *judgment*, which is issued by a common law court.

Distribution The giving out or division of the remainder of an estate, after payment of debts and charges, to those legally entitled to it.

Execution The legal process of enforcing judgments for payment of money, usually by seizing and selling the property of the debtor.

Exemptions The privilege created via constitution or statute by which a debtor's property, up to a certain amount or in certain categories, is protected from the possibility of seizure and sale by creditors.

Forced sale A sale to satisfy a debt made by virtue of execution or other legal process.

Homestead The fixed residence of the family or of a single person, which is exempt from seizure and sale for the satisfaction of debt. In Texas there are two kinds, rural and urban. A *rural* homestead consists of a maximum of 200 acres for a family and 100 acres for a single person. An *urban* homestead consists of 1 acre, which may be split between residential and business homestead.

Insolvent As used in the Probate Code, a deficiency of assets to pay all claims. Exempt property is not considered to be a part of the assets for the purpose of determining insolvency.

Joint control The requirement by bonding companies that they, or someone they choose, co-sign all estate checks or other withdrawals of money and approve expenditures before they will commit to issue a bond on the representative.

Sale An entry into an executory contract between two parties, the seller (*vendor*) and the buyer (*purchaser*), in which the seller agrees to sell real or personal property to the buyer.

Securities Stocks, bonds, notes, and warrants. These are evidence of obligations to pay money or of rights to participate in the earnings of corporations.

Surety One who undertakes to pay money should another (the principal) fail to do some act or meet some duty that the principal is legally compelled to do.

Verified Having made a formal oath to the truth of a pleading, account, or other paper. Used interchangeably with *sworn*.

INTRODUCTION

The major difference between dependent administration and independent administration is that following the filing and approval of the inventory, appraisement, and list of claims, very few actions can be taken in the dependent administration without the prior approval of the Probate Court, which must be obtained through a hearing and sometimes two hearings. The independent administrator can pay creditors, sell property for administration purposes, make **distribution** to devisees and heirs, and choose whether to close the probate proceedings, all without first seeking the approval of the Probate Court. On the other hand, the dependent administrator must file documents with the Probate Court requesting the approval of such actions and must set hearings at which the Probate Court hears evidence and determines whether to approve the procedures.

Because of the large amount of paperwork, the frequent contact with clients and others, and the number of hearings before the Probate Court, dependent administration is a fertile area for the use of legal assistants. The legal assistant may be called on to perform the following tasks, among others:

1. Preparing the application for letters of administration.
2. Filing the application (together with the original will, if one exists).
3. Setting the hearing to consider the application.

4. Preparing the order to be signed by the court at the application hearing, the written proof, the oath, and sometimes the bond.

5. Preparing and filing the inventory, appraisement, and list of claims.

6. Arranging for the publication of the notice to creditors required in Probate Code Section 294.

7. Preparing and mailing notices to secured creditors as required by Probate Code Section 295(a).

8. Preparing and mailing notices to general creditors as required by Section 295(b) of the Probate Code.

9. Receiving and handling the claims of creditors.

10. Participating in the determination of whether to allow or reject the claims of creditors.

11. Classifying the claims of creditors.

12. Preparing the orders to approve or disapprove the claims of creditors to be executed by the court, and obtaining the setting for hearing so that the claims can be approved or disapproved by the court.

13. Setting up estate bank accounts, and supervising them as the claims of creditors are paid pursuant to the orders of the court.

14. Preparing the applications and orders concerning the setting apart of the **homestead** or other exempt property or fixing family allowances, and the setting of hearings to consider these.

15. Preparing the documentation necessary to sell assets belonging to the estate for the purposes authorized by the Probate Code and for setting of hearings to consider the application for **sale** and the report of sale.

16. Preparing documents similar to those just mentioned concerning the leasing of real or personal property belonging to the estate or the entering into of mineral leases or pooling and unitization agreements.

17. Preparing the legal documents requesting and effectuating the partition and distribution of the estate.

18. Preparing and filing annual accounts.

19. Preparing and filing final accounts.

In addition to these, it will be necessary, just as in any other estate, for the legal assistant to:

1. Gather all information on the assets and liabilities of the estate.

2. See that final tax returns of the decedent and fiduciary tax returns for the estate are filed.

3. See that estate tax returns are filed, including gathering all the information concerning lifetime gifts needed to file the returns.

4. Transfer assets of the estate for purposes of obtaining money to pay creditors or other expenses of the estate.

5. Effectuate the distribution to the heirs or devisees.

6. Maintain adequate records, including receipts for disbursements, in order to perform other mandatory **accountings**.

7. Prepare accountings demanded by any party interested in the estate.

8. Deal with the administrator concerning gathering information and giving instructions.

A dependent administration will be necessary if there is no will, the will fails to appoint an executor, the will does not make the executor independent, or the named executors are incapable of or refuse to serve and the estate is not made independent under Probate Code Section 145, as discussed in Chapter 10.

Although the number of dependent administrations has decreased significantly since the amendment of Probate Code Section 145 in 1977, and again in 1979, there are still many instances where only a dependent administration will solve the problems of the estate. This can come about: (a) because devisees or heirs are unknown or cannot be located to give their consent to an independent administration; (b) when the prospective administrator knows or believes that there will be conflict between the heirs or devisees; (c) where the heirs or devisees refuse to consent to an independent administration because of discord; or (d) when anyone interested in the estate objects to the creation of an independent administration and there is no will requiring one and the court refuses to grant an independent administration. The legal assistant must be equipped to handle these situations when they arise.

APPLICATION

Before preparing an application for letters of administration in a dependent administration, the legal assistant must review the rules on venue to determine in which county the application must be filed. Then the legal assistant must consider the proposed applicant to see that he is in the proper order of persons qualified to serve, as required by Section 77 of the Probate Code and that he is not disqualified to serve, as provided in Section 78. If the proposed applicant is not a resident of Texas, an appointment of resident agent for the purpose of service of notices must be prepared. Inasmuch as the administrator will be required to file a bond, an estimate of the amount of the bond should be made, and the applicant should be sent to his insurance agent to determine whether he can qualify for such a bond. This may require negotiation with the underwriter who will issue the bond concerning the placing of liquid assets of the estate in restricted bank accounts or the granting of **joint control** in which the insurance agent or another will be required to execute checks written by the administrator. (A more complete discussion of bonds is found later in this chapter.)

Once these preliminary matters are disposed of, the application should be prepared in accordance with Section 82 of the Probate Code, which requires, at a minimum, the following information:

1. The name and domicile of the applicant, his relationship to the decedent, and a statement that he is not disqualified to act as administrator under Section 78.

2. The name and fact of intestacy, and the name of the decedent, and the fact, time, and place of death.

3. The venue.

4. Whether the decedent owned real or personal property, along with a statement of its probable value. (For a fuller discussion concerning this requirement, see the discussion in Chapter Ten concerning the same allegation in an application for probate of a written will and for letters testamentary.)

5. The name, age, marital status, address, if known, and relationship, if any, of each heir to the decedent.

6. Whether children were born to or adopted by the decedent, along with the name, date, and place of birth of each.

7. Whether the decedent was ever divorced and, if so, when and from whom.

8. That a necessity exists for administration of the estate, alleging the facts that show this necessity. (For a fuller discussion of this allegation, see the discussion in Chapter 10 concerning an application for probate of a will and for letters of administration with will annexed.

9. The social security numbers of the applicant and the decedent, if known.

The application, including the original will and any codicils, if a dependent administration with will annexed, and a check for court cost (as discussed in Chapter Ten) should be delivered or forwarded to the clerk of the county-level courts having probate jurisdiction. As soon as the application has been filed and the citation issued, the legal assistant should obtain a setting for the hearing on the application. (This was more fully discussed in Chapter Ten.) An example of an application is found at the end of this chapter at Form 11-1.

THE HEARING

Prior to the hearing the legal assistant should prepare the order granting letters of administration (an example is attached as Form 11-3), a written proof (an example is attached as Form 11-2), and the oath (an example of which is attached as Form 11-4).

THE BOND

The court must require a bond in a dependent administration. The Probate Code sections dealing with bonds are found in Part 2 of Chapter VII starting at Section 193. Section 194(4) of the Probate Code stipulates that the bond shall be fixed by the court in an amount equal to the estimated value of all personal property, together with an additional amount to cover revenue anticipated to be derived from any source during the following 12 months. The legal assistant should have prepared prior to the date appointed for the probate hearing a summary of the estimated value of personal property, together with an estimate of revenues to be received in the succeeding 12 months. The attorney will use the summary to discuss the amount of the bond with the probate judge.

Note that real estate is not considered in setting the bond. But, as will be seen later in this chapter, when real estate is sold it is converted to personal property, that is, money. If it is anticipated that real estate will be sold fairly soon after the opening of administration, then to save the necessity of filing a new bond or a supplemental bond at that time, the anticipated proceeds of the sale of that real estate should also be considered by the probate judge when he sets the amount of the bond.

In addition, the legal assistant will have arranged with the applicant and any other necessary witnesses to attend the hearing on the application for letters of administration.

Immediately following the hearing, the legal assistant will aid the applicant in completing arrangements to obtain a bond. For this, most fidelity companies have their own form for bonds that are acceptable in Texas. Often, the oaths of the administrator or other personal representative appear on the back of the bond form. If this is the case, then no bond or oath need be prepared by the legal assistant; if not, the legal assistant will have to prepare the bond form, as stipulated by Section 196 of the Probate Code. (The form for the oath has been discussed in Chapter Ten.)

The Probate Code sections dealing with bonds contain provisions for bonds with personal **sureties**; that is sureties who are individual persons rather than insurance or fidelity companies. Although the use of personal surety bonds at one time was fairly prevalent, the courts are now reluctant to accept them without creating liens on real property owned by the personal sureties to secure the bonds. Because of this, it is difficult to get someone who has sufficient properties to agree to act as a personal surety. If a personal surety bond is used, the personal sureties must execute an affidavit stating the amount of their assets that are not exempt and are reachable by creditors. These assets must be worth more than the liabilities, at least double the amount of the bond. Then, if the judge of the Probate Court finds that the estimated value of the personal property of the estate cannot be deposited or held in safekeeping and that the personal sureties cannot be accepted without creating liens on specific real property, he has a responsibility to order each surety to designate real property that is subject to **execution** and on which a lien shall be imposed to secure the estate and those interested in the estate.

If the corporate surety—that is, the fidelity company or insurance company—requires joint control, then the court may require the administrator to agree with the sureties to deposit cash and other assets in banks, savings and loans, etc. in such a fashion that the money or other assets cannot be withdrawn without the written consent of the surety.

In addition, the amount of the bond may be reduced by depositing cash or placing **securities** or other personal assets in safekeeping, subject to withdrawal only by order of the court. The bond must be approved by the Probate Court and then filed, and is subject to being increased or decreased by order of the court.

In addition to the provisions already discussed, Part 2 of Chapter VII also contains provisions by which the court may require an executor or guardian serving without bond to give a bond. If a complaint in writing is filed with the court to the effect that the executor or guardian is wasting, mismanaging, or misapplying the estate and that a creditor may thereby lose his debt or some other person's interest in the estate may be diminished or lost, and the court so finds, then the court is required to enter an order directing the executor or guardian to give bond within 10 days. Failure to do so constitutes grounds for removal. Prior to the adoption of Sections 149(a), (b), and (c) these provisions, together with Section 149 (which specifically required an independent executor to give bond), were the only way to remove an independent administrator.

INVENTORY AND APPRAISEMENT

The discussion in Chapter Ten concerning the preparation, filing, and approving of an inventory, appraisement, and list of claims is applicable to the dependent administration. There are no differences between dependent and independent administrations regarding what must be included within an inventory, appraisement, and list of claims, nor in the provisions for filing and approving them.

EXEMPTIONS AND ALLOWANCES

Perhaps the first thing the legal assistant will have to concern himself with in the dependent administration, other than perhaps the publication of the notice to creditors, will be obtaining the orders setting apart homestead and other exempt property or fixing allowances in lieu of exempt property or fixing the family allowance. The relevant provisions are found in Part 3 of Chapter VII. These procedures generally are only applicable to estates, whether dependent or independent, that are **insolvent** or where the testate decedent has devised all or a substantial part of his assets to someone other than his spouse or dependent children. Obviously, the former is more prevalent than the latter, although many attorneys have had to represent estates in which the latter occurred.

This is not an appropriate forum for a full discussion of Texas homestead or the personal property **exemptions** from **forced sale** or seizure. Suffice it to say that the exemptions created by the Texas Constitution and the statutes concerning homestead and exempt personal property continue after the death of one or more of the claimants. In fact, Section 271 of the Probate Code requires the probate court to set aside for the use and benefit of the surviving spouse, minor children and any unmarried children, remaining with the family of the deceased all of the property of the estate that is exempt from execution or forced sale by the Constitution and laws of this state.

Sections 273-276 provide that if the decedent did not own any of the articles that are exempted from execution for sale by the Constitution of Texas, the court shall instead make a reasonable allowance to be paid to the surviving spouse and children. This means cash money in lieu of the exempt articles not found among the decedent's assets. Section 273 stipulates that the allowance in lieu of the homestead not exceed $15,000 and that the allowance in lieu of exempt property not exceed $5,000. This means that the surviving spouse or dependent children or unmarried children remaining with a family can receive from the estate up to $20,000 in lieu of exempt property, even when the estate is insolvent.

To these allowances is added the family allowance. Sections 286-293 provide a procedure by which the probate court can determine, and order paid to the surviving spouse and minor children, an amount of money sufficient for their support for a period of one year from the time of death of the decedent. This can be paid in either a lump sum or installments, but cannot be paid to the surviving spouse if the surviving spouse has separate property adequate for his maintenance, or to the minor children if they have property in their own right adequate for their maintenance. The family allowance is paid before all other debts of the estate, except for the expenses of funeral and last illness. Estate property may be sold to raise the funds for the allowance, or property may be transferred to the spouse and minor children in satisfaction of the allowance. Examples of forms are found at Forms 11-5, 11-6, and 11-7.

THE CLAIMS PROCEDURE

The requirement of giving notice to creditors was discussed in Chapter Ten, and examples of forms were given there. A notice with a publisher's affidavit is found at Form 11-8. The preparation of these notices, however, is not the last contact in a dependent administration that the legal assistant will have with claims. The independent administrator does not have to follow the claim procedure, although he can. On the other hand, the dependent administrator cannot pay any debts of the estate unless the creditor has filed a **verified** claim in accordance with Section 301 of the Probate Code and that claim has been allowed or rejected by the administrator and approved or disapproved by the Probate Court. An example of a verified claim is found at Form 11-9.

The claims procedure requires each creditor to present his claim within six months after the original grant of letters testamentary to have the claim paid in the due course of administration. If the claim is not presented within six months, then it is not to be paid until all other claims presented within the six months have been paid.

The claims can be presented either to the executor/administrator or by filing them, or depositing them, with the clerk of the court. If the latter, the clerk is required to advise the representative of the deposit by letter mailed to the last known address.

The claim must be authenticated—that is, supported by an affidavit that the claim is just and that all legal offsets, payments, and credits known to the creditor have been allowed. If the claim is founded on a written instrument, a photostatic copy of the written instrument must be attached; if it is not, then the affidavit must state the facts on which the claim is founded.

There is a special manner of handling secured claims, provided for in Section 306 of the Probate Code, and which will not be further discussed here.

Once the claim has been presented to the executor/administrator or deposited with the clerk, the representative must endorse on the claim or annex to the claim a memorandum, signed by him, stating the time of presentation or filing and that the administrator either allows or rejects it or what portion of it he allows or rejects. Failure to do this within 30 days after presentation of the claim constitutes an absolute rejection of the claim that cannot be retracted.

If the claim is rejected, then within 90 days from the rejection the claimant must file a lawsuit in either the Probate Court in which the estate is pending or any other court of proper jurisdiction, or the claim will be barred. This is referred to as a *suit for establishment*. If the rejected claim or part thereof is established by the suit, the judgment is certified to the Probate Court if rendered by a court other than the Probate Court and handled as if originally allowed and approved.

If the claim is allowed by the personal representative, it cannot be paid until it has been approved by the Probate Court. At the time of approval, the Probate Court will also classify the claim according to the requirements of Section 322 of the Probate Code. Section 320 provides for an order of payment. It requires the representative, when he has funds in hand and the claims have been approved, to pay claims in the following order:

1. Funeral expenses and expenses of last illness not exceeding $5,000, provided the claims had been presented within 60 days. If not, the payment is postponed until allowances made to the widow and children are paid.

2. Allowances paid to the widow or children or either, as discussed in the prior section.

3. Expenses of administration and expenses incurred in preserving, safekeeping, and managing the estate. Notice that the fees payable to the attorney representing the estate are paid after the allowance to widows and orphans.

4. Other claims against the estate, in order of their classification, are provided by Section 322, which describes eight classes of claims. Attorney fees are postponed until after payment of funeral expenses and expenses of last illness, not to exceed $5,000. Another way of saying this is that undertakers and doctors, as well as widows and orphans, get paid before attorneys.

If the estate is insolvent or does not possess sufficient funds to pay all in the claims of all of the classes, even though more funds may become available in the future, then the claims that have been allowed and approved will be paid pro rata. In other words, one would pay class one claims, then class-two claims, then class-three claims, etc., through class seven, which is all other claims legally exhibited within six months after the original grant of letters testamentary or of administration, until there are insufficient monies available now or in the future to pay all such claims. The legal assistant then establishes a percentage based on the total amount of class seven claims allowed and approved in relation to the amount of money available for the payment of claims, and pays that percentage of each claim to the creditor owning the claim.

For example, assume the estate assets are valued at $100,000 and consist of the homestead, exempt personal property, and cash assets equal to $25,000. The funeral bills exceed $5,000 and the costs of administration total $2,500. No claim is made for family allowances or for class-four, -five, or -six creditors. Class-seven claims total $32,000. The percentage is obtained by dividing $17,500 (nonexempt property minus class one and class three claims) by $25,000 and moving the decimal point two places to the right, for a result of 54.69%. Thus, the estate is required to pay 54.69% of each of the class-seven claims, and there are no funds remaining to pay any class-eight claims.

Failure to follow this procedure exactly may result in the liability of the executor or administrator to the estate and those persons interested in it, and result in a malpractice claim against the attorney representing the estate. Form 11-10 is an application for authority to pay a claim that has been allowed and approved.

SALE OF ESTATE PROPERTY

Section 331 of the Texas Probate Code states: "No sale of any property of an estate shall be made without an order of the court authorizing the same." The term *sale* is often misinterpreted by attorneys and laypersons alike. It refers to the entry into a contract of sale rather than completion of the transaction. The sales procedures as provided for in this section must be carried out in full before title may be transferred to the purchaser.

There are two exceptions to the requirement of Section 331 requiring an order of the court authorizing a sale. The first, contained in Section 332, provides that whenever an executor, by the terms of a will, is authorized to sell property of the testator, no order of the court shall be necessary to authorize the executor to make the sale. This refers to specific authorization directing that the sale be without court order. The intentions of the Legislature when they adopted Section 332 are unknown. Although Section 332 has not had wide influence in matters concerning wills probated in the Texas, it does have importance for wills probated in a sister state, referred to as *foreign wills*. Chapter Twelve will discuss the procedure for giving effect to wills probated elsewhere than in Texas. However, although most states do not provide for an independent administration, or at least did not until adoption of the Uniform Probate Code, they do provide statutory authority for an executor to sell property without order of the court if authorized by the will of the decedent. A lot of foreign wills given effect in Texas contain an explicit provision authorizing the sale by the executor of real property belonging to the estate and dispensing with the requirement that he first obtain an order of sale from the court.

The second exception is in the case of independent administrations. By the terms of the Probate Code sections creating independent administrations, such administrations do not have to seek approval of the court before selling property belonging to the estate. However, as discussed in Chapters Five and Ten, the authority of an independent administrator is restricted to sales of property necessary to the administration of the estate, such as paying claims against the estate. The executor may not sell property of the estate other than in administering of the estate, unless authorized to do so by a specific provision of the will allowing the discretionary sale of the property or granting to the executor the powers of trustee under the Texas Trust Code.

The sections dealing with the sale of property of the estate are found in Part 5 of Chapter VIII of the Probate Code, commencing with Section 331 and concluding with Section 358. In addition, Part 6 deals with the hiring and renting real and personal property of the estate, and Part 7 deals with mineral leases, pooling, unitization agreements, and other matters relating to mineral properties.

Part 5, dealing with sales, is divided into provisions concerning personal property and provisions concerning real property. However, Section 339 makes the procedure for gaining authorization for the sale of personal property the same as that for the sale of real estate, other than that no conveyance is necessary in the case of personal property. Title to all personal property, except branded cattle and personal property subject to a certificate of title act such as aircraft, automobiles, trucks, trailers, and boats is transferred by transfer of possession. Section 339 does, however, authorize the representative of an estate to deliver a bill of sale if requested by the purchaser, at the expense of the purchaser. A bill of sale shows the transfer of title to personal property but is not necessary except in the case of branded animals.

The first step in the sale of either personal or real property is the filing of an application with the court. The application must describe the property being sold and must be accompanied by an exhibit, under oath, showing the condition of the estate, the charges and claims that have been approved or established by suit or that have been rejected and may still be established by suit, the amount of each claim, the property of the estate remaining on hand liable for the payment of such claims, and any other facts tending to show the necessity or advisability of the sale.

The administrator cannot just sell property for whatever reason he may desire. Personal property may be sold, and in fact must be sold, only if it is to subject to waste or deterioration, or it may be sold if it is established that it is in the best interest of the estate in order to pay expenses of administration, funeral expenses, expenses of last illness, allowances or claims against the estate.

Real property belonging to the estate may be sold only if it appears necessary or advisable in order to pay expenses of administration, funeral expenses, expenses of last illness of decedents, allowances, or claims against the estate of the decedents or to dispose of any interest in real property in the estate of the decedent when it is deemed to be in the best interest of the estate to do so. To gain approval of the court for the sale, it will be necessary to allege and establish one of these reasons for selling the property.

When the application for sale of real estate is filed, an order must also be presented to the judge for the setting of a hearing on the application for sale. Inasmuch as the filing of an application for sale in effect begins a new lawsuit and requires citation, the hearing date should be on or after the Monday following the expiration of 10 days from the date of citation. Citation will be issued by the clerk and served by posting. On the date of the hearing or thereafter, if the court is satisfied that the sale of the property is necessary or advisable, the court orders the sale to be made.

Section 346 requires that the order of sale to specify the land to be sold, giving a description; to state whether the property is to be sold at public auction or at private sale; and if at public auction, to give the time and place of the auction. The order is also required to show the necessity and advisability of the sale, and, except in cases where no bond is required, the court must either find the existing bond to be sufficient or require a supplemental or increased bond in an amount to be specified by the court. Further, the order must require the sale to be carried out, and a report of sale returned, in accordance with the law. It also must determine the terms of the sale.

Section 348 gives the permissible terms for the sale of real estate: The sale may be for either cash or credit or for part cash and part credit, and the equity in land may be sold subject to the indebtedness on it or with an assumption of the indebtedness on it at either private or public sale, whichever appears to be in the best interest of the estate. If the real estate is sold partially on credit, the down payment is to be not less than 20% of the purchase price, and the purchaser is required to execute a note for the deferred payments in installments of such amounts and bearing such interest as the court determines to be in the best interest of the estate. The note must be secured by a vendor's lien retained in the deed and by a deed of trust on the property with normal provisions. In regard to personal property, no more than six months credit can be allowed, and apparently a bond must be delivered unless delivery of the personal property will not be made until the note with interest has been paid.

The order of sale then authorizes the executor/administrator to begin looking for someone who will enter into an acceptable contract of sale with the estate. In most situations a contract of sale was entered into before the application of sale was filed. Hopefully, the person who prepared the contract did it properly, so that the contract was made subject to the sale proceedings required by the Code and provided that if the court did not approve the sale, then the contract would become null and void.

Within 30 days after the sale, the representative is required to file a report of sale, in writing and under oath, that shows the date of the order of sale, the property sold, the time and place of sale, the name of the purchaser, the purchase price, the terms of sale, whether the sale was made at public auction or privately, and whether the purchaser is ready to comply with the order of sale. This report must be on file for a full five days before the court can take any further action.

At the hearing on the report of sale, the court will again consider whether the bond, if any is required, is sufficient. The court will further consider whether the sale was for a fair price properly made in conformity with the law, and whether any additional or increased bond found necessary has been filed. If the court finds all this to be the case, the court will enter a **decree** confirming the sale. This decree is a final judgment and is appealable. It authorizes the representative of the estate to transfer title to the property being sold upon compliance by the purchaser with the terms of the sale.

With regard to real estate, Section 357 requires that, after the sale has been confirmed, the representative execute and deliver to the purchaser a proper deed conveying the property. The deed is required by Section 356 to refer to and identify the decree of court confirming the sale. If the sale is made partly on credit, the vendor's lien must be retained in the deed, and the purchaser must execute and deliver to the representative a promissory note and a deed of trust, and the deed must be recorded in the official public real property records of the county in which the land is situated.

Part 6 deals with hiring and renting. *Hiring* relates to personal property and *renting* to real property. The same procedure as required for the sale of real estate and personal property is required for the hiring or renting of property belonging to the estate.

Part 7 deals with mineral leases, the entry into pooling or unitization agreements, and the entry into certain other agreements relating to minerals. The procedure required for the leasing for minerals is identical to that required for sale of real or personal property.

Examples of an application for sale of real estate, an order setting searing, an order of sale, a report of sale, a decree confirming sale, and a deed are found at Forms 11-11 through 11-16, respectively.

ANNUAL ACCOUNTING

Part 11 of Chapter VIII of the Probate Code stipulates that, pending closing of an estate, and after 12 months from the date of qualification and receipt of letters, the personal representative must file an annual account. This is accomplished by returning to the court an exhibit, in writing and under oath, setting forth a list of all claims presented within the period covered by the account, and specifying which claims had been allowed, which had been paid, which had been rejected, the date of rejection, which claims have been sued upon, and the condition of the suit. The account must also show the information listed in Sections 399(a)(1) through (6). These annual reports must be filed every 12 months until the estate is finally closed. Section 399(d) requires supporting vouchers, letters of verification from banks or depositories, and proof of possession of securities to be attached to the account, all of them sworn to. It should be noted that in addition to being removed, a representative may be fined up to $500 for failure to file annual accounts. An example of an annual account is found at Form 11-17; forms to verify accounts and safekeeping are found at Forms 11-18 and 11-19, respectively.

CLOSING THE ESTATE

The Probate Code is not as clear concerning the procedure for closing the estate as it is with other matters. It is a two-step proceeding. Step one is the filing of an application for partition and distribution (often unnecessary). Step two is the filing of a final account. Though the Probate Code is somewhat unclear, Section 408(b) seems to indicate that the final account is filed first and that the court will order partition and distribution as a part of the procedural process relating to the final accounting. Once the final account has been approved, an application for distribution, as detailed in Section 373 of the Probate Code, should be filed. Then the procedure for partition and distribution will go forward. Upon its completion, the court will order the estate closed.

Many attorneys follow another procedure, however. They file an application for partition and distribution before filing a final account.

After the partition and distribution procedures are complete and distribution has in fact been made, a final accounting is filed showing, among other things, the distribution. Then the estate is closed.

Either procedure is probably effective. The legal assistant should follow whichever of these two procedures is normal at the firm for which he works.

Partition and Distribution

Partition and distribution is another small lawsuit requiring an application and citation and resulting in a final and appealable judgment.

The application for partition and distribution may not be filed until the expiration of 12 months from the original grant of letters testamentary or of administration. It may be filed either by the personal representative or by the heirs, devisees, or legatees of the estate. There is no provision in the Probate Code allowing the heirs or devisees to enter into an agreement of partition and distribution between the heirs or devisees, and no provision for approval of such by the Probate Court. Still, this is commonly done. The courts assume, and justifiably so, that they have the right to approve a compromise and settlement agreement to any form of a lawsuit, including, though not specifically statutorily authorized, a probate matter with regard to partition and distribution. Also, the heirs may receive the estate property in undivided interests, which is what is probably most often done. No partition is needed in this instance. Because of these factors and because the estate often consists only of money, the need to go through partition and discharge procedure is infrequent.

The contents required of such an application are stipulated in Section 373(b). The application and procedures for partition and distribution as set out in the Probate Code are extremely similar to those required for the equitable partition of real estate not owned by an estate. Upon the filing of the application, citation will issue that must be personally served on each person residing in the state who is entitled to a share of the estate and whose address is known. Citation for those whose address or identities are unknown or who are not residents of this state or who are absent from the state is served by publication. Guardians ad litem must be appointed to represent minors or incompetents, and attorneys ad litem must be appointed to represent those who are cited by publication. At an appropriate time, a hearing is held on the application for partition and distribution at which the court is required to find the names and addresses of those entitled to a share of the estate and the proportional part of the estate to which each is entitled. The court at that time will also determine whether the executor/administrator should retain any money for the payment of debts, taxes, and expenses of administration not yet paid, specifying the exact.

If the estate consists only of money and debts due to the estate, then the courts will determine the amount to which each distributee is entitled and order payment by the personal representative. It is a waste of estate funds even to file an application for partition and distribution in this situation.

If, on the other hand, the estate does not consist entirely of money or debts, the court will determine whether the estate or any part of it is incapable of partition. The court will then order sold the portion of the estate determined to be incapable of partition. The sale procedure is precisely the same as the procedures of sale discussed in the previous section.

If the property is capable of partition, the probate court is required to appoint three or more discreet and disinterested persons as **commissioners**. These commissioners make a fair, just, and impartial partition and distribution of the estate by allotting to each distributee a share in each parcel of land or other property, or, if that is not possible, by allotting to one or more of the distributees a portion of the money or other personal property to supply any deficiency. The commissioners then make a like division of money and personal property. Once the commissioners have divided up the estate into shares equaling the percentages as found for each distributee by the court, the shares will be apportioned to the respective heirs. If there are multiple equal shares, apportionment is determined by lot, usually by drawing a piece of paper out of a hat or the like.

When all this has been accomplished, the commissioners make a sworn report to the court, notice issues, and the court, at a hearing, examines the report to determine whether it is fair and just, hearing any objections to it and any evidence in favor of it. If the court determines that the division has been fairly made, the court will approve it and enter a decree vesting title in the distributees of their respective shares or portions. If not, the court will set aside the report and order a new partition to be made.

A similar procedure is available when the estate owns an undivided interest either with community property or with jointly owned property.

Even though partition and distribution of the estate cannot occur until the expiration of 12 months, Section 373(c) allows for partial distributions at any time after the original grant of letters testamentary or of administration and the filing and approval of an inventory. This requires (a) the filing of a written application by either the personal representative of the heirs, the devisees, or the legatees of the estate, (b) citation personally served, and (c) a hearing. The court may distribute any portion of the estate it deems advisable. If, however, it distributes to some but not all of the heirs and devisees, a refunding bond will be required of those heirs or devisees receiving a portion, thereby securing their obligation to refund any overage in distribution they have received.

If there is no partition and distribution and, consequently, no declaration regarding who the heirs are and what their interests are, heirship must be declared within the dependent administration. Forms to do so are found at Forms 11-20, 11-20A, and 11-21.

Final Accounting

The procedure for final accounting found in Part 12 of Chapter VIII of the Probate Code, provides that the administration of the estate of a decedent may be closed when all debts known to exist against the estate have been paid, at least insofar as assets in the hands of the personal representative permit, and when there is no further need for administration. The procedure involves filing a final account, or an account for final settlement: an example is found at Form 11-22.

The final account is a verified account that must show the property that came into the hands of the executor, the disposition that was made of the property, the debts that have been paid, the debts and expenses still owing, the property still remaining on hand, the persons entitled to receive the estate, and all advancements or payments made by the administrator. This may be shown in the final account by reference to the inventory and any prior proceedings during the administration. For instance, the property of this estate remaining on hand may be shown in an allegation such as "The property of the estate remaining on hand is that shown in the inventory, appraisement and list of claims filed herein on the _____ day of _____, 19___, less sales as shown in decree confirming sale dated the ____ day of _____, 19___, and decree confirming sale dated the ____ day of _____, 19___."

This too is a little lawsuit, and requires citation. Citation is by certified mail, return receipt requested, unless another type of notice is directed by the court. The notice must include a copy of the account for final settlement, and must be served on each heir or devisee. A waiver of such a notice is found at Form 11-22A.

At the hearing, the court examines the account for final settlement, and hears exceptions or objections to it, and either approves it or orders it restated if necessary. If there is any estate remaining in the hands of the personal representative, the court orders it delivered to the persons legally entitled to it. If there is no such property or when such property is reported as being delivered, then an order is entered closing the estate and discharging the representative from the trust. Section 410 requires that the final account cannot be approved nor the estate closed unless the final account shows and the court finds that all inheritance taxes due and owing to the State of Texas have been paid. An example of such an order is found at Form 11-23. A report of distribution and application to close the estate is found at Form 11-24, and an order closing the estate is found at Form 11-25.

CHAPTER QUESTIONS AND EXERCISES

1. Is there more work for a legal assistant with reference to dependent administrations than with independent administrations? If your answer is yes, explain why.

2. How is exempt property treated under the Probate Code when one of the owners dies?

3. What is an allowance in lieu of exempt property?

4. What is the family allowance, and when is it allowed?

5. When and how must a claim be filed?

6. Who allows and rejects claims? How is this done?

7. What do you do in the following circumstances, and how much of each creditor's bill can you pay? The estate has $7,000 in cash and owes $10,000 to class-seven creditors. The creditors are demanding payment immediately.

8. What documents have to be prepared in order to sell property belonging to an estate?

9. How is an estate closed?

10. When is the first annual account due?

11. Supplying any additional information needed, prepare an application for letters of administration and a letter enclosing the application to the clerk, for the following situation:

   Dan Durwood left a wife and four adult children. He had no will. He owned as community property two automobiles, a house and lot, one checking account, one savings account, a substantial certificate of deposit, a mutual fund account, furniture, personal effects, and clothes of a total value of over $250,000. He died January of this year in your county, where he resided prior to his death.

12. Prepare all documents needed to qualify the administrator under the facts of Exercise 11. He has found two very wealthy family members who will act as personal sureties. To complete this exercise, you will need to ascertain the requirements regarding personal surety bonds and find forms for the bond and related documents in form books in the law library.

13. Set aside the exempt property to those entitled to it as provided in the fact situation in Exercise 11. Dan also has a retirement account, payable directly to his wife upon death, worth $121,230 and life insurance payable to her in the amount of $321,000. To complete this assignment, you will have to locate and read the Texas statute that exempts personal property from forced sale.

14. Charlie Creditor, the local loan shark, was owed $2,313.26 by Dan on a personal loan that is represented by a promissory note. Charlie is going to bring you the note tomorrow. However, since it is getting close to six months from Dan's death, he wants you to have a claim ready, so a copy of the note can be quickly attached and he can hand-deliver it to the courthouse. Prepare the claim.

15. Dan's wife has received an offer for the house that she cannot refuse. It is about $10,000 above appraised evaluation. The prospective buyer, Sam Specter, has heard that Dan's ghost is haunting the house, and he has always wanted to own a haunted house. By the same token, Dan's wife has never wanted to own a haunted house; besides, she had enough of Dan when he was alive. Sam is offering

$275,000 in cash. Prepare all documents necessary to sell the house. All orders of the courts should have dates filled in. Remember to check the various time limitations and provisions. Apply the format for a legal description used in the documents in Chapter Ten.

16. Prepare an annual account for the year in which Charlie (from Exercise 14) files and is paid his claim and in which the house is sold to Sam (from Exercise 15). Both events occur in the same accounting period.

17. Prepare a final account incorporating the facts in Exercises 11-16. Make up any additional needed facts.

Form 11-1: Application for Letters of Administration

NO. _____

ESTATE OF	§	IN THE COUNTY COURT
PETER SMITH,	§	AT LAW NO. TWO
DECEASED	§	ROUGH RIDER COUNTY, TEXAS

APPLICATION FOR LETTERS OF ADMINISTRATION

PAULA SMITH, Applicant, Social Security No. 420-26-4340, represents the following concerning the Estate of **PETER PROBATE**, Deceased, Social Security 280-92-4242.

1. Applicant is an individual interested in this Estate, is domiciled in and resides at 1412 Bullmoose, San Juan Hill, Rough Rider County, Texas, is entitled to Letters of Administration, is not disqualified by law, and is Decedent's surviving spouse.

2. Decedent died intestate on March 3, 1992 in San Juan Hill, Rough Rider County, Texas.

3. This Court has jurisdiction and venue because Decedent was domiciled and had a fixed place of residence in this county on the date of death.

4. Decedent owned property of a probate value in excess of $100,000.00, which property is described generally as home, cash, securities, automobiles, household goods, personal effects, etc.

5. There is no need for the appointment of appraisers.

6. A necessity exists for administration of this Estate because there are at least two debts against the Estate and because the Court should partition the Estate among the heirs.

7. Applicant request that citation issue as required by law to all persons interested in this Estate, that Applicant be appointed Administrator of this Estate, that Letters of Administration be issued to Applicant, that appraisers not be appointed, and that such other orders be entered as the Court may deem proper.

Respectfully submitted,

TEDDY & FRANKLIN

_____

JOHN TEDDY
State Bar No. 00000100
5155 Teton Pkwy., Suite 206
P.O. Box 186
Corpus Christi, TX 79421
(512) 555-1234 Telephone
(512) 555-5678 FAX

ATTORNEY FOR THE ESTATE

Form 11-2: Proof of Death and Other Facts

(Reprinted from <u>Texas Probate System</u>, copyright State Bar of Texas, with permission.)

NO. 23814-2

ESTATE OF	§	**IN THE COUNTY COURT**
PETER SMITH,	§	**AT LAW NO. TWO**
DECEASED	§	**ROUGH RIDER COUNTY, TEXAS**

PROOF OF DEATH AND OTHER FACTS

On this day, **PAULA SMITH**, Affiant, personally appeared in Open Court, and after being duly sworn, deposes and says that:

1. "**PETER SMITH**, Decedent, died on March 3, 1992, in San Juan Hill, Rough Rider County, Texas, at the age of 87 years and four years have not elapsed since the date of Decedent's death.

2. "Decedent was domiciled and had a fixed place of residence in this County at the date of death.

3. "So far as I know and believe, Decedent did not leave a will.

4. "A necessity exists for the administration of this Estate.

5. "The Applicant for Letters of Administration is not disqualified by law from accepting Letters of Administration or from serving as Administrator and is qualified and entitled to such Letters."

SIGNED this _____ day of May, 1992.

_____
PAULA SMITH

SWORN TO AND SUBSCRIBED BEFORE ME by **PAULA SMITH** this _____ day of May, 1992, to certify which witness my hand and seal of office.

CLERK OF THE COUNTY COURT
Rough Rider County, Texas

By: _____
Deputy

Form 11-3: Order Granting Letters of Administration

NO. 23814-2

ESTATE OF	§	IN THE COUNTY COURT
PETER SMITH,	§	AT LAW NO. TWO
DECEASED	§	ROUGH RIDER COUNTY, TEXAS

ORDER GRANTING LETTERS OF ADMINISTRATION

On this day the Court heard and considered the Application for Letters of Administration filed by **PAULA SMITH**, Applicant, in the Estate of **PETER SMITH**, Deceased, and after hearing the Application, the Court finds that Decedent is dead and four (4) years have not elapsed since the date of Decedent's death; the Court has jurisdiction and venue over this Estate; citation has been served and returned as required by law; there exists a necessity for an administration of this Estate; the Application for Letters of Administration should be granted; Applicant is entitled by law to be appointed Administrator of this Estate and is not disqualified from acting as such Administrator; no interested person has applied for the appointment of appraisers, and the Court does not deem an appraisal necessary.

It is therefore, ORDERED, ADJUDGED, and DECREED that **PAULA SMITH** Is hereby appointed Administrator of this Estate and shall give Bond in the sum of $_____, conditioned as required by law, and the Clerk of the Court shall issue Letters of Administration when the Administrator has qualified according to law, and no appraisers are appointed in this Estate

SIGNED AND ENTERED this _____ day of May, 1992.

_____
JUDGE PRESIDING

Form 11-4: Oath of Administrator

NO. 23814-2

ESTATE OF	§	**IN THE COUNTY COURT**
PETER SMITH,	§	**AT LAW NO. TWO**
DECEASED	§	**ROUGH RIDER COUNTY, TEXAS**

OATH OF ADMINISTRATOR

I do solemnly swear that **PETER SMITH**, Decedent, died without leaving a will, so far as I know or believe, and that I will well and truly perform all of the duties of Administrator of Decedent's Estate.

_____
PAULA SMITH

SWORN TO AND SUBSCRIBED BEFORE ME by **PAULA SMITH** this _____ day of May, 1992, to certify which witness my hand and seal of office.

_____
CLERK OF THE COUNTY COURT
Court of Rough Rider County, Texas

By: _____
Deputy

Form 11-5: Application to Set Aside Exempt Property

NO. 23814-2

ESTATE OF	§	IN THE COUNTY COURT
PETER SMITH,	§	AT LAW NO. TWO
DECEASED	§	ROUGH RIDER COUNTY, TEXAS

APPLICATION TO SET ASIDE EXEMPT PROPERTY

PAULA SMITH, Applicant, the Administratrix of this Estate, represents to the Court as follows:

1. **PETER SMITH**, Decedent, was survived by his widow, **PAULA SMITH**, and by **PETER SMITH, JR.** and **PENELOPE SMITH** minor children. Decedent's widow is the mother of such children.

2. The following described property, belonging to the Estate, is exempt from execution or forced sale under the constitution and laws of the State of Texas:

    Lot Two (2), Block One (1), Sunnyside Addition, an addition in the City of San Juan Hill, Texas, as shown by the map or Plat Records of Rough Rider County in Volume 12, at page 334 of the map records of Rough Rider County, Texas

    Decedent owned personal property as part of the community estate described generally as household goods, personal effects, clothing, cash, tools, and 1991 Chevrolet Lumina APV, vehicle I.D. #3CZL42810M213. All of such property has a probate value of in excess of FIVE HUNDRED THOUSAND AND 00/100 DOLLARS ($500,000.00).

3. The Property should be set apart for the use and benefit of Decedent's Widow and the minor children pursuant to Section 271 of the Texas Probate Code.

4. The Property should be delivered to Decedent's Widow.

5. Applicant request the Court to enter an Order setting apart the Property for the use and benefit of Decedent's Widow and the minor children and directing the Administrator to deliver such property to Decedent's Widow.

Respectfully submitted,

PAULA SMITH
Administratrix

By: _____
Attorney for Applicant

ORDER

On this day the foregoing Application to Set Aside Exempt Property was heard by this Court, and the Court finds that such Application is true and correct and should be granted;

IT IS, THEREFORE, ORDERED, ADJUDGED AND DECREED that the following described property is hereby set apart for the use and benefit of Decedent's Widow and minor children and such property shall be delivered by the Administratrix, without delay, to Decedent's Widow, **PAULA PROBATE**:

Lot Two (2), Block One (1), Sunnyside Addition, an addition in the City of San Juan Hill, Texas, as shown by the map or Plat Records of Rough Rider County in Volume 12, at page 334 of the map records of Rough Rider County, Texas

Decedent owned personal property as part of the community estate described generally as household goods, personal effects, clothing, cash, tools, and 1991 Chevrolet Lumina APV, vehicle I.D. #3CZL42810M213. All of such property has a probate value of in excess of FIVE HUNDRED THOUSAND AND 00/100 DOLLARS ($500,000.00).

SIGNED AND ENTERED this _____ day of June, 1992.

_____
Judge Presiding

Form 11-6: Application for Allowance in Lieu of Exempt Property

(Reprinted from <u>Texas Probate System</u>, copyright State Bar of Texas, with permission.)

NO. 23814-2

ESTATE OF	§	IN THE COUNTY COURT
PETER SMITH,	§	AT LAW NO. TWO
DECEASED	§	ROUGH RIDER COUNTY, TEXAS

APPLICATION FOR ALLOWANCE IN LIEU OF EXEMPT PROPERTY

PAULA SMITH, Applicant, the Administratrix of this Estate, represents as follows:

1. The Inventory, Appraisement and List of Claims of this Estate has been approved.

2. **PETER SMITH**, Decedent and his wife, **PAULA SMITH** had two minor children at the time of Decedent's death, but they did not own a homestead at such time.

3. Pursuant to Section 273 of the Texas Probate Code, the Court should make a reasonable allowance in lieu of the homestead to be paid to Decedent's widow, the sum of TEN THOUSAND AND 00/100 DOLLARS ($10,000.00) is a reasonable allowance for such purpose.

4. The allowance should be paid in a lump sum out of funds belonging to the Estate.

5. Applicant requests the Court to enter an Order making a reasonable allowance in lieu of homestead and directing such allowance to be paid to Decedent's widow out of the funds belonging to the Estate.

PAULA SMITH

Administratrix

By: _____

Attorney for Applicant

ORDER

On this day the foregoing Application For Allowance In Lieu of Exempt Property was heard by this Court, and the Court finds that such Application is true and correct and should be granted;

IT IS, THEREFORE, ORDERED, ADJUDGED AND DECREED that the Administratrix of this Estate shall pay to Decedent's widow, **PAULA SMITH**, an allowance in lieu of exempt property in the sum of TEN THOUSAND AND 00/100 DOLLARS ($10,000.00), in a lump sum, out of the funds belonging to the Estate.

SIGNED and ENTERED this _____ day of June, 1992.

_____

Judge Presiding

Form 11-7: Application for Allowance

(Reprinted from <u>Texas Probate System</u>, copyright State Bar of Texas, with permission.)

NO. 23814-2

ESTATE OF	§	IN THE COUNTY COURT
PETER SMITH,	§	AT LAW NO. TWO
DECEASED	§	ROUGH RIDER COUNTY, TEXAS

APPLICATION FOR FAMILY ALLOWANCE

PAULA SMITH, Applicant, Administratrix of this Estate, represents the following:

1. The Inventory, Appraisement and List of Claims has been approved.
2. **PETER SMITH**, Decedent was survived by his wife **PAULA SMITH** and two minor children. Decedent's Widow and minor children do not have separate property adequate for their maintenance.
3. The amount of the family allowance should be determined by the facts and circumstances now existing and those anticipated to exist during the first year after Decedent's death, and such allowance should be in the amount of TWELVE THOUSAND AND 00/100 DOLLARS ($12,000.00) in monthly installments of ONE THOUSAND 00/100 DOLLARS ($1,000.00) each.

Applicant request the Court to set the amount of the family allowance, and specify the fund or other property from which such allowance should be paid.

Respectfully submitted,

PAULA SMITH
Administratrix

By: _____
Attorney for Applicant

ORDER

On this day the foregoing Application for Family Allowance was heard and considered by the Court and the Court finds that a fair and reasonable allowance be paid for the support of Decedent's Widow and minor children, based upon the facts now existing and those expected to exist during the first year after the death of the Decedent, is the sum of TWELVE THOUSAND AND 00/100 DOLLARS ($12,000.00).

IT IS, THEREFORE, ORDERED, ADJUDGED AND DECREED that family allowance of TWELVE THOUSAND AND 00/100 DOLLARS ($12,000.00), payable in monthly installments of ONE THOUSAND AND 00/100 DOLLARS ($1,000.00) each shall be paid to Decedent's Widow, **PAULA SMITH**, and that the Administratrix pay such allowance from the funds belonging to the Estate.

SIGNED and ENTERED this _____ day of June, 1992.

_____
Judge Presiding

Form 11-8: Notice to Creditors with Publisher's Affidavit

NO. 23814-2

ESTATE OF	§	IN THE COUNTY COURT
PETER SMITH,	§	AT LAW NO. TWO
DECEASED	§	ROUGH RIDER COUNTY, TEXAS

NOTICE TO ALL PERSONS HAVING CLAIMS AGAINST
THE ESTATE OF PETER SMITH, DECEASED

Notice is hereby given that original Letters of Administration for the Estate of **PETER SMITH** were issued on June 3, 1992, in Cause No. 23814-2, pending in the County Court at Law No. Two, Rough Rider County, Texas, to:

PAULA SMITH

The residence of such **PAULA SMITH** is Rough Rider County, Texas. The post office address is:

C/O JOHN TEDDY

P.O. Box 186

San Juan Hill, Texas 79421

The persons having claims against this Estate which is currently being administered are required to present them within the time and in the manner prescribed by law.

DATED the 10th day of June, 1992.

PAULA SMITH

Administratrix

By: _____

Attorney for the Estate

PUBLISHER'S AFFIDAVIT

I solemnly swear that the above notice was published in Rough Rider Gazette, a newspaper printed in Rough Rider, Rough Rider County, Texas, and of general circulation in said county, as provided in the Texas Probate Code for the service of citation or notice by publication, and the date that the issue of said newspaper bore in which said notice was published was June 11, 1992. A copy of the notice as published, clipped from the newspaper, is attached hereto.

_____

PUBLISHER

SWORN TO AND SUBSCRIBED BEFORE ME by_____
this ____ day of _____, 19___, to certify which witness my hand and seal of office.

_____

Notary Public, State of Texas

Form 11-9: Authenticated Unsecured Claim

(Reprinted from <u>Texas Probate System</u>, copyright State Bar of Texas, with permission.)

NO. 23814-2

ESTATE OF	§	IN THE COUNTY COURT
PETER SMITH,	§	AT LAW NO. TWO
DECEASED	§	ROUGH RIDER COUNTY, TEXAS

AUTHENTICATED UNSECURED CLAIM

1. **CHARLES CREDITOR** is the owner of an unsecured claim against the Estate in the sum of ONE THOUSAND ONE HUNDRED SEVENTY-NINE AND 20/100 DOLLARS ($1,179.20). This claim is founded upon the following:

Loans and advances of money made by me to **PETER PROBATE** on September 11, 1992 in the original amount of ONE THOUSAND AND 00/100 DOLLARS ($1,000.00) said amount bearing interest at the agreed rate of eight percent (8%).

2. Claimant requests allowance and payment of this claim.

_____
CHARLES CREDITOR
Claimant

Claimant's Name   CHARLES CREDITOR
Address 134   Jones Avenue
City, State, ZIP   San Juan Hill, Texas 79321

STATE OF TEXAS   §
COUNTY OF ROUGH RIDER   §

BEFORE ME, the undersigned authority, on this day personally appeared **CHARLES CREDITOR**, and after being duly sworn by me, stated that the foregoing unsecured claim is just and that all legal offsets, payments and credits known to Claimant have been allowed.

_____
CHARLES CREDITOR
Claimant

SUBSCRIBED AND SWORN TO BEFORE ME by **CHARLES CREDITOR** this _____ day of July, 1992, to certify which witness my hand and seal of office.

_____
Notary Public, State of Texas

MEMORANDUM OF ALLOWANCE

The foregoing Authenticated Unsecured Claim was presented to me on the _____ day of July, 1992, and is by me _____.

_____
PAULA SMITH
Administratrix of the Estate of
PETER SMITH, Deceased.

ORDER

The foregoing Authenticated Unsecured Claim was allowed by the Administratrix this Estate and has been on the Claim Docket of this Court for more than ten (10) days. It is hereby by this Court this _____ day of _____, 1992.

_____
JUDGE PRESIDING

Form 11-10: Application for Authority to Expend Funds

(Reprinted from <u>Texas Probate System</u>, copyright State Bar of Texas, with permission.)

NO. 23814-2

ESTATE OF	§	IN THE COUNTY COURT
PETER SMITH,	§	AT LAW NO. TWO
DECEASED	§	ROUGH RIDER COUNTY, TEXAS

APPLICATION FOR AUTHORITY TO EXPEND FUNDS

PAULA SMITH, Applicant, Administratrix of this Estate, respectfully represents as follows:

1. The following claims against the Estate have been allowed by the Administratrix and approved by the Court and should be paid by Applicant:

   Claim of **CHARLES CREDITOR** in the amount of ONE THOUSAND ONE HUNDRED SEVENTY-NINE AND 20/100 DOLLARS ($1,179.20).

2. Sufficient funds are on hand to pay these amounts.

3. Applicant requests the Court to enter an Order authorizing Applicant to pay these amounts.

_____

PAULA SMITH

Administratrix

ORDER

On this day the foregoing Application was heard and considered by this Court and the Court finds that such payments should be made and that the Application should be granted.

It is therefore ORDERED, ADJUDGED and DECREED that the Applicant pay out the funds belonging to this Estate the claims listed in the foregoing Application.

SIGNED AND ENTERED this ____ day of July, 1993.

_____

JUDGE PRESIDING

Form 11-11: Application for Sale of Real Property

(Reprinted from <u>Texas Probate System</u>, copyright State Bar of Texas, with permission.)

NO. 23814-2

ESTATE OF	§	IN THE COUNTY COURT
PETER SMITH,	§	AT LAW NO. TWO
DECEASED	§	ROUGH RIDER COUNTY, TEXAS

APPLICATION FOR SALE OF REAL PROPERTY

PAULA SMITH, Administratrix of this Estate respectfully represents the following:

1. The Inventory, Appraisement and List of Claims of this Estate has been approved.

2. A full legal description of the real property sought to be sold and a description of the Estate's ownership interest in such property is attached to this Application, designated for identification as Exhibit A, and made a part hereof for all purposes.

3. A statement, verified by affidavit, which shows fully and in detail the condition of the Estate, the charges and claims that have been approved or established by suit or that have been reflected and may yet be established, the amount of each claim, the property of the Estate remaining on hand and liable for the payment of such claims and all other facts tending to show the necessity and advisability of this proposed sale, is attached to this Application, designated for identification as Exhibit B, and made a part hereof for all purposes.

4. It is necessary and advisable to sell the Estate's interest in the Property in order to pay allowances and claims against the estate.

5. It will be in the best interests of the Estate for the Property to be sold at a private sale.

Applicant requests that citation be issued to all persons interested in the Estate, as required by law, and that upon a hearing on this Application, the court enter an Order authorizing Applicant to sell the Estate's interest in the Property described in Exhibit A at a private sale on the terms set forth above.

Respectfully submitted,

PAULA SMITH
Administratrix

By: _____
Attorney for Applicant

Form 11-11: (continued)

EXHIBIT A

(Description of real estate to be sold)

Lot Two (2), Block One (1), Sunnyside Addition, an addition in the City of San Juan Hill, Texas, as shown by the map or Plat Records of Rough Rider County in Volume 12, at page 334 of the map records of Rough Rider County, Texas

Form 11-11: (continued)

EXHIBIT B

VERIFIED EXHIBIT SHOWING CONDITION

OF THE ESTATE

STATE OF TEXAS	§
COUNTY OF ROUGH RIDER	§

BEFORE ME, the undersigned authority, on this day personally appeared PAULA SMITH, Affiant, who after being duly sworn by me, on oath stated that:

1. "Affiant is the duly appointed and qualified Administratrix of the Estate of PETER SMITH, Deceased, and in support of Affiant's Application For Sale of Property, Affiant submits this Exhibit to the Court showing fully and in detail the condition of the Estate, as follows:

   A. Charges and Claims

   The following are all of the charges and claims against the Estate that have been approved or established by suit or have been rejected and may yet be established:

Nature of Claim or Charge	Amount
CHARLES CREDITOR	$ 1,179.20
PAULA SMITH	$12,00.00
Total Amount of Unpaid Charges and Claims	$13,179.20

   B. Property Remaining On Hand

   The following is a full and complete list, to the best of the Affiant's knowledge and belief, of all property owned by the Estate still remaining on hand and liable for the payment of the above charges and claims:

Description of Property	Value of Property
Real Estate Described in Exhibit B	$125,000.00
Total Value of Property Remaining on Hand	$125,000.00

2. "The sale sought in the foregoing Application For Sale of Property is necessary and advisable in order to pay allowances, and claims against the Estate."

_____

PAULA SMITH

Administratrix

SWORN TO AND SUBSCRIBED BEFORE ME by PAULA SMITH, Administratrix this _____ day of July, 1992, to certify which witness my hand and seal of office.

_____

Notary Public, State of Texas

Form 11-12: Order Setting Hearing on Application for Sale of Real Property

(Reprinted from <u>Texas Probate System</u>, copyright State Bar of Texas, with permission.)

NO. 23814-2

ESTATE OF	§	IN THE COUNTY COURT
PETER SMITH,	§	AT LAW NO. TWO
DECEASED	§	ROUGH RIDER COUNTY, TEXAS

ORDER SETTING HEARING ON APPLICATION
FOR SALE OF REAL PROPERTY

On this day the Application for Sale of Real Property belonging to this Estate was called to the attention of the Court, and it is ORDERED that such Application shall be heard by this Court on the 13th day of July, 1992, at 10:00 o'clock a.m., and the Clerk of this Court shall issue and serve citation as required by law.

SIGNED this ____ day of June, 1992.

_____
JUDGE PRESIDING

Form 11-13: Order of Sale of Real Property

(Reprinted from <u>Texas Probate System</u>, copyright State Bar of Texas, with permission.)

NO. 23814-2

ESTATE OF	§	IN THE COUNTY COURT
PETER SMITH,	§	AT LAW NO. TWO
DECEASED	§	ROUGH RIDER COUNTY, TEXAS

ORDER OF SALE OF REAL PROPERTY

On this day the Application For Sale of Real Property was heard and considered by the Court, and after hearing the evidence in support of the Application, the Court finds that citation has been issued and served as required by law; the Application is accompanied by an Exhibit, verified by affidavit, showing the condition of the Estate, and the Application and Exhibit meet all requirements of law; the real property to be sold is fully described in Exhibit A attached to and made a part of this Offer; the general bond is sufficient as required by law; the Application should be granted and the sale of the Property should be made; the sale is necessary and advisable in order to pay allowances and claims against the Estate.

IT IS, THEREFORE, ORDERED, ADJUDGED AND DECREED that the Property described in the attached Exhibit A shall be sold at a private sale.

IT IS FURTHER ORDERED, ADJUDGED AND DECREED that no additional bond shall be required at this time, and that after the sale has been made, a Report of Sale shall be filed and returned in accordance with law.

Signed and entered this _____ day of July , 1992.

_____
JUDGE PRESIDING

Form 11-14: Report of Sale of Real Property

(Reprinted from <u>Texas Probate System</u>, copyright State Bar of Texas, with permission.)

NO. 23814-2

ESTATE OF	§	IN THE COUNTY COURT
PETER SMITH,	§	AT LAW NO. TWO
DECEASED	§	ROUGH RIDER COUNTY, TEXAS

REPORT OF SALE OF REAL PROPERTY

PAULA SMITH, Administratrix of this Estate, reports the following:

1. The Offer of Sale of Real Property in this Estate is dated July 13, 1992.
2. A description of the property sold is contained in the attached Exhibit A.
3. The property was sold at a private sale on July 20, 1992.
4. The name of the purchaser is EDWARD GONZALES.
5. The total sales price of the property sold was $126,000.00, less estimated costs and expenses of sale in the sum of $7,416.00, leaving a net sales price $118,584.00.
6. This sale was made as specified in the contract, a copy of which is attached as Exhibit B.
7. The purchaser is ready to comply with the Order of Sale of Real Property.

_____
PAULA SMITH
Administratrix

SWORN TO AND SUBSCRIBED BEFORE ME by **PAULA SMITH** this day of _____, 19___, to certify which witness my hand and seal of office.

_____
Notary Public, State of Texas

Form 11-15: Decree Confirming Sale of Real Property

(Reprinted from <u>Texas Probate System</u>, copyright State Bar of Texas, with permission.)

NO. 23814-2

ESTATE OF	§	IN THE COUNTY COURT
PETER SMITH,	§	AT LAW NO. TWO
DECEASED	§	ROUGH RIDER COUNTY, TEXAS

DECREE CONFIRMING SALE OF REAL PROPERTY

On this day the Court heard and considered the Report of Sale of Real Property, and the Court finds that five (5) days have expired since the filing of the Report; the general bond is sufficient to protect the Estate and is in compliance with this Court's previous Order of Sale of Real Property and with the law; the real property has been sold for a fair price and such sale was properly made and in conformity with the law. Such property is described in Exhibit A, which is attached hereto and made a part of this Decree.

IT IS, THEREFORE, ORDERED, ADJUDGED AND DECREED that the sale described in the Report is hereby APPROVED AND CONFIRMED, and conveyance of the property is authorized upon compliance by the Purchaser with the terms of sale.

SIGNED this ____ day of July, 1992.

_____
JUDGE PRESIDING

Form 11-16: Deed Pursuant to Decree Confirming Sale

(Reprinted from <u>Texas Probate System</u>, copyright State Bar of Texas, with permission.)

DEED

THE STATE OF TEXAS   §

              KNOW ALL MEN BY THESE PRESENTS THAT:

COUNTY OF ROUGH RIDER   §

  Whereas, the Estate of **PETER SMITH**, Deceased, now pending the County Court at Law No. 2 of Rough Rider County, Texas, No. 23814-2, owns an interest in the real property described on the page attached and designated as Exhibit A; and

  Whereas, the undersigned, **PAULA SMITH**, the duly appointed, qualified and acting Administratrix of the Estate, made Application to the Court for an order to sell the Property; and

  Whereas, the Court made and entered an Order, dated June 23, 1992, directing the sale of the Property, after which and on July 20, 1992, the undersigned, pursuant to such Order, sold the Property at private sale to **EDWARD GONZALES**, a single man(hereinafter called Grantee); and

  Whereas, the undersigned filed the Report of Sale in this proceeding on July 21, 1992 after which date such sale was in all respects confirmed by a Decree of the Court entered on July 29, 1992; and

  Whereas, the Grantee has complied with the terms of such sale.

  NOW THEREFORE, I, **PAULA SMITH**, Individually and as Administratrix of such Estate for and in consideration of the sum of TWO HUNDRED FIFTY-TWO THOUSAND AND 00/100 DOLLARS ($252,000.00), paid to me by the Grantee, the receipt of which is hereby acknowledged, have GRANTED, SOLD AND CONVEYED and by these presents do GRANT, SELL AND CONVEY unto the Grantee, all of the real property in Rough Rider County, Texas, described in the attached Exhibit A.

  TO HAVE AND TO HOLD the above described premises, together with all and singular the rights and appurtenances thereto in anywise be to the said Grantee, his heirs and administrators forever.

  EXECUTED this ____ day of July, 1992.

_____

PAULA SMITH
Individually and as Administratrix
of the Estate of PETER PROBATE

THE STATE OF TEXAS   §
COUNTY OF ROUGH RIDER   §

  BEFORE ME, the undersigned authority, on this day personally appeared **PAULA SMITH**, known to me to be the person whose name is subscribed to the foregoing instrument, and acknowledged to me that she executed the same Individually and as Administratrix of the Estate of PETER SMITH, Deceased, for the purpose and consideration therein expressed and in the capacity therein set forth.

  GIVEN UNDER MY HAND AND SEAL OF OFFICE this ____ day of July, 1992.

_____

Notary Public, State of Texas

Form 11-17: Annual Account

(Reprinted from <u>Texas Probate System</u>, copyright State Bar of Texas, with permission.)

NO. 23814-2

ESTATE OF	§	IN THE COUNTY COURT
PETER SMITH,	§	AT LAW NO. TWO
DECEASED	§	ROUGH RIDER COUNTY, TEXAS

ANNUAL ACCOUNT

PAULA SMITH, Administratrix of this Estate, respectfully presents this verified exhibit pursuant to the provisions of Section 399 of the Texas Probate Code:

1. This Account covers the twelve month period from May 1, 1992 to May 1, 1993.

2. The following claims against the Estate have been presented and the following action has been taken with respect to each:

    The Claim of CHARLES CREDITOR in the amount of ONE THOUSAND ONE HUNDRED SEVENTY-NINE AND 20/100 DOLLARS ($1,179.20) was presented, allowed, approved and paid pursuant to order dated July 29, 1992.

3. The following property which has come to my knowledge or into my possession and which was not previously listed or inventoried is as follows:

    None

4. The following changes have occurred in property of the estate but have not been reported.

    Real Property was sold pursuant to sale procedures culminating in decree confirming sale dated July 29, 1992.

5. The receipts of the estate are as follows:

    EIGHTEEN THOUSAND FIVE HUNDRED EIGHTY-FOUR AND 00/100 DOLLARS ($18,584.00) received July 30, 1992 as proceeds of sale described in No. 5 above.

6. The disbursements of the Estate have been as follows:

    A. ONE THOUSAND ONE HUNDRED SEVENTY-NINE 20/100 DOLLARS ($1,179.20) to CHARLES CREDITOR as described above.

    B. ELEVEN THOUSAND AND 00/100 DOLLARS ($11,000.00) to PAULA SMITH as authorized in order approving application for family allowance.

7. The description of the property being administered is the same as the property shown in the Inventory previously filed herein except as otherwise specified herein.

8. The following cash belonging to the Estate is on hand:

    ONE HUNDRED EIGHTEEN THOUSAND FIVE HUNDRED SIXTY-SEVEN AND 20/100 DOLLARS ($118,567.29) deposited a passbook savings account #124912 in the Rough Rider Savings Bank, F.S.B. subject to order of the Court.

9. Attached to this account are proper vouchers for each item of credit claimed in this Account.

10. Attached to this Account are Verifications from all depositories where money or other personal property belonging to this Estate are being held in safekeeping.

    The undersigned requests the Court to hear and approve this Annual Account and enter such other orders as may be proper.

Respectfully submitted,

_____
PAULA SMITH
Administratrix

Form 11-17: (continued)

AFFIDAVIT OF PAULA SMITH

THE STATE OF TEXAS   §
COUNTY OF ROUGH RIDER   §

   BEFORE ME, the undersigned authority, on this day personally appeared **PAULA SMITH**, known to me to be the Administratrix of the Estate of **PETER SMITH**, and to be the person whose name is subscribed to the foregoing Annual Account, who after being duly sworn by me, on oath stated that the Annual account and all vouchers and other attachments thereto are true, correct, and complete in every respect.

_____
PAULA SMITH
Administratrix

   SWORN TO AND SUBSCRIBED BEFORE ME by **PAULA SMITH** this ____ day of May, 1993, to certify which witness my hand and seal of office.

_____
Notary Public, State of Texas

ORDER

   On this day the foregoing Annual Account was heard and considered by the Court and the Court finds that it has jurisdiction and venue of this proceeding; that such Annual Account has remained on file for a full ten (10) days before being considered; that the Court is fully advised as to all the items of such Account, possession of cash and other assets kept in safekeeping, as well as those on deposit, that all vouchers were produced and filed for each item of credit claimed in such Account and that satisfactory evidence has been presented as to the status and existence of the assets of this estate; and that the facts stated in such Account are true, correct and complete and that his Account should be approved.

   It is therefore ORDERED, ADJUDGED and DECREED that the foregoing Annual Account is APPROVED.

   SIGNED AND ENTERED this ____ day of May, 1992.

_____
JUDGE PRESIDING

Form 11-18: Verification of Funds on Deposit

(Reprinted from <u>Texas Probate System</u>, copyright State Bar of Texas, with permission.)

NO. 23814-2

ESTATE OF	§	IN THE COUNTY COURT
PETER SMITH,	§	AT LAW NO. TWO
DECEASED	§	ROUGH RIDER COUNTY, TEXAS

VERIFICATION OF FUNDS ON DEPOSIT

The undersigned, an officer of the financial institution named below, hereby certifies that **PAULA PROBATE**, Administratrix of this Estate, has on deposit with this institution, in Passbook account number 124912, funds belonging to this Estate, and that as of May 1, 1994 the balance in such account is the sum of $118,567.29.

The undersigned further certifies that under no circumstances will any of the funds, including any subsequent deposits or any interest or dividends credited to such account, in such account be delivered by this institution to anyone without written authority for such payment from the Court.

SIGNED this ____ day of May, 1994.

ROUGH RIDER SAVINGS BANK, FSB

By: _____

Form 11-19: Confirmation of Safekeeping

(Reprinted from Texas Probate System, copyright State Bar of Texas, with permission.)

NO. 23814-2

ESTATE OF	§	IN THE COUNTY COURT
PETER SMITH,	§	AT LAW NO. TWO
DECEASED	§	ROUGH RIDER COUNTY, TEXAS

CONFIRMATION OF SAFEKEEPING

The undersigned hereby certifies that as of May 1, 1994, **PAULA PROBATE**, Administratrix of this Estate, has on deposit with this office the following described securities or other assets held subject to orders of the Court:

10 shares of IBM as represented by Certificate No. 1218792

The undersigned further certifies that under no circumstances will any of such securities or other assets be delivered to anyone without written authority therefor from the Court.

SIGNED this ____ day of May, 1994.

ROUGH RIDER SAVINGS BANK, FSB

By: _____

Form 11-20: Application to Declare Heirship

NO. 23814-2

ESTATE OF	§	IN THE COUNTY COURT
PETER SMITH,	§	AT LAW NO. TWO
DECEASED	§	ROUGH RIDER COUNTY, TEXAS

APPLICATION TO DECLARE HEIRSHIP

PAULA SMITH, Administratrix of this Estate, Applicant, who resides at 1412 Bullmoose, San Juan Hill, shows the Court the following:

1. **PETER SMITH**, Decedent died on March 3, 1992 at San Juan Hill, Rough Rider County, Texas.

2. An administration is pending upon Decedent's Estate in the above numbered and entitled cause, and it is necessary and in the best interest of the Estate for the Court to determine who are the heirs and only heirs of Decedent.

3. Applicant claims to be the owner of a part of Decedent's Estate.

4. At the time of Decedent's death, Decedent owned the following property:

   Lot Two (2), Block One (1), Sunnyside Addition, an addition in the City of San Juan Hill, Texas, as shown by the map or Plat Records of Rough Rider County in Volume 12, at page 334 of the map records of Rough Rider County, Texas

   of claims however since then the real property has been sold.

5. The names and residences of the heirs of Decedent are as follows:

NAME	RESIDENCE	SHARE OF ESTATE
PETER SMITH,JR.	252 Yellowstone Parkway San Juan Hill, TX 79231	50%

NAME	RESIDENCE	SHARE OF ESTATE
PENELOPE SMITH	721 Monolle Drive San Juan Hill, TX 79231	50%

6. Decedent was married to and survived by **PAULA SMITH** on the date of death.

7. Decedent had two children born to him, **PETER SMITH, JR.**, an adult who resides at 252 Yellowstone Parkway, San Juan Hill, Texas and **PENELOPE SMITH**, an adult, who resides at 721 Monolle Drive, San Juan Hill, Texas.

Applicant prays that citation be issued in accordance with law, that upon hearing hereof, this Court determine who are the heirs and their respective shares and interests in such Estate, and that all other orders be entered as the Court may deem proper.

PAULA SMITH
Administratrix

By: _____
Attorney for Applicant

JOHN TEDDY
State Bar No. 00000100
5155 Teton Pkwy., Suite 206
P.O. Box 186
Corpus Christi, TX 79421
(512) 555-1234 Telephone
(512) 555-5678 FAX

Form 11-20: (continued)

THE STATE OF TEXAS   §

            KNOW ALL MEN BY THESE PRESENTS:

COUNTY OF ROUGH RIDER   §

 I, the undersigned, having been duly sworn, hereby state on oath that insofar as is known to me, all the allegations of the foregoing Application are true in substance and in fact and that no material fact or circumstance has, within my knowledge, been omitted from the Application.

_____

PAULA SMITH

 SUBSCRIBED AND SWORN TO BEFORE ME, the undersigned authority, by the said PAULA SMITH this ____ day of August, 1992, to certify which witness my hand and seal of office.

_____

Notary Public, State of Texas

Form 11-20A: Waiver of Citation

NO. 23814-2

ESTATE OF	§	IN THE COUNTY COURT
PETER SMITH,	§	AT LAW NO. TWO
DECEASED	§	ROUGH RIDER COUNTY, TEXAS

WAIVER OF CITATION

| STATE OF TEXAS | § |
| COUNTY OF ROUGH RIDER | § |

BEFORE ME, the undersigned authority, on this day personally appeared **PETER SMITH, JR.** who, being by me duly sworn, upon oath states:

"I, **PETER SMITH, JR.**, am the adult son and heir of **PETER SMITH**, and a respondent in the above-entitled and -numbered cause. My mailing address is 137 Heir Ave, San Juan Hill, Texas numbered cause. I have been given a copy of the Application for Declaration of Heirship that has been filed in this cause, and I have read it and understand it. I hereby waive the issuance and personal service of citation in accordance with Rule 35 of the Texas Probate Code. I agree to all that is stated therein and that the matter may be taken up and considered by the Court without further notice to me."

_____
PETER SMITH, JR.

SUBSCRIBED AND SWORN TO BEFORE ME this ____ day of August, 1992.

_____
Notary Public, State of Texas

Form 11-21: Judgment Declaring Heirship

NO. 23814-2

ESTATE OF	§	IN THE COUNTY COURT
PETER SMITH,	§	AT LAW NO. TWO
DECEASED	§	ROUGH RIDER COUNTY, TEXAS

JUDGMENT DECLARING HEIRSHIP

On this day came on to be heard the sworn Application to Declare Heirship of the Estate of **PETER SMITH**, Deceased, wherein **PAULA SMITH** is the Applicant and Decedent's living heirs names and whereabouts are known and have waived issuance and service of citation, and it appears to the Court, and the Court so finds that all parties interested in the Estate of Decedent have been duly and legally served with citation or have waived such as required by law; and that all parties have appeared in person herein; that this Court has jurisdiction of the subject matter and all persons and parties; that the evidence presented and admitted fully and satisfactorily proves each and every issue presented to the Court; that Decedent died intestate and that the heirship of Decedent has been fully and satisfactorily proved as well as the identity of the nature of Decedent's property as being separate or community and the interest and shares of each of the heirs therein.

It is therefore, ORDERED, ADJUDGED and DECREED by the court that the names and places of residence of the heirs of Decedent and their respective shares and interests in the real and personal property of Decedent is as follows:

Form 11-21: (continued)

NAMES	RESIDENCE	SHARE & DESCRIPTION OF REAL PROPERTY	SHARE & DESCRIPTION OF PERSONAL PROPERTY
PETER SMITH, JR.	137 Heir Ave San Juan Hill Texas	None	1/2 of the Decedent's 1/2 Community
PENELOPE SMITH	1414 Dollar St. San Juan Hill Texas	None	1/2 of the Decedent's 1/2 Community

_____
JUDGE PRESIDING

APPROVED:

PAULA SMITH
Applicant

By_____
    Attorney for Applicant

JOHN TEDDY
State Bar No. 00000100
5155 Teton Pkwy., Suite 206
P.O. Box 186
Corpus Christi, TX 79421
(512) 555-1234 Telephone
(512) 555-5678 FAX

APPROVED:

_____
PETER SMITH, JR.

_____
PENELOPE SMITH

Form 11-22: Account for Final Settlement

NO. 23814-2

ESTATE OF	§	IN THE COUNTY COURT
PETER SMITH,	§	AT LAW NO. TWO
DECEASED	§	ROUGH RIDER COUNTY, TEXAS

ACCOUNT FOR FINAL SETTLEMENT

PAULA SMITH, Administratrix of this Estate, respectfully presents this verified Account For Final Settlement pursuant to the provisions of the Texas Probate Code:

1. There is no further need of administration of this Estate. Except as may be provided below, all debts known to exist against this Estate have been paid.

2. The property belonging to the Estate which has come into my hands is that property listed and described in the Inventory, Appraisement, and List of Claims previously filed herein, reference to which is here made for the purposes."

3. The following debts of the estate have been paid by authorization of the Court and are as follows:
    As shown by Annual Account dated May 5, 1993.

4. The previously unreported receipts of the estate are as follows:
    None

5. The previously unreported disbursements of the estate have been as follows:
    None

6. The debts and expenses still owing by the estate are as follows:
    None

7. The property of the estate remaining on hand is as follows:
    Cash in the amount of $118,567.29 as shown in annual account, plus accrued interest in amount of $2,192.20.

8. Attached to this Account are proper vouchers for each item of credit claimed in this Account.

9. Attached to this Account are Verifications from all depositories where money or other personal property belonging to this Estate are being held in safekeeping.

10. With respect to Inheritance Taxes due and owing to the State of Texas, none are due. No other tax returns have been filed with any governmental entity and no taxes are due.

11. The persons entitled to receive the property remaining on hand after the payment of all debts and expenses have been determined pursuant to the Judgment Declaring Heirship previously entered in this Estate, and are as follows:

    A. **PETER SMITH, JR.** son of Decedent, 137 Heir Ave., San Juan Hill, Texas, an adult is entitled to 50% of Estate as shown by Judgment Declaring Heirship.

    B. **PENELOPE SMITH**, daughter to Decedent, 1414 Dollar Street, San Juan Hill, Texas, an adult is entitled to 50% of Estate as shown by Judgment Declaring Heirship.

12. Citation should be served as required by law, following which the Court should audit, settle, and approve this Account and authorize the payment of all unpaid debts and expenses and the distribution of the property remaining on hand to the persons entitled to receive such property, and enter such orders as may be proper.

Respectfully submitted,

PAULA SMITH
Administratrix

By: _____
Attorney for Applicant

JOHN TEDDY
State Bar No. 00000100
5155 Teton Pkwy., Suite 206
P.O. Box 186
Corpus Christi, TX 79421
(512) 555-1234 Telephone
(512) 555-5678 FAX

Form 11-22: (continued)

AFFIDAVIT OF PAULA SMITH

THE STATE OF TEXAS   §
COUNTY OF ROUGH RIDER   §

    BEFORE ME, the undersigned authority, on this day personally appeared **PAULA SMITH**, known to me to be the Administratrix of the Estate of **PETER SMITH**, and to be the person whose name is subscribed to the foregoing Account For Final Settlement, who after being duly sworn to me, on oath stated that the Account and all vouchers and other attachments thereto are true, correct, and complete in every respect.

                                                      _____
                                                      PAULA SMITH
                                                      Administratrix

    SWORN TO AND SUBSCRIBED BEFORE ME by _____this
_____ day of August 1993, to certify which witness my hand and seal of office.

                                                      _____
                                                    Notary Public, State of Texas

Form 11-22A: Waiver of Citation

NO. 23814-2

ESTATE OF	§	IN THE COUNTY COURT
PETER SMITH,	§	AT LAW NO. TWO
DECEASED	§	ROUGH RIDER COUNTY, TEXAS

WAIVER OF CITATION

STATE OF TEXAS	§
COUNTY OF ROUGH RIDER	§

BEFORE ME, the undersigned authority, personally appeared **PETER SMITH, JR.**, who by me duly sworn, on oath says:

"I, **PETER SMITH, JR.** am an heir in the above-entitled and -numbered cause. I have been given a copy of the Account for Final Settlement which has been filed in this cause, and I have read it and understand it. I hereby enter my appearance in this cause for all purposes and waive the issuance, service and return of process. I agree that the account may be amended and that the cause may be taken up and considered by the Court without further notice to me."

SIGNED on the _____ day of _____, 1993.

_____
PETER SMITH, JR.

SWORN TO AND SUBSCRIBED before me by **PETER SMITH, JR.** on _____, 1993.

_____
Notary Public, State of Texas

Form 11-23: Order Approving Final Account

NO. 23814-2

ESTATE OF	§	**IN THE COUNTY COURT**
PETER SMITH,	§	**AT LAW NO. TWO**
DECEASED	§	**ROUGH RIDER COUNTY, TEXAS**

**ORDER APPROVING ACCOUNT FOR FINAL SETTLEMENT
AND AUTHORIZING DISTRIBUTION OF THE ESTATE**

On this day the Account for Final Settlement of this Estate was heard and considered by the Court, and after examining the Account and the vouchers accompanying the same and hearing the evidence in support of same, the Court finds that citation has been duly served upon all persons interested in this Estate; that the Court has jurisdiction of this proceeding and of the subject matter as required by law; that the Account For Final Settlement has been audited and settled by the Court, complies with the law in every respect, and should be approved as filed; that all claims, debts and expenses have been paid or are approved and should be paid; that this Estate has been fully administered; that the property remaining on hand in this Estate should be delivered to the persons named in the Account For Final Settlement, and that these persons are the persons entitled to receive such property.

It is therefore, ORDERED, ADJUDGED and DECREED that the Account For Final Settlement is hereby APPROVED, that the debts and expenses remaining unpaid, as set forth in the Account For Final Settlement shall be paid, and that all of the property belonging to the Estate and still remaining on hand after payment of all debts and expenses shall be delivered to persons who are entitled to receive such property as Decedent's heirs at law pursuant to the Judgment Declaring Heirship previously heard and considered by the Court, and after examining the Account and the vouchers accompanying the same and hearing the evidence in support of same, the Court finds that citation has been duly served upon all persons interested in this Estate; that the Court has jurisdiction of this proceeding and of the subject matter as required by law; that the Account For Final Settlement has been audited and settled by the Court, complies with the law in every respect, and should be approved as filed; that all claims, debts and expenses have been paid or are approved and should be paid; that all inheritance taxes due and owing to the State of Texas have been paid; that this Estate has been fully administered; that the property remaining on hand in this Estate should be delivered to the persons named in the Account for Final Settlement, and that these persons are the persons entitled to receive such property.

It is therefore, ORDERED, ADJUDGED and DECREED that the Account for Final Settlement is hereby APPROVED, that the debts and expenses remaining unpaid, as set forth in the Account For Final Settlement shall be paid, and that all property belonging to the Estate and still remaining on hand after payment of all debts and expenses shall be delivered to persons who are entitled to receive such property as Decedent's heirs at law pursuant to the Judgment Declaring Heirship previously entered in this Estate, and who are as follows:

With respect to Inheritance Taxes due and owing to the State of Texas, none are due.

It is further ORDERED that upon the distribution of the estate to such persons and the filing of proper receipts therefore, the Administratrix of this Estate shall apply to the Court for an Order of Discharge and for a declaration that this Estate is closed.

SIGNED AND ENTERED this _____ day of September, 1993.

                                                             _____
                                                             JUDGE PRESIDING

Form 11-24: Application to Close Estate

(Reprinted from <u>Texas Probate System</u>, copyright State Bar of Texas, with permission.)

NO. 23814-2

ESTATE OF	§	IN THE COUNTY COURT
PETER SMITH,	§	AT LAW NO. TWO
DECEASED	§	ROUGH RIDER COUNTY, TEXAS

APPLICATION TO CLOSE ESTATE AND TO
DISCHARGE PERSONAL REPRESENTATIVE

PAULA SMITH, Administratrix of this Estate, respectfully represents as follows:

1. This Court has previously entered its Order approving the Account For Final Settlement of this Estate and ordering Applicant to deliver the property remaining on hand to the persons entitled to receive such property.

2. Applicant has fully complied with such Order and there is no property belonging to this Estate remaining in the hands of Applicant.

3. Applicant requests this Court to enter an Order discharging Applicant from this trust, discharging the surety on Applicant's Bond from further liability, and declaring this Estate closed.

_____
PAULA PROBATE
Administratrix

Form 11-25: Order Closing Estate

(Reprinted from <u>Texas Probate System</u>, copyright State Bar of Texas, with permission.)

NO. 23814-2

ESTATE OF	§	IN THE COUNTY COURT
PETER SMITH,	§	AT LAW NO. TWO
DECEASED	§	ROUGH RIDER COUNTY,
TEXAS		

**ORDER CLOSING ESTATE AND DISCHARGING
PERSONAL REPRESENTATIVE**

On this day the Court heard and considered the Application to Close Estate and Discharge Personal Representative, filed by the Administratrix of this Estate, and after hearing the evidence in support of such Application, the Court finds that this Estate has been fully administered; that the Administrator has delivered all of the property of the Estate remaining on hand to the persons entitled to receive the same; and that this Estate should be closed.

It is therefore, ORDERED, ADJUDGED, and DECREED that **PAULA SMITH**, Administratrix of this Estate, is hereby discharged from this trust; that ABC Insurance Co., Surety on the Bond of the **PAULA SMITH** hereby discharged from further liability under such Bond; and this Estate is hereby declared to be closed.

SIGNED AND ENTERED this ____ day of September, 1993.

_____
JUDGE PRESIDING

---

12 PROBATE ADMINISTRATION– MISCELLANEOUS AND ALTER- NATIVE PROBATE PROCEDURES

CHAPTER OBJECTIVES

Upon completion of this chapter, the student should be able to:

1. Compare and contrast, with each other and with independent and dependent administrations, the procedures for the muniment of title, determination of heirship, foreign wills, small estates, community administration, temporary administration, and informal probate.

2. Determine when probate as a muniment of title is applicable to a client's fact situation.

3. Prepare all documents necessary to probate a will as a muniment of title.

4. Prepare all documents relevant to a determination of heirship.

5. Know when an estate may be settled by use of a small estate affidavit and prepare all relevant documents.

CHAPTER GLOSSARY

Ancillary administration An administration or probate taken out in a second jurisdiction to conduct some business in that second jurisdiction or to clear title to estate property. (*Ancillary* means "auxiliary" or "subordinate.")

Authentication A proper officer's attestation certifying that a record is in due form of law and that she is the person appointed to so certify.

Declaratory judgment The judgment that results from a suit brought when parties are in doubt as to their rights, to

declare those rights even though no relief is awarded.

Domiciliary jurisdiction Jurisdiction when the party to a suit is domiciled in the state whose courts exercise jurisdiction over that party. The decedent had his or her legal home in the state in which the will was probated.

Exemplification See *Authentication*.

Foreign will A will admitted to probate in a sister state or in a foreign nation.

Full faith and credit The obligation (created in Article 4, Section 1, of the U.S.

Constitution) of states in the United States to recognize the legislative acts, public records, and judicial decisions of all other states.

Informal probate A procedure, taken from the Uniform Probate Code, enacted by the Texas legislature as Sections 501-510 of the Texas Probate Code, effective September 1, 1993, allowing the probating of the will and the issuance of limited letters testamentary. Under the limited letters testamentary, which can be issued to a devisee as well as to an executor, the only action that can be taken is the transfer of property designated for transfer in the inventory and the letters to the distributees.

Judicial action An adjudication of the rights and duties of parties who are properly before a court by notice or voluntary appearance. Final judgment (subject to appeal) is rendered on those rights and duties.

Judicial notice Knowledge of facts that need not be proved because they are so notorious that everyone is presumed to know them. Also called *judicial knowledge*.

Lien Security for a debt, duty, or other obligation; an ownership interest in property created in favor of a creditor to secure her right to the debt's repayment. If she is not repaid, she may foreclose the lien and either obtain possession of the property or have it sold in satisfaction of the debt.

Title The right of ownership of property.

INTRODUCTION

This chapter deals with certain procedures created in the Texas Probate Code that provide quick, simple, or less costly alternatives to the probate procedures discussed in the previous two chapters. All, with the exception of the temporary administration and the **foreign wills** procedure, are often referred to as "procedures in lieu of administration," because they dispense with the necessity of appointing an executor or administrator and with most of the formalities involved in a formal administration of an estate.

There are regional preferences with regards to the use of these procedures. Lawyers in a particular locale may make heavy use of one procedure and rarely use another or any of the others. For instance, the legal assistant may find that local lawyers hardly ever use the determination of heirship and small-estate procedure because of the general acceptance of affidavits of heirship (discussed in Chapter Two), or that they seldom use the muniment of **title** procedure, for whatever reason.

The procedures for muniment of title, determination of heirship, small estates, community administration, and **informal probate** are alternative probate procedures; therefore, the choice of whether to use them is the lawyer's. Although the foreign will procedures are necessary when there is a foreign will, even then a choice exists of which procedure to use. However, the client's facts determine whether a temporary administration is required.

MUNIMENT OF TITLE   REQUIRES A WILL

Section 89A of the Texas Probate Code creates a procedure commonly referred to as "probate as a muniment of title." This procedure can decrease both the cost and the complexity of the estate and, in some cases, the length of time the estate is open. Section 89A begins by stating that upon the completion of a hearing on an application for probate of a will, if the court is satisfied that the will should be admitted to probate and there are no unpaid debts (other than debts secured by liens on real estate) and no other reason for the administration of the estate, the court shall enter an order admitting the will to probate as a muniment of title. *Muniment* is a legal term meaning "evidence"; thus a muniment of title is written evidence of title. A deed is a muniment of title. In this Code section, then, a procedure is created by which a will is admitted to probate but no administration is opened on the estate. This requires proof that there are no unpaid debts owing by the estate other than debts secured by liens on real property, and that there is no other reason for administering the estate. Then the order entered by the court omits the portion of the order that appoints an executor. No executor is appointed, and no letters testamentary are issued.

Section 89A(b), added in 1993, provides that the court may include in the order admitting the will to probate as a muniment of title a **declaratory judgment** construing the will or determining the persons who are entitled to receive the property under the will and what their respective shares of the estate are. This is to be used in the event that a question exists concerning the construction of the will or if the persons entitled to the estate cannot be determined solely by reference to the will. Such declaratory judgment requires application and notice, just as for declaratory judgments under the Civil Practices and Remedies Code.

Section 89A(c) stipulates that the order admitting a will to probate as muniment of title constitutes legal authority to anyone who owes money to, has custody of property of, or is purchasing from or otherwise dealing with the estate to pay, transfer, or deal with the persons described in the will as entitled to receive the assets without administration. The persons entitled to the properties under the provisions of the will may deal with and treat the properties as if record title was vested in their name. This is a common clause in the Probate Code. There has already been reference to it in the preceding chapters. It also shows up in the procedures for determination of heirship and for small estates.

By this statute, then, the order probating the will, while not creating an administration, has the effect of transferring title from the decedent to the devisees named in the will to receive **title**. It is self-effectuating, and no executor/administrator is needed to carry out the terms of the will.

When this procedure was originally created, the probating of the will was the final step. All that needed to be done was to file an application, issue citation, and hold a hearing at which proof was introduced and a written proof of will executed and filed. The court would then enter an order admitting the will to probate, and that would be the end of the entire procedure.

In 1983, the legislature added Section 89A(d), which requires that unless the court waives it, the applicant who filed the probate procedure must file a sworn affidavit with the clerk stating the terms of the will that have been fulfilled and those that have not. Unless otherwise extended by the court, this affidavit must be filed before the 181st day after the date the will is admitted to probate. There is no statement as to the effect of failure to do so, although it does state that any such failure will not affect the passage of title. The courts can waive the filing of the affidavit and do so with frequency, particularly where only one heir exists.

The benefit of the procedures for muniment of title is that it does away with the need for an executor, which then relieves the attorney from preparing an oath and also does away with the need to file an inventory and appraisement or any other procedure required in dependent administrations. It saves money for the estate, both in attorney's fees and in court costs, though normally not more than several hundred dollars.

The problem with muniment of title is that the estate cannot owe any debts other than debts secured by real estate. Few estates are debt-free at the death of the testator. If nothing else, the estate owes the testator's current utility bills, but usually much more. It is not what is owed at the time of death that is relevant; rather, it is what is owed at the time of the hearing to probate the will. However, estates only infrequently have the funds to pay off all debts. Some attorneys solve this problem by delaying filing an application until insurance on the life of the testator has paid off. They use the funds to pay the existing indebtedness, and then file the application for probate as a muniment.

Another problem is that no other state has a procedure for muniment of title (see later discussion under "Informal Probate"). Consequently out-of-state transfer agents often initially refuse to accept the procedure. Generally, sending a copy of Section 89A, with pertinent provisions highlighted, along with exemplified copies of the will and the order admitting it to probate will solve the problem.

Forms 12-1 through 12-5 present, respectively, an application for probate as a muniment of title, an order admitting a will to probate as a muniment of title, a waiver of the affidavit, proof of death and other facts, and an affidavit in the event the court refuses to waive the requirement.

FOREIGN WILLS

The **judicial actions** of a sister state have no legal effect on title to real property located in the State of Texas unless recognized by the State of Texas under the **"full faith and credit"** provisions of the U.S. Constitution. There are procedures set out for the recognition of out-of-state judgments in normal civil cases.

With regard to judgments of other states that probate wills, there are special provisions for recognition in the Texas Probate Code in Part 2 of Chapter V, beginning at Section 95. These sections are difficult to understand, primarily because they provide two separate procedures and do not adequately differentiate between the two. One of these is a muniment of title procedure and the other is a procedure by which the foreign probate judgment is given recognition under the "full faith and credit" provisions. The latter is referred to as an **ancillary administration**.

The decision as to which of the two to use depends on whether the services of an executor or administrator will be required, in other words, on whether there is a need for administration. If the devisees named in the will are of age, competent, locatable, and in agreement, muniment of title is by far the easiest and cheapest procedure to use. On the other hand, if the services of an executor are going to be needed in order to transfer title of land because devisees are minors or incompetents, are not located, or are simply unable to agree, then the more expensive procedure of an ancillary administration is required.

There is a third alternative concerning a foreign will, and that is to probate it originally in this state. This is permissible if the will either has been probated in another state or has not been probated in another state but where the reason for nonprobate is not that it was rejected from probate in that other state. This is covered in Sections 103 and 104 of the Probate Code. Section 104 seems to indicate that the will is not admissible to probate in this state unless the will meets all the requirements of a valid will under the laws of the State of Texas.

The muniment of title procedure is presented in Probate Code Sections 96-99. To comply with these provisions the will must have been probated in any state or territory of the United States or in some foreign country. A copy of the will and the order admitting it to probate that bears the attestation, seal, and certificate required by Section 95(c) may be filed and recorded in the official real property records of any county in which real estate owned by the estate is located. Section 98 states that if the will has been properly authenticated and recorded, it takes effect and is valid and effectual as a deed of conveyance, and serves as notice of the will to all existing persons. That is, a will, properly authenticated and filed of record, acts as a muniment of title.

Routinely, certified copies of Texas judgments and other Texas court documents are recorded in the real property records. "Certified" here means that the clerk attaches a certification, either via stamp or by on separate page, that the document is a true and correct copy of the original, which is on file in her office. Nothing further is needed inasmuch as the courts of this state take **judicial notice** of who the clerk of a court in Texas is and therefore they judicially know that the proper person certified the document.

When dealing with out-of-state documents, there is no similar provision of law requiring the courts to take judicial notice of which out-of-state officer certifies the document. Through custom and tradition at common law, a procedure has evolved for the **authentication**, or **exemplification**, of foreign judicial records. First, the clerk certifies the document or attaches a certification that it is a true and correct copy of the original, which is of record in her office. Then the judge of the court, in this case the probate judge, certifies that the person signing the certificate is the clerk of the court and that the certification is in due form. Then the clerk certifies that the judge is the judge of the court. Almost all clerks, both of Texas counties and in foreign states, have preprinted forms or stamps containing these three certifications.

Ancillary administration, provided for in Section 95, requires that an application, together with an authenticated copy of the foreign probate proceedings (which consists of a copy of the will and the decree by which it was admitted to probate), be filed with the clerk in whatever county land is located. The form of the application and the procedure vary slightly, depending on whether the will was probated in a state in which the decedent was domiciled at the time of death or in a state in which the decedent was not domiciled at the time of death.

With regard to a will probated in an **domiciliary jurisdiction**, the application need only state that probate is requested on the basis of the authenticated copy, and no citation or notice of any kind is required. With regard to a will probated in a nondomiciliary jurisdiction, the application for probate must contain all the information required in an application for the probate of a domestic will. In addition, it must set out the name and address of each devisee and heir. Citations then must be served on each devisee and heir by registered or certified mail. In either case, if no will contest is received, the clerk simply records the will and the evidence of probate on minutes of the court, and no order of the probate court is necessary. When the will has been thus filed and recorded, it is considered admitted to probate in the State of Texas. So far, however, it only serves as a muniment of title.

In order for letters to be issued to the executor of that will, proof must be made to the court under Section 105 of the Probate Code that the executor named in the foreign will has duly qualified as such in the jurisdiction in which the will was admitted to probate and is not disqualified to serve as executor in this state. After proof is received by the court, the court will enter an order directing that ancillary letters testamentary be issued to the executor. The executor will not be required to give bond if the will appointing her so provides; however, if it does not, she will be ordered to give bond in Texas. Effect is given here, as discussed earlier, to those provisions of foreign wills that authorize executors to sell real or personal property without order of the court. The executor or trustee appointed by the will has such authority in this state also. Sections 100-102 present procedures by which the foreign will may be contested.

DETERMINATION OF HEIRSHIP  *INTESTATE*

The proceedings known as determination of heirship," and their related procedures, are found in Chapter 3 of the Probate Code, Sections 48-56. This procedure, which resembles an action for declaratory judgment in ordinary civil suits, results in a declaration by the Probate Court regarding who the heirs of the decedent are.

The proceedings to determine heirship are available (a) if a person dies intestate and there has been no administration in this state upon her estate, (b) when a will has been probated in this state or elsewhere and an administration opened in this state and real or personal property in this state has been omitted from the will or no final disposition of the property has been made in the administration, and (c) where no will has been admitted to probate in this state.

An application for determination of heirship may be filed even after four years from the date of the death of the decedent. If filed *within* four years of that date, the applicant may request the court to determine whether a necessity of administration exists. The application may be filed by a qualified personal representative of the estate, by any person claiming to be a secured creditor, by the owner of the whole or part of the estate of the decedent, or by the guardian of an estate of a ward. The application must contain:

1. The name of the decedent and the time and place of death.

2. The names and residence of the decedent's heirs, the relationship of each heir to the decedent, and the true interest of the applicant and each of the heirs.

3. Any material facts and circumstances that might tend to show the time and place of death or the names and residence of heirs if exact information is not known to the applicant.

4. A statement that all children born to or adopted by the decedent have been listed.

5. A statement that each marriage of decedent has been listed, along with the date of marriage, the name of the spouse, the date and place of termination, and any other facts that show whether a spouse has an interest in the property of the decedent.

6. A statement about whether the decedent died testate and, if so, what dispositions were admitted in the will.

7. A general description of all real and personal property belonging to the estate.

8. An explanation for the omission of any of the foregoing information. The application must be supported by an affidavit as provided for in Section 49(b).

Notice is served by registered or certified mail on everybody shown as a possible heir in the application. Citation by personal service is permitted. The Texas Probate System (published by the State Bar of

Texas) suggests that personal service is preferable to service by mail. If there are unknown heirs or heirs whose addresses are unknown, they are served by publication. Unless there is service of citation by publication in addition to the personal notice, citation is posted in the county in which the proceedings are commenced and in the county of the decedent's last residence.

The court is required to hear evidence concerning the facts of heirship. The evidence may be in the form of a family history or an affidavit of heirship that has been of record for at least five years in the deed records. Alternatively, the evidence may be by testimony of witnesses, with the evidence reduced to writing and subscribed and sworn to by the witnesses.

Section 54 says that the judgment in a proceeding to declare heirship is to declare the names and places of residence of the heirs of the decedent and their respective shares and interest of the real and personal property of the decedent. Section 55 says that any such judgment is a final judgment that protects the bona fide purchaser for value.

If the court further states in the judgment that it has found no necessity for administration, then the judgment has the effect of a muniment of title. Section 56 authorizes the filing of a certified copy of the judgment in the office of the county clerk in any county in which real property described in the judgment is situated.

An application is found at Form 12-6, a statement sworn to and signed by the witnesses is located at Form 12-9, and an order determining heirship is found at Form 12-10.

SMALL ESTATES NO will

Section 137 of the Probate Code provides for the collection of small estates upon an affidavit. This procedure is applicable when no petition for the appointment of a personal representative is pending or has been granted, at least 30 days have lapsed since the death of the decedent, and the value of all assets of the estate, not including homestead and exempt property, does not exceed $50,000. This last requirement probably encompasses a majority of estates, since if the home and exempt personal property valued under $60,000 are excluded, many persons have little other property, except maybe $10,000-$15,000 worth of insurance and a couple of thousand dollars of savings.

The small-estates procedure does not affect the disposition of property under the terms of the will, nor does it transfer title to real property, other than homestead. A 1993 amendment to Section 137 provides that the small-estates procedure is effective as to homestead, if an affidavit that meets the requirement of the section is filed in the Deed Records (apparently, the Legislature forgot that it did away with the Deed Records at the preceding legislative session and replaced them with Official Real Property Records). The amendment also protects anyone who purchases the property for value. The small-estates procedure should be used only where there is no real property, other than homestead, or where the real property can be conveyed through other methods. It should not be used where there is a will, except when the only property involved is homestead. Unfortunately, this procedure has been employed in both instances by lawyers who have not taken the time to read the statutes carefully.

The procedure simply requires filing the equivalent to the affidavit of heirship, with the additional stipulation that it include a list of assets and liabilities, which must be sworn to by all of the heirs or devisees who are of age and by two disinterested witnesses. The affidavit must also be examined by the judge and, if approved by her, recorded in the Small Estate Records. Apparently, no such approval is necessary in regard to homestead. Under Section 138, any person making payment, delivery, or transfer of property to someone named in the affidavit may rely on the affidavit and is not required to inquire into the truth of any statement made in the affidavit.

If the value of all assets, not including homestead and exempt property, doesn't exceed the amount to which the surviving spouse and minor children would be entitled as a family allowance, then in addition, an application for an order of no administration may be filed. This application must include, in addition to information already discussed, a list of creditors of the estate, together with the amounts of their claims. If the court finds that the expenses of last illness, funeral charges, and expenses of the proceeding have been paid, then the court makes a family allowance. If that allowance uses up all the assets of the estate, than the court enters an order that no administration is to be had on the estate and assigns the entire estate to the surviving spouse and minor children in the same manner and with the same effect as already discussed concerning the making of family allowances. Section 141 says that this order constitutes a muniment of title. A small-estates affidavit and order are found at the end of this chapter as Form 11-12.

COMMUNITY ADMINISTRATION

Under the marital property laws of Texas, a surviving spouse remains liable for community indebtedness and has the right, as does a partner in a partnership, to have community property applied to the satisfaction of the community liability. Because of this, some special rules are found in Part 5 of Chapter 6 of the Probate Code, Sections 155-177.

There are two situations covered concerning a decedent's estate. The first is when a husband or wife dies intestate and the community property passes to the survivor. In this case no administration, community or otherwise, is necessary. The community property continues to be subject to community liabilities. If no one has qualified as executor or administrator, then the surviving spouse, as surviving partner of the marital partnership, has the power, without having to file anything with the court, to sue and to be sued, to sell, mortgage, lease, or dispose of community assets for the purposes of paying community debts, and to collect claims due to the community estate. She also has any other powers as may be necessary to preserve community property, discharge community obligations, and wind up community affairs. If, on the other hand, an executor or administrator has qualified, then the surviving spouse has only the power to retain possession and control of the community property that was under her sole management during the marriage, referred to as the *survivor's special community property*. The executor or administrator has power over the separate property of the deceased spouse, the special community property of the deceased spouse, and the general community property (the community property that was under the joint control of the spouses during their marriage).

The second situation is when an interest passes to someone other than the spouse: The surviving spouse must be appointed and must qualify as community administrator. She will be appointed if the deceased spouse failed to name an executor in her will, the executor named in the will of the deceased spouse is unable or unwilling to qualify as such, or the deceased spouse died intestate.

In order to open a formal community administration, the surviving spouse must, within four years of the death of the other spouse, file a written application (a form of which is found at Form 10-13) in a court having venue over the estate of the deceased spouse. This application must state:

1. The fact, time, and place of death.
2. The name and residence of each heir or devisee.
3. That a community estate exists and such facts as authorize the survivor to be appointed as community administrator.
4. That the court has venue.
5. Whether the applicant desires appraisers to be appointed, in which case not less than one or more than three appraisers is to be appointed. If appraisers are requested by the applicant or by any interested person, then the judge is required, without notice or citation, to appoint an appraiser.

In a slightly backwards procedure, the surviving spouse then is required to file a complete inventory, appraisement, and list of claims (in regard to the community property only) within 90 days. At the time of filing the inventory and appraisement, the community administrator is also required to present to the court a bond payable to the judge conditioned that the surviving spouse will faithfully administer the community estate and, after payment of community debts, will deliver the property to the persons entitled to it. There is no provision in the community administration sections regarding the amount of the bond, nor is there any procedure for the court to set the bond. The inventory and appraisement and the bond must be filed with the court before the court has a hearing authorizing the survivor, as community administrator, to manage, control, and dispose of community property. Most attorneys schedule a hearing prior to the return of the inventory, appraisement, and list of claims and the bond, and make the order appointing the community administrator subject to the filing and approval of the inventory, appraisement, and list of claims and the bond.

Section 167 then provides that once this order has been entered, the survivor has the power to control, manage, and dispose of community property as fully as if she were the sole owner and to sue and be sued with regard to it. Section 167 further states that a certified copy of the order is the equivalent of letters. Once the community administrator has paid all community debts, the qualified community administrator may carry on as a statutory trustee for those who inherited or received by devise until the community estate terminates as provided in the code.

Section 175 provides that any time after 12 months from the filing of the bond, the community administration may be terminated whenever termination is desired by either the surviving spouse or the persons entitled to a share of the deceased spouse's community property. Partition and distribution may be had and the administration closed either by proceedings as in other independent administrations or by proceedings in the appropriate district court.

Sections 157 and 158 create a form of community administration in the case of incompetency. Section 157 provides that whenever a husband or wife is judicially declared to be incompetent, the other spouse, in the capacity as surviving partner of the marital partnership, acquires full power to manage, control, and dispose of the entire community estate. No administration, community or otherwise, is necessary. Although this probably means that no guardianship is necessary; the problem is that the only procedure for judicial declaration of incompetency in Texas is in a guardianship. The statute goes on to say that if a guardian is appointed, the guardian must immediately deliver all community property to the spouse upon demand. The qualification of a guardian does not deprive the competent spouse of the right to manage, control, and dispose of the entire community estate. This little-used provision is generally not acceptable to title insurance underwriters for the purpose of conveying title to property that is to be insured.

TEMPORARY ADMINISTRATION

Infrequently, there is some reason why an administrator has to be appointed immediately without time for the passage of the period of citation and awaiting a hearing on a full administration. This procedure is not needed as much as it once was, when it was impossible to get access to safe-deposit boxes except through the Probate Court. The only way to do this was to have a temporary administrator appointed with authority to enter the safe-deposit box and remove the last will and testament of the decedent. The temporary administration would be closed at that time and an application for probate of the will and letters testamentary would be filed.

Although temporary administration is no longer needed for those purposes, it may become necessary for other purposes, generally involving some emergency action to safeguard the assets of the estate. For example, if the decedent owned a business, it may be crucial to get authority to operate the business pending the opening of an ordinary administration. In addition, temporary administrations are created pending the contest of wills or the appointment of an executor/ administrator, as provided for in Section 132.

Section 131(a) is the prime statute dealing with temporary administration; it requires that if the Probate Court determines that the interests of the estate require the immediate appointment of a personal representative, the judge may, by written order, appoint a temporary administrator with limited powers based on the circumstances of the need. The order must specify the duration of the appointment, not to exceed 180 days unless the appointment is made permanent. It requires the filing of a written application, which must be sworn to and must include the information required in Section 82. In addition, it must allege the facts showing an immediate necessity for the appointment of a temporary administrator and a statement of the requested powers and duties of the temporary administrator. The order of appointment must designate the appointee as temporary administrator, must define the powers conferred on the appointee, and must set a bond. The bond is to be filed on the date of the order, although this is not critical. The clerk then issues letters of appointment specifying the powers to be exercised, and posts a notice of appointment at the courthouse door.

On the date of the issuance of the letters, the appointee is required to notify known heirs by certified mail, return receipt requested. The notices must advise the interested persons or heirs of their right to contest the appointment not later than the 15th day after the date on which letters are issued and that if no contest is made within that period, the appointment will continue for the time specified in the order of the appointment and may be made permanent. Under Section 131A(j), the temporary administration may be rolled directly into a permanent administration. This occurs without further citation, inasmuch as citation is given in reference to the temporary administration that it may be made permanent. However, if a permanent administration is desired, the application must contain all allegations required for such application in addition to those required for a temporary administration.

During the existence of the temporary administration, the temporary administrator can exercise only those rights and powers specifically expressed in the order of the court appointing her or as may be expressed in subsequent orders of the court. At the expiration of the temporary appointment, the appointee is required to file with the clerk a sworn list of all property of the estate that has come into her hands and of all sales made by her, and a full exhibit and account of all her acts. Upon such filing, the court enters an order requiring the temporary appointee to deliver the estate to the persons or person legally entitled to it. Upon proof of delivery, the appointee is discharged. Forms for an application for temporary administration and for an order of temporary administration are included as Forms 12-14 and 12-15, respectively.

INFORMAL PROBATE  *Repealed*

Effective September 1, 1993, the Texas legislature adopted from the Uniform Probate Code a procedure referred to as "informal probate." This procedure is covered in Chapter XII, Sections 501-524. Somehow the legislature managed to create two Chapters 12 in 1993 (the other is the Durable Power of Attorney Act), and both contain Sections numbered 501-506. Since the procedure is new, it is difficult to ascertain what effect it will have on probate practice. It appears to be duplicitous of the probate as a procedure for muniment of title, although it would certainly be more easily accepted by out-of-state transfer agents who, though unaware of the unique-to-Texas procedure of probate as a muniment of title, are very familiar with informal probates.

The informal probate procedures allow the filing of a will for informal probate not earlier than 30 days or later than four years after the death of the testator. It is available only if all debts have been paid, all debts that are unpaid are secured by liens, or all creditors have been notified by certified or registered mail. In addition, no application under the other provisions of the Code must be pending.

The application must be sworn to and contain the following information:

1. That 30 days have elapsed since the death of the testator.
2. Facts showing compliance with the rule concerning debts.
3. That the total assets of the estate do not exceed $50,000, exclusive of homestead and exempt property.
4. That the court has venue.
5. That the will has never been revoked.
6. The social security number and address of the applicant and the social security number and last address of the deceased.
7. That no one has objected to the offer of the will for informal probate.

The application must be accompanied by the original will, an affidavit of a disinterested witness complying with the proof of facts necessary to probate a will under Section 88 of the Probate Code, and, if the will is not self-proved, an affidavit of a witness to the will. In addition, an inventory, appraisement, and list of claims must be filed with the application. Although the statute does not explicitly require a list of claims, the inventory must include all of the information required by Sections 250 and 251, which includes a list of claims.

Prior to the filing of the application, the applicant must have given notice to all persons named in the will and to the surviving spouse and children of the decedent, if any. Notice to minors may be sent to their natural guardian (parent) and to incompetents by sending it to the guardian of their person. The notices must be sent by certified or registered mail, and proof of mailing, in the form of the return receipts or the original returned notices, must be filed with the application.

After 11 days from the filing of the application, the clerk is supposed to present the application to the judge, who, after making certain required findings, may deny the application if a personal representative has been appointed in another county, another will of the decedent has been the subject of a previous probate order in this state, or the court, in its discretion, determines that formal probate is necessary.

If the court approves the informal administration, it admits the will for informal probate and may issue limited letters testamentary, if requested in the application. The letters testamentary are limited to the transfer of any assets identified in the inventory, and the letters themselves must either list the assets or have attached a certified copy of the inventory. It is presumed that the word *transfer* as used in the statute means transfer to the distributees and not sale to third parties, because the purposes of the informal probate procedure is limited to the probating of the will and the distribution of assets. However, Section 509(d) states that if a devisee is a minor or an incompetent, the representative must convert the assets to cash and deposit it either in the registry of the court until a guardian of the estate is appointed or under Section 144 (discussed in Chapter 14). How the estate can be converted to cash without selling assets is difficult to comprehend.

Sections 520-524 of the Probate Code, which were created along with the informal probate sections, provide for emergency intervention procedures for approval of the payment of funeral, burial, or storage locker expenses.

CHAPTER QUESTIONS AND EXERCISES

1. When may a will be probated as a muniment of title?
2. What is the benefit of probating a will as a muniment of title?
3. What steps are necessary in a probate as a muniment of title?
4. Why does the Probate Code have provisions relating to foreign wills?
5. Summarize the procedures by which a foreign will is given recognition in Texas.
6. When may the "determination of heirship" procedure be used?
7. Summarize the "determination of heirship" procedure.
8. What is the small-estate procedure? When may it be used? When should it not be used?
9. What is a community administration? Under what circumstances is it available?
10. What is a temporary administration? When is it used? How long can it last?

11. George Grady, Jr., wants to probate his father's will. The will names George as independent executor and devises George Sr.'s property to Jr. and his sister, Petunia. There was a small insurance policy, which has been paid. George Jr. and Petunia paid all of the funeral and burial expenses, expenses of last illness, and other bills owned by George Sr. out of the proceeds of the insurance, with the exception of the mortgage of George Sr.'s house. They want to probate the will in the cheapest manner. Your employer has determined that an affidavit of heirship will not work and that probate as a muniment of title is appropriate. She instructs you to prepare all documents, assuming that the court will waive the affidavit requirement. Do so.

12. A woman is referred to your office by the Legal Aid Society. They have determined that she is unable to pay for legal services. Your employer has agreed to represent her in partial fulfillment of his obligation pro bono publico. She and her deceased spouse acquired a house, which they had been buying on a contract for deed, some furniture, and a middle-aged car. All of a sudden, her deceased husband's brothers and sisters have descended on her, demanding that she sell the house and pay them "their share." Your employer has decided that determination of heirship, followed by a letter from him to the in-laws, would be the best route.

    Prepare the necessary documents to accomplish the determination of heirship. Provide all the other facts and the names that may be necessary.

13. Use the same information as in Exercise 12, except assume the home is clearly the surviving spouse's separate property, and decedent and surviving spouse had $21,122.39 in the bank, the car is worth $2,530, furniture is worth $1,000 and clothes and personal effects are worth $750. Your employer instead chooses to use a Small Estate Affidavit. Do it, supplying any additional needed information. Remember the protection in regard the homestead in favor of the surviving wife.

Form 12-1: Application for Probate of Will as Muniment of Title

NO. _____

THE ESTATE OF	§	IN THE COUNTY COURT
PETER SMITH,	§	AT LAW NO. TWO
DECEASED	§	ROUGH RIDER COUNTY, TEXAS

APPLICATION FOR PROBATE OF WILL AS MUNIMENT OF TITLE

TO THE HONORABLE COURT OF NUECES COUNTY, TEXAS:

Your Applicant, **PAULA SMITH**, Social Security No. 420-26-4340, of Rough Rider County, Texas, appearing herein by and through her attorney, respectfully shows unto the Court the following:

I.

That **PAULA SMITH** resides and is domiciled at 1412 Bullmoose, San Juan Hill, Rough Rider County, Texas.

II.

That **PETER SMITH**, Social Security No. 280-92-4242, is dead, that he died at the age of 87 years on March 3, 1992 in Rough Rider County, Texas, having maintained his principal residence in said county and state.

III.

That at the time of his death the said **PETER SMITH** was seized and possessed of real and personal property of the probable value of less than ONE HUNDRED FIFTY THOUSAND AND 00/100 DOLLARS ($150,000.00). He left a written will, duly executed on June 19, 1964, which is attached hereto and filed herewith, and in which your Applicant, **PAULA SMITH**, was appointed Independent Executrix.

IV.

That Applicant **PAULA SMITH**, is the sole beneficiary under the will. Neither the State of Texas or any governmental entity of the State of Texas nor any charitable organization is named by the will as devisee.

V.

After making of such will no child of said decedent was born to or adopted who survived him.

VI.

That decedent has never been divorced since the making of this will.

VII.

That there is no necessity for administration of Decedent's estate, as there are no unpaid debts owing by the estate of the testator, excluding debts secured by liens on real estate.

WHEREFORE, on this the _____ day of May, 1994, your Applicant prays that citation be issued as required by law; that said will be admitted to probate, for the purposes of a Muniment of Title only; and that such other and further orders be made as the Court may deem proper.

Respectfully submitted,

PAULA SMITH

By: _____

JOHN TEDDY
State Bar No. 00000100
5155 Teton Pkwy., Suite 206
P.O. Box 186
Corpus Christi, TX 79421
(512) 555-1234 Telephone
(512) 555-5678 FAX

ATTORNEY FOR THE ESTATE

Form 12-2: Order Admitting Will to Probate as a Muniment of Title

NO. 23814-2

THE ESTATE OF	§	IN THE COUNTY COURT
PETER SMITH,	§	AT LAW NO. TWO
DECEASED	§	ROUGH RIDER COUNTY, TEXAS

ORDER ADMITTING WILL TO PROBATE AS A MUNIMENT OF TITLE

On June 3, 1994 came on to be heard the application of **PAULA SMITH**, filed in the above-entitled and numbered estate, for the probate of the will of **PETER SMITH**, deceased, as a muniment of title.

The Court, after having heard and considered the evidence and the will of **PETER SMITH**, deceased, finds that the allegations set forth in the application of **PAULA SMITH** are true; that notice and citation herein have been given in the manner and for the length of time required by law; that **PETER SMITH**, deceased, died on March 3, 1992 at San Juan Hill, Texas; that this Court has jurisdiction and venue of the estate of **PETER SMITH**, deceased; that the decedent died testate, leaving a will dated June 19, 1964; that said will was executed with the formalities and solemnities and under the circumstances required by law to make it a valid will; that on the date of said will the decedent was more than 18 years of age and was of sound mind; that the decedent never revoked said will; that no objection to or contest of the probate of said will has been filed herein; that the proof required for the probate of said will has been made and said will is entitled to probate; that there are no unpaid debts owing by the Estate of **PETER SMITH**, deceased, other than debts secured by liens on real estate; and no necessity exists for the administration of deceased's estate.

IT, THEREFORE, ORDERED, ADJUDGED, and DECREED that said will of **PETER SMITH**, deceased by and it is hereby admitted to probate as a muniment of title only, and the Clerk of this Court is ordered to record said will, together with the application of **PAULA SMITH** in the minutes of this Court; and this order shall constitute sufficient legal authority to all persons owing money, having custody of any property, or acting as registrar or agent of any evidence of interest, indebtedness, property, or right belonging to the Estate of **PETER SMITH**, deceased, and to persons purchasing from or otherwise dealing with the Estate of **PETER PROBATE**, deceased, for payment or transfer to **PAULA SMITH**, the sole beneficiary of said Estate.

SIGNED and ENTERED this _____ day of June, 1994.

_____
JUDGE PRESIDING

PREPARED BY:
JOHN TEDDY
State Bar No. 00000100
5155 Teton Pkwy., Suite 206
P.O. Box 186
Corpus Christi, TX 79421
(512) 555-1234 Telephone
(512) 555-5678 FAX

ATTORNEY FOR THE ESTATE

Form 12-3: Waiver of Affidavit of Distribution

NO. 23814-2

THE ESTATE OF	§	IN THE COUNTY COURT
PETER SMITH,	§	AT LAW NO. TWO
DECEASED	§	ROUGH RIDER COUNTY, TEXAS

ORDER WAIVING AFFIDAVIT REQUIREMENT

This the _____ day of June, 1994, came on to be heard the oral application of **PAULA SMITH**, Applicant and sole beneficiary herein, for waiver of the requirement for Affidavit set forth in V.A.T.S. Probate Code Section 89 and, it appearing that there is no particular need for such affidavit in this particular cause and that the need therefore should be waived,

IT IS THEREFORE ORDERED, the Applicant herein, **PAULA SMITH**, is not required to file an Affidavit stating which terms of the will have been fulfilled or unfulfilled, as set out in V.A.T.S. Probate Code Section 89, and that such requirement is specifically waived herein.

SIGNED this _____ day of June, 1994.

_____
JUDGE PRESIDING

Form 12-4: Proof of Death and Other Facts

NO. 23814-2

THE ESTATE OF	§	**IN THE COUNTY COURT**
PETER SMITH,	§	**AT LAW NO. TWO**
DECEASED	§	**ROUGH RIDER COUNTY, TEXAS**

PROOF OF DEATH AND OTHER FACTS

On this day, **PAULA SMITH**, Affiant personally appeared in Open Court, and after being duly sworn, stated the following:

1. **PETER SMITH**, Decedent died on March 3, 1994 in San Juan Hill, Rough Rider County, Texas, at the age of 87 years and four years have not elapsed since the date of Decedent's death.

2. Decedent was domiciled and had a fixed place of residence in this County at the date of death.

3. The document dated June 19, 1964, now shown to me and which purports to be Decedent's will was never revoked so far as I know.

4. No necessity exists for the administration of this Estate.

5. Decedent was never divorced.

SIGNED this _____ day of June, 1994.

_____
PAULA SMITH

SUBSCRIBED AND SWORN TO BEFORE ME by **PAULA SMITH**, this _____ day of June, 1994.

Clerk of the County Court at Law
No. Two, Rough Rider County, Texas

By: _____
Deputy

Form 12-5: Affidavit of Fulfillment of Terms of Will

NO. 23814-2

THE ESTATE OF	§	IN THE COUNTY COURT
PETER SMITH,	§	AT LAW NO. TWO
DECEASED	§	ROUGH RIDER COUNTY, TEXAS

AFFIDAVIT OF FULFILLMENT OF TERMS OF WILL

On the 3rd day of June, 1994, the application of **PAULA SMITH**, Applicant, was heard and granted, and the will of **PETER SMITH**, Deceased, was admitted to probate as a muniment of title only.

The Applicant, **PAULA SMITH**, has executed this affidavit and states that all terms of the will have been fulfilled, in accordance with Section 89, Texas Probate Code.

SIGNED this _____ day of July, 1994.

_____
PAULA SMITH
Applicant

SWORN TO AND SUBSCRIBED before me by **PAULA SMITH**, on July _____ , 1994.

_____
Notary Public, State of Texas

Form 12-6: Application to Determine Heirship

(Reprinted from <u>Texas Probate System</u>, copyright State Bar of Texas, with permission.)

NO. 23814-2

THE ESTATE OF	§	IN THE COUNTY COURT
PETER SMITH,	§	AT LAW NO. TWO
DECEASED	§	ROUGH RIDER COUNTY, TEXAS

APPLICATION TO DETERMINE HEIRSHIP

PAULA SMITH, Applicant who resides at 1412 Bullmoose, San Juan Hill, Rough Rider County, Texas furnished the following information to the Court:

1. **PETER SMITH**, Decedent, died on March 3, 1992, at San Juan Hill, Rough Rider County, Texas.

2. No administration is pending upon Decedent's Estate and none appears necessary. It is necessary and in the best interest of the Estate for the Court to determine who are the heirs and only heirs of Decedent.

3. Applicant claims to be the owner of a part of Decedent's Estate. The names and residences of all of Decedent's heirs, the relationship of each heir to Decedent, and the true interest of the Applicant and of each of the heirs in the Estate of Decedent are as follows:

NAME	RESIDENCE	SHARE OF ESTATE
PETER SMITH, JR.	252 Yellowstone Parkway San Juan Hill, TX 79231	50%
PENELOPE SMITH	721 Monolle Drive San Juan Hill, TX 79231	50%

4. At the time of Decedent's death, Decedent owned the following property:

   Lot Two (2), Block One (1), Sunnyside Addition, an addition in the City of San Juan Hill, Texas, as shown by the map or Plat Records of Rough Rider County in Volume 12, at page 334 of the map records of Rough Rider County, Texas

5. Decedent was married to and survived by **PAULA SMITH** on the date of death.

6. Only two children, **PETER SMITH, JR.** and **PENELOPE SMITH**, were born to or adopted by Decedent.

7. All children born to or adopted by Decedent have been listed. Each marriage of Decedent has been listed.

8. To the best of my knowledge, Decedent died intestate.

9. This Application does not omit any information required by Probate Code, Section 49.

10. There are no debts owed by Decedent that are not secured by liens upon real estate and there is no necessity for an administration of this Estate.

   Applicant prays that citation issue as required by law; that an attorney ad litem be appointed to represent Decedent's living heirs whose names and whereabouts are unknown; that upon hearing hereof, this Court determine who are the heirs and only heirs of Decedent and their respective shares and interests in this Estate and that no necessity exists for an administration of Decedent's Estate.

Respectfully submitted,

PAULA SMITH

By: _____
   JOHN TEDDY
   State Bar No. 00000100
   5155 Teton Pkwy., Suite 206
   P.O. Box 186
   Corpus Christi, TX 79421
   (512) 555-1234 Telephone
   (512) 555-5678 FAX

   ATTORNEY FOR THE ESTATE

Form 12-6: (continued)

STATE OF TEXAS   §   KNOW ALL MEN BY THESE PRESENTS:
COUNTY OF ROUGH RIDER   §

BEFORE ME, the undersigned authority, on this day personally appeared **PAULA SMITH**, and after being duly sworn, stated that:

Insofar as is known to me, all the allegations of the foregoing Application are true in substance and in fact and that no material fact or circumstances has, within my knowledge, been omitted from the Application.

_____
PAULA SMITH

SUBSCRIBED AND SWORN TO BEFORE ME, the undersigned authority, by **PAULA SMITH** on this _____ day of _____, 19_____, to certify which witness my hand and seal of office.

_____
Notary Public, State of Texas

STATE OF TEXAS   §   KNOW ALL MEN BY THESE PRESENTS:
COUNTY OF ROUGH RIDER   §

BEFORE ME, the undersigned authority, on this day personally appeared **PETER SMITH, JR.**, and after being duly sworn, stated that:

"Insofar as is known to me, all the allegations of the foregoing Application are true in substance and in fact and that no material fact or circumstances has, within my knowledge, been omitted from the Application."

_____
PETER SMITH, JR.

SUBSCRIBED AND SWORN TO BEFORE ME, the undersigned authority, by **PETER SMITH, JR.** on this _____ day of _____, 19_____, to certify which witness my hand and seal of office.

_____
Notary Public, State of Texas

STATE OF TEXAS   §   KNOW ALL MEN BY THESE PRESENTS:
COUNTY OF ROUGH RIDER   §

BEFORE ME, the undersigned authority, on this day personally appeared **PENELOPE SMITH**, and after being duly sworn, stated that:

"Insofar as is known to me, all the allegations of the foregoing Application are true in substance and in fact and that no material fact or circumstances has, within my knowledge, been omitted from the Application."

_____
PENELOPE SMITH

SUBSCRIBED AND SWORN TO BEFORE ME, the undersigned authority, by **PENELOPE SMITH** on this _____ day of _____, 19_____, to certify which witness my hand and seal of office.

_____
Notary Public, State of Texas

Form 12-7: Motion to Appoint Attorney Ad Litem

(Reprinted from <u>Texas Probate System</u>, copyright State Bar of Texas, with permission.)

NO. 42264-2

THE ESTATE OF	§	IN THE COUNTY COURT
PETER SMITH,	§	AT LAW NO. TWO
DECEASED	§	ROUGH RIDER COUNTY, TEXAS

MOTION TO APPOINT ATTORNEY AD LITEM

PAULA SMITH, Applicant for the determination of heirship herein, requests the Court to appoint an attorney ad litem to represent Decedent's heirs whose names and/or whereabouts are unknown and heirs who are suffering legal disability.

Respectfully submitted,

PAULA SMITH
Applicant

By: _____
Attorney for Applicant

ORDER

On this day, the foregoing Application was heard by this Court and the Court finds that the heirs of **PETER SMITH,** Deceased, whose names and/or whereabouts are unknown and heirs suffering legal disability, have not answered or entered an appearance herein, and that an attorney ad litem should be appointed.

It is ORDERED that WET BEHINEARS, an attorney licensed to practice before this Court, is appointed to defend the interests of those Defendants and that this suit proceed and be defended by this attorney as in other causes where service is made by publication.

SIGNED this _____ day of June, 1992.

_____
JUDGE PRESIDING

Form 12-8: Answer of Attorney Ad Litem

(Reprinted from <u>Texas Probate System</u>, copyright State Bar of Texas, with permission.)

NO. 42264-2

THE ESTATE OF	§	IN THE COUNTY COURT
PETER SMITH,	§	AT LAW NO. TWO
DECEASED	§	ROUGH RIDER COUNTY, TEXAS

ANSWER OF ATTORNEY AD LITEM

NOW COMES the undersigned duly appointed attorney ad litem for the living heirs of **PETER SMITH**, Deceased, whose names and/or whereabouts are unknown and for heirs who are suffering legal disability, and denies each and every allegation in the Application to Determine Heirship and demands strict proof thereof.

The undersigned prays that the Applicant take nothing and that all costs of Court be adjudged against the Applicant.

WET BEHINEARS
State Bar No. 00000300
5000 Flynn Pkwy., Suite 800
P.O. Box 4567
Corpus Christi, TX 79421
(512) 555-1234 Telephone
(512) 555-5678 FAX

Form 12-9: Statement of Facts

(Reprinted from <u>Texas Probate System</u>, copyright State Bar of Texas, with permission.)

NO. 42264-2

THE ESTATE OF	§	IN THE COUNTY COURT
PETER PROBATE,	§	AT LAW NO. TWO
DECEASED	§	ROUGH RIDER COUNTY, TEXAS

STATEMENT OF FACTS

On this day GOODIE JONES, Affiant personally appeared in open Court, and after being duly sworn, stated that:

I am well acquainted with the family history of **PETER SMITH**, Decedent, who died in San Juan Hill, Rough Rider County, Texas, on March 3, 1992. To the best of my knowledge, Decedent died intestate.

Decedent was married to and survived by **PAULA SMITH** on the date of death.

Only two children, **PETER SMITH, JR.** and **PENELOPE SMITH**, were born to or adopted by Decedent.

I have no interest in the Estate of Decedent and am not related to Decedent under the laws of descent and distribution of the State of Texas.

SIGNED this _____ day of July, 1992.

_____
GOODIE JONES
Affiant

SUBSCRIBED AND SWORN TO BEFORE ME by GOODIE JONES in open Court on this _____ day of July, 1992, to certify which witness my hand and seal of office.

_____
Clerk of the County Court at Law No. Two,
Rough Rider County, Texas

By: _____
Deputy

NOTE: Inasmuch as the Probate Code requires two witnesses a like statement of facts must be signed by a second witness.

Form 12-10: Judgment Declaring Heirship

(Reprinted from <u>Texas Probate System</u>, copyright State Bar of Texas, with permission.)

NO. 42264-2

THE ESTATE OF	§	IN THE COUNTY COURT
PETER SMITH,	§	AT LAW NO. TWO
DECEASED	§	ROUGH RIDER COUNTY, TEXAS

JUDGMENT DECLARING HEIRSHIP

On this day came on to be heard the sworn Application to Determine Heirship of the Estate of **PETER SMITH**, Deceased, wherein **PAULA SMITH** is the Applicant and Decedent's living heirs are Defendants, and it appears to the Court, and the Court so finds that all parties interested in the Estate of Decedent have been duly and legally served with citation as required by law; the Defendants have appeared; that this Court has jurisdiction of the subject matter and all persons and parties; that the evidence presented and admitted fully and satisfactorily proves each and every issue presented to the Court; that Decedent died intestate and that the heirship of Decedent has been fully and satisfactorily proved as well as the identity of the nature of Decedent's property as being separate or community and the interest and shares of each of the heirs therein; and that no administration is necessary.

The Court finds and it is ORDERED and DECREED by the Court that the names and places of residence of the heirs of Decedent and their respective shares and interests in the real and personal property of Decedent are as follows:

NAMES	RESIDENCE	SHARE & DESCRIPTION OF REAL PROPERTY	SHARE & DESCRIPTION OF PERSONAL PROPERTY
PETER SMITH, JR.	137 Heir Ave San Juan Hill Texas	None	1/2 of the Decedent's 1/2 Community
PENELOPE SMITH	1414 Dollar St. San Juan Hill Texas	None	1/2 of the Decedent's 1/2 Community

The Court finds that there exists no necessity for administration of the Estate of Decedent, none is ordered, and upon payment of all costs of Court no further proceedings be had in this cause.

SIGNED this _____ day of July, 1992.

_____
JUDGE PRESIDING

APPROVED:

_____
PAULA SMITH

_____
PETER SMITH, JR.

_____
PENELOPE SMITH

By: _____
     Attorney for Applicant

Form 12-11: Judgment Declaring Heirship (In Event of Citation by Publication)

(Reprinted from <u>Texas Probate System</u>, copyright State Bar of Texas, with permission.)

(In Event of Citation by Publication)

NO. 42264-2

THE ESTATE OF	§	IN THE COUNTY COURT
PETER SMITH,	§	AT LAW NO. TWO
DECEASED	§	ROUGH RIDER COUNTY, TEXAS

JUDGMENT DECLARING HEIRSHIP

On this day came on to be heard the sworn Application to Determine Heirship of the Estate of **PETER SMITH**, Deceased, wherein **PAULA SMITH** is the Applicant and Decedent's living heirs whose names and/or whereabouts are unknown and heirs suffering legal disability are Defendants, and it appears to the Court, and the Court so finds that all parties interested in the Estate of Decedent have been duly and legally served with citation as required by law; that the Court appointed an attorney ad litem to appear and answer and to represent Defendants and such attorney ad litem did so appear and filed an answer for Defendants; that this Court has jurisdiction of the subject matter and all persons and parties; that the evidence presented and admitted fully and satisfactorily proves each and every issue presented to the Court; that Decedent died intestate and that the heirship of Decedent has been fully and satisfactorily proved as well as the identity of the nature of Decedent's property as being separate or community and the interest and shares of each of the heirs therein; and that no administration is necessary.

The Court finds and it is ORDERED and DECREED by the Court that the names and places of residence of the heirs of Decedent and their respective shares and interests in the real and personal property of Decedent are as follows:

NAMES	RESIDENCE	SHARE & DESCRIPTION OF REAL PROPERTY	SHARE & DESCRIPTION OF PERSONAL PROPERTY
PETER SMITH, JR.	137 Heir Ave San Juan Hill Texas	None	1/2 of the Decedent's 1/2 Community
PENELOPE SMITH	1414 Dollar St. San Juan Hill Texas	None	1/2 of the Decedent's 1/2 Community

It is ORDERED and DECREED that the attorney ad litem appointed to represent the interests of the Defendants is allowed a fee of $_____ to be paid out of the assets of Decedent.

The Court finds that there exists no necessity for administration of the Estate of Decedent, none is ordered, and upon payment of all costs of Court no further proceedings be had in this cause.

SIGNED this _____ day of July, 1992.

_____

JUDGE PRESIDING

APPROVED:

PAULA SMITH

By: _____
    Attorney for Applicant

JOHN TEDDY
State Bar No. 00000100
5155 Teton Pkwy., Suite 206
P.O. Box 186
Corpus Christi, TX 79421
(512) 555-1234 Telephone
(512) 555-5678 FAX

ATTORNEY FOR THE ESTATE

Form 12-12: Small Estate Affidavit and Order

NO. 50,331-2

THE ESTATE OF	§	IN THE COUNTY COURT
PETER SMITH,	§	AT LAW NO. TWO
DECEASED	§	ROUGH RIDER COUNTY, TEXAS

SMALL ESTATE AFFIDAVIT AND ORDER

PETER SMITH, JR., and **PENELOPE SMITH** furnish the following information to the Court:

1. **PETER SMITH**, Decedent, died on March 3, 1992, in San Juan Hill, Rough Rider County, Texas.
2. Decedent's domicile was in Rough Rider County, Texas, where the principal part of Decedent's property at the time of death was situated.
3. No petition for the appointment of a personal representative is pending or has been granted for Decedent's estate.
4. More than thirty days have elapsed since the death of Decedent.
5. The value of the entire assets of Decedent as of the date of death, exclusive of homestead and exempt property, does not exceed $50,000.00 and those non-exempt assets exceed the known liabilities of the estate.
6. The names and addresses of all the distributees, heirs, devisees, or assigns of the money or property of the estate of Decedent, and their right to receive the same are as follows:

NAME	RELATIONSHIP TO D	SHARE OF ESTATE
PETER SMITH, JR.	Son	50%
PENELOPE SMITH	Daughter	50%

7. The Known assets and Liabilities of Decedent's estate are as follows:

ASSETS

Description	Estimated Value	Encumbrances
Furniture	$ 1,000.00	None
1989 Plymouth	3,500.00	None
Cash in Account #12-510-8		
Rough Rider National	37,121.00	None

LIABILITIES

Creditor	Amount of Claim
None	

Distributees state that the facts contained in this Affidavit are true and pray that this Affidavit and application be filed in the Small Estate Records; that the same be approved by the Court; and that the Clerk issue certified copies thereof in order to allow the Distributees to present the same to persons owing money to the estate, having custody or possession of property of the estate, or acting as registrar, fiduciary, or transfer agent of anyone having evidences of interest, indebtedness, property, or other right belonging to said estate:

_____
PETER SMITH, JR.
Distributee

SUBSCRIBED AND SWORN TO BEFORE ME by the said **PETER SMITH, JR.**, on this _____ day of July, 1992, to certify which, witness my hand and seal of office.

_____
Notary Public, State of Texas

_____
PENELOPE SMITH
Distributee

Form 12-12: (continued)

SUBSCRIBED AND SWORN TO BEFORE ME by the said **PENELOPE SMITH**, on this day of July, 1992, to certify which, witness my hand and seal of office.

_____
Notary Public, State of Texas

I have no interest in the estate of Decedent and am not related to Decedent under the laws of descent and distribution of the State of Texas. The facts contained in this Affidavit are true.

_____
JOAN EDWARDS

_____
ED BROWN

SUBSCRIBED AND SWORN TO BEFORE ME by the said JOAN EDWARDS and ED BROWN, on this _____ day of _____, 19____, to certify which, witness my hand and seal of office.

_____
Notary Public State of Texas

ORDER

On this day the Court considered the Affidavit of the Distributees of this Estate and the Court finds that the above Affidavit complies with the terms and provisions of the Texas Probate Code, that this Court has jurisdiction and venue, that this Estate qualifies under the provisions of the Probate Code as a Small Estate, and that the Affidavit should be approved.

It is ORDERED and DECREED by the Court that the foregoing Affidavit be and the same is hereby APPROVED, and shall forthwith be recorded in the Small Estates Records of this County, and the Clerk of this Court shall issue certified copies thereof to all persons entitled thereto.

SIGNED this _____ day of July, 1992.

_____
JUDGE PRESIDING

Form 12-13: Application for Community Administration

NO. _____

THE ESTATE OF	§	IN THE COUNTY COURT
PETER SMITH,	§	AT LAW NO. TWO
DECEASED	§	ROUGH RIDER COUNTY, TEXAS

APPLICATION FOR COMMUNITY ADMINISTRATION

TO THE HONORABLE JUDGE OF SAID COURT:

PAULA SMITH, applicant, makes this application for formal community administration of the Estate of **PETER SMITH**, deceased, and furnishes the following information to the court:

I.

Applicant is the surviving spouse of **PETER SMITH** and is an individual domiciled in and residing at 1412 Bullmoose, San Juan Hill, Rough Rider, County, Texas.

II.

PETER SMITH died on March 3, 1992, in San Juan Hill, Rough Rider County, Texas, at the age of 87 years. **PETER SMITH** died intestate.

III.

This Court has jurisdiction and venue because the deceased was domiciled in and had a fixed place of residence in this county at the time of death.

IV.

There is a community estate between the deceased, **PETER SMITH**, and the applicant, **PAULA PROBATE**, surviving spouse, and **PETER SMITH** died intestate thus authorizing the applicant to be appointed as community administratrix.

V.

The name, age, and address, if known, and the relationship to the deceased of each person to whom an interest in community property has passed by the laws of intestacy are as follows:

PETER SMITH, JR. (Adult)
137 Heir Ave, San Juan Hill, Texas
Surviving child

PENELOPE SMITH
1414 Dollar St., San Juan Hill, Texas
Surviving child

No necessity exists for the appointment of appraisers.

WHEREFORE, applicant requests that citation be issued to all persons interested in this estate as required by law, and that **PAULA SMITH** be appointed community administratrix of the estate of **PETER SMITH**, and that such other and further orders be made as the Court may deem proper.

Respectfully submitted,

TEDDY & FRANKLIN

_____

JOHN TEDDY
State Bar No. 00000100
5155 Teton Pkwy., Suite 206
P.O. Box 186
Corpus Christi, TX 79421
(512) 555-1234 Telephone
(512) 555-5678 FAX

ATTORNEY FOR THE ESTATE

ORDER SETTING HEARING DATE

IT IS ORDERED that the hearing on the foregoing application be and the same is hereby scheduled for _____ o'clock ___.m., on the _____ day of _____, 1992, in the courtroom of the County Court at Law No. Two, San Juan Hill, Rough Rider, Texas.

SIGNED this _____ day of July, 1992.

_____

JUDGE PRESIDING

Form 12-14: Application for Temporary Administration

NO. 60301-2

THE ESTATE OF	§	IN THE COUNTY COURT
PETER SMITH,	§	AT LAW NO. TWO
DECEASED	§	ROUGH RIDER COUNTY, TEXAS

APPLICATION FOR TEMPORARY ADMINISTRATION

PAULA SMITH, Applicant, furnishes the following information to the Court for the appointment of Applicant as temporary Administrator and for the issuance of Letters of Temporary Administration:

1. **PETER SMITH**, Decedent, died on March 3, 1992, in San Juan Hill, Rough Rider County, Texas.

2. This Court has jurisdiction and venue because Decedent was domiciled and had a fixed place of residence in this county on the date of death.

3. The interest of Decedent's estate requires immediate appointment of a personal representative because Rough Rider National Bank has frozen the community checking accounts of Decedent and Applicant. Applicant has not other funds to pay her necessary costs of living. She should be given immediate authority to write checks on such account, at least up to one half of the amount on deposit.

4. Applicant would be a suitable temporary representative and is domiciled and resides at 1412 Bullmoose, San Juan Hill, Rough Rider County, Texas. Applicant is not disqualified by law from serving as Temporary Administrator of this Estate.

5. The Temporary Administrator of this Estate should be given the following powers:

    (a) To have authority to withdraw funds from Account #124808 at Rough Rider National Bank for the reasonable and necessary living expenses of applicant until the will of Decedent is probate but in no account to exceed 60 days from date of qualification as temporary administratrix.

Applicant requests the Court to make an immediate appointment of Applicant as Temporary Administrator of Decedent's Estate to serve as such until discharged by order of this Court.

_____
PAULA SMITH
Applicant

By: _____
JOHN TEDDY
State Bar No. 00000100
5155 Teton Pkwy., Suite 206
P.O. Box 186
Corpus Christi, TX 79421
(512) 555-1234 Telephone
(512) 555-5678 FAX

ATTORNEY FOR THE ESTATE

Form 12-15: Order Appointing Temporary Administrator

NO. 60301-2

THE ESTATE OF	§	IN THE COUNTY COURT
PETER SMITH,	§	AT LAW NO. TWO
DECEASED	§	ROUGH RIDER COUNTY, TEXAS

ORDER APPOINTING TEMPORARY ADMINISTRATOR

On this day this Court heard and considered the Application for Temporary Administration filed by **PAULA SMITH**, Applicant, and after hearing the evidence in support of the Application, the Court finds that **PETER SMITH**, Decedent is dead and four (4) years have not elapsed since the date of Decedent's death; the Court has jurisdiction and venue over this Estate, and the interest of this Estate requires the immediate appointment of a personal representative; the Application For Letters of Temporary Administration should be granted and Applicant would be a suitable temporary representative, is not disqualified from acting as such, and should be appointed Temporary Administrator of this Estate.

It is ORDERED that **PAULA SMITH** is hereby appointed Temporary Administrator of this Estate and shall give Bond in the sum of $3,000.00, conditioned as required by law; that unless this appointment is contested after service of citation, it shall be continued in force for such period of time as the Court shall deem in the interest of this Estate, or it shall be made permanent, if found by the Court to be necessary; that the Clerk of this Court shall issue Letters of Temporary Administration when the Temporary Administrator has qualified according to law; and that the Temporary Administrator shall have the following powers:

To have authority to withdraw funds for the reasonable and necessary living expenses of applicant until the will of Decedent is probated but in no account to exceed 60 days from date of qualification as temporary administratrix.

SIGNED this _____ day of June, 1992.

_____
JUDGE PRESIDING

13

PROBATE ADMINISTRATION– POSTMORTEM ESTATE PLANNING, CHECKLISTS, AND THE TRANSFER OF ESTATE ASSETS

CHAPTER OBJECTIVES

Upon completion of this chapter, the student should be able to:

1. Understand postmortem elections and decisions applicable to estates.

2. Prepare checklists and critical or significant date lists.

3. Know the steps necessary to effectuate the transfer of assets commonly owned by estates.

4. Prepare documents and correspondence relevant to the transfer of estate assets.

CHAPTER GLOSSARY

Affidavit of domicile An affidavit usually required in connection with the transfer of stocks and bonds in which the owner of the stock or bond states, under oath, the state of his domicile.

Certificate of title A document that evidences ownership. It is commonly used in connection with automobiles, although boats and trailers/trailer houses in Texas also have certificates of title.

Distributable net income (DNI) Taxable income received by an estate or trust.

Fiduciary income tax return The form of tax return required to be filed by an estate or a trust from the date of death (estate) or the effective date (trust) until final distribution.

Final return The income tax return, filed by an executor, administrator, or surviv-

ing spouse, that reports income received by the decedent from the beginning of the tax year in which the decedent died until the date of death.

Income in respect to a decedent (IRD) Income to which the decedent was entitled at the time of death. It is subject to both income tax and estate tax.

Proof of loss A written statement, made by an owner of a policy of insurance, to the underwriter, notifying it of a claim and giving it information from which it can determine the extent of its liability under the policy.

Recapture Recovery by the Internal Revenue Service of a deduction or credit previously taken by a taxpayer.

Stock power A power of attorney that allows someone other than the current owner to transfer the ownership of corporate stocks or bonds.

Tax assessor-collector An official in each taxing district who traditionally was charged with assessing and collecting that district's taxes. Though much of the assessment function has been taken over by countywide appraisal districts, this official also handles the administrative procedures relating both to the transfer of certificates of title for automobiles and trailers and to the issuance of license plates.

Widow's election The election that a surviving spouse has either to accept the benefits, if any, in the will of the deceased spouse or to take the half of the community property that he already owns.

INTRODUCTION

This chapter deals with many of the many things done in or through an attorney's office or that have to be coordinated by the attorney's office with the client or with the client's stockbroker or some other financial advisor. The first portion deals with postmortem estate planning elections and other steps required of the executor, trustee or surviving spouse. Some elections also may be made by the devisees. These elections are much more numerous than one might believe, and some of them are extremely technical and complicated and relate only to a limited number of estates. Some of the more technical and limited exceptions will be mentioned but not dealt with in any detail.

The second section of the chapter covers the use of checklists and critical or significant date lists for ensuring that necessary actions are taken and by the date mandated by law. Once the decedent dies, there are many significant dates and some very critical dates. Also, a number of lawyers and, for want of a better term, efficiency experts believe that at the beginning of representation all tasks to be undertaken should have at least a target date by which the planner believes that he can and should complete the given tasks. This chapter will discuss the use and formulation of these checklists and significant date lists and provide an example in the Forms Appendix.

The third section deals with the transfer of estate assets. Some law offices handle all such transfers for the clients; others handle them on request of the clients; and yet others, in order to hold down the costs of probate, merely give the client directions on how to handle the transfer of estate assets other than real estate. However, at the very least, the legal assistant should know some of the problems inherent in transferring estate assets so he can give factual advice to the clients and because such problems affect the choice of probate procedures. This section will discuss the transfer of some of the more common estate assets and the procedures generally required for such transfers.

POSTMORTEM ESTATE PLANNING

As briefly referred to in Chapter Three, estate planning does not cease with the death of the testator or settlor. A number of choices and/or elections are either required or permitted by the Internal Revenue Code and, to a limited extent, by the Texas Probate Code that can affect the amount of estate taxes due and when they become due, the amount of the generation-skipping transfer tax and when it becomes due, and the amount of federal income tax due on the decedent's **final return**. There also can be a choice or election by the surviving spouse, often called the **widow's election**, that can affect what property he will end up owning after administration of the estate is complete. This decision also will affect other devisees in regard to how much or what specific property they will end up with upon distribution.

Income Tax Elections

An executor can elect to claim administration expenses as defined under Internal Revenue Code Section 2053(a)(2) and losses during administration as defined under Internal Revenue Code Section 2054 for the purpose of computing the final income tax obligation instead of the estate tax. Treasury Regulation 1.642(g)-1 states that these deductions are not allowed for computing the estate's taxable income unless the executor elects and files a statement that the items have not and will not be taken as a deduction for estate tax purposes. This statement must, in addition, include a waiver of the estate's right to deduct the items on the estate tax return. In effect, the executor chooses to deduct these expenses on the **fiduciary income tax return** for the particular year in which the expenditures were made, thereby reducing the income tax payable by the estate but increasing the estate tax, if in fact the estate owes any tax. Obviously, if the estate is not going to be subject to estate tax, it is more beneficial to take these expenses as deductions from the income tax, since in that manner some benefit will be derived from the deductions whereas none will be derived as a deduction against estate tax.

If there is estate tax, the person preparing these various tax returns or giving advice must be aware that an election to deduct on the income tax has the following effects:

1. It increases the estate tax while decreasing the income tax. This may increase the liability for proportionate shares of the estate tax as against specific devisees and life insurance beneficiaries while decreasing the liability or responsibility for estate taxes and increasing the ultimate income tax savings received by residuary beneficiaries.

2. It increases the income in the estate while reducing the principal. This would then shift the tax savings attributable to the deductions from principal beneficiaries or remainder beneficiaries to income beneficiaries.

3. It increases the marital share, if the marital share is provided for by a residuary bequest, and decreases the bypass or credit shelter gift.

Medical and dental expenses are deductible as debts of the estate under Internal Revenue Code Section 2053(a)(3). However, Treasury Regulation Section 1.213-1(d)(1) provides that medical and dental expenses paid out of the estate within one year after the date of death of the decedent can be deducted on the decedent's final income tax return.

To be deductible on the final return, these expenses may not be deducted on the estate tax return, and a statement must be filed, generally with the final return, declaring this as so and waiving the estate's right to do so in the future. This election has the same effect as deducting administration expenses on income tax returns rather than on estate tax returns.

The executor of a decedent's estate can elect to report on the decedent's final income tax return any interest earned on series E or EE bonds that had accrued by the date of the decedent's death. If this is done, the estate will pay the income tax attributable to the interest. On the other hand, if this election is not made, then (a) the income will be distributed with the bonds to whomever receives them under a will or trust, (b) there will be no recognition of the unrecognized income, and (c) the distributee will receive the income as **income in respect to a decedent**, or **IRD**. This election, then, determines who pays the income tax attributable to the accrued interest—the estate, or the beneficiary actually receiving the assets. Also, an additional conflict exists because, although the income tax on the decedent's final income tax return is deductible against estate tax liability, the election will increase the amount of income tax payable by the surviving spouse if he joins with the executor on a joint final return.

An election to file the final return for the year of the decedent's death as a joint return with the decedent's spouse must be made when the return is filed. If, however, the surviving spouse files this joint return prior to the appointment of a personal representative, the personal representative after appointment may disaffirm the joint return, as long as he does so on or before one year from the date prescribed for the filing of the return. The filing of a joint return can affect the amount of income tax paid for the final year on the part of either the surviving spouse or the estate or both.

An estate may also adopt a taxable year other than the calendar year if it does so on or before the last day prescribed for filing of the first fiduciary return. This refers not to the final return filed for the year of the decedent's death but rather to the fiduciary income tax returns filed by the executor concerning estate income. An income tax return for an estate is due on or before the 15th day of the fourth month following the close of its taxable year.

Finally, Internal Revenue Code Section 643(e) permits a fiduciary, including an executor, to elect to recognize gain or loss on any distribution, except in the case of the distribution of a specific bequest or if appreciated property is used to satisfy a pecuniary bequest. The latter case refers to a situation such as where there is a devise to a beneficiary of $10,000 and, instead of paying the $10,000 in cash, the executor agrees with the beneficiary to transfer estate property worth $10,000 but whos taxable basis (adjusted basis) is less than $10,000.

This election becomes extremely complicated to explain because of the many relevant income tax regulations and revenue rulings. However, contrary to the common belief that a distribution from an estate is entirely tax free, a distribution may carry with it **distributable**

net income (DNI). Such an election means the estate, rather than the ultimate beneficiary, pays income tax on the gain or receives an income tax deduction on the loss.

Obviously, with all these elections, the possibility for conflict is great. The law firm advising the executor should be extremely cautious, not only because of the executor's possible exposure to a lawsuit by an embittered beneficiary, but also because of possible malpractice liability.

Estate Tax Elections

Several elections must be made either on or with a timely filed estate tax return. One that has already been discussed is the QTIP election required in Section 2056(b)(7) of the Internal Revenue Code, which allows the executor to exclude from the gross estate any estate property that qualifies for the marital deduction. The right to this deduction is claimed simply by deducting it on the estate tax return. However, if the property is passing in the form of qualified terminable interest property, then the executor is required to elect QTIP status by indicating this at the appropriate location on the federal estate tax return. Also, the QTIP election may be partial. This was discussed in connection with funding a bypass or exemption-equivalent trust by making a partial election disclaiming through a formula deduction an amount equal to the exemption equivalent of $600,000. Many estate planners suggest that, in drafting a will or trust providing for a marital deduction QTIP, specific instructions be included as to whether the QTIP election will be required by the executor or will be discretionary with the executor. If discretionary, guidance should be given to the executor how to make the election. In addition, there should be some negation of liability when the executor exercises his discretion one way or another.

The executor is also allowed to choose alternate evaluation dates (Section 2032 of the Internal Revenue Code). In lieu of the date of death, the executor may elect to value the gross estate as of a day six months after the date of death. Next, the executor is permitted to elect a special-use valuation of real property (mostly farm and ranch) meeting the requirements of Section 2032A of the Internal Revenue Code. This will reduce the value for federal estate tax purposes, up to a maximum of $750,000. Such an election can create ongoing complications, including the possibility of a **recapture** tax being assessed. Because the recaptured tax does not come within the definition of estate tax, the beneficiary who received the property could possibly have no claim back against the estate for reimbursement of any portion of the recapture tax.

Finally, in connection with qualified retirement plans, there are some elections concerning excess distributions and accumulations.

As already mentioned, an election is made to defer federal estate tax when a marital deduction is claimed. In addition to that type of deferment, there is also a provision under Section 6166 of the Internal Revenue Code to defer payment of estate taxes and, for that matter, generation-skipping transfer taxes attributable to a closely held business. The problem with this deferral is that interest is charged against the amount deferred until paid. In addition, the estate cannot be closed until the deferred amount is paid.

Generation-Skipping Transfer Taxes

There is an election concerning allocation of the transfer tax that must be made by the executor on or before the due date for filing the estate tax return. Each individual is entitled to an exemption of $1 million from generation-skipping transfer tax. This exemption may be allocated by the individual, or by his executor or trustee after death, to any property transferred by the individual. Once made, the allocation is irrevocable. If no allocation is made, then the IRS will deem allocations. Since the source for payment of the tax is the property constituting the transfer, beneficiaries of the generation-skipping transfer are going to be affected by how the executor allocates the decedent's generation skipping transfer tax exemption. Again, it is suggested that the estate planner provide in the estate planning document some directions to the executor or trustee on how to override the deemed allocation rules. Additionally, the planner might want to include instructions to the executor to make proportionate allocations to all beneficiaries in order to avoid an executor's or trustee's favoring one beneficiary over another or to give beneficiaries any basis for arguing with the executor or trustee concerning the allocations.

There are other elections provided for under the Texas Probate Code concerning disclaimers by devisees or heirs that can affect taxes and certainly can affect who gets what property from the estate and how much. As discussed in prior chapters, a surviving spouse can be forced to elect to take under the will or to keep his half of the community property in what is often referred to as a widow's election will.

CHECKLISTS AND SIGNIFICANT DATE LISTS

It is suggested that at the outset of each new representation, in connection with either probate proceedings or proceedings in lieu of probate, the legal assistant or the attorney draft a checklist or a list of significant dates and critical dates. The checklists could also combine critical dates imposed by the probate code or by tax law or by other outside influences with target dates set by the persons who are actually going to be working with the file.

There are a lot of deadlines set by various provisions of law that affect probate administration, for instance:

1. Executors and administrators have to qualify within 20 days of the order appointing them.

2. The inventory, appraisement, and list of claims has to be filed within 90 days of qualification.

3. Notice to creditors must be published in the newspaper within one month after receiving letters.

4. Notice to each person having a secured claim and to each other creditor must be given within four months after the issuance of letters.

5. For creditors to preserve their priority, claims for funeral expenses and expenses of last illness must be presented within 60 days after the issuance of letters, and other secured claims must be presented within six months after the grant of letters.

6. Elections by secured creditors must be made within six months of the original grant of letters.

7. Personal representatives must approve or reject claims within 30 days after presentment.

8. Suits on a rejected claim must be filed within 90 days after rejection.

9. Federal estate tax returns must be filed within nine months after the date of the decedent's death, unless extended for a term of no more than six months, with the extension having to be filed prior to nine months from the date of the decedent's death. Texas Inheritance Tax returns are due and any inheritance tax is payable nine months after the date of the decedent's death, unless the due date for filing the federal return is extended.

Some of these other deadlines talked about in the preceding section are crucial, and others are not. Regardless, all deadlines should be observed, because any deadline can become crucial in a given set of facts. A lot of the deadline dates depend on the date of something else that occurs in the estate and that may not be known at the time the critical or significant date checklist is prepared. The idea is to enter all dates in the original checklist and then, as events occur that affect them, to fill in the dates of the new deadlines. A good checklist should also provide space to note the date the deadline was met or the task carried out, plus the initials of the person responsible.

One of the best publications to use in preparing checklists and lists of significant or critical dates is the State Bar of Texas' Texas Probate System, 2nd revised edition, edited by James E. Brill and Linda D. Woodal. The problem with these published lists is that they are generic, that is, meant to fit any estate that falls within a particular classification. For example, for a probate as a muniment of title, the checklist is designed to cover any possible estate that might be probated as a muniment of title. Thus, a lot of information called for in the checklist and the list of dates will not be applicable to any given estate. In fact, the checklists are sometimes a quarter- to a half-inch thick. It is better to use the checklist as a guide and to prepare a separate checklist tailored to each individual estate. One way to accomplish this is to set up the checklist as a shell document in a word processing program. This eliminates the possibility of overlooking something that needs to be done because there are so many pages and such a long list of items in the prepared checklist that are not applicable to the particular estate. It also forces the legal assistant or the lawyer to consider what actions are necessary in the particular estate. An example for independent administrations from Texas Probate System is found at Form 13-1.

It is therefore suggested that at the beginning of representation, the legal assistant list, using one of the significant dates lists or checklists provided by the state system or some other source, all of the deadlines that either are already applicable or will later become applicable, with a column for the dates to be inserted and another column to put in the date on which the action is carried out, together perhaps with the initials of the person who does so. In addition, the legal assistant should list each of the assets that will need to be transferred, and note down all of the actions necessary to carry out the transfer. For instance, for stock, someone is going to need to find out the high and low selling prices on the date of the decedent's death and on the date exactly six months after. Someone will then have to find out who the transfer agent is for the stock, write the transfer agent requesting information regarding its requirements and any forms required by it, fill out the forms, have them properly executed, resubmit them to the transfer agent, and finally await receipt of the newly issued stock. Each of these steps should be listed, with a space for a target date and a date of completion, together with the initials of the responsible party. There should be enough space to write notes concerning to whom the asset will be transferred, where it is to be mailed, etc. There should also be spaces to write in the name and address of the transfer agent when located or perhaps a date to follow up on letters written to the transfer agent.

Something like this should be done for each and every asset the estate owns, even those that will not be transferred by the law firm. For assets that are not going to be transferred by the law firm, some notation should be made as to who is going to effectuate the transfer.

Other actions may need to be taken in the estate. For instance, if the elections talked about in the preceding section are applicable, they should be included within the checklist or list of significant dates.

When thought out and formulated with care, these lists can serve two very important purposes. First, they help make sure that all information necessary to the representation of the estate will be obtained. Second, they help ensure that all necessary actions are carried out in a timely manner. Preparation and use of such checklists is important in average estates, but essential in more complicated estates.

TRANSFER OF ESTATE PROPERTY

Too many different types of assets owned in limited numbers of estates exist even to begin to discuss all of them. Some estates own airplanes, oil or gas interests, works of art, etc. This discussion is limited to the types of assets found in the great majority of estates.

Real Estate

With regard to the transfer of real estate during administration, it is necessary to discuss three different types of administrations. First, come independent administrations. There are two fact situations which will affect the procedure of transfer in an independent administration. The first is when the estate is transferring the real estate to a third party in the event of the sale of the property by the estate. The requirements in this case depend on whether the will contains a power of sale. (This subject was discussed in Chapters Five and Ten.) If there is a power of sale, the independent executor may execute an ordinary deed tailored to the particular transaction on behalf of the estate. He will execute the deed as "Independent Executor of the Estate of, _____ deceased." If the executor is also a beneficiary of the property being sold, he must execute the deed individually and as independent executor of the estate in order to convey his individual interest. The other devisees or beneficiaries under the will do not need to join in the deed unless the estate is relatively old, in which case some title insurers require that the beneficiaries also join in the conveyance. If there is no power of sale contained in the will, the general consensus is that either the executor must prove to the satisfaction of the purchaser or title insurer that the property is being sold to pay debts of the estate, or all devisees who receive an interest under the will must also execute the deed.

The second situation involving the independent administration is when the transfer by the independent executor or administrator is to the devisees/heirs entitled to the property. Generally speaking, as long as the independent administration has not been closed by the filing of a closing affidavit, the independent executor/administrator must execute a deed to the devisees or heirs in order to vest in them title to the property free from the right of possession by the estate. If the devisees or heirs entitled to such real property want to sell the property, a deed from the independent executor/administrator to the devisees and/or heirs must first be executed. This will be a cash deed and generally should be a special warranty deed. An example is attached to Chapter Ten.

If the will has been probated as a muniment of title, the legal assistant should file a certified copy of the will and the order admitting it to probate in the official real property records of each county in which the estate owns real property other than the county in which the estate is being probated. This will adequately reflect the vesting of title in the devisees named in the will to receive title to the real property. No other action need be taken to reflect the passage of title to those named in the will to receive it, and if they want to sell the property, they may do so simply by executing a deed in their individual capacity.

For a dependent administration, deeds may be executed by the administrator only in two circumstances. The first is after a decree confirming sale has been entered by the Probate Court in a sale proceeding. (This procedure is discussed, and a deed form found, in Chapter Eleven.) The second circumstance is upon distribution of the estate. Again, this can only be done with an appropriate order of the court, which might come in an action for partition and distribution or in an order approving a final account.

Automobiles and Boats

The transfer of title to automobiles has to be done on forms furnished by the Texas Department of Transportation. The transfer of boats, which are not documented by the U.S. Coast Guard, must be on forms furnished by the Texas Parks and Wildlife Commission. These forms change so rapidly that it is difficult to keep current forms on file and therefore many law firms clients to the office of the **tax assessor-**

collector at the county courthouse or to the Texas Parks and Wildlife Commission's local office to handle the transfer on their own.

If title to the automobile or boat is in the name of a deceased person, the tax assessor-collector or the Parks and Wildlife Commission will require one of the following:

1. Letters testamentary or letters of administration. A substantial number of tax assessor-collectors accept either form of letters without any further order from the court. If it is a dependent administration, the administrator should not be transferring an automobile without a decree confirming sale in the event of a sale or an order directing the dependent administrator to distribute the asset to a particular named heir.

2. A certified copy of a will and an order admitting it to probate in a muniment of title proceeding. If the order provides the names of the devisees, the Department of Transportation will usually not require a certified copy of the will.

3. An affidavit of heirship prepared on the form required by the Department of Transportation or the Department of Parks and Wildlife. This form also has a place for the heirs to sign, to designate into whose name the title shall be placed, which can be a third party.

In order to transfer the title, one must possess the original **certificate of title** or obtain a duplicate through the procedures required by either office.

The procedure discussed for automobiles also relates to trailers, including travel trailers and house trailers. It does not cover manufactured homes, which generally have been attached to the land on which they are situated and are therefore recognized by the law as real estate.

Stocks and Bonds

It will be necessary to acquire the original stock and bond certificates. There are two choices with regard to the transfer of the stocks and bonds. The representative may have the stocks and bonds transferred into his own name as personal representative and then later transfer the stocks and bonds to the beneficiaries entitled to them. Or, he may simply leave them in the name of the decedent until the stocks and bonds are either sold or distributed to the beneficiaries. Which is done depends on many circumstances, including the length of time it is anticipated the administration will be open, whether the stocks are likely to be sold to pay debts or other expenses of the estate rather than be distributed to beneficiaries, and the stability of the stock.

In order to transfer the stock, it will be necessary to communicate with a transfer agent representing each of the issuers of the stocks or bonds. The transfer agent is a company who, for a fee, handles the transfer of stock for the company issuing it. Many transfer agents are banks, although many are just companies in the business of acting as transfer agents. Often, the stock certificates give the name and address of the transfer agent on their face. However, there is some degree of change in transfer agents, and it would probably be best to determine who the present transfer agent is, information available from any stock broker. Also, both Prentice Hall and Commerce Clearing House have publications that list transfer agents. In rare cases, the company may serve as its own transfer agent.

It is best to write to the transfer agent to determine what its requirements are and to obtain its forms. Although some transfer agents will accept any forms, others require that their own forms be used. A letter to the transfer agent requesting such information is found as Form 13-2.

Generally, in order to transfer stocks and bonds, transfer agents will require:

1. The original stock certificate or bond.

2. A certified copy of the will and sometimes the order admitting it to probate.

3. An originally certified death certificate.

4. Letters testamentary (see discussion under "Muniment of Title" in Chapter Twelve).

5. An **affidavit of domicile** in which the personal representative swears that the decedent was a resident of a certain jurisdiction at the time of death. A form for an affidavit of domicile is found at the end of this chapter as Form 13-3.

6. A stock or bond power, with the signature of the personal representative guaranteed by either an officer of a national bank or a registered stock broker. A form of a **stock power** is found at Form 13-4 and that of a bond power at Form 13-5.

These materials should be sent to the transfer agent by registered mail. A sample of a letter to send to the transfer agent enclosing the original stock or bond certificate and the other documents listed above is found at Form 13-6.

On some occasions, companies will have changed their names since the stock certificates were issued. If these were publicly traded stocks, the legal assistant can contact the New York Stock Exchange Public Information Office, the American Stock Exchange Rulings and Inquiries Department, or the National Association of Securities Dealers. In addition, if the legal assistant knows the state of incorporation, which he should if he has the original certificate, he can contact the secretary of state of the particular state of incorporation. For municipal bonds, the legal assistant can contact the comptroller or city secretary of the city or town, or in the case of state-issued bonds, the treasurer of the state. In addition, some private agencies will do research on corporations.

United States Savings Bonds generally may be transferred at any commercial bank. The bank will require to be sent with the original certificate, original letters testamentary, an originally certified death certificate, a certified copy of the will, and sometimes the order admitting it to probate. The bank will require the Social Security number of the heir or deviser.

Bank Accounts

Generally, a personal representative either will set up new accounts in his name as independent executor of the estate or will have the bank change the existing accounts from the decedent's name to the personal representative's name. The bank will require, when paying to the personal representative the balances of an existing account or changing the name from the decedent to the personal representative, original letters testamentary, an originally certified death certificate, a certified copy of the will, and often the order admitting it to probate. In addition, the personal representative will have to furnish to the bank the taxpayer identification number of the estate, which is obtained by filing a Form SS-4 with the Internal Revenue Service. (This procedure will be discussed in Chapter Fifteen.)

If tax returns are to be filed, while setting up the bank accounts the personal representative should also obtain the style of each account, the name and location of the bank or other financial institution, the account number, the type of account, and the balance on the date of the death of the testator after the payment of any checks that were presented on that date.

Other Personal Property

The personal representative should obtain all of the personal property belonging to the estate, as well as an inventory of any safe-deposit box in which the decedent had an interest. In addition, the personal representative should examine closely any documents in the safe-deposit box to see whether they present any information relevant to the probate or revealing an asset previously unknown.

Title, upon distribution to the beneficiaries (except for items of personal property subject to certificate of title acts, such as automobiles, boats, and planes), is transferred simply by placing the beneficiary in possession of the personal property.

COLLECTING LIFE INSURANCE PROCEEDS

Many times, the attorney will either assist with or handle, for the named beneficiaries, the collection of the proceeds of insurance policies that were payable upon the death of the decedent to those beneficiaries. The first step is to write the insurance company to advise them of the death of the insured and to request claim forms. An example of such a letter is attached as Form 13-7.

Insurance companies generally require a certified copy of the death certificate, the original insurance policy, and completed **proof of loss** using their form. If the original insurance policy has been lost, the personal representative or beneficiary will have to execute a lost policy affidavit and furnish a bond. The insurance company will make arrangements to obtain the bond at the estate's or beneficiaries' costs. When these items are sent to the insurance company, the letter should also request that the insurance company send Internal Revenue Service Forms 712. These are required to be attached to the federal estate tax return, and, even if no return is contemplated to be filed, it may become necessary later. A form for such a letter is included at Form 13-8.

Sometimes the address of the insurance company is on the insurance policy. If not, one can look in the phone book to determine if there is a local agent for that particular insurance company. If there is, the legal assistant may call that agent to get the address of the home office. Many agents have a list or directory of insurance underwriters, and if the legal assistant is on friendly terms with an agent, he may be called to obtain the address.

The Department of Insurance of the State of Texas has, as a part of its records, the name and address of any insurance company authorized to issue insurance in the state. If the insurance company is not registered with the Texas Department of Insurance because the insurance policy was purchased in some other state and that particular company has never desired to issue policies in Texas, then the legal assistant can contact the Insurance Commission or the Department of Insurance of the state that is shown on the policy as the insurance company's home state.

CHAPTER QUESTIONS AND EXERCISES

1. Name, with a short explanation, two postmortem elections in connection with income tax.

2. Name, with a short explanation, two postmortem elections in connection with estate tax. Do not use any of the elections you named in answer to Question 1.

3. Describe a significant date list stating what information is to be found in it. How is it used?

4. Explain how real estate belonging to an estate is transferred to the heirs or devisees.

5. List, with a short explanation, the steps necessary to collect life insurance proceeds payable either to the estate or to a named beneficiary.

6. List, with a short explanation, the steps that a legal assistant might take to effectuate the transfer of stock from the estate to the heirs or devisees.

7. How are U.S. Savings Bonds transferred by the estate? What documents will the representative be required to produce in order to transfer them?

8. What documents are necessary to transfer the ownership of automobiles from the estate to the heirs or devisees?

9. How are bank accounts that were in existence prior to the death of the decedent handled? Who must do this? What documents will be needed, and what information should be obtained?

Form 13-1: Independent Administration Checkplan and Significant Date List

(Reprinted from <u>Texas Probate System</u>, copyright State Bar of Texas, with permission.)

Explanatory Comments

In the Second Revised Edition of the <u>Texas Probate System</u>, released in late 1993, the editors changed the format of both the checkplan and the significant date list. In the prior edition there were individual checkplans and significant date lists for each probate procedure covered. The current edition consolidates all of the checkplans into a single checkplan with individual sections and all of the significant date lists into a combined significant date list.

The checkplan is organized into relevant topics, with each topic beginning on a new page. This allows the user to assemble a checkplan which is more or less tailored to the current probate matter which he or she is working on. The entire checkplan is 131 pages long. The first 20 pages would apply to any estate. Thereafter, however, the legal assistant would make copies of the only those sections which apply to the current probate matter and put them in the file.

The significant date list is only 10 pages long. Consequently, the fact that it may contain matters not relevant to the current case is not especially burdensome.

On the following page is the table of contents of the checkplan. It is followed by the portion of the checkplan that relates to independent administrations. This would not be the only section used in an independent administration, as one can determine by looking at the table of contents. It is included as an example of how the checkplan is organized and is not intended for actual use. Following the checkplan is the Combined Significant Date List.

Form 13-1: (continued)

Form 13-1: (continued)

INDEPENDENT ADMINISTRATION (IA)

	NA	L	S	DATE	INITIALS
19. If Independent Administration (IA) is the proper probate procedure, go to Items 22 through 37 of this Checkplan and indicate that they are not applicable, and do the following:					
a. See Special Instruction 68 - Independent Administration (IA).					
b. See Special Instruction 5 - Qualification of and Priority Rights To Be Appointed an Administrator or an Executor to determine that Applicant qualifies to serve as Executor.					
c. See Special Instruction 15 - Jurisdiction and Venue and prepare Application For Probate of Will and Issuance of Letters Testamentary (Form 5).					
d. Prepare Waiver and Renunciation of Right to Letters Testamentary (Form 96) for those preferentially entitled to serve as Executor who do not wish to serve and arrange for proper signature before a notary.					
e. Determine amount of filing fee, issue check for filing fee, and charge to client's account.					
f. Take D's original Will and Codicil(s) and original Application for Probate of Will and Issuance of Letters Testamentary (Form 5) and file with clerk of court. If Waiver and Renunciation of Right to Letters Testamentary (Form 96) was prepared and has been signed, file original with clerk of court. Enter date of this filing as Item 16 of SDL and as Item 6.23 of MIL. NOTE: When Application for Probate of Will and Issuance of Letters Testamentary (Form 5) is filed with the clerk of court, it must be accompanied by D's original Will and Codicil(s), but the Will and Codicil(s) are left in their own manuscript covers or "blue backs" and are not put in the same manuscript cover with the Application for Probate of Will and Issuance of Letters Testamentary (Form 5).					
g. If a docket number has not been previously assigned to proceedings in this estate, obtain the court docket number, enter it on the Probate Chart, on the cover page of the MIL and as Item 6.01 of MIL, and conform office file copies.					
h. Calculate the return date for the citation and enter as Item 18 of SDL (see Special Instruction 16 - Citation and Hearing Date).					
i. Arrange for time and date of hearing on the Application for Probate of Will and Issuance of Letters Testamentary (Form 5) and enter as Item 22 of SDL. Complete Item 23 of SDL and Item 6.24 of MIL. If proof of proper execution must be made by alternate methods (see Item 38 of this Checkplan), it will be necessary to wait until all required proof has been assembled before the hearing can be scheduled.					
(1) Prepare Proof of Death and Other Facts (Form 7) and place in file folder entitled "Court Proceedings."					

Form 13-1: (continued)

	NA	L	S	DATE	INITIALS
(2) If witness for Proof of Death and Other Facts (Form 7) is <u>not</u> the named Executor, prepare and send Letter 13 to witness together with a copy of the Proof of Death and Other Facts (Form 7) to advise of the date and time of the hearing and of the need for the witness to appear in court.					
j. If D's Will is self-proven, skip to Item 19n of this Checkplan.					
k. If D's Will is not self-proven or attested, but is holographic, skip to Item 19m of this Checkplan.					
l. If D's Will is attested, refer to Item 2.11 of MIL to determine the identity of the attesting witness who will testify as to the proper execution of the Will and determine if that witness will be available to testify in court.					
(1) If the witness will be available, do the following:					
(a) Prepare Proof by Subscribing Witness (Form 8) and place in file folder entitled "Court Proceedings."					
(b) Prepare and send Letter 14 to witness together with a copy of the Proof by Subscribing Witness (Form 8) and a copy of D's Will to advise of the date of the hearing and of the need for the witness to appear in court.					
(2) If the witness will not be available to testify in court, determine an alternate method of proving D's Will. If D's Will is to be proved by written interrogatories, see Item 38 of this Checkplan and take appropriate action.					
(3) Repeat procedures in this Item 19 l for each attested codicil.					
m. If D's Will is holographic and is neither attested nor self-proven, refer to Item 2.04 of MIL to determine the identity of the two witnesses who will testify as to D's handwriting and also determine if each witness will be available to testify in court.					
(1) For <u>both</u> of these witnesses who will testify in court, do the following:					
(a) Prepare Proof of Decedent's Handwriting and Signature (Form 14) for each witness and place in file folder entitled "Court Proceedings."					
(b) Prepare and send Letter 17 to each witness together with a copy of the Proof of Decedent's Handwriting and Signature (Form 14) for that witness and a copy of D's Will to advise witness of the date and time of the hearing and of the need for the witness to appear in court.					
(2) For each witness who will not be available to testify in court, determine an alternate method of proving D's Will. If D's Will is to be proved by written interrogatories, see Item 38 of this Checkplan and take appropriate action.					
(3) Repeat procedures in this Item 19m for each holographic codicil.					

Form 13-1: (continued)

	NA	L	S	DATE	INITIALS
n. Determine if any proposed Executor is a nonresident of Texas. If so, do the following:					
(1) Prepare Appointment of Resident Agent (Form 15 for each nonresident individual Executor and Form 16 for each nonresident corporate Executor) and place in file folder entitled "Court Proceedings."					
(2) Prepare and send Letter 18 to each nonresident Executor together with the original and one copy of Appointment of Resident Agent (Form 15 or Form 16).					
(3) When Appointment of Resident Agent (Form 15 or Form 16) is received, place in file folder entitled "Court Proceedings."					
o. Prepare and send Letter 19 to each named Executor together with a copy of the Application For Probate of Will and Issuance of Letters Testamentary (Form 5) to advise of the date and time of hearing.					
p. Prepare Order Admitting Will to Probate and Authorizing Letters Testamentary (Form 17) and place in file folder entitled "Court Proceedings."					
q. Review Item 2.58 of MIL, determine whether proposed Executor will sign oath in court or before a notary, prepare Oath (Form 18 for each individual Executor and Form 19 for each corporate Executor), and place in file folder entitled "Court Proceedings."					
r. If hearing must be rescheduled, enter rescheduled date as Item 6.24 of MIL and as Item 24 of SDL, revise Item 23 of SDL, and notify all Executors and other witnesses of new date.					
s. One business day before the hearing, call to remind all Executors and all witnesses of the time, date, and place of hearing.					
20. For the hearing itself, do the following:					
a. Assemble the following documents and take to hearing:					
(1) Original copy of Proof of Death and Other Facts (Form 7) for person who will testify as to death, etc.					
(2) Original copy of Proof by Subscribing Witness (Form 8) or Proof of Decedent's Handwriting and Signature (Form 14) for each appropriate witness who will appear in court.					
(3) Original copies of Appointment of Resident Agent (Form 15 or Form 16).					
(4) Original copy of Order Admitting Will to Probate and Authorizing Letters Testamentary (Form 17).					
(5) Original copies of Oath (Form 18 or Form 19) for each Executor who will sign Oath in court.					
b. Determine whether local rules of court require different or additional documents or procedures and if so, take appropriate action.					
c. Attend hearing (see Special Instruction 18 - What To Do at Hearing) and enter actual date of hearing as Item 6.25 of MIL and Item 25 of SDL.					

Form 13-1: (continued)

		NA	L	S	DATE	INITIALS
d.	Enter the date the Order Admitting Will to Probate and Autho-rizing Letters Testamentary (Form 17) was signed by judge as Item 6.26 of MIL and as Item 26 of SDL. Complete Items 27, 28, 30, 32 and 33 of SDL. If appraisers were appointed, complete Items 6.42 through 6.46 of MIL.					
e.	Have Executors who attend hearing sign their Oath (Form 18 or Form 19) before appropriate court official and file with clerk of court. If these are the only Executors, complete Item 6.38 and 6.39 of MIL and Item 34 of SDL.					
f.	Order two Letters Testamentary from clerk of court and, if you paid for them, charge to client's account. If ordering by mail, deter-mine appropriate number of Letters and the correct charge, issue check for payment, charge to client's account, and prepare and send Letter 2 to clerk of court. When received, place in file folder enti-tled "Letters Testamentary."					
	NOTE: In Harris County this letter must be signed by the attorney and not by a staff member.					
21.	Follow-up. Refer to Item 2.58 of MIL. For each Oath (Form 18 or Form 19) that was not signed before a court official, prepare and send Letter 20 to each Executor who did not sign the Oath in court together with the original and one copy of Oath (Form 18 or Form 19).					
a.	When all Oaths are signed and returned, prepare and send Letter 21 to clerk of court together with the original Oaths (Form 18 or Form 19).					
b.	Determine the date on which the last Oath (Form 18 or Form 19) was filed and enter this date as Items 6.38 and 6.39 of MIL, and as Item 34 of SDL. Also complete Items 37 through 47 of SDL and complete Items 6.85, 6.145, 7.35 and 21.23 of MIL.					
c.	If there were governmental and charitable beneficiaries, by the date shown in Item 6.26 of MIL and Item 28 of SDL (30 days after Will admitted to probate), do the following:					
(1)	Prepare and send by registered or certified mail, return receipt requested, Letter 67 to the entity together with appropriate enclosures.					
(2)	Attach mailing receipt to file copy of Letter 67.					
(3)	When received, attach return receipt to file copy of Letter 67.					
(4)	Prepare and send Letter 21 to clerk of court along with photo-copy of Letter 67 and of return receipt for each such entity.					
d.	Prepare and send Letter 22 to thank each witness other than Exec-utor(s) who appeared in court.					
e.	Prepare and send Letter 23 to Executor(s) to advise of nature and extent of the duties of office and actions which will follow.					
f.	Conform file copies of all documents for dates and signatures.					
g.	Collect all of D's records, books, title papers, and business papers. If anyone refuses to deliver the same, file a complaint pursuant to Probate Code, Section 75.					
h.	Skip to Item 39 of this Checkplan.					

Form 13-1: (continued)

REMEMBER: When date for future action has been determined, be sure to enter it in your calendar or other tickler system. Those marked with an asterisk (*) are critical dates. We recommend that you also prepare reminders for one month, one week and one day before due dates for Inventory, inheritance, estate and income tax returns and reminders for selection of fiscal year end 3, 6 and 9 months following date of D's death. As a date is determined, it should also be entered at the indicated place in the Master Information List (MIL) and on the Probate Chart.

COMBINED SIGNIFICANT DATE LIST (SDL)

NAME OF DECEDENT (D)_____

Determination of Date of Document, Event, or Action   **Actual Date**

1. Date of Will--as shown on Will itself (Item 2.02 of MIL).   _____

    NOTE: ITEM 1 IS NOT APPLICABLE TO RDA OR PDII

2. Date of Codicil--as shown on Codicil itself (Item 2.17 of MIL).   _____

    NOTE: ITEM 2 IS NOT APPLICABLE TO RDA OR PDII

3. Date of death--as shown on death certificate (Item 1.07 of MIL).   _____

4. Date exactly ten years before date of D's death--This is the beginning date of the period for credit for previously taxed property.   _____

5. Date exactly three years before date of D's death--This is the beginning date for including taxable gifts made by D and the gift tax thereon, into the gross valuation of D's estate for federal estate tax purposes.   _____

6. Date five days (actually 120 hours) after date of D's death--This is the date to which D's heirs and beneficiaries (including life insurance beneficiaries) must have survived or they will be deemed to have predeceased D unless D's Will directs otherwise.   _____

7. Date thirty days after date of D's death--This is the earliest date on which the Small Estate Affidavit may be filed with clerk of court.   _____

8. Date six months after date of D's death--Enter this date as Item 26.22 of MIL. This is the date for: _____

    a. Determining the alternate valuation of D's assets for state inheritance and federal estate tax purposes.

    b. Beginning to prepare Texas Inheritance Tax Return - Federal Estate Tax Credit (FF 12) and United States Estate (and Generation-Skipping Transfer) Tax Return (FF 20).

    c. Determining whether necessary to prepare and file Application For Extension of Time to File a Return and/or Pay U.S. Estate (and Generation-Skipping Transfer) Taxes (FF 11).

        NOTE: This Application should be filed at least forty days prior to due date (Item 26.28 of MIL).

    d. Determining whether necessary to prepare and file application for extension of time to file Texas Inheritance Tax Return - Federal Estate Tax Credit (FF 12).

        NOTE: This application should be filed at least forty days prior to due date (Item 26.19 of MIL).

Form 13-1: (continued)

*9. Date nine months after date of D's death--Enter this date as Items 26.19 and 26.28 of MIL. This is the date for: _____

   a. Filing a disclaimer or renunciation of bequest or inheritance and receipt of copy by each Executor or Administrator.

   b. Filing Schedule S for increased estate tax on excess retirement accumulations and paying the tax unless an extension is granted.

     (1) First extended date (Item 26.29 MIL) _____

   c. Filing the United States Estate (and Generation-Skipping Transfer) Tax Return (FF 20) and paying the taxes unless an extension is granted.

     (1) First extended date (Item 26.29 of MIL) _____

   d. Filing D's final gift tax return unless due on an earlier date (Refer to Items 55 and 56 of this SDL).

   e. Filing the Texas Inheritance Return - Federal Estate Tax Credit (FF 12) and paying the taxes unless an extension is granted.

     (1) First extended date (Item 26.20 of MIL) _____

10. Date one year from last day of calendar month prior to date of D's death--This is the last possible date for the end of the first fiscal year for D's Estate. _____

11. Date one year from end of first fiscal year for D's Estate--If D's Estate has not been closed by this date, estimated income tax payments may be required for all future years. _____

12. Date one year after date of D's death--This is the last date for obtaining Family Allowance and the earliest date on which the statutes of limitation are no longer suspended for suits by or against D. _____

13. Date two years after date of D's death--Payment of estimated income taxes by Estate will be required for all fiscal years ending after this date. _____

14. Date three years and nine months after date of D's death--This is the date on which the statute of limitations runs with respect to a timely filed United States Estate (and Generation-Skipping Transfer) Tax Return (FF 20). _____

15. Date four years after date of D's death--This is the last date on which original Letters Testamentary (IA or ADE) or Letters of Administration (AWA or RDA) can be authorized and the last date on which a request can be filed for the court to determine whether a necessity for administration exists (PDH). _____

16. Date of filing Application (IA, MT, PDH, ADE, AWA, or RDA) or Small Estate Affidavit and Order (SE) --as shown on receipt issued by clerk of the court (Item 6.23 of MIL). _____

   NOTE: For SE, this date must be after the date shown in Item 7 of this SDL.

17. Date ninety days after filing Application--This is the date following which fees must be paid for all instruments filed with the clerk of the court. _____

18. Return date for Citation by Posting--First Monday following expiration of ten days' notice by posting. _____

19. Date of newspaper in which Application to Determine Heirship is published if there is citation by publication--as shown in newspaper. _____

20. Return date for Citation by Publication--First Monday following expiration of ten days from date of publication in newspaper. _____

Form 13-1: (continued)

21. Date which is the latest of Items 18 and 20--no hearing may be held before this date. _____

22. Date scheduled for hearing on Application--as scheduled by clerk of the court (Item 6.24 of MIL). _____

23. One business day before scheduled date for hearing on Application--Call witnesses on this date. _____

24. If hearing on Application is rescheduled--Enter new date and remember to remind witnesses one business day before new date. _____

25. Actual date of hearing on Application--as furnished by attorney who appeared in court (Item 6.25 of MIL). _____

26. Date of Order or Judgment--as shown in Order or Judgment signed by judge (Item 6.26 of MIL). _____

*27. Date twenty days after date of Order or Judgment--All Oaths and Bonds must be filed with the clerk of the court by this date. _____

28. Date thirty days after date of Probate--This is the date to give notice to the State of Texas, each governmental agency of the State of Texas, and each charity named as a devisee under D's Will. _____

    a. Date of giving notice to such a beneficiary--as shown on return receipt. _____

    b. Date that is nine months after date of receipt as shown in Item 28a--This is the last date by which a governmental or charitable entity can file a disclaimer. _____

29. Date ninety days after date D's Will was admitted to probate as MT as shown in Item 26--This is the due date for filing the Inventory (if required by the court) unless the time is extended. Complete Item 6.85 of MIL. If time is extended, enter new date(s) below: _____

    a. First extended due date (Complete Item 6.86 of MIL). _____

    b. Second extended due date (Revise Item 6.86 of MIL). _____

    c. Third extended due date (Revise Item 6.86 of MIL). _____

30. Date four months after date D's Will was admitted to probate as MT as shown in Item 26-- This is the last date for giving notice by certified or registered mail to secured creditors (Item 7.35 of MIL). _____

31. Date one hundred eighty-one days after date D's Will was admitted to probate as MT as shown in Item 26--This is the last date to file a sworn affidavit stating the terms of the will that have been fulfilled and those that have not been fulfilled. If time is extended, enter new date below: _____

    a. First extended due date. _____

32. Date fifteen months after date D's Will was admitted to probate--This is the date following which an Independent Executor can be required to make an accounting under Probate Code, Section 149A. _____

    a. Date one year following above date. This is the next opportunity for an interested party to demand an accounting. _____

    b. Date two years following above date. This is the next opportunity for an interested party to demand an accounting. _____

33. Date two years after date D's Will was admitted to probate--This is the date following which an Independent Executor can be required to make an accounting and distribution under Probate Code, Section 149B. _____

34. Date of filing all Oaths--as shown by clerk's file stamp (Item 6.38 of MIL). _____

    NOTE: This is the date of qualification for Independent Executors.

Form 13-1: (continued)

35. Date of filing Bond--as shown by clerk's file stamp (Item 6.36 of MIL). _____

36. Date of approval of Bond by judge--as shown in Order signed by judge (Item 6.37 of MIL). _____

37. Date which is the latest of Items 34, 35, and 36--This is the date of qualification of Executor or Administrator (Item 6.39 or MIL). _____

38. Date of initial grant of Letters Testamentary or Letters of Administration if different from Item 34--as determined from clerk of court. _____

*39. Date thirty days after Date of Qualification shown in Item 37--This is the last date for giving Notice of Fiduciary Relationship on IRS Form 56 (Item 21.23 of MIL). _____

40. Date one month after Date of Qualification shown in Item 37--This is the last date for publishing Notice to Creditors and furnishing copy to Comptroller of Public Accounts (Item 21.23 of MIL). _____

41. Date sixty days after Date of Qualification shown in Item 37--This is the last date for Class 1 claims (funeral expenses and expenses of last sickness) retaining priority status. _____

42. Date ninety days after Date of Qualification shown in Item 37 (Item 6.39 of MIL)--This is the due date for filing the Inventory unless the time is extended. Complete Item 6.85 of MIL. If time is extended, enter new date(s) below:

    a. First extended due date (Complete Item 6.86 of MIL). _____

    b. Second extended due date (Revise Item 6.86 of MIL). _____

    c. Third extended due date (Revise Item 6.86 of MIL). _____

43. Date four months after receiving Letters Testamentary or Letters of Administration (normally the Date of Qualification shown in Item 37) (Item 6.39 of MIL)--This is the last date for giving certified or registered mail notice to secured creditors (Item 7.35 of MIL) and the last date for giving notice to each person known to have an outstanding claim for money against D's estate. _____

44. Date six months after Date of Qualification shown in Item 37 (Item 6.39 of MIL)--This is the last date for a creditor to present a claim and to retain priority status. _____

45. Date one year from Date of Qualification shown in Item 37 (Item 6.39 of MIL)--This is the last date for:

    a. Obtaining an award of the Family Allowance. _____

    b. Filing the first Annual Account with the court (Item 6.145 of MIL). See also Item 72 of this SDL. _____

    c. Ending the suspension of the statutes of limitation for suits by or against D. _____

46. Date two years from Date of Qualification in Item 37 (Item 6.39 of MIL)--This is the due date for the second Annual Account if the estate has not been closed (Item 6.145 of MIL). See also Item 73 of this SDL. _____

47. Date three years from Date of Qualification shown in Item 37 (Item 6.39 of MIL)--This is the due date for the third Annual Account if the estate has not been closed (Item 6.145 of MIL) and is the date on which the Executor or Administrator can be removed if final settlement of the estate has not been made. See also Item 74 of this SDL. _____

48. Ending date of fiscal year for Estate--as established by Executor or Administrator and as used on the initial federal income tax return filed for the Estate on IRS Form 1041 (Item 26.14 of MIL). _____

*49. Fifteenth day of fourth month following end of first fiscal year for Estate (April 15th if tax year is calendar year)--This is the last date to file the first federal income tax return for the Estate on IRS Form 1041. Note that payment of tax in quarterly installments is no longer permitted. _____

Form 13-1: (continued)

    a. Date one year following above date. This is the due date for the return for the following year.   ————

    b. Date one year following date in "a" above. This is the due date for the return for the next following year.   ————

    c. Date one year following date in "b" above. This is the doe date for the return for the next following year.   ————

50. <u>Ending Date of Second Fiscal Year for Estate (one year after date shown in Item 48)</u>--For fiscal years commencing after this date, estimated tax payments are required. If fiscal year is a calendar year, these payments will be due on April 15, June 15, September 15, and January 15 next following this ending date. If fiscal year is not a calendar year, corresponding months of the fiscal year are substituted.   ————

    a. First installment due (15th day of 4th month)   ————

    b. Second installment due (15th day of 6th month)   ————

    c. Third installment due (15th day of 9th month)   ————

    d. Fourth installment due (15th day of 13th month)   ————

51. <u>Date of expiration of D's leases.</u>

    a. Residence   ————

    b. Office   ————

    c. Other   ————

52. <u>Date of current fiscal year end of a Subchapter S corporation in which D was a shareholder</u> (Item 10.12 of MIL).   ————

53. <u>Date two months and fifteen days after date of current fiscal year end of Subchapter S corporation as shown in Item 52</u>--This is normally the last date for a majority of shareholders to revoke a previously filed Subchapter S election for that fiscal year (see Item 10.81 of MIL).   ————

•54. <u>Date for filing D's income tax and gift tax returns for tax year before year of death</u>--(Fifteenth day of fourth month following end of tax year--April 15th if tax year is calendar year). (Refer to Item 9 of this SDL). If time is extended, enter new date below: ————

    a. First extended due date   ————

•55. <u>Date for filing D's income tax and gift tax returns for tax year of D's death</u>--(Fifteenth day of fourth month following end of D's tax year--April 15th if tax year is calendar year). If time is extended, enter new date below: ————

    a. First extended due date.   ————

Form 13-1: (continued)

56. Date Inventory is approved--as shown on Order signed by judge (Item 6.88 of MIL). This is the date following which fees must be paid for all instruments filed with the clerk of the court. It also is the earliest date on which proper applications may be made to the court to do the following: _____

    a. Set aside exempt property.

    b. Obtain allowance in lieu of exempt property.

    c. Obtain family allowance.

    d. Dispose of items with no commercial value.

    e. Dispose of personal property which is likely to perish, etc.

    f. Sell personal property.

    g. Sell real property.

    h. Enter into mineral and other leases.

    i. Obtain approval of Final Account.

57. Date disposition of personal property having no commercial value is authorized by court--as shown by Order signed by the judge (Item 6.91 of MIL). _____

58. Date sale of perishable property is authorized by court--as shown by Order signed by the judge. _____

59. If there is a sale of personal property and court approval is required, complete the following:

    a. Date scheduled for hearing on Sale of Personal Property--as scheduled by clerk of court. _____

    b. Date of Order of Sale of Personal Property--as shown on Order signed by the judge (Item 6.91 of MIL). _____

    c. Date of "Concluding Sale" of Personal Property--as furnished by attorney handling sale (Item 6.92 of MIL). _____

    d. Date of filing Report of Sale of Personal Property--as shown by clerk's file stamp (Item 6.98 of MIL). _____

    e. Date five days after Report of Sale has been filed. _____

    f. Date one day later than the date shown in Item 59e above--This is the earliest date on which the Decree Confirming Sale may be presented for judge's approval. _____

    g. Date of Decree Confirming Sale--as shown on Decree signed by the judge (Item 6.99 of MIL). _____

60. If there is a sale of Real Property and court approval is required, complete the following:

    a. Date scheduled for hearing on Sale of Real Property--as scheduled by clerk of court. _____

    b. Date of Order of Sale of Real Property--as shown on the Order signed by the judge (Item 6.107 of MIL). _____

    c. Date of "Concluding Sale" of Real Property--as to be shown on Report of Sale (Item 6.108 of MIL). _____

    d. Date thirty days after "Concluding Sale" as shown in Item 60c above--This is the date by which the Report of Sale must be filed. _____

Form 13-1: (continued)

    e. Date of filing Report of Sale of Real Property--as shown by clerk's file stamp (Item 6.110 of MIL).   _____

    f. Date five days after Report of Sale has been filed.   _____

    g. Date one day later than the date shown in Item 60f above--This is the earliest date on which Decree Confirming Sale may be presented for judge's approval.   _____

    h. Date of entry of Decree Confirming Sale--as shown on the Decree signed by the judge (Item 6.116 of MIL).   _____

    i. Date of Deed to Real Property--as furnished by attorney handling sale.   _____

61. If there is to be an oil, gas, and mineral lease by private sale and court approval is required, complete the following:

    a. Date of filing Application To Lease--as shown by clerk's file stamp.   _____

    b. Date five days after date of filing Application To Lease as shown in Item 61a above--This is the earliest date on which a hearing may be held.   _____

    c. Date ten days after date of filing Application To Lease as shown in Item 61a above--This is the latest date on which a hearing may be held.   _____

    d. Date scheduled for hearing on Application to Lease--as scheduled by clerk of court (NOTE: This date must not be earlier than the date shown in Item 61b or later than the date shown in Item 61c).   _____

    e. Date of Order Granting Application To Lease--as shown on the Order signed by the judge.   _____

    f. Date thirty days later than the date shown in Item 61e above--This is the latest date by which the lease can be executed without an additional order from the court.   _____

    g. Date of mineral lease--as furnished by attorney handling lease (if the lease approved by the court was not dated, the date shown in Item 61e is the date of the lease for all purposes).   _____

62. Date nine months after federal estate tax return was filed (Refer to Item 9 or 9c(1) of this SDL)--This is the date on which Executor, Administrator, or client can be discharged from personal liability for payment of federal estate taxes if request for early assessment has been filed.   _____

63. Date four years after federal estate tax return was filed (Refer to Item 9 or 9c(1) of this SDL)--This is the date on which proof of payment of all inheritance, estate or succession taxes due to any state or foreign country must be submitted to the IRS.   _____

64. Date IRS determines D's estate qualifies for special use valuation where protective election was filed--as furnished by attorney.   _____

65. Date sixty days after date shown in Item 64--This is the last date to file an amended federal estate tax return with a complete election under IRC Section 2032A.   _____

66. Date IRS determines D's estate qualifies for deferred payment of estate taxes where protective election was filed under IRS Section 6166--As furnished by attorney.   _____

67. Date sixty days after date shown in Item 66--This is the last date to make a complete election under IRC Section 6166 and pay tax and accrued interest then due.   _____

68. Date "closing letter" or notice of final assessment of federal estate taxes was received.   _____

69. Date thirty days following the date shown in Item 68--This is the last date to report the final determination of federal estate taxes to the Comptroller of Public Accounts of the State of Texas, and is also the last day to pay additional federal estate tax assessment without penalty.   _____

70. Date ninety days following the date shown in Item 68--This is the last date to initiate necessary action to collect apportioned death taxes.   _____

Form 13-1: (continued)

71. If claims are presented by creditors, complete the following for each claimant:

   a. Date claim was filed by creditor--as furnished by Executor or Administrator, as shown by clerk's file stamp, or when received in lawyer's office as the case may be. _____

   b. Date thirty days after the date a claim was filed--This is date by which a claim will be automatically disallowed unless allowed by Executor or Administrator. _____

   c. Date claim is allowed by Executor or Administrator--as endorsed on claim itself. _____

   d. Date of filing claim allowed by Executor or Administrator--as shown by clerk's file stamp. _____

   e. Date of Order approving payment of claim--as shown on the Order signed by the judge. _____

   f. Date of disallowance of a claim, if applicable--as furnished by attorney. _____

   g. Date ninety days after claim is disallowed as shown in Item 71b or 71f if applicable--This is the date by which suit must be filed to collect a disallowed claim or it will be barred. _____

72. First Annual Account

   a. Date of filing Account--as shown by clerk's receipt. _____

   b. Date 10 days after filing Account--This is the earliest date that the Account can be acted upon by the court. _____

   c. Date scheduled for hearing on Annual Account--as set by clerk of court. _____

   d. Date of Order Approving Annual Account--as shown on the Order signed by the judge. This date must be later than the date shown in Item 72b above. _____

73. Second Annual Account

   a. Date of filing Account--as shown by clerk's receipt. _____

   b. Date 10 days after filing Account--This is the earliest date that the Account can be acted upon by the court. _____

   c. Date scheduled for hearing on Annual Account--as set by clerk of court. _____

   d. Date of Order Approving Annual Account--as shown on the Order signed by the judge. This date must be later than the date shown in Item 73b above. _____

74. Third Annual Account

   a. Date of filing Account--as shown by clerk's receipt. _____

   b. Date 10 days after filing Account--This is the earliest date that the Account can be acted upon by the court. _____

   c. Date scheduled for hearing on Annual Account--as set by clerk of court. _____

   d. Date of Order Approving Annual Account--as shown on the Order signed by the judge. This date must be later than the date shown in Item 74b above. _____

75. Determination of Heirship in RDA

   a. Date of filing Application to Declare Heirship--as shown by clerk's file stamp. _____

   b. Return date for citation by posting--first Monday following expiration of ten days' notice by posting. _____

   c. Date of newspaper in which citation is published if there is citation by publication--as shown on newspaper. _____

Form 13-1: (continued)

d. Return date for citation by publication--first Monday following expiration of ten days from date of publication.   _____

e. Date which is the latest of Items 75b and 75d--no hearing may be held before this date.   _____

f. Date scheduled for hearing on Application to Declare Heirship--as scheduled by clerk of court.   _____

g. One business day before date of hearing--call witnesses on this day.   _____

h. If hearing rescheduled--enter new date and remember to remind witnesses one business day before new date.   _____

i. Actual date of hearing on Application--as furnished by attorney who appeared in court.   _____

j. Date of Judgment Declaring Heirship--as shown in Order signed by judge.   _____

76. If a Temporary Administration is created, complete the following:

a. Date of filing Application--as shown on receipt issued by clerk of court (Item 6.23 of MIL).   _____

b. Date scheduled for hearing on Application--as scheduled by clerk of the court (Item 6.24 of MIL).   _____

c. One business day before scheduled date for hearing on Application--call witnesses on this date.   _____

d. If hearing on Application is rescheduled--Enter new date and remember to remind witnesses one business day before new date.   _____

e. Actual date of hearing--as furnished by attorney who appeared in Court (Item 6.25 of MIL).   _____

f. Date of Order Appointing Temporary Administrator--as shown in Order signed by judge (Item 6.26 of MIL)--This is the date on which the bond of the Temporary Administrator must be filed.   _____

g. Date three days after date of Order Appointing Temporary Administrator--This is the date by which clerk of court must issue Letters of Temporary Administration and post notice.   _____

h. Date of filing bond--as shown by clerk's file stamp (Item 6.36 of MIL). This date must be the same as the date shown in Item 76f above.   _____

i. Date of filing Oath--as shown by clerk's file stamp (Item 6.38 of MIL).   _____

j. Date which is latest of Items 76h and 76i--This is the date of qualification of Temporary Administrator (Item 6.39 of MIL).   _____

k. Date set by court for expiration of Temporary Administration--as shown in Order signed by judge (Item 6.157 of MIL).   _____

l. Date 180 days after date of Order Appointing Temporary Administrator (Item 76f above)--This is the latest date for expiration of Temporary Administration.   _____

m. Date on which clerk of court first issues Letters of Temporary Administration (Item 6.156 of MIL)--This is the date on which Temporary Administrator must give notice to all heirs.   _____

n. Date on which Temporary Administrator gave notice to heirs--as shown by letter(s) sent to heirs.   _____

o. Date fifteen days after clerk issues Letters of Temporary Administration--Contest of appointment of Temporary Administrator must be filed by this date.   _____

p. Date heir files a request for hearing to contest appointment--as shown by clerk's file stamp.   _____

Form 13-1: (continued)

    q. Date ten days after date on which heir files a request for hearing--This is the date by. which a hearing must be held. _____

    r. Actual date of hearing on contest--as furnished by attorney who appeared in court. _____

77. Account For Final Settlement

    a. Date of filing Account For Final Settlement--as shown by clerk's file stamp (Item 6.146 of MIL). _____

    b. Return date for citation by posting--first Monday following expiration of ten days' notice by posting. _____

    c. Date scheduled for hearing on Account--as scheduled by clerk of court. _____

    d. Date of Order Approving Account and Authorizing Distribution of Estate--as shown in Order signed by judge (Item 6.149 of MIL). _____

78. Closing Estate

    a. Date scheduled for hearing on Application to Close Estate--as scheduled by clerk of court. _____

    b. Date for filing closing report--as set by judge. _____

    c. Actual date of filing closing report--as shown by clerk's file stamp. _____

    d. Date of Order Closing Estate and Discharging Executor or Administrator and Sureties--as shown in Order signed by judge. _____

79. Date all steps have been concluded and Estate is closed--as indicated by attorney. _____

Form 13-2: Letter to Transfer Agent

(Reprinted from <u>Texas Probate System</u>, copyright State Bar of Texas, with permission.)

August 21, 1993

Last National Bank
2400 North Central Expressway
Dallas, Texas 77012-4492

Re: Estate of Paul Smith, Dec'd
Date of death:July 2, 1993
1000 shares of stock in
Anaconda Copper, Inc

Gentlemen:

This letter is to advise you that Decedent died on the above date, the apparent owner of the above described stock.

Please advise me of your requirements for transferring this stock, and forward copies of any forms which must be completed. Thank you very much.

Yours very Truly,

John Teddy

Form 13-3: Affidavit of Domicile

(Reprinted from <u>Texas Probate System</u>, copyright State Bar of Texas, with permission.)

AFFIDAVIT OF DOMICILE

STATE OF TEXAS   ) (

COUNTY OF ROUGH RIDER   ) (

PAULA SMITH, Independent Executrix of the Estate of Paul Smith, Deceased, after being duly sworn, stated that:

My address is 1212 Bullmoose, San Juan Hill, Rough Rider County, Texas. I am personally familiar with the Estate of Paul Smith, Deceased. At the time of death the domicile and legal residence of said decedent was at 1212 Bullmoose. San Juan Hill, Texas. Decedent was domiciled in the State of Texas and was not domiciled in any other state at the time of death.

The transfer of the securities being made by the undersigned is not a sale or exchange but is a distribution of assets of the estate.

It is hereby certified that the delivery and transfer of the attached certificate is not subject to the New York Stock Transfer Tax under Section 28(d) of the Securities Exchange Act of 1934 and that no transaction subject to tax has occurred.

_____

Paula Smith, Independent
Executrix of the Estate
of Paul Smith, Deceased

SUBSCRIBED AND SWORN TO BEFORE ME this _____ day of 1993.

_____

Notary Public, State of Texas

Form 13-4: Form to Transfer Stock

(Reprinted from <u>Texas Probate System</u>, copyright State Bar of Texas, with permission.)

<u>IRREVOCABLE STOCK POWER</u>

For value received, the undersigned does hereby sell assign and transfer to Paul Smith, Jr., 500 shares of Anaconda Copper, Inc. represented by Certificate No. 0002 standing in the name of Peter Smith on the books of said company.

The undersigned does hereby irrevocably constitute and appoint _____ attorney to transfer the said stock on the books of said Company, with full power of substitution in the premises.

Dated: _____

In Presence of: _____

_____
Paula Smith, Independent
Executrix of the Estate
of Paul Smith. Deceased

Form 13-5: Form to Transfer Bonds

(Reprinted from <u>Texas Probate System</u>, copyright State Bar of Texas, with permission.)

IRREVOCABLE BOND POWER

For value received, the undersigned does hereby sell, assign and transfer to Paul Smith, Jr., one bond of Anaconda Copper, Inc. in the principal amount of $20,000.00, No. 123456 standing in the name of Paul Smith on the books of said company.

The undersigned does hereby irrevocably constitute and appoint _____ attorney to transfer the said bond on the books of said Company, with full power of substitution in the premises.

Dated: _____

In Presence of: _____

_____
Paula Smith, Independent
Executrix of the Estate
of Paul Smith. Deceased

Form 13-6: Letter to Transfer Agent to Forward Securities

(Reprinted from <u>Texas Probate System</u>, copyright State Bar of Texas, with permission.)

August 21, 1993

Last National Bank
2400 North Central Expressway
Dallas, Texas 77234-4098

Re; Estate of Paul Smith

Gentlemen:

We enclose the following documents in support of the transfer of securities:
  Power with signature properly guaranteed
  Decedent's death certificate
  Affidavit of domicile
  Original certificate number 0002
  Letters testamentary
  Certified copies of will and order admitting will to probate

Please register the securities as follows:
  Paul Smith, Jr., Social Security No. 466-34-8475
  212 Yellowstone Parkway
  San Juan Hill, Texas 12345

Upon the completion of this transfer, please forward the new certificate <u>in care of this office</u>.
Thank you very much.

Yours very truly,

John Teddy

REGISTERED MAIL, RETURN RECEIPT REQUESTED

Form 13-7: Letter to Insurance Company to Request Claim Forms

(Reprinted from <u>Texas Probate System</u>, copyright State Bar of Texas, with permission.)

August 21, 1993

Nopay Mutual Insurance Company
3456 South Lamar Boulevard
Austin, Texas 77401

Re: Your Policy No. 34559872209844-12
      Insured: Paul Smith
      Date of Death: July 2, 1993

Gentlemen:

This letter is to advise of the fact and date of death of the above named insured. Please advise me of your requirements to effect payment of the policy benefits and send any required forms. Thank you very much.

Yours very truly,

John Teddy

Form 13-8: Letter to Insurance Company to Collect Benefits
(Reprinted from <u>Texas Probate System</u>, copyright State Bar of Texas, with permission.)

August 21, 1993

CERTIFIED MAIL, Return Receipt Requested

Nopay Mutual Insurance Company
2345 S. Lamar Boulevard
Austin, Texas 12345

Re: Your Policy Number 289467485057873948376
       Insured: Paul Smith
       Date of Death: July 2, 1993

Gentlemen:

In accordance with your instructions you will find the following items enclosed with this letter:

1. Certified copy of death certificate
2. Original insurance policy
3. Proof of loss forms

You should make payment to the beneficiary in care of this office. Please furnish this office with three properly completed copies of IRS Form 712 for use in the preparation of the death tax returns. Thank you very much.

Yours very truly,

John Teddy

Enclosures
       Death Certificate
       Policy
       Proof of Loss

14 PROBATE ADMINISTRATION– GUARDIANSHIPS

CHAPTER OBJECTIVES

Upon completion of this chapter, the student should be able to:

1. Understand the laws relating to the guardianship of incapacitated persons.

2. Apply such laws in order to determine which procedures to use in a particular situation, to interview clients, and to obtain necessary information.

3. Prepare an application for guardianship, for both minors and incapacitated adults.

4. Prepare the order of the court in such matters.

5. Convert the inventory, appraisement, and list of claims, sale of estate property, claims, annual accounting, and final accounting documents from previous chapters for use in guardianships.

6. Prepare the documentation necessary to carry out a Section 889 sale of a minor's interest in real or personal property.

CHAPTER GLOSSARY

Attorney ad litem As used in of this chapter, an attorney appointed by the court in guardianship proceedings to represent and advocate on behalf of a proposed ward, incapacitated person, or unborn child.

Court visitor A person appointed by a Probate Court to visit a ward or proposed ward in order to evaluate the ward's living conditions, social, intellectual, physical, and emotional condition, and medical prognosis. In addition, this person may make recommendations regarding modifications in the guardianship or proposed guardianship.

Guardian ad litem A special guardian appointed by the court to represent the interests of a ward in reference to pending litigation. The guardian ad litem only has authority with reference to the litigation.

Guardianship program A local, county, or regional program that provides guardianship and related services to incapacitated persons or other persons who need assistance making decisions concerning their own welfare or financial affairs.

Management trust A trust created by order of the court in a guardianship proceeding. A bank having trust powers must be the trustee. The assets of the estate are put in the trust, thereby allowing the guardianship to be closed.

Missing person A person reported by an executive department of the United States to be a prisoner of war or missing in the course of public service to the United States.

Nonresident guardian A guardian of incapacitated persons appointed by a foreign jurisdiction (one other than Texas) who qualifies to act as guardian in Texas under Section 881 of the Probate Code.

Private professional guardian A person, other than an attorney or corporate fiduciary, who is in the business of providing guardianship services.

Temporary guardian A guardian appointed with limited powers for a limited period of time, not to exceed 60 days, because there appears to be imminent danger to the person or property of the proposed ward and no time to create a permanent guardianship.

INTRODUCTION

In the 1993 legislative session, the Texas Legislature created, in House Bill 2685, what is being referred to as the Texas Guardianship Code. In reality, it is Chapter XIII, Sections 601-892, of the Texas Probate Code. The act creating the new sections concerning the guardianship of **incapacitated persons** and related matters also eliminates references to guardianships or guardians in over 60 sections of the Probate Code and then reenacts almost every one of those sections as part of the sections on guardianship. Several attorneys have expressed the opinion that House Bill 2685 not only was unnecessary (although some amendment to existing guardianship sections was necessary) but also unduly lengthens and complicates the Probate Code and adds costs and attorney's fees to guardianships. Quantitatively, the Guardianship Code changes the laws relating to guardianships, both procedural and substantive, only slightly, despite its great length. Whether there are any significant qualitative changes remains to be seen.

Since the Guardianship Code is so recent, there are still many unanswered questions to be resolved, particularly in reference to **guardianship programs**, **court visitors**, and **private professional guardians**. These are new concepts created by the guardianship code. The necessity of renewing letters of guardianship by filing annual accounts, the requirement of specification of the powers of a guardian, the proof required before a guardianship is created, and other procedural changes may very well produce more problems than are solved.

Section 108 of the Texas Probate Code has been repealed. It had stated that the provisions, rules, and regulations governing estates of decedents also applied to guardianships, whenever not inconsistent with any provisions specifically regulating guardianships. Much of what has already been discussed in this text concerning the procedures of the probate of a decedent's estate, such as the inventory and appraisement, sale of real property, claims procedure, and filing of accounts also was applied to the administration of an estate of a minor or incompetent.

THE GUARDIAN

As for the estates of decedents, Section 676 gives an order of preference of persons qualified to serve as guardians. Section 681 lists the persons who are disqualified to serve as guardians. Section 676 begins by saying that, if the parents live together, both parents, by the marriage, are the natural guardians of the person of the minor, and one of the parents is entitled to be appointed guardian of the child's estate. Parents need not be appointed as guardians of the person of a minor child; they already are such by virtue of the parent/child relationship. As to the estate, parents, like anyone else, must be appointed by the Probate Court; but they are given a prior right to be appointed. Section 676(b) goes on to discuss what occurs in the event of disagreement between the parents regarding which of them should be appointed, what occurs if one parent is dead, and what happens if the parents do not live together.

Section 676(c) then specifies the order of preference concerning the guardians of minors, the first order of preference being to the person appointed by the last surviving parent. Section 676(d) provides that the surviving parent of a minor may by will or other written declaration appoint any qualified person to be guardian of the person of her minor child or children. If the person appointed is not disqualified, she shall also be entitled to be appointed guardian of the estate of the child after the death of the last surviving parent. Next in order of preference comes the nearest ascendent in the direct line, a grandparent or perhaps a great-grandparent. After that comes the nearest of kin; and if there are two or more in the same degree, guardianship is to be based on the best interest of the orphan. Finally, if there is no relative, any qualified person may apply for guardianship; if no one applies, then the court is to appoint a qualified person.

Section 677 stipulates the order of preference concerning the appointment of guardians for incompetents, and someone for whom a guardian needs to be appointed to receive funds due from a governmental source. The first order of preference here is the spouse, then the nearest of kin, then any qualified person.

Section 680 states that if a minor has reached the age of 14, she may by writing choose the guardian, subject to the court's approval. Even when another guardian has been appointed, the minor, upon reaching the age of 14, may select another person; if the court finds that person suitable and that the appointment is in the best interest of the minor, the court is required to remove the existing guardian by revoking the old letters of guardianship and appointing the new person.

In addition, Section 689 says that the court is to make a reasonable effort to consider the incapacitated person's preference concerning the person to be guardian.

Section 679 allows adults to designate by written declaration a person or persons to serve as guardian of the person and/or estate of that adult if she becomes incompetent. Further, the declaration may disqualify persons from serving as guardian of the declarant's person or estate.

Section 681 and, for some reason, Section 110 deal with persons who are disqualified to serve as guardians. They list:

1. Minors.

2. Persons whose conduct is notoriously bad.

3. Incapacitated persons.

4. Persons who are themselves parties to, or whose mother or father is a party to, a lawsuit involving the welfare or estate of the **ward** (subject to two exceptions).

5. Those who are indebted to the ward or to the estate of the ward, unless they first pay the debt.

6. Those asserting an adverse claim on the ward as to the ward's property.

7. Those who are shown to be incapable of properly and prudently managing and controlling the ward or estate by reason of inexperience or lack of education.

8. A person disqualified in a declaration made pursuant to Section 679.

9. A nonresident, unless she designates a resident agent for service.

10. A person disqualified for any other good reason.

APPLICATION

The legal assistant's role in gathering information and preparing the applicable legal documents does not differ much from that already discussed in connection with decedent's estates. Section 682 sets out the requirements of the application for the appointment of guardian. It must be filed in the appropriate county having venue over the guardianship, and must state:

1. The name, sex, date of birth, and address of the person for whom appointment of a guardian is sought.

2. The name, relationship, and address of the person whom the applicant desires to have appointed.

3. The Social Security number of the applicant and of the person, if different, for whom the appointment of guardian is sought.

4. Whether the guardianship is of the person and estate or of either the person or the estate.

5. The nature and degree of the alleged incapacity, the specific areas of protection, and the limitation of rights requested to be included in the order of appointment.

6. The facts that require a guardian to be appointed.

7. The nature and description of any guardianship existing in Texas or any other state.

8. The name and address of any person or entity having the care and custody of the proposed ward.

9. A general description of the property comprising the estate, if guardianship of the estate is sought.

10. The name and address of any person known to hold a power of attorney signed by the proposed ward and a description of the type of powers held by the person.

11. If the person is a minor, the names of the parents, next of kin, whether either or both of the parents are dead, and whether the proposed ward has been the subject of a legal or conservatorship proceeding in the preceding two years, together with the result thereof.

12. If the proposed ward is of the age of 60 or more, the name and address of the proposed ward's spouse, siblings, and children, and if none, the next of kin.

13. If the proposed ward is a **missing person**:

    a. Her last known address.

    b. The name of the executive department, date of report, and last known whereabouts.

    c. Names and addresses of spouse, children, and parents, and if there are none, the next of kin.

14. Facts showing that the court has venue.

15. If applicable, that the person sought to be appointed is a private professional guardian who has complied with Section 697.

Citation is required to issue, and is served by posting. In addition, citation is to be personally served upon the proposed ward (unless a missing person) and the parent (or parents) with whom a minor under age 14 resides. Further, notice by certified or registered mail, return receipt requested, with instructions to deliver to addressee only, must be sent by the applicant to a spouse, all siblings and children of the proposed ward, and any person known to hold a power of attorney by the applicant, or the applicant can request the clerk to send it (probably intended to apply only to wards who are over 60). These requirements are found in Probate Code Section 111, which is not part of the

Guardianship Code. Notice must also be sent to the Veteran's Administration at the regional office by mail if the proposed ward is receiving any benefits from the Veteran's Administration. Any person, other than the ward, may waive service of citation by a written waiver filed with the clerk.

Section 646 requires that the court appoint an **attorney ad litem** to represent the interest of the ward, except in the case of a missing person. To be eligible for appointment, the attorney must be certified by the State Bar as having completed a four-hour course of instruction in guardianship law and procedure as provided for in Section 81.118 of the Government Code. Section 647 lists the duties of the attorney ad litem. An order appointing the attorney ad litem should be prepared at the same time as the application and will usually be signed by the judge at the same time or immediately after the application is filed. Section 645 provides that the court *may* appoint a **guardian ad litem** (not required to be licensed to practice law), but may instead appoint an attorney ad litem in the interest of saving the estate some money.

As an additional protection of the ward or proposed ward, Section 648 requires that each statutory Probate Court operate a court visitor program to assess the condition of wards and proposed wards. It provides that the court visitors be volunteers, insofar as possible. It requires a written report by the court visitor to be filed within 14 days of evaluation, and specifies the contents of the report.

An application in the case of minors is found at Form 14-1 and for an adult incapacitated person at Form 14-3. An order appointing an attorney ad litem is attached as Form 14-5.

THE HEARING

The hearing will be set just as has been discussed in the sections concerning hearings for the probate of a will and the issuance of letters testamentary.

Section 642 of the Probate Code provides that any person has the right to appear and contest the appointment of a particular person as guardian or to contest any proceeding she deems injurious to the ward. This contrasts with the language dealing with the estates of decedents, which says that any interested person has the right to appear and contest. The reason for this difference is that the law presumes that every person is interested in the welfare of minors and incompetents. However, Section 642(b) prohibits a person who has an interest adverse to the ward from contesting the creation of a guardianship or the appointment of a guardian.

At the hearing, the court must find that the person for whom a guardian is to be appointed is incapacited. In addition, the court must find that it has venue; that the person to be appointed is eligible; that the rights of persons and property will be protected by the appointment of a guardian; that if the guardianship is of a minor the guardianship is not done primarily to enable the minor to establish residency for an enrollment in a school or school district to which she would otherwise not be entitled to enroll; and if the proposed ward is a missing person, that she was reported missing at least six months prior to the filing of the application.

The court must require strict proof of each element. A determination of incapacity of an adult, other than a missing person or one who must have a guardian appointed to receive funds from a governmental source, must be based on evidence of recurring acts or occurrences within the preceding six months and not be isolated instances of negligence or bad judgment.

The proposed ward is entitled, on request, to a jury trial; and, except for a missing person, the proposed ward's presence in court is mandatory, unless the court determines that appearance is unnecessary. The court can, at the request of the proposed ward, close the hearing to the public.

Section 112A requires that no guardianship be opened unless the applicant presents to the court a letter or certificate from a physician licensed in Texas stating:

1. That the proposed ward, in the opinion of the physician, is incapacitated.

2. The general nature of the incapacity.

In addition, it allows the court to appoint physicians to examine the proposed ward and to require reports by such physicians. If the basis for a determination of incapacity is mental retardation, then such an examination is necessary, along with additional requirements.

Section 112A makes no exception for minors, missing persons, or persons who need a guardian appointed for the purpose of receiving funds from governmental sources. (One might be slightly curious concerning how to obtain an examination of a missing person or why one might be necessary for a minor or, for that matter, for a person who must have a guardian in order to continue receiving funds from the Veteran's Administration.)

At the hearing, the court is required to:

1. Inquire into the ability of any allegedly incapacitated person to feed, clothe, and shelter herself, to care for her own physical health, and to manage her property and financial affairs.

2. Ascertain the age of any proposed ward who is a minor.

3. Inquire into the governmental reports concerning any missing person or persons who must have a guardian appointed to receive funds from a governmental source.

4. Determine the qualifications, abilities, and capabilities of the person seeking to be appointed as guardian.

Section 690 states that only one person can be appointed as guardian of the person or estate, but one person may be appointed guardian of the person and another guardian of the estate. Excepted from this rule is the joint appointment of husband and wife, and of coguardians who are duly appointed by the law of some sister state, country, or the District of Columbia.

Section 676(a) provides that the surviving parent of a minor may by a will or other written declaration appoint any qualified person to be guardian of the person of her children after her death; if the person appointed as guardian is not disqualified, then she is entitled to be appointed as guardian of the estate also.

Section 693 states that if the court finds that an adult possesses the capacity to care for herself and manage her property as would a reasonably prudent person, then the application is to be dismissed. If the ward is found to be totally without capacity, the court must recite this finding in its order and may appoint a person with full authority over the incapacitated person. If, on the other hand, the court finds that the ward lacks capacity to do some, but not all, of the tasks necessary to care for herself, the court is to appoint an individual with limited powers, and to permit the ward to care for herself or manage her property to the extent of her abilities.

Sections 692 and 693 both state what must be included in the order appointing a guardian:

1. The name of the person appointed.
2. The name of the ward.
3. Whether the guardian is of the person or estate, or both.
4. The amount of any bond required.
5. If the guardianship is of an estate, and the court deems that an appraisal is necessary, the names of one or more, but not more than three, disinterested persons to appraise the estate.
6. That the clerk issue letters of guardianship to the person appointed once that person qualifies.
7. The specific powers, limitations, or duties of the guardian.
8. If necessary, the amount of funds from the corpus of the estate that the court will allow the guardian to spend for the education and maintenance of the ward, as provided for in Section 776.

Upon application, the powers, limitations, or duties may be changed based on a change in the ward's incapacity.

Sections 696, 697, and 698 provide for the appointment and registration of private professional guardians. This is a concept created by the Guardianship Code and yet to be tested on a statewide basis.

Section 881 presents a procedure for the recognition of **nonresident guardians** appointed in foreign jurisdictions. This resembles the procedures dealing with the probate of a foreign will, although there are differences.

Examples of orders are included as Forms 14-2 and 14-4.

PROCEDURES DURING ADMINISTRATION

The procedures concerning oaths and bonds are virtually unchanged by the Guardianship Code and are the same as those for executors and administrators. However, rather than the oaths and bonds of guardians being dealt with in connection with the other personal representatives, the sections dealing with other representatives were duplicated as Sections 699-706. Bonds are mandatory, except where the guardian is a corporate fiduciary or has been appointed in a will by a last surviving parent and the will waives the requirement of a bond.

The procedure for presentation of claims against the estate is virtually the same as with the estates of decedents. The guardian is required to give the same forms of notice as is the executor/administrator of an estate. However, not many attorneys give the required notices, to judge by the legal notices in the newspapers. When the legislature copied the claims procedures and renumbered them as Sections 783-809, they failed to make a number of necessary changes. For instance, Section 783 refers to the requirement of giving notice to the comptroller if the "decedent" had been paying state taxes prior to death.

It makes no difference when the claim is presented to the guardian, as long as this is prior to the time the estate is closed and prior to the barring of the claim under the applicable statute of limitations. Also, claims against an estate of a ward are not classified, but rather paid in the following order:

1. Expenses for the care, maintenance and education of the ward or her dependents.

2. Funeral expenses or expenses of last illness if the guardianship is kept open after the death of the ward, provided that claims that have been allowed and approved prior to death are paid prior to the funeral expenses and expenses of last illness.

3. Expenses of administration.

4. Other claims against the estate.

With regard to the sale of real and personal property belonging to the estate of a ward, the only difference in the procedure between that carried out in the case of the estate of a ward and that in the case of a decedent is in the permissible reasons for sale. Section 820 holds that application may be made by a guardian to sell property of the estate in order to:

1. Pay expenses of administration, allowances, and claims against the ward, and pay funeral expenses upon the ward's death.

2. Make up the deficiency when the income of a ward's estate and the personal property of it and the proceeds from previous sales are insufficient for the education and maintenance of the ward or to pay debts against the estate.

3. Dispose of the property of an estate of a ward that consists of an undivided interest in real estate.

4. Dispose of real estate of a ward, any part of which is not productive or does not produce sufficient revenues to make a fair return.

5. Conserve the estate of a ward by selling mineral interest or royalties of minerals and place.

The new Guardianship Code makes some substantial changes with regard to the annual accounting practice. This has always been a problem with guardianships. In a majority of guardianships, the requirements concerning the filing of annual accounts are ignored unless the probate judge is unusually vigilant.

Section 659(b) now provides that letters of guardianship expire one year plus 120 days after their issuance. Section 659(c) stipulates that the clerk is to renew letters of guardianship upon the receipt and approval by the court of the annual accounting. Hence, the guardian's authority automatically expires unless annual accounting requirements are complied with.

In regard to the account itself, in addition to the information already required as discussed in Chapter Eleven, the guardian must certify that the bond premium has been paid and that the guardian has filed all tax returns and paid all taxes, along with the amount of the tax, the date it was paid, and the name of the governmental agency to which it was paid. The court can waive the requirement of filing annual accounts where the estate produces negligible or fixed income.

Section 743 sets out requirements concerning the filing of an annual account by a guardian of the person where there is a separate guardian (or no guardian) of the estate.

The procedure for closing an estate is the same as with decedent's estates. A guardianship must be closed when:

1. The minor ward dies or becomes an adult, except that, upon death, the guardian must make all funeral arrangements and pay the funeral expenses and the expenses of last illness before closing by filing a final account.

2. A ward dies, after payment of funeral and last illness expenses, or has been restored to sound mind or sober habits.

3. The spouse of a married ward has qualified as a survivor in community and the ward owns no separate property.

4. The estate of a ward has become exhausted.

5. The foreseeable income accruing to a ward or her estate is so negligible that to maintain a guardianship would be burdensome.

6. All of the assets have been placed in a **management trust** and the court decides that the guardianship is no longer necessary.

7. The court determines for any reason that the guardianship is no longer necessary.

The new concept of management trusts is found in Sections 867-873; which state that the court may enter an order creating a trust for the benefit of the ward, if the court finds this to be in the best interests of the ward. The order is to direct that the assets of the estate be transferred to a state or national bank having trust powers and is to include the terms and conditions of the trust as provided in Section 868. The order can continue the trust until a minor's 25th birthday.

The guardian of a ward does two things during the pendency of the guardianship that have no real parallel in the estates of decedents. One is to expend funds for the benefit of the ward; the other is to invest the assets of the estate. Section 776 requires the guardian to have the court's approval to spend more than the net income of the estate. There has been some question regarding the interpretation of the predecessor section to Section 236(a), which was basically worded identically. However, the case law seems to indicate that the guardian has the right to spend the income from the assets of the estate without prior approval of the court, provided it is spent for the education and maintenance of the ward. To the extent, however, that it is necessary to expend the principal of the estate, the guardian must have prior court approval. An exception to the requirement of prior court approval is found in Section 776(b), which says that the guardian may spend during an annual accounting period up $5,000 from corpus without first obtaining the approval of the court if it is not convenient or possible to first secure approval. If thereafter the guardian proves by clear and convincing evidence that the expenditures were reasonable and proper, and the court would have granted the authority to make such expenditures out of the principle of the estate, then the courts may approve the same.

With regard to the investment of estate assets, the guardian of a ward has responsibilities that do not extend to the executor/administrator of an estate. The guardian is obligated to manage the estate as well as to take care of it. Section 768 says that the personal representative of an estate "shall take care of and manage the property of the estate as a prudent person would manage the person's own property." Section 768 also states that the guardian "is entitled to the possession and management of all properties belonging to the ward." The guardian is required to account for all rents, profits, and revenues that the estate would have produced by such prudent management.

The permissible investments both with and without court approval are found in subpart K of Chapter XIII, Sections 853-864.

APPLICATION TO SELL PROPERTY UNDER SECTION 889

Section 889 provides a method by which a natural or adoptive parent of a minor may receive from the court an order to sell either real or personal property of the minor without first being appointed guardian. This section is applicable when the value of the minor's interest in the property does not exceed $25,000. It requires the parent to make application under oath for the sale of the property. Venue for the application is the same as for an application for the appointment of a guardian of a minor. The application must contain the following information:

1. The legal description of the real property or a description of the personal property.

2. The name of the minor or minors and their interest in the property.

3. The name of the prospective purchaser.

4. A statement that the sale of the minor's interest is for cash.

5. A statement that all funds received by the parent will be used for the use and benefit of the minor.

Once the application has been filed, the court is required to set a hearing for a date not less than five days from the date of application and, if the court deems necessary, to order a citation to be issued. If at the hearing the court is satisfied from the evidence that the sale is in the best interest of the minor, it orders the sale of the property and may require an independent appraisal of the property to be sold to establish a minimum sales price.

Once the property has been sold pursuant to the order of sale and the transaction has been completely closed, the purchaser of the property is required to pay the proceeds of the sale belonging to the minor into the registry of the court. This is normally done in the form of a check in which the payee is:

> The Clerk of the _____ County Court for the use and benefit of _____ and _____, minors, under order of sale issued in cause no. _____, style the Estate of _____ and _____ and _____, Minors."

Finally, Section 889 states that the monies may be withdrawn from the registry of the court under Section 885 of the Texas Probate Code; which provides that the father or mother or unestranged spouse of a ward or a child whose interest in real property or personal property has been sold pursuant to Section 889 may withdraw up to $25,000 upon the filing with the clerk of a written application and bond approved by the county judge. The bond is to be for double the amount of money withdrawn payable to the judge or his successors in office, and is to stipulate that the money will be used for the benefit of the minor. When the custodian has expended the money and otherwise complied with the terms of the bond, she is required to file with the county clerk a sworn report accounting for expenditures of the funds. Forms for sale of a minor's interest and withdrawal of funds are included as Forms 14-6 through 14-9.

TEMPORARY GUARDIANSHIP

As with the estates of decedents, a temporary administration may be opened for the persons or estates of minors incapacitated adults. Section 875 gives this procedure. It first states that a guardian may be appointed for the person or estate of a minor or an incapacitated person, referred to as *respondent* in these sections. A **temporary guardian** can be appointed either with or without the filing of an application. If appointed without the filing of written application, then a written application must be filed no later than the end of the next court business day after the appointment. The application is required to state:

1. The name and address of the subject of the guardianship procedure.
2. The alleged imminent danger to the person or property.
3. The type of appointment and the particular protection and assistance being requested.
4. The facts and reasons supporting the allegations and requests.
5. The name, address, and qualifications of the proposed temporary guardian.
6. The name, address, and interest of the applicant.
7. The Social Security numbers of the applicant and the respondent.
8. If applicable, that the proposed temporary guardian is a private professional guardian who has complied with the requirements of Section 667.

An attorney is to be appointed either upon the filing of the application or at the appointment of the guardian if done before an application is filed. This is only where the respondent has not engaged independent counsel.

A hearing must be held within 10 days of the filing, and the temporary guardianship will expire at the hearing unless the respondent or her attorney consents that the order be extended for a longer period (not to exceed 60 days from the date of the filing of the application). At the hearing, if the court determines that there is an imminent danger to the physical health or safety of the respondent or that the respondent's estate will be seriously damaged or dissipated unless immediate action is taken, it will appoint a temporary guardian by written order, assigning to the guardian only those duties and powers necessary to protect against the dangers shown. The order must describe the duties and the powers to be exercised by the guardian. No temporary guardianship may remain in effect for longer than 60 days, except as provided in Section 875(k).

For some reason, Section 875 fails to cover the transmutation of the temporary guardianship into a permanent guardianship, although it does mention this in subsection k. Regardless, that procedure is customarily used by attorneys and approved by courts.

Finally, Sections 883 and 884 provide for an informal community administration by the spouse of an incapacitated person.

CHAPTER QUESTIONS AND EXERCISES

1. What is the order of preference concerning the appointment of a guardian of a minor?

2. What requirement is made for citation for the guardianship of minors or incapacitated persons?

3. Are the Probate Code sections applicable to the estates of decedents in any way applicable to guardianships? If so, how?

4. When must a guardianship be closed?

5. Describe the procedures necessary to sell property of a minor without the creation of a guardianship. When property of a minor is sold under Section 889, what happens to the proceeds or money derived from the sale?

6. When may a temporary guardianship be created, and how long may it last?

7. Sam Chavez has died without a will. He is survived by his wife, Juana, and two minor children, Sam, Jr., and Juanita (his child by a former marriage which ended in the death of Juanita's mother; Juanita has been left in the custody of Juana). He left a home, some money in the bank, two automobiles, personal effects and furniture. His surviving spouse needs to sell the house and to get control of the bank accounts in order to move and to have funds to support her and the children. After consultation with the spouse, your attorney directs you to prepare an application for guardianship, an oath, and an order granting the guardianship. Do so.

8. Sydney Sain's father, who is a widower, has begun to act bizarre. She has taken him to his doctor, who says that he is incapable of managing his affairs and is in need of close supervision. Father, who is 57 years of age and resides in your county, has a house, some money in the bank, and other things that need to be managed, which Father is incompetent to do.

   Your attorney instructs you to prepare the application, oath, and order necessary to open a guardianship for the father. Do so.

9. Ima Widder's husband is dead. Ima's husband's parents have died without a will, and he was an only child. The only real asset is the grandparent's home, which Ima needs to sell. There was money in the bank, but it was in joint survivorship accounts and consequently was paid to Ima upon the death of the grandparents. The home is valued at $42,500. Ima has two minor children and she

desperately needs to sell the property because she cannot afford to make the payments.

After your attorney talks to Ima, she tells you he believes it would be cheapest to sell the minor's property under Section 889 of the Probate Code and that a guardianship should be unnecessary. He proposes to use an affidavit of heirship to reflect the children's right as the sole heirs of the grandparents. Supplying any other information you might need, prepare all documents to accomplish this task.

Form 14-1: Application for Appointment of Guardian (Minors)

NO._____

IN THE MATTER OF	§	IN THE PROBATE COURT
	§	
PETER SMITH, JR. and	§	OF
PENELOPE SMITH,	§	
	§	
MINORS	§	ROUGH RIDER COUNTY, TEXAS

APPLICATION FOR APPOINTMENT OF GUARDIAN

TO THE HONORABLE COURT:

PAULA SMITH, Applicant, makes this her application for the appointment of a guardian of the person and estate of **PETER SMITH, JR.** and **PENELOPE SMITH**, and in support thereof respectfully shows:

I.

That said **PETER SMITH, JR.**, a male, born on March 17, 1990 and **PENELOPE SMITH**, a female, born September 2, 1991, are minors, and respectively, reside at 252 Yellowstone Parkway San Juan Hill, Rough Rider County, Texas 79231, and are without a guardian of their person or estate.

II.

That Applicant desires to be appointed as guardian of the persons and estates of **PETER SMITH, JR.** and **PENELOPE SMITH**.

III.

That a general description of the property comprising the estate of the said **PETER SMITH, JR.** and **PENELOPE SMITH** is as follows: An undivided one-half (1/2) interest in the Northwest 30 feet of Lot Eleven (11), all of Lot Eighteen (18), and the Southeast 15.5 feet of Lot Twelve (12), Block 83, of White Cliffs, an Addition to the City of San Juan Hill, Rough Rider County, Texas, as shown by the map or plat thereof, recorded in Volume 4, Page 107, Map Records, Rough Rider County, Texas, and it is of the probable value of less than ONE HUNDRED THOUSAND AND 00/100 DOLLARS ($100,000.00).

IV.

That a guardian should be appointed, and that there is a necessity that one be appointed, because of the following facts: **PETER SMITH, JR.** and **PENELOPE SMITH** are minors. That Applicant **PAULA SMITH** is the mother of **PETER SMITH, JR.** and **PENELOPE SMITH** and said minors have inherited certain property from their grandfather **PAVLOV PROBATE**, Deceased, and that said property should be managed by a guardian for the use and benefit of said minors. That **PAULA SMITH**, whom Applicant desires to be appointed as guardian of the persons and estates of **PETER SMITH, JR.** and **PENELOPE SMITH** is proper person to act as such guardian and is entitled to be so appointed; and that her address is 252 Yellowstone Parkway, San Juan Hill, Rough Rider County, Texas 79231.

V.

That a guardianship of both the persons and estates of **PETER SMITH, JR.** and **PENELOPE SMITH** is sought. No other guardianships existing this or any other county.

VI.

That this Court has venue over this proceeding because the residence of Applicant is Rough Rider County, Texas and Applicant has custody of said minors.

VII.

Neither of said minors have been the subject of any legal or conservatorship proceeding within the proceeding two-year period.

VIII.

Applicant's social security no. is 420-26-4340, **PETER SMITH, JR.'s** social security no. is 454-20-5555, and **PENELOPE SMITH's** social security no. is 453044-2222.

THEREFORE, Applicant prays that notice be given as required by law, and that the said **PAULA SMITH** be appointed guardian of the persons and estates of **PETER SMITH JR.** and **PENELOPE SMITH**.

Respectfully submitted,

PAULA SMITH

JOHN TEDDY
State Bar No. 00000100
5155 Teton Pkwy., Suite 206
P.O. Box 186
Corpus Christi, TX 79421
(512) 555-1234 Telephone
(512) 555-5678 FAX

ATTORNEY FOR THE ESTATE

Form 14-2: Order Appointing Guardian (Minors)

NO. 20990-3

IN THE MATTER OF	§	IN THE PROBATE COURT
	§	
PETER SMITH, JR. and	§	OF
PENELOPE SMITH,	§	
	§	
MINORS	§	ROUGH RIDER COUNTY, TEXAS

ORDER APPOINTING GUARDIAN

This the _____ day of _____, 19____, came on to be heard in the above-entitled and numbered proceeding, the application of **PAULA SMITH**, for Letters of Guardianship of the persons and estates of **PETER SMITH JR.** and **PENELOPE SMITH**, minors, and it appearing to the Court, and the Court being satisfied after due hearing, that notice of said application has been given as required by law, and that **PETER SMITH JR.** and **PENELOPE SMITH** have no lawful guardian of their estates or persons, and the said **PAULA SMITH** is not disqualified to act as guardian and is entitled to be appointed such guardian, that it will be to the benefit and interest of said **PETER SMITH JR.** and **PENELOPE SMITH** that she be so appointed, in that **PETER SMITH JR.** and **PENELOPE SMITH** must be cared for and their rights of person and property protected, and that this Court has venue and jurisdiction of the proceeding and subject matter and of all persons of who the law requires that jurisdiction be had.

It is therefore ORDERED that the said **PAULA SMITH** be, and she is hereby, appointed guardian of the persons and estates of the said **PETER SMITH JR.** and **PENELOPE SMITH**, with full authority subject to no limitations, and that letters issue to her on her giving bond in the sum of _____ dollars which is the proper sum hereby ordered and fixed in accordance with the requirements of the law, payable and conditioned as required by law, and taking the oath required by law, each within twenty (20) days.

It is further ORDERED that such security and any cash or other security in lieu or addition thereof, shall be subject to the further orders of this Court.

It is further ORDERED that there being no need for appraisers the guardian herein appointed is directed to return an inventory and appraisement.

It is further ORDERED that the clerk of this Court issue letters of guardianship to the said **PAULA SMITH** when she has qualified according to law.

SIGNED AND ORDERED ENTERED this _____ day of _____, 1993.

_____
JUDGE PRESIDING

Form 14-3: Application for Appointment of Guardian (Incapacitated Person)

NO._____

IN THE MATTER OF	§	IN THE PROBATE COURT
PETER SMITH	§	OF
AN INCAPACITATED	§	ROUGH RIDER COUNTY, TEXAS

APPLICATION FOR APPOINTMENT OF GUARDIAN

TO THE HONORABLE COURT:

PAULA SMITH, social security no. 420-26-4340, makes this her application for the appointment of a guardian of the person and estate of **PETER SMITH**, and in support thereof respectfully shows:

I.

That said **PETER SMITH**, Social Security No. 280-92-4242, is a incapacitated male person, was born on the 25th day of March, 1905, resides at San Juan Hill Nursing Home at 123 Teton Street, Rough Rider County, Texas, and is without a guardian of his person or estate.

II.

That Applicant desires to be appointed as guardian of the person and estate of **PETER SMITH**.

III.

That a general description of the property comprising the estate of the said **PETER SMITH** is as follows: An undivided one-half (1/2) interest in the Northwest 30 feet of Lot Eleven (11), all of Lot Eighteen (18), and the Southeast 15.5 feet of Lot Twelve (12), Block 83, of White Cliffs, an Addition to the City of San Juan Hill, Rough Rider County, Texas, as shown by the map or plat thereof, recorded in Volume 4, Page 107, Map Records, Rough Rider County, Texas, cash in banks miscellaneous personal property, and an interest in a pension or retirement plan at Kansas City Paint Co. of the probable value of more than ONE HUNDRED THOUSAND AND 00/100 DOLLARS ($100,000.00).

IV.

That a guardian should be appointed, and that there is a necessity that one be appointed, because of the following facts: **PETER SMITH** is incapacitated and completely is unable to manage his own affairs and property or to care for himself. That **PAULA SMITH**, whom Applicant desires to be appointed as guardian of the person and estate of **PETER SMITH** is the spouse of said **PETER SMITH** and is a proper person to act as such guardian and is entitled to be so appointed; and that her address is 1412 Bullmoose, San Juan Hill, Rough Rider County, Texas.

V.

That a guardianship of both the person and estate of **PETER SMITH** is sought.

VI.

That this court has venue over this proceeding because the residence of **PETER SMITH** is Rough Rider County, Texas and the principal portion of his estate is situated in Rough Rider County, Texas.

VII

PETER SMITH has had only two children born to him:

a. **PETER SMITH JR.**, 252 Yellowstone Parkway, San Juan Hill, Rough Rider County, Texas 79231.

b. **PENELOPE SMITH**, 721 Monolle Drive, San Juan Hill, Rough Rider County, Texas 79231.

PETER SMITH has one living brother and no sisters. The brother's name is **PAUL SMITH** and his address is 1317 Havana Street, San Juan Hill, Rough Rider County, Texas.

THEREFORE, applicant prays that notice be given as required by law, and that the said **PAULA SMITH** be appointed guardian of the person and estate of said **PETER SMITH**.

Respectfully submitted,

PAULA SMITH

By: _____
Attorney for Applicant

Form 14-4: Order Appointing Guardian

NO. 19,900-2

IN THE MATTER OF	§	IN THE PROBATE COURT
PETER SMITH	§	OF
AN INCAPACITATED PERSON	§	ROUGH RIDER COUNTY, TEXAS

ORDER APPOINTING GUARDIAN

This the _____ day of June, 1992, came on to be heard in the above-entitled and numbered proceeding, the application of **PAULA SMITH** for Letters of Guardianship of the person and estate of **PETER SMITH**, an Incapacitated Person, and it appearing to the Court, and the Court being satisfied after due hearing, that due notice of said application has been given as required by law, and that said **PETER SMITH** has no lawful guardian of his estate or person, and the said **PAULA SMITH** is not disqualified to act as guardian and is entitled to be appointed such guardian, that it will be to the benefit and interest of such **PETER SMITH** that she be so appointed, in that **PETER SMITH** is mentally incapable of caring for himself or managing his property and financial affairs, and that this Court has venue and jurisdiction of the proceeding and subject matter and of all persons of whom the law requires that jurisdiction be had.

It is therefore ORDERED that the said **PAULA SMITH** be, and she is hereby, appointed guardian of the person and estate of the said **PETER SMITH**, with complete authority, and that letters issue to her on her giving bond in the sum of _____ dollars which is the proper sum hereby ordered and fixed in accordance with the requirements of the law, payable and conditioned as required by law, and taking the oath required by law, each within twenty (20) days.

It is further ORDERED that such security and any cash or other security in lieu or addition thereto, shall be subject to the further orders of this Court.

It is further ORDERED that there being no need for appraisers the guardian herein appointed is directed to return an inventory and appraisement.

It is further ORDERED that the clerk of this Court issue letters of guardianship to the said **PAULA SMITH** when she has qualified according to law.

SIGNED AND ORDERED ENTERED this _____ day of June, 1992.

_____
JUDGE PRESIDING

Form 14-5: Order Appointing Attorney Ad Litem

NO. 20,990-3

IN THE MATTER OF	§	IN THE PROBATE COURT
	§	
PETER SMITH, JR. and	§	OF
PENELOPE SMITH,	§	
	§	
MINORS	§	ROUGH RIDER COUNTY, TEXAS

ORDER APPOINTING ATTORNEY AD LITEM

It having come to the attention of the Court that the above named minors are without representation in this cause, **DONALD SPAIN**, Attorney at Law, is hereby appointed as Attorney Ad Litem for said minors, to represent and defend their interest in proceedings before this Court.

SIGNED AND ORDERED ENTERED, this the _____ day of June, 1992.

_____
JUDGE PRESIDING

Form 14-6: Section 889 Sale of Minor's Interest in Real Estate

NO._____

IN THE MATTER OF	§	IN THE PROBATE COURT
	§	
PETER SMITH, JR. and	§	OF
PENELOPE SMITH,	§	
	§	
MINORS	§	ROUGH RIDER COUNTY, TEXAS

APPLICATION FOR SALE OF REAL ESTATE

This Application for Sale of Real Estate under the provisions of Section 889 of Texas Probate Code, is made by **PAULA SMITH**, as mother, and on behalf of her minor children, **PETER SMITH, JR.** and **PENELOPE SMITH**, and in this connection Applicant will show the following:

I.

The legal description of the property sought to be sold is Lot Thirty-nine (39), Block Four (4), CUBAN TERRACE, a Subdivision in the City of San Juan Hill, Rough Rider County, Texas, as shown by map or plat thereof, recorded in volume 23, Page 80, Map Records, Rough Rider County, Texas.

II.

The name of the minors owning an interest in said property are **PETER SMITH, JR.** and **PENELOPE SMITH** who each own an undivided one-fourth (1/4) interest in the property.

III.

The property is being purchased by JOHN E. and ANNIE S. KING who are paying said minors cash for their interest, which amount will be less than TWENTY FIVE THOUSAND AND 00/100 DOLLARS ($25,000.00).

IV.

Applicant will use all funds received from the sale of such property for the use and benefit of such minors.

V.

The sale of such undivided interest is deemed advisable and to the best interest of the minor.

Applicant respectfully requests that a hearing be set upon this Application and an Order of Sale be entered for such minors' interest pursuant to the terms and under the authority of Section 339-A, Texas Probate Code.

Respectfully submitted,

By: _____
Attorney for Applicant

STATE OF TEXAS	§
COUNTY OF ROUGH RIDER	§

Before me, the undersigned authority, on this day personally appeared **PAULA SMITH**, to me well known, and after by me being first duly sworn, on her oath deposes and says:

My name is **PAULA SMITH**. I am the same person who makes the above and foregoing Application for Appointment for Sale of Real Estate and I have read the same and all assertions and allegations therein are true and correct.

_____
PAULA SMITH

SUBSCRIBED AND SWORN TO BEFORE me, this the _____ day of _____, 1992.

_____
Notary Public, State of Texas

Form 14-7: Order of Sale (Section 889)

NO. 25352-1

IN THE MATTER OF	§	IN THE PROBATE COURT
	§	
PETER SMITH, JR. and	§	OF
PENELOPE SMITH,	§	
	§	
MINORS	§	ROUGH RIDER COUNTY, TEXAS

ORDER OF SALE

This day of June, 1992, came on to be considered the Application for Sale of Real Estate by **PAULA SMITH**, as Mother, and on behalf of her minor children, **PETER SMITH, JR.** and **PENELOPE SMITH**, and come the Applicant in person and by her attorney.

It being determined no notice is required and the matter is before the Court and the Court has jurisdiction of the proceedings, parties and property, the Court proceeded to hear evidence in the matter and makes the following findings and conclusions:

1. The minor children of applicant are **PETER SMITH, JR.** and **PENELOPE SMITH**, and they are presently residing with and under the custody of applicant, **PAULA SMITH**.

2. The grandfather of said minor children, **PAVLOV SMITH**, died March 3, 1992, in Rough Rider County, Texas, intestate, and said minors, inherited a (1/2) interest in the real estate hereinafter described.

3. That said minors each own an individual one-fourth (1/4) interest in the following described real property, to-wit:

   Lot Thirty-nine (39), Block Four (4), CUBAN TERRACE, a Subdivision in the City of San Juan Hill, Rough Rider County, Texas, as shown by map or plat thereof, recorded in volume 23, Page 80, Map Records, Rough Rider County, Texas.

4. Applicant has a bona fide sale of said property to JOHN E. and ANNIE S. KING, under and by virtue of the terms of which sale said minors will receive approximately FIVE THOUSAND TWO HUNDRED FORTY-TWO AND 20/100 ($5,242.20) each, and the Court is satisfied and it is herein determined that such sale is to the best interest of said minors.

IT IS THEREFORE ORDERED, ADJUDGED and DECREED that **PAULA SMITH**, sell said property, and that the proceeds of such sale belonging to said minors be paid into the registry of this Court, and that **PAULA SMITH** be allowed to withdraw such funds upon making application and bond, in accordance with Article 144, Probate Code, State of Texas.

It is FURTHER ORDERED that a certified copy of this Order by filed in the Deed Records of Rough Rider County, Texas.

SIGNED and ORDER ENTERED this _____ day of June, 1992.

_____
JUDGE PRESIDING

Form 14-8: Motion to Withdraw Funds Deposited

NO. 25352-1

IN THE MATTER OF	§	IN THE PROBATE COURT
	§	
PETER SMITH, JR. and	§	OF
PENELOPE SMITH,	§	
	§	
MINORS	§	ROUGH RIDER COUNTY, TEXAS

MOTION TO WITHDRAW FUNDS DEPOSITED

Now comes, **PAULA SMITH**, the natural mother of **PETER SMITH, JR.** and **PENELOPE SMITH**, and on behalf of her minor children, **PETER SMITH, JR.** and **PENELOPE SMITH**, requests the Court for permission to withdraw the funds so deposited heretofore and for such would show the Court the following:

HERETOFORE, the sum of FIVE THOUSAND TWO HUNDRED FORTY-TWO AND 20/100 DOLLARS ($5,242.20) was deposited for the benefit of **PETER SMITH, JR.** and **PENELOPE SMITH**, the said minor children. **PAULA SMITH** as the natural mother of such children now requests that she be allowed to withdraw the funds from the Registry of the County Clerk and to use them for the use and benefit of said minors as their interest might lie under the control and direction of the Court and does hereby bind herself so to do.

WHEREFORE, PREMISES CONSIDERED, **PAULA SMITH** requests permission of the Court to withdraw said funds from the Registry of the Court.

PAULA SMITH

By: _____
  Attorney for Applicant

ORDER OF THE COURT

On this _____ day of June, 1992, the Court having had presented to it the above motion and bond in double the amount of monies now on deposit with the Clerk of this Court; finds that said motion is in order and said bond is sufficient.

It is accordingly ORDERED that said Motion be granted, said bond filed and the Clerk of this Court shall disburse such funds to **PAULA SMITH** for the use and benefit of the minors.

_____
JUDGE PRESIDING

Form 14-9: Bond to Withdraw Minor's Funds

NO. 25352-1

IN THE MATTER OF	§	IN THE PROBATE COURT
	§	
PETER SMITH, JR. and	§	OF
PENELOPE SMITH,	§	
	§	
MINORS	§	ROUGH RIDER COUNTY, TEXAS

KNOW ALL MEN BY THESE PRESENTS:

That we **PAULA SMITH**, as Principal and Continental Assurance Co., as surety, are firmly bound unto the County Judge of Rough Rider County, Texas, to his or their successors in office, in the amount of TWENTY THOUSAND FOUR HUNDRED NINETY-SIX AND 80/100 ($20, 496.80) to the payment which well and truly to be made, we do hereby bind ourselves, our heirs, executors and administrators, firmly by these presents:

The condition of the above obligation is such that whereas said above described minor children, **PETER SMITH, JR.** and **PENELOPE SMITH**, received as proceeds of the sale of real estate in which they had an interest, the amount of FIVE THOUSAND TWO HUNDRED FORTY-TWO AND 20/100 ($5,242.20) each, in the above styled and numbered cause in this Court, and that upon approval of this bond the said **PAULA SMITH** will pay said money, with lawful interest thereon, to the person entitled to receive the same, when ordered by the Court and that she will use such money for the benefit of the owners thereof under the direction of the court.

NOW, THEREFORE, if the said **PAULA SMITH**, her heirs, executors and administrators, shall well and truly pay said money, with lawful interest thereon, to the persons entitled to receive the same, when ordered by the Court to do so, and shall use such money for the use and benefit of the owners under the direction of the Court, then the above obligation shall be null and void; otherwise, it shall remain in full force and effect.

WITNESS OUR HAND, this the _____ day of _____ , 1992.

_____
PAULA SMITH

_____
SURETY

15 PROBATE ADMINISTRATION– TAXATION

CHAPTER OBJECTIVES

Upon completion of this chapter, the student should be able to:

1. Answer questions on the Certified Legal Assistant examination concerning the 1976 Tax Reform Act, the 1981 Economic Recovery Tax Act, the 1986 Tax Reform Act and current estate and gift taxation.
2. Prepare and file a notice of fiduciary relationship.
3. Prepare Form SS-4, and request an employer's identification number by telephone or mail.
4. Prepare and file Form 706, United States Estate Tax Return.
5. Prepare and file Form 709, United States Gift Tax Return.
6. Answer questions on the Certified Legal Assistant examination concerning the generation-skipping transfer tax.

CHAPTER GLOSSARY

Alternate valuation date The date exactly six months from the date of death, or the date on which the estate sells the property, whichever comes first. The executor or administrator of an estate may elect to have estate property valued for estate tax purposes either on the date of death or the on alternate valuation date.

Causa mortis An act done in contemplation of impending death.

Closely-held business A business, generally in corporate form, in which the ownership is held by a few related (not necessarily by blood) individuals.

CUSIP Acronym for Committee on Uniform Security Identification Procedure. The CUSIP number is a number assigned to all stocks traded on recognized exchanges and to many over-the-counter stocks.

Economic Recovery Tax Act (ERTA) The name of the collective tax laws enacted by Congress in 1981, which finetuned many of the changes of the Tax Reform Act of 1976. Specifically, it increased the Unified Transfer Tax credit and the annual gift tax exclusion to their present levels.

Incidents of ownership An IRS concept that affects estate taxation. If a decedent or settlor retains some degree of control or right in property, the IRS treats the property as if he still owned it at the time of death, for example, the right to change beneficiaries in a life insurance policy and the right to revoke a trust.

Kiddie tax A tax created by the Tax Reform Act of 1986 to stop income-splitting as between parent and child. It taxes unearned income to the child at the parent's highest rate, subject to some exceptions.

Non-skip person A person who is a member of the generations that are skipped, for example, a child, spouse, or niece of the grantor.

QDOT Acronym for qualified domestic trust. A trust that allows the benefit of the marital deduction even though the surviving spouse in not a U.S. citizen. The trustee is required to withhold the estate tax from distributions of corpus. In some other states the abbreviation is *QDT*.

Reversionary interest The same as a remainder interest, except, whereas the remainder interest passes to a third party, a reversionary interest comes back to the original grantor.

Skip person A person two or more generations below the settlor's generation. A trust constitutes a skip person if all beneficiaries are skip persons.

Special use valuation Allows a farm or closely held business to be valued for estate tax purposes at its use value rather than at its highest and best-use value. For example, a farm located in the midst of a shopping district would be valued at its use as a farm rather than at its highest and best use as a shopping mall.

Tax Reform Act of 1976 The name of the collective tax laws passed by the U.S. Congress in 1976, which made significant changes in income, estate, and gift taxation and created the present scheme of estate and gift taxation.

INTRODUCTION

This chapter is included in this book for three reasons. First, it will aid any legal assistants intending to take the Certified Legal Assistant examination. The optional section of that exam that deals with the subject of this book emphasizes estate and gift taxation and, particularly, the history of estate and gift tax law since 1976 and the generation skipping transfer tax (GSTT). Second, the chapter is of benefit to both the estate planning legal assistants and probate legal assistants in fulfilling their tasks and helping clients avoid tax liability. Last, the chapter provides instructions on preparing tax returns relating to gifts and decedent's estates.

ESTATE AND GIFT TAX HISTORY

Estate and gift taxation has undergone dramatic change in the last nearly 20 years. Prior to January 1, 1977, the federal tax laws relating to estate and gift taxation stipulated that a donor could make up to $30,000 in gifts during the donor's lifetime to any donees, and the gifts would be exempt from gift tax. And each donee could get up to $3,000 annually. The tax rates applicable to gifts were lower than those applicable at the time of death. There was benefit in making lifetime gifts inasmuch as the gift removed the asset from the donor's estate at a tax rate less than would be imposed if the donor still owned the asset at the time of the donor's death. The federal estate tax provided for a $60,000 exemption. That is, $60,000 of the total assets of the decedent were exempt from federal estate taxation.

The **Tax Reform Act of 1976** began an avalanche of tax changes by eliminating both the estate and gift tax exemptions and replacing them with a Unified Transfer Tax credit, which was phased in over a five-year period beginning in 1977. The phase-in is illustrated in Example 15-1.

In addition, the 1976 Tax Reform Act unified the tax rates for gift and estate tax.

Example 15-1

Year	Unified Credit	Exemption Equivalent
1977	$30,000	$120,666
1978	$34,000	$134,000
1979	$38,000	$147,333
1980	$42,500	$161,563
1981	$47,000	$175,225

By the 1976 Tax Reform Act, all gifts made within three years of the death of the decedent, regardless of the intent of the decedent, were to be added back to the decedent's gross estate for the purpose of calculating federal estate taxes. In the event any gift taxes had been paid on such gifts, the tax would be allowed as a credit; that is, the amount of the gift tax paid would be subtracted from the federal estate tax owed by the estate. The act did retain the $3,000 annual exclusion per donee. Which was ultimately increased to $10,000 in the Economic Recovery Tax Act of 1981. The $10,000 annual exclusion per donee remains in effect.

In 1981, the U.S. Congress enacted the **Economic Recovery Tax Act (ERTA)**, which extended the phase-in of the flat-rate Unified Transfer Tax credit, gradually increasing the credit to $192,800 by 1987, and producing an exemption equivalent of $600,000. (The phase-in schedule under the ERTA is shown in upcoming Example 15-2.) In addition, however, the ERTA stipulated that all taxable gifts made after December 31, 1976, are included in the decedent's gross estate and are subject to federal estate tax, while retaining the credit for federal fift taxes previously paid. This eliminated the luck factor for donors who died within three years of the date of a gift, and also removed most of the estate-tax-saving benefits of lifetime gifts. Although the 1981 ERTA generally eliminated the carryback for gifts within three years of death, this was retained for gifts of life insurance in which the insured policy holder retained **incidents of ownership**. The value of a life insurance policy at the time of a gift is based upon its cash surrender value, which might be only several thousand dollars or perhaps even zero. If incidents of ownership are retained and the donor dies within three years, the face value payable upon death is included within the assets subject to federal estate tax. This can have a substantial impact on estate tax liability.

In addition, the 1981 ERTA radically changed the marital deduction for both gift and estate tax. Under the 1976 Tax Reform Act, the marital deduction for estate tax purposes was limited to the greater of $250,000 or one-half the adjusted gross estate. For gift tax purposes under the 1976 Tax Reform Act, the first $100,000 a person gave to his spouse was not subject to tax, the second $100,000 was, and one-half of any gifts that exceeded $200,000 were not subject to gift tax. Under the Economic Recovery Tax Act, the marital deduction for both gift and estate tax purposes is unlimited.

Example 15-2

Year	Unified Credit	Exemption Equivalent
1982	$62,800	$225,000
1983	$79,300	$275,000
1984	$96,300	$325,000
1985	$121,800	$400,000
1986	$155,800	$500,000
1987	$192,800	$600,000

The 1976 Tax Reform Act also imposed for the first time something called the generation skipping tax, now known as the generation-skipping transfer tax. The act, however, did not impose the generation-skipping tax upon direct transfers (direct skips) to grandchildren or great-grandchildren.

The 1986 Tax Reform Act has had major impact on estate planning by imposing a tax on the direct skip and in other modifications in the GSTT. It also substantially reduced the ability to shift taxable income between family members by effectively doing away with the so-called Clifford Trust and creating the **kiddie tax**. The 1986 Tax Reform Act also has had impact on grantor-retained income trusts and to the use of trusts in estate planning.

More recent tax acts have made primarily technical corrections and changes or altered the tax rates. Although a few of the changes have been significant, they are too technical for this book.

DUTY OF THE PERSONAL REPRESENTATIVE TO FILE RETURNS AND PAY TAXES

The personal representative of an estate is obligated by federal tax laws to file a final tax return for the portion of the year of death that the decedent was alive, unless the decedent was survived by a spouse who elects to file a joint return with the deceased spouse for that portion of the year. This is accomplished by filing the same tax form the decedent would have been required to file had he survived the year, normally IRS Form 1040 or 1040A.

The only difference in the tax return is that the fact and date of death is to be shown on the final tax return and the tax return covers only that portion of the year in which the decedent was alive.

If the final tax return is to be filed by a personal representative, then with it, or prior to filing it, a Notice of Fiduciary Relationship on Internal Revenue, IRS Form 56 must be filed. An example of Form 56 is attached to this chapter as Form 15-1. With this notice, the fiduciary is required to furnish proof of his fiduciary authority.

The final tax return must be filed, under the decedent's Social Security number, by the 15th day of the fourth month (normally April 15th) following the year of the decedent's death. Failure to file the return or to pay the tax can make the personal representative personally liable for the tax owed or for any penalties for late filing or late payment.

In addition to the final return, the personal representative must file IRS Form 1041, U.S. Fiduciary Income Tax Return, by the 15th day of the fourth month following each year in which the estate or trust had income in excess of $600 or has a beneficiary who is a nonresident alien. Prior to or simultaneous with the filing of the first return (provided the fiduciary did not file a final return), the fiduciary must file Form 56, Notice of Fiduciary Relationship.

In addition, every estate or trust must have an employer identification number (EIN). The personal representative applies for an EIN by filing Form SS-4, Application for Employer Identification Number. Form SS-4, instructions for completing form SS-4, and instructions for obtaining an EIN by telephone are included at the end of this chapter as Form 15-2. IRS Form 1041 is included with this chapter as Form 15-3. Schedules D, J, and K-1, which are commonly filed in connection with the 1041, are included as Forms 15-4, 15-5, and 15-6, respectively.

The personal representative is also required to file a Form 709 U.S. Gift (and Generation-Skipping Transfer) Tax Return, on any taxable gifts or generation-skipping transfers subject to tax made by the decedent in the year of the decedent's death or not previously reported by the decedent. Form 709 is included at the end of the chapter as Form 15-7.

Finally, the personal representative is obligated to file on behalf of the estate Form 706, U.S. Estate (and Generation-Skipping Transfer) Tax Return, on or before nine months from the date of the decedent's death (unless extended) if the gross estate, plus adjusted taxable gifts, is more than $600,000 (for decedent's dying after 1986). This form is included at chapter's end as Form 15-8. Form 712, which is used to report either information concerning proceeds of life insurance payable upon the decedent's death or certain information relating to insurance owned by the decedent at the time of death but payable upon the death of someone other than the decedent, is found at Form 15-9. Form 712 must be completed by each insurance company paying or issuing such a policy.

UNITED STATES ESTATE TAX AND PREPARATION OF FORM 706

An understanding of estate tax concepts is important in many practice areas and especially in estate planning and probate administration. Also, a growing number of attorneys leave the preparation of estate tax returns to certified public accountants and others. Consequently, although the discussion to follow is sufficient to obtain a working knowledge of estate taxation concepts, the legal assistant who is to prepare estate tax returns will also need to study the instructions for the preparation of Form 706, which may be obtained by calling the toll-free number listed in the telephone book under U.S. Government or by visiting the local office of the IRS.

Unified Transfer Tax Credit

As stated earlier, prior to the Tax Reform Act of 1976, the then-existing estate tax laws provided for a federal estate tax exemption of $60,000. This meant that no tax was owed until the estate exceeded $60,000. The 1976 Tax Reform Act replaced this exemption with a credit, known as the Unified Transfer Tax credit. In tax law, a credit is subtracted directly from the tax due. This is referred to as a Unified Transfer Tax credit because the transfer tax credit is applicable to both estate and gift taxation. Each individual has a flat-rate tax credit of $192,800 against the tax owed by reason of cumulative taxable gifts and that tax imposed against the gross estate upon death. During life the individual may elect to claim all or part of this credit by subtracting it from the gift tax shown due on Form 709, United States Gift (and Generation-Skipping Transfer) Tax Return. To the extent that an individual does not claim such credit, either because he makes no taxable gifts or because he elects not to claim the credit on Form 709, then this may be claimed as a credit on Form 706, United States Estate (and Generation-Skipping Transfer) Tax Return. Any portion of the unified credit claimed to reduce gift tax reduces the amount of the credit available as against estate tax.

For estates exceeding $10 million, there is a recapture of the unified credit by the assessment of an additional 5 percent tax on all amounts exceeding $10 million but less than $21,040,000.

United States Gift and Estate Tax Rates

The unified tax rates for gifts made at death and inter vivos gifts are shown on the tax table in the Instructions for Form 706, a copy of which is given at Example 15-3. These rates are cumulative as to gifts.

In Form 709, United States Gift Tax Return, tax is calculated based on the total gifts made during the preceding year *and* during prior years, with a credit given for gift tax paid in the prior years. As cumulative taxable gifts rise, so does the applicable tax rate. When the federal estate tax is computed, all prior taxable gifts are added to the gross estate for the purposes of calculating federal estate tax, and a credit is then given for gift tax already paid. As can be seen from the rate schedules, the tax rate is progressive. That is, as the amount of the gift and/or gross estate increases, so does the applicable percentage of tax, up to a maximum of 55 percent. This maximum rate is not applied to the entire gift or gross estate but only to the amount over $3 million. Thus, the effective tax rate is less than 55 percent. Also, the Unified Transfer Tax credit is subtracted from the total tax due.

Example 15-3

Table A—Unified Rate Schedule

Column A	Column B	Column C	Column D
Taxable amount over	Taxable amount not over	Tax on amount in column A	Rate of tax on excess over amount in column A
			(Percent)
0	$10,000	0	18
$10,000	20,000	$1,800	20
20,000	40,000	3,800	22
40,000	60,000	8,200	24
60,000	80,000	13,000	26
80,000	100,000	18,200	28
100,000	150,000	23,800	30
150,000	250,000	38,800	32
250,000	500,000	70,800	34
500,000	750,000	155,800	37
750,000	1,000,000	248,300	39
1,000,000	1,250,000	345,800	41
1,250,000	1,500,000	448,300	43
1,500,000	2,000,000	555,800	45
2,000,000	2,500,000	780,800	49
2,500,000	3,000,000	1,025,800	53
3,000,000	....	1,290,800	55

Form 706

Before dealing directly with Form 706, it is necessary to understand how federal estate tax is imposed—that is, what assets are included within the estate, what deductions are allowed, and what credits may be taken against the tax. For this purpose, let us examine the first page of Form 706.

After the identifying information, the first calculation is the total gross estate, that is, the sum of the assets shown on schedules A through I of Form 706. On these schedules are listed all the real estate, stocks and bonds, mortgages, notes and cash, insurance on the decedent's life, jointly owned property, miscellaneous property, transfers during the decedent's life, powers of appointment, and annuities. From the total gross estate is subtracted the deductions shown on Schedules J through O, including funeral expenses, mortgages and liens owed by the decedent or by the estate, net losses, expenses incurred in administering the estate, the marital deduction, and bequests to charities or public institutions. This yields the taxable estate.

Next, any adjusted taxable gifts made after December 31, 1976, are added. The worksheets in the instructions to Form 706 aid in calculating the amount of adjusted taxable gifts, which are added at this point.

Next, the tentative tax is calculated from Table A, page 9, of the instructions for Form 706. If the taxable estate, plus any adjusted taxable gifts, exceeds $10 million, 5 percent of the excess, up to $21,040,000, is added. Then any gift tax payable on previously unreported gifts made by the decedent is added. The sum of these amounts equals the gross estate tax. Subtracted from the gross estate tax is the unified credit, credit for state death taxes (calculated using Table B and the instructions), the credit for gift taxes and the credit for foreign death taxes paid. This gives the net estate tax.

Form 706 must be filed within nine months after the date of the decedent's death, unless the personal representative applies for and receives an extension of time to file via Form 4768, Application for Extension of Time to File a Return and/or Pay U.S. Estate (and Generation-Skipping Transfer) Tax. If an extension is obtained, a copy of it must be attached to Form 706.

Form 706 must be signed by all executors if there is more than one. *Executor* here includes administrators. Schedules A through I must be attached to Form 706 unless a zero is shown in the recapitulation of page 3 in regard to the omitted schedules. Schedules J-O must be filed with the form for any deduction claimed in the recapitulation on page 3 of Form 706. If credits for foreign death taxes or for taxes paid on prior transfers are claimed, schedule P and/or schedule Q must be attached also.

In preparing the return, the preparer is allowed to round off to the nearest dollar and to omit filling in applicable blanks that would otherwise be zero, except for the recapitulation, in which either a sum of money or a zero must be entered in each blank.

Part 3 on page 2 contains four elections to be made by the executor by checking either yes or no. If an **alternate valuation date** is elected, the values shown for all assets in the estate tax return will be the value as of a date exactly six months after the date of the decedent's death.

The second election deals with **special-use valuation**, which is applicable to certain farm or **closely held business** real property. Under this election, the executor may choose to base the property value on its actual use rather than at fair market value.

The installment election provided for in number 3 is applicable under certain conditions to closely held businesses. If applicable, then the tax can be deferred for up to five years and paid in 10 installments at a relatively low interest rate.

The fourth election relates to postponing payment of taxes attributable to a **reversionary interest** owned by the estate until the contingency occurs and title actually reverts to the estate.

Part 4 deals with general information on the estate and requires attaching of a certified copy of the will (if there is one), an original death certificate, and certain documents listed in the instructions if the decedent was a U.S. citizen but not a resident of the United States.

If the executor desires someone to receive tax information or to represent the estate before the Internal Revenue Service, the name of that person must be listed in the opening portion of Part 4. The rest of the information required by Part 4 is fairly self-explanatory, at least with help from the instructions for Form 706. A yes answer to many of the questions on Part 4 requires attaching additional information. For example, 7A asks whether federal gift tax returns have been filed; if the answer is yes, copies of the returns must be attached.

Part 5, the recapitulation previously referred to, involves carrying forward the totals from applicable schedules. If any of the schedules are not applicable to the particular estate, either because the estate does not own any of the type of asset or because no deduction is claimed, then a zero should be placed in the appropriate blank. *Both* the alternate value and the value at date of death must be shown if an alternate valuation date is chosen.

Schedule A deals with all real property owned by the estate, except that required to be reported on either Schedule E, Schedule F, Schedule G, or Schedule H. The instructions for Schedule A are found on the back of Schedule A, together with examples of how the real property should be described. If no alternate valuation date is adopted, the alternate valuation date and the value column need not be filled in, and the totals of those columns aren't carried over to the recapitulation. A full legal description and address should be used in describing each specific piece of real property. For Texas property, this would include either lot number, block number, subdivision name, city, and county or a metes and bounds description, including the county in which the property is located. Each specific piece of real property should be supported by attaching a copy of a written appraisal to Form 706.

Schedule A-1 is only applicable if yes has been answered to question 2 in Part 3 of Form 706. If such special valuation is chosen, all heirs or beneficiaries of the estate are required to indicate approval by executing the agreement shown as Part 3 of schedule A-1.

Schedule B requires a listing of all stocks, bonds, and U.S. Savings Bonds. On pages 8 and 10 of the instructions for Form 706 are examples of how to describe such stocks or bonds and any interest or dividends that have accrued to them. Notice in the example the number referred to as **CUSIP**, which stands for Committee on Uniform Security Identification Procedure. This is a nine-digit number assigned to all stocks and bonds that are traded on major exchanges and to many over-the-counter stocks. Usually, the CUSIP number is found on the face of the stock certificate. If not, it can be obtained through the transfer agent for the company or through any stock broker. The value to be listed is the fair market value, which is defined by the IRS as the mean between the highest and lowest selling prices quoted on the valuation date. The instructions provide alternate methods of ascertaining value if in fact there was no highest and lowest selling price on the date of death or the alternate valuation date.

Schedule C lists mortgages, notes, and cash owned by the decedent or in which the decedent had an interest at the time of death. The instructions for completing Schedule C are found on the reverse of Schedule C. With regard to cash in banks or other financial organizations, although the instructions do not require attaching a statement from a financial organization to Form 706, it is probably best to do so.

Schedule D relates to insurance on the decedent's life. Any such insurance that is receivable by or for the benefit of the estate or that is receivable by a beneficiary other than the estate must be listed on Schedule D. Further information, together with instructions regarding describing the insurance policies is found on the back of Schedule D. For each insurance policy listed on the schedule, a Form 712, Life Insurance Statement, must be obtained from the company that issued the policy. The companies usually will mail these out as a matter of course when paying the proceeds. If the law firm is filing the claims for the payment of life insurance, a request of Form 712 should be made to each insur-ance company. If the law firm is not handling the claims, then whoever is should be notified to request Form 712 and to furnish it to the law firm when received, or, if not received, to advise the lawyer or legal assistant so that the form can be requested from the insurance company.

Schedule E requires a listing of all jointly owned property. Part 1 deals with qualified joint interests, which, in the case of Texas residents, is applicable only to property held by the decedent and his spouse as joint tenants with right of survivorship. The reason this is listed separately is that only one-half the value of the jointly held property will be included within the decedent's gross estate. Part 2 deals with any other joint interest, that is, any real property or personal property in which the decedent owned an undivided interest. This property must be described in the same way as other property, together with the percentage of ownership and the name and address of each co-owner. Community property interests are not shown on Schedule E, but rather on the other forms. It is usually identified by a statement such as "one-half community property interest."

Schedule F lists all assets not reported on Schedules A-E (the instructions are on the back of Schedule F), including debts other than notes and mortgages, any interest in a business (including partnerships and sole proprietorships), insurance on the life of another (for which a Form 712 must be obtained), royalty interests, lease hold interests, reversionary or remainder interests, shares in trusts, household goods, personal effects, wearing apparel and other personal property, foreign products, machinery, and automobiles. Also included is any real estate owned for business purposes. If the decedent owned any interest in a partnership or a sole proprietorship, a statement of assets and liabilities, not only for the valuation date but for the five prior years, and a statement of net earnings for the five prior years must be attached.

According to the instructions for Schedule F, if the decedent owned any items with artistic or intrinsic value, the yes box of line 1 of the schedule must be checked, and full details must be given. If any of those articles is valued at more than $3,000 or a collection of similar articles at more than $10,000, an appraisal by an expert under oath must be attached, together with a statement regarding the appraiser's qualifications: an affidavit by the executor that he believes the appraiser is qualified to express an opinion concerning the value of the specific types of personal property.

Schedule G must be filed if the decedent made any of five types of transfers. These types are listed in the instructions for Schedule G found on page 11 of the instructions for Form 706.

Schedule H is required if the question on line 13 of part 4 of Form 706 was answered yes. This question asks if the decedent ever possessed, exercised, or released any general power of appointment. Power of appointment was defined earlier, and is defined in the instructions for Schedule H found on page 12 of the instructions for Form 706. The value shown will be the value of the property over which the decedent possessed the general power of appointment.

Schedule I is applicable only if the executor is excluding the value of a lump sum distribution from an approved plan. This is generally not applicable to the estate of decedents who died after December 31, 1984, and is dealt with in more detail in the instructions for Form 706, beginning on page 12.

Schedule J is for listing deductions for funeral expenses and expenses incurred in administering property subject to claims of creditors. Property not subject to claims of creditors is listed in Schedule L. Permissible deductions include executor's commissions and attorney's fees. Once these expenses have been claimed as a deduction for estate tax purposes, the expenses may not thereafter be claimed as a deduction for federal income tax purposes. If such expenses are claimed as an income tax deduction, they should not be listed in Schedule J or L, and a waiver executed by the beneficiaries should be filed with Form 1041.

Schedule K is where all of the debts of the decedent, including mortgages or liens, owed at the time of death are claimed as deductions. Instructions for Schedule K are found on page 14 in the instructions to Form 706, including the information to be given in the description column on each item claimed as a deduction.

Schedule L is for listing net losses during administration and expenses incurred in administering property that is not subject to claims. Instructions are found on page 15 of the instructions to Form 706.

Schedule M is where the marital deduction is claimed. It is also where the election to take property under a QTIP is made. Further information can be found in "Election to Deduct Qualified Terminable Interest (QTIP)" on page 28 of Form 706. Line 3 deals with a qualified domestic trust election, also referred to as a **QDOT**. This covers surviving spouses who are not U.S. citizens. The Internal Revenue Code allows a marital deduction for such a surviving spouse only if the property passes in a qualified domestic trust or if the property was transferred or assigned to a qualified domestic trust prior to the filing of the decedent's estate tax return. The requirements for a QDOT are shown on page 28 under the caption on line 3—qualified domestic trust election. In Schedule M is to be listed each property interest for which a marital deduction is claimed. If the property that is the subject of the marital deduction is as a result of the residuary clause or of a general bequest, a lump-sum designation may be made on Schedule M, and a supporting document showing how this figure was reached may be attached.

Schedule O deals with a deduction for charitable, public, and similar gifts and bequests. The instructions are found on page 15 of the instructions to Form 706.

Schedule P must be filed if a credit for foreign death taxes is claimed. This will be applicable only if the decedent was a citizen of the United States but resident in another country, or vice versa. As to U.S. residents who are not citizens, the credit is allowable only if the decedent's country of citizenship allows a similar credit to U.S. citizens residing there. There is a blank in which to insert the word "statute" or the name of the particular treaty. There is a general statute that allows a credit for foreign death taxes. In certain cases, however, particular treaties between the United States and other countries allow higher amounts of credit. If this is the case, the name of the specific treaty must be included.

Schedule Q is for claiming a credit for a tax on prior transfers, if the decedent received property from someone else who died within 10 years before or two years after the decedent for whom this return is being filed. A credit is allowable for all or a portion of the federal estate tax paid on the estate of the person from whom the decedent received the property. There is no credit allowable if the decedent received the property from his spouse and a marital deduction was allowed in regard to the property. Instructions begin on page 16 of the instructions for Form 706. On page 17 is a schedule for computing the credit. The percentage of the credit diminishes with the number of years since the death of the prior deceased person.

Schedules R and R-1 deal with the generation-skipping transfer tax and will be discussed in connection with that subject later in this chapter.

Schedule S is used to calculate the increased tax imposed by Section 4980A(d) of the Internal Revenue Code on excess accumulations in qualified employee plans and individual retirement plans. If there are excess accumulations, the estate must file Schedule S with an estate tax return regardless of the size of the gross estate. Section 4980A(d) provides that an accumulation is excessive if there are pension distributions of more than $750,000. It levies a 15 percent tax on the excess, in addition to any estate or gift taxes.

Finally, attached to Form 706 is a continuation schedule to be used if any schedule is insufficient to list all applicable property. This continuation schedule must be photocopied and a separate continuation schedule must be used for each main schedule that is being continued. Instructions are included on the back of the continuation schedule on page 41 of Form 706.

SPECIAL ESTATE AND GIFT TAX CONSIDERATIONS

Although previously dealt with in general, the subjects of the marital deduction, lifetime gifts (including in trust), and the GSTT are too vital to estate planning to be passed by so lightly. It is important, however, to understand the federal estate tax and gift tax in order to comprehend these subjects, which is why a full explanation has been held until this point. These subjects are covered in the Certified Legal Assistant examination in some detail.

Marital Deduction

The marital deduction provisions of the 1981 Economic Recovery Tax Act have been discussed in several prior chapters. Under the 1976 Tax Reform Act, the maximum marital deduction for property passing from a decedent to a surviving spouse was the greater of $250,000 or one-half of the decedent's adjusted gross estate. It was limited to the amount actually left to the spouse.

The Economic Recovery Tax Act of 1981 provided for an unlimited marital deduction for transfers between spouses. It also made the marital deduction applicable not only to property passing upon the death of a spouse but also to gifts between spouses. Prior to 1982, there was a $100,000 marital deduction on gifts between spouses plus 50 percent of any gift in excess of $200,000. For gifts since 1982, the marital deduction is unlimited in regard both to gifts and to property passing to a spouse by reason of the death of a spouse.

The marital deduction must be claimed either on a gift tax return or on an estate tax return, and is mainly a tax-deferral provision rather than a tax-saving provision. Although no tax has to be paid on a gift or a bequest to a spouse by the spouse first dying, to the extent that any of the assets given or devised are still possessed by the surviving spouse's estate at the time of his death, they will be included in that spouse's estate for the purpose of calculating estate taxes.

For example, if a husband dies leaving his entire half of community property, valued at $1 million, to his wife, and the marital deduction is claimed, no tax will be due on his estate. If, however, the surviving wife spends none of the inherited portion nor her half of the community estate during her life, assuming she spends all of the interest or other income from it, then her estate will be valued at $2 million upon her death. Federal estate tax will have to be paid on the full amount less the unified credit. This example assumes that no bypass or exemption-equivalent trust was used in the husband's estate.

On the other hand, if a bypass or exemption equivalent trust was created in the husband's will, $600,000 of the $1 million in the husband's half of community interest will never become part of the assets of the surviving wife's estate. The marital deduction would then be applied to the remaining $400,000, leaving no tax owed on the husband's estate. Upon the death of the wife, the $600,000 in the exemption-equivalent trust passes directly to the named beneficiaries. However, the $400,000 remaining from the husband's estate is added to the wife's half of the community property, creating a gross estate of $1.4 million. From this figure is subtracted the unified credit attributable to the wife's estate, reducing the taxable estate to $800,000. In most estates, there would be other deductions and perhaps additional credits that would reduce the taxable estate and the tax even further.

The Economic Recovery Tax Act of 1981 also added the qualified terminable interest property, or QTIP, which is used only in connection with the marital deduction. It allows property that does not pass outright to the surviving spouse but in which the spouse only has a life-time interest to qualify for the marital deduction. The eligible property, called *qualified terminable interest property*, is property passing from the deceased spouse in which the surviving spouse has only an income interest for life. In order to qualify, a surviving spouse has to have the right to receive all of the income, which must be payable at least annually, for life. Further, no one must have a power of appointment concerning any of the property except for the surviving spouse. After the death of the surviving spouse, the personal representative of the deceased spouse's estate must elect to treat the property as QTIP property on the decedent's federal estate tax return. The QTIP can be either in the form of a trust or in the form of a legal life estate to the surviving spouse, with remainder to others, generally the children.

Lifetime Gifts

A *gift* is defined as a transfer of property from one person to another for less than full or adequate compensation. Federal gift tax is levied on this right to transfer as against the person who makes the gift, normally referred to as the *donor*. Sometimes a donor is also referred to as a *grantor* or *transferor*. Federal gift tax is assessed against the donor and not against the donee, transferee, grantee or recipient of the gift. Prior to 1976, the gift tax rates were considerably lower than the federal estate tax rates. The Tax Reform Act unified or equalized the rates.

Under the 1976 Tax Reform Act, any gift made within three years of the decedent's death was included in the decedent's gross estate at the time of the decedent's death. Prior to 1976, only gifts made in contemplation of death by the decedent were included in the gross estate. The Economic Recovery Tax Act of 1981 stipulated that all gifts made after December 31, 1976, are included in the decedent's gross estate and therefore subject to federal estate tax. A credit for federal gift tax paid is allowed. The gift tax is levied and a gift tax return must be filed if a donee makes a gift in excess of $10,000 (annual exclusion amount) to any one donee (including a spouse) in any tax year.

If the donor is married, then the donor or spouse may join in the gift. Since there are now two donors and each is allowed a $10,000 exclusion, a total exclusion of $20,000 is allowed per year to each donee. This is called *gift-splitting.* Such a gift may be made by the spouses, either from community property or from the separate property of either spouse, provided that there is evidence that both spouses are joining in the making of the gift. If this gift is to be made out of the separate property of one of the spouses, there must be a document, which both spouses sign, that evidences their joint intent to make a gift. For instance, if the gift is to be made from one spouse's separate bank account, the other spouse should sign the check even though his signature is not only unnecessary but not authorized in the bank records. Further, the check itself and the stub should be referenced to reflect that it is a gift from both spouses. For other forms of gifts, a bill of sale (in the case of personal property) or a deed (in the case of real property) should be used and altered to show that the consideration is as a gift and not as a sale.

A valid gift requires delivery by the donor to the donee. Although acceptance by the donee is normally presumed, the IRS does require that an adult donee know of the gift. If the knowledge of the donee is not otherwise indicated, such as by the endorsement of the check, then a letter informing the donee of the gift should be delivered to the donee.

Although a lot of incentives regarding lifetime gifts were removed, first by the Tax Reform Act of 1976 and then by the Economic Recovery Tax Act of 1981, some incentives for lifetime giving remain. The $10,000 annual exclusion ($20,000 in the case of a joint spousal gift) allows an individual to transfer out of his potential estate annual sums of money (or the equivalent value in assets) that are not subject to federal gift tax and not included in the donor's estate upon death. Also, since the value for gift tax purposes is fixed at the date of the gift, it will be that value rather than the value at the time of death that is included in the decedent's gross estate for estate tax purposes.

When a gift to a single donee exceeds $10,000 (or $20,000 in the case of a joint spousal gift), a gift tax return on IRS Form 709 must be filed for the year of the gift. The tax is imposed cumulatively, meaning that each time a donor is required to file Form 709, all prior taxable gifts are added to the amount of the present year's gift, tax is calculated as if both the prior gifts and the present gift were made in the year of tax, and a credit is given for gift tax paid on prior years' gifts.

If the marital deduction is to be claimed in order to reduce the taxable amount of the gift to zero in the event of an interspousal gift, then a Form 709 must be filed. In addition, if the unified credit is to be claimed for a lifetime gift, a Form 709 must be filed, which also will document the diminution of the amount of the credit available upon the death of the donor.

The United States Gift (and Generation-Skipping Transfer) Tax Return, or Form 709, is not very complex, and the instructions are complete. Consequently, no further discussion on filling out the form is necessary.

There is a short-form gift tax return, Form 709-A, which is usable only when gift-splitting between spouses amounts to $20,000 or less.

Trusts

If not already clear, it should be understood by the legal assistant that the inter vivos creation of a trust or a transfer into an existing trust involves a gift and is therefore subject to federal gift taxation. In addition, income earned by a trust is subject to federal income taxation when it exceeds $600 per year. Such income must be reported on the United States Fiduciary Income Tax Return.

Someone who transfers property into a trust must file a United States Gift Tax Return when the transfer exceeds $10,000 ($20,000 in the case of spousal gift splitting), and the trustee of the trust must annually file a fiduciary income tax return when the trust has income in excess of $600.

A problem can arise in trusts concerning future versus present gifts: In order for an inter vivos lifetime gift to be effective, some present interest in the property must be transferred to the donee. Inasmuch as trusts deal primarily with future interests, in order for a transfer to qualify as a gift the beneficiary must receive some present interest. In the case of adult beneficiaries, this normally means the right to withdraw at least the income and often the principal of the trust. With to minors, it means the trustee must be given, at a minimum, the discretionary right to expend funds for the health, safety, and well-being of the minors. There are many discussions in estate planning texts and seminar materials concerning the wording necessary to create a present interest when the trustee is not required to expend funds for the benefit of the minors but has the discretion to expend funds for the benefit of minors. In drafting such a trust, one must be very careful in wording the grant of authority to the trustee. Not using the proper language can result in the IRS's failing to recognize the attempted gift as an effective lifetime gift and including it within the decedent's estate at its value then rather than its value at the time of the attempted gift.

Generation Skipping Transfers

The original generation-skipping transfer tax was created in the 1976 Tax Reform Act in order to plug a loophole whereby an individual could create a trust that would exist, for example for the benefit of the surviving spouse, then the children, then the grandchildren, then perhaps even the great-grandchildren of the original trustor or testator. This created a situation, subject to the rule against perpetuities, that allowed an estate to be maintained intact, benefiting successive generations subject to estate tax only upon the death of the original creator and the ultimate beneficiaries, but not the interim beneficiaries.

In the Tax Reform Act of 1986, a new GSTT was created to replace the original GSTT as enacted in 1976. The current GSTT applies to "direct skips" as well as "taxable distributions" and "taxable terminations." A *direct skip* is a transfer for the benefit of a person who is at least two generations below the transferor, and can be either a present gift or a transfer in trust. The person who receives the benefit of such a transfer is called the **skip person**. Probably the best example is the grandchildren of the transferor or donor. A spouse, regardless of age difference, is in the same generation as the transferor. Children of the transferor are one generation below the transferor, and grandchildren are two generations below the transferor. If an inter vivos gift is made, either in trust or outright, to the grandchildren of the transferor or donor at a time when there are children of the donor or transferor alive, the transfer is subject to the GSTT. If, on the other hand, there are no children of the transferor alive at the time of the gift, that generation is eliminated for the purpose of calculation, and grandchildren are only one generation below the transferor; consequently, there is no skip.

The GSTT is applicable only to otherwise-taxable gifts under federal gift taxation. The $10,000 annual exclusion is also applicable to the GSTT. In addition, there is a lifetime $1 million exemption on generation-skipping transfers. That is, each transferor (doubled in the case of gift-splitting between spouses) may make generation-skipping transfers of no more than $1 million ($2 million in the case of gift-splitting) that are not subject to the GSTT. The GSTT only comes into effect when gifts in excess of the exempt amount and the annual exclusion are made to individuals at least two generations below the transferor.

Imposition of the GSTT differs depending on whether the generation-skipping transfer is a direct skip or either a taxable distribution or a taxable termination. The estate planner or the person representing either the trustee of the trust or the personal representative of an estate involving generation-skipping transfers must understand the difference. This necessitates understanding the terminology in the 1986 Tax Reform Act, the most important of which is skip persons versus **nonskip persons**. A *skip person* is an individual to whom a transfer is made and who is two or more generations below the generation of the transferor. Examples are grandchildren, grandchildren of a sibling, grandchildren of a spouse and great-grandchildren of a parent. Grandchildren are two or more generations below the generation of the grandparent. A trust can be a skip person if all present beneficiaries are skip persons or if there is no present beneficiary and if no distribution, including terminating distributions, can ever be made to a nonskip person by the trust. A *nonskip person* is any person, whether an individual or a trust, who is not a skip person. Examples are parents, grandparents, spouse, and children of the transferor, as well as charities.

The 1986 act defines a generation-skipping transfer as including taxable distributions, taxable terminations, and direct skips. *Taxable termination* involves a termination, either by death, lapse of time, specific provision, release of a power of appointment, or otherwise, of an interest in property held in trust, unless immediately after termination a nonskip person has an interest in the property. An example is the common situation where an individual creates a trust in which the income is payable to children during the life of the children and, upon the death of the children, vests in the grandchildren. In this example, there is no direct skip inasmuch as the present interest in the trust property is held by a nonskip person. However, when the children die, there is no longer any interest held by a nonskip person and the entirety of the trust property is owned by skip persons. At the time of this termination, the assets passing to the grandchildren (skip persons) are subject to the GSTT.

A *taxable distribution* is the distribution to a skip person of any portion of a trust, whether income or principal. Using the preceding example—a trust with income to or children during the life of the children, with the remainder to the grandchildren—let us assume the trustee is given the discretionary power to expend either income or principal during the life of the children of the transferor for the benefit of a grandchild also. When the trustee then expends funds from the trust estate for the benefit of the skip person (the grandchild), there is a taxable distribution, and the GSTT is imposed on the amount received by the skip persons.

Both taxable terminations and taxable distributions are reportable on Form 709, United States Gift Tax Return. The applicable rate of tax is a flat rate equal to the maximum federal gift and estate tax rate. This tax rate is then multiplied by a fraction created by considering the amount of the generation-skipping tax exemption allocated to the transfer or direct skip.

A *direct skip*, which can be either inter vivos or **causa mortis**, is the transfer to a skip person of an asset that is otherwise subject to gift or estate tax.

If the transfer is inter vivos, it is reported on Form 709, United States Gift (and Generation-Skipping Transfer) Tax Return. The GSTT as calculated earlier is then paid in addition to gift tax. If the transfer is testamentary or occurs only upon the death of the transferor, the report is filed on Form 706, United States Estate (and Generation-Skipping Transfer) Tax Return, and the GSTT is payable in addition to any federal estate taxes due.

The $1 million GSTT exemption may be allocated by the transferor or, if not by the transferor, by the personal representative of his estate or any trustee of any trust created by him. An important part of the preparation of estate planning documents can be instructions by the settlor or testator to the personal representative or trustee concerning the allocation of the GSTT exemption.

The subject of the GSTT is more complex than is dealt with in this chapter, particularly with reference to the allocation of the exemption and calculation of the rate itself. Since it is assumed that only a few legal assistants will have to deal with generation skipping transfers that exceed $1 million in value, and even then only infrequently, no more discussion will be allotted to the subject in this text.

CHAPTER QUESTIONS AND EXERCISES

1. Discuss the effects of the 1976 Tax Reform Act, the 1981 Economic Recovery Act, and the 1986 Tax Reform Act on estate and gift taxation.

2. Prepare an IRS Form 56, Notice of Fiduciary Administration for the Estate of Peter Smith, as per Form 10-1 in the Forms Appendix to Chapter 10.

3. Prepare IRS Form SS-4 for the estate in Question 2, and explain how to obtain an EIN for the estate over the telephone.

4. Read IRS Form 1041 and the instructions for its preparation. Be prepared to enter into a class discussion as to when it must be filed, where it must be filed, and how it is prepared.

5. Using the instructions in this book and the instructions for preparation of IRS Form 706, prepare a United States Estate Tax Return for the Estate of Peter Smith. Use the information found in Forms 10-1, 10-7, and 10-16. Assume there have been no lifetime gifts that exceed the annual exclusion. Make up any additional information needed.

6. Read IRS Form 709 and the instructions for its preparation. Be prepared to enter into a class discussion about it.

7. Explain the procedure for imposing the GSTT.

8. Discuss an estate's liability for federal estate tax under current law. Include in your discussion the Unified Transfer Tax credit and the effect of lifetime gifts.

9. Discuss gift taxation. Include who is liable for it, when liability occurs, the annual exclusion, and the effects of gift tax on estate tax.

10. What are the obligations, responsibilities, and liabilities of the heirs, devisees, surviving spouse, and/or executors, administrators, or trustees under federal tax laws.

Form 15-1: Notice Concerning Fiduciary Relationship

Form **56** (Rev. January 1992) Department of the Treasury Internal Revenue Service	**Notice Concerning Fiduciary Relationship** (Internal Revenue Code sections 6036 and 6903)	OMB No. 1545-0013 Expires 1-30-94

Part I   Identification

Name of person for whom you are acting (as shown on the tax return)	Identifying number

Address of person for whom you are acting (number, street, and room or suite no.)

City or town, state, and ZIP code. (If a foreign address, enter city, province or state, postal code, and country.)

Fiduciary's name

Address of fiduciary (number, street, and room or suite no.)

City or town, state, and ZIP code	Telephone number (optional) ( )

Part II   Authority

1 Evidence of fiduciary authority (check applicable boxes):
 a ☐ Certified copy of will and codicils (or court order appointing the fiduciary) attached . . Date of death ....
 b ☐ Certified copy of court order appointing the fiduciary attached . . . . Date (see instructions) ....
 c ☐ Copy of valid trust instrument and amendments attached
 d ☐ Other evidence of creation of fiduciary relationship (describe) ▶ ....

Part III   Tax Notices

Send to the fiduciary listed in Part I all notices and other written communications involving the following tax matters:
 2 Type of tax (estate, gift, generation-skipping transfer, income, excise, etc.) ....
 3 Federal tax form number (706, 1040, 1041, 1120, etc.) ....
 4 Year(s) or period(s) (if estate tax, date of death)

Part IV   Revocation or Termination of Notice

Section A—Total Revocation or Termination

5 Check this box if you are revoking or terminating all prior notices concerning fiduciary relationships on file with the Internal Revenue Service for the same tax matters and years or periods covered by this notice concerning fiduciary relationship . ▶ ☐
 Evidence of termination of fiduciary authority (check applicable boxes):
 a ☐ Certified copy of court order revoking fiduciary authority attached
 b ☐ Copy of certificate of dissolution or termination of a business entity attached
 c ☐ Other evidence of termination of fiduciary relationship (describe) ▶

Section B—Partial Revocation

6a Check this box if you are revoking earlier notices concerning fiduciary relationships on file with the Internal Revenue Service for the same tax matters and years or periods covered by this notice concerning fiduciary relationship . . . . ▶ ☐
 b Specify to whom granted, date, and address, including ZIP code, or refer to attached copies of earlier notices and authorizations.
 ....

Section C—Substitute Fiduciary

7 Check this box if a new fiduciary or fiduciaries have been or will be substituted for the revoking or terminating fiduciary(ies) and specify the name(s) and address(es), including ZIP code(s), of the new fiduciary(ies) . . . . ▶ ☐

Part V   Court and Administrative Proceedings

Name of court (if other than a court proceeding, identify the type of proceeding and name of agency)	Date proceeding initiated

Address of court	Docket number of proceeding

City or town, state, and ZIP code	Date	Time	a.m. p.m.	Place of other proceedings

I certify that I have the authority to execute this notice concerning fiduciary relationship on behalf of the taxpayer.

| Please Sign Here | ▶ Fiduciary's signature | (Title, if applicable) | Date |
| | ▶ Fiduciary's signature | (Title, if applicable) | Date |

For Paperwork Reduction Act and Privacy Act Notice, see back page.   Cat. No. 16375I   Form **56** (Rev. 1-92)

Form 15-1: (continued)

General Instructions

(Section references are to the Internal Revenue Code unless otherwise noted.)

Paperwork Reduction Act and Privacy Act Notice

We ask for the information on this form to carry out the Internal Revenue laws of the United States. Form 56 is provided for your convenience and its use is voluntary. Under section 6109 you must disclose the social security number or employer identification number of the individual or entity for which you are acting. The principal purpose of this disclosure is to secure proper identification of the taxpayer. We also need this information to gain access to the tax information in our files and properly respond to your request. If you do not disclose this information, we may suspend processing the notice of fiduciary relationship and not consider this as proper notification until you provide the information.

The time needed to complete and file this form will vary depending on individual circumstances. The estimated average time is:

Recordkeeping . . . . . . 8 min.
Learning about the
law or the form . . . . . 32 min.
Preparing the form . . . . . 46 min.
Copying, assembling, and
sending the form to the IRS . . 15 min.

If you have comments concerning the accuracy of these time estimates or suggestions for making this form more simple. we would be happy to hear from you. You can write to both the **Internal Revenue Service,** Washington. DC 20224. Attention: IRS Reports Clearance Officer. T:FP: and the **Office of Management and Budget,** Paperwork Reduction Project (1545-0013). Washington. DC 20503. DO NOT send the form to either of these offices. Instead. see **When and Where To File** on this page.

Purpose of Form

Form 56 may be used to notify the IRS of the creation or termination of a fiduciary relationship under section 6903: and to give notice of qualification under section 6036.

Who Should File

Form 56 is used by the fiduciary (see **Definitions**) to notify the IRS of the creation. or termination. of a fiduciary relationship under section 6903. For example. if you are acting as fiduciary for an individual. a decedent's estate. or a trust. you may file Form 56. If notification is not given to the IRS. notices sent to the last known address of the taxable entity. transferee. or other person subject to tax liability are considered sufficient to satisfy the requirements of the Internal Revenue Code.

Form 56 is also used by receivers and assignees for the benefit of creditors to give notice of qualification under section 6036. However. a bankruptcy trustee. debtor in possession. or other like fiduciary in a bankruptcy proceeding is not required

to give notice of qualification under section 6036. Trustees. etc.. in bankruptcy proceedings are subject to the notice requirements under title 11 of the United States Code (Bankruptcy Rules).

Definitions

Fiduciary.—A fiduciary is any person acting in a fiduciary capacity for any other person (or terminating entity). such as an administrator. conservator. designee. executor. guardian. receiver. trustee of a trust. trustee in bankruptcy. personal representative. person in possession of property of a decedent's estate. or debtor in possession of assets in any bankruptcy proceeding by order of the court.

Person.—A person is any individual. trust. estate. partnership. association. company or corporation.

Decedent's Estate.—An estate of a deceased person is a taxable entity separate from the decedent. It generally continues to exist until the final distribution of the assets of the estate is made to the heirs and other beneficiaries.

Terminating Entities.—A terminating entity. such as a corporation. partnership. trust. etc.. only has the legal capacity to establish a fiduciary relationship while it is in existence. Establishing a fiduciary relationship prior to termination of the entity allows the fiduciary to represent the entity on all tax matters after it is terminated.

When and Where To File

1. Notice of Fiduciary Relationship.— Generally. Form 56 should be filed when you create (or terminate) a fiduciary relationship. To receive tax notices upon creation of a fiduciary relationship. Form 56 should be filed with the IRS service center where the person for whom you are acting is required to file tax returns. However. when a fiduciary relationship is first created. a fiduciary who is required to file a return can file Form 56 with the first tax return filed.

2. Proceedings (Other Than Bankruptcy) and Assignments for the Benefit of Creditors.—A fiduciary who is appointed or authorized to act as:

● A receiver in a receivership proceeding or similar fiduciary (including a fiduciary in aid of foreclosure). or

● An assignee for the benefit of creditors must file Form 56 on or within 10 days of the date of appointment with the Chief. Special Procedures Staff. of the District office of the IRS having jurisdiction over the person for whom you are acting.

The receiver or assignee may also file a separate Form 56 with the service center where the person for whom the fiduciary is acting is required to file tax returns to provide the notice required by section 6903.

Specific Instructions

Part I.—Identification

Provide all the information called for in this part.

Identifying Number.—If you are acting for an individual. an individual debtor. or other person whose assets are controlled. the

identifying number is the social security number (e.g.. decedent's social security number shown on his or her final Form 1040). If you are acting for a person other than an individual. including an estate or trust. the identifying number is the employer identification number.

Address.—Include the suite. room. or other unit number after the street address.

If the postal service does not deliver mail to the street address and the fiduciary (or person) has a P.O. box. show the P.O. box number instead of the street address.

Part II.—Authority

Line 1a.—Testate Decedent.—Check the box on line 1a if the decedent died testate and enter the date of the decedent's death.

Line 1b.—Intestate Decedent.—Enter the decedent's date of death and write "Date of Death" next to the date.

Assignment for the Benefit of Creditors.—Enter the date the assets were assigned to you and write "Assignment Date" after the date.

Proceedings Other Than Bankruptcy.— Enter the date you were appointed or took possession of the assets of the debtor or other person whose assets are controlled.

Part III.—Tax Notices

Complete this part if you want the IRS to send you tax notices regarding the person for whom you are acting.

Line 2.—Specify the type of tax involved. This line should also identify a transferee tax liability under section 6901 or fiduciary tax liability under 31 U.S.C. 3713(b) when either exists.

Part IV.—Revocation or Termination of Notice

Complete this part only if you are revoking or terminating a prior notice concerning a fiduciary relationship. Completing this part will relieve you of any further duty or liability if used as a notice of termination.

Part V.—Court and Administrative Proceedings

Complete this part only if you have been appointed a receiver. trustee. or a fiduciary by a court or other governmental unit in a proceeding other than a bankruptcy proceeding.

If proceedings are scheduled for more than one date. time or place. attach a separate schedule of the proceedings.

Assignment for the Benefit of Creditors.—You must attach the following information:

1. A brief description of the assets that were assigned. and

2. An explanation of the action to be taken regarding such assets. including any hearings. meetings of creditors. sale or other scheduled action.

Signature

Sign Form 56 and enter a title describing your role as a fiduciary (e.g.. assignee: guardian: trustee: personal representative: receiver; or conservator).

*U.S. Government Printing Office: 1992 — 618-993/40519

Form 15-2: Application for Employer Identification Number

Form **SS-4** (Rev. December 1993) Department of the Treasury Internal Revenue Service	**Application for Employer Identification Number** (For use by employers, corporations, partnerships, trusts, estates, churches, government agencies, certain individuals, and others. See instructions.)	EIN OMB No. 1545-0003 Expires 12-31-96

Please type or print clearly.

1 Name of applicant (Legal name) (See instructions.)

2 Trade name of business, if different from name in line 1 | **3** Executor, trustee, "care of" name

4a Mailing address (street address) (room, apt., or suite no.) | **5a** Business address, if different from address in lines 4a and 4b

4b City, state, and ZIP code | **5b** City, state, and ZIP code

6 County and state where principal business is located

7 Name of principal officer, general partner, grantor, owner, or trustor—SSN required (See instructions.) ▶

8a Type of entity (Check only one box.) (See instructions.)
- ☐ Sole Proprietor (SSN) _____
- ☐ REMIC   ☐ Personal service corp.
- ☐ State/local government   ☐ National guard
- ☐ Other nonprofit organization (specify) _____
- ☐ Other (specify) ▶ _____
- ☐ Estate (SSN of decedent) _____
- ☐ Plan administrator-SSN _____
- ☐ Other corporation (specify) _____
- ☐ Federal government/military   ☐ Church or church controlled organization
- ☐ Trust
- ☐ Partnership
- ☐ Farmers' cooperative

(enter GEN if applicable) _____

8b If a corporation, name the state or foreign country (if applicable) where incorporated ▶ | State | Foreign country

9 Reason for applying (Check only one box.)
- ☐ Started new business (specify) ▶ _____
- ☐ Hired employees
- ☐ Created a pension plan (specify type) ▶ _____
- ☐ Banking purpose (specify) ▶
- ☐ Changed type of organization (specify) ▶ _____
- ☐ Purchased going business
- ☐ Created a trust (specify) ▶ _____
- ☐ Other (specify) ▶

10 Date business started or acquired (Mo., day, year) (See instructions.) | **11** Enter closing month of accounting year. (See instructions.)

12 First date wages or annuities were paid or will be paid (Mo., day, year). **Note:** *If applicant is a withholding agent, enter date income will first be paid to nonresident alien. (Mo., day, year)* . . . . ▶

13 Enter highest number of employees expected in the next 12 months. **Note:** *If the applicant does not expect to have any employees during the period, enter "0."* . . . . ▶ | Nonagricultural | Agricultural | Household

14 Principal activity (See instructions.) ▶

15 Is the principal business activity manufacturing? . . . . ☐ Yes   ☐ No
If "Yes," principal product and raw material used ▶

16 To whom are most of the products or services sold? Please check the appropriate box.   ☐ Business (wholesale)
☐ Public (retail)   ☐ Other (specify) ▶   ☐ N/A

17a Has the applicant ever applied for an identification number for this or any other business? . . . . ☐ Yes   ☐ No
Note: *If "Yes," please complete lines 17b and 17c.*

17b If you checked the "Yes" box in line 17a, give applicant's legal name and trade name, if different than name shown on prior application.

Legal name ▶   Trade name ▶

17c Enter approximate date, city, and state where the application was filed and the previous employer identification number if known.

Approximate date when filed (Mo., day, year) | City and state where filed | Previous EIN

Under penalties of perjury, I declare that I have examined this application, and to the best of my knowledge and belief, it is true, correct, and complete. | Business telephone number (include area code)

Name and title (Please type or print clearly.) ▶

Signature ▶   Date ▶

Note: *Do not write below this line.*   For official use only.

Please leave blank ▶	Geo.	Ind.	Class	Size	Reason for applying

For Paperwork Reduction Act Notice, see attached instructions.   Cat. No. 16055N   Form **SS-4** (Rev. 12-93)

Form 15-2: (continued)

Form SS-4 (Rev. 12-93)   Page **2**

General Instructions

(Section references are to the Internal Revenue Code unless otherwise noted.)

Purpose

Use Form SS-4 to apply for an employer identification number (EIN). An EIN is a nine-digit number (for example, 12-3456789) assigned to sole proprietors, corporations, partnerships, estates, trusts, and other entities for filing and reporting purposes. The information you provide on this form will establish your filing and reporting requirements.

Who Must File

You must file this form if you have not obtained an EIN before and
• You pay wages to one or more employees.
• You are required to have an EIN to use on any return, statement, or other document, even if you are not an employer.
• You are a withholding agent required to withhold taxes on income, other than wages, paid to a nonresident alien (individual, corporation, partnership, etc.). A withholding agent may be an agent, broker, fiduciary, manager, tenant, or spouse, and is required to file **Form 1042**, Annual Withholding Tax Return for U.S. Source Income of Foreign Persons.
• You file **Schedule C**, Profit or Loss From Business, or **Schedule F**, Profit or Loss From Farming, of **Form 1040**, U.S. Individual Income Tax Return, and have a Keogh plan or are required to file excise, employment, or alcohol, tobacco, or firearms returns.

The following must use EINs even if they do not have any employees:
• Trusts, except the following:

1. Certain grantor-owned revocable trusts (see the instructions for Form 1040).
2. Individual Retirement Arrangement (IRA) trusts, unless the trust has to file **Form 990-T**, Exempt Organization Business Income Tax Return (See the Instructions for Form 990-T.)
• Estates
• Partnerships
• REMICs (real estate mortgage investment conduits) (See the instructions for **Form 1066**, U.S. Real Estate Mortgage Investment Conduit Income Tax Return.)
• Corporations
• Nonprofit organizations (churches, clubs, etc.)
• Farmers' cooperatives
• Plan administrators (A plan administrator is the person or group of persons specified as the administrator by the instrument under which the plan is operated.)

Note: *Household employers are not required to file Form SS-4 to get an EIN. An EIN may be assigned to you without filing Form SS-4 if your only employees are household employees (domestic workers) in your private home. To have an EIN assigned to you, write "NONE" in the space for the EIN on Form 942, Employer's Quarterly Tax Return for Household Employees, when you file it.*

When To Apply for A New EIN

New Business.—If you become the new owner of an existing business, **DO NOT** use the EIN of the former owner. If you already have an EIN, use that number. If you do not have an EIN, apply for one on this form. If you become the "owner" of a corporation by acquiring its stock, use the corporation's EIN.

Changes in Organization or Ownership.—If you already have an EIN, you may need to get a new one if either the organization or ownership of your business changes. If you incorporate a sole proprietorship or form a partnership, you must get a new EIN. However, **DO NOT** apply for a new EIN if you change only the name of your business.

File Only One Form SS-4.—File only one Form SS-4, regardless of the number of businesses operated or trade names under which a business operates. However, each corporation in an affiliated group must file a separate application.

EIN Applied For, But Not Received.—If you do not have an EIN by the time a return is due, write "Applied for" and the date you applied in the space shown for the number. **DO NOT** show your social security number as an EIN on returns.

If you do not have an EIN by the time a tax deposit is due, send your payment to the Internal Revenue service center for your filing area. (See **Where To Apply** below.) Make your check or money order payable to Internal Revenue Service and show your name (as shown on Form SS-4), address, kind of tax, period covered, and date you applied for an EIN.

For more information about EINs, see **Pub. 583**, Taxpayers Starting a Business and Pub. 1635, EINs Made Easy.

How To Apply

You can apply for an EIN either by mail or by telephone. You can get an EIN immediately by calling the Tele-TIN phone number for the service center for your state, or you can send the completed Form SS-4 directly to the service center to receive your EIN in the mail.

Application by Tele-TIN.—Under the Tele-TIN program, you can receive your EIN over the telephone and use it immediately to file a return or make a payment. To receive an EIN by phone, complete Form SS-4, then call the Tele-TIN phone number listed for your state under **Where To Apply**. The person making the call must be authorized to sign the form (see **Signature block** on page 3).

An IRS representative will use the information from the Form SS-4 to establish your account and assign you an EIN. Write the number you are given on the upper right-hand corner of the form, sign and date it.

You should mail or FAX the signed SS-4 within 24 hours to the Tele-TIN Unit at the service center address for your state. The IRS representative will give you the FAX number. The FAX numbers are also listed in Pub. 1635.

Taxpayer representatives can receive their client's EIN by phone if they first send a facsimile (FAX) of a completed **Form 2848**, Power of Attorney and Declaration of Representative, or **Form 8821**, Tax Information Authorization, to the Tele-TIN unit. The Form 2848 or Form 8821 will be used solely to release the EIN to the representative authorized on the form.

Application by Mail.—Complete Form SS-4 at least 4 to 5 weeks before you will need an EIN. Sign and date the application and mail it to the service center address for your state. You will receive your EIN in the mail in approximately 4 weeks.

Where To Apply

The Tele-TIN phone numbers listed below will involve a long-distance charge to callers outside of the local calling area, and should be used only to apply for an EIN. THE NUMBERS MAY CHANGE WITHOUT NOTICE. Use 1-800-829-1040 to verify a number or to ask about an application by mail or other Federal tax matters.

If your principal business, office or agency, or legal residence in the case of an individual, is located in:	Call the Tele-TIN phone number shown or file with the Internal Revenue Service center at:
Florida, Georgia, South Carolina	Attn: Entity Control Atlanta, GA 39901 (404) 455-2360
New Jersey, New York City and counties of Nassau, Rockland, Suffolk, and Westchester	Attn: Entity Control Holtsville, NY 00501 (516) 447-4955
New York (all other counties), Connecticut, Maine, Massachusetts, New Hampshire, Rhode Island, Vermont	Attn: Entity Control Andover, MA 05501 (508) 474-9717
Illinois, Iowa, Minnesota, Missouri, Wisconsin	Attn: Entity Control Stop 57A 2306 E. Bannister Rd. Kansas City, MO 64131 (816) 926-5999
Delaware, District of Columbia, Maryland, Pennsylvania, Virginia	Attn: Entity Control Philadelphia, PA 19255 (215) 574-2400

Form 15-2: (continued)

Indiana, Kentucky, Michigan, Ohio, West Virginia	Attn: Entity Control Cincinnati, OH 45999 (606) 292-5467
Kansas, New Mexico, Oklahoma, Texas	Attn: Entity Control Austin, TX 73301 (512) 462-7843
Alaska, Arizona, California (counties of Alpine, Amador, Butte, Calaveras, Colusa, Contra Costa, Del Norte, El Dorado, Glenn, Humboldt, Lake, Lassen, Marin, Mendocino, Modoc, Napa, Nevada, Placer, Plumas, Sacramento, San Joaquin, Shasta, Sierra, Siskiyou, Solano, Sonoma, Sutter, Tehama, Trinity, Yolo, and Yuba), Colorado, Idaho, Montana, Nebraska, Nevada, North Dakota, Oregon, South Dakota, Utah, Washington, Wyoming	Attn: Entity Control Mail Stop 6271-T P.O. Box 9950 Ogden, UT 84409 (801) 620-7645
California (all other counties), Hawaii	Attn: Entity Control Fresno, CA 93888 (209) 452-4010
Alabama, Arkansas, Louisiana, Mississippi, North Carolina, Tennessee	Attn: Entity Control Memphis, TN 37501 (901) 365-5970

If you have no legal residence, principal place of business, or principal office or agency in any state, file your form with the Internal Revenue Service Center, Philadelphia, PA 19255 or call (215) 574-2400.

Specific Instructions

The instructions that follow are for those items that are not self-explanatory. Enter N/A (nonapplicable) on the lines that do not apply.

Line 1.—Enter the legal name of the entity applying for the EIN exactly as it appears on the social security card, charter, or other applicable legal document.

Individuals.—Enter the first name, middle initial, and last name.

Trusts.—Enter the name of the trust.

Estate of a decedent.—Enter the name of the estate.

Partnerships.—Enter the legal name of the partnership as it appears in the partnership agreement.

Corporations.—Enter the corporate name as set forth in the corporation charter or other legal document creating it.

Plan administrators.—Enter the name of the plan administrator. A plan administrator who already has an EIN should use that number.

Line 2.—Enter the trade name of the business if different from the legal name. The trade name is the "doing business as" name.

Note: *Use the full legal name on line 1 on all tax returns filed for the entity. However, if you enter a trade name on line 2 and choose to use the trade name instead of the legal name, enter the trade name on all returns you file. To prevent processing delays and errors, always use either the legal name only or the trade name only on all tax returns.*

Line 3.—Trusts enter the name of the trustee. Estates enter the name of the executor, administrator, or other fiduciary. If the entity applying has a designated person to receive tax information, enter that person's name as the "care of" person. Print or type the first name, middle initial, and last name.

Line 7.—Enter the first name, middle initial, last name, and social security number (SSN) of a principal officer if the business is a corporation; of a general partner if a partnership; and of a grantor owner, or trustor if a trust.

Line 8a.—Check the box that best describes the type of entity applying for the EIN. If not specifically mentioned, check the "other" box and enter the type of entity. Do not enter N/A.

Sole proprietor.—Check this box if you file Schedule C or F (Form 1040) and have a Keogh plan, or are required to file excise, employment, or alcohol, tobacco, or firearms returns. Enter your SSN (social security number) in the space provided.

Plan administrator.—If the plan administrator is an individual, enter the plan administrator's SSN in the space provided.

Withholding agent.—If you are a withholding agent required to file Form 1042, check the "other" box and enter "withholding agent."

REMICs.—Check this box if the entity has elected to be treated as a real estate mortgage investment conduit (REMIC). See the Instructions for Form 1066 for more information.

Personal service corporations.—Check this box if the entity is a personal service corporation. An entity is a personal service corporation for a tax year only if:

● The principal activity of the entity during the testing period (prior tax year) for the tax year is the performance of personal services substantially by employee-owners.

● The employee-owners own 10 percent of the fair market value of the outstanding stock in the entity on the last day of the testing period.

Personal services include performance of services in such fields as health, law, accounting, consulting, etc. For more information about personal service corporations, see the instructions to **Form 1120,** U.S. Corporation Income Tax Return, and **Pub. 542,** Tax Information on Corporations.

Other corporations.—This box is for any corporation other than a personal service corporation. If you check this box, enter the type of corporation (such as insurance company) in the space provided.

Other nonprofit organizations.—Check this box if the nonprofit organization is

other than a church or church-controlled organization and specify the type of nonprofit organization (for example, an educational organization.)

If the organization also seeks tax-exempt status, you must file either **Package 1023 or Package 1024,** Application for Recognition of Exemption. Get **Pub. 557,** Tax-Exempt Status for Your Organization, for more information.

Group exemption number (GEN).—If the organization is covered by a group exemption letter, enter the four-digit GEN. (Do not confuse the GEN with the nine-digit EIN.) If you do not know the GEN, contact the parent organization. Get Pub. 557 for more information about group exemption numbers.

Line 9.—Check only **one** box. Do not enter N/A.

Started new business.—Check this box if you are starting a new business that requires an EIN. If you check this box, enter the type of business being started. **DO NOT** apply if you already have an EIN and are only adding another place of business.

Changed type of organization.—Check this box if the business is changing its type of organization, for example, if the business was a sole proprietorship and has been incorporated or has become a partnership. If you check this box, specify in the space provided the type of change made, for example, "from sole proprietorship to partnership."

Purchased going business.—Check this box if you purchased an existing business. DO NOT use the former owner's EIN. Use your own EIN if you already have one.

Hired employees.—Check this box if the existing business is requesting an EIN because it has hired or is hiring employees and is therefore required to file employment tax returns. **DO NOT** apply if you already have an EIN and are only hiring employees. If you are hiring household employees, see **Note** under **Who Must File** on page 2.

Created a trust.—Check this box if you created a trust, and enter the type of trust created.

Note: *DO NOT file this form if you are the individual-grantor/owner of a revocable trust. You must use your SSN for the trust. See the instructions for Form 1040.*

Created a pension plan.—Check this box if you have created a pension plan and need this number for reporting purposes. Also, enter the type of plan created.

Banking purpose.—Check this box if you are requesting an EIN for banking purposes only and enter the banking purpose (for example, a bowling league for depositing dues, an investment club for dividend and interest reporting, etc.).

Form 15-2: (continued)

Other (specify).—Check this box if you are requesting an EIN for any reason other than those for which there are checkboxes, and enter the reason.

Line 10.—If you are starting a new business, enter the starting date of the business. If the business you acquired is already operating, enter the date you acquired the business. Trusts should enter the date the trust was legally created. Estates should enter the date of death of the decedent whose name appears on line 1 or the date when the estate was legally funded.

Line 11.—Enter the last month of your accounting year or tax year. An accounting or tax year is usually 12 consecutive months, either a calendar year or a fiscal year (including a period of 52 or 53 weeks). A calendar year is 12 consecutive months ending on December 31. A fiscal year is either 12 consecutive months ending on the last day of any month other than December or a 52-53 week year. For more information on accounting periods, see **Pub. 538,** Accounting Periods and Methods.

Individuals.—Your tax year generally will be a calendar year.

Partnerships.—Partnerships generally must adopt the tax year of either (1) the majority partners; (2) the principal partners; (3) the tax year that results in the least aggregate (total) deferral of income; or (4) some other tax year. (See the Instructions for **Form 1065,** U.S. Partnership Return of Income, for more information.)

REMICs.—Remics must have a calendar year as their tax year.

Personal service corporations.—A personal service corporation generally must adopt a calendar year unless:

• It can establish a business purpose for having a different tax year, or

• It elects under section 444 to have a tax year other than a calendar year.

Trusts.—Generally, a trust must adopt a calendar year except for the following:

• Tax-exempt trusts,

• Charitable trusts, and

• Grantor-owned trusts.

Line 12.—If the business has or will have employees, enter the date on which the business began or will begin to pay wages. If the business does not plan to have employees, enter N/A.

Withholding agent.—Enter the date you began or will begin to pay income to a nonresident alien. This also applies to individuals who are required to file Form 1042 to report alimony paid to a nonresident alien.

Line 14.—Generally, enter the exact type of business being operated (for example, advertising agency, farm, food or beverage establishment, labor union, real estate agency, steam laundry, rental of coin-operated vending machine, investment club, etc.). Also state if the business will involve the sale or distribution of alcoholic beverages.

Governmental.—Enter the type of organization (state, county, school district, or municipality, etc.).

Nonprofit organization (other than governmental).—Enter whether organized for religious, educational, or humane purposes, and the principal activity (for example, religious organization—hospital, charitable).

Mining and quarrying.—Specify the process and the principal product (for example, mining bituminous coal, contract drilling for oil, quarrying dimension stone, etc.).

Contract construction.—Specify whether general contracting or special trade contracting. Also, show the type of work normally performed (for example, general contractor for residential buildings, electrical subcontractor, etc.).

Food or beverage establishments.—Specify the type of establishment and state whether you employ workers who receive tips (for example, lounge—yes).

Trade.—Specify the type of sales and the principal line of goods sold (for example, wholesale dairy products, manufacturer's representative for mining machinery, retail hardware, etc.).

Manufacturing.—Specify the type of establishment operated (for example, sawmill, vegetable cannery, etc.).

Signature block.—The application must be signed by: (1) the individual, if the applicant is an individual, (2) the president, vice president, or other principal officer, if the applicant is a corporation, (3) a responsible and duly authorized member or officer having knowledge of its affairs, if the applicant is a partnership or other unincorporated organization, or (4) the fiduciary, if the applicant is a trust or estate.

Some Useful Publications

You may get the following publications for additional information on the subjects covered on this form. To get these and other free forms and publications, call 1-800-TAX-FORM (1-800-829-3676).

Pub. 1635, EINs Made Easy

Pub. 538, Accounting Periods and Methods

Pub. 541, Tax Information on Partnerships

Pub. 542, Tax Information on Corporations

Pub. 557, Tax-Exempt Status for Your Organization

Pub. 583, Taxpayers Starting A Business

Pub. 937, Employment Taxes and Information Returns

Package 1023, Application for Recognition of Exemption

Package 1024, Application for Recognition of Exemption Under Section 501(a) or for Determination Under Section 120

Paperwork Reduction Act Notice

We ask for the information on this form to carry out the Internal Revenue laws of the United States. You are required to give us the information. We need it to ensure that you are complying with these laws and to allow us to figure and collect the right amount of tax.

The time needed to complete and file this form will vary depending on individual circumstances. The estimated average time is:

Recordkeeping	7 min.
Learning about the law or the form	18 min.
Preparing the form	44 min.
Copying, assembling, and sending the form to the IRS	20 min.

If you have comments concerning the accuracy of these time estimates or suggestions for making this form more simple, we would be happy to hear from you. You can write to both the **Internal Revenue Service,** Attention: Reports Clearance Officer, PC:FP, Washington, DC 20224; and the **Office of Management and Budget,** Paperwork Reduction Project (1545-0003), Washington, DC 20503. **DO NOT** send this form to either of these offices. Instead, see **Where To Apply** on page 2.

Form 15-3: U.S. Fiduciary Income Tax Return

Form 1041

Department of the Treasury—Internal Revenue Service

U.S. Fiduciary Income Tax Return 1993

OMB No. 1545-0092

For the calendar year 1993 or fiscal year beginning _____ , 1993, and ending _____ , 19 ____

A Type of Entity	Name of estate or trust (grantor type trust, see instructions)	C Employer identification number
☐ Decedent's estate		
☐ Simple trust		D Date entity created
☐ Complex trust		
☐ Grantor type trust	Name and title of fiduciary	E Nonexempt charitable and split-interest trusts, check applicable boxes (see instructions):
☐ Bankruptcy estate–Chpt. 7		
☐ Bankruptcy estate–Chpt. 11	Number, street, and room or suite no. (If a P.O. box, see page 5 of instructions.)	
☐ Pooled income fund		☐ Described in section 4947(a)(1)
B Number of Schedules K-1 attached (see instructions). ▶	City, state, and ZIP code	☐ Not a private foundation
		☐ Described in section 4947(a)(2)

F Check applicable boxes:	☐ Initial return ☐ Final return ☐ Amended return	G Pooled mortgage account (see instructions)
	Change in Fiduciary's ▶ ☐ Name ☐ Address	☐ Bought ☐ Sold Date:

Income

			Sold	Date:
1	Interest income	1		
2	Dividends	2		
3	Business income or (loss) (attach Schedule C or C-EZ (Form 1040))	3		
4	Capital gain or (loss) (attach Schedule D (Form 1041))	4		
5	Rents, royalties, partnerships, other estates and trusts, etc. (attach Schedule E (Form 1040))	5		
6	Farm income or (loss) (attach Schedule F (Form 1040))	6		
7	Ordinary gain or (loss) (attach Form 4797)	7		
8	Other income (state nature of income)	8		
9	**Total income** (combine lines 1 through 8) ▶	9		

Deductions

10	Interest. (Check if Form 4952 is attached ▶ ☐)	10	
11	Taxes	11	
12	Fiduciary fees	12	
13	Charitable deduction (from Schedule A, line 7)	13	
14	Attorney, accountant, and return preparer fees	14	
15a	Other deductions NOT subject to the 2% floor (attach schedule)	15a	
b	Allowable miscellaneous itemized deductions subject to the 2% floor.	15b	
16	**Total** (add lines 10 through 15b)	16	
17	Adjusted total income or (loss) (subtract line 16 from line 9). Enter here and on Schedule B, line 1 ▶	17	
18	Income distribution deduction (from Schedule B, line 17) (see instructions) (attach Schedules K-1 (Form 1041))	18	
19	Estate tax deduction (including certain generation-skipping taxes) (attach computation)	19	
20	Exemption	20	
21	**Total deductions** (add lines 18 through 20) ▶	21	

Tax and Payments

22	Taxable income of fiduciary (subtract line 21 from line 17).	22	
23	**Total tax** (from Schedule G, line 7)	23	
24	Payments: a 1993 estimated tax payments and amount applied from 1992 return	24a	
b	Estimated tax payments allocated to beneficiaries (from Form 1041-T)	24b	
c	Subtract line 24b from line 24a	24c	
d	Tax paid with extension of time to file: ☐ Form 2758 ☐ Form 8736 ☐ Form 8800	24d	
e	Federal income tax withheld	24e	
	Credits: f Form 2439 .... ; g Form 4136 .... ; h Other .... ; Total ▶	24i	
25	**Total payments** (add lines 24c through 24e, and 24i) ▶	25	
26	**Penalty** for underpayment of estimated tax (see instructions)	26	
27	**Tax Due.** If line 25 is smaller than the total of lines 23 and 26, enter amount owed	27	
28	**Overpayment.** If line 25 is larger than the total of lines 23 and 26, enter amount overpaid	28	
29	Amount of line 28 to be: a Credited to 1994 estimated tax ▶ _____ ; b Refunded ▶	29	

Please Sign Here

Under penalties of perjury, I declare that I have examined this return, including accompanying schedules and statements, and to the best of my knowledge and belief, it is true, correct, and complete. Declaration of preparer (other than fiduciary) is based on all information of which preparer has any knowledge.

▶		
Signature of fiduciary or officer representing fiduciary	Date	EIN of fiduciary (see instructions)

Paid Preparer's Use Only

Preparer's signature ▶	Date	Check if self-employed ▶ ☐	Preparer's social security no.
Firm's name (or yours if self-employed) and address ▶		E.I. No. ▶	
		ZIP code ▶	

For Paperwork Reduction Act Notice, see page 1 of the separate instructions.   Cat. No. 11370H   Form **1041** (1993)

Form 15-3: (continued)

Form 1041 (1993)   Page **2**

Schedule A   Charitable Deduction—Do not complete for a simple trust or a pooled income fund.

1	Amounts paid for charitable purposes from current year's gross income	1	
2	Amounts permanently set aside for charitable purposes from current year's gross income	2	
3	Add lines 1 and 2	3	
4	Tax-exempt income allocable to charitable contribution (see instructions)	4	
5	Subtract line 4 from line 3	5	
6	Amounts paid or set aside for charitable purposes other than from the current year's income	6	
7	**Total** (add lines 5 and 6). Enter here and on page 1, line 13	7	

Schedule B   Income Distribution Deduction (see instructions)

1	Adjusted total income (from page 1, line 17) (see instructions)	1	
2	Adjusted tax-exempt interest	2	
3	Net gain shown on Schedule D (Form 1041), line 17, column (a). (see instructions)	3	
4	Enter amount from Schedule A, line 6	4	
5	Long-term capital gain included on Schedule A, line 3	5	
6	Short-term capital gain included on Schedule A, line 3	6	
7	If the amount on page 1, line 4, is a capital loss, enter here as a positive figure	7	
8	If the amount on page 1, line 4, is a capital gain, enter here as a negative figure	8	
9	Distributable net income (combine lines 1 through 8)	9	
10	Accounting income for the tax year as determined under the governing instrument	10	
11	Income required to be distributed currently	11	
12	Other amounts paid, credited, or otherwise required to be distributed	12	
13	Total distributions (add lines 11 and 12). (If greater than line 10, see instructions.)	13	
14	Enter the amount of tax-exempt income included on line 13	14	
15	Tentative income distribution deduction (subtract line 14 from line 13)	15	
16	Tentative income distribution deduction (subtract line 2 from line 9)	16	
17	Income distribution deduction. Enter the smaller of line 15 or line 16 here and on page 1, line 18	17	

Schedule G   Tax Computation (see instructions)

1	Tax: a ☐ Tax rate schedule or ☐ Schedule D (Form 1041)	1a	
	b Other taxes	1b	
	c Total (add lines 1a and 1b) ▶	1c	
2a	Foreign tax credit (attach Form 1116)	2a	
b	Check: ☐ Nonconventional source fuel credit ☐ Form 8834	2b	
c	General business credit. Enter here and check which forms are attached:		
	☐ Form 3800 or ☐ Form (specify) ▶	2c	
d	Credit for prior year minimum tax (attach Form 8801)	2d	
3	**Total** credits (add lines 2a through 2d) ▶	3	
4	Subtract line 3 from line 1c	4	
5	Recapture taxes. Check if from: ☐ Form 4255 ☐ Form 8611	5	
6	Alternative minimum tax (from Schedule H, line 39)	6	
7	**Total tax** (add lines 4 through 6). Enter here and on page 1, line 23 ▶	7	

Other Information (see instructions)

		Yes	No
1	Did the estate or trust receive tax-exempt income? (If "Yes," attach a computation of the allocation of expenses.) Enter the amount of tax-exempt interest income and exempt-interest dividends ▶ $		
2	Did the estate or trust have any passive activity losses? (If "Yes," get **Form 8582**, Passive Activity Loss Limitations, to figure the allowable loss.)		
3	Did the estate or trust receive all or any part of the earnings (salary, wages, and other compensation) of any individual by reason of a contract assignment or similar arrangement?		
4	At any time during the tax year, did the estate or trust have an interest in or a signature or other authority over a bank, securities, or other financial account in a foreign country? (See the instructions for exceptions and filing requirements for Form TD F 90-22.1.)		
	If "Yes," enter the name of the foreign country ▶		
5	Was the estate or trust the grantor of, or transferor to, a foreign trust which existed during the current tax year, whether or not the estate or trust has any beneficial interest in it? (If "Yes," you may have to file Form 3520, 3520-A, or 926.)		
6	Did the estate or trust receive, or pay, any seller-financed mortgage interest?		
7	If this entity has filed or is required to file **Form 8264**, Application for Registration of a Tax Shelter, check here ▶ ☐		
8	If this is a complex trust making the section 663(b) election, check here ▶ ☐		
9	To make a section 643(e)(3) election, attach Schedule D (Form 1041), and check here ▶ ☐		
10	If the decedent's estate has been open for more than 2 years, check here ▶ ☐		

Form 15-3: (continued)

Schedule H   Alternative Minimum Tax (see instructions)—To Be Completed by any Decedent's Estate, or Simple or Complex Trust

Part I—Fiduciary's Share of Alternative Minimum Taxable Income

1	Adjusted total income or (loss) (from page 1, line 17)	**1**	
2	Net operating loss deduction (Enter as a positive amount.)	**2**	
3	Add lines 1 and 2	**3**	
4a	Interest	**4a**	
b	Taxes	**4b**	
c	Miscellaneous itemized deductions (from page 1, line 15b)	**4c**	
d	Refund of taxes	**4d** ( )	
e	Combine lines 4a through 4d	**4e**	
5	Adjustments:		
a	Depreciation of property placed in service after 1986	**5a**	
b	Circulation and research and experimental expenditures paid or incurred after 1986	**5b**	
c	Mining exploration and development costs paid or incurred after 1986	**5c**	
d	Long-term contracts entered into after February 28, 1986	**5d**	
e	Pollution control facilities placed in service after 1986	**5e**	
f	Installment sales of certain property	**5f**	
g	Adjusted gain or loss (including incentive stock options)	**5g**	
h	Certain loss limitations	**5h**	
i	Tax shelter farm activities	**5i**	
j	Passive activities	**5j**	
k	Beneficiaries of other trusts or decedent's estates	**5k**	
l	Combine lines 5a through 5k	**5l**	
6	Tax preference items:		
a	Tax-exempt interest from specified private activity bonds	**6a**	
b	Depletion	**6b**	
c	Combine lines 6a and 6b	**6c**	
7	Other items of tax preference:		
a	Accelerated depreciation of real property placed in service before 1987	**7a**	
b	Accelerated depreciation of leased personal property placed in service before 1987	**7b**	
c	Intangible drilling costs	**7c**	
d	Combine lines 7a through 7c	**7d**	
8	Add lines 3, 4e, 5l, 6c, and 7d	**8**	
9	Alternative tax net operating loss deduction (see instructions for limitations)	**9**	
10	Adjusted alternative minimum taxable income (subtract line 9 from line 8). Enter here and on line 13	**10**	
	Note: *Complete Part II before proceeding with line 11.*		
11a	Income distribution deduction from line 27	**11a**	
b	Estate tax deduction (from page 1, line 19)	**11b**	
c	Add lines 11a and 11b	**11c**	
12	Fiduciary's share of alternative minimum taxable income (subtract line 11c from line 10)	**12**	

Note: *If line 12 is more than $22,500, proceed to Part III. If line 12 is $22,500 or less, stop here, as you are not liable for the alternative minimum tax.*

(continued on page 4)

Form 15-3: (continued)

Form 1041 (1993)   Page **4**

Part II—Income Distribution Deduction on a Minimum Tax Basis

13	Adjusted alternative minimum taxable income (from line 10)	**13**	
14	Adjusted tax-exempt interest (other than amounts included in line 6a)	**14**	
15	Net capital gain from Schedule D (Form 1041), line 17, column (a) (If a loss, enter -0-.)	**15**	
16	Capital gains allocable to corpus paid or set aside for charitable purposes (from Schedule A, line 6)	**16**	
17	Capital gains paid or permanently set aside for charitable purposes from current year's income (see instructions)	**17**	
18	Capital gains computed on a minimum tax basis included in line 10	**18**	( )
19	Capital losses computed on a minimum tax basis included in line 10 (Enter as a positive amount.)	**19**	
20	Distributable net alternative minimum taxable income (DNAMTI) (combine lines 13 through 19).	**20**	
21	Income required to be distributed currently (from Schedule B, line 11)	**21**	
22	Other amounts paid, credited, or otherwise required to be distributed (from Schedule B, line 12)	**22**	
23	Total distributions (add lines 21 and 22)	**23**	
24	Tax-exempt income included on line 23 (other than amounts included in line 6a)	**24**	
25	Tentative income distribution deduction on a minimum tax basis (subtract line 24 from line 23).	**25**	
26	Tentative income distribution deduction on a minimum tax basis (subtract line 14 from line 20).	**26**	
27	Income distribution deduction on a minimum tax basis. Enter the smaller of line 25 or line 26. Enter here and on line 11a	**27**	

Part III—Alternative Minimum Tax Computation

28	Enter amount from line 12 (If at least $165,000, but not more than $175,000, skip lines 29a through 33. If more than $175,000, skip lines 29a through 34.)		**28**	
29a	Exemption amount	**29a** $22,500		
b	Phase-out of exemption amount	**29b** $75,000		
30	Subtract line 29b from line 28 (If zero or less, enter -0-.)		**30**	
31	Multiply line 30 by 25% (.25)		**31**	
32	Subtract line 31 from line 29a (If zero or less, enter -0-.)		**32**	
33	Subtract line 32 from line 28		**33**	
34	Multiply line 33 by 26% (.26). (If line 28 is at least $165,000, but not more than $175,000, multiply line 28 by 26% (.26).) Enter the result here, and skip line 35.		**34**	
35	If line 28 is $175,000 or more, subtract $175,000 from line 28. Multiply the difference by 28% (.28). Add the result to $45,500 and enter the result here		**35**	
36	Alternative minimum tax foreign tax credit (see instructions)		**36**	
37	Tentative minimum tax (subtract line 36 from line 34 or 35, whichever applies)		**37**	
38a	Regular tax before credits (see instructions)	**38a**		
b	Section 644 tax (see instructions)	**38b**		
c	Add lines 38a and 38b		**38c**	
39	**Alternative minimum tax.** (subtract line 38c from line 37). (If zero or less, enter -0-.) Enter here and on Schedule G, line 6.		**39**	

♻ Printed on recycled paper   *U.S. Government Printing Office: 1993 — 345-252

Form 15-4: Schedule D to Form 1041

SCHEDULE D (Form 1041)	Capital Gains and Losses	OMB No. 1545-0092

SCHEDULE D (Form 1041)
Department of the Treasury
Internal Revenue Service

Capital Gains and Losses
▶ Attach to Form 1041 (or Form 5227). See the separate instructions for Form 1041 (or Form 5227).

OMB No. 1545-0092

1993

Name of estate or trust | Employer identification number

Note: *Form 5227 filers need to complete ONLY Parts I and II.*

Part I   Short-Term Capital Gains and Losses—Assets Held 1 Year or Less

(a) Description of property (Example, 100 shares 7% preferred of "Z" Co.)	(b) Date acquired (mo., day, yr.)	(c) Date sold (mo., day, yr.)	(d) Gross sales price	(e) Cost or other basis (see instructions)	(f) Gain or (loss) (col. (d) less col. (e))
1					

2 Short-term capital gain or (loss) from Form 6252 and Form 8824	**2**	
3 Net short-term gain or (loss) from partnerships, S corporations, and other trusts or estates . . .	**3**	
4 Net gain or (loss) (combine lines 1 through 3)	**4**	
5 Short-term capital loss carryover from 1992 Schedule D, line 28	**5** (	)
6 Net short-term gain or (loss) (combine lines 4 and 5). Enter here and on line 15 below . . . ▶	**6**	

Part II   Long-Term Capital Gains and Losses—Assets Held More Than 1 Year

7					

8 Long-term capital gain or (loss) from Form 6252 and Form 8824	**8**	
9 Net long-term gain or (loss) from partnerships, S corporations, and other trusts or estates . . .	**9**	
10 Capital gain distributions	**10**	
11 Enter gain, if applicable, from Form 4797	**11**	
12 Net gain or (loss) (combine lines 7 through 11)	**12**	
13 Long-term capital loss carryover from 1992 Schedule D, line 35	**13** (	)
14 Net long-term gain or (loss) (combine lines 12 and 13). Enter here and on line 16 below . . . ▶	**14**	

Part III Summary of Parts I and II		(a) Beneficiaries (see instructions)	(b) Fiduciary	(c) Total
15 Net short-term gain or (loss) from line 6, above	**15**			
16 Net long-term gain or (loss) from line 14, above . . .	**16**			
17 Total net gain or (loss) (combine lines 15 and 16) . . . ▶	**17**			

If line 17, column (c), is a net gain, enter the gain on Form 1041, line 4. If lines 16 and 17, column (b) are net gains, go to Part VI, and DO NOT complete Parts IV and V. If line 17, column (c), is a net loss, complete Parts IV and V, as necessary.

For Paperwork Reduction Act Notice, see page 1 of the Instructions for Form 1041.   Cat. No. 11376V   **Schedule D (Form 1041) 1993**

Form 15-4: (continued)

Schedule D (Form 1041) 1993   Page **2**

Part IV   **Computation of Capital Loss Limitation**

18 Enter here and enter as a (loss) on Form 1041, line 4, the smaller of:
   (i) The net loss on line 17, column (c); or
   (ii) $3,000 . . . .   **18** (   )

If the net loss on line 17, column (c) is more than $3,000, OR if the taxable income on line 22, page 1, of Form 1041 is zero or less, complete Part V to determine your capital loss carryover.

Part V   **Computation of Capital Loss Carryovers From 1993 to 1994**

Section A.—Computation of Carryover Limit

19	Enter taxable income or (loss) for 1993 from Form 1041, line 22.	**19**	
20	Enter loss from line 18 as a positive amount	**20**	
21	Enter amount from Form 1041, line 20	**21**	
22	Adjusted taxable income (Combine lines 19, 20, and 21, but do not enter less than zero.) . . .	**22**	
23	Enter the lesser of lines 20 or 22	**23**	

Section B.—Short-Term Capital Loss Carryover
(Complete this part only if there is a loss on line 6, and line 17, column (c).)

24	Enter loss from line 6 as a positive amount	**24**	
25	Enter gain, if any, from line 14. (If that line is blank or shows a loss, enter -0-.)	**25**	
26	Enter amount from line 23	**26**	
27	Add lines 25 and 26	**27**	
28	Subtract line 27 from line 24. If zero or less, enter -0-. This is the fiduciary's short-term capital loss carryover from 1993 to 1994. If this is the final return of the trust or decedent's estate, also enter on line 12b, Schedule K-1 (Form 1041)	**28**	

Section C.—Long-Term Capital Loss Carryover
(Complete this part only if there is a loss on line 14 and line 17, column (c).)

29	Enter loss from line 14 as a positive amount . . . . : . . .	**29**	
30	Enter gain, if any, from line 6. (If that line is blank or shows a loss, enter -0-.)	**30**	
31	Enter amount from line 23	**31**	
32	Enter amount, if any, from line 24	**32**	
33	Subtract line 32 from line 31. If zero or less, enter -0-	**33**	
34	Add lines 30 and 33	**34**	
35	Subtract line 34 from line 29. If zero or less, enter -0-. This is the fiduciary's long-term capital loss carryover from 1993 to 1994. If this is the final return of the trust or decedent's estate, also enter on line 12c, Schedule K-1 (Form 1041)	**35**	

Part VI   **Tax Computation Using Maximum Capital Gains Rate** *(Complete this part only if lines 16 and 17, column (b) are net capital gains for 1993.)*

36	Taxable income (from Form 1041, line 22)	**36**	
37a	Net capital gain for 1993 (Enter the smaller of line 16 or 17, column (b).)	**37a**	
b	If you completed Form 4952, enter the amount from line 4e of Form 4952	**37b**	
c	Subtract line 37b from line 37a. If zero or less, stop here. You cannot use Part VI to figure the tax for the estate or trust. Instead, use the 1993 Tax Rate Schedule	**37c**	
38	Subtract line 37c from line 36. If zero or less, enter -0-.	**38**	
39	Enter the greater of line 38 or $1,500	**39**	
40	Tax on amount on line 39 from the 1993 Tax Rate Schedule. If line 39 is $1,500, enter $225.00 .	**40**	
41	Subtract line 39 from line 36. If zero or less, enter -0-	**41**	
42	Multiply line 41 by (.28)	**42**	
43	Maximum capital gains tax (add lines 40 and 42)	**43**	
44	Regular tax on amount on line 36 from the 1993 Tax Rate Schedule	**44**	
45	**Tax.** (Enter the smaller of line 43 or line 44.) Enter here and on line 1a of Schedule G, Form 1041	**45**	

U.S. GPO : 1993 – 345-254

Printed on recycled paper

Form 15-5: Schedule J to Form 1041

SCHEDULE J (Form 1041)	Accumulation Distribution for a Complex Trust	OMB No. 1545-0092
Department of the Treasury Internal Revenue Service	▶ File with Form 1041. ▶ See the separate Form 1041 Instructions.	1993

Name of trust	Employer identification number

Part I   Accumulation Distribution in 1993

See the Form 4970 instructions for certain income that minors may exclude and special rules for multiple trusts.

1 Other amounts paid, credited, or otherwise required to be distributed for 1993 (from Schedule B of Form 1041, line 12) **1**

2 Distributable net income for 1993 (from Schedule B of Form 1041, line 9) . . .   **2**

3 Income required to be distributed currently for 1993 (from Schedule B of Form 1041, line 11) **3**

4 Subtract line 3 from line 2. If zero or less, enter -0- **4**

5 Accumulation distribution for 1993. (Subtract line 4 from line 1.) **5**

Part II   Ordinary Income Accumulation Distribution (Enter the applicable throwback years below.)

If the distribution is thrown back to more than five years (starting with the earliest applicable tax year beginning after December 31, 1968), attach additional schedules. (If the trust was a simple trust, see Regulations section 1.665(e)-1A(b).)		Throwback year ending 19	Throwback year ending 19	Throwback year ending 19	Throwback year ending 19	Throwback year ending 19 ....
6 Distributable net income (see instructions)	**6**					
7 Distributions (see instructions) .	**7**					
8 Subtract line 7 from line 6 .	**8**					
9 Enter amount from page 2, line 25 or line 31, as applicable	**9**					
10 Undistributed net income (Subtract line 9 from line 8.) .	**10**					
11 Enter amount of prior accumulation distributions thrown back to any of these years	**11**					
12 Subtract line 11 from line 10	**12**					
13 Allocate the amount on line 5 to the earliest applicable year first. Do not allocate an amount greater than line 12 for the same year (see instructions) .	**13**					
14 Divide line 13 by line 10 and multiply result by amount on line 9	**14**					
15 Add lines 13 and 14 . . .	**15**					
16 Tax-exempt interest included on line 13 (see instructions) .	**16**					
17 Subtract line 16 from line 15	**17**					

For Paperwork Reduction Act Notice, see page 1 of the Instructions for Form 1041.   Cat. No. 11382Z   Schedule J (Form 1041) 1993

Form 15-5: (continued)

Schedule J (Form 1041) 1993   Page **2**

Part III   Taxes Imposed on Undistributed Net Income (Enter the applicable throwback years below.) (see instructions)
If more than five throwback years are involved, attach additional schedules. If the trust received an accumulation distribution from another trust, see Regulations section 1.665 (d)-1A.

		Throwback year ending 19	Throwback year ending 19	Throwback year ending 19	Throwback year ending 19	Throwback year ending 19 ....
If the trust elected the alternative tax on capital gains, SKIP lines 18 through 25 AND complete lines 26 through 31.						
(The alternative tax on capital gains was repealed for tax years beginning after December 31, 1978.)						
18 Regular tax	**18**					
19 Trust's share of net short-term gain	**19**					
20 Trust's share of net long-term gain	**20**					
21 Add lines 19 and 20. . . .	**21**					
22 Taxable income	**22**					
23 Enter percent (divide line 21 by line 22, but not more than 100%)	**23**	%	%	%	%	%
24 Multiply line 18 by the percentage on line 23. . .	**24**					
25 Tax on undistributed net income. (Subtract line 24 from line 18. Enter here and on page 1, line 9.)	**25**					
Complete lines 26 through 31 only if the trust elected the alternative tax on long-term capital gain.						
26 Tax on income other than long-term capital gain . .	**26**					
27 Trust's share of net short-term gain	**27**					
28 Trust's share of taxable income less section 1202 deduction	**28**					
29 Enter percent (divide line 27 by line 28, but not more than 100%)	**29**	%	%	%	%	%
30 Multiply line 26 by the percentage on line 29. . .	**30**					
31 Tax on undistributed net income. (Subtract line 30 from line 26. Enter here and on page 1, line 9.)	**31**					

Part IV   Allocation to Beneficiary
Note: *Be sure to complete Form 4970, Tax on Accumulation Distribution of Trusts.*

Beneficiary's name		Identifying number	

Beneficiary's address (number and street including apartment number or P.O. box)		(a) This beneficiary's share of line 13	(b) This beneficiary's share of line 14	(c) This beneficiary's share of line 16
City, state, and ZIP code				
32 Throwback year 19	**32**			
33 Throwback year 19	**33**			
34 Throwback year 19	**34**			
35 Throwback year 19	**35**			
36 Throwback year 19	**36**			
37 Total (Add lines 32 through 36. Enter here and on the appropriate lines of Form 4970.)	**37**			

Printed on recycled paper

Form 15-6: Schedule K-1 to Form 1041

SCHEDULE K-1 (Form 1041) Department of the Treasury Internal Revenue Service	Beneficiary's Share of Income, Deductions, Credits, etc. for the calendar year 1993, or fiscal year beginning .... , 1993, ending .... , 19 .... ► Complete a separate Schedule K-1 for each beneficiary.	OMB No. 1545-0092 19**93**

Name of trust or decedent's estate

☐ Amended K-1
☐ Final K-1

Beneficiary's identifying number ►

Trust's or Decedent's Estate's employer identification number ►

Beneficiary's name, address, and ZIP code

Fiduciary's name, address, and ZIP code

(a) Allocable share item	(b) Amount	(c) Calendar year 1993 Form 1040 filers enter the amounts in column (b) on:
1 Interest		Schedule B, Part I, line 1
2 Dividends		Schedule B, Part II, line 5
3a Net short-term capital gain		Schedule D, line 5, column (g)
b Net long-term capital gain		Schedule D, line 13, column (g)
4a Business income and other nonpassive income before directly apportioned deductions. (see instructions)		Schedule E, Part III
b Depreciation		
c Depletion		
d Amortization		
5a Rental, rental real estate, and other passive income before directly apportioned deductions. (see instructions)		
b Depreciation		
c Depletion		
d Amortization		
6 Income for minimum tax purposes		
7 Income for regular tax purposes (add lines 1 through 3b, 4a. and 5a)		
8 Adjustment for minimum tax purposes (subtract line 7 from line 6) (see instructions)		Form 6251, line 12
9 Estate tax deduction (including certain generation-skipping transfer taxes)		Schedule A, line 25
10 Foreign taxes (list on a separate sheet)		Form 1116 or Schedule A (Form 1040), line 7
11 Tax preference items (itemize):		
a Accelerated depreciation		⎰ Include on the applicable ⎱
b Depletion		⎱ line of Form 6251 ⎰
c Amortization		
d Exclusion items		1994 Form 8801
12 Distributions in the final year of trust or decedent's estate:		
a Excess deductions on termination (see instructions)		Schedule A, line 20
b Short-term capital loss carryover		Schedule D, line 5, column (f)
c Long-term capital loss carryover		Schedule D, line 13, column (f)
d Net operating loss (NOL) carryover for regular tax purposes		Form 1040, line 22
e Net operating loss carryover for minimum tax purposes		⎰ Include on the applicable line ⎱
f		⎱ of appropriate tax form ⎰
g		
13 Other (itemize):		
a Payments of estimated taxes credited to you		Form 1040, line 55
b Tax-exempt interest		Form 1040, line 8b
c		
d		
e		⎰ Include on the applicable line ⎱
f		⎱ of appropriate tax form ⎰
g		
h		

For Paperwork Reduction Act Notice, see page 1 of the Instructions for Form 1041.   Cat. No. 11380D   Schedule K-1 (Form 1041) 1993

Form 15-6: (continued)

Instructions for Beneficiary Filing Form 1040

General Instructions

Purpose of form.—The fiduciary of a trust or decedent's estate, uses Schedule K-1 to report your share of the trust's or estate's income, credits, deductions, etc. **Keep it for your records. Do not file it with your tax return.** A copy has been filed with the IRS.

Name, address, and identifying number.—The fiduciary should have entered your name, address, and identifying number, the trust's or decedent's estate's identifying number, and the fiduciary's name and address on the Schedule K-1 you received.

Tax shelters.—If you receive a copy of **Form 8271,** Investor Reporting of Tax Shelter Registration Number, and other tax shelter information from the trust or estate, see the instructions for Form 8271 to determine your reporting requirements.

Errors.—If you think the fiduciary has made an error on your Schedule K-1, notify the fiduciary and ask for an amended or a corrected Schedule K-1. Do not change any items on your copy. Be sure that the fiduciary sends a copy of the amended Schedule K-1 to the IRS.

Beneficiaries of generation-skipping trusts.—If you received **Form 706GS(D-1),** Notification of Distribution From a Generation-Skipping Trust, and paid a generation-skipping transfer (GST) tax on **Form 706GS(D),** Generation-Skipping Transfer Tax Return for Distributions, you can deduct the GST tax paid on income distributions on Schedule A (Form 1040) (or Form 1041 if a trust).

To compute the deduction, look at column d of Form 706GS(D-1), Part II, that was filed in 1993. If the inclusion ratio is the same for all items, compute a fraction. The numerator of the fraction is the total of all income items from your Schedule(s) K-1 (Form 1041) whose values are included in column e of Form 706GS(D-1), Part II. The denominator of the fraction is the total of all the fair market values in column e. Multiply the amount on line 11, Form 706GS(D), by this fraction. Include this amount with any other taxes on Schedule A (Form 1040), line 7 (or on line 11, page 1 of Form 1041, if a trust).

If the distributions are from trusts that have different inclusion ratios, compute the GST tax attributable to income distributions from each trust separately in the following manner:

Step 1. Compute the portion of the total GST tax attributable to total distributions from the trust under consideration. To do this, multiply the total GST tax shown on line 11, Form 706GS(D) by a fraction. The numerator of the fraction is the amount in column f of Form 706GS(D-1), Part II, for that particular trust. The denominator of the fraction is line 3 of Form 706GS(D).

Step 2. Multiply the GST tax attributable to the particular trust (from Step 1 above) by a different fraction. The numerator of this fraction is the income from that particular trust as shown on Schedule K-1 (Form 1041), which is also included in column e of Form 706GS(D-1), Part II; and the denominator of this fraction is the total amount shown in column e of Form 706GS(D-1) for that particular trust.

Attach a schedule to your income tax return showing your computations.

Note: All references to Forms 706GS(D) and 706GS(D-1) are to the November 1992 versions.

Specific Instructions

Line 1. Interest.—Report the amount from line 1 (Schedule K-1) on your Schedule B (Form 1040), Part I, line 1.

Line 2. Dividends.—Report the amount from line 2 (Schedule K-1) on your Schedule B (Form 1040), Part II, line 5.

Lines 3a and 3b. Capital gains.—Report the amount from line 3a (Schedule K-1) on your Schedule D (Form 1040), line 5, column (g). Report the amount from line 3b (Schedule K-1) on your Schedule D (Form 1040), line 13, column (g). If there is an attachment to this Schedule K-1 reporting a disposition of a rental, rental real estate, or passive business activity, see the instructions to **Form 8582,** Passive Activity Loss Limitations, for information on the treatment of dispositions of interests in a passive activity.

Lines 5a–5d.—Caution: *The limitations on passive activity losses and credits under section 469 apply to trusts and decedent's estates. Rules for treating a beneficiary's share of income and directly apportionable deductions from a trust or decedent's estate, and other rules for applying the passive loss and credit limitations to beneficiaries, have not yet been issued.*

Code section 469 provides rules limiting deductions from passive activities to the income from passive activities and credits from passive activities to the tax imposed on any net income from passive activities.

Line 11d.—If you pay alternative minimum tax in 1993, the amount on line 11d will help you figure any minimum tax credit for 1994. See the 1994 **Form 8801,** Credit for Prior Year Minimum Tax—Individuals and Fiduciaries, for more information.

Lines 12a–12d.—If the fiduciary checked the "Final K-1" box at the top, you may be allowed to deduct excess deductions from the final year of the trust or decedent's estate and certain unused carryovers (subject to limitations) on your individual tax return.

Line 13a.—For purposes of computing any underpayment and penalty on **Form 2210,** Underpayment of Estimated Tax by Individuals and Fiduciaries, you should treat the amount entered on line 13a as an estimated tax payment made on January 17, 1994.

Line 13b.—If any tax-exempt interest is entered on this line by the trust or decedent's estate, report it on Form 1040, line 8b.

Lines 13c–13h.—The amount of gross farming and fishing income is included in lines 4a and 5a. This income is also separately stated on line 13 to help you determine if you are subject to a penalty for underpayment of estimated tax.

● *Individual Beneficiaries.*—Report the amount of gross farming and fishing income on Schedule E (Form 1040), line 41.

● *Beneficiaries That Are Trusts or Decedent's Estates.*—Beneficiaries that are trusts or decedent's estates must pass through the amount of gross farming and fishing income included on line 13 of their Schedules K-1 to line 13 of their beneficiaries' Schedules K-1 on a pro rata basis.

Note: You can find the fiduciary's instructions for completing Schedule K-1 in the Form 1041 instructions.

Form 15-7: U.S. Gift Tax Return

Form 709
(Rev. November 1993)

Department of the Treasury
Internal Revenue Service

United States Gift (and Generation-Skipping Transfer) Tax Return

(Section 6019 of the Internal Revenue Code) (For gifts made after December 31, 1991)

Calendar year 19 ....

▶ See separate instructions. For Privacy Act Notice, see the Instructions for Form 1040.

OMB No. 1545-0020
Expires 5-31-96

Part 1—General Information

1 Donor's first name and middle initial	2 Donor's last name	3 Donor's social security number
4 Address (number, street, and apartment number)		5 Legal residence (Domicile) (county and state)
6 City, state, and ZIP code		7 Citizenship

	Yes	No
8 If the donor died during the year, check here ▶ ☐ and enter date of death.................., 19		
9 If you received an extension of time to file this Form 709, check here ▶ ☐ and attach the Form 4868, 2688, 2350, or extension letter		
10 Enter the total number of separate donees listed on Schedule A—count each person only once . . . . ☐		
11a Have you (the donor) previously filed a Form 709 (or 709-A) for any other year? If the answer is "No," do not complete line 11b .		
11b If the answer to line 11a is "Yes," has your address changed since you last filed Form 709 (or 709-A)?		
12 Gifts by husband or wife to third parties.—Do you consent to have the gifts (including generation-skipping transfers) made by you and by your spouse to third parties during the calendar year considered as made one-half by each of you? (See instructions.) (If the answer is "Yes," the following information must be furnished and your spouse must sign the consent shown below. If the answer is "No," skip lines 13–18 and go to Schedule A.)		
13 Name of consenting spouse	14 SSN	
15 Were you married to one another during the entire calendar year? (see instructions)		
16 If the answer to 15 is "No," check whether ☐ married ☐ divorced or ☐ widowed, and give date (see instructions) ▶		
17 Will a gift tax return for this calendar year be filed by your spouse?		

18 **Consent of Spouse**—I consent to have the gifts (and generation-skipping transfers) made by me and by my spouse to third parties during the calendar year considered as made one-half by each of us. We are both aware of the joint and several liability for tax created by the execution of this consent.

Consenting spouse's signature ▶   Date ▶

Part 2—Tax Computation

1	Enter the amount from Schedule A, Part 3, line 15	1	
2	Enter the amount from Schedule B, line 3	2	
3	Total taxable gifts (add lines 1 and 2)	3	
4	Tax computed on amount on line 3 (see Table for Computing Tax in separate instructions) . .	4	
5	Tax computed on amount on line 2 (see Table for Computing Tax in separate instructions) . .	5	
6	Balance (subtract line 5 from line 4)	6	
7	Maximum unified credit (nonresident aliens, see instructions)	7	192,800 00
8	Enter the unified credit against tax allowable for all prior periods (from Sch. B, line 1, col. C)	8	
9	Balance (subtract line 8 from line 7)	9	
10	Enter 20% (.20) of the amount allowed as a specific exemption for gifts made after September 8, 1976, and before January 1, 1977 (see instructions)	10	
11	Balance (subtract line 10 from line 9)	11	
12	Unified credit (enter the smaller of line 6 or line 11)	12	
13	Credit for foreign gift taxes (see instructions)	13	
14	Total credits (add lines 12 and 13)	14	
15	Balance (subtract line 14 from line 6) (do not enter less than zero)	15	
16	Generation-skipping transfer taxes (from Schedule C, Part 3, col. H, total)	16	
17	Total tax (add lines 15 and 16).	17	
18	Gift and generation-skipping transfer taxes prepaid with extension of time to file	18	
19	If line 18 is less than line 17, enter BALANCE DUE (see instructions)	19	
20	If line 18 is greater than line 17, enter AMOUNT TO BE REFUNDED	20	

Under penalties of perjury, I declare that I have examined this return, including any accompanying schedules and statements, and to the best of my knowledge and belief it is true, correct, and complete. Declaration of preparer (other than donor) is based on all information of which preparer has any knowledge.

Donor's signature ▶   Date ▶

Preparer's signature
(other than donor) ▶   Date ▶

Preparer's address
(other than donor) ▶

Attach check or money order here.

For Paperwork Reduction Act Notice, see page 1 of the separate instructions for this form.   Cat. No. 16783M   Form **709** (Rev. 11-93)

Form 15-7: (continued)

Form 709 (Rev. 11-93)   Page **2**

SCHEDULE A   Computation of Taxable Gifts

Part 1—Gifts Subject Only to Gift Tax. *Gifts less political organization, medical, and educational exclusions—see instructions*

A Item number	B • Donee's name and address • Relationship to donor (if any) • Description of gift • If the gift was made by means of a trust, enter trust's identifying number and attach a copy of the trust instrument • If the gift was of securities, give CUSIP number	C Donor's adjusted basis of gift	D Date of gift	E Value at date of gift
1				

Part 2—Gifts That are Direct Skips and are Subject to Both Gift Tax and Generation-Skipping Transfer Tax. You must list the gifts in chronological order. *Gifts less political organization, medical, and educational exclusions—see instructions. (Also list here direct skips that are subject only to the GST tax at this time as the result of the termination of an "estate tax inclusion period." See instructions.)*

A Item number	B • Donee's name and address • Relationship to donor (if any) • Description of gift • If the gift was made by means of a trust, enter trust's identifying number and attach a copy of the trust instrument • If the gift was of securities, give CUSIP number	C Donor's adjusted basis of gift	D Date of gift	E Value at date of gift
1				

Part 3—Taxable Gift Reconciliation

1	Total value of gifts of donor (add column E of Parts 1 and 2)	1	
2	One-half of items .... attributable to spouse (see instructions)	2	
3	Balance (subtract line 2 from line 1)	3	
4	Gifts of spouse to be included (from Schedule A, Part 3, line 2 of spouse's return—see instructions)	4	
	If any of the gifts included on this line are also subject to the generation-skipping transfer tax, check here ▶ ☐ and enter those gifts also on Schedule C, Part 1.		
5	Total gifts (add lines 3 and 4)	5	
6	Total annual exclusions for gifts listed on Schedule A (including line 4, above) (see instructions)	6	
7	Total included amount of gifts (subtract line 6 from line 5)	7	

Deductions (see instructions)

8	Gifts of interests to spouse for which a marital deduction will be claimed, based on items .... of Schedule A	8		
9	Exclusions attributable to gifts on line 8	9		
10	Marital deduction—subtract line 9 from line 8	10		
11	Charitable deduction, based on items ......to ......less exclusions	11		
12	Total deductions—add lines 10 and 11		12	
13	Subtract line 12 from line 7		13	
14	Generation-skipping transfer taxes payable with this Form 709 (from Schedule C, Part 3, col. H, Total)		14	
15	Taxable gifts (add lines 13 and 14). Enter here and on line 1 of the Tax Computation on page 1		15	

(If more space is needed, attach additional sheets of same size.)

Form 15-7: (continued)

SCHEDULE A	Computation of Taxable Gifts *(continued)*

16 Terminable Interest (QTIP) Marital Deduction. (See instructions for line 8 of Schedule A.)

If a trust (or other property) meets the requirements of qualified terminable interest property under section 2523(f), and

   a. The trust (or other property) is listed on Schedule A, and

   b. The value of the trust (or other property) is entered in whole or in part as a deduction on line 8, Part 3 of Schedule A,

then the donor shall be deemed to have made an election to have such trust (or other property) treated as qualified terminable interest property under section 2523(f).

   If less than the entire value of the trust (or other property) that the donor has included in Part 1 of Schedule A is entered as a deduction on line 8, the donor shall be considered to have made an election only as to a fraction of the trust (or other property). The numerator of this fraction is equal to the amount of the trust (or other property) deducted on line 10 of Part 3. The denominator is equal to the total value of the trust (or other property) listed in Part 1 of Schedule A.

   If you make the QTIP election (see instructions for line 8 of Schedule A), the terminable interest property involved will be included in your spouse's gross estate upon his or her death (section 2044). If your spouse disposes (by gift or otherwise) of all or part of the qualifying life income interest, he or she will be considered to have made a transfer of the entire property that is subject to the gift tax (see Transfer of Certain Life Estates on page 3 of the instructions).

17 Election out of QTIP Treatment of Annuities

☐ ◄ Check here if you elect under section 2523(f)(6) **NOT** to treat as qualified terminable interest property any joint and survivor annuities that are reported on Schedule A and would otherwise be treated as qualified terminable interest property under section 2523(f). (See instructions.) Enter the item numbers (from Schedule A) for the annuities for which you are making this election ►

SCHEDULE B	Gifts From Prior Periods

If you answered "Yes" on line 11a of page 1, Part 1, see the instructions for completing Schedule B. If you answered "No," skip to the Tax Computation on page 1 (or Schedule C, if applicable).

A Calendar year or calendar quarter (see instructions)	B Internal Revenue office where prior return was filed	C Amount of unified credit against gift tax for periods after December 31, 1976	D Amount of specific exemption for prior periods ending before January 1, 1977	E Amount of taxable gifts

1 Totals for prior periods (without adjustment for reduced specific exemption)	**1**		
2 Amount, if any, by which total specific exemption, line 1, column D, is more than $30,000		**2**	
3 Total amount of taxable gifts for prior periods (add amount, column E, line 1, and amount, if any, on line 2). (Enter here and on line 2 of the Tax Computation on page 1.)		**3**	

(If more space is needed, attach additional sheets of same size.)

Form 15-7: (continued)

Form 709 (Rev. 11-93)   Page **4**

SCHEDULE C   Computation of Generation-Skipping Transfer Tax

Note: *Inter vivos direct skips that are completely excluded by the GST exemption must still be fully reported (including value and exemptions claimed) on Schedule C.*

Part 1—Generation-Skipping Transfers

A Item No. (from Schedule A, Part 2, col. A)	B Value (from Schedule A, Part 2, col. E)	C Split Gifts (enter ½ of col. B) (see instructions)	D Subtract col. C from col. B	E Nontaxable portion of transfer	F Net Transfer (subtract col. E from col. D)
1					
2					
3					
4					
5					
6					

If you elected gift splitting and your spouse was required to file a separate Form 709 (see the instructions for "Split Gifts"), you must enter all of the gifts shown on Schedule A, Part 2, of your spouse's Form 709 here. In column C, enter the item number of each gift in the order it appears in column A of your spouse's Schedule A, Part 2. We have preprinted the prefix "S-" to distinguish your spouse's item numbers from your own when you complete column A of Schedule C, Part 3. In column D, for each gift, enter the amount reported in column C, Schedule C, Part 1, of your spouse's Form 709.	Split gifts from spouse's Form 709 (enter item number)	Value included from spouse's Form 709	Nontaxable portion of transfer	Net transfer (subtract col. E from col. D)
	S-			
	S-			
	S-			
	S-			
	S-			
	S-			
	S-			
	S-			

Part 2—GST Exemption Reconciliation (Code section 2631) and Section 2652(a)(3) Election

Check box ► ☐ if you are making a section 2652(a)(3) (special QTIP) election (see instructions)

Enter the item numbers (from Schedule A) of the gifts for which you are making this election ► ....

1	Maximum allowable exemption	1	$1,000,000
2	Total exemption used for periods before filing this return	2	
3	Exemption available for this return (subtract line 2 from line 1)	3	
4	Exemption claimed on this return (from Part 3, col. C total, below)	4	
5	Exemption allocated to transfers not shown on Part 3, below. You must attach a Notice of Allocation. (See instructions.)	5	
6	Add lines 4 and 5	6	
7	Exemption available for future transfers (subtract line 6 from line 3)	7	

Part 3—Tax Computation

A Item No. (from Schedule C, Part 1)	B Net transfer (from Schedule C, Part 1, col. F)	C GST Exemption Allocated	D Divide col. C by col. B	E Inclusion Ratio (subtract col. D from 1.000)	F Maximum Estate Tax Rate	G Applicable Rate (multiply col. E by col. F)	H Generation-Skipping Transfer Tax (multiply col. B by col. G)
1					55% (.55)		
2					55% (.55)		
3					55% (.55)		
4					55% (.55)		
5					55% (.55)		
6					55% (.55)		
					55% (.55)		
					55% (.55)		
					55% (.55)		
					55% (.55)		

Total exemption claimed. Enter here and on line 4, Part 2, above. May not exceed line 3, Part 2, above	Total generation-skipping transfer tax. Enter here, on line 14 of Schedule A, Part 3, and on line 16 of the Tax Computation on page 1	

(If more space is needed, attach additional sheets of same size.)   *U.S. Government Printing Office: 1993 — 301-828/80256

Form 15-8: U.S. Estate Tax Return

| Form **706** (Rev. August 1983) Department of the Treasury Internal Revenue Service | **United States Estate (and Generation-Skipping Transfer) Tax Return** Estate of a citizen or resident of the United States (see separate instructions). To be filed for decedents dying after October 8, 1990. For Paperwork Reduction Act Notice, see page 1 of the instructions. | OMB No. 1545-0015 Expires 12-31-95 |

Part 1.—Decedent and Executor

1a Decedent's first name and middle initial (and maiden name, if any)	1b Decedent's last name	2 Decedent's social security no.
3a Domicile at time of death (county and state, or foreign country)	3b Year domicile established	4 Date of birth	5 Date of death
6a Name of executor (see instructions)	6b Executor's address (number and street including apartment or suite no. or rural route; city, town, or post office; state; and ZIP code)
6c Executor's social security number (see instructions)	
7a Name and location of court where will was probated or estate administered	7b Case number

8 If decedent died testate, check here ▶ ☐ and attach a certified copy of the will. 9 If Form 4768 is attached, check here ▶ ☐

10 If Schedule R-1 is attached, check here ▶ ☐

Part 2.—Tax Computation

1	Total gross estate (from Part 5, Recapitulation, page 3, item 10)	1
2	Total allowable deductions (from Part 5, Recapitulation, page 3, item 20)	2
3	Taxable estate (subtract line 2 from line 1)	3
4	Adjusted taxable gifts (total taxable gifts (within the meaning of section 2503) made by the decedent after December 31, 1976, other than gifts that are includible in decedent's gross estate (section 2001(b))	4
5	Add lines 3 and 4	5
6	Tentative tax on the amount on line 5 from Table A in the instructions	6
7a	If line 5 exceeds $10,000,000, enter the lesser of line 5 or $21,040,000. If line 5 is $10,000,000 or less, skip lines 7a and 7b and enter -0- on line 7c . . [7a]	
b	Subtract $10,000,000 from line 7a . . . . [7b]	
c	Enter 5% (.05) of line 7b	7c
8	Total tentative tax (add lines 6 and 7c)	8
9	Total gift tax payable with respect to gifts made by the decedent after December 31, 1976. Include gift taxes by the decedent's spouse for such spouse's share of split gifts (section 2513) only if the decedent was the donor of these gifts and they are includible in the decedent's gross estate (see instructions)	9
10	Gross estate tax (subtract line 9 from line 8)	10
11	Maximum unified credit against estate tax . . . . . . [11] 192,800 00	
12	Adjustment to unified credit. (This adjustment may not exceed $6,000. See page 6 of the instructions.) . . . . [12]	
13	Allowable unified credit (subtract line 12 from line 11)	13
14	Subtract line 13 from line 10 (but do not enter less than zero)	14
15	Credit for state death taxes. Do not enter more than line 14. Compute the credit by using the amount on line 3 less $60,000. See Table B in the instructions and attach credit evidence (see instructions)	15
16	Subtract line 15 from line 14	16
17	Credit for Federal gift taxes on pre-1977 gifts (section 2012) (attach computation) [17]	
18	Credit for foreign death taxes (from Schedule(s) P). (Attach Form(s) 706CE) [18]	
19	Credit for tax on prior transfers (from Schedule Q) . . . . . . [19]	
20	Total (add lines 17, 18, and 19)	20
21	Net estate tax (subtract line 20 from line 16)	21
22	Generation-skipping transfer taxes (from Schedule R, Part 2, line 10)	22
23	Section 4980A increased estate tax (from Schedule S, Part I, line 17) (see instructions) . . .	23
24	Total transfer taxes (add lines 21, 22, and 23)	24
25	Prior payments. Explain in an attached statement . . . . . [25]	
26	United States Treasury bonds redeemed in payment of estate tax . . [26]	
27	Total (add lines 25 and 26)	27
28	Balance due (or overpayment) (subtract line 27 from line 24)	28

Under penalties of perjury, I declare that I have examined this return, including accompanying schedules and statements, and to the best of my knowledge and belief, it is true, correct, and complete. Declaration of preparer other than the executor is based on all information of which preparer has any knowledge.

Signature(s) of executor(s)   Date

Signature of preparer other than executor   Address (and ZIP code)   Date

Cat. No. 20548R

Form 15-8: (continued)

Form 706 (Rev. 8-93)

Estate of:

Part 3.—Elections by the Executor

Please check the "Yes" or "No" box for each question.

	Yes	No
1 Do you elect alternate valuation?		
2 Do you elect special use valuation? . . . . If "Yes," you must complete and attach Schedule A–1		
3 Do you elect to pay the taxes in installments as described in section 6166? . . . . If "Yes," you must attach the additional information described in the instructions.		
4 Do you elect to postpone the part of the taxes attributable to a reversionary or remainder interest as described in section 6163?		

Part 4.—General Information (Note: *Please attach the necessary supplemental documents. You must attach the death certificate.*)

Authorization to receive confidential tax information under Regulations section 601.504(b)(2)(i), to act as the estate's representative before the Internal Revenue Service, and to make written or oral presentations on behalf of the estate if return prepared by an attorney, accountant, or enrolled agent for the executor:

Name of representative (print or type)	State	Address (number, street, and room or suite no., city, state, and ZIP code)

I declare that I am the ☐ attorney/ ☐ certified public accountant/ ☐ enrolled agent (you must check the applicable box) for the executor and prepared this return for the executor. I am not under suspension or disbarment from practice before the Internal Revenue Service and am qualified to practice in the state shown above.

Signature	CAF number	Date	Telephone number

1   Death certificate number and issuing authority (attach a copy of the death certificate to this return).

2   Decedent's business or occupation. If retired, check here ▶ ☐ and state decedent's former business or occupation.

3   Marital status of the decedent at time of death:
   ☐ Married
   ☐ Widow or widower—Name, SSN, and date of death of deceased spouse ▶ ....
   ☐ Single
   ☐ Legally separated
   ☐ Divorced—Date divorce decree became final ▶

4a Surviving spouse's name	4b Social security number	4c Amount received (see instructions)

5   Individuals (other than the surviving spouse), trusts, or other estates who receive benefits from the estate (do not include charitable beneficiaries shown in Schedule O) (see instructions). For Privacy Act Notice (applicable to individual beneficiaries only), see the Instructions for Form 1040.

Name of individual, trust, or estate receiving $5,000 or more	Identifying number	Relationship to decedent	Amount (see instructions)

All unascertainable beneficiaries and those who receive less than $5,000 . . . . ▶

Total . . . .

(Continued on next page)   **Page 2**

Form 15-8: (continued)

Form 706 (Rev. 8-93)

Part 4.—General Information (continued)

Please check the "Yes" or "No" box for each question.

		Yes	No
6	Does the gross estate contain any section 2044 property (qualified terminable interest property (QTIP) from a prior gift or estate) (see page 5 of the instructions)?		
7a	Have Federal gift tax returns ever been filed? If "Yes," please attach copies of the returns, if available, and furnish the following information:		

7b Period(s) covered	7c Internal Revenue office(s) where filed

If you answer "Yes" to any of questions 8–16, you must attach additional information as described in the instructions.

		Yes	No
8a	Was there any insurance on the decedent's life that is not included on the return as part of the gross estate?		
b	Did the decedent own any insurance on the life of another that is not included in the gross estate?		
9	Did the decedent at the time of death own any property as a joint tenant with right of survivorship in which (a) one or more of the other joint tenants was someone other than the decedent's spouse, and (b) less than the full value of the property is included on the return as part of the gross estate? If "Yes," you must complete and attach Schedule E		
10	Did the decedent, at the time of death, own any interest in a partnership or unincorporated business or any stock in an inactive or closely held corporation?		
11	Did the decedent make any transfer described in section 2035, 2036, 2037, or 2038 (see the instructions for Schedule G)? If "Yes," you must complete and attach Schedule G		
12	Were there in existence at the time of the decedent's death:		
a	Any trusts created by the decedent during his or her lifetime?		
b	Any trusts not created by the decedent under which the decedent possessed any power, beneficial interest, or trusteeship?		
13	Did the decedent ever possess, exercise, or release any general power of appointment? If "Yes," you must complete and attach Schedule H		
14	Was the marital deduction computed under the transitional rule of Public Law 97-34, section 403(e)(3) (Economic Recovery Tax Act of 1981)? If "Yes," attach a separate computation of the marital deduction, enter the amount on item 18 of the Recapitulation, and note on item 18 "computation attached."		
15	Was the decedent, immediately before death, receiving an annuity described in the "General" paragraph of the instructions for Schedule I? If "Yes," you must complete and attach Schedule I		
16	Did the decedent have a total "excess retirement accumulation" (as defined in section 4980A(d)) in qualified employer plans and individual retirement plans? If "Yes," you must complete and attach Schedule S		

Part 5.—Recapitulation

Item number	Gross estate	Alternate value	Value at date of death
1	Schedule A—Real Estate		
2	Schedule B—Stocks and Bonds		
3	Schedule C—Mortgages, Notes, and Cash		
4	Schedule D—Insurance on the Decedent's Life (attach Form(s) 712)		
5	Schedule E—Jointly Owned Property (attach Form(s) 712 for life insurance)		
6	Schedule F—Other Miscellaneous Property (attach Form(s) 712 for life insurance)		
7	Schedule G—Transfers During Decedent's Life (attach Form(s) 712 for life insurance)		
8	Schedule H—Powers of Appointment		
9	Schedule I—Annuities		
10	Total gross estate (add items 1 through 9). Enter here and on line 1 of the Tax Computation		

Item number	Deductions	Amount
11	Schedule J—Funeral Expenses and Expenses Incurred in Administering Property Subject to Claims	
12	Schedule K—Debts of the Decedent	
13	Schedule K—Mortgages and Liens	
14	Total of items 11 through 13	
15	Allowable amount of deductions from item 14 (see the instructions for item 15 of the Recapitulation)	
16	Schedule L—Net Losses During Administration	
17	Schedule L—Expenses Incurred in Administering Property Not Subject to Claims	
18	Schedule M—Bequests, etc., to Surviving Spouse	
19	Schedule O—Charitable, Public, and Similar Gifts and Bequests	
20	Total allowable deductions (add items 15 through 19). Enter here and on line 2 of the Tax Computation	

Page 3

Form 15-8: (continued)

Form 706 (Rev. 8-93)

Estate of:

SCHEDULE A—Real Estate

(For jointly owned property that must be disclosed on Schedule E, see the instructions for Schedule E.)

(Real estate that is part of a sole proprietorship should be shown on Schedule F. Real estate that is included in the gross estate under section 2035, 2036, 2037, or 2038 should be shown on Schedule G. Real estate that is included in the gross estate under section 2041 should be shown on Schedule H.)

(If you elect section 2032A valuation, you must complete Schedule A and Schedule A-1.)

Item number	Description	Alternate valuation date	Alternate value	Value at date of death
1				

Total from continuation schedule(s) (or additional sheet(s)) attached to this schedule . .

TOTAL. (Also enter on Part 5, Recapitulation, page 3, at item 1.) . . . .

(If more space is needed, attach the continuation schedule from the end of this package or additional sheets of the same size.)

(See the instructions on the reverse side.)

Schedule A—Page 4

Form 15-8: (continued)

Form 706 (Rev. 8-93)

Instructions for Schedule A—Real Estate

If the total gross estate contains any real estate, you must complete Schedule A and file it with the return. On Schedule A list real estate the decedent owned or had contracted to purchase. Number each parcel in the left-hand column.

Describe the real estate in enough detail so that the IRS can easily locate it for inspection and valuation. For each parcel of real estate, report the area and, if the parcel is improved, describe the improvements. For city or town property, report the street and number, ward, subdivision, block and lot, etc. For rural property, report the township, range, landmarks, etc.

If any item of real estate is subject to a mortgage for which the decedent's estate is liable, that is, if the indebtedness may be charged against other property of the estate that is not subject to that mortgage, or if the decedent was personally liable for that mortgage, you must report the full value of the property in the value column.

Enter the amount of the mortgage under "Description" on this schedule. The unpaid amount of the mortgage may be deducted on Schedule K. If the decedent's estate is NOT liable for the amount of the mortgage, report only the value of the equity of redemption (or value of the property less the indebtedness) in the value column as part of the gross estate. Do not enter any amount less than zero. Do not deduct the amount of indebtedness on Schedule K.

Also list on Schedule A real property the decedent contracted to purchase. Report the full value of the property and not the equity in the value column. Deduct the unpaid part of the purchase price on Schedule K.

Report the value of real estate without reducing it for homestead or other exemption, or the value of dower, curtesy, or a statutory estate created instead of dower or curtesy.

Explain how the reported values were determined and attach copies of any appraisals.

Schedule A Examples

In this example, the alternate valuation is not adopted; the date of death is January 1, 1993.

Item number	Description	Alternate valuation date	Alternate value	Value at date of death
1	House and lot, 1921 William Street NW, Washington, DC (lot 6, square 481). Rent of $2,700 due at end of each quarter, February 1, May 1, August 1, and November 1. Value based on appraisal, copy of which is attached			108,000
	Rent due on item 1 for quarter ending November 1, 1992, but not collected at date of death			2,700
	Rent accrued on item 1 for November and December 1992			1,800
2	House and lot, 304 Jefferson Street, Alexandria, VA (lot 18, square 40). Rent of $600 payable monthly. Value based on appraisal, copy of which is attached			96,000
	Rent due on item 2 for December 1992, but not collected at date of death . . .			600

In this example, alternate valuation is adopted; the date of death is January 1, 1993.

Item number	Description	Alternate valuation date	Alternate value	Value at date of death
1	House and lot, 1921 William Street NW, Washington, DC (lot 6, square 481). Rent of $2,700 due at end of each quarter, February 1, May 1, August 1, and November 1. Value based on appraisal, copy of which is attached. Not disposed of within 6 months following death	7/1/93	90,000	108,000
	Rent due on item 1 for quarter ending November 1, 1992, but not collected until February 1, 1993	2/1/93	2,700	2,700
	Rent accrued on item 1 for November and December 1992, collected on February 1, 1993	2/1/93	1,800	1,800
2	House and lot, 304 Jefferson Street, Alexandria, VA (lot 18, square 40). Rent of $600 payable monthly. Value based on appraisal, copy of which is attached. Property exchanged for farm on May 1, 1993	5/1/93	90,000	96,000
	Rent due on item 2 for December 1992, but not collected until February 1, 1993 .	2/1/93	600	600

Schedule A—Page 5

Form 15-8: (continued)

Form 706 (Rev. 8-93)

Instructions for Schedule A-1.—Section 2032A Valuation

The election to value certain farm and closely held business property at its special use value is made by checking "Yes" to line 2 of Part 3, Elections by the Executor, Form 706. Schedule A-1 is used to report the additional information that must be submitted to support this election. In order to make a valid election, you must complete Schedule A-1 and attach all of the required statements and appraisals.

For definitions and additional information concerning special use valuation, see section 2032A and the related regulations.

Part 1.—Type of Election

Estate and GST Tax Elections.—If you elect special use valuation for the estate tax, you must also elect special use valuation for the GST tax and vice versa.

You must value each specific property interest at the same value for GST tax purposes that you value it at for estate tax purposes.

Protective Election.—To make the protective election described in the separate instructions for line 2 of Part 3, Elections by the Executor, you must check this box, enter the decedent's name and social security number in the spaces provided at the top of Schedule A-1, and complete line 1 and column A of lines 3 and 4 of Part 2. For purposes of the protective election, list on line 3 all of the real property that passes to the qualified heirs even though some of the property will be shown on line 2 when the additional notice of election is subsequently filed. You need not complete columns B–D of lines 3 and 4. You need not complete any other line entries on Schedule A-1. Completing Schedule A-1 as described above constitutes a Notice of Protective Election as described in Regulations section 20.2032A-8(b).

Part 2.—Notice of Election

Line 10.—Because the special use valuation election creates a potential tax liability for the recapture tax of section 2032A(c), you must list each person who receives an interest in the specially valued property on Schedule A-1. If there are more than eight persons who receive interests, use an additional sheet that follows the format of line 10. In the columns "Fair market value" and "Special use value," you should enter the total respective values of all the specially valued property interests received by each person.

GST Tax Savings

To compute the additional GST tax due upon disposition (or cessation of qualified use) of the property, each "skip person" (as defined in the instructions to Schedule R) who receives an interest in the specially valued property must know the total GST tax savings on all of the interests in specially valued property received. This GST tax savings is the difference between the total GST tax that was imposed on all of the interests in specially valued property received by the skip person valued at their special use value and the total GST tax that would have been imposed on the same interests received by the skip person had they been valued at their fair market value.

Because the GST tax savings depends on the executor's allocation of the GST exemption and the grandchild exclusion, the skip person who receives the interests is unable to compute this GST tax savings. Therefore, for each skip person who receives an interest in specially valued property, you must attach worksheets showing the total GST tax savings attributable to all of that person's interests in specially valued property.

How To Compute the GST Tax Savings.—Before computing each skip person's GST tax savings, you must complete Schedules R and R-1 for the entire estate (using the special use values).

For each skip person, you must complete two Schedules R (Parts 2 and 3 only) as worksheets, one showing the interests in specially valued property received by the skip person at their special use value and one showing the same interests at their fair market value.

If the skip person received interests in specially valued property that were shown on Schedule R-1, show these interests on the Schedule R, Parts 2 and 3 worksheets, as appropriate. Do not use Schedule R-1 as a worksheet.

Completing the Special Use Value Worksheets.—On lines 2–4 and 6, enter -0-.

Completing the Fair Market Value Worksheets.—Lines 2 and 3, fixed taxes and other charges.—If valuing the interests at their fair market value (instead of special use value) causes any of these taxes and charges to increase, enter the increased amount (only) on these lines and attach an explanation of the increase. Otherwise, enter -0-.

Line 6—GST exemption.—If you completed line 10 of Schedule R, Part 1, enter on line 6 the amount shown for the skip person on the *line 10 special use allocation schedule* you attached to Schedule R. If you did not complete line 10 of Schedule R, Part 1, enter -0- on line 6.

Total GST Tax Savings.—For each skip person, subtract the tax amount on line 10, Part 2 of the special use value worksheet from the tax amount on line 10, Part 2 of the fair market value worksheet. This difference is the skip person's total GST tax savings.

Part 3.—Agreement to Special Valuation Under Section 2032A

The agreement to special valuation by persons with an interest in property is required under section 2032A(a)(1)(B) and (d)(2) and must be signed by all parties who have any interest in the property being valued based on its qualified use as of the date of the decedent's death.

An interest in property is an interest that, as of the date of the decedent's death, can be asserted under applicable local law so as to affect the disposition of the specially valued property by the estate. Any person who at the decedent's death has any such interest in the property, whether present or future, or vested or contingent, must enter into the agreement. Included are owners of remainder and executory interests; the holders of general or special powers of appointment; beneficiaries of a gift over in default of exercise of any such power; joint tenants and holders of similar undivided interests when the decedent held only a joint or undivided interest in the property or when only an undivided interest is specially valued; and trustees of trusts and representatives of other entities holding title to, or holding any interests in the property. An heir who has the power under local law to caveat (challenge) a will and thereby affect disposition of the property is not, however, considered to be a person with an interest in property under section 2032A solely by reason of that right. Likewise, creditors of an estate are not such persons solely by reason of their status as creditors.

If any person required to enter into the agreement either desires that an agent act for him or her or cannot legally bind himself or herself due to infancy or other incompetency, or due to death before the election under section 2032A is timely exercised, a representative authorized by local law to bind the person in an agreement of this nature may sign the agreement on his or her behalf.

The Internal Revenue Service will contact the agent designated in the agreement on all matters relating to continued qualification under section 2032A of the specially valued real property and on all matters relating to the special lien arising under section 6324B. It is the duty of the agent as attorney-in-fact for the parties with interests in the specially valued property to furnish the IRS with any requested information and to notify the IRS of any disposition or cessation of qualified use of any part of the property.

Schedule A-1—Page 6

Form 15-8: (continued)

Form 706 (Rev. 8-93)

Checklist for Section 2032A Election—*If you are going to make the special use valuation election on Schedule A-1, please use this checklist to ensure that you are providing everything necessary to make a valid election.*

To have a valid special use valuation election under section 2032A, you must file, in addition to the Federal estate tax return, **(a)** a notice of election (Schedule A-1, Part 2), and **(b)** a fully executed agreement (Schedule A-1, Part 3). You must include certain information in the notice of election. To ensure that the notice of election includes all of the information required for a valid election, use the following checklist. The checklist is for your use only. Do not file it with the return.

1. Does the notice of election include the decedent's name and social security number as they appear on the estate tax return?

2. Does the notice of election include the relevant qualified use of the property to be specially valued?

3. Does the notice of election describe the items of real property shown on the estate tax return that are to be specially valued and identify the property by the Form 706 schedule and item number?

4. Does the notice of election include the fair market value of the real property to be specially valued and also include its value based on the qualified use (determined without the adjustments provided in section 2032A(b)(3)(B))?

5. Does the notice of election include the adjusted value (as defined in section 2032A(b)(3)(B)) of **(a)** all real property that both passes from the decedent and is used in a qualified use, without regard to whether it is to be specially valued, and **(b)** all real property to be specially valued?

6. Does the notice of election include **(a)** the items of personal property shown on the estate tax return that pass from the decedent to a qualified heir and that are used in qualified use and **(b)** the total value of such personal property adjusted under section 2032A(b)(3)(B)?

7. Does the notice of election include the adjusted value of the gross estate? (See section 2032A(b)(3)(A).)

8. Does the notice of election include the method used to determine the special use value?

9. Does the notice of election include copies of written appraisals of the fair market value of the real property?

10. Does the notice of election include a statement that the decedent and/or a member of his or her family has owned all of the specially valued property for at least 5 years of the 8 years immediately preceding the date of the decedent's death?

11. Does the notice of election include a statement as to whether there were any periods during the 8-year period preceding the decedent's date of death during which the decedent or a member of his or her family **(a)** did not own the property to be specially valued, **(b)** use it in a qualified use, or **(c)** materially participate in the operation of the farm or other business? (See section 2032A(e)(6).)

12. Does the notice of election include, for each item of specially valued property, the name of every person taking an interest in that item of specially valued property and the following information about each such person: **(a)** the person's address, **(b)** the person's taxpayer identification number, **(c)** the person's relationship to the decedent, and **(d)** the value of the property interest passing to that person based on both fair market value and qualified use?

13. Does the notice of election include affidavits describing the activities constituting material participation and the identity of the material participants?

14. Does the notice of election include a legal description of each item of specially valued property?

(In the case of an election made for qualified woodlands, the information included in the notice of election must include the reason for entitlement to the woodlands election.)

Any election made under section 2032A will not be valid unless a properly executed agreement (Schedule A-1, Part 3) is filed with the estate tax return. To ensure that the agreement satisfies the requirements for a valid election, use the following checklist.

1. Has the agreement been signed by each and every qualified heir having an interest in the property being specially valued?

2. Has every qualified heir expressed consent to personal liability under section 2032A(c) in the event of an early disposition or early cessation of qualified use?

3. Is the agreement that is actually signed by the qualified heirs in a form that is binding on all of the qualified heirs having an interest in the specially valued property?

4. Does the agreement designate an agent to act for the parties to the agreement in all dealings with the IRS on matters arising under section 2032A?

5. Has the agreement been signed by the designated agent and does it give the address of the agent?

Form 15-8: (continued)

Form 706 (Rev. 8-93)

Estate of:

| | Decedent's Social Security Number |

SCHEDULE A-1—Section 2032A Valuation

Part 1.—Type of Election (Before making an election, see the checklist on page 7.):

☐ **Protective election (Regulations section 20.2032A-8(b)).**—Complete Part 2, line 1, and column A of lines 3 and 4. (See instructions.)

☐ **Regular election.**—Complete all of Part 2 (including line 11, if applicable) and Part 3. (See instructions.)

Before completing Schedule A-1, see the checklist on page 7 for the information and documents that must be included to make a valid election.

The election is not valid unless the agreement (i.e., Part 3-Agreement to Special Valuation Under Section 2032A)—

● Is signed by each and every qualified heir with an interest in the specially valued property, and

● Is attached to this return when it is filed.

Part 2.—Notice of Election (Regulations section 20.2032A-8(a)(3))

Note: *All real property entered on lines 2 and 3 must also be entered on Schedules A, E, F, G, or H, as applicable.*

1 Qualified use—check one ▶ ☐ Farm used for farming, or

▶ ☐ Trade or business other than farming

2 Real property used in a qualified use, passing to qualified heirs, and to be specially valued on this Form 706.

A Schedule and item number from Form 706	B Full value (without section 2032A(b)(3)(B) adjustment)	C Adjusted value (with section 2032A(b)(3)(B) adjustment)	D Value based on qualified use (without section 2032A(b)(3)(B) adjustment)

Totals . . . .

Attach a legal description of all property listed on line 2.

Attach copies of appraisals showing the column B values for all property listed on line 2.

3 Real property used in a qualified use, passing to qualified heirs, but not specially valued on this Form 706.

A Schedule and item number from Form 706	B Full value (without section 2032A(b)(3)(B) adjustment)	C Adjusted value (with section 2032A(b)(3)(B) adjustment)	D Value based on qualified use (without section 2032A(b)(3)(B) adjustment)

Totals . . . .

If you checked "Regular election," you must attach copies of appraisals showing the column B values for all property listed on line 3.

(Continued on next page)   **Schedule A-1—Page 8**

Form 15-8: (continued)

Form 706 (Rev. 8-93)

4 Personal property used in a qualified use and passing to qualified heirs.

A Schedule and item number from Form 706	B Adjusted value (with section 2032A(b)(3)(B) adjustment)	A (continued) Schedule and item number from Form 706	B (continued) Adjusted value (with section 2032A(b)(3)(B) adjustment)
		"Subtotal" from Col. B, below left	....

Subtotal . . . .

Total adjusted value . . .

5 Enter the value of the total gross estate as adjusted under section 2032A(b)(3)(A). ▶ _____

6 Attach a description of the method used to determine the special value based on qualified use.

7 Did the decedent and/or a member of his or her family own all property listed on line 2 for at least 5 of the 8 years immediately preceding the date of the decedent's death? . . . . ☐ Yes ☐ No

8 Were there any periods during the 8-year period preceding the date of the decedent's death during which the decedent or a member of his or her family:

	Yes	No
a Did not own the property listed on line 2 above?		
b Did not use the property listed on line 2 above in a qualified use?		
c Did not materially participate in the operation of the farm or other business within the meaning of section 2032A(e)(6)?.		

If "Yes" to any of the above, you must attach a statement listing the periods. If applicable, describe whether the exceptions of sections 2032A(b)(4) or (5) are met.

9 Attach affidavits describing the activities constituting material participation and the identity and relationship to the decedent of the material participants.

10 Persons holding interests. Enter the requested information for each party who received any interest in the specially valued property. (Each of the qualified heirs receiving an interest in the property must sign the agreement, and the agreement must be filed with this return.)

	Name	Address
A		
B		
C		
D		
E		
F		
G		
H		

	Identifying number	Relationship to decedent	Fair market value	Special use value
A				
B				
C				
D				
E				
F				
G				
H				

You must attach a computation of the GST tax savings attributable to direct skips for each person listed above who is a skip person. (See Instructions.)

11 Woodlands election.—Check here ▶ ☐ If you wish to make a woodlands election as described in section 2032A(e)(13). Enter the Schedule and item numbers from Form 706 of the property for which you are making this election ▶................................
You must attach a statement explaining why you are entitled to make this election. The IRS may issue regulations that require more information to substantiate this election. You will be notified by the IRS if you must supply further information.

Schedule A-1—Page 9

Form 15-8: (continued)

Form 706 (Rev. 8-93)

Part 3.—Agreement to Special Valuation Under Section 2032A

Estate of:	Date of Death	Decedent's Social Security Number

There cannot be a valid election unless:

● The agreement is executed by each and every one of the qualified heirs, and

● The agreement is included with the estate tax return when the estate tax return is filed.

We (list all qualified heirs and other persons having an interest in the property required to sign this agreement)

_____

_____ ,

being all the qualified heirs and _____ ,

being all other parties having interests in the property which is qualified real property and which is valued under section 2032A of the Internal Revenue Code, do hereby approve of the election made by _____ ,

Executor/Administrator of the estate of _____ ,

pursuant to section 2032A to value said property on the basis of the qualified use to which the property is devoted and do hereby enter into this agreement pursuant to section 2032A(d).

The undersigned agree and consent to the application of subsection (c) of section 2032A of the Code with respect to all the property described on line 2 of Part 2 of Schedule A-1 of Form 706, attached to this agreement. More specifically, the undersigned heirs expressly agree and consent to personal liability under subsection (c) of 2032A for the additional estate and GST taxes imposed by that subsection with respect to their respective interests in the above-described property in the event of certain early dispositions of the property or early cessation of the qualified use of the property. It is understood that if a qualified heir disposes of any interest in qualified real property to any member of his or her family, such member may thereafter be treated as the qualified heir with respect to such interest upon filing a Form 706-A and a new agreement.

The undersigned interested parties who are not qualified heirs consent to the collection of any additional estate and GST taxes imposed under section 2032A(c) of the Code from the specially valued property.

If there is a disposition of any interest which passes or has passed to him or her or if there is a cessation of the qualified use of any specially valued property which passes or passed to him or her, each of the undersigned heirs agrees to file a Form 706-A, United States Additional Estate Tax Return, and pay any additional estate and GST taxes due within 6 months of the disposition or cessation.

It is understood by all interested parties that this agreement is a condition precedent to the election of special use valuation under section 2032A of the Code and must be executed by every interested party even though that person may not have received the estate (or GST) tax benefits or be in possession of such property.

Each of the undersigned understands that by making this election, a lien will be created and recorded pursuant to section 6324B of the Code on the property referred to in this agreement for the adjusted tax differences with respect to the estate as defined in section 2032A(c)(2)(C).

As the interested parties, the undersigned designate the following individual as their agent for all dealings with the Internal Revenue Service concerning the continued qualification of the specially valued property under section 2032A of the Code and on all issues regarding the special lien under section 6324B. The agent is authorized to act for the parties with respect to all dealings with the Service on matters affecting the qualified real property described earlier. This authority includes the following:

● To receive confidential information on all matters relating to continued qualification under section 2032A of the specially valued real property and on all matters relating to the special lien arising under section 6324B.

● To furnish the Service with any requested information concerning the property.

● To notify the Service of any disposition or cessation of qualified use of any part of the property.

● To receive, but not to endorse and collect, checks in payment of any refund of Internal Revenue taxes, penalties, or interest.

● To execute waivers (including offers of waivers) of restrictions on assessment or collection of deficiencies in tax and waivers of notice of disallowance of a claim for credit or refund.

● To execute closing agreements under section 7121.

(continued on next page)

Schedule A-1—Page 10

Form 15-8: (continued)

Form 706 (Rev. 8-93)

Part 3.—Agreement to Special Valuation Under Section 2032A *(Continued)*

Estate of:	Date of Death	Decedent's Social Security Number

● Other acts (specify) ▶ _____

By signing this agreement, the agent agrees to provide the Service with any requested information concerning this property and to notify the Service of any disposition or cessation of the qualified use of any part of this property.

_____   _____   _____
Name of Agent   Signature   Address

The property to which this agreement relates is listed in Form 706, United States Estate (and Generation-Skipping Transfer) Tax Return, and in the Notice of Election, along with its fair market value according to section 2031 of the Code and its special use value according to section 2032A. The name, address, social security number, and interest (including the value) of each of the undersigned in this property are as set forth in the attached Notice of Election.

IN WITNESS WHEREOF, the undersigned have hereunto set their hands at _____,

this _____ day of _____ .

SIGNATURES OF EACH OF THE QUALIFIED HEIRS:

_____   _____
Signature of qualified heir   Signature of qualified heir

_____   _____
Signature of qualified heir   Signature of qualified heir

_____   _____
Signature of qualified heir   Signature of qualified heir

_____   _____
Signature of qualified heir   Signature of qualified heir

_____   _____
Signature of qualified heir   Signature of qualified heir

_____   _____
Signature of qualified heir   Signature of qualified heir

_____
Signatures of other interested parties

_____
Signatures of other interested parties

Schedule A-1—Page 11

Form 15-8: (continued)

Form 706 (Rev. 8-93)

Estate of:

SCHEDULE B—Stocks and Bonds
(For jointly owned property that must be disclosed on Schedule E, see the instructions for Schedule E.)

Item number	Description including face amount of bonds or number of shares and par value where needed for identification. Give CUSIP number if available.	Unit value	Alternate valuation date	Alternate value	Value at date of death
1					

Total from continuation schedule(s) (or additional sheet(s)) attached to this schedule . .

TOTAL. (Also enter on Part 5, Recapitulation, page 3, at item 2.) . . . .

(If more space is needed, attach the continuation schedule from the end of this package or additional sheets of the same size.)
(The instructions to Schedule B are in the separate instructions.)   **Schedule B—Page 12**

Form 15-8: (continued)

Form 706 (Rev. 8-93)

Estate of:

SCHEDULE C—Mortgages, Notes, and Cash
(For jointly owned property that must be disclosed on Schedule E, see the instructions for Schedule E.)

Item number	Description	Alternate valuation date	Alternate value	Value at date of death
1				
	Total from continuation schedule(s) (or additional sheet(s)) attached to this schedule .			
	TOTAL. (Also enter on Part 5, Recapitulation, page 3, at item 3.).			

(If more space is needed, attach the continuation schedule from the end of this package or additional sheets of the same size.)
(See the instructions on the reverse side.)

Schedule C—Page 13

Form 15-8: (continued)

Form 706 (Rev. 8-93)

Instructions for Schedule C.— Mortgages, Notes, and Cash

If the total gross estate contains any mortgages, notes, or cash, you must complete Schedule C and file it with the return.

On Schedule C list mortgages and notes *payable to* the decedent at the time of death. (Mortgages and notes *payable by* the decedent should be listed (if deductible) on Schedule K.) Also list on Schedule C cash the decedent had at the date of death.

Group the items in the following categories and list the categories in the following order:

1. Mortgages.—List: (a) the face value and unpaid balance; (b) date of mortgage; (c) date of maturity; (d) name of maker; (e) property mortgaged; and (f) interest dates and rate of interest. For example: bond and mortgage of $50,000, unpaid balance $24,000; dated January 1, 1980; John Doe to Richard Roe; premises 22 Clinton Street, Newark, NJ; due January 1, 1993, interest payable at 10% a year January 1 and July 1.

2. Promissory notes.—Describe in the same way as mortgages.

3. Contract by the decedent to sell land.—List: (a) the name of the purchaser; (b) date of contract; (c) description of property; (d) sale price; (e) initial payment; (f) amounts of installment payment; (g) unpaid balance of principal; and (h) interest rate.

4. Cash in possession.—List separately from bank deposits.

5. Cash in banks, savings and loan associations, and other types of financial organizations.—List: (a) the name and address of each financial organization; (b) amount in each account; (c) serial number; and (d) nature of account, indicating whether checking, savings, time deposit, etc. If you obtain statements from the financial organizations, keep them for IRS inspection.

Schedule C—Page 14

Form 15-8: (continued)

Form 706 (Rev. 8-93)

Estate of:

SCHEDULE D—Insurance on the Decedent's Life

You must list **all** policies on the life of the decedent and attach a Form 712 for each policy.

Item number	Description	Alternate valuation date	Alternate value	Value at date of death
1				
	Total from continuation schedule(s) (or additional sheet(s)) attached to this schedule .			
	TOTAL. (Also enter on Part 5, Recapitulation, page 3, at item 4.)			

(If more space is needed, attach the continuation schedule from the end of this package or additional sheets of the same size.)

(See the instructions on the reverse side.)

Schedule D—Page 15

Form 15-8: (continued)

Form 706 (Rev. 8-93)

Instructions for Schedule D.—Insurance on the Decedent's Life

If there was any insurance on the decedent's life, whether or not included in the gross estate, you must complete Schedule D and file it with the return.

Insurance you must include on Schedule D.—Under section 2042 you must include in the gross estate:

- Insurance on the decedent's life receivable by or for the benefit of the estate; and
- Insurance on the decedent's life receivable by beneficiaries other than the estate, as described below.

The term "insurance" refers to life insurance of every description, including death benefits paid by fraternal beneficiary societies operating under the lodge system, and death benefits paid under no-fault automobile insurance policies if the no-fault insurer was unconditionally bound to pay the benefit in the event of the insured's death.

Insurance in favor of the estate.—Include on Schedule D the full amount of the proceeds of insurance on the life of the decedent receivable by the executor or otherwise payable to or for the benefit of the estate. Insurance in favor of the estate includes insurance used to pay the estate tax, and any other taxes, debts, or charges that are enforceable against the estate. The manner in which the policy is drawn is immaterial as long as there is an obligation, legally binding on the beneficiary, to use the proceeds to pay taxes, debts, or charges. You must include the full amount even though the premiums or other consideration may have been paid by a person other than the decedent.

Insurance receivable by beneficiaries other than the estate.—Include on Schedule D the proceeds of all insurance on the life of the decedent not receivable by or for the benefit of the decedent's estate if the decedent possessed at death any of the incidents of ownership, exercisable either alone or in conjunction with any person.

Incidents of ownership in a policy include:

- The right of the insured or estate to its economic benefits;
- The power to change the beneficiary;
- The power to surrender or cancel the policy;
- The power to assign the policy or to revoke an assignment;
- The power to pledge the policy for a loan;
- The power to obtain from the insurer a loan against the surrender value of the policy;
- A reversionary interest if the value of the reversionary interest was more than 5% of the value of the policy immediately before the decedent died. (An interest in an insurance policy is considered a reversionary interest if, for example, the proceeds become payable to the insured's estate or payable as the insured directs if the beneficiary dies before the insured.)

Life insurance not includible in the gross estate under section 2042 may be includible under some other section of the Code. For example, a life insurance policy could be transferred by the decedent in such a way that it would be includible in the gross estate under section 2036, 2037, or 2038. (See the instructions to Schedule G for a description of these sections.)

Completing the Schedule

You must list every policy of insurance on the life of the decedent, whether or not it is included in the gross estate.

Under "Description" list:

- Name of the insurance company and
- Number of the policy.

For every policy of life insurance listed on the schedule, you must request a statement on **Form 712,** Life Insurance Statement, from the company that issued the policy. Attach the Form 712 to the back of Schedule D.

If the policy proceeds are paid in one sum, enter the net proceeds received (from Form 712, line 24) in the value (and alternate value) columns of Schedule D. If the policy proceeds are not paid in one sum, enter the value of the proceeds as of the date of the decedent's death (from Form 712, line 25).

If part or all of the policy proceeds are not included in the gross estate, you must explain why they were not included.

Schedule D—Page 16

Form 15-8: (continued)

Form 706 (Rev. 8-93)

Estate of:

SCHEDULE E—Jointly Owned Property
(If you elect section 2032A valuation, you must complete Schedule E and Schedule A-1.)

PART 1.—Qualified Joint Interests—Interests Held by the Decedent and His or Her Spouse as the Only Joint Tenants (Section 2040(b)(2))

Item number	Description For securities, give CUSIP number, if available.	Alternate valuation date	Alternate value	Value at date of death
	Total from continuation schedule(s) (or additional sheet(s)) attached to this schedule			

1a Totals . . . .

1b Amounts included in gross estate (one-half of line 1a) . . . .

PART 2.—All Other Joint Interests

2a State the name and address of each surviving co-tenant. If there are more than three surviving co-tenants, list the additional co-tenants on an attached sheet.

	Name	Address (number and street, city, state, and ZIP code)
A.		
B.		
C.		

Item number	Enter letter for co-tenant	Description (including alternate valuation date if any) For securities, give CUSIP number, if available.	Percentage includible	Includible alternate value	Includible value at date of death
	Total from continuation schedule(s) (or additional sheet(s)) attached to this schedule				

2b Total other joint interests . . . .

3 Total includible joint interests (add lines 1b and 2b). Also enter on Part 5, Recapitulation, page 3, at item 5 . . . .

(If more space is needed, attach the continuation schedule from the end of this package or additional sheets of the same size.)
(See the instructions on the reverse side.) **Schedule E—Page 17**

Form 15-8: (continued)

Form 706 (Rev. 8-93)

Instructions for Schedule E.—Jointly Owned Property

You must complete Schedule E and file it with the return if the decedent owned any joint property at the time of death, whether or not the decedent's interest is includible in the gross estate.

Enter on this schedule all property of whatever kind or character, whether real estate, personal property, or bank accounts, in which the decedent held at the time of death an interest either as a joint tenant with right to survivorship or as a tenant by the entirety.

Do not list on this schedule property that the decedent held as a tenant in common, but report the value of the interest on Schedule A if real estate, or on the appropriate schedule if personal property. Similarly, community property held by the decedent and spouse should be reported on the appropriate Schedules A through I. The decedent's interest in a partnership should not be entered on this schedule unless the partnership interest itself is jointly owned. Solely owned partnership interests should be reported on Schedule F, "Other Miscellaneous Property."

Part 1.—Qualified joint interests held by decedent and spouse.—Under section 2040(b)(2), a joint interest is a qualified joint interest if the decedent and the surviving spouse held the interest as:

- Tenants by the entirety, or
- Joint tenants with right of survivorship if the decedent and the decedent's spouse are the only joint tenants.

Interests that meet either of the two requirements above should be entered in Part 1. Joint interests that do not meet either of the two requirements above should be entered in Part 2.

Under "Description," describe the property as required in the instructions for Schedules A, B, C, and F for the type of property involved. For example, jointly held stocks and bonds should be described using the rules given in the instructions to Schedule B.

Under "Alternate value" and "Value at date of death," enter the full value of the property.

Note: *You cannot claim the special treatment under section 2040(b) for property held jointly by a decedent and a surviving spouse who is not a U.S. citizen. You must report these joint interests on Part 2 of Schedule E, not Part 1.*

Part 2.—Other joint interests.—All joint interests that were not entered in Part 1 must be entered in Part 2.

For each item of property, enter the appropriate letter A, B, C, etc., from line 2a to indicate the name and address of the surviving co-tenant.

Under "Description," describe the property as required in the instructions for Schedules A, B, C, and F for the type of property involved.

In the "Percentage includible" column, enter the percentage of the total value of the property that you intend to include in the gross estate.

Generally, you must include the full value of the jointly owned property in the gross estate. However, the full value should not be included if you can show that a part of the property originally belonged to the other tenant or tenants and was never received or acquired by the other tenant or tenants from the decedent for less than adequate and full consideration in money or money's worth, or unless you can show that any part of the property was acquired with consideration originally belonging to the surviving joint tenant or tenants. In this case, you may exclude from the value of the property an amount proportionate to the consideration furnished by the other tenant or tenants. Relinquishing or promising to relinquish dower, curtesy, or statutory estate created instead of dower or curtesy, or other marital rights in the decedent's property or estate is not consideration in money or money's worth. See the Schedule A instructions for the value to show for real property that is subject to a mortgage.

If the property was acquired by the decedent and another person or persons by gift, bequest, devise, or inheritance as joint tenants, and their interests are not otherwise specified by law, include only that part of the value of the property that is figured by dividing the full value of the property by the number of joint tenants.

If you believe that less than the full value of the entire property is includible in the gross estate for tax purposes, you must establish the right to include the smaller value by attaching proof of the extent, origin, and nature of the decedent's interest and the interest(s) of the decedent's co-tenant or co-tenants.

In the "Includible alternate value" and "Includible value at date of death" columns, you should enter only the values that you believe are includible in the gross estate.

Schedule E—Page 18

Form 15-8: (continued)

Form 706 (Rev. 8-93)

Estate of:

SCHEDULE F—Other Miscellaneous Property Not Reportable Under Any Other Schedule

(For jointly owned property that must be disclosed on Schedule E, see the instructions for Schedule E.)
(If you elect section 2032A valuation, you must complete Schedule F and Schedule A-1.)

		Yes	No
1	Did the decedent at the time of death own any articles of artistic or collectible value in excess of $3,000 or any collections whose artistic or collectible value combined at date of death exceeded $10,000? . . . . If "Yes," submit full details on this schedule and attach appraisals.		
2	Has the decedent's estate, spouse, or any other person, received (or will receive) any bonus or award as a result of the decedent's employment or death? . . . . If "Yes," submit full details on this schedule.		
3	Did the decedent at the time of death have, or have access to, a safe deposit box? . . . . If "Yes," state location, and if held in joint names of decedent and another, state name and relationship of joint depositor.		

If any of the contents of the safe deposit box are omitted from the schedules in this return, explain fully why omitted.

Item number	Description For securities, give CUSIP number, if available.	Alternate valuation date	Alternate value	Value at date of death
1				
	Total from continuation schedule(s) (or additional sheet(s)) attached to this schedule. .			
	TOTAL. (Also enter on Part 5, Recapitulation, page 3, at item 6.)			

(If more space is needed, attach the continuation schedule from the end of this package or additional sheets of the same size.)
(See the instructions on the reverse side.)

Schedule F—Page 19

Form 15-8: (continued)

Form 706 (Rev. 8-93)

Instructions for Schedule F.—Other Miscellaneous Property

You must complete Schedule F and file it with the return.

On Schedule F list all items that must be included in the gross estate that are not reported on any other schedule, including:

● Debts due the decedent (other than notes and mortgages included on Schedule C)

● Interests in business

● Insurance on the life of another (obtain and attach **Form 712,** Life Insurance Statement, for each policy)

Note for single premium or paid-up policies: *In certain situations, for example where the surrender value of the policy exceeds its replacement cost, the true economic value of the policy will be greater than the amount shown on line 56 of Form 712. In these situations, you should report the full economic value of the policy on Schedule F. See Rev. Rul. 78-137, 1978-1 C.B. 280 for details.*

● Section 2044 property

● Claims (including the value of the decedent's interest in a claim for refund of income taxes or the amount of the refund actually received)

● Rights

● Royalties

● Leaseholds

● Judgments

● Reversionary or remainder interests

● Shares in trust funds (attach a copy of the trust instrument)

● Household goods and personal effects, including wearing apparel

● Farm products and growing crops

● Livestock

● Farm machinery

● Automobiles

If the decedent owned any interest in a partnership or unincorporated business, attach a statement of assets and liabilities for the valuation date and for the 5 years before the valuation date. Also attach statements of the net earnings for the same 5 years. You must account for goodwill in the valuation. In general, furnish the same information and follow the methods used to value close corporations. See the instructions for Schedule B.

All partnership interests should be reported on Schedule F unless the partnership interest, itself, is jointly owned. Jointly owned partnership interests should be reported on Schedule E.

If real estate is owned by the sole proprietorship, it should be reported on Schedule F and not on Schedule A. Describe the real estate with the same detail required for Schedule A.

Line 1.—If the decedent owned at the date of death articles with artistic or intrinsic value (e.g., jewelry, furs, silverware, books, statuary, vases, oriental rugs, coin or stamp collections), check the "Yes" box on line 1 and provide full details. If any one article is valued at more than $3,000, or any collection of similar articles is valued at more than $10,000, attach an appraisal by an expert under oath and the required statement regarding the appraiser's qualifications (see Regulations section 20.2031-6(b)).

Schedule F—Page 20

Form 15-8: (continued)

Form 706 (Rev. 8-93)

Estate of:

SCHEDULE G—Transfers During Decedent's Life
(If you elect section 2032A valuation, you must complete Schedule G and Schedule A-1.)

Item number	Description For securities, give CUSIP number, if available.	Alternate valuation date	Alternate value	Value at date of death
A.	Gift tax paid by the decedent or the estate for all gifts made by the decedent or his or her spouse within 3 years before the decedent's death (section 2035(c))	X X X X X		
B.	Transfers includible under section 2035(a), 2036, 2037, or 2038:			
1				
	Total from continuation schedule(s) (or additional sheet(s)) attached to this schedule .			
	TOTAL. (Also enter on Part 5, Recapitulation, page 3, at item 7.).			

SCHEDULE H—Powers of Appointment
(Include "5 and 5 lapsing" powers (section 2041(b)(2)) held by the decedent.)
(If you elect section 2032A valuation, you must complete Schedule H and Schedule A-1.)

Item number	Description	Alternate valuation date	Alternate value	Value at date of death
1				
	Total from continuation schedule(s) (or additional sheet(s)) attached to this schedule .			
	TOTAL. (Also enter on Part 5, Recapitulation, page 3, at item 8.).			

(If more space is needed, attach the continuation schedule from the end of this package or additional sheets of the same size.)
(The instructions to Schedules G and H are in the separate instructions.)

Schedules G and H—Page 21

Form 15-8: (continued)

Form 706 (Rev. 8-93)

Estate of:

SCHEDULE I—Annuities

Note: *Generally, no exclusion is allowed for the estates of decedents dying after December 31, 1984 (see instructions).*

		Yes	No
A	Are you excluding from the decedent's gross estate the value of a lump-sum distribution described in section 2039(f)(2)? . . . . If "Yes," you must attach the information required by the instructions.		

Item number	Description Show the entire value of the annuity before any exclusions.	Alternate valuation date	Includible alternate value	Includible value at date of death
1				

Total from continuation schedule(s) (or additional sheet(s)) attached to this schedule .

TOTAL. (Also enter on Part 5, Recapitulation, page 3, at item 9.) . . . .

(If more space is needed, attach the continuation schedule from the end of this package or additional sheets of the same size.)

Schedule I—Page 22

(The instructions to Schedule I are in the separate instructions.)

Form 15-8: (continued)

Form 706 (Rev. 8-93)

Estate of:

SCHEDULE J—Funeral Expenses and Expenses Incurred in Administering Property Subject to Claims

Note: *Do not list on this schedule expenses of administering property not subject to claims. For those expenses, see the instructions for Schedule L.*

If executors' commissions, attorney fees, etc., are claimed and allowed as a deduction for estate tax purposes, they are not allowable as a deduction in computing the taxable income of the estate for Federal income tax purposes. They are allowable as an income tax deduction on Form 1041 if a waiver is filed to waive the deduction on Form 706 (see the Form 1041 instructions).

Item number	Description	Expense amount	Total Amount
1	**A. Funeral expenses:**		
	Total funeral expenses		. . . .
	B. Administration expenses:		
1	Executors' commissions—amount estimated/agreed upon/paid. (Strike out the words that do not apply.)		. . . .
2	Attorney fees—amount estimated/agreed upon/paid. (Strike out the words that do not apply.) . .		. . . .
3	Accountant fees—amount estimated/agreed upon/paid. (Strike out the words that do not apply.) . .		. . . .
4	Miscellaneous expenses:	Expense amount	
	Total miscellaneous expenses from continuation schedule(s) (or additional sheet(s)) attached to this schedule		
	Total miscellaneous expenses		
	TOTAL. (Also, enter on Part 5, Recapitulation, page 3, at item 11.)		

(If more space is needed, attach the continuation schedule from the end of this package or additional sheets of the same size.)
(See the instructions on the reverse side.) **Schedule J—Page 23**

Form 15-8: (continued)

Form 706 (Rev. 8-93)

Instructions for Schedule J.—
Funeral Expenses and Expenses Incurred in Administering Property Subject to Claims

General.—You must complete and file Schedule J if you claim a deduction on item 11 of Part 5, Recapitulation.

On Schedule J, itemize funeral expenses and expenses incurred in administering property subject to claims. List the names and addresses of persons to whom the expenses are payable and describe the nature of the expense. **Do not list expenses incurred in administering property not subject to claims on this schedule. List them on Schedule L instead.**

Funeral Expenses.—Itemize funeral expenses on line A. Deduct from the expenses any amounts that were reimbursed, such as death benefits payable by the Social Security Administration and the Veterans Administration.

Executors' Commissions.—When you file the return, you may deduct commissions that have actually been paid to you or that you expect will be paid. You may not deduct commissions if none will be collected. If the amount of the commissions has not been fixed by decree of the proper court, the deduction will be allowed on the final examination of the return, provided that:

● The District Director is reasonably satisfied that the commissions claimed will be paid;

● The amount entered as a deduction is within the amount allowable by the laws of the jurisdiction where the estate is being administered;

● It is in accordance with the usually accepted practice in that jurisdiction for estates of similar size and character.

If you have not been paid the commissions claimed at the time of the final examination of the return, you must support the amount you deducted with an affidavit or statement signed under the penalties of perjury that the amount has been agreed upon and will be paid.

You may not deduct a bequest or devise made to you instead of commissions. If, however, the decedent fixed by will the compensation payable to you for services to be rendered in the administration of the estate, you may deduct this amount to the extent it is not more than the compensation allowable by the local law or practice.

Do not deduct on this schedule amounts paid as trustees' commissions whether received by you acting in the capacity of a trustee or by a separate trustee. If such amounts were paid in administering property not subject to claims, deduct them on Schedule L.

Note: *Executors' commissions are taxable income to the executors. Therefore, be sure to include them as income on your individual income tax return.*

Attorney Fees.—Enter the amount of attorney fees that have actually been paid or that you reasonably expect to be paid. If on the final examination of the return the fees claimed have not been awarded by the proper court and paid, the deduction will be allowed provided the District Director is reasonably satisfied that the amount claimed will be paid and that it does not exceed a reasonable payment for the services performed, taking into account the size and character of the estate and the local law and practice. If the fees claimed have not been paid at the time of final examination of the return, the amount deducted must be supported by an affidavit, or statement signed under the penalties of perjury, by the executor or the attorney stating that the amount has been agreed upon and will be paid.

Do not deduct attorney fees incidental to litigation incurred by the beneficiaries. These expenses are charged against the beneficiaries personally and are not administration expenses authorized by the Code.

Miscellaneous Expenses.—Miscellaneous administration expenses necessarily incurred in preserving and distributing the estate are deductible. These expenses include appraiser's and accountant's fees, certain court costs, and costs of storing or maintaining assets of the estate.

The expenses of selling assets are deductible only if the sale is necessary to pay the decedent's debts, the expenses of administration, or taxes, or to preserve the estate or carry out distribution.

Schedule J—Page 24

Form 15-8: (continued)

Form 706 (Rev. 8-93)

Estate of:

SCHEDULE K—Debts of the Decedent, and Mortgages and Liens

Item number	Debts of the Decedent—Creditor and nature of claim, and allowable death taxes	Amount unpaid to date	Amount in contest	Amount claimed as a deduction
1				

Total from continuation schedule(s) (or additional sheet(s)) attached to this schedule . . . .

TOTAL. (Also enter on Part 5, Recapitulation, page 3, at item 12.) . . . .

Item number	Mortgages and Liens—Description	Amount
1		

Total from continuation schedule(s) (or additional sheet(s)) attached to this schedule . . . .

TOTAL. (Also enter on Part 5, Recapitulation, page 3, at item 13.) . . . .

(If more space is needed, attach the continuation schedule from the end of this package or additional sheets of the same size.)
(The instructions to Schedule K are in the separate instructions.)　　　**Schedule K —Page 25**

Form 15-8: (continued)

Form 706 (Rev. 8-93)

Estate of:

SCHEDULE L—Net Losses During Administration and Expenses Incurred in Administering Property Not Subject to Claims

Item number	Net losses during administration (Note: Do not deduct losses claimed on a Federal income tax return.)	Amount
1		
	Total from continuation schedule(s) (or additional sheet(s)) attached to this schedule	
	TOTAL. (Also enter on Part 5, Recapitulation, page 3, at item 16.)	

Item number	Expenses incurred in administering property not subject to claims (Indicate whether estimated, agreed upon, or paid.)	Amount
1		
	Total from continuation schedule(s) (or additional sheet(s)) attached to this schedule	
	TOTAL. (Also enter on Part 5, Recapitulation, page 3, at item 17.)	

(If more space is needed, attach the continuation schedule from the end of this package or additional sheets of the same size.)

Schedule L —Page 26   (The instructions to Schedule L are in the separate instructions.)

Form 15-8: (continued)

Form 706 (Rev. 8-93)

Estate of:

SCHEDULE M—Bequests, etc., to Surviving Spouse

Election To Deduct Qualified Terminable Interest Property Under Section 2056(b)(7).—If a trust (or other property) meets the requirements of qualified terminable interest property under section 2056(b)(7), and

   a. The trust or other property is listed on Schedule M, and

   b. The value of the trust (or other property) is entered in whole or in part as a deduction on Schedule M,

then unless the executor specifically identifies the trust (all or a fractional portion or percentage) or other property to be excluded from the election the executor shall be deemed to have made an election to have such trust (or other property) treated as qualified terminable interest property under section 2056(b)(7).

   If less than the entire value of the trust (or other property) that the executor has included in the gross estate is entered as a deduction on Schedule M, the executor shall be considered to have made an election only as to a fraction of the trust (or other property). The numerator of this fraction is equal to the amount of the trust (or other property) deducted on Schedule M. The denominator is equal to the total value of the trust (or other property).

Election To Deduct Qualified Domestic Trust Property Under Section 2056A.—If a trust meets the requirements of a qualified domestic trust under section 2056A(a) and this return is filed no later than 1 year after the time prescribed by law (including extensions) for filing the return, and

   a. The entire value of a trust or trust property is listed on Schedule M, and

   b. The entire value of the trust or trust property is entered as a deduction on Schedule M,

then unless the executor specifically identifies the trust to be excluded from the election, the executor shall be deemed to have made an election to have the entire trust treated as qualified domestic trust property.

		Yes	No
1	Did any property pass to the surviving spouse as a result of a qualified disclaimer?		
	If "Yes," attach a copy of the written disclaimer required by section 2518(b).		
2a	In what country was the surviving spouse born? _____		
b	What is the surviving spouse's date of birth? _____		
c	Is the surviving spouse a U.S. citizen?		
d	If the surviving spouse is a naturalized citizen, when did the surviving spouse acquire citizenship? _____		
e	If the surviving spouse is not a U.S. citizen, of what country is the surviving spouse a citizen? _____		
3	**Election out of QTIP Treatment of Annuities.**—Do you elect under section 2056(b)(7)(C)(ii) **not** to treat as qualified terminable interest property any joint and survivor annuities that are included in the gross estate and would otherwise be treated as qualified terminable interest property under section 2056(b)(7)(C)? (see instructions)		

Item number	Description of property interests passing to surviving spouse	Amount
1		

	Total from continuation schedule(s) (or additional sheet(s)) attached to this schedule		
4	**Total** amount of property interests listed on Schedule M	**4**	
5a	Federal estate taxes (including section 4980A taxes) payable out of property interests listed on Schedule M	5a	
b	Other death taxes payable out of property interests listed on Schedule M . . .	5b	
c	Federal and state GST taxes payable out of property interests listed on Schedule M	5c	
d	Add items a, b, and c	5d	
6	Net amount of property interests listed on Schedule M (subtract 5d from 4). Also enter on Part 5, Recapitulation, page 3, at item 18	**6**	

(If more space is needed, attach the continuation schedule from the end of this package or additional sheets of the same size.)

(See the instructions on the reverse side.)

                                                              Schedule M—Page 27

Form 15-8: (continued)

Form 706 (Rev. 8-93)

Examples of Listing of Property Interests on Schedule M

Item number	Description of property interests passing to surviving spouse	Amount
1	One-half the value of a house and lot, 256 South West Street, held by decedent and surviving spouse as joint tenants with right of survivorship under deed dated July 15, 1957 (Schedule E, Part I, item 1)	$ 32,500
2	Proceeds of Gibraltar Life Insurance Company policy No. 104729, payable in one sum to surviving spouse (Schedule D, item 3)	20,000
3	Cash bequest under Paragraph Six of will	100,000

Instructions for Schedule M.—Bequests, etc., to Surviving Spouse (Marital Deduction)

General

You must complete Schedule M and file it with the return if you claim a deduction on item 18 of Part 5, Recapitulation.

The marital deduction is authorized by section 2056 for certain property interests that pass from the decedent to the surviving spouse. You may claim the deduction only for property interests that are included in the decedent's gross estate (Schedules A through I).

Note: *The marital deduction is generally not allowed if the surviving spouse is not a U.S. citizen. The marital deduction is allowed for property passing to such a surviving spouse in a "qualified domestic trust" or if such property is transferred or irrevocably assigned to such a trust before the estate tax return is filed. The executor must elect qualified domestic trust status on this return. See the instructions on pages 27, 29, and 30 for details on the election.*

Property Interests That You May List on Schedule M

Generally, you may list on Schedule M all property interests that pass from the decedent to the surviving spouse and are included in the gross estate. However, you should not list any "Nondeductible terminable interests" (described below) on Schedule M unless you are making a QTIP election. The property for which you make this election must be included on Schedule M. See "Qualified Terminable Interest Property" on the following page.

For the rules on common disaster and survival for a limited period, see section 2056(b)(3).

You may list on Schedule M only those interests that the surviving spouse takes:

1. As the decedent's legatee, devisee, heir, or donee;

2. As the decedent's surviving tenant by the entirety or joint tenant;

3. As an appointee under the decedent's exercise of a power or as a taker in default at the decedent's nonexercise of a power;

Page 28

4. As a beneficiary of insurance on the decedent's life;

5. As the surviving spouse taking under dower or curtesy (or similar statutory interest); and

6. As a transferee of a transfer made by the decedent at any time.

Property Interests That You May Not List on Schedule M

You should not list on Schedule M:

1. The value of any property that does not pass from the decedent to the surviving spouse.

2. Property interests that are not included in the decedent's gross estate.

3. The full value of a property interest for which a deduction was claimed on Schedules J through L. The value of the property interest should be reduced by the deductions claimed with respect to it.

4. The full value of a property interest that passes to the surviving spouse subject to a mortgage or other encumbrance or an obligation of the surviving spouse. Include on Schedule M only the net value of the interest after reducing it by the amount of the mortgage or other debt.

5. Nondeductible terminable interests (described below).

6. Any property interest disclaimed by the surviving spouse.

Terminable Interests

Certain interests in property passing from a decedent to a surviving spouse are referred to as *terminable interests.* These are interests that will terminate or fail after the passage of time, or on the occurrence or nonoccurrence of some contingency. Examples are: life estates, annuities, estates for terms of years, and patents.

The ownership of a bond, note, or other contractual obligation, which when discharged would not have the effect of an annuity for life or for a term, is not considered a terminable interest.

Nondeductible terminable interests.— A terminable interest is *nondeductible,* and should not be entered on Schedule M (unless you are making a QTIP election) if:

1. Another interest in the same property passed from the decedent to some other person for less than adequate and full consideration in money or money's worth; and

2. By reason of its passing, the other person or that person's heirs may enjoy part of the property after the termination of the surviving spouse's interest.

This rule applies even though the interest that passes from the decedent to a person other than the surviving spouse is not included in the gross estate, and regardless of when the interest passes. The rule also applies regardless of whether the surviving spouse's interest and the other person's interest pass from the decedent at the same time. Property interests that are considered to pass to a person other than the surviving spouse are any property interest that: (a) passes under a decedent's will or intestacy; (b) was transferred by a decedent during life; or (c) is held by or passed on to any person as a decedent's joint tenant, as appointee under a decedent's exercise of a power, as taker in default at a decedent's release or nonexercise of a power, or as a beneficiary of insurance in the decedent's life.

For example, a decedent devised real property to his wife for life, with remainder to his children. The life interest that passed to the wife does not qualify for the marital deduction because it will terminate at her death and the children will thereafter possess or enjoy the property.

However, if the decedent purchased a joint and survivor annuity for himself and his wife who survived him, the value of the survivor's annuity, to the extent that it is included in the gross estate, qualifies for the marital deduction because even though the interest will terminate on the wife's death, no one else will possess or enjoy any part of the property.

The marital deduction is not allowed for an interest that the decedent directed the executor or a trustee to convert, after death, into a terminable interest for the surviving spouse. The marital deduction is not allowed for such an interest even if there was no interest

Form 15-8: (continued)

Form 706 (Rev. 8-93)

in the property passing to another person and even if the terminable interest would otherwise have been deductible under the exceptions described below for life estate and life insurance and annuity payments with powers of appointment. For more information, see Regulations sections 20.2056(b)-1(f) and 20.2056(b)-1(g), Example (7).

If any property interest passing from the decedent to the surviving spouse may be paid or otherwise satisfied out of any of a group of assets, the value of the property interest is, for the entry on Schedule M, reduced by the value of any asset or assets that, if passing from the decedent to the surviving spouse, would be nondeductible terminable interests. Examples of property interests that may be paid or otherwise satisfied out of any of a group of assets are a bequest of the residue of the decedent's estate, or of a share of the residue, and a cash legacy payable out of the general estate.

Example: A decedent bequeathed $100,000 to the surviving spouse. The general estate includes a term for years (valued at $10,000 in determining the value of the gross estate) in an office building, which interest was retained by the decedent under a deed of the building by gift to a son. Accordingly, the value of the specific bequest entered on Schedule M is $90,000.

Life Estate With Power of Appointment in the Surviving Spouse.—A property interest, whether or not in trust, will be treated as passing to the surviving spouse, and will not be treated as a nondeductible terminable interest if: (a) the surviving spouse is entitled to all of the income from the entire interest; (b) the income is payable annually or at more frequent intervals; (c) the surviving spouse has the power, exercisable in favor of the surviving spouse or the estate of the surviving spouse, to appoint the entire interest; (d) the power is exercisable by the surviving spouse alone and (whether exercisable by will or during life) is exercisable by the surviving spouse in all events; and (e) no part of the entire interest is subject to a power in any other person to appoint any part to any person other than the surviving spouse (or the surviving spouse's legal representative or relative if the surviving spouse is disabled. See Rev. Rul. 85-35 1985-1 C.B. 328). If these five conditions are satisfied only for a specific portion of the entire interest, see the section 2056(b) regulations to determine the amount of the marital deduction.

Life Insurance, Endowment, or Annuity Payments, With Power of Appointment in Surviving Spouse.—A property interest consisting of the entire proceeds under a life insurance, endowment, or

annuity contract is treated as passing from the decedent to the surviving spouse, and will not be treated as a nondeductible terminable interest if: (a) the surviving spouse is entitled to receive the proceeds in installments, or is entitled to interest on them, with all amounts payable during the life of the spouse, payable only to the surviving spouse; (b) the installment or interest payments are payable annually, or more frequently, beginning not later than 13 months after the decedent's death; (c) the surviving spouse has the power, exercisable in favor of the surviving spouse or of the estate of the surviving spouse, to appoint all amounts payable under the contract; (d) the power is exercisable by the surviving spouse alone and (whether exercisable by will or during life) is exercisable by the surviving spouse in all events; and (e) no part of the amount payable under the contract is subject to a power in any other person to appoint any part to any person other than the surviving spouse. If these five conditions are satisfied only for a specific portion of the proceeds, see the section 2056(b) regulations to determine the amount of the marital deduction.

Charitable Remainder Trusts.—An interest in a charitable remainder trust will not be treated as a nondeductible terminable interest if:

1. The interest in the trust passes from the decedent to the surviving spouse; and

2. The surviving spouse is the only beneficiary of the trust other than charitable organizations described in section 170(c).

A "charitable remainder trust" is either a charitable remainder annuity trust or a charitable remainder unitrust. (See section 664 for descriptions of these trusts.)

Election To Deduct Qualified Terminable Interests (QTIP)

You may elect to claim a marital deduction for qualified terminable interest property or property interests. You make the QTIP election simply by listing the qualified terminable interest property on Schedule M and deducting its value. You are presumed to have made the QTIP election if you list the property and deduct its value on Schedule M. If you make this election, the surviving spouse's gross estate will include the value of the "qualified terminable interest property." See the instructions for line 6 of General Information for more details. **The election is irrevocable.**

If you file a Form 706 in which you do not make this election, you may not file an amended return to make the election

unless you file the amended return on or before the due date for filing the original Form 706.

The effect of the election is that the property (interest) will be treated as passing to the surviving spouse and will not be treated as a nondeductible terminable interest. All of the other marital deduction requirements must still be satisfied before you may make this election. For example, you may not make this election for property or property interests that are not included in the decedent's gross estate.

Qualified Terminable Interest Property is property (a) that passes from the decedent, and (b) in which the surviving spouse has a qualifying income interest for life.

The surviving spouse has a *qualifying income interest for life* if the surviving spouse is entitled to all of the income from the property payable annually or at more frequent intervals, or has a usufruct interest for life in the property, and during the surviving spouse's lifetime no person has a power to appoint any part of the property to any person other than the surviving spouse. An annuity is treated as an income interest regardless of whether the property from which the annuity is payable can be separately identified.

The QTIP election may be made for all or any part of a qualified terminable interest property. A partial election must relate to a fractional or percentile share of the property so that the elective part will reflect its proportionate share of the increase or decline in the whole of the property when applying sections 2044 or 2519. Thus, if the interest of the surviving spouse in a trust (or other property in which the spouse has a qualified life estate) is qualified terminable interest property, you may make an election for a part of the trust (or other property) only if the election relates to a defined fraction or percentage of the entire trust (or other property). The fraction or percentage may be defined by means of a formula.

Qualified Domestic Trust Election (QDOT)

The marital deduction is allowed for transfers to a surviving spouse who is not a U.S. citizen only if the property passes to the surviving spouse in a "qualified domestic trust" (QDOT) or if such property is transferred or irrevocably assigned to a QDOT before the decedent's estate tax return is filed.

A QDOT is any trust:

1. That requires at least one trustee to be either an individual who is a citizen of the United States or a domestic corporation;

Form 15-8: (continued)

Form 706 (Rev. 8-93)

2. That requires that no distribution of corpus from the trust can be made unless such a trustee has the right to withhold from the distribution the tax imposed on the QDOT;

3. That meets the requirements of any applicable regulations; and

4. For which the executor has made an election on the estate tax return of the decedent.

You make the QDOT election simply by listing the qualified domestic trust or the **entire value** of the trust property on Schedule M and deducting its value. You are presumed to have made the QDOT election if you list the trust or trust property and deduct its value on Schedule M. **Once made, the election is irrevocable.**

If an election is made to deduct qualified domestic trust property under section 2056A(d), the following information should be provided for each qualified domestic trust on an attachment to this schedule:

1. The name and address of every trustee;

2. A description of each transfer passing from the decedent that is the source of the property to be placed in trust; and

3. The employer identification number for the trust.

The election must be made for an entire QDOT trust. In listing a trust for which you are making a QDOT election, unless you specifically identify the trust as not subject to the election, the election will be considered made for the entire trust.

The determination of whether a trust qualifies as a QDOT will be made as of the date the decedent's Form 706 is filed. If, however, judicial proceedings are brought before the Form 706's due date (including extensions) to have the trust revised to meet the QDOT requirements, then the determination will not be made until the court-ordered changes to the trust are made.

Line 1

If property passes to the surviving spouse as the result of a qualified disclaimer, check "Yes" and attach a copy of the written disclaimer required by section 2518(b).

Line 3

Section 2056(b)(7) creates an automatic QTIP election for certain joint and survivor annuities that are includible in the estate under section 2039. To qualify, only the surviving spouse can have the right to receive payments before the death of the surviving spouse.

The executor can elect out of QTIP treatment, however, by checking the "Yes" box on line 3. Once made, the election is irrevocable. If there is more than one such joint and survivor annuity, you are not required to make the election for all of them.

If you make the election out of QTIP treatment by checking "Yes" on line 3, you cannot deduct the amount of the annuity on Schedule M. If you do not make the election out, you must list the joint and survivor annuities on Schedule M.

Listing Property Interest on Schedule M

List each property interest included in the gross estate that passes from the decedent to the surviving spouse and for which a marital deduction is claimed. This includes otherwise nondeductible terminable interest property for which you are making a QTIP election. Number each item in sequence and describe each item in detail. Describe the instrument (including any clause or paragraph number) or provision of law under which each item passed to the surviving spouse. If possible, show where each item appears (number and schedule) on Schedules A through I.

In listing otherwise nondeductible property for which you are making a QTIP election, unless you specifically identify a fractional portion of the trust or other property as not subject to the election, the election will be considered made for all of the trust or other property.

Enter the value of each interest before taking into account the Federal estate tax or any other death tax. The valuation dates used in determining the value of the gross estate apply also on Schedule M.

If Schedule M includes a bequest of the residue or a part of the residue of the decedent's estate, attach a copy of the computation showing how the value of the residue was determined. Include a statement showing:

• The value of all property that is included in the decedent's gross estate (Schedules A through I) but is not a part of the decedent's probate estate, such as lifetime transfers, jointly owned property that passed to the survivor on decedent's death, and the insurance payable to specific beneficiaries.

• The values of all specific and general legacies or devises, with reference to the applicable clause or paragraph of the decedent's will or codicil. (If legacies are made to each member of a class, for example, $1,000 to each of decedent's employees, only the number in each class and the total value of property received by them need be furnished.)

• The date of birth of all persons, the length of whose lives may affect the value of the residuary interest passing to the surviving spouse.

• Any other important information such as that relating to any claim to any part of the estate not arising under the will.

Lines 5a, b, and c.—The total of the values listed on Schedule M must be reduced by the amount of the Federal estate tax, the Federal GST tax, and the amount of state or other death and GST taxes paid out of the property interest involved. If you enter an amount for state or other death or GST taxes on lines 5b or 5c, identify the taxes and attach your computation of them. For additional information, see Pub. 904, Interrelated Computations for Estate and Gift Taxes.

Attachments.—If you list property interests passing by the decedent's will on Schedule M, attach a certified copy of the order admitting the will to probate. If, when you file the return, the court of probate jurisdiction has entered any decree interpreting the will or any of its provisions affecting any of the interests listed on Schedule M, or has entered any order of distribution, attach a copy of the decree or order. In addition, the District Director may request other evidence to support the marital deduction claimed.

Page 30

Form 15-8: (continued)

Form 706 (Rev. 8-93)

Estate of:

SCHEDULE O—Charitable, Public, and Similar Gifts and Bequests

		Yes	No
1a If the transfer was made by will, has any action been instituted to have interpreted or to contest the will or any of its provisions affecting the charitable deductions claimed in this schedule? . . . . If "Yes," full details must be submitted with this schedule.			
b According to the information and belief of the person or persons filing this return, is any such action planned? If "Yes," full details must be submitted with this schedule.			
2 Did any property pass to charity as the result of a qualified disclaimer? . . . . If "Yes," attach a copy of the written disclaimer required by section 2518(b).			

Item number	Name and address of beneficiary	Character of institution	Amount
1			

Total from continuation schedule(s) (or additional sheet(s)) attached to this schedule . . . .

3 Total	**3**	
4a Federal estate tax (including section 4980A taxes) payable out of property interests listed above	**4a**	
b Other death taxes payable out of property interests listed above	**4b**	
c Federal and state GST taxes payable out of property interests listed above	**4c**	
d Add items a, b, and c	**4d**	
5 Net value of property interests listed above (subtract 4d from 3). Also enter on Part 5, Recapitulation, page 3, at item 19	**5**	

(If more space is needed, attach the continuation schedule from the end of this package or additional sheets of the same size.)
(The instructions to Schedule O are in the separate instructions.)

Schedule O—Page 31

Form 15-8: (continued)

Form 706 (Rev. 8-93)

Estate of:

SCHEDULE P—Credit for Foreign Death Taxes

List all foreign countries to which death taxes have been paid and for which a credit is claimed on this return.

If a credit is claimed for death taxes paid to more than one foreign country, compute the credit for taxes paid to one country on this sheet and attach a separate copy of Schedule P for each of the other countries.

The credit computed on this sheet is for the ....
(Name of death tax or taxes)

.... imposed in ....
(Name of country)

Credit is computed under the ....
(Insert title of treaty or "statute")

Citizenship (nationality) of decedent at time of death

(All amounts and values must be entered in United States money)

1 Total of estate, inheritance, legacy, and succession taxes imposed in the country named above attributable to property situated in that country, subjected to these taxes, and included in the gross estate (as defined by statute)	
2 Value of the gross estate (adjusted, if necessary, according to the instructions for item 2)	
3 Value of property situated in that country, subjected to death taxes imposed in that country, and included in the gross estate (adjusted, if necessary, according to the instructions for item 3)	
4 Tax imposed by section 2001 reduced by the total credits claimed under sections 2010, 2011, and 2012 (see instructions)	
5 Amount of Federal estate tax attributable to property specified at item 3. (Divide item 3 by item 2 and multiply the result by item 4.)	
6 Credit for death taxes imposed in the country named above (the smaller of item 1 or item 5). Also enter on line 18 of Part 2, Tax Computation	

SCHEDULE Q—Credit for Tax on Prior Transfers

Part 1.—Transferor Information

	Name of transferor	Social security number	IRS office where estate tax return was filed	Date of death
A				
B				
C				

Check here ▶ ☐ if section 2013(f) (special valuation of farm, etc., real property) adjustments to the computation of the credit were made (see instructions).

Part 2.—Computation of Credit (see instructions)

Item	Transferor			Total A, B, & C
	A	**B**	**C**	
1 Transferee's tax as apportioned (from worksheet, (line 7 ÷ line 8) × line 35 for each column) . .				
2 Transferor's tax (from each column of worksheet, line 20)				
3 Maximum amount before percentage requirement (for each column, enter amount from line 1 or 2, whichever is smaller)				
4 Percentage allowed (each column) (see instructions)	%	%	%	
5 Credit allowable (line 3 × line 4 for each column)				
6 TOTAL credit allowable (add columns A, B, and C of line 5). Enter here and on line 19 of Part 2, Tax Computation				

Schedules P and Q—Page 32   (The instructions to Schedules P and Q are in the separate instructions.)

Form 15-8: (continued)

Form 706 (Rev. 8-93)

SCHEDULE R—Generation-Skipping Transfer Tax

Note: *To avoid application of the deemed allocation rules, Form 706 and Schedule R should be filed to allocate the GST exemption to trusts that may later have taxable terminations or distributions under section 2612 even if the form is not required to be filed to report estate or GST tax.*

The GST tax is imposed on taxable transfers of interests in property located outside the United States as well as property located inside the United States.

Part 1.—GST Exemption Reconciliation (Section 2631) and Section 2652(a)(3) (Special QTIP) Election

Check box ▶ ☐ If you are making a section 2652(a)(3) (special QTIP) election (see instructions)

1	Maximum allowable GST exemption	**1** \$1,000,000
2	Total GST exemption allocated by the decedent against decedent's lifetime transfers	**2**
3	Total GST exemption allocated by the executor, using Form 709, against decedent's lifetime transfers	**3**
4	GST exemption allocated on line 6 of Schedule R, Part 2	**4**
5	GST exemption allocated on line 6 of Schedule R, Part 3	**5**
6	Total GST exemption allocated on line 4 of Schedule(s) R-1	**6**
7	Total GST exemption allocated to intervivos transfers and direct skips (add lines 2–6)	**7**
8	GST exemption available to allocate to trusts and section 2032A interests (subtract line 7 from line 1)	**8**

9 Allocation of GST exemption to trusts (as defined for GST tax purposes):

A Name of trust	B Trust's EIN (if any)	C GST exemption allocated on lines 2–6, above (see instructions)	D Additional GST exemption allocated (see instructions)	E Trust's inclusion ratio (optional—see instructions)

9D Total. May not exceed line 8, above	**9D**	

10 GST exemption available to allocate to section 2032A interests received by individual beneficiaries (subtract line 9D from line 8). You must attach special use allocation schedule (see instructions) | **10**

(The instructions to Schedule R are in the separate instructions.)

Schedule R—Page 33

Form 15-8: (continued)

Form 706 (Rev. 8-93)

Estate of:

Part 2.—Direct Skips Where the Property Interests Transferred Bear the GST Tax on the Direct Skips

Name of skip person	Description of property interest transferred	Estate tax value

1 Total estate tax values of all property interests listed above **1**

2 Estate taxes, state death taxes, and other charges borne by the property interests listed above . **2**

3 GST taxes borne by the property interests listed above but imposed on direct skips other than those shown on this Part 2. (See instructions.) **3**

4 Total fixed taxes and other charges. (Add lines 2 and 3.) **4**

5 Total tentative maximum direct skips. (Subtract line 4 from line 1.) **5**

6 GST exemption allocated **6**

7 Subtract line 6 from line 5 . . . . **7**

8 GST tax due. (Divide line 7 by 2.818182) **8**

9 Enter the amount from line 8 of Schedule R, Part 3 . . . . **9**

10 Total GST taxes payable by the estate. (Add lines 8 and 9.) Enter here and on line 22 of the Tax Computation on page 1 . . . . **10**

Schedule R—Page 34

Form 15-8: (continued)

Form 706 (Rev. 8-93)

Estate of:

Part 3.—Direct Skips Where the Property Interests Transferred Do Not Bear the GST Tax on the Direct Skips

Name of skip person	Description of property interest transferred	Estate tax value

1 Total estate tax values of all property interests listed above	**1**	
2 Estate taxes, state death taxes, and other charges borne by the property interests listed above .	**2**	
3 GST taxes borne by the property interests listed above but imposed on direct skips other than those shown on this Part 3. (See instructions.)	**3**	
4 Total fixed taxes and other charges. (Add lines 2 and 3.)	**4**	
5 Total tentative maximum direct skips. (Subtract line 4 from line 1.)	**5**	
6 GST exemption allocated	**6**	
7 Subtract line 6 from line 5	**7**	
8 GST tax due (multiply line 7 by .55). Enter here and on Schedule R, Part 2, line 9	**8**	

Schedule R—Page 35

Form 15-8: (continued)

SCHEDULE R-1 **(Form 706)** (August 1993) Department of the Treasury Internal Revenue Service	**Generation-Skipping Transfer Tax** Direct Skips From a Trust Payment Voucher	OMB No. 1545-0015 Expires 12-31-95

Executor: File one copy with Form 706 and send two copies to the fiduciary. Do not pay the tax shown. See the separate instructions.
Fiduciary: See instructions on following page. Pay the tax shown on line 6.

Name of trust	Trust's EIN

Name and title of fiduciary	Name of decedent	

Address of fiduciary (number and street)	Decedent's SSN	Service Center where Form 706 was filed

City, state, and ZIP code	Name of executor	

Address of executor (number and street)	City, state, and ZIP code	

Date of decedent's death	Filing due date of Schedule R, Form 706 (with extensions)	

Part 1.—Computation of the GST Tax on the Direct Skip

Description of property interests subject to the direct skip	Estate tax value

1 Total estate tax value of all property interests listed above	**1**
2 Estate taxes, state death taxes, and other charges borne by the property interests listed above.	**2**
3 Tentative maximum direct skip from trust. (Subtract line 2 from line 1.)	**3**
4 GST exemption allocated	**4**
5 Subtract line 4 from line 3	**5**
6 **GST tax due from fiduciary. (Divide line 5 by 2.818182) (See instructions if property will not bear the GST tax.)**	**6**

Under penalties of perjury, I declare that I have examined this return, including accompanying schedules and statements, and to the best of my knowledge and belief, it is true, correct, and complete.

Signature(s) of executor(s)   Date

Date

Signature of fiduciary or officer representing fiduciary   Date

Schedule R-1 (Form 706)—Page 36

Form 15-8: (continued)

Form 706 (Rev. 8-93)

Instructions for Fiduciary

Purpose of Schedule R-1

Code section 2603(a)(2) provides that the Generation-Skipping Transfer (GST) tax imposed on a direct skip from a trust is to be paid by the trustee. Schedule R-1 (Form 706) serves as a payment voucher for the trustee to remit the GST tax to the IRS. See the instructions for Form 706 as to when a direct skip is from a trust.

How To Pay the GST Tax

The executor will compute the GST tax, complete Schedule R-1, and give you two copies. You should pay the GST tax using one copy and keep the other copy for your records.

The GST tax due is the amount shown on line 6. Make your check or money order for this amount payable to "Internal Revenue Service," write "GST tax" and the trust's EIN on it, and send it and one copy of the completed Schedule R-1 to the IRS Service Center where the Form 706 was filed, as shown on the front of the Schedule R-1.

When To Pay the GST Tax

The GST tax is due and payable 9 months after the decedent's date of death (entered by the executor on Schedule R-1). Interest will be charged on any GST taxes unpaid as of that date. However, you have an automatic extension of time to file Schedule R-1 and pay the GST tax due until 2 months after the due date (with extensions) for filing the decedent's Schedule R, Form 706. This Schedule R, Form 706 due date is entered by the executor on Schedule R-1. Thus, while interest will be due on unpaid GST taxes, no penalties will be charged if you file Schedule R-1 by this extended due date.

Signature

You, as fiduciary, must sign the Schedule R-1 in the space provided.

Schedule R-1 (Form 706)—Page 37

Form 15-8: (continued)

Form 706 (Rev. 8-93)

Estate of:

SCHEDULE S—Increased Estate Tax on Excess Retirement Accumulations
(Under section 4980A(d) of the Internal Revenue Code)

Part I Tax Computation

1 Check this box if a section 4980A(d)(5) spousal election is being made. . . . . ▶ ☐
   You must attach the statement described in the instructions.
2 Enter the name and employer identification number (EIN) of each qualified employer plan and individual retirement account in
   which the decedent had an interest at the time of death:

	Name	EIN
Plan #1		
Plan #2		
Plan #3		
IRA #1		
IRA #2		
IRA #3		

		A Plan #1	B Plan #2	C Plan #3	D All IRAs
3	Value of decedent's interest	▨	▨	▨	
4	Amounts rolled over after death	▨	▨	▨	
5	Total value (add lines 3 and 4)				
6	Amounts payable to certain alternate payees (see instructions)				▨
7	Decedent's investment in the contract under section 72(f)				
8	Excess life insurance amount.				▨
9	Decedent's interest as a beneficiary				
10	Total reductions in value (add lines 6, 7, 8, and 9) . . .				
11	Net value of decedent's interest (subtract line 10 from line 5)				

12 Decedent's aggregate interest in all plans and IRAs (add columns A–D of line 11) . . . . . . ▶ | 12 | ▨

13 Present value of hypothetical life annuity (from Part III, line 4) . . . . . | 13 | |

14 Remaining unused grandfather amount (from Part II, line 4) . . . . . | 14 | |

15 Enter the greater of line 13 or line 14 . . . . | 15 |

16 Excess retirement accumulation (subtract line 15 from line 12) . . . . | 16 |

17 Increased estate tax (multiply line 16 by 15%). Enter here and on line 23 of the Tax Computation on page 1 . . . . | 17 |

(The instructions to Schedule S are in the separate instructions.)

Schedule S —Page 38

Form 15-8: (continued)

Form 706 (Rev. 8-93)

Part II — Grandfather Election

1 Was a grandfather election made on a previously filed Form 5329? . . . . ▶ ☐ Yes ☐ No
If "Yes," complete lines 2–4 below. You may not make or revoke the grandfather election after the due date (with extensions) for filing the decedent's 1988 income tax return. If "No," enter -0- on line 4 and skip to Part III.

2 Initial grandfather amount **2**

3 Total amount previously recovered **3**

4 Remaining unused grandfather amount (subtract line 3 from line 2). Enter here and on Part I, line 14, on page 38 . . . . **4**

Part III — Computation of Hypothetical Life Annuity

1 Decedent's attained age at date of death (in whole years, rounded down) **1**

2 Applicable annual annuity amount (see instructions) **2**

3 Present value multiplier (see instructions) **3**

4 Present value of hypothetical life annuity (multiply line 2 by line 3). Enter here and on Part I, line 13, on page 38 . . . . **4**

Schedule S—Page 39

Form 15-8: (continued)

Form 706 (Rev. 8-93)   (Make copies of this schedule before completing it if you will need more than one schedule.)

Estate of:

CONTINUATION SCHEDULE

Continuation of Schedule _____
(Enter letter of schedule you are continuing.)

Item number	Description For securities, give CUSIP number, if available.	Unit value (Sch B, E, or G only)	Alternate valuation date	Alternate value	Value at date of death or amount deductible

TOTAL. (Carry-forward to main schedule.) . . . .

See the instructions on the reverse side.   **Continuation Schedule—Page 40**

Form 15-8: (continued)

Form 706 (Rev. 8-93)

Instructions for Continuation Schedule

The Continuation Schedule on page 40 provides a uniform format for listing additional assets from Schedules A, B, C, D, E, F, G, H, and I and additional deductions from Schedules J, K, L, M, and O. Use the Continuation Schedule when you need to list more assets or deductions than you have room for on one of the main schedules.

Use a separate Continuation Schedule for each main schedule you are continuing. For each schedule of Form 706, you may use as many Continuation Schedules as needed to list all the assets or deductions to be reported. Do not combine assets or deductions from different schedules on one Continuation Schedule. Because there is only one Continuation Schedule in this package, you should make copies of the schedule before completing it if you expect to need more than one.

Enter the letter of the schedule you are continuing in the space provided at the top of the Continuation Schedule. Complete the rest of the Continuation Schedule as explained in the instructions for the schedule you are continuing. Use the *Unit value* column only if you are continuing Schedules B, E, or G. For all other schedules, you may use the space under the *Unit value* column to continue your description.

To continue Schedule E, Part 2, you should enter the *Percentage includible* in the *Alternate valuation date* column of the Continuation Schedule.

To continue Schedule K, you should use the *Alternate valuation date* and *Alternate value* columns of the Continuation Schedule as *Amount unpaid to date* and *Amount in contest* columns, respectively.

To continue Schedules J, L, and M, you should use the *Alternate valuation date* and *Alternate value* columns of the Continuation Schedule to continue your description of the deductions. You should enter the amount of each deduction in the *amount deductible* column of the Continuation Schedule.

To continue Schedule O, you should use the space under the *Alternate valuation date* and *Alternate value* columns of the Continuation Schedule to provide the *Character of institution* information required on Schedule O. You should enter the amount of each deduction in the *amount deductible* column of the Continuation Schedule.

Carry the total from the Continuation Schedule(s) forward to the appropriate line of the main schedule.

For sale by the U.S. Government Printing Office
Superintendent of Documents, Mail Stop: SSOP, Washington, DC 20402-9328

Form 15-9: Life Insurance Statement

Form **712** (Rev. November 1991) Department of the Treasury Internal Revenue Service	**Life Insurance Statement**	OMB No. 1545-0022 Expires 11-30-94

Part I   Decedent—Insured (To Be Filed With United States Estate Tax Return, Form 706)

1 Decedent's first name and middle initial	2 Decedent's last name	3 Decedent's social security number (if known)	4 Date of death

5 Name and address of insurance company

6 Type of policy	7 Policy number

8 Owner's name. If decedent is not owner, please attach copy of application.	9 Date issued	10 Assignor's name. Please attach copy of assignment.	11 Date assigned

12 Value of the policy at the time of assignment	13 Amount of premium (see instructions)	14 Name of beneficiaries

15 Face amount of policy	$
16 Indemnity benefits	$
17 Additional insurance	$
18 Other benefits.	$
19 Principal of any indebtedness to the company that is deductible in determining net proceeds . . .	$
20 Interest on indebtedness (item 19) accrued to date of death	$
21 Amount of accumulated dividends	$
22 Amount of post-mortem dividends	$
23 Amount of returned premium	$
24 Amount of proceeds if payable in one sum	$
25 Value of proceeds as of date of death (if not payable in one sum)	$

26 Policy provisions concerning deferred payments or installments.

Note: *If other than lump-sum settlement is authorized for a surviving spouse, please attach a copy of the insurance policy.*

....

....

27 Amount of installments	$

28 Date of birth, sex, and name of any person the duration of whose life may measure the number of payments.

....

....

29 Amount applied by the insurance company as a single premium representing the purchase of installment benefits	$

30 Basis (mortality table and rate of interest) used by insurer in valuing installment benefits.

....

31 Was the insured the annuitant or beneficiary of any annuity contract issued by the company? . . . .   ☐ Yes   ☐ No

32 Names of companies with which decedent carried other policies and amount of such policies if this information is disclosed by your records.

....

....

The undersigned officer of the above-named insurance company hereby certifies that this statement sets forth true and correct information.

Signature ▶   Title ▶   Date of Certification ▶

Instructions

Paperwork Reduction Act Notice.—We ask for the information on this form to carry out the Internal Revenue laws of the United States. You are required to give us the information. We need it to ensure that you are complying with these laws and to allow us to figure and collect the right amount of tax.

The time needed to complete and file this form will vary depending on individual circumstances. The estimated average time is:

Form	Recordkeeping	Preparing the form
712	18 hrs., 25 min.	18 min.

If you have comments concerning the accuracy of these time estimates or suggestions for making this form more simple, we would be happy to hear from you. You can write to both the IRS and

the Office of Management and Budget at the addresses listed in the instructions of the tax return with which this form is filed. DO NOT send the tax form to either of these offices. Instead. return it to the executor or representative who requested it.

Statement of Insurer.—This statement must be made, on behalf of the insurance company that issued the policy, by an officer of the company having access to the records of the company. For purposes of this statement. a facsimile signature may be used in lieu of a manual signature and if used, shall be binding as a manual signature.

Separate Statements.—A separate statement must be filed for each policy.

Line 13.—Report on line 13 the annual premium, not the cumulative premium to date of death. If death occurred after the end of the premium period. report the last annual premium.

Cat. No. 10170V   Form **712** (Rev. 11-91)

Form 15-9: (continued)

Form 712 (Rev. 11-91)   Page **2**

Part II **Living Insured**
(File With United States Gift Tax Return, Form 709. May Be Filed With United States Estate Tax Return, Form 706, Where Decedent Owned Insurance on Life of Another)

SECTION A—General Information

33 First name and middle initial of donor (or decedent)	34 Last name	35 Social security number

36 Date of gift for which valuation data submitted . . . . ▶

37 Date of decedent's death for which valuation data submitted . . . . ▶

SECTION B—Policy Information

38 Name of insured	39 Sex	40 Date of birth

41 Name and address of insurance company

42 Type of policy	43 Policy number	44 Face amount	45 Issue date

46 Gross premium	47 Frequency of payment

48 Assignee's name	49 Date assigned

50 If irrevocable designation of beneficiary made. name of beneficiary	51 Sex	52 Date of birth. if known	53 Date designated

54 If other than simple designation. quote in full. (Attach additional sheets if necessary.)

55 If policy is not paid up:

 a Interpolated terminal reserve on date of death. assignment, or irrevocable designation of beneficiary . . . .

 b Add proportion of gross premium paid beyond date of death. assignment. or irrevocable designation of beneficiary . . . .

 c Add adjustment on account of dividends to credit of policy. . . . .

 d Total (add lines a. b. and c) . . . .

 e Outstanding indebtedness against policy . . . .

 f Net total value of the policy (for gift or estate tax purposes) (subtract line e from line d) . . . .

56 If policy is either paid up or a single premium:

 a Total cost. on date of death. assignment. or irrevocable designation of beneficiary. of a single-premium policy on life of insured at attained age. for original face amount plus any additional paid-up insurance (additional face amount $ _____)

 (If a single-premium policy for the total face amount would not have been issued on the life of the insured as of the date specified. nevertheless. assume that such a policy could then have been purchased by the insured and state the cost thereof. using for such purpose the same formula and basis employed. on the date specified. by the company in calculating single premiums.)

 b Adjustment on account of dividends to credit of policy . . . .

 c Total (add lines a and b) . . . .

 d Outstanding indebtedness against policy . . . .

 e Net total value of policy (for gift or estate tax purposes) (subtract line d from line c) . . . .

The undersigned officer of the above-named insurance company hereby certifies that this statement sets forth true and correct information

Signature ▶   Title ▶   Date of Certification ▶

INDEX_____